The Planning
of Change

The Planning of Change

SECOND EDITION

Edited by

Warren G. Bennis
State University of New York at Buffalo

Kenneth D. Benne
Boston University

Robert Chin
Boston University

HOLT, RINEHART AND WINSTON, INC.
New York · Chicago · San Francisco · Atlanta · Dallas
Montreal · Toronto · London · Sydney

PREFACE

The first edition of *The Planning of Change* was published in 1961. This current edition shows both continuities with the first and departures from it.

Both have sought to contribute to the unfinished task of merging and reconciling the arts of social practice and the sciences of human behavior. This task, we believe, should be seen as at once an intellectual and a practical moral challenge. Living in an age whose single constant is radical change, all men are in urgent need of whatever resources may be made available as they seek to understand and manage themselves and their environment, to understand and solve the unprecedented personal and social problems confronting them.

The intellectual challenge comes from the necessity of developing an adequate theory of the processes through which knowledge is applied. More particularly, a theory of applying and adapting theories of social and personal dynamics to the special and important case of planned changing is required. Both editions have sought to bring together some of the best current conceptualizations of different aspects of application and change process.

The practical challenge lies in inventing and developing social technologies, consistent with our best social and behavioral knowledge and adequate to the practical and moral requirements of contemporary change situations. Both editions have sought to present discussions and evaluations of a growing body of change technologies, viewed not as isolated methods for achieving change, but rather in their intellectual, practical, and moral bearings and implications.

Another part of the practical challenge is the development of persons who can function effectively and responsibly as agents of planned change. Both editions have been prepared as material aids in the education of such persons. Change agents are now being educated within various departments of behavioral and social science and within various professional schools as well. In both editions, we have tried to keep the needs of this scattered academic audience in mind. We hope that, as in the case of the first edition, this edition will prove useful in courses in departments of psychology, sociology, and anthropology and in schools of business administration, social work, education, theology, nursing, and public health as well.

How do the two editions differ? About nine-tenths of the readings in the second edition are new. This change reflects the current rapid expansion and development of theory building, research, and practical experimentation in applied behavioral science in this country and abroad. A field of study and professional training in applied behavioral science is taking shape. We have tried to reflect the contours of this developing field of study in our second edition.

In the first edition, we included a special emphasis upon the dynamics of the face-to-face group. The second edition does not contain this special emphasis. This editorial decision reflects no derogation of the importance of applied group dynamics in processes of planned change. Rather, it was based on a recognition that professional literature on applied group dynamics outside this volume is readily available to students of planned change and on a wish to give a more balanced treatment of change processes at various levels of human organization.

Finally, the second edition is shorter than the first. This adjustment represents greater clarity on our part concerning the boundaries of the developing field of study known as applied behavioral science. Our first edition was a pioneer attempt to define such a field of study. Our subsequent experiences, along with those of our colleagues, have helped us to define these boundaries more accurately, and this has made our task of selection easier.

It is hard to know where to begin and where to end in acknowledging the contributions of the many people who have helped us, directly and indirectly, in preparing this book. Our most direct debt is to those contributors whose work we have reprinted. Specific acknowledgment of our obligation to each of them and to their publishers is made at the beginning of each selection.

The index shows many names in addition to those of our contributors. In a number of cases, these writers have published work that we wished to include. Space limitations made its inclusion impossible. We are nevertheless grateful for their very real help to us in maturing our own thinking.

We wish to acknowledge a debt to three environments in which we have worked before and during the preparation of this edition—Boston University's Human Relations Center, the Massachusetts Institute of Technology's Alfred P. Sloan School of Management, and the National Training Laboratories now in transition to a new form of organization—the NTL Institute of Applied Behavioral Science. All of these environments have offered the challenge of continual work with colleagues and students in theory building, research, and practical experimentation within the field of study to which this book is devoted.

Shirley Frobes gave valuable editorial and bibliographical assistance throughout the preparation of this second edition. Morton and Shelley Elfenbein, Susan Salsburg, and Gregory O'Brien assisted in the final preparation of the volume.

W. G. B.
K. D. B.
R. C.

State University of New York at Buffalo
Boston University
November 1968

CONTENTS

notes diff. to maint. "new changes" in the old organiz. setting — something else is at work!

INTRODUCTION

In an important sense this world of ours is a new world, in which the unity of knowledge, the nature of human communities, the order of society, the order of ideas, the very notions of society and culture have changed and will not return to what they have been in the past. What is new is new not because it has never been there before, but because it has changed in quality. One thing that is new is the prevalence of newness, the changing scale and scope of change itself, so that the world alters as we walk in it, so that the years of man's life measure not some small growth or rearrangement or moderation of what he learned in childhood, but a great upheaval. What is new is that in one generation our knowledge of the natural world engulfs, upsets, and complements all knowledge of the natural world before. The techniques, among and by which we live, multiply and ramify, so that the whole world is bound together by communication, blocked here and there by the immense synapses of political tyranny. The global quality of the world is new: our knowledge of and sympathy with remote and diverse peoples, our involvement with them in practical terms, and our commitment to them in terms of brotherhood. What is new in the world is the massive character of the dissolution and corruption of authority, in belief, in ritual, and in temporal order. Yet this is the world that we have to live in. The very difficulties which it presents derive from growth in understanding, in skill, in power. To assail the changes that have unmoored us from the past is futile,

1

and in a deep sense, I think, it is wicked. We need to recognize the change and learn what resources we have.

Robert Oppenheimer[1]

THE PROBLEM

Richard Weaver has remarked recently that the ultimate term in contemporary rhetoric, the "god term," is "progress" or "change":[2] the world, as Oppenheimer remarks, alters as we walk in it. It would appear, then, that we are beyond debating the inevitability of change; most students of our society agree that the one major invariant is the tendency toward movement, growth, development, process: change. The contemporary debate has swung from change versus no change to the methods employed in controlling and directing forces in change. Dewey has remarked that ". . . history in being a process of change generates change not only in details but also in the *method of directing social change*."[3] The predicament we confront, then, concerns method; methods that maximize freedom and limit as little as possible the potentialities of growth; methods that will realize man's dignity as well as bring into fruition desirable social goals.

Concerning the methods of change, we can observe two idea systems in the contemporary scene that are directly counterposed: the law of nonintervention and the law of radical intervention. The former stems from the natural-law and "invisible-hand" ideology of the laissez-faire doctrine—part economic analysis and part ideology. Tampering and social tinkering with man's natural and social universe interferes with the homeostatic forces, which if left unfettered, will bring about the perfectly maximized good life. Keynesian and welfare economics, as well as the monopolistic structure of contemporary society, have all exposed the weaknesses in the natural-equilibrium position. (Keynes once remarked that classical economic doctrines may well work in the long run; but, he poignantly added, in the long run we'll all be dead.)

Marxian analysis, with its emphasis on conflict, inevitable class struggle, and radical intervention—occasionally at the price of human freedom—represents the other extreme. Although Marxian theory was developed as an indispensable antidote to the elegant rationalizations of the laissez-faire doctrine, it now also suffers from an obsolescence wrought by the accelerating changes of the world, including the Marxian world, which its basic theory could not predict or encompass.

Planned change, as we view it, emerges as the only feasible alternative to these methods; that is, a method which self-consciously and experimentally employs social technology to help solve the problems of men and societies. One may

---

[1] Robert Oppenheimer, "Prospects in the Arts and Sciences," *Perspectives USA*, II (Spring 1955), 10–11.

[2] Richard Weaver, "Ultimate Terms in Contemporary Rhetoric," *Perspectives USA*, II (Spring 1955), 123.

[3] John Dewey, *Liberalism and Social Action* (New York: G. P. Putnam's Sons, 1935), p. 83 (our italics).

approve or deplore the concept of planned change—or look on it with scientific detachment. But no one will deny its importance. And this book was designed to bring about greater understanding of its developing methods, the social processes bearing on its use, its potentialities, its consequences, both ethical and pragmatic, as well as its limitations.

NATURE OF THIS BOOK

There is an old parable that has made the rounds about the grasshopper who decided to consult the hoary consultant of the animal kingdom, the owl, about a personal problem. The problem concerned the fact that the grasshopper suffered each winter from severe pains due to the savage temperature. After a number of these painful winters, in which all of the grasshopper's known remedies were of no avail, he presented his case to the venerable and wise owl. The owl, after patiently listening to the grasshopper's misery, so the story goes, prescribed a simple solution. "Simply turn yourself into a cricket and hibernate during the winter." The grasshopper jumped joyously away, profusely thanking the owl for his wise advice. Later, however, after discovering that this important knowledge could not be transformed into action, the grasshopper returned to the owl and asked him how he could perform this metamorphosis. The owl replied rather curtly, "Look, I gave you the principle. It's up to you to work out the details!"

All parables, supposedly, contain a moral, and the moral here provides one of the main cornerstones of this volume: How can the man of knowledge utilize his hard-won knowledge to help clients and lay personnel? And conversely, how can the lay public provide information and insight that will aid the man of knowledge, the expert, in his role as helper as well as theory builder?

These are not very simple questions, and unfortunately ways of answering them are not easily arrived at or even certainly known. And the condition of the world today—with the often noted communication gap between practitioners and scientists, clients and professional helpers—and the ever increasing specialization and technocracy of the sciences, tend to exacerbate the problem. In another part of the essay quoted above, Oppenheimer states eloquently what can be taken as a central leitmotiv of this book of readings and text:

The specialization of science is an inevitable accompaniment of progress; yet it is full of dangers, and it is cruelly wasteful, since so much that is beautiful and enlightening is cut off from most of the world. Thus it is proper io the role of the scientist that he not merely find new truth and communicate it to his fellows, but that he teach, that he try to bring the most honest and intelligible account of new knowledge to all who will try to learn. This is one reason—it is the decisive organic reason—why scientists belong in universities. It is one reason why the patronage of science by and through universities is its most proper form; for it is here, in teaching, in the association of scholars, and in the friendships of teachers and taught, of men who by profession must themselves be both teachers and taught, that the narrowness of scientific life can best be moderated, and that the analogies, insights, and harmonies of scientific discovery can find their way into the wider life of man.[4]

Putting the problem a little differently, we can say that the major foundation of this book is the *application of systematic and appropriate knowledge in human affairs for the purpose of creating intelligent action and change.* Thus, this is a book that focuses on *planned change*; a conscious, deliberate, and collaborative effort to improve the operations of a human system, whether it be self-system, social system, or cultural system, through the utilization of scientific knowledge.[5]

Let us review briefly some of the organizing features of this volume. First, what is meant by systematic and appropriate knowledge? The parable, of course, burlesques just this point. Yet we find that a substantial body of social science literature suffers an owlish deficiency. Whitehead, commenting pungently on this matter said: "In this modern world the celibacy of the medieval learned class has been replaced by a celibacy of the intellect which is divorced from the concrete contemplation of complete facts."[6]

The relationship between theory and practice must constantly be kept within the same field of vision in order for both to cope with the exigencies of reality. We have developed a substantial body of theory and certainly a rich body of practice, but somehow our failure has been to provide the transformations and bridging between the two. Kurt Lewin, one of the intellectual forebears of this volume, was preoccupied with this issue of the relationship between the abstract and concrete. He once compared this task to the building of a bridge across the gorge separating theory from full reality. "The research worker can achieve this only if, as a result of a constant intense tension, he can keep both theory and reality fully within his field of vision."[7] We seem, quite often, to become lost at the crossroads of a false dichotomy; the purity and virginity of theory on the one hand and the anti-intellectualism of some knowledge-for-what adherents on the other. This division oversimplifies the issue. The issue is far more complicated; it concerns the transformations and developmental conceptualizing that have to be undertaken before theory can become practical.[8]

a problem of interests also

[4] Oppenheimer, p. 9.

[5] Ronald Lippitt *et al., Dynamics of Planned Change* (New York: Harcourt, Brace & World, Inc., 1958). This book would undoubtedly serve as an excellent companion text to this volume. Any book of readings, by definition, suffers from a lack of systematic integration of its content; Lippitt's book may provide a welcome format for readers of this text. On the other hand, *Dynamics* represents a more constricted view of change than the present volume.

[6] Alfred North Whitehead, *Science and the Modern World* (New York: Mentor Books).

[7] Remark attributed to Lewin by his wife, Getrud Weiss Lewin, in her introduction to *Resolving Social Conflicts* (New York: Harper & Row, Publishers, 1948).

[8] Harold Guetzkow writes about the conversion barriers in using the social sciences. "Little attention has been given," he says, "to the way the very structure of knowledge affects its conversion for application. In the social sciences the role of scientist, engineer, technician, practitioner, and policy-maker has not been well differentiated. It may be useful to sketch how the knowledge that the scientist develops may be converted by others for use and then to examine the impact of certain characteristics of basic knowl-

Once these intellectual linkages between theory and practice are effectively established, we have to be concerned further with the social processes that bear on the infusion of knowledge into action and policy decisions. These two foci— practical theory and the social dynamics of utilizing knowledge in effecting change —make up two of the dominant themes in this volume.

One other meaning that has implications for the organization of this book can be drawn from our parable. The grasshopper, suppliant, comes to the expert owl for help. The owl listens to the problem, prescribes a remedy, and terminates the relationship. The owl did not discuss implementation or consequences of his therapy, nor did he seem to understand the *dependence* of the client, nor did he recognize the *transference* in the relationship. The owl simply proffered a rational *"solution."* The meaning, then, that now emerges from our parable has to do with the nature of the relationship between the man of knowledge, the expert, and his client. Our conviction, which is reflected in a number of articles in this volume, is that the extent to which knowledge can be effectively utilized by practitioners and clients—especially knowledge provided for social change— depends to a great extent on the nature of the relationship between the client and change agent.[9] In other words, we do not view science in and of itself as the panacea. This naïve technocratic viewpoint does not take into account the importance of the existential relationship between the man of knowledge (change agent) and the client system. Dewey once said that "Mankind now has in its possession a new method, that of cooperative and experimental science which expresses the method of intelligence."[10] In this book on the theory and practice of planned change we aim to stress the cooperative and collaborative aspects of the various relationships implicated in change—change agent to client, among clients, and among change agents—as well as the scientific findings related to change. (Too often social scientists neglect as legitimate inquiry the collaborative process and the interpersonal and methodological norms and rules distinctively required in the practices of an action science.)

We are now in a better position to express succinctly the nature of this book. Perhaps our greatest emphasis is on the processes of planned changing, on how

---

edge upon the application process." This conversion process is one of the main concerns of this volume. See "Conversion Barriers in Using the Social Sciences," *Administrative Science Quarterly*, IV (1959), 68–81.

[9] These terms have been developed in conjunction with the National Training Laboratories and used by Lippitt *et al.* in *Dynamics of Planned Change* (New York: Harcourt, Brace & World, Inc., 1958). Client refers to the person or group being helped, thus client system whether it be person, group, organization, community, culture, family, club, or whatever. Change agent refers to the helper, the person or group who is attempting to effect change. These are fairly clumsy terms but we cannot think of ready substitutes, and they are coming into wider usage.

We might point out now that Lippitt *et al.* restrict the role of the change agent by defining him as exogenous to the client system, a person from the outside who attempts to effect change. We believe this is too narrow a view, and we have encompassed in our definition the idea that the change agent may be either in or outside the client system.

[10] Dewey, p. 83.

change is created, implemented, evaluated, maintained, and resisted. The processes of change take us, given its enormous scope, into many fields. The exploration fans out into the various dimensions of change processes (from brainwashing to introducing change in a classroom or a factory), into the social and psychological consequences of change, into the antecedent conditions for effectively planning change, into strategic leverage points for effecting change. Included, also, are some of the major instruments which have been developed for creating and maintaining change: training, consulting, and applied research.

Focusing on the processes and instruments of change, however, does not provide an adequate picture of the complications of change and changing. We have to illuminate the targets or systems to which the change is directed. In this book we make a strong effort to keep in mind four types (or levels) of systems: self, role, interpersonal or group, and larger systems such as formal organizations, communities, and in some cases, cultural systems. "The educational task," Dewey once said, "cannot be accomplished merely by working on men's minds without action that effects actual changes in institutions."[11] We cannot overemphasize the importance of keeping the fact in mind that human behavior is like a centipede, standing on many legs. Nothing that we do has a single determinant. We emphasize this now because we believe there is a danger in focusing too narrowly on personality factors; elements in addition to the *personal* equipment of the client must be considered.

In addition to the change processes and the various client systems, we will present material, touched on earlier, relevant to the nature of the collaborative processes in planned-change programs. Moreover, some attention will be given to the strategy and methodology of planned change, its complexities, vicissitudes, and outcomes.

George Santayana once observed that in our changing world we no longer salute our ancestors but bid them good-bye. The temptations to ungrateful impiety are great for all men but perhaps particularly great for practitioners and theorists of planned change with their typical present and future orientation to human affairs. We have tried to resist this temptation to impiety in ourselves by giving attention to the historical roots of contemporary ideas about deliberate changing of men and societies. We have sought to salute our ancestors in this field of intellectual and moral endeavor, both ancestors who have fed our own chosen orientation and those who have nourished variant contemporary orientations. Statements about change become shrill and hollow, when they do not include attention to the conditions of stability and continuity in human life.

No discussion of planned change would be complete without some attention to the perplexing philosophical issues, axiological and ethical, which this subject generates. In these times of "hidden persuaders," brainwashing, "payola," conformity, and manipulation, lay and intellectual publics alike are exceedingly wary lest social and psychological knowledge bring into actuality the specter of predictable—and thereby helpless—man. We share this concern, as a number

---

[11] Dewey, p. 4.

of articles in this volume attest; but we also join Spinoza in saying that our job as men of knowledge is not to weep or laugh, but to understand.

One of our problems here is that our ethical-value positions are intimately related to our pragmatic positions. For example, when we postulate that collaboration is a *sine qua non* of effective planned change, we are insisting on an ethical imperative as well as on a scientific objective. Value orientations color almost every statement in the book. The best we can hope to do is make our own values as explicit as we can. Throughout the course of the book we have attempted to do this.

A brief word about the outline of this volume is now in order. What is the outline of this edition of the book, and how does it compare and contrast with the first edition? The present edition contains four parts. Part I focuses on the evolution of planned change and presents articles on current notions about changing of human systems and on the historical development of these notions. The first volume had a similar beginning, but it tended to rely more heavily on abstract and speculative writings than the present volume does. It is also true, as one of the readers of our manuscript tactfully said, that writings by the editors seem to dominate Part I. The reason for this is we have been thinking for sometime about preparing a textbook in the field of planned change, and some of our writings represent initial conceptions of parts of this textbook. In addition, we feel we know much more about these topics than we did in 1960 when the first edition was prepared. Perhaps this feeling accounts for our zeal in putting our new knowledge into print here.

Part II of the present volume deals with the elements of planned change, classified into four areas: utilization of scientific knowledge, collaboration and conflict, relevant theories of change, influence and systems in change. In general, we think this is a much stronger section than Part II of the first edition. First of all, there are now more and better theories of changing; for example, an active, manipulative, direct kind of theory which takes into account *strategic variables*. In our earlier volume, we had to rely more on theories of changing that were comparatively passive, contemplative, and indirect. We invite the reader to compare, for example, the article by McClelland in the present volume with the change articles in the first edition.

Another significant difference between the two volumes is our relative inattention in the present volume to small group theory and research. The predecessor of the first edition was Benne and Muntyan, *Human Relations in Curriculum Change* (1950), which emphasized the small group as a medium of changing. It seems to us that a more balanced treatment of client systems is now desirable and possible. This has led to greater emphasis in the present volume upon organizational contexts and variables as factors in projects and programs of planned change. Nevertheless, the Lewinian conceptual basis is still very much with us and furnishes material for the present edition as well as the first.

This can be seen best in Part III, Chapter 7, of the present volume, which includes articles on Lewinian "force-field" theory and analysis. Tacit acknowledgment of the influence of Lewin's theories of change is present throughout

Chapters 8 and 9 on instrumentation and resistance, respectively. The part of the first edition which corresponds to Part III in the present book dealt with fewer actual cases of planned changing. We remember our difficulty in finding concrete examples that illustrated adequately the theory we were evolving. Now there is a surfeit and we hope to publish a book of cases within the next year or so. In addition, discussions of the principal tools of planned change: consulting, training, and applied research—although identical in name to the ones we presented in the first edition—appear to be more sophisticated, subtle, and differentiated in the present edition.

Part IV in the first edition dealt with the programs and technologies of planned change, a subject which is covered in the present volume in Part III. In this edition, we have inserted a new section on the value and goal dilemmas in planned change, a topic we all felt remiss in slighting the first time around. The reason for this was basically our inability to find good articles. The present volume is more satisfactory from this point of view, but we still are seeking more seminal articles relevant to the ethical-value issues surrounding the uses of scientific knowledge.

This, in a very general way, depicts the nature of this volume. We think that the reader will recognize the editors' dilemma in constructing a book of readings and text that is of so enormous a range and that draws from the major disciplines of the behavioral sciences, from the history of these sciences, from philosophy of science, from ethical and moral theory, and from theories of application. However, that is, as we see it, the scope of the topic, and hence this book of readings.

Good philosophical references –
Move away from small group – inter relational
    explanations – to organizations – structural analyses

Lewenian "force fields"

don't organizations reflect "interests"?

PART ONE

The Evolution
of Planned Change

Chapter 1

THE ROOTS OF
PLANNED CHANGE

THE explanation of the place of experts in a society is compounded in difficulty when the expertise is about man and society itself. Expertness about things has been supplemented by expertness about people and their social arrangements, differentiated further into expertness about actions required to create, maintain, or alter these arrangements, and expertness in knowledge about what these arrangements actually are. These two kinds of experts, the man of action and the man of knowledge, are interdependent and yet in conflict with each other. Conflicts arise from the role requirements of each form of expertness and in a realistic sense from incompatibilities in the roles of the man of action and the man of knowledge, both as self-defined and as socially defined.

A review of the historical antecedents of present ways in which expert knowledge becomes related to action shows persistent themes. First of all, the legitimacy of a role for men of knowledge in influencing action has been in dispute. Critics and social philosophers have alternately lamented the infrequent use of men of knowledge and the domination of action by theoretical experts. The man of knowledge himself also has displayed uneasiness over his own role in practical affairs. His ambivalence about his position of influence and the proper exercise of his functions shows up in discussions of moral issues, value judgments, impartiality of scholarship, subversion of the purity of knowledge, and many other related questions. In addition, there have been tensions about the proper functioning of the role itself: freedom versus planning, technocratic control versus individuality, expertise versus political and ideological commitment, manipulation versus openness of choice, rational efficiency versus human needs, crisis versus normal operations, and so forth. These themes often become polarized into either-or forms, though in more recent times efforts have been made to reconceptualize the issues and to restate them in a more integrative fashion. The new versions of the old themes are: freedom under planning, creativity and individuality within technologically sophisticated environments, existential value confrontations by both change agents and clients, optimum power balance between change agent and client systems, and so forth. Furthermore, the imperatives of action have often been met by feelings of inadequacy on the part of men of knowledge. With the increasing complexity and rapidity of change, the ever rising urgency of people's expectations for solutions to their problems, the necessity for some kind of participation by men of knowledge in action becomes imperative. Yet, when the expert tries to make use of the present accumulation of applicable knowledge, too often he gets feedbacks of failure. He is not sure whether he has used too little or too much knowledge, or whether he has succeeded or failed in using his knowledge in the right ways.

Men of action have discomforts too. These arise from feelings that the forms and methods of their action may be obsolescent or obsolete under changing conditions. In recent times, discomforts have also arisen from the haunting possibility that sustained collaboration with men of knowledge might have produced more desirable outcomes.

There *are* incompatibilities between the orientations of the man of action and the man of knowledge. These incompatibilities have to do with time perspective, the comparative values of specific and general knowledge, ways in which dependable generalizations are reached, the degree of surety with respect to expected outcomes on which action should be based, as well as with such issues as the degree of responsibility felt for the particular case, caring for the person and issue at hand as compared to watching things work themselves out. Can the gulf be bridged? Yes. Can it be bridged to the extent that there is no noticeable difference? Of course not. It is more in keeping with current wisdom to insist that there is a conflict in role, a conflict which should not dissuade efforts to bring the man of action into working relationships with the man of knowledge. Indeed, it is from this very conflict of interests that some of the growth possibilities for both men of action and men of knowledge arise, if the conflict can be managed wisely.

There is a final and more optimistic point. As specific technologies and procedures of changing are evolved and utilized, these may obviate the more difficult processes of articulating the efforts of knowledge experts and action leaders. We have not yet taken full advantage of accumulated technologies for deliberate interadaptation of individuals, of groups, of organizations, and of communities and nations. Some of these technologies have been derived from academic scholarship; others have been developed from inventions in particular fields of practice. Like Topsy, the roles of social technologists and the technologies have grown,

*Micro/Macro refers to the unit and point of reference—
Comte's was "The society"
a better analogy would be temporary/utopian*

[margin right, vertical]: Just whenever Macro elsewhere is used as a temporal measure in "class-theories" this is not a logical necessity Macro = temporal

13   THE ROOTS OF PLANNED CHANGE

both in scope and in significance. We need to assess their significance in more general terms.

The roots of planned change can be seen developmentally as representing three sets of entangled issues: the role of the expert in practice and action; the uses of knowledge of man and his relationships, including knowledge of change and changing; and newly emerging definitions of the collaborative relationship between the agent of change and those being changed.

The dilemmas of the expert are expressed well by George A. Kelly in "The Expert as Historical Actor," the lead article in this chapter. Despite his own statement that "never have the unifying principles of knowledge and action been more obscure," Kelly posits for the expert "his right of trespass in politics." Out of a welter of historical contexts, Kelly sees, in the responses of men of knowledge, inherent dilemmas in mediating between systems of knowledge and systems of power. The distinction between *macroexpertise* and *microexpertise* is used to illuminate the contemporary state of the expert. Macroexpertise is a con- *[margin: this is not a proper analogy]* stellation of particular types of advice given to secular authorities without any implication that its application shall become universal. This form, says Kelly, is vastly enhanced because nations have been deeply involved in vast and periodic crises. Microexpertise, on the other hand, relates to the "sociological vision": *[margin: micro—]* building systems of thought and principles, and making use of utopias, thus bordering on technocracy in administering societies. This type of expertise is *[margin: w/d Comte]* not as frequently used as the former. However, in our view, it may be possible to transpose the size of the unit system to which expertise is applied; macroexpertise may be applied to communities, organizations, small groups, and individuals in crisis.

Within the development of the social sciences, there has been similar debate. Benne, Chin, and Bennis in "Planned Change in America," demonstrate that debates about planned change have shifted from an ideological form to a technical one. The shift has been from "should we seek to plan change" to "how to plan particular changes for particular people in particular settings."

In "General Strategies for Effecting Changes in Human Systems," Chin and Benne attempt two tasks. They try to develop a three-way classification of the strategies of changing in current use. The authors of this volume are committed to one of these families of strategies, the "normative-re-educative," as most appropriate to the conditions of contemporary life and to the advancement of scientific and democratic values in human society. But this commitment does not mean that the authors reject any place for the other two families of strategies— the "rational-empirical" and the "power-coercive," as Chin and Benne name them—in the armamentarium of change agents and change strategists in our time. It is probably safe to predict that all three kinds of strategies will continue to be used in action programs. However, we believe that continuing research, development, and training in the applied behavioral sciences will extend the use of normative-re-educative strategies in national and world society. *[margin: ✳ Position of authors clearly stated]*

Chin and Benne also attempt to place the three classes of general strategies within the recent historical streams of thought about man and society, which have fed these strategies and their sustaining and supporting rationales. This tracing of the intellectual roots of contemporary ways of thinking about planned change is designed to establish continuities with our past as well as to place alternative contemporary approaches to changing into clearer relief. Although this final piece was prepared primarily for an audience of leaders in public education, it should have meaning for change strategists in other institutional settings as well.

1.1 THE EXPERT AS HISTORICAL ACTOR

George A. Kelly

Society rises to its challenges, abates its fears, and calms its nerves with expertise. At moments of great stress it may also use experts to transcribe its protests and inspire its revolutions. New knowledge or new ways of putting the old, whether forbidden or public, sacred or secular, are the province of the expert, who "sees combinations we do not see," and by his vocation, as we presently define it, helps to translate them into action. He pronounces anathemas and justifications that serve us but are beyond our skill. Experts are revered or reviled; but they have been indispensable in history.

The expert as policy counsellor has been available to societies from earliest times, wearing among other transitory costumes those of magician, tax collector, confessor, constitution-writer, strategist, and economic planner. The form has changed with convenience, values on the scale of knowledge, morale, and culture; but the function has stayed rather constant. If not always enlisted

From George A. Kelly, "The Expert as Historical Actor," reprinted by permission from *Daedalus*, published by the American Academy of Arts and Sciences, Boston, Massachusetts. Vol. 92, No. 3, "Themes in Transition." Some footnotes omitted.

as a guide to salvation or the millennium, the expert has at least been the confidant of dark secrets or the pathfinder toward some ancillary truth. This role seems little abridged even in a "scientific age" when an expert may be implored not to "take sides" but to remain the neutral judge of contingencies. The expert proposes, he does not dispose; but we must assume that his neutrality is a discretionary one.

Today much attention is focused upon the expert's collaboration with political authority. This is not new: in former times experts had been closely woven into the fabric of state councils as soothsayers, lawyers, confessors, private secretaries, etc. The fundamental novelty is, rather, that the form of official expertise seems finally to have caught up with the needs of a complicated bureaucracy and been assimilated to it. This contributes to a rather high *esprit de corps* among experts of the moment.

Yet the expert is essentially a lonely figure. Never have the unifying principles of knowledge and action been more obscure, both because of the multiplication of particular fact and the alienation of the intellectual disciplines from each other. We must dwell on the idea of a world steadily reduced to conceptual particles if we are to grasp the evolution of the expert function. It may be that the expert is learning to be content with his crumb. But many believe that the fragmentation of knowledge, together with the splitting of the atom, of the psyche, and of existential man from his fellow creatures, has produced a condition—our modern ethical philosophers have said it—where man (experts included) is *forlorn.* Not only does the expert fail to grasp a unity which, if it ever existed, seems to be slipping further away; but he despairs that men find it impossible to collaborate effectively in seeking one.

An immediate problem of expertise is then suggested, that of communicating knowledge upward to those who make history, collegiately, and downward to the uninitiated so that it will arrive on time, with the proper impact, and ungarbled. This problem is eloquently illustrated by the frequency of questions of the following order: Does Khrushchev *know* we mean business in Berlin? Does the President *believe* counterforce strategy will work? Can the people be *persuaded* that fallout shelters are important?

The modern expert has often reacted to this modern form of despair by becoming deeply preoccupied with his channels of communication, especially with others who labor with scraps of expertise. This effect is sometimes represented as deadening committee-system procedure or even as social extravagance subsidized by a plethora of willing sponsors. But the diagnosis should go much deeper. Since the modern expert is *forlorn*, he does not thunder, heroic and alone, with rolling Carlylean

periods, but manages modestly and monotonously in the jargon of his discipline. He needs certainty, even microscopic certainty, and the assurance his colleagues can provide. And so he worries about communication, and he perceives that others, more powerful than he, are troubled with the same problem.

The modern expert is generally more willing and eager to render his services to the secular authority, long regarded with deep suspicion by the purer type of intellectual. There are various reasons—personal, moral, and political—that drive the expert to the bosom of the state. There is the anguished concern at human imperfection and social dilemma. There is the hyperdramatic issue of physical survival and the control of the forces which place it in irrevocable jeopardy. And there is the feel for the spotlight, the Faustian temptation to translate knowledge into power. Henry Adams was only the first to reflect: "Though Washington belonged to a different world, and the two worlds could not live together, he was not sure that he enjoyed the Boston world most."[1]

But there is, above all, *forlornness* and the dream of a rational order which must, after all, be built of crumbs if these are all you have. Today the nation-state—though some experts are avidly building "Europe"—appears uniquely capable of the range of power that might command any sane reconstitution of a partitioned world. It also seems the single and best confraternity, perhaps more so than the fabled "international brotherhood of learning" where the personally wrought pieces of the knowledge machine can be brought together and assembled.

But the state must also be understood as the field of action where knowledge and power collide and where the most explicit faults of expertise—of understanding, communication, or execution—come to light. Knowledge alone is something held and challenged only by academic inquisition; knowledge as power is released and exposed, a scapegoat of its own and other failures. Several troubles may occur. The uses of power may easily become confused with the cognitive presuppositions assigned to them. The furious drive, under time pressure, to integrate semidigested bits of knowledge, far from blasting new channels of contact, may block existing ones.

There are, to be sure, moral imperatives that yoke the expert to the state, and they are important ones. But although the state has considerable advantages as a matrix for collaborative expertise, it can take outrageous liberties with the orderly solution of problems. The expert has no cause for complaint. Expertise, like the affiliated technique of divination, has rarely—unless among its own sects—been construed as an end in itself. It demands a patron and becomes the marriage knot between knowledge and power. If it were a true art and not a function, it could glory in all its shades and colors. "Let there be Maecenases, and there will be no lack of Virgils." But authority demands consistency and obedience from its technicians, not a giddy plurality of options.

The expert also has several problems of a subjective order. First, what does being an "expert" imply about his personal thoughts and opinions? Shall he be neutral in his testimony and "engaged" in his life? Obviously, under the pressure of some events, he not only can but must because new occasions teach new duties. The physicist Hans Bethe, who led the United States delegation to the Second Technical Conference on the Detection of Nuclear Testing in 1959, had the responsibility of presenting "new evidence" on the difficulty of underground detection; he later wrote in a magazine article that this was one of the most distasteful things he had ever had to do.[2] Here was one man's response to his predicament; but it does not point the way to any universal solution.

Secondly, the expert is at least vaguely aware that he occupies a certain position in the social order. He shares various reflexes with other professionals, though he may deplore some of their attitudes. He sometimes imagines himself either as an individual or part of a cohesive class, and he may attempt to work out his own rules of life on this basis. Reality usually intrudes bitterly on this self-portrait, for in most cases he shares the prejudice and reason of other groups of human beings. He may bring his sacks of grain to be ground into grist at the mill of power, but he knows he is not the miller; neither is he the bureaucrat who bakes nor the consumer who buys and eats. This functional limitation is often a source of annoyance which affects the expert's view of the social order. Indispensable as part of a functioning system, he would prefer to be defined as the wisest part of it.

Thirdly, the expert is confronted, as we have suggested, by personal judgments regarding the development and transmission of knowledge. He must argue and debate, interpret, prevail, concede, and conciliate. And above all, throughout history, he has been part of a permanent panel to decide on the scope of useful knowledge, worthless knowledge, and dangerous knowledge. A great deal of expert knowledge in all periods of violent change and shifting premises has been pretty strong medicine. The Egyptian priestly cult was, after all, a panel of experts; so, too, one must suppose, is a committee that grants security clearances.

Fourthly, the expert must be drastically concerned with the implications of the knowledge he provides. In this sense he is a secondary agent of power. A human drama accompanies the transmission of knowledge. Even if, in the words of Burke, it is up to the statesmen to decide which matters "they will leave to a wise and salutary neglect," the expert knows that increments of power have a habit of being used and not neglected. How can he control his own destiny as an agent of change?

Power attracts advice. Where a measure of centralized power exists, there, too, is the expert, sometimes more in sun, sometimes more in shade; in harmony with the rationale of power or working to change it; sometimes the "lion beneath the throne," sometimes the god Thoth handing the sacred letters to the temporal ruler and adding to his divinity. Leader of a priestly cult or sponsor of a busy corps of technocrats, the expert stands with a foot in knowledge and a foot in power, and prepares the arcane for practical use. He must define useful knowledge in terms of the capacities of power and in terms of the understanding and belief of his age. Now in addition— though units of society have been faced before with times of famine, flood, and conquest—he must gloom over the data

of survival and measure this ominous quantity against other concerns. He must establish priorities. He must cultivate the unscientific talent of persuasion for use among his fellows and in the ante rooms of power.

Some of the most serious matters which the expert faces, consciously or not, are his historical role in the construction of knowledge systems, his collaboration with the state in crisis periods, his mediation between the systems of knowledge and the systems of power, and his right of trespass in politics. We shall try to comment on these dilemmas in the paragraphs to follow.

The Question of Useful Knowledge

"A man's nature runs either to herbs or weeds," wrote Francis Bacon. "Therefore let him seasonably water the one and destroy the other." The expert must come to feel somewhat this way about the details of knowledge which abound so infinitely. If he cannot practice Socratic surgery on this mass, he must at least exercise a measure of discrimination. In so doing he implies a structure of knowledge, even if he does not attempt to build one outright. Decision-makers act on skeletal constructs which have been fleshed out. Each skeleton incorporates a bias, and the greatest structures of all, by their pattern, establish the unique flavor of a civilization.

But every growing civilization is, at prime moments, in a kind of Hobbesian civil war when the great issues of architecture are debated. Here, the involved experts must choose sides, which is to say, they must contend over the directions in which knowledge itself is to be developed. They must become moral philosophers, if this is not already their vocation, for upon their judgment and means of persuasion will depend results destined to dominate the human condition. . . .

Although the glories of pure experiment—we call it pure research—are widely acknowledged by our present intellectual society, no one can fail to see what difficulties this approach raises in defining useful knowledge or in rendering any qualitative judgment about knowledge at all. We owe much of our magnificent advance and our confusion to the same source. The English Royal Society, chartered in 1662, made no bones about its intentions; ". . . this Society will not own any hypothesis, system, or doctrine of the principles of natural philosophy, proposed or mentioned by any philosopher ancient or modern, nor the explication of any phenomenon whose recourse must be had to originall causes. . . ."[3] By the twentieth century the feeling would grow among experts that their task ended when the last equations had been inscribed and submitted to the secular authority. The "neutrality" of science, indeed of all rigorous expertise, became a moral goal in itself.[4] It was difficult, anyway, to draw ethical conclusions from scraps of a fragmented knowledge system; only the combinations, which were the responsibility of power, could prove deadly or beneficent.

Today's experts, with the scientists in the forefront, are not so sanguine about their intellectual acts: The familiar questions of survival are raised, together with other doubts about economy and utility: Is it better to clear slums or put a man on the moon? Is not the world population problem more menacing than nuclear weapons? Shall we have to eat seaweed in 2050? But the thrust is still outward, and all the avenues of experimentalism are still precious. No fact is to be taken too lightly; no problem can contain too many facts. Few experts in communication with authority, unless perhaps they are spiritual advisors, will be found to say, with John Locke:

Our business here is not to know all things, but those which concern our conduct. If we can find out those measures whereby a rational creature, put in that state in which man is in this world, may and ought to govern his opinions, and actions depending thereon, we need not be troubled that some other things escape our knowledge.[5]

Yet as the years go by, expertise, though still experimental, may be seeking more and more the cover of an ethical umbrella. Wary of the sociological visions which have rent his civilization in the past, but still fragmented and *forlorn*, the expert searches for new ways of galvanizing his scraps of knowledge even if the king's horses and men cannot reassemble them. It may even fall to him to create drastic controls for the technology inspired by the vision of his ancestors.

On Macroexpertise

Keynesian economics has been described as a new science developed for the use of policy-makers. Another term often applied to it is *macroeconomics*, which means simply that its conceptual starting point is the society at large, its wants and needs. By contrast, *microeconomics*, the "classical" economics of Adam Smith and his successors, begins with the study of the individual or individual firm as an economic unit and argues that practices efficient and rewarding to him or it will be good for the entire society. Viewed in another fashion, microeconomics is "classical" because it presumes to hold true at all places and in all times, whereas macroeconomics is a tool developed for present emergency, temporally and geographically defined: it is not "cosmopolitan" but expedient and empirical. Our circle of definition may be closed by noting Keynes's assertion that once an economy can be brought back into equilibrium, the laws of classical economics will generally apply.

Can we approach the problem of expertise usefully by making the distinction between *microexpertise* and *macroexpertise*? Surely, as we have suggested above, there is a relevance to the two terms as they regard the economic expert. We presume also that a wider application of the idea is appropriate. Macroexpertise is a constellation of particular types of advice given to the secular authority to meet situations of crisis without any implication that its application shall become universal. It will perhaps not endure into calmer times nor be relevant to the next crisis.

Emergency planning or, as we have called it, macroexpertise will face a number of special problems and betray certain distinct characteristics. The ageless goals of the society may have to be set aside in the face of a present danger. Whether we speak of the Renaissance Italian city-state or World War I America, the planning in time of crisis becomes more rigorous: men must be impressed into military service or hired; the mechanical or commercial supports of war must be mobilized; a

patriotic sensibility must be intensified. Or, as with Keynes, a humanitarian revulsion against factories lying idle, people going jobless and hungry, and the uncontrolled downward spiral of consumption and production spurs the conviction that something must be done.

Up to the present crisis of survival, the vision of the international system has compelled the attention of the macroexpert less acutely. The essential became the here-and-now, the vitality of the society to which he felt himself belonging. Generally in history as a crisis has deepened, planning and expertise, with all their formulas of unaccustomed coercion and "interference with the natural order," have expanded, but at the same time they have become much less cosmopolitan in scope. "Classical" theory may have been fortified with the impression that its range was broad and timeless; but its challenger, born in the sweat and tears of emergency, is like a fireman rushing to a conflagration, little caring whether his hoses will operate for the next alarm. Yet the fireman must block off streets, forbid private interference, and establish his law within the precinct where the blaze is being fought. The "classicist" will tend to noninterference since his vision, either because it is liberal or automatic, can depend only on the cautionary counselling of individuals about acts that might transgress against another's rights as defined by ordinary law. He will not seek to substitute policy for the law. In the one case the theorist may seem powerful; but in the other the macroexpert will gather into his hands specific powers which seemed unimaginable in the palmier days of normalcy. At the same time the main thrust of his effort will become limited to the arena of the crisis.

This is but one of the jousts between freedom and coercion in which the expert becomes an accomplice. In general, it is the one in which he may be least accused of power-grabbing: both people and authority literally implore the expert to settle their worst crises. Bankers, workers, scholars and statesmen join in the unanimous howl to summon the specialist. This is not to say that societies frequently emerge from their black moments by the intervention of calculating expertise or that the expert enjoys a pleasant reception once he appears. There is, nonetheless, a much greater willingness to let the expert roll up his sleeves and tinker while politics takes a holiday.

The practical curtailments of this process are all too evident, as a simple example should suffice to illustrate. In 1933 virtually all Americans, perhaps 90 per cent, ranging from the United States Chamber of Commerce to socialist ideologues, felt that some steps toward government control over the economy had to be taken. The field of action was thus quite favorable for macroexpertise; and, aside from the bewildering variety of emergency plans submitted to the government privately or corporately, it found its locus in the loose group of economic advisors that was to become known as the "brain trust." Some members of this group were known to favor solutions comprehending national, though not specifically socialist, planning, usually organized through a National Economic Council with *ipso facto* legislative power. In the economic literature of the time it was not exceptional to read

statements such as: "the basic industries must be taken from the sphere of political manipulation and carried on purely as a scientific and technological enterprise."[6] A whole school of economists began to speak of the inadequacy and inaccuracy of earlier premises and "laws." In many circles, there was a confidence in expertise and pure technique, or a willingness to recur to them, never before identified in America.

Of course residual political attitudes made such a solution extremely unlikely, even if President Roosevelt had had much doctrinaire faith in it. Wisely he accepted as much efficient pragmatic control as the traffic would bear, but justified it to the nation on grounds of humanitarianism, fair play, and the moral value of employment, not in terms of a technocratic Utopia. A reading of his address introducing the National Industrial Recovery Act cannot fail to impress by its abstinence from all dogmatism and its cultivation of traditionally American themes. If we did not recognize the peculiar political development of our country, our surprise might be great at the envenomed backlash from some quarters which was to greet the President's modest emergency measures.

Even in severe emergency, macroexpertise, or the hint of it, confronts many antagonistic interests which attack its "purity" on grounds of politics, precedent, or fear of coercion. At the opposite pole from the American manufacturers and Stock Exchange, Simone Weil, from her unorthodox and deeply felt anarcho-revolutionary tradition, was writing in France:

The most significant movement [in curtailing liberty] is the technocratic movement which has, allegedly, in a short space of time covered the surface of the United States; as we know, within the boundaries of a closed national economy, it aims at the abolition of competition and markets, and an economic dictatorship sovereignly exercised by the technicians.[7]

Macroexpertise in America has foundered whenever it was possible to rationalize it as a political threat to a generally conservative order. But putting aside for the moment the position of American expertise today, we should consider why America is so sensitive on the subject. Chiefly, there seem to be two reasons. The first is that in a bountiful, complacent, and sheltered country, we have been led to place untold reliance on the operation of a system that is very purely political. Secondly, and this is the point I should like to develop, because of our youth as a nation, our traditions and habits are mainly those of the nineteenth century. Concepts peculiar to a brief segment of history tend to seem like a norm to us, whereas older nations may not be similarly affected. The nineteenth century was much more an age of deeds and acts—and of heroes and villains—than of expertise. If it was an age of crisis in the social order, it was still not the time in which that crisis was made most explicit. Americans learned in the nineteenth century to say with Carlyle: "By nature [Man] has a strength for learning, for imitating; but also a strength for acting, for knowing on his own account."[8] They continued to say it in the twentieth to a very great degree and were inclined to express skepticism or outrage when events challenged the noble axiom.

The seventeenth and eighteenth centuries had known their share of technical tinkering: it was probably a complement of the growth of centralized monarchy. Mercantilist economics, especially in France, is almost a symbol of this condition. Colbert and his school, as well as later financial innovators like John Law, exercised a degree of control over the national wealth which the nineteenth century would have found immoral and the twentieth, in the democracies, at least unnatural. In the disappearance of this system of regulation a number of factors are evident. But one which is too often overlooked is that the growth of national enterprise had outrun the possibilities of technocratic control. As one historian writes: "This partial abandonment of internal mercantilism [by the British after 1660] was no doubt largely due to the fact that the monarchy no longer had an administrative system effective enough to maintain national regulation of economic life."[9]

Today expertise seems resurgent not because technocratic talent has again caught up with the ever-accelerating spread of national activity, but rather because our crisis is so deep that, despite serious obstacles, the rational ordering of this activity seems a *sine qua non* if our precarious system is not to collapse. In many instances it is being done *à contre-coeur*. Some of our most ponderous difficulties now arise from our having, for the first time in history, it seems, to apply wide resources of macroexpertise to what looks suspiciously like a cosmopolitan situation. But we have developed no "laws" beyond the imperatives of crisis, nor perhaps can we. "As long as governments protect the learned, in theory and practice, one remains in the old regime," wrote Henri Saint-Simon. "But from the moment the learned protect governments one really begins the new regime." Pragmatic appeals to the expert may grow more and more preponderant; they do not necessarily usher in the new order.

The Sociological Vision*

If the nineteenth century was not the great age of practicing expertise, it was the great *atelier* for theories of total expertise, or what is generally called technocracy. But we must be careful to distinguish between license for technocratic direction and the more inclusive realm of sociological system-building. Basically we may say that there are two predominant strains of system-building proceeding out of nineteenth-century theory. There is, first of all, the tradition of ideal utopian constructs, like those of Comte and the Positivists, proceeding from the general belief that man can capture the secrets of nature —including his own nature—and bend them to his will, thereby achieving the just and harmonious society in which he can expect peace, stability, and the due reward for rational effort. In this school of thought the nineteenth century combines three strains: historical utopianism or the wish for a rational order, as manifested in the schemes of Plato, More, Campanella, Bacon, etc.; the distillation of the philosophy of the *Aufklärung*, whose most important premise was that man's inherent reason was capable of liberating him from disorder; and the growing observation of social inequity and class struggle following the turbulence of the French Revolution. Many of the solutions of

* I have obtained many ideas from the brilliant posthumous work of Georges Duveau, *Sociologie de l'Utopie*, Paris, 1961.

the "utopian" school tended to become attached to the rise of socialism, just as their proponents became described as socialists; but it was less a socialism of class apocalypse than one of efficiency and control with production publicly or technocratically organized.

The contrary method of system-building may be generally described as German historicism, with Hegel as its most refined exponent. In historicism the idea of Utopia loses its vigor, not because it ceases to be a goal but because men cease to build it; it is not achieved through the agency of men but under the supervision of historical will. Not surprisingly, elements of this kind of determinism periodically infect the utopian school, which is mainly French, thereby contributing to the difficulty of generalization. Marx—who, for these and other purposes, belongs to the Hegelians—postulates, as is well known, a societal perfection in which struggle dies and the state "withers away." This might be classified as a Utopia; but it actually is so marginal compared to the business that counts—class struggle, dictatorship of the proletariat—that we may be forgiven for awarding it a very humble prominence in the system of that great Protestant and prophet.

The two schools discussed seem to present the following characteristics. *Struggle* is the essence of the system proposed by the revolutionary historicists: the end-product is rather sketchy. *Organization* is the essence of the utopian system, without a great deal of attention paid to process. The latter can apparently be legislated or enforced (e.g., by Napoleon, as Saint-Simon hoped). *Expertise* is central to the vision of the utopists. Technological experts will regulate the activities of society; they will indeed be more important than customary government in this respect. *Expertise* is negligible, theoretically, in the Marxist or any other system deriving from the premises of historicism. In the case of Marxism, the mission of history is entrusted to a class that gains its pedigree from the bias of history, not from any demonstrated capability to exercise and enforce technocratic judgment.

Expertise, then, cleaves to the utopian school of systems, which probably had its most capacious and profound exponent in the person of Saint-Simon, the patron saint of technocrats. "Imagine," said Saint-Simon, "that the nation loses Monsieur, princes, cardinals, bishops, judges, and in addition, ten thousand of the richest property owners among those who live off their incomes without producing. What would the result be? This accident would certainly afflict all the French because they are good . . . but no political harm to the state would result." On the other hand, if France were to lose a fraction of this number of producers, whether of the learned or managerial kind, it "would become a body without a soul" and would need "at least a generation to repair the damage."[10]

The historical lines formulated and then advanced by Saint-Simon, which have led through Comte and Durkheim to Jean Monnet and even, in certain respects, to General De Gaulle, need no defense as a continuing tradition that retains political vitality—to say that Marx was a more influential socialist is to miss the point entirely. The aristocratic French technocrat was the first to say, with detail, that the state should be given over to the experts. In his own time, he was willing to operate

as the *soi-disant* advisor of Napoleon, perceiving that technocratic unity is most easily imposed by a conqueror, but also having that amazing insight, unavailable to Marx and the historicists, that unity is, in fact, plural and permissive. "Human conduct is intelligent and enlightened only to the degree it is directed by theory—though theory cannot be productive except on condition of its not being limited to pursuit of practical ends,"[11] comments Durkheim, interpreting his master.

Many have remarked on the Saint-Simonian lineage of aspects of European integration. But if Saint-Simon is indirectly responsible for some of our most promising successes in the West, he also carries the banner of technocracy into battle against liberal politics. There is no sense in pointing to the fact that the other side has stifled parties and parliaments already. We should instead make the distinction that the one side believes chiefly in the power of historical momentum and that the other believes in human cunning. This is surely a prime difference.

Let us look for a moment at the image of *pax perpetua* which a variety of eighteenth-century philosophers so optimistically constructed. One contention was that this could be achieved through some radical surgery on human nature; this, in economic terms, was at the basis of the Communist belief, although limited success led them to succumb to the easier solution of *imperium*.

The Western belief hovers between trust in a controlled liberal chaos and the cultivation of a dedicated technocratic elite (Saint-Simonianism) which might have both the ardor and intelligence to lead us out of our difficulties.

We elude the main issue if we speak naively of a world struggle between two types of socialism: the question of socialism as such has, frankly, been superseded. But we may be very right in questioning the axioms of control which our advancing choices impose on us.

We are indeed faced with the choice of believing either that final problems can be finally solved or that they cannot. Expertise, though by no means every expert, is committed to the idea that they can; this type of expert is constant throughout the last several hundred years of Western history—whether or not God or magic or science is invoked. A recent and highly intelligent commentator on the political avatars of modern science has had the following observation to make: "The scientist's quest for certainty and his confidence that reason and new methods can solve man's problems are reinforced by his conviction that something which is theoretically possible is also most likely to be politically possible."[12] The eternal question is posed. If this were true, would it be worth the sacrifices of traditional liberty to follow reason's dictates toward a promised land which no man has ever quite imagined, much less tasted and enjoyed?

Freedom, Power, and Expertise*

Whether we like it or not, the existence of collegial expertise in close relationship with the state raises the prob-

* I have found some useful hints in Isaiah Berlin's lecture-monograph *Two Concepts of Liberty* (Oxford, 1958), though his arguments have only an oblique bearing on the substance of these paragraphs.

lem of freedom and coercion. Few experts wish to prevail, to *become* the power—indeed their temperament and inclination are usually otherwise—but their function demands that they should wish their ideas to prevail. Perhaps it is desirable that, in the words of Saint-Simon, "the learned should protect governments" from their ignorance and vulgar errors, from their biases, from their inaccuracy and abuses of power. But it is just possible that governments will not wish to be thus protected, and it is especially likely that governments which claim, rightly or wrongly, to derive their authority from the people will look askance at this fundamental contradiction of their *raison d'être*.

But let us not confuse the model with the reality. History begets ingenious compromises which bear little resemblance to the philosophical controversies raging in its soul. Thus all regimes are, more or less, mixtures of license and coercion, chance and planning, expertise and ignorance. What counts, then, is probably not so much the results obtained as the fundamental doctrine by which an organized society sets about its business. Were a national society to commit itself to the proposition that "the learned should protect governments, and consequently the governed," the repercussions on our political value system would be tremendous. If, however, the same doctrine is introduced pragmatically, inch by inch and never far in excess of current crisis requirements for expertise, a society may learn to live with it, just as republican Rome "saw its ancient liberties stripped away" but turned into a tolerably well functioning Empire.

Our current notions of political liberty, however jealously we cling to them, are historical upstarts. Previous societies went without them and prospered, at least for a time.

No man is thereby prevented from making a value judgment about wanting liberty and wanting it more than any conceivable kind of "scientific regimentation." Deeds and opinions involving human alternatives do create history; science, still in quest of the *just city*, has not done so up to this date, unless one considers history itself a science, albeit one that can neither be proved nor disproved. We must, it seems, deal first with the question: can science make history and make it orderly, provided that human beings are persuaded or coerced to act according to the precepts of order? Is proper technocratic organization, in effect, nothing less than the general will itself and a guarantee against the worst forms of coercion?

Perhaps all this is just to play cruel tricks with the pros and cons of voluntarism. One starts with the hypothesis that man is free, or he is not. Certain consequences follow if we accept the electrifying analysis of Georg Buechner: "I find in human nature a shocking equality, in man's fate an ineluctable power granted to all and to none. The individual is nothing but spume on the wave, greatness is a simple accident, and the force of genius a puppet's dance, a laughable struggle against a brazen law."[13] If this *cri de coeur* is true, then it would seem to make rather little difference if man's activities are highly ordered and organized; in fact there may be a positive advantage in giving power to those whose intelligences are more apt to be in communication with the ineluctable pattern of human destiny.

But if man is free, at least within the spectrum that his social relations will decide, then any man could be led to construct exhaustive and confusing catalogues of legitimate freedoms. The expert re-enters the political picture in the possible role of adjudicating among conflicting freedoms. But this is a different kind of expert from the one who uses the whip of science to drive governments and peoples toward the gleaming turrets of the just city. The "liberal" expert is in fact, as Walter Lippmann has correctly perceived, the judge and not the technocrat.[14]

There is a third solution, politically much more familiar, which defines the expert's oscillation between knowledge and power. This is the notion of crisis counsel, or, as we have previously termed it, macroexpertise. In this image, the expert guides power only to the extent that crisis requires the abrogation of accepted political function. Macroexpertise implies that the expert's hold on the reins slackens as the crisis recedes, that the expert's power is at all times politically revocable, and that the expert is concerned purely with the diagnosis and cure of functional disorder and not with commanding the construction of the just society. The possible criticisms of this solution are apparent, from both sides.

On the one hand, the expert may be badgered by incessant review and interference, and rendered unable to do his job properly. On the other hand, he may covet power discreetly and devise ways for increasing his hold on it or for perpetuating his usefulness. He may become a pawn or ally of political elements themselves contending for a greater share of power. Probably, however, he will not build the just city and impose it on his fellows. The question is one of measure, and measure is an instinctual talent.

We should underscore the element of revocability, for this mechanism joins expertise squarely to the political process. There is the danger it might be used capriciously—politicians are not, after all, supreme metaphysicians—but the danger is greater in theory if the instrument is not available. Let us not ignore, however, that as crisis lengthens and new political relations become customary, revocability could become a dead letter. Since many believe that the invention of nuclear weapons has, in fact, ushered in an era of perpetual crisis, this possibility may be worth considering. In such a situation entrenched expertise might be expected to cultivate the natural belief that it was not merely a salvationary convenience but a real improvement over what had gone before. Thus "Utopia" might be reached without even having first been spied in the distance and admired.

The practical question is one of priorities and personnel. Societies must always decide between their principles and their security. Today's expert, from all observation, stands ready to help and not to take power. The political resistances against even the modest exercise of his talent are tremendous, especially in the Anglo-Saxon countries. In fact, he normally acts in such a way as to demonstrate his political humility, as before committees of the Congress. Furthermore, he is often at odds with his own peers over scholarly and political issues, and he does not especially cherish his capacity for collective action. Who can fear him?

Only the long-range history of our world's crises, the changing sociology of the expert group, and the acts and abnegations of statesmen can ultimately decide whether the learned will one day protect governments and whether or not this will be, in Simone Weil's words, "oppression exercised in the name of function."

In Place of a Conclusion

Today the position of the expert is vastly enhanced in his function of macroexpertise because nations have been deeply involved in vast and periodic crises. But the Saint-Simonian dream of the "administration of things" has not been fulfilled. The expert is neither the Party in the Soviet Union, nor is he the government apparatus in the democracies. He may, however, be moving increasingly into these spheres, by a mode of adaptation that is not altogether clear, as crisis succeeds to crisis and generates an atmosphere of perpetual emergency.

In three areas his expanded role particularly stands out. The first of these regards the critical problem of bringing the ex-colonial nations into the world community and animating their economies. This process is still too young to be much more than speculative, but the penchant of the new nations for "arriving in a hurry" via the planned society and the customary requirement of a national plan as the prerequisite for economic aid are straws in the wind.

The second area where the expert is especially involved—with the United

States leading the way—is military strategy and corollary notions such as arms control. Military planning has become an arcane subject increasingly detached from the political process—as such slogans as "push-button war" and "command and control system" eloquently indicate. Few pretend that this hypothetical disparity between action and consultation is going to diminish or that the role of the expert will be any less significant in establishing doctrine. The American people place great faith in the delegation of political power where the matter of security is concerned—a willingness they certainly do not show in the economic field. But the question must be raised: is there a point beyond which the learned will indeed be protecting the government? The concept of disarmament with heavy doses of control and inspection presents some analogous problems and prospects for the expert.

Thirdly, amid some juvenile disorders and national recriminations, an entity called "Europe" seems to be emerging. There is an undercurrent of controversy as to whether it shall be a "planned Europe," as emphasis on function might indicate, and to what degree it will inevitably have to be planned. Brussels has become the city of experts, perhaps even more so than Washington. "Europeans" are debating these questions; and many believe that it is here that Saint-Simon has the greatest chance of achieving success. The pure political tradition shared by ourselves and some of the Commonwealth nations does not act as so great a counterforce on the Continent, though diplomacy may, and the polytechnician—"the man who knows every-thing, and nothing else"—is held in higher esteem. One Belgian analyst has written: "The act of decision itself should remain completely the prerogative of the politician, himself the technician of that *ars artium*, the government of men."[15] Others are far from agreeing. But the quality that perhaps strikes one most forcibly about the technicians of the "new Europe" is that they are workers first and visionaries only second. Despite the vast temptation to construct their edifice on notions of the *just city* and to spin a sociological myth thereon, it is precisely they who are most aware of practical limitations and the concurrent demands of policy and action outside of Europe. This realism could not be a more hopeful sign.

What, finally, of the expert in power: that goal of the utopians, bugbear of the liberals, and conceivable recourse of the zealous and discouraged alike? We have already hinted that the traditions of this civilization militate heavily against such a solution, short of the incidence of all-out catastrophe, in which case the experts are as apt to be executed as summoned. But there seems also to be a radical discontinuity between the application of knowledge and the exercise of power that cannot be totally explained away as administrative imperfection. Power relies upon an unbalanced formula of knowledge in which expertise is never fundamentally at home. Its abuses may be attributed to this imbalance; but so, then, must be its successes. One may doubt that any crisis, even the ultimate one, will be construed as grave enough to consecrate the millennial reign of the expert in our society.

REFERENCES

1. Henry Adams, *The Education of Henry Adams* (New York: Modern Library, Inc., 1931), p. 45.
2. "The Case for Ending Nuclear Tests," *The Atlantic* (August 1960), p. 48.
3. Quoted from C. R. Weld, *History of the Royal Society* (Cambridge, England, 1848), I, p. 146.
4. See, for example, Percy W. Bridgman, "Scientists and Society," *Bulletin of the Atomic Scientists* (March 1948), pp. 69–72.
5. John Locke, *Essay Concerning Human Understanding* (London: Ward, Lock, n.d.), I, i, 6, p. 4.
6. Harold Rugg, *The Great Technology: Social Chaos and the Public Mind* (New York: The John Day Company, Inc., 1933), p. 175.
7. The essay "Perspectives: Allons-nous vers la révolution prolétarienne?" was first published in *Révolution prolétarienne*, No. 158 (25 August 1933). It is contained in the collection *Oppression et liberté* (Paris: Gallimard, 1955). Citation from p. 20.
8. Thomas Carlyle, "Characteristics," in *Critical and Miscellaneous Essays*, 5 Vols. (New York: Charles Scribner's Sons, 1899), III, pp. 37–38.
9. Charles Woolsey Cole, *French Mercantilism, 1683–1700* (New York: Columbia University Press, 1943), p. 283.
10. Henri, Comte de Saint-Simon, "Organisateur," in *Oeuvres*, IV, pp. 22–23, in *Oeuvres de Saint-Simon et d'Enfantin*, 47 Vols. (Paris: E. Dentu, 1865–1878).
11. Emile Durkheim, *Socialism and Saint-Simon* (*Le socialisme*), editor A. W. Gouldner (Yellow Springs, Ohio: The Antioch Press, 1958), p. 144.
12. Robert Gilpin, *American Science and Nuclear Weapons Policy* (Princeton: Princeton University Press, 1962), p. 30.
13. Quoted from Georges Duveau, *Sociologie de l'Utopie* (Paris: Presses Universitaires Françaises, 1961), p. 112.
14. Walter Lippmann, *The Good Society* (New York: Universal paperback, n.d.).
15. Léo Moulin, "Le Sociologue devant l'Intégration Européenne," in *Sciences humaines et Intégration Européenne* (Leyden: Sythoff, 1961), p. 113.

1.2 PLANNED CHANGE IN AMERICA

Kenneth D. Benne
Warren G. Bennis
Robert Chin

Policy makers, social scientists and social practitioners in America are not

Reprinted from the first edition of *The Planning of Change: Readings in the Applied Behavioral Sciences*, edited by Warren G. Bennis, Kenneth D. Benne, and Robert Chin. Copyright © 1961 by Holt, Rinehart and Winston, Inc.

more agreed about the proper direction and management of social change in 1960 than they were at the turn of the present century. But the focus of the controversy has shifted. In 1900—in America at least—the issue was typically stated in sweeping ideological terms. Should or should not men seek, through deliberate and collaborative forethought in the present, to mold the shape of their collective future? Or should confidence rather be placed in a principle of automatic adjustment, operating within the processes of history to reequilibrate, without human forethought yet in the interest of progress and human welfare, the inescapable human upsets and dislocations of changing society?

This issue raised a corollary issue concerning the proper relations of the emerging social sciences of the time, and of social scientists, to the guidance and management of practical affairs. In general, the "planners" saw an important place for social science in informing policies and in rendering social practice more intelligent and reality-oriented. Proponents of "automatic adjustment" tended to relegate social scientists to an observer role and to deny them participation or leadership in influencing the direction or the form of practical affairs. This conception of "nonintervening" social science fitted the main-line traditions of the natural sciences and of the older social studies —history, economics, and political theory. This view of the proper relationships between social science and social action was further reenforced by aspirations of the younger and more behavior-oriented sciences—psychology and sociology—to achieve and maintain their autonomy and "purity" within the academic world in which they were parvenus. The issue concerning "science" and "practice" has been raised anew as "applied social science" has been encouraged and supported by many policy-makers and social practitioners, and actively promoted by some

social scientists. But intervening events have given to it, as to the more general issue of "planning," a new form and focus within discussions among students of human affairs.

Lester F. Ward was one of the earliest social scientists in America to proclaim that modern men must extend scientific approaches into the planning of changes in the patterns of their behaviors and relationships. He was well aware that men were already utilizing their accumulating collective and scientific intelligence deliberately to induce changes in their nonhuman environment. And he saw a major role for the emerging sciences of man in extending a similar planning approach into the management of human affairs.

Man's destiny is in his own hands. Any law that he can comprehend he can control. He cannot increase or diminish the powers of nature, but he can direct them . . . His power over nature is unlimited. He can make it his servant and appropriate to his own use all the mighty forces of the universe . . . Human institutions are not exempt from this all-pervading spirit of improvement. They, too, are artificial, conceived in the ingenious brain and wrought with mental skill born of inventive genius. The passion for their improvement is of a piece with the impulse to improve the plow or the steam engine . . . Intelligence, heretofore a growth, is destined to become a manufacture . . . The origination and distribution of knowledge can no longer be left to chance or to nature. They are to be systematized and erected into true arts.[1]

Ward's proclamation seemed foolish boasting, if not downright sacrilege, to

[1] Quoted in Henry Commager, *The American Mind*, New Haven, Conn.: Yale University Press, 1950, pp. 208, 210, 213–214.

many among his contemporaries. William Graham Sumner was one of the leaders in sociology who emphasized both the folly and sacrilege of prophecies like Ward's.

If we can acquire a science of society based on observation of phenomena and study of forces, we may hope to gain some ground slowly toward the elimination of old errors and the re-establishment of a sound and natural social order. Whatever we gain that way will be by growth, never in the world by any reconstruction of society on the plan of some enthusiastic social architect. The latter is only repeating the old error over again, and postponing all our chances of real improvement. Society needs first of all to be free from these meddlers— that is, to be let alone. Here we are, then, once more back at the old doctrine *laissez faire*. Let us translate it into blunt English, and it will read—Mind your own business. It is nothing but the doctrine of liberty. Let every man be happy in his own way.[2]

It may be fortunate or unfortunate that American controversies today over the direction and management of social change seldom take the form of sweeping societal prescriptions and counter-prescriptions or ideological debates—a form which Ward and Sumner, along with their contemporaries, gave to them. In any event, the form of the controversies has shifted. In large measure subsequent events have foreclosed the factual basis for Sumner's argument. *Laissez faire* has been widely abandoned in practice as a principle of social management, whatever ghostly existence it yet enjoys in political platforms and pronunciamentos. Human interventions designed to shape and modify the institutionalized behaviors

of men are now familiar features of our social landscape. "Helping professions" have proliferated since Ward's and Sumner's day. Professions of industrial and public management have taken shape. The reasons for being of all of these is deliberately to induce and coach changes in the future behaviors and relationships of their various "client" populations. This is most apparent in "new" professions such as psychiatry, social work, nursing, counseling, management, and consultation in its manifold forms. But older professions too, such as medicine, law, teaching, and the clergy, have been pressed increasingly to become agencies of social change rather than of social conservation. Resistances to assuming the new role have, of course, developed along with the situational pressures to enact it.

Behavioral scientists, neo-Sumnerians among others, have been drawn, with varying degrees of eagerness and resistance, into activities of "changing," such as consultation and applied research. "Helping professionals," "managers," and "policy-makers" in various fields of practice increasingly seek and employ the services of behavioral scientists to anticipate more accurately the consequences of prospective social changes and to inform more validly the processes of planning designed to control these consequences.

We are widely seeking to plan social changes in the sixties. And both the products and the methods of social research are being more and more widely utilized in the processes of such planning. Sumner's ideological advice has been widely rejected in practice.

But it is equally true that Ward's millennial hope seems far—indeed very

[2] Quoted, *op. cit.*, pp. 201–202.

far—from realization today. Attempts to apply social knowledge in planning and controlling changes tend to be fragmented by the division of contemporary agents of change into specialized and largely noncommunicating professions. These attempts are thwarted too by noncommunication and noncollaboration among policy-makers and action planners in the various institutional settings where planning has become familiar practice—industry, government, welfare, health, and education. Advocates and students of planned change have become more cautious in their claims, less millennial in their hopes than Ward tended to be. The modal question has shifted from "should we seek to plan change?" to "how plan particular changes in particular settings and situations?" Where the wider societal view has not been entirely lost the question is raised— "how interrelate the various forms which the planning of change has taken in conventionally isolated but actually interdependent settings of social action and practice?"

Men today have thus widely come to believe that they have no actual choice as to whether somebody will seek to plan continuing changes in the patterns of their lives. Men must try to plan their changing futures and this necessity is seen to be determined by cultural conditions, not primarily by the ideology men happen to hold. "Democratic," "communistic," and "fascist" peoples must alike try to plan social changes. This helps to account for the shift of many questions about planned change from an "ideological" to a "technical" form. This does not mean, as some who would reduce all questions of planning to purely tech-

nical form might believe, that questions about the values which should guide planners can or should disappear from discussions about planning or from the processes of planning. It means rather that these questions too have taken new forms.

Both Ward and Sumner worked within a framework of common assumptions about the actuality and desirability, if not the inevitability, of Progress. Their ideological differences centered on varying ways of achieving the Progress which both generally assumed to be, in some way, America's destiny, and by patriotic extension, human destiny as well. (The pessimism of Sumner grown old came more from despair over the course of events about him than from relinquishment of this ideal.) Differing means of achieving progress, of course, if carefully analyzed, meant different meanings of Progress as well. But the values of "rationality," "freedom," and the "extension through science of human control over the natural environment" were, in general, values acceptable to "planners" and "anti-planners" as well. Both sought to settle value issues by an appeal to living traditions of "liberalism" and "democracy," traditions not clearly distinguished one from the other.

Today this living tradition can no longer be assumed. Intellectually and practically, the core values of "liberalism" and "democracy" have been challenged and eroded, both in America and outside it. The actuality as well as the desirability of Progress, as defined and revered within this tradition, have been questioned and challenged. "Liberal" theology has been attacked by religious neoorthodoxies of various types. "Liberal" politics has been denounced as unrealistic by nationalists and communists alike. "Progressive" education is inveighed against by conservative critics as negligent of "fundamentals" in knowledge and morality. Neoconservative attacks against "liberalism" in its various forms are thus alike in seeking a reaffirmation of "sound" traditions. ("Liberalism" is denounced just as roundly by Marxist "planners," though out of a different set of assumptions about man and society.) But different neoconservatives appeal to different "sound" traditions and betray in the very variety of the "authoritative" traditions to which they appeal the fragmentation and disruption of the community of values that once characterized American life. It is this fragmentation of traditional bases of community that forces the value-dilemmas of American planners

of the sixties to a new and deeper level as compared with the planners of 1900.

As planners of change face conflicts about the proper direction of change among various segments of our population today, they encounter of necessity the question of the basis or bases upon which one value-orientation can be judged better than another. Indeed, they must face the deeper question, which various philosophers and depth psychologists have raised widely and vigorously in our time—can value and ideological differences be settled rationally at all? Is there an irreducible surd of irrationality that dogs all of the choices of men? More specifically, do "scientific methods" extend to the evaluation of the competing ends of human action or only to the evaluation of alternative means for reaching ends chosen on arbitrary and rationally "inarbitrable" grounds?

1.3   GENERAL STRATEGIES FOR EFFECTING CHANGES IN HUMAN SYSTEMS

Robert Chin
Kenneth D. Benne

Discussing general strategies and procedures for effecting change requires that we set limits to the discussion. For, under a liberal interpretation of the title, we would need to deal with

much of the literature of contemporary social and behavioral science, basic and applied.

Therefore, we shall limit our discussion to those changes which are planned

Prepared especially for this volume and used by permission. This paper is adapted from a paper by Robert Chin prepared for "Designing Education for the Future—An Eight State Project" (Denver, Colo., 1967). Kenneth D. Benne joined in revising and expanding sections of the original paper for inclusion in this volume. In the process of revision, what is in

several respects a new paper emerged. The original focus on changing in education has been maintained. Historical roots of ideas and strategies have been explored. The first person style of the original has also been maintained. Citations have been modified to include articles contained in this volume, along with other references.

changes—in which attempts to bring about change are conscious, deliberate, and intended, at least on the part of one or more agents related to the change attempt. We shall also attempt to categorize strategies and procedures which have a few important elements in common but which, in fact, differ widely in other respects. And we shall neglect many of these differences. In addition, we shall look beyond the description of procedures in common sense terms and seek some genotypic characteristics of change strategies. We shall seek the roots of the main strategies discussed, including their variants, in ideas and idea systems prominent in contemporary and recent social and psychological thought.

One element in all approaches to planned change is the conscious utilization and application of knowledge as an instrument or tool for modifying patterns and institutions of practice. The knowledge or related technology to be applied may be knowledge of the nonhuman environment in which practice goes on or of some knowledge-based "thing technology" for controlling one or another feature of the practice environment. In educational practice, for example, technologies of communication and calculation, based upon new knowledge of electronics—audio-visual devices, television, computers, teaching machines—loom large among the knowledges and technologies that promise greater efficiency and economy in handling various practices in formal education. As attempts are made to introduce these new thing technologies into school situations, the change problem shifts to the human problems of dealing with the resistances, anxieties, threats to morale, con-

flicts, disrupted interpersonal communications, and so on, which prospective changes in patterns of practice evoke in the people affected by the change. So the change agent, even though focally and initially concerned with modifications in the thing technology of education, finds himself in need of more adequate knowledge of human behavior, individual and social, and in need of developed "people technologies," based on behavioral knowledge, for dealing effectively with the human aspects of deliberate change.

The knowledge which suggests improvements in educational practice may, on the other hand, be behavioral knowledge in the first instance—knowledge about participative learning, about attitude change, about family disruption in inner-city communities, about the cognitive and skill requirements of new careers, and so forth. Such knowledge may suggest changes in school grouping, in the relations between teachers and students, in the relations of teachers and principals to parents, and in counseling practices. Here change agents, initially focused on application of behavioral knowledge and the improvement of people technologies in school settings, must face the problems of using people technologies in planning, installing, and evaluating such changes in educational practice. The new people technologies must be experienced, understood, and accepted by teachers and administrators before they can be used effectively with students.

This line of reasoning suggests that, whether the focus of planned change is in the introduction of more effective thing technologies or people technologies into institutionalized practice, processes of introducing such changes must be based on behavioral knowledge of change and must utilize people technologies based on such knowledge.

A. Types of Strategies for Changing

Our further analysis is based on three types or groups of strategies. The first of these, and probably the most frequently employed by men of knowledge in America and Western Europe, are those we call empirical-rational strategies. One fundamental assumption underlying these strategies is that men are rational. Another assumption is that men will follow their rational self-interest once this is revealed to them. A change is proposed by some person or group which knows of a situation that is desirable, effective, and in line with the self-interest of the person, group, organization, or community which will be affected by the change. Because the person (or group) is assumed to be rational and moved by self-interest, it is assumed that he (or they) will adopt the proposed change if it can be rationally justified and if it can be shown by the proposer(s) that he (or they) will gain by the change.

A second group of strategies we call normative-re-educative. These strategies build upon assumptions about human motivation different from those underlying the first. The rationality and intelligence of men are not denied. Patterns of action and practice are supported by sociocultural norms and by commitments on the part of individuals to these norms. Sociocultural norms are supported by the attitude and value systems of individuals—normative outlooks which undergird their commitments. Change in a pattern of practice

or action, according to this view, will occur only as the persons involved are brought to change their normative orientations to old patterns and develop commitments to new ones. And changes in normative orientations involve changes in attitudes, values, skills, and significant relationships, not just changes in knowledge, information, or intellectual rationales for action and practice.

The third group of strategies is based on the application of power in some form, political or otherwise. The influence process involved is basically that of compliance of those with less power to the plans, directions, and leadership of those with greater power. Often the power to be applied is legitimate power or authority. Thus the strategy may involve getting the authority of law or administrative policy behind the change to be effected. Some power strategies may appeal less to the use of authoritative power to effect change than to the massing of coercive power, legitimate or not, in support of the change sought.[1]

[1] Throughout our discussion of strategies and procedures, we will not differentiate these according to the size of the target of change. We assume that there are similarities in processes of changing, whether the change affects an individual, a small group, an organization, a community, or a culture. In addition, we are not attending to differences among the aspects of a system, let us say an educational system, which is being changed—curriculum, audio-visual methods, team teaching, pupil grouping, and so on. Furthermore, because many changes in communities or organizations start with an individual or some small membership group, our general focus will be upon those strategies which lead to and involve individual changes.

We will sidestep the issue of defining

1. EMPIRICAL-RATIONAL STRATEGIES

A variety of specific strategies are included in what we are calling the empirical-rational approach to effecting change. As we have already pointed out, the rationale underlying most of these is an assumption that men are guided by reason and that they will utilize some rational calculus of self-interest in determining needed changes in behavior.

It is difficult to point to any one person whose ideas express or articulate the orientation underlying commitment to empirical-rational strategies of changing. In Western Europe and America, this orientation might be better identified with the general social orientation of the Enlightenment and of classical liberalism than with the ideas of any one man. On this view, the chief foes to human rationality and to change or progress based on rationality were ignorance and superstition. Scientific investigation and research represented the chief ways of extending knowledge and reducing the limitations of ignorance. A corollary of this optimistic view of man and his future was an advocacy of education as a way of disseminating scientific knowledge and of freeing men and women from the shackles of superstition. Although elitist notions played a part in the thinking of many classic liberals, the increasing trend during the nineteenth century was toward the universalization of educational opportunity. The common and universal school, open to all men and women, was the principal instrument by which knowledge would replace ignorance and superstition in the minds of people and become a principal agent in the spread of reason, knowledge, and knowledge-based action and practice (progress) in human society. In American experience, Jefferson may be taken as a principal, early advocate of research and of education as agencies of human progress. And Horace Mann may be taken as the prophet of progress through the institutionalization of universal educational opportunity through the common school.[2]

a. Basic Research and Dissemination of Knowledge through General Education

The strategy of encouraging basic knowledge building and of depending on general education to diffuse the results of research into the minds and thinking of men and women is still by far the most appealing strategy of change to most academic men of knowledge and to large segments of the American population as well. Basic researchers are quite likely to appeal for

---

change in this paper. As further conceptual work progresses in the study of planned change, we shall eventually have to examine how different definitions of change relate to strategies and procedures for effecting change. But we are not dealing with these issues here.

[2] We have indicated the main roots of ideas and idea systems underlying the principal strategies of changing and their sub-variants on a chart which appears as figure 1 at the end of this essay. It may be useful in seeing both the distinctions and the relationships between various strategies of changing in time perspective. We have emphasized developments of the past twenty-five years more than earlier developments. This makes for historical foreshortening. We hope this is a pardonable distortion, considering our present limited purpose.

time for further research when confronted by some unmet need. And many people find this appeal convincing. Both of these facts are well illustrated by difficulties with diseases for which no adequate control measures or cures are available—poliomyelitis, for example. Medical researchers asked for more time and funds for research and people responded with funds for research, both through voluntary channels and through legislative appropriations. And the control measures were forthcoming. The educational problem then shifted to inducing people to comply with immunization procedures based on research findings.

This appeal to a combination of research and education of the public has worked in many areas of new knowledge-based thing technologies where almost universal readiness for accepting the new technology was already present in the population. Where such readiness is not available, as in the case of fluoridation technologies in the management of dental caries, general strategy of basic research plus educational (informational) campaigns to spread knowledge of the findings do not work well. The cases of its inadequacy as a single strategy of change have multiplied, especially where "engineering" problems, which involve a divided and conflicting public or deep resistances due to the threat by the new technology to traditional attitudes and values, have thwarted its effectiveness. But these cases, while they demand attention to other strategies of changing, do not disprove the importance of basic research and of general educational opportunity as elements in a progressive and self-renewing society.

We have noted that the strategy under discussion has worked best in grounding and diffusing generally acceptable thing technologies in society. Some have argued that the main reason the strategy has not worked in the area of people technologies is a relative lack of basic research on people and their behavior, relationships, and institutions and a corresponding lack of emphasis upon social and psychological knowledges in school and college curricula. It would follow in this view that increased basic research on human affairs and relationships and increased efforts to diffuse the results of such research through public education are the ways of making the general strategy work better. Auguste Comte with his emphasis on positivistic sociology in the reorganization of society and Lester F. Ward in America may be taken as late nineteenth century representatives of this view. And the spirit of Comte and Ward is by no means dead in American academia or in influential segments of the American public.

b. Personnel Selection and Replacement

Difficulties in getting knowledge effectively into practice may be seen as lying primarily in the lack of fitness of persons occupying positions with job responsibilities for improving practice. The argument goes that we need the right person in the right position, if knowledge is to be optimally applied and if rationally based changes are to become the expectation in organizational and societal affairs. This fits with the liberal reformers' frequently voiced and enacted plea to drive the unfit from office and to replace them with those more fit as a condition of social progress.

That reformers' programs have so often failed has sobered but by no means destroyed the zeal of those who regard personnel selection, assessment, and replacement as a major key to program improvement in education or in other enterprises as well. This strategy was given a scientific boost by the development of scientific testing of potentialities and aptitudes. We will use Binet as a prototype of psychological testing and Moreno as a prototype in sociometric testing, while recognizing the extensive differentiation and elaboration which have occurred in psychometrics and sociometrics since their original work. We recognize too the elaborated modes of practice in personnel work which have been built around psychometric and sociometric tools and techniques. We do not discount their limited value as actual and potential tools for change, while making two observations on the way they have often been used. First, they have been used more often in the interest of system maintenance rather than of system change, since the job descriptions personnel workers seek to fill are defined in terms of system requirements as established. Second, by focusing on the role occupant as the principal barrier to improvement, personnel selection and replacement strategies have tended not to reveal the social and cultural system difficulties which may be in need of change if improvement is to take place.

c. Systems Analysts as Staff and Consultants

Personnel workers in government, industry, and education have /typically worked in staff relations to line management, reflecting the bureaucratic, line-staff form of organization which has flourished in the large-scale organization of effort and enterprise in the twentieth century. And other expert workers—systems analysts—more attuned to system difficulties than to the adequacies or inadequacies of persons as role occupants within the system, have found their way into the staff resources of line management in contemporary organizations.

There is no reason why the expert resources of personnel workers and systems analysts might not be used in nonbureaucratic organizations or in processes of moving bureaucratic organizations toward nonbureaucratic forms. But the fact remains that their use has been shaped, for the most part, in the image of the scientific management of bureaucratically organized enterprises. So we have placed the systems analysts in our chart under Frederick Taylor, the father of scientific management in America.

The line management of an enterprise seeks to organize human and technical effort toward the most efficient service of organizational goals. And these goals are defined in terms of the production of some mandated product, whether a tangible product or a less tangible good or service. In pursuing this quest for efficiency, line management employs experts in the analysis of sociotechnical systems and in the laying out of more efficient systems. The experts employed may work as external consultants or as an internal staff unit. Behavioral scientists have recently found their way, along with mathematicians and engineers, into systems analysis work.

It is interesting to note that the role of these experts is becoming embroiled in discussions of whether or not behavioral science research should be used to sensitize administrators to new organizational possibilities, to new goals, or primarily to implement efficient operation within perspectives and goals as currently defined. Jean Hills has raised the question of whether behavioral science when applied to organizational problems tends to perpetuate established ideology and system relations because of blinders imposed by their being "problem centered" and by their limited definition of what is "a problem."[3]

We see an emerging strategy, in the use of behavioral scientists as systems analysts and engineers, toward viewing the problem of organizational change and changing as a wide-angled problem, one in which all the input and output features and components of a large-scale system are considered. It is foreseeable that with the use of high-speed and high-capacity computers, and with the growth of substantial theories and hypotheses about how parts of an educational system operate, we shall find more and more applications for systems analysis and operations research in programs of educational change. In fact, it is precisely the quasi-mathematical character of these modes of research that will make possible the rational analysis of qualitatively different aspects of educational work and will bring them into the range of rational planning—masses of students, massive problems of poverty and educational and cultural deprivation, and so on. We see no necessary incompatibility between an ideology which emphasizes the individuality of the student and the use of systems analysis and computers in strategizing the problems of the total system. The actual incompatibilities may lie in the limited uses to which existing organizers and administrators of educational efforts put these technical resources.

*d. Applied Research and
Linkage Systems for
Diffusion of Research Results*

The American development of applied research and of a planned system for linking applied researchers with professional practitioners and both of these with centers for basic research and with organized consumers of applied research has been strongly influenced by two distinctive American inventions—the land-grant university and the agricultural extension system. We, therefore, have put the name of Justin Morrill, author of the land-grant college act and of the act which established the cooperative agricultural extension system, on our chart. The land-grant colleges or universities were dedicated to doing applied research in the service of agriculture and the mechanic arts. These colleges and universities developed research programs in basic sciences as well and experimental stations for the development and refinement of knowledge-based technologies for use in engineering and agriculture. As the extension services developed, county agents—practitioners—were attached to the state land-grant college or university that received financial support from both state and federal governments. The county agent and his staff developed local organizations of adult farm men and women and of farm youth

[3] Jean Hills, "Social Science, Ideology and the Purposes of Educational Administration," *Education Administration Quarterly* I (Autumn 1965), 23–40.

to provide both a channel toward informing consumers concerning new and better agricultural practices and toward getting awareness of unmet consumer needs and unsolved problems back to centers of knowledge and research. Garth Jones has made one of the more comprehensive studies of the strategies of changing involved in large-scale demonstration.[4]

All applied research has not occurred within a planned system for knowledge discovery, development, and utilization like the one briefly described above. The system has worked better in developing and diffusing thing technologies than in developing and diffusing people technologies, though the development of rural sociology and of agricultural economics shows that extension workers were by no means unaware of the behavioral dimensions of change problems. But the large-scale demonstration, through the land-grant university cooperative extension service, of the stupendous changes which can result from a planned approach to knowledge discovery, development, diffusion, and utilization is a part of the consciousness of all Americans concerned with planned change.[5]

1) Applied research and development is an honored part of the tradition of engineering approaches to problem identification and solution. The pioneering work of E. L. Thorndike in applied research in education should be noted on our chart. The processes and slow tempo of diffusion and utilization of research findings and inventions in public education is well illustrated in studies by Paul Mort and his students.[6] More recently, applied research, in its product development aspect, has been utilized in a massive way to contribute curriculum materials and designs for science instruction (as well as in other subjects). When we assess this situation to find reasons why such researches have not been more effective in producing changes in instruction, the answers seem to lie both in the plans of the studies which produced the materials and designs and in the potential users of the findings. Adequate linkage between consumers and researchers was frequently not established. Planned and evaluated demonstrations and experimentations connected with the use of materials were frequently slighted. And training of consumer teachers to use the new materials adaptively and creatively was frequently missing.

Such observations have led to a fresh spurt of interest in evaluation research addressed to educational programs. The fear persists that this too may lead to disappointment if it is not focused for two-way communication between researchers and teachers and if it does not involve collaboratively the ultimate consumers of the results of such re-

---

[4] Garth Jones, "Planned Organizational Change, a Set of Working Documents," Center for Research in Public Organization, School of Public Administration (Los Angeles: University of Southern California, 1964).

[5] For a review, see Ronald G. Havelock and Kenneth D. Benne, "An Exploratory Study of Knowledge Utilization," in this volume, Chap. 3, p. 124.

[6] Paul R. Mort and Donald R. Ross, *Principles of School Administration* (New York: McGraw-Hill, Inc., 1957). Paul R. Mort and Francis G. Cornell, *American Schools in Transition: How our Schools Adapt their Practices to Changing Needs* (New York: Bureau of Publications, Teachers College, Columbia University Press, 1941).

search—the students. Evaluation researches conducted in the spirit of justifying a program developed by expert applied researchers will not help to guide teachers and students in their quest for improved practices of teaching and learning, if the concerns of the latter have not been taken centrally into account in the evaluation process.[7]

2) Recently, attempts have been made to link applied research activities in education with basic researchers on the one hand and with persons in action and practice settings on the other through some system of interlocking roles similar to those suggested in the description of the land grant–extension systems in agriculture or in other fields where applied and development researches have flourished.

The linking of research-development efforts with diffusion-innovation efforts has been gaining headway in the field of education with the emergence of federally supported Research and Development Centers based in universities, Regional Laboratories connected with state departments of education, colleges and universities in a geographic area, and with various consortia and institutes confronting problems of educational change and changing. The strategy of change here usually includes a well-researched innovation which seems feasible to install in practice settings. Attention is directed to the question of whether or not the innovation will bring about a desired result, and with what it can accomplish, if given a trial in one or more practice settings.

The questions of *how* to get a fair trial and *how* to install an innovation in an already going and crowded school system are ordinarily not built centrally into the strategy. The rationalistic assumption usually precludes research attention to these questions. For, if the invention can be rationally shown to have achieved desirable results in some situations, it is assumed that people in other situations will adopt it once they know these results and the rationale behind them. The neglect of the above questions has led to a wastage of much applied research effort in the past.

Attention has been given recently to the roles, communication mechanisms, and processes necessary for innovation and diffusion of improved educational practices.[8] Clark and Guba have formulated very specific processes related to and necessary for change in educational practice following upon research. For them, the necessary processes are: *development*, including invention and design; *diffusion*, including dissemination and demonstration; *adoption*, includ-

---

[7] Robert Chin, "Research Approaches to the Problem of Civic Training," in F. Patterson (ed.), *The Adolescent Citizen* (New York: The Free Press, 1960).

[8] Matthew B. Miles, *Some Propositions in Research Utilization in Education* (March 1965), in press. Kenneth Wiles, unpublished paper for seminar on Strategies for Curriculum Change (Columbus, Ohio, Ohio State University). Charles Jung and Ronald Lippitt, "Utilization of Scientific Knowledge for Change in Education," in *Concepts for Social Change* (Washington, D.C.: National Educational Association, National Training Laboratories, 1967). Ronald G. Havelock and Kenneth D. Benne, "An Exploratory Study of Knowledge Utilization," in this volume, Chap. 3, p. 124. David Clark and Egon Guba, "An Examination of Potential Change Roles in Education," seminar on Innovation in Planning School Curricula (Columbus, Ohio: Ohio State University, 1965).

ing trial, installation, and institutionalization. Clark's earnest conviction is summed up in this statement: "In a sense, the educational research community will be the educational community, and the route to educational progress will self-evidently be research and development."[9]

The approach of Havelock and Benne is concerned with the intersystem relationships between basic researchers, applied researchers, practitioners, and consumers in an evolved and evolving organization for knowledge utilization. They are concerned especially with the communication difficulties and role conflicts that occur at points of intersystem exchange. These conflicts are important because they illuminate the normative issues at stake between basic researchers and applied researchers, between applied researchers and practitioners (teachers and administrators), between practitioners and consumers (students). The lines of strategy suggested by their analysis for solving role conflicts and communication difficulties call for transactional and collaborative exchanges across the lines of varied organized interests and orientations within the process of utilization. This brings their analysis into the range of normative-re-educative strategies to be discussed later.

The concepts from the behavioral sciences upon which these strategies of diffusion rest come mainly from two traditions. The first is from studies of

the diffusion of traits of culture from one cultural system to another, initiated by the American anthropologist, Franz Boas. This type of study has been carried on by Rogers in his work on innovation and diffusion of innovations in contemporary culture and is reflected in a number of recent writers such as Katz and Carlson.[10] The second scientific tradition is in studies of influence in mass communication associated with Carl Hovland and his students.[11] Both traditions have assumed a *relatively passive recipient of input* in diffusion situations. And actions within the process of diffusion are interpreted from the standpoint of an observer of the process. Bauer has pointed out that scientific studies have exaggerated the effectiveness of mass persuasion since they have compared the total number in the audience to the communications with the much smaller proportion of the audience persuaded by the communication.[12] A clearer view of processes of diffusion must include the actions of

[10] Elihu Katz, "The Social Itinerary of Technical Change: Two Studies on the Diffusion of Innovation," in this volume, Chap. 5, p. 230. Richard Carlson, "Some Needed Research on the Diffusion of Innovations," paper at the Washington Conference on Educational Change (Columbus, Ohio: Ohio State University). Everett Rogers, "What are Innovators Like?" in *Change Processes in the Public Schools*, Center for the Advanced Study of Educational Administration (Eugene, Oregon: University of Oregon, 1965). Everett Rogers, *Diffusion of Innovations* (New York: The Free Press, 1962).

[11] Carl Hovland, Irving Janis, and Harold Kelley, *Communication and Persuasion* (New Haven: Yale University Press, 1953).

[12] Raymond Bauer, "The Obstinate Audience: The Influence Process from the Point of View of Social Communication," in this volume, Chap. 9, p. 507.

[9] David Clark, "Educational Research and Development: The Next Decade," in *Implications for Education of Prospective Changes in Society*, a publication of "Designing Education for the Future—an Eight State Project" (Denver, Colo., 1967).

the receiver as well as those of the transmitter in the transactional events which are the units of diffusion process. And strategies for making diffusion processes more effective must be transactional and collaborative by design.

e. Utopian Thinking as a Strategy of Changing

It may seem strange to include the projection of utopias as a rational-empirical strategy of changing. Yet inventing and designing the shape of the future by extrapolating what we know of in the present is to envision a direction for planning and action in the present. If the image of a potential future is convincing and rationally persuasive to men in the present, the image may become part of the dynamics and motivation of present action. The liberal tradition is not devoid of its utopias. When we think of utopias quickened by an effort to extrapolate from the sciences of man to a future vision of society, the utopia of B. F. Skinner comes to mind.[13] The title of the Eight State Project, "Designing Education for the Future" for which this paper was prepared, reveals a utopian intent and aspiration and illustrates an attempt to employ utopian thinking for practical purposes.[14]

Yet it may be somewhat disheartening to others as it is to us to note the absence of rousing and beckoning normative statements of what both can and ought to be in man's future in most current liberal-democratic utopias,

whether these be based on psychological, sociological, political, or philosophical findings and assumptions. The absence of utopias in current society, in this sense, and in the sense that Mannheim studied them in his now classical study,[15] tends to make the forecasting of future directions a problem of technical prediction, rather than equally a process of projecting value orientations and preferences into the shaping of a better future.

f. Perceptual and Conceptual Reorganization through the Clarification of Language

In classical liberalism, one perceived foe of rational change and progress was superstition. And superstitions are carried from man to man and from generation to generation through the agency of unclear and mythical language. British utilitarianism was one important strand of classical liberalism, and one of utilitarianism's important figures, Jeremy Bentham, sought to purify language of its dangerous mystique through his study of fictions.

More recently, Alfred Korzybski and S. I. Hayakawa, in the general semantics movement, have sought a way of clarifying and rectifying the names of things and processes.[16] While their main applied concern was with personal therapy, both, and especially Hayakawa, were also concerned to

---

[13] B. F. Skinner, *Walden Two* (New York: Crowell-Collier and Macmillan, Inc., 1948).

[14] "Designing Education for the Future —an Eight State Project" (Denver, Colo., 1967).

[15] Karl Mannheim, *Ideology and Utopia* (New York: Harcourt, Brace & World, Inc., 1946).

[16] Alfred Korzybski, *Science and Sanity* (3d ed.; International Non-Aristotelian Library Publishing Company, 1948). S. I. Hayakawa, *Language in Thought and Action* (New York: Harcourt, Brace & World, Inc., 1941).

bring about changes in social systems as well. People disciplined in general semantics, it was hoped, would see more correctly, communicate more adequately, and reason more effectively and thus lay a realistic common basis for action and changing. The strategies of changing associated with general semantics overlap with our next family of strategies, the normative-re-educative, because of their emphasis upon the importance of interpersonal relationships and social contexts within the communication process.

2.   NORMATIVE-RE-EDUCATIVE STRATEGIES OF CHANGING

We have already suggested that this family of strategies rests on assumptions and hypotheses about man and his motivation which contrast significantly at points with the assumptions and hypotheses of those committed to what we have called rational-empirical strategies. Men are seen as inherently active, in quest of impulse and need satisfaction. The relation between man and his environment is essentially transactional, as Dewey[17] made clear in his famous article on "The Reflex-Arc Concept." Man, the organism, does not passively await given stimuli from his environment in order to respond. He takes stimuli as furthering or thwarting the goals of his ongoing action. Intelligence arises in the process of shaping organism-environmental relations toward more adequate fitting and joining of organismic demands and environmental resources.

Intelligence is social, rather than nar-

[17] John Dewey, *Philosophy, Psychology and Social Practice*, Joseph Ratner (ed.) (Capricorn Books, 1967).

rowly individual. Men are guided in their actions by socially funded and communicated meanings, norms, and institutions, in brief by a normative culture. At the personal level, men are guided by internalized meanings, habits, and values. Changes in patterns of action or practice are, therefore, changes, not alone in the rational informational equipment of men, but at the personal level, in habits and values as well and, at the sociocultural level, changes are alterations in normative structures and in institutionalized roles and relationships, as well as in cognitive and perceptual orientations.

For Dewey, the prototype of intelligence in action is the scientific method. And he saw a broadened and humanized scientific method as man's best hope for progress if men could learn to utilize such a method in facing all of the problematic situations of their lives. *Intelligence*, so conceived, rather than *Reason* as defined in classical liberalism, was the key to Dewey's hope for the invention, development, and testing of adequate strategies of changing in human affairs.

Lewin's contribution to normative-re-educative strategies of changing stemmed from his vision of required interrelations between research, training, and action (and, for him, this meant collaborative relationships, often now lacking, between researchers, educators, and activists) in the solution of human problems, in the identification of needs for change, and in the working out of improved knowledge, technology, and patterns of action in meeting these needs. Man must participate in his own re-education if he is to be re-educated at all. And re-education is a normative change as well as a cognitive and perceptual change. These convictions led Lewin[18] to emphasize action research as a strategy of changing, and participation in groups as a medium of re-education.

Freud's main contributions to normative-re-educative strategies of changing are two. First, he sought to demonstrate the unconscious and preconscious bases of man's actions. Only as a man finds ways of becoming aware of these non-conscious wellsprings of his attitudes and actions will he be able to bring them into conscious self-control. And Freud devoted much of his magnificent genius to developing ways of helping men to become conscious of the main springs of their actions and so capable of freedom. Second, in developing therapeutic methods, he discovered and developed ways of utilizing the relationship between change agent (therapist) and client (patient) as a major tool in re-educating the client toward expanded self-awareness, self-understanding, and self-control. Emphasis upon the collaborative relationship in therapeutic change was a major contribution by Freud and his students and colleagues to normative-re-educative strategies of changing in human affairs.[19]

Normative-re-educative approaches to effecting change bring direct interventions by change agents, interventions based on a consciously worked out theory of change and of changing, into the life of a client system, be that system a person, a small group, an organization, or a community. The theory of changing is still crude but it is probably as explicitly stated as possible, granted our present state of knowledge about planned change.[20]

Some of the common elements among variants within this family of change strategies are the following. First, all emphasize the client system and his (or its) involvement in working out programs of change and improvement for himself (or itself). The way the client sees himself and his problem must be brought into dialogic relationship with the way in which he and his problem are seen by the change agent, whether the latter is functioning as researcher, consultant, trainer, therapist, or friend in relation to the client. Second, the problem confronting the client is not assumed *a priori* to be one which can be met by more adequate technical information, though this possibility is not ruled out. The problem may lie rather in the attitudes, values, norms, and the external and internal relationships of the client system and may require alteration or re-education of these as a condition of its solution. Third, the change agent must learn to intervene mutually and collaboratively along with the client into efforts to define and solve the client's problem(s). The here and now experience of the two provide an important basis for

[18] Kurt Lewin, *Resolving Social Conflicts* (New York: Harper & Row Publishers, 1948). Kurt Lewin, *Field Theory in Social Science* (New York: Harper & Row Publishers, 1951).

[19] For Freud, an interesting summary is contained in Otto Fenichel, *Problems of Psychoanalytic Technique* (Albany: NT Psychoanalytic Quarterly Inc., 1941).

[20] W. Bennis, K. Benne, and R. Chin, *The Planning of Change* (1st ed.; New York: Holt, Rinehart and Winston, Inc., 1961). R. Lippitt, J. Watson and B. Westley, *The Dynamics of Planned Change* (New York: Harcourt, Brace & World, Inc., 1958). W. Bennis, *Changing Organizations* (New York: McGraw-Hill, Inc., 1966).

diagnosing the problem and for locating needs for re-education in the interest of solving it. Fourth, nonconscious elements which impede problem solution must be brought into consciousness and publicly examined and reconstructed. Fifth, the methods and concepts of the behavioral sciences are resources which change agent and client learn to use selectively, relevantly, and appropriately in learning to deal with the confronting problem and with problems of a similar kind in the future.

These approaches center in the notion that people technology is just as necessary as thing technology in working out desirable changes in human affairs. Put in this bold fashion, it is obvious that for the normative-re-educative change agent, clarification and reconstruction of values is of pivotal importance in changing. By getting the values of various parts of the client system along with his own, openly into the arena of change and by working through value conflicts responsibly, the change agent seeks to avoid manipulation and indoctrination of the client, in the morally reprehensible meanings of these terms.

We may use the organization of the National Training Laboratories in 1947 as a milestone in the development of normative-re-educative approaches to changing in America. The first summer laboratory program grew out of earlier collaborations among Kurt Lewin, Ronald Lippitt, Leland Bradford, and Kenneth Benne. The idea behind the laboratory was that participants, staff, and students would learn about themselves and their back-home problems by collaboratively building a laboratory in which participants would become both experimenters and subjects in the study of their own developing interpersonal and group behavior within the laboratory setting. It seems evident that the five conditions of a normative-re-educative approach to changing were met in the conception of the training laboratory. Kurt Lewin died before the 1947 session of the training laboratory opened. Ronald Lippitt was a student of Lewin's and carried many of Lewin's orientations with him into the laboratory staff. Leland Bradford and Kenneth Benne were both students of John Dewey's philosophy of education. Bradford had invented several technologies for participative learning and self-study in his work in WPA adult education programs and as training officer in several agencies of the federal government. Benne came out of a background in educational philosophy and had collaborated with colleagues prior to 1943 in developing a methodology for policy and decision making and for the reconstruction of normative orientations, a methodology which sought to fuse democratic and scientific values and to translate these into principles for resolving conflicting and problematic situations at personal and community levels of human organization.[21] Benne and his colleagues had been much influenced by the work of Mary Follett,[22] her studies of integrative solutions to conflicts in settings of public and business administration, and by the

[21] Raup, Benne, Smith, and Axtelle, *The Discipline of Practical Judgment in a Democratic Society*, Yearbook No. 28 of the National Society of College Teachers of Education (Chicago: University of Chicago Press, 1943).

[22] Mary Follett, *Creative Experience and Dynamic Administration* (New York: David McKay Company, Inc., 1924).

work of Karl Mannheim[23] on the ideology and methodology of planning changes in human affairs, as well as by the work of John Dewey and his colleagues.

The work of the National Training Laboratories has encompassed development and testing of various approaches to changing in institutional settings, in America and abroad, since its beginning. One parallel development in England which grew out of Freud's thinking should be noted. This work developed in efforts at Tavistock Clinic to apply therapeutic approaches to problems of change in industrial organizations and in communities. This work is reported in statements by Elliot Jaques[24] and in this volume by Eric Trist. Another parallel development is represented by the efforts of Roethlisberger and Dickson to use personal counseling in industry as a strategy of organizational change.[25] Roethlisberger and Dickson had been strongly influenced by the pioneer work of Elton Mayo in industrial sociology[26] as well as by the counseling theories and methodologies of Carl Rogers.

Various refinements of methodologies for changing have been developed and tested since the establishment of the National Training Laboratories in 1947, both under its auspices and under other auspices as well. For us, the modal developments are worthy of further discussion here. One set of approaches is oriented focally to the improvement of the problem-solving processes utilized by a client system. The other set focuses on helping members of client systems to become aware of their attitude and value orientations and relationship difficulties through a probing of feelings, manifest and latent, involved in the functioning and operation of the client system.[27] Both approaches use the development of "temporary systems" as a medium of re-education of persons and of role occupants in various ongoing social systems.[28]

a. Improving the Problem-solving Capabilities of a System

This family of approaches to changing rests on several assumptions about change in human systems. Changes in a system, when they are reality oriented, take the form of problem solving. A system to achieve optimum reality orientation in its adaptations to its changing internal and external environments must develop and institutionalize its own problem-solving structures and processes. These structures and processes must be tuned both to human

[23] Karl Mannheim, *Man and Society in an Age of Reconstruction* (New York: Harcourt, Brace & World, Inc., 1940).

[24] Elliot Jaques, *The Changing Culture of a Factory* (New York: Holt, Rinehart and Winston, Inc., 1952).

[25] William J. Dickson and F. J. Roethlisberger, *Personal Counseling in an Organization. A Sequel to the Hawthorne Researches* (Boston: Harvard Business School, 1966).

[26] Elton Mayo, *The Social Problems of an Industrial Civilization* (Cambridge, Mass., Harvard University Press, 1945).

[27] Leland Bradford, Jack R. Gibb, and Kenneth D. Benne, *T-Group Theory and Laboratory Method* (New York: John Wiley & Sons, Inc., 1964).

[28] Matthew B. Miles, "On Temporary Systems," in M. B. Miles (ed.), *Innovation in Education* (New York: Bureau of Publications, Teachers College, Columbia University Press, 1964), pp. 437–492.

problems of relationship and morale and to technical problems of meeting the system's task requirements, set by its goals of production, distribution, and so on.[29] System problems are typically not social *or* technical but actually sociotechnical.[30] The problem-solving structures and processes of a human system must be developed to deal with a range of sociotechnical difficulties, converting them into problems and organizing the relevant processes of data collection, planning, invention, and tryout of solutions, evaluation and feedback of results, replanning, and so forth, which are required for the solution of the problems.

The human parts of the system must learn to function collaboratively in these processes of problem identification and solution and the system must develop institutionalized support and mechanisms for maintaining and improving these processes. Actually, the model of changing in these approaches is a cooperative, action-research model. This model was suggested by Lewin and developed most elaborately for use in educational settings by Stephen M. Corey.[31]

The range of interventions by outside change agents in implementing this approach to changing is rather wide. It has been most fully elaborated in relation to organizational development programs. Within such programs, intervention methods have been most comprehensively tested in industrial settings. Some of these more or less tested intervention methods are listed below. A design for any organizational development program, of course, normally uses a number of these in succession or combination.

1. Collection of data about organizational functioning and feedback of data into processes of data interpretation and of planning ways of correcting revealed dysfunctions by system managers and data collectors in collaboration.[32]

2. Training of managers and working organizational units in methods of problem solving through self-examination of present ways of dealing with difficulties and through development and tryout of better ways with consultation by outside and/or inside change agents. Usually, the working unit leaves its working place for parts of its training. These laboratory sessions are ordinarily interspersed with on-the-job consultations.

3. Developing acceptance of feedback (research and development) roles and functions within the organization, training persons to fill these roles, and relating such roles strategically to the ongoing management of the organization.

4. Training internal change agents to function within the organization

[29] Robert R. Blake and Jane S. Mouton, *The Managerial Grid* (Houston: The Gulf Publishing Company, 1961).

[30] Jay W. Lorsch and Paul Lawrence, "The Diagnosis of Organizational Problems," in this volume, Chap. 8, p. 468.

[31] Stephen M. Corey, *Action Research to Improve School Practices* (New York: Bureau of Publications, Teachers College, Columbia University Press, 1953).

[32] See contributions by Miles *et al.*, "Data Feedback and Organizational Change in a School System," in this volume, Chap. 8, p. 457, and Jay W. Lorsch, and Paul Lawrence, "The Diagnosis of Organizational Problems," in this volume, Chap. 8, p. 468.

in carrying on needed applied research, consultation, and training.[33]

Whatever specific strategies of intervention may be employed in developing the system's capabilities for problem solving, change efforts are designed to help the system in developing ways of scanning its operations to detect problems, of diagnosing these problems to determine relevant changeable factors in them, and of moving toward collaboratively determined solutions to the problems.

b. Releasing and Fostering Growth in the Persons Who Make Up the System to be Changed

Those committed to this family of approaches to changing tend to see the person as the basic unit of social organization. Persons, it is believed, are capable of creative, life-affirming, self- and other-regarding and respecting responses, choices, and actions, if conditions which thwart these kinds of responses are removed and other supporting conditions developed. Rogers has formulated these latter conditions in his analysis of the therapist-client relationship—trustworthiness, empathy, caring, and others.[34] Maslow has worked out a similar idea in his analysis of the hierarchy of needs in persons.[35] If lower needs are met, higher need-meeting actions will take place. Mc-

Gregor[36] has formulated the ways in which existing organizations operate to fixate persons in lower levels of motivation and has sought to envision an organization designed to release and support the growth of persons in fulfilling their higher motivations as they function within the organization.

Various intervention methods have been designed to help people discover themselves as persons and commit themselves to continuing personal growth in the various relationships of their lives.

1. One early effort to install personal counseling widely and strategically in an organization has been reported by Roethisberger and Dickson.[37]

2. Training groups designed to facilitate personal confrontation and growth of members in an open, trusting, and accepting atmosphere have been conducted for individuals from various back-home situations and for persons from the same back-home setting. The processes of these groups have sometimes been described as "therapy for normals."[38]

3. Groups and laboratories designed to stimulate and support personal

[33] C. Argyris, "Explorations in Consulting-Client Relationships," in this volume, Chap. 8, p. 434. See also Richard Beckhard, "The Confrontation Meeting," in this volume, Chap. 8, p. 478.

[34] Carl Rogers, "The Characteristics of a Helping Relationship," in this volume, Chap. 4, p. 153.

[35] Abraham Maslow, *Motivation and Personality* (New York: Harper & Row, Publishers, 1954).

[36] Douglas M. McGregor, "The Human Side of Enterprise," in W. Bennis, K. Benne, and R. Chin *The Planning of Change* (1st ed.; New York: Holt, Rinehart and Winston, Inc., 1961), pp. 422–431.

[37] Dickson and Roethisberger, cited above.

[38] James V. Clark "A Healthy Organization," in this volume, Chap. 6, p. 282. Irving Weschler, Fred Massarik, and Robert Tannenbaum, "The Self in Process: A Sensitivity Training Emphasis," in I. R. Weschler and E. Schein (eds.), *Issues in Training*, Selected Reading Series No. 5 (Washington, D.C., National Training Laboratories).

growth have been designed to utilize the resources of nonverbal exchange and communication among members along with verbal dialogue in inducing personal confrontation, discovery, and commitment to continuing growth.

4. Many psychotherapists, building on the work of Freud and Adler, have come to use groups, as well as two-person situations, as media of personal re-education and growth. Such efforts are prominent in mental health approaches to changing and have been conducted in educational, religious, community, industrial, and hospital settings. While these efforts focus primarily upon helping individuals to change themselves toward greater self-clarity and fuller self-actualization, they are frequently designed and conducted in the hope that personal changes will lead to changes in organizations, institutions, and communities as well.

We have presented the two variants of normative-re-educative approaches to changing in a way to emphasize their differences. Actually, there are many similarities between them as well, which justify placing both under the same general heading. We have already mentioned one of these similarities. Both frequently use temporary systems—a residential laboratory or workshop, a temporary group with special resources built in, an ongoing system which incorporates a change agent (trainer, consultant, counselor, or therapist) temporarily—as an aid to growth in the system and/or in its members. More fundamentally, both approaches emphasize experience-based learning as an ingredient of all enduring changes in human systems. Yet both accept the principle that people must learn to learn from their experiences if self-directed change is to be maintained and continued. Frequently, people have learned to defend against the potential lessons of experience when these threaten existing equilibria, whether in the person or in the social system. How can these defenses be lowered to let the data of experience get into processes of perceiving the situation, of constructing new and better ways to define it, of inventing new and more appropriate ways of responding to the situation as redefined, of becoming more fully aware of the consequences of actions, of rearticulating value orientations which sanction more responsible ways of managing the consequences of actions, and so forth? Learning to learn from ongoing experience is a major objective in both approaches to changing. Neither denies the relevance or importance of the noncognitive determinants of behavior—feelings, attitudes, norms, and relationships—along with cognitive-perceptual determinants, in effecting behavioral change. The problem-solving approaches emphasize the cognitive determinants more than personal growth approaches do. But exponents of the former do not accept the rationalistic biases of the rational-empirical family of change strategies, already discussed. Since exponents of both problem-solving and personal growth approaches are committed to re-education of persons as integral to effective change in human systems, both emphasize norms of openness of communication, trust between persons, lowering of status barriers between parts of the system, and mutuality between parts as necessary conditions of the re-educative process.

Great emphasis has been placed recently upon the releasing of creativity in persons, groups, and organizations as requisite to coping adaptively with accelerated changes in the conditions of modern living. We have already stressed the emphasis which personal growth approaches put upon the release of creative responses in persons being re-educated. Problem-solving approaches also value creativity, though they focus more upon the group and organizational conditions which increase the probability of creative responses by persons functioning within those conditions than upon persons directly. The approaches do differ in their strategies for releasing creative responses within human systems. But both believe that creative adaptations to changing conditions may arise *within* human systems and do not have to be imported from *outside* them as in innovation-diffusion approaches already discussed and the power-compliance models still to be dealt with.

One developing variant of normative-re-educative approaches to changing, not already noted, focuses upon effective conflict management. It is, of course, common knowledge that differences within a society which demand interaccommodation often manifest themselves as conflicts. In the process of managing such conflicts, changes in the norms, policies, and relationships of the society occur. Can conflict management be brought into the ambit of planned change as defined in this volume? Stemming from the work of the Sherifs in creating intergroup conflict and seeking to resolve it in a field-laboratory situation,[39] training in intergroup conflict and conflict resolution found its way into training laboratories through the efforts of Blake and others. Since that time, laboratories for conflict management have been developed under NTL and other auspices and methodologies for conflict resolution and management, in keeping with the values of planned change, have been devised. Blake's and Walton's work represent some of the findings from these pioneering efforts.[40]

Thus, without denying their differences in assumption and strategy, we believe that the differing approaches discussed in this section can be seen together within the framework of normative-re-educative approaches to changing. Two efforts to conceptualize planned change in a way to reveal the similarities in assumptions about changing and in value orientations toward change underlying these variant approaches are those by Lippitt, Watson, and Westley and by Bennis, Benne, and Chin.[41]

Another aspect of changing in human organizations is represented by efforts to conceive human organization in forms that go beyond the bureaucratic form which captured the imagination and fixed the contours of think-

[39] Muzafer and Carolyn Sherif, *Groups in Harmony and Tension* (New York: Harper & Row, Publishers, 1953).

[40] Robert Blake *et al.*, "The Union Management Inter-Group Laboratory," in this volume, Chap. 4, p. 176. Richard Walton, "Two Strategies of Social Change and Their Dilemmas," in this volume, Chap. 4, p. 167.

[41] R. Lippitt, J. Watson, and B. Westley, *Dynamics of Planned Change* (New York: Harcourt, Brace & World, Inc., 1958). W. Bennis, K. Benne, R. Chin, *The Planning of Change* (1st ed.; New York: Holt, Rinehart and Winston, Inc., 1961).

ing and practice of organizational theorists and practitioners from the latter part of the nineteenth through the early part of the twentieth century. The bureaucratic form of organization was conceptualized by Max Weber and carried into American thinking by such students of administration as Urwick.[42] On this view, effective organization of human effort followed the lines of effective division of labor and effective establishment of lines of reporting, control, and supervision from the mass base of the organization up through various levels of control to the top of the pyramidal organization from which legitimate authority and responsibility stemmed.

The work of industrial sociologists like Mayo threw doubt upon the adequacy of such a model of formal organization to deal with the realities of organizational life by revealing the informal organization which grows up within the formal structure to satisfy personal and interpersonal needs not encompassed by or integrated into the goals of the formal organization. Chester Barnard may be seen as a transitional figure who, in discussing the functions of the organizational executive, gave equal emphasis to his responsibilities for task effectiveness and organizational efficiency (optimally meeting the human needs of persons in the organization).[43] Much of the development of subsequent organizational theory and practice has centered on problems of integrating the actualities,

criteria, and concepts of organizational effectiveness and of organizational efficiency.

A growing group of thinkers and researchers have sought to move beyond the bureaucratic model toward some new model of organization which might set directions and limits for change efforts in organizational life. Out of many thinkers, we choose four who have theorized out of an orientation consistent with what we have called a normative-re-educative approach to changing.

Rensis Likert has presented an intergroup model of organization. Each working unit strives to develop and function as a group. The group's efforts are linked to other units of the organization by the overlapping membership of supervisors or managers in vertically or horizontally adjacent groups. This view of organization throws problems of delegation, supervision, and internal communication into a new light and emphasizes the importance of linking persons as targets of change and re-education in processes of organizational development.[44]

We have already stressed McGregor's efforts to conceive a form of organization more in keeping with new and more valid views of human nature and motivation (Theory Y) than the limited and false views of human nature and motivation (Theory X) upon which traditional bureaucratic organization has rested. In his work he sought to move thinking and practice relevant to organization and organizational change beyond the limits of traditional forms. "The essential task of manage-

[42] Lyndall Urwick, *The Pattern of Management* (Minneapolis: University of Minnesota Press, 1956).

[43] Chester I. Barnard, *The Functions of the Executive* (Cambridge: Harvard University Press, 1938).

[44] Rensis Likert *New Patterns of Management* (New York: McGraw-Hill, Inc., 1961).

ment is to arrange organizational conditions and methods of operation so that people can achieve their own goals best by directing their own efforts toward organizational objectives."[45]

Bennis has consciously sought to move beyond bureaucracy in tracing the contours of the organization of the future.[46] And Shephard has described an organizational form consistent with support for continual changing and self-renewal, rather than with a primary mission of maintenance and control.[47]

3. POWER-COERCIVE APPROACHES TO EFFECTING CHANGE

It is not the use of power, in the sense of influence by one person upon another or by one group upon another, which distinguishes this family of strategies from those already discussed. Power is an ingredient of all human action. The differences lie rather in the ingredients of power upon which the strategies of changing depend and the ways in which power is generated and applied in processes of effecting change. Thus, what we have called rational-empirical approaches depend on knowledge as a major ingredient of power. In this view, men of knowledge are legitimate sources of power and the desirable flow of influence or power is from men who know to men who don't know through processes of education and of dissemination of valid information.

Normative-re-educative strategies of

changing do not deny the importance of knowledge as a source of power, especially in the form of knowledge-based technology. Exponents of this approach to changing are committed to redressing the imbalance between the limited use of behavioral knowledge and people technologies and the widespread use of physical-biological knowledge and related thing technologies in effecting changes in human affairs. In addition, exponents of normative-re-educative approaches recognize the importance of noncognitive determinants of behavior as resistances or supports to changing—values, attitudes, and feelings at the personal level and norms and relationships at the social level. Influence must extend to these noncognitive determinants of behavior if voluntary commitments and reliance upon social intelligence are to be maintained and extended in our changing society. Influence of noncognitive determinants of behavior must be exercised in mutual processes of persuasion within collaborative relationships. These strategies are oriented against coercive and nonreciprocal influence, both on moral and on pragmatic grounds.

What ingredients of power do power-coercive strategies emphasize? In general, emphasis is upon political and economic sanctions in the exercise of power. But other coercive strategies emphasize the utilization of moral power, playing upon sentiments of guilt and shame. Political power carries with it legitimacy and the sanctions which accrue to those who break the law. Thus getting a law passed against racial imbalance in the schools brings legitimate coercive power behind efforts

[45] McGregor, pp. 422–431.
[46] W. G. Bennis, "Changing Organizations," in this volume, Chap. 10, p. 568.
[47] H. A. Shephard, "Innovation-Resisting and Innovation-Producing Organizations," in this volume, Chap. 9, p. 519.

to desegregate the schools, threatening those who resist with sanctions under the law and reducing the resistance of others who are morally oriented against breaking the law. Economic power exerts coercive influence over the decisions of those to whom it is applied. Thus federal appropriations granting funds to local schools for increased emphasis upon science instruction tends to exercise coercive influence over the decisions of local school officials concerning the emphasis of the school curriculum. In general, power-coercive strategies of changing seek to mass political and economic power behind the change goals which the strategists of change have decided are desirable. Those who oppose these goals, if they adopt the same strategy, seek to mass political and economic power in opposition. The strategy thus tends to divide the society when there is anything like a division of opinion and of power in that society.

When a person or group is entrenched in power in a social system, in command of political legitimacy and of political and economic sanctions, that person or group can use power-coercive strategies in effecting changes, which they consider desirable, without much awareness on the part of those out of power in the system that such strategies are being employed. A power-coercive way of making decisions is accepted as in the nature of things. The use of such strategies by those in legitimate control of various social systems in our society is much more widespread than most of us might at first be willing or able to admit. This is true in educational systems as well as in other social systems.

When any part of a social system becomes aware that its interests are not being served by those in control of the system, the coercive power of those in control can be challenged. If the minority is committed to power-coercive strategies, or is aware of no alternatives to such strategies, how can they make headway against existing power relations within the system? They may organize discontent against the present controls of the system and achieve power outside the legitimate channels of authority in the system. Thus teachers' unions may develop power against coercive controls by the central administrative group and the school board in a school system. They may threaten concerted resistance to or disregard of administrative rulings and board policies or they may threaten work stoppage or a strike. Those in control may get legislation against teachers' strikes. If the political power of organized teachers grows, they may get legislation requiring collective bargaining between organized teachers and the school board on some range of educational issues. The power struggle then shifts to the negotiation table and compromise between competing interests may become the expected goal of the intergroup exchange. Whether the augmented power of new, relevant knowledge or the generation of common power through joint collaboration and deliberation are lost in the process will depend on the degree of commitment by all parties to the conflict to a continuation and maintenance of power-coercive strategies for effecting change.

What general varieties of power-coercive strategies to be exercised either by those in control as they seek to maintain their power or to be used by those now outside a position of control and seeking to enlarge their power can be identified?

a. Strategies of Nonviolence

Mahatma Gandhi may be seen as the most prominent recent theorist and practitioner of nonviolent strategies for effecting change, although the strategies did not originate with him in the history of mankind, either in idea or in practice. Gandhi spoke of Thoreau's *Essay on Civil Disobedience* as one important influence in his own approach to nonviolent coercive action. Martin Luther King was perhaps America's most distinguished exponent of nonviolent coercion in effecting social change. A minority (or majority) confronted with what they see as an unfair, unjust, or cruel system of coercive social control may dramatize their rejection of the system by publicly and nonviolently witnessing and demonstrating against it. Part of the ingredients of the power of the civilly disobedient is in the guilt which their demonstration of injustice, unfairness, or cruelty of the existing system of control arouses in those exercising control or in others previously committed to the present system of control. The opposition to the disobedient group may be demoralized and may waver in their exercise of control, if they profess the moral values to which the dissidents are appealing.

Weakening or dividing the opposition through moral coercion may be combined with economic sanctions— like Gandhi's refusal to buy salt and other British manufactured commodities in India or like the desegregationists' economic boycott of the products of racially discriminating factories and businesses.

The use of nonviolent strategies for opening up conflicts in values and demonstrating against injustices or inequities in existing patterns of social control has become familiar to educational leaders in the demonstrations and sitins of college students in various universities and in the demonstrations of desegregationists against *de facto* segregation of schools. And the widened use of such strategies may be confidently predicted. Whether such strategies will be used to extend collaborative ways of developing policies and normative-reeducative strategies of changing or whether they will be used to augment power struggles as the only practical way of settling conflicts, will depend in some large part upon the strategy commitments of those now in positions of power in educational systems.

b. Use of Political Institutions to Achieve Change

Political power has traditionally played an important part in achieving changes in our institutional life. And political power will continue to play an important part in shaping and reshaping our institutions of education as well as other institutions. Changes enforced by political coercion need not be oppressive if the quality of our democratic processes can be maintained and improved.

Changes in policies with respect to education have come from various departments of government. By far the most of these have come through legislation on the state level. Under legislation, school administrators have various degrees of discretionary powers, and policy and program changes are frequently put into effect by administrative rulings. Judicial decisions have played an important part in shaping educational policies, none more dramatically than the Supreme Court decision declaring laws and policies supporting school segregation illegal. And the federal courts have played a central part in seeking to implement and enforce this decision.

Some of the difficulty with the use of political institutions to effect changes arises from an overestimation by change agents of the capability of political action to effect changes in practice. When the law is passed, the administrative ruling announced, or the judicial decision handed down legitimizing some new policy or program or illegitimizing some traditional practice, change agents who have worked hard for the law, ruling, or decision frequently assume that the desired change has been made.

Actually, all that has been done is to bring the force of legitimacy behind some envisioned change. The processes of re-education of persons who are to conduct themselves in new ways still have to be carried out. And the new conduct often requires new knowledge, new skills, new attitudes, and new value orientations. And, on the social level, new conduct may require changes in the norms, the roles, and the relationship structures of the institutions involved. This is not to discount the importance of political actions in legitimizing changed policies and practices in educational institutions and in other institutions as well. It is rather to emphasize that normative-re-educative strategies must be combined with po-

litical coercion, both before and after the political action, if the public is to be adequately informed and desirable and commonly acceptable changes in practice are to be achieved.

c. Changing through the Recomposition and Manipulation of Power Elites

The idea or practice of a ruling class or of a power elite in social control was by no means original with Karl Marx. What was original with him was his way of relating these concepts to a process and strategy of fundamental social change. The composition of the ruling class was, of course, for Marx those who owned and controlled the means and processes of production of goods and services in a society. Since, for Marx, the ideology of the ruling class set limits to the thinking of most intellectuals and of those in charge of educational processes and of communicating, rationales for the existing state of affairs, including its concentration of political and economic power, is provided and disseminated by intellectuals and educators and communicators within the system.

Since Marx was morally committed to a classless society in which political coercion would disappear because there would be no vested private interests to rationalize and defend, he looked for a counterforce in society to challenge and eventually to overcome the power of the ruling class. And this he found in the economically dispossessed and alienated workers of hand and brain. As this new class gained consciousness of its historic mission and its power increased, the class struggle could be effectively joined. The outcome of this struggle was victory for those best able to organize and maximize the productive power of the instruments of production—for Marx this victory belonged to the now dispossessed workers.

Many of Marx's values would have put him behind what we have called normative-re-educative strategies of changing. And he recognized that such strategies would have to be used after the accession of the workers to state power in order to usher in the classless society. He doubted if the ruling class could be re-educated, since re-education would mean loss of their privileges and coercive power in society. He recognized that the power elite could, within limits, accommodate new interests as these gained articulation and power. But these accommodations must fall short of a radical transfer of power to a class more capable of wielding it. Meanwhile, he remained committed to a power-coercive strategy of changing until the revolutionary transfer of power had been effected.

Marxian concepts have affected the thinking of contemporary men about social change both inside and outside nations in which Marxism has become the official orientation. His concepts have tended to bolster assumptions of the necessity of power-coercive strategies in achieving fundamental redistributions of socioeconomic power or in recomposing or manipulating power elites in a society. Democratic, re-educative methods of changing have a place only after such changes in power allocation have been achieved by power-coercive methods. Non-Marxians as well as Marxians are often committed to this Marxian dictum.

In contemporary America, C. Wright Mills has identified a power elite, essentially composed of industrial, military, and governmental leaders, who direct and limit processes of social change and accommodation in our society. And President Eisenhower warned of the dangerous concentration of power in substantially the same groups in his farewell message to the American people. Educators committed to democratic values should not be blinded to the limitations to advancement of those values, which are set by the less than democratic ideology of our power elites. And normative-re-educative strategists of changing must include power elites among their targets of changing as they seek to diffuse their ways of progress within contemporary society. And they must take seriously Marx's questions about the re-educability of members of the power elites, as they deal with problems and projects of social change.

The operation of a power elite in social units smaller than a nation was revealed in Floyd Hunter's study of decision making in an American city. Hunter's small group of deciders, with their satellite groups of intellectuals, front men, and implementers, is in a real sense a power elite. The most common reaction of educational leaders to Hunter's "discovery" has been to seek ways in which to persuade and manipulate the deciders toward support of educational ends which educational leaders consider desirable—whether bond issues, building programs, or anything else. This is non-Marxian in its acceptance of power relations in a city or community as fixed. It would be Marxian if it sought to build counter power to offset and reduce the power of the presently deciding group where this power interfered with the achievement of desirable educational goals. This latter strategy, though not usually Marxian inspired in the propaganda sense of that term, has been more characteristic of organized teacher effort in pressing for collective bargaining or of some student demonstrations and sit-ins. In the poverty program, the federal government in its insistence on participation of the poor in making policies for the program has at least played with a strategy of building countervailing power to offset the existing concentration of power in people not iden-tified with the interests of the poor in reducing their poverty.

Those committed to the advancement of normative-re-educative strategies of changing must take account of present actual concentrations of power wherever they work. This does *not* mean that they must develop a commitment to power-coercive strategies to change the distribution of power except when these may be necessary to effect the spread of their own democratically and scientifically oriented methods of changing within society.

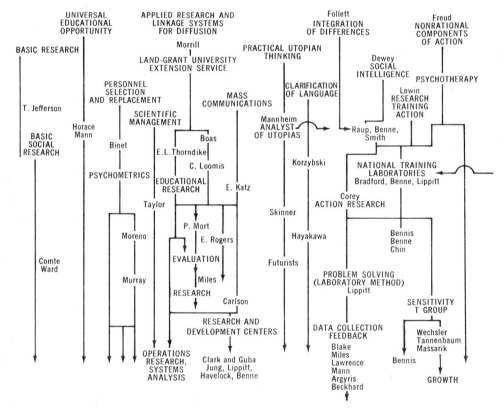

A. RATIONAL—EMPIRICAL

VIEWS OF THE ENLIGHTENMENT AND CLASSICAL LIBERALISM

B. NORMATIVE—

VIEWS OF THERAPISTS,

FIGURE 1.

RE-EDUCATIVE

C. POWER—COERCIVE

TRAINERS, AND SITUATION CHANGERS

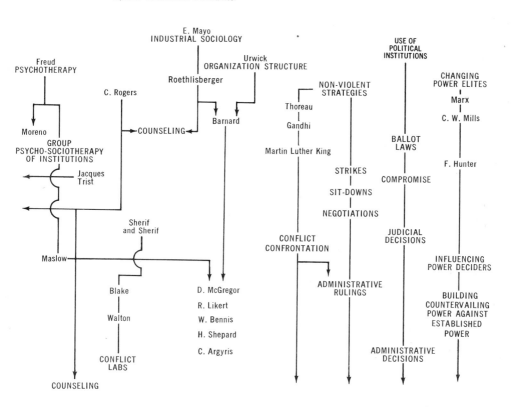

Strategies of Deliberate Changing

Chapter 2

CURRENT
AND EMERGENT NOTIONS
ABOUT PLANNED CHANGE

NOTIONS and ideas invented and developed to guide practitioners of planned change have grown and spread widely during the past twenty years, and new notions continue to be invented and developed both by researchers and practitioners concerned with planned change. We use the term "notions" rather than "theory" advisedly. For the body of notions now available does not constitute a theory in any of the accepted usages of that term in contemporary philosophies of science.

Yet we believe these notions about planned change are important not alone as guides to consultants, trainers, and researchers of processes of changing, but as elements in a theory of applied behavioral science still largely to be developed. The epistemological requirements for such a science are different from those of a pure science. Some of the differences are noted by Bennis in his article in this chapter. In applied behavioral science, a value position needs to be taken more clearly and explicitly, and ideas about strategic accessibility to the change agent of levers of action must be focal in the framework of the theory. A theory of changing will thus probably never be as conceptually elegant as a theory of change can be.

Let us back away from the imposing challenge of developing a full-fledged theory of changing to note a few trends and issues in current thinking about planned change. Planned change is used by some writers as a generic term for *any* deliberate effort at changing. We prefer to use the term more restrictively for processes of deliberate changing which meet criteria, already noted, such as the use of valid knowledge and the cultivation of collaborative relationships between the change agent and client system. Yet we do not propose to legislate any official definition for planned change. And we hope to learn from students of deliberate changing who embrace value orientations different from our own, as we hope they will be able and willing to learn from us. Similar ambiguities hold for current usage of the term, change agent. Here again, we choose to use the term in a special sense.

The principal bases for our chosen criteria and requirements for planned change and change agent are clinically evaluated experiences in changing, value preferences, and researched knowledge of human behavior.

It would be desirable to be able to justify our definition of planned change by carefully researched knowledge of processes of changing. But, for the most part, this research base has yet to be developed. We hope and believe that it will develop in the future. But we feel that future theories of planned change, like other practitioner theories, will continue to rest not on one base but upon three—criticized values, evaluated practical experience, and research knowledge.

In our more optimistic moods, we believe that current notions are becoming more rationalized and coherent and are thus providing an increasingly useful conceptual scheme for the analysis of behavioral processes in changing. But, as we mentioned before, we do not yet have a theory of changing which embodies testable hypotheses for the adequate guidance of empirical inquiry and research. What do these limitations of current theory mean? Conceptual schemes are never right or wrong; they are only useful or not for some specified purpose. In this view, current conceptual schemes of planned change may be judged as of some use for observers and students of its processes and of even greater use for steering the activities of change agents in the practice of their roles.

Issues concerning applied behavioral science remain. These issues are concerned both with *what* we know is to be applied and with *how* the process of application takes place. In the view of many laymen, and of some behavioral scientists as well, what is to be applied is any or all presently available knowledge from the behavioral sciences. But when the issue is examined further, a more precise question emerges: what kinds of behavioral science knowledge can be applied?

Bennis' "Applying Behavioral Science" summarizes the kinds of change programs now in use. He seeks to operationalize the defining criteria of planned change—the use of valid knowledge and collaborative relationships and describes three major forms of change programs: training, consulting, and research. He contrasts planned change with operations research—an attempt to apply knowledge derived from systems engineering and mathematics to technical management and efficient organization.

Barnes' "Approaches to Organizational Change" lists several varieties of current programs for initiating and conducting change programs in organizations and threads these program varieties along the dimension of "power equalization" to "power hierarchy."

One kind of applicable knowledge is knowledge that gives a change agent leverage upon the human system(s) he is seeking to change, whether in terms of strategic points of entry into the system or in terms of effective methods of intervention into the processes of the system. Gouldner examines such issues in his "Theoretical Requirements of Applied Social Sciences." Throughout this landmark article, he insists that applied social science "emerges from the deepest tap-roots" of the basic disciplines of the social sciences. For Gouldner, the question of how we apply social or behavioral science is partly answered by the inherent nature of social science and social process, not just by the accumulating body of research knowledge.

Lewin's three-step process of change—unfreezing, moving, and refreezing—is presented, and each stage illuminated in the terms of social psychological mechanisms and ego psychology in "Personal Change through Interpersonal Relationships" by Edgar Schein. Schein clarifies some of the important problems for future research which will provide a more adequate knowledge base for a theory of changing.

2.1 THEORY AND METHOD IN APPLYING BEHAVIORAL SCIENCE TO PLANNED ORGANIZATIONAL CHANGE[1]

Warren G. Bennis

Three assumptions underlie this paper: (1) that the proportion of contemporary change that is planned or that issues from deliberate innovation is much higher than in former times; (2) that man's wisdom and mundane behavior are somewhat short of perfection insofar as they regulate the fate and selective adaptation of complex human organizations; (3) that behavioral scientists in increasing numbers are called upon to influence organizational functioning and effectiveness. The paper is concerned with the strategic, methodological, and conceptual issues brought about by the emergence of the action role of the behavioral scientist.

What we have witnessed in the past two or three decades has been called the "Rise of the Rational Spirit"—the belief that science can help to better the human condition. The focus of this paper is on one indication of this trend: the emerging role for the behavioral scientist and, more specifically, the at-

From Warren G. Bennis, "Theory and Method in Applying Behavioral Science to Planned Organizational Change," *The Journal of Applied Behavioral Science*, I, No. 4 (1965), 337–359. Used by permission.

[1] Drawn from keynote address presented at International Conference on Operational Research and the Social Sciences, Cambridge, England, September 1964.

tempts by behavioral scientists to apply knowledge (primarily sociological and psychological) toward the improvement of human organizations.

The Emergence
of the Action Role

Many signs and activities point toward an emerging action role for the behavioral scientist. The *manipulative standpoint*, as Lasswell calls it, is becoming distinguishable from the *contemplative standpoint* and is increasingly ascendant insofar as knowledge utilization is concerned.[2] Evidence can be found in the growing literature on planned change through the uses of the behavioral sciences (Bennis, Benne, & Chin, 1961; Freeman, 1963; Zetterberg, 1962; Gibb & Lippitt, 1959; Leeds & Smith, 1963; Likert & Hayes, 1957; Glock, Lippitt, Flanagan, Wilson, Shartle, Wilson, Croker, & Page, 1960) and in such additions to the vocabulary of the behavioral scientist as action research, client system, change agent, clinical sociology, knowledge centers, social catalysts. The shift is also reflected in increased emphasis on application in annual meeting time of the professional associations or in the formation of a Center for Research on the Utilization of Scientific Knowledge within The University of Michigan's Institute for Social Research.

It is probably true that in the United

[2] For an excellent discussion of the "value" issues in this development, see Kaplan, A. *The conduct of inquiry.* San Francisco: Chandler, 1964, Chapter 10; and Benne, K. D., & Swanson, G. (Eds.) Values and the social scientist. *J. Soc. Issues,* 1960, 6.

States there is a more practical attitude toward knowledge than anywhere else. When Harrison Salisbury (1960) traveled over Europe he was impressed with the seeming disdain of European intellectuals for practical matters. Even in Russia he found little interest in the "merely useful." Salisbury saw only one great agricultural experiment station on the American model. In that case professors were working in the fields. They told him, "People call us Americans."

Not many American professors may be found working in the fields, but they can be found almost everywhere else: in factories, in the government, in underdeveloped countries, in mental hospitals, in educational systems. They are advising, counseling, researching, recruiting, developing, consulting, training. Americans may not have lost their deep ambivalence toward the intellectual, but it is clear that the academic intellectual has become *engagé* with spheres of action in greater numbers, with more diligence, and with higher aspirations than at any other time in history.

It may be useful to speculate about the reasons for the shift in the intellectual climate. Most important, but trickiest to identify, are those causative factors bound up in the warp and woof of "our times and age," the *Zeitgeist.* The apparently growing disenchantment with the moral neutrality of the scientist may be due, in C. P. Snow's phrase, to the fact that "scientists cannot escape their own knowledge." In any event, though "impurity" is still implied, action research as distinguished from pure research does not carry the opprobrium it once did.

Perhaps the crucial reason for the

shift in emphasis toward application is simply that we know more.[3] Since World War II we have obtained large bodies of research and diverse reports on application. We are today in a better position to assess results and potentialities of applied social science.

Finally, there is a fourth factor having to do with the fate and viability of human organization, particularly as it has been conceptualized as "bureaucracy." I use the term in its sociological, Weberian sense, not as a metaphor à la Kafka's *The Castle* connoting "red tape," impotency, inefficiency, despair. In the past three decades Weber's vision has been increasingly scrutinized and censured. Managers and practitioners, on the one hand, and organizational theorists and researchers on the other, are more and more dissatisfied with current practices of organizational behavior and are searching for new forms and patterns of organizing for work. A good deal of activity is being generated.

The Lack of a
Viable Theory of Social Change

Unfortunately, no viable theory of social change has been established. Indeed it is a curious fact about present theories that they are strangely silent on matters of *directing* and *implementing* change. What I particularly object to—and I include the "newer" theories of neo-conflict (Coser, 1956; Dahrendorf, 1961), neo-functionalism (Boskoff, 1964), and neo-revolutionary theories—

is that they tend to explain the dynamic interactions of a system without providing one clue to the identification of strategic leverages for alteration. They are suitable for *observers* of social change, not for practitioners. They are theories of *change*, and not of *changing*.

It may be helpful to suggest quickly some of the prerequisites for a theory of changing. I am indebted here to my colleague Robert Chin (1961, 1963):

a. A theory of changing must include manipulable variables—accessible levers for influencing the direction, tempo, and quality of change and improvement.

b. The variables must not violate the client system's values.

c. The cost of usage cannot be prohibitive.

d. There must be provided a reliable basis of diagnosing the strength and weakness of conditions facing the client system.

e. Phases of intervention must be clear so that the change agent can develop estimates for termination of the relationship.

f. The theory must be communicable to the client system.

g. It must be possible to assess appropriateness of the theory for different client systems.

Such a theory does not now exist, and this probably explains why change agents appear to write like "theoretical orphans" and, more important, why so many change programs based on theories of social change have been inadequate. This need should be kept in mind as we look at models of knowledge utilization.

---

[3] For a recent inventory of scientific findings of the behavioral sciences, see Berelson, B., & Steiner, G. A. *Human behavior.* New York: Harcourt, Brace & World, Inc., 1964.

The Notion of Planned Change

Planned change can be viewed as a linkage between theory and practice, between knowledge and action. It plays this role by converting variables from the basic disciplines into strategic instrumentation and programs. Historically, the development of planned change can be seen as the resultant of two forces: complex problems requiring expert help and the growth and viability of the behavioral sciences. The term "behavioral sciences" itself is of post-World War II vintage coined by the more empirically minded to "safeguard" the social disciplines from the nonquantitative humanists and the depersonalized abstractions of the econometricists. The process of planned change involves a *change agent*, a *client system*, and the collaborative attempt to apply *valid knowledge* to the client's problems.[4]

Elsewhere I have attempted a typology of change efforts in which planned change is distinguished from other types of change in that it entails mutual goal setting, an equal power ratio (eventually), and deliberateness on both sides (Bennis et al., 1961, p. 154).

It may further help in defining planned change to compare it with another type of deliberate change effort, Operations Research. I enter this with a humility bordering on fear and a rueful sense of kinship in our mutual incapacity to explain to one another the nature of our work. There are these similarities. Both are World War II

[4] For a fuller discussion, see Lippitt, R., Watson, J., & Westley, B. *The dynamics of planned change.* New York: Harcourt, Brace & World, Inc., 1961; and Bennis et al., 1961.

products; both are problem-centered (though both have also provided inputs to the concepts and method of their parent disciplines). Both emphasize improvement and to that extent are *normative* in their approach to problems. Both rely heavily on empirical science; both rely on a relationship of confidence and valid communication with clients; both emphasize a *systems* approach to problems—that is, both are aware of interdependence within the system as well as boundary maintenance with its environment; and both appear to be most effective when working with systems which are complex, rapidly changing, and probably science-based.

Perhaps the most crucial difference between OR and planned change has to do with the identification of strategic variables, that is, with those factors which appear to make a difference in the performance of the system. Planned change is concerned with such problems as (1) the identification of mission and values, (2) collaboration and conflict, (3) control and leadership, (4) resistance and adaptation to change, (5) utilization of human resources, (6) communication, (7) management development. OR practitioners tend to select economic or engineering variables which are more quantitative, measurable, and linked to profit and efficiency. Ackoff and Rivett (1963), for example, classify OR problems under (1) inventory, (2) allocation, (3) queuing, (4) sequencing, (5) routing, (6) replacement, (7) competition, (8) search.

A second major difference has to do with the perceived importance of the relationship with the client. In planned change, the quality and nature of the relationship are used as indicators for the measure of progress and as valid sources of data and diagnosis. Undoubtedly, the most successful OR practitioners operate with sensitivity toward their clients; but if one looks at what they *say* about their work, they are clearly less concerned with human interactions.

A third major difference is that the OR practitioner devotes a large portion of his time to research, to problem solving. The change agent tends to spend somewhat more time on implementation through counseling, training, management development schemes, and so forth. Fourth, planned-change agents tend to take less seriously the idea of the *system* in their approaches. Finally, the idea of an interdisciplinary team, central to OR, does not seem to be a part of most planned-change programs.

One thing that emerges from this comparison is a realization of the complexity of modern organization. Look through the kaleidoscope one way, and a configuration of the economic and technological factors appears; tilt it, and what emerges is a pattern of internal human relations problems. It is on these last problems and their effects upon performance of the system that practitioners of planned organizational change tend to work.

A Focus of Convenience

To develop what George Kelly refers to as a "focus of convenience" for planned organizational change, I want to make two key aspects clearer: the notions of "collaborative relationships" and of "valid knowledge." I see the outcome of planned-change efforts as depending to some considerable extent on the relationship between client and agent. To optimize a collaborative relationship, there need to be a "spirit of inquiry," with data publicly shared, and equal freedom to terminate the relationship and to influence the other.

As to valid knowledge, the criteria are based on the requirements for a viable applied behavioral science research—an applied behavioral science that:

a. Takes into consideration the behavior of persons operating within their specific institutional environments;

b. Is capable of accounting for the interrelated levels (person, group, role, organization) within the context of the social change;

c. Includes variables that the policy maker and practitioner can understand, manipulate, and evaluate;

d. Can allow selection of variables appropriate in terms of its own values, ethics, moralities;

e. Accepts the premise that groups and organizations as units are amenable to empirical and analytic treatment;

f. Takes into acount external social processes of change as well as interpersonal aspects of the collaborative process;

g. Includes propositions susceptible to empirical test focusing on the dynamics of change.

These criteria must be construed as an arbitrary goal, not as an existing reality. To my knowledge, there is no program which fulfills these requirements fully. In this focus of convenience, I have arbitrarily selected change agents working on organizational dynamics partly because of my greater familiarity with their work but also because they seem to fulfill the criteria outlined to a greater extent than do other change agents. My choice of emphasis is also based on the belief that changes in the sphere of organizations—primarily industrial—in patterns of work and relationship, structure, technology, and administration promise some of the most significant changes in our society. Indeed it is my guess that industrial society, at least in the United States, is more radical, innovative, and adventurous in adapting new ways of organizing than the government, the universities, and the labor unions, who appear rigid and stodgy in the face of rapid change. If space permitted, however, I would refer also to change agents working in a variety of fields—rural sociology, economics, anthropology—and in such settings as communities, hospitals, cultural-change programs.

Let us turn now to some of the "traditional" models of knowledge utilization.

Eight Types of Change Programs

It is possible to identify eight types of change programs if we examine their strategic rationale: exposition and propagation, élite corps, human relations training, staff, scholarly consultations, circulation of ideas to the élite, developmental research, and action research.

I should like to look at each of these programs quickly and then refer to four biases which seem to me to weaken their impact.

Exposition and propagation, perhaps the most popular type of program, assumes that knowledge is power. It follows that the men who possess "Truth" will lead the world.

Elite corps programs grow from the realization that ideas by themselves do not constitute action and that a strategic *role* is a necessity for ideas to be implemented (e.g., through getting scientists into government as C. P. Snow suggests).

Human relations training programs are similar to the élite corps idea in the attempt to translate behavioral science concepts in such ways that they take on personal referents for the men in power positions.

Staff programs provide a source of intelligence within the client system, as in the work of social anthropologists advising military governors after World War II. The strategy of the staff idea is to observe, analyze, and to plan rationally (Myrdal, 1958).

Scholarly consultation, as defined by Zetterberg (1962), includes exploratory inquiry, scholarly understanding, confrontation, discovery of solutions, and scientific advice to client.

Circulation of ideas to the élite builds on the simple idea of influencing change by getting to the people with power or influence.

Developmental research has to do with seeing whether an idea can be brought to an engineering stage. Unlike Zetterberg's scholarly confrontation, it is directed toward a particular problem, not necessarily a client, and is concerned with implementation and program. (I would wager that *little* development research is being done today in the behavioral sciences.)

Action research, the term coined by Kurt Lewin, undertakes to solve a problem for a client. It is identical to applied research generally except that in action research the roles of researcher and subject may change and reverse, the subjects becoming researchers and the researchers engaging in action steps.

These eight programs, while differing in objectives, values, means of influence, and program implications, are similar in wanting to use knowledge to gain some socially desirable end. Each seems successful or promising; each has its supporters and its detractors. Intrinsic to them all, I believe, is some bias or flaw which probably weakens their full impact. Four biases are particularly visible.

RATIONALISTIC BIAS: NO IMPLEMENTATION OF PROGRAM

Most of the strategies rely almost totally on rationality. But knowledge *about* something does *not* lead automatically to intelligent action. Intelligent action requires commitment and programs as well as truth.

TECHNOCRATIC BIAS: NO SPIRIT OF COLLABORATION

Change typically involves risk and fear. Any significant change in human organization involves rearrangement of patterns of power, association, status, skills, and values. Some may benefit, others may lose. Thus change typically involves risk and fear. Yet change efforts sometimes are conducted as if there were no need to discuss and "work through" these fears and worries (e.g., F. W. Taylor's failure to consider the relationship between the engineer with the stopwatch and the worker, or Freud's early work when he considered it adequate to examine the unconscious of his patients and tell them what he learned—even to the extent on occasion of analyzing dreams by mail).

INDIVIDUALIST BIAS: NO ORGANIZATION STRATEGY IS INVOLVED

This refers to strategies which rely on the individual while denying the organizational forces and roles surrounding him. There is, however, simply no guarantee that a wise individual who attains power will act wisely. It may be that *role corrupts*—both the role of power and the role of powerlessness. In any event, there is no guarantee that placing certain types of people in management—or training them or psychoanalyzing them or making scientists of them—leads to more effective action. Scientists act like administrators when they gain power. And graduates of human relations training programs tend to act like nonalumni shortly after their return to their organizational base.

The staff idea, proposed by Myrdal, is limited by the unresolved tensions in the staff-line dilemma noted by students of organizational behavior and by the conflicts derived from the role of the intellectual working in bureaucratic structures. The élite strategy has serious drawbacks, primarily because it focuses on the individual and not the organization.

INSIGHT BIAS: NO MANIPULABILITY

My major quarrel here is not with the formulation: insight leads to change, though this can be challenged, but with the lack of provision of variables accessible to control. It is not obvious that insight leads directly to sophistication in rearranging social systems or making strategic organizational interventions. Insight provides the relevant variables for planned change as far as personal manipulation goes, but the question remains: How can that lead directly to the manipulation of external factors?

The Elements of Planned Organizational Change

In the October 7, 1963, edition of the *New York Times*, a classified ad announced a search for change agents. It read:

WHAT'S A CHANGE AGENT? A result-oriented individual able to accurately and quickly resolve complex tangible and intangible problems. Energy and ambition necessary for success . . .

The change agents I have in mind need more than "energy and ambition." They are *professionals* who, for the most part, hold doctorates in the behavioral sciences. They are not a very homogeneous group, but they do have some similarities.

They are alike in that they take for granted the *centrality of work* in our culture to men and women in highly organized instrumental settings; in their concern with improvement, development, and measurement of *organizational effectiveness*; in their *preoccupation with people* and the process of human interaction; in their interest in changing the relationships, perceptions, and values of *existing personnel*. They may be members of the client system,

arguing that inside knowledge is needed, or external agents, arguing that perspective, detachment, and energy from outside are needed. They intervene at different structural points in the organization and at different times.

Though each change agent has in mind a set of unique goals based on his own theoretical position and competencies as well as the needs of the client system, there are some general aims. In a paradigm developed by Chris Argyris (1962), bureaucratic values tend to stress the rational, task aspects of work and to ignore the basic human factors which, if ignored, tend to reduce task competence. Managers brought up under this system of values are badly cast to play the intricate human roles now required of them. Their ineptitude and anxieties lead to systems of discord and defense which interfere with the problem-solving capacity of the organization.

Generally speaking, the normative goals of change agents derive from this paradigm. They include: improving interpersonal competence of managers; effecting a change in values so that human factors and feelings come to be considered legitimate; developing increased understanding among and within working groups to reduce tensions; developing "team management"; developing better methods of "conflict resolution" than suppression, denial, and the use of unprincipled power; viewing the organization as an organic system of relationships marked by mutual trust, interdependence, multigroup membership, shared responsibility, and conflict resolution through training or problem solving.

Programs for Implementing Planned Organizational Change

TRAINING

Discussion here will focus on three broad types of change programs that seem to be most widely used, frequently in some combination: training, consultation, and research. Training is an inadequate word in this context, as its dictionary meaning denotes "drill" and "exercise." I refer to what has been called laboratory training, sensitivity or group dynamics training, and most commonly, T-Group training.[5] The idea originated in Bethel, Maine, under the guidance of Leland Bradford, Kenneth Benne, and Ronald Lippitt, with initial influence from the late Kurt Lewin. The T Group has evolved since 1947 into one of the main instruments for organizational change. Bradford has played a central role in this development as director of the National Training Laboratories. Growth has been facilitated through the active participation of a number of university-based behavioral scientists and practitioners. Tavistock Institute has played a similar role in England, and recently a group of European scientists set up a counterpart to the National Training Laboratories.

The main objective at first was *personal change* or *self-insight*. Since the

[5] For a popular account of laboratory training, see Argyris, C. T-groups for organizational effectiveness. *Harvard bus. Rev.*, 1964, 42, 60–74. For a theoretical background, see Bradford, L. P., Gibb, J. R., & Benne, K. D. (Eds.) *T-group theory and laboratory method.* New York: John Wiley & Sons, Inc., 1964; and Schein, E. H., & Bennis, W. G. *Personal and organizational change via group methods.* New York: John Wiley & Sons, Inc., 1965).

fifties the emphasis has shifted to *organizational development*, a more precise date being 1958, when the Esso Company inaugurated a series of laboratories at refineries over the country under the leadership of Blake and Shepard (Shepard, 1960).

Briefly, laboratory training unfolds in an unstructured group setting where participants examine their interpersonal relationships. By examining data generated by themselves, members attempt to understand the dynamics of group behavior, e.g., decision processes, leadership and influence, norms, roles, communication distortions, effects of authority on behavioral patterns, coping mechanisms. T-Group composition is itself a strategic issue. Thus the organization may send an executive to a "stranger laboratory" which fills a "seeding" function; "cousin laboratories" may be conducted for persons of similar rank and occupational responsibilities within the company but from different functional groups; "diagonal slices" may be composed of persons of different rank but not in the same work group or in direct relationship; and "family laboratories" may be conducted for functional groups. The more the training groups approach a "family," the more the total organization is affected.

CONSULTING

The change agent *qua* consultant, perhaps best exemplified in the work of the Tavistock Institute, operates in a manner very like the practicing physician or psychoanalyst: that is, he starts from the chief "presenting symptom" of the client, articulates it in such a way that causal and underlying mechanisms of the problem are understood, and then takes remedial action. Heavy emphasis is placed on the strategy of *role model* because the main instrument is the change agent himself. Sofer (1961) reveals this when he suggests that psychotherapy or some form of clinical experience is necessary preparation for the change agent. Argyris, as consultant, confronts the group with their behavior toward him as an analogue of their behavior *vis-à-vis* their own subordinates.

If the role of the consultant sounds ambiguous and vague, this probably reflects reality. Certainly in the consultant approach the processes of change and the change agent's interventions are less systematic and less programmed than in training or applied research programs. A word about the latter.

APPLIED RESEARCH

I refer here to research in which the results are used systematically as an *intervention*. Most methods of research application collect information and report it. Generally, the relationship ends there. In the survey-feedback approach, as developed primarily by Floyd Mann (1957) and his associates at The University of Michigan's Institute for Social Research, this is only the beginning. Data are reported in "feedback" meetings where subjects become clients and have a chance to review the findings, test them against their own experience, and even ask the researchers to test some of their hypotheses. Instead of being submitted "in triplicate" and probably ignored, research results serve to activate involvement and participation in the planning, collection, analysis, and interpretation of more data.

Richard Beckhard, too, utilizes data

as the first step in his work as change agent (in press). In his procedure the data are collected through formal, nonstructured interviews which he then codes by themes about the managerial activities of the client for discussion at an off-site meeting with the subjects.

It should be stressed that most planned-change inductions involve all three processes—training, consulting, researching—and that both agent and client play a variety of roles. The final shape of the change agent's role is not as yet clear, and it is hazardous to report exactly what change agents do on the basis of their reports. Many factors, of course, determine the particular intervention the change agent may choose: cost, time, degree of collaboration required, state of target system, and so on.

Strategic Models Employed by Change Agents

More often than not, change agents fail to report their strategy or to make it explicit. It may be useful to look at two quite different models that are available: one developed by Robert Blake in his "Managerial Grid" system, and one with which I was associated at an Esso refinery and which Chris Argyris evaluated some years later.

Blake has developed a change program based on his analytic framework of managerial styles (Blake, Mouton, Barnes, & Greiner, 1964). Figure 1 shows the grid for locating types of managerial strategies. Blake and his colleagues attempt to change the organization in the direction of "team management" (9, 9 or high concern for people and high concern for production). Based on experience with 15 dif-

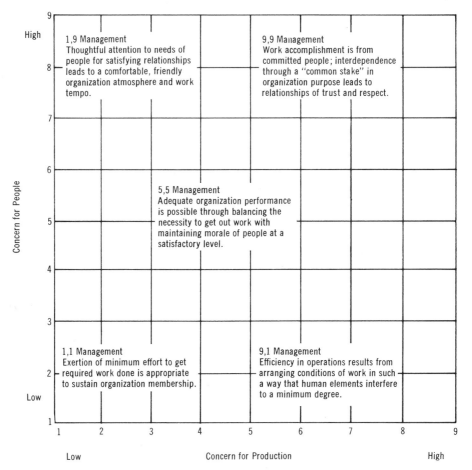

FIGURE 1. The Managerial Grid®. [From *The Managerial Grid* by Dr. Robert R. Blake and Dr. Jane S. Mouton. Copyright 1964, Gulf Publishing Company, Houston, Texas. Used with permission.]

ferent factories, the Blake strategy specifies six phases: off-site laboratory for "diagonal slice" of personnel; off-site program focused on team training for "family" groups; training in the plant location designed to achieve better integration between functional groups; goal-setting sessions for groups of 10 to 12 managers.

Blake and his colleagues estimate that these four phases may require two years or longer. The next two, implementing plans and stabilizing changes,

may require an additional two years.

Figure 2 (Argyris, 1960) presents another strategy: a change program used in a large oil company to improve the functioning of one of its smaller refineries. A new manager was named and sent to a T-Group training session to gain awareness of the human problems in the refinery. The Headquarters Organizational Development staff then conducted a diagnosis through a survey and interview of the managerial staff (70) and a sample of hourly employees

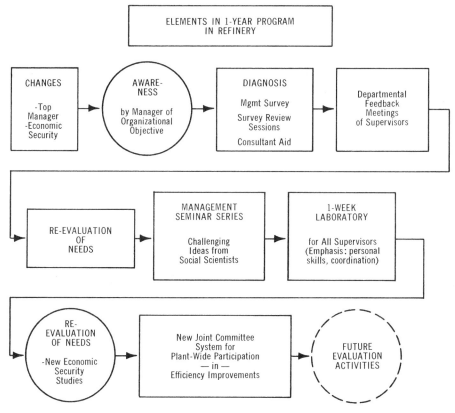

FIGURE 2.   A Change Program

(40/350). About that time the author was brought in to help the headquarters staff and the new manager.

It was decided that a laboratory program of T Groups might be effective but premature, with the result that weekly seminars that focused on new developments in human relations were held with top management (about 20). A one-week laboratory training program followed for all supervisors in diagonal slices, and then another re-evaluation of needs was undertaken. Some structural innovations were suggested and implemented. During the last phase of the program (not shown in the figure), the Scanlon Plan was adapted and installed (incidentally, for the first time in a "process" industry and for the first time that a union agreed to the Plan without a bonus automatically guaranteed).

Though it cannot be said with any assurance that these two strategies are typical, it may be helpful to identify certain features: (a) *length of time* (Blake estimates five years; the refinery program took two years up to the Scanlon Plan); (b) *variety of programs* utilized (research, consulting, training, teaching, planning); (c) *necessity of cooperation* with top management and the parent organization; (d) approaching the organization *as a system* rather than as a collection of individuals; (e) *phasing program* from individual to group to intergroup to overall organization; (f) intellectual *and* emotional content.

Power and the Role of the Change Agent

How and why do people and organizations change, and what is the nature and source of the power exerted by the change agent? We have to make inferences because change agents themselves tend to be silent on this. It is not *coercive power*, for the change agent generally does not have the ability to reward or punish. Moreover, he would prefer, at least intellectually, not to wield power at variance with his normative goals. Further, there is some evidence that coercive power is less durable than are other kinds of power, except under conditions of vigilant surveillance.

Traditional power? Almost certainly not. The change agent is, in fact, continually working without legitimization. *Expert power?* Possibly some, but it is doubtful whether his knowledge is considered "expert" enough—in the sense that an engineer or doctor or lawyer is seen as expert. *Referent* or *identification power?* Apparently so. Sofer, for example, attributes some influence to the client system's ability and desire to emulate the change agent. Still, this will vary from a considerable degree to not at all.

This leaves us with *value power* as the likeliest candidate of the possible sources of power. Most change agents do emit cues to a consistent value system. These values are based on Western civilization's notion of a scientific humanism: concern for our fellow man, experimentalism, openness and honesty, flexibility, cooperation, democracy. If what I have said about power is correct, it is significant (at least in the United States) that this set of values seems to be potent in influencing top management circles.

Characteristics of Client System

For the most part, the client systems appear to be subsystems of relatively large-scale international operations who find themselves in increasingly competitive situations, in rapidly changing environments, subjected to what have been called "galloping variables." Often the enterprise was founded through an innovation or monopolistic advantage which is thought to be in jeopardy.

Then there is some tension—some discrepancy between the ideal and the actual—which seems to activate the change program.

Finally, there is some faith in the idea that an intermediate proportion of organizational effectiveness is determined by social and psychological factors and that improvement here, however vague or immeasurable, may improve organizational effectiveness.

The Measurement of Effects

Until very recently, change agents, if they did any evaluation research at all, concentrated almost exclusively on attitudinal and subjective factors. Even so-called "hard" behavioral variables, like absentee rates, sickness and accident rates, personnel turnover, and so forth, were rarely investigated. Relating change programs to harder criteria, like productivity and economic and cost factors, was rarely attempted and never, to my knowledge, successful.

And again, the research that was conducted—even on the attitudinal measures—was far from conclusive. Roger Harrison attempted an evaluation study of Argyris' work and found that while there was a significant improvement in the individual executive's interpersonal ability compared with a control group, there was no significant "transfer" of this acuity to the real-life organizational setting. In short, there was a fairly rapid "fade-out" of effects obtained in T-Group training upon return to the organization (Harrison, 1962). This study also shows that new tensions were generated between those individuals who attended the training program and those who' did not—an example of the lack of a *systems* approach. Shepard's evaluation on the Esso organization shows that the impact of laboratory training was greatest on personal and interpersonal learnings, but "slightly more helpful than useless" in changing the organization.

More recently, though, some studies have been undertaken which measure more meaningful, less subjective variables of organizational effectiveness. Blake, Mouton, Barnes, and Greiner (1964), for example, conducted an evaluation study of their work in a very large (4,000 employees) petrochemical plant. Not only did they find significant changes in the values, morale, and interpersonal behavior of the employees, but significant improvements in productivity, profits, and cost reduction. David (in press), a change agent working on a program that attempts to facilitate a large and complicated merger, attributed the following effects to the programs: increased produc-

tivity, reduced turnover and absenteeism, in addition to a significant improvement in the area of attitudes and subjective feelings.

While these new research approaches show genuine promise, much more has to be done. The research effort has somehow to equal all the energy that goes into developing the planned-change programs themselves.

Some Criticisms and Qualifications

The work of the change agents reported here is new and occurs without the benefit of methodological and strategic precedents. The role of the change agent is also new, its final shape not fully emerged. Thus it has both the advantage of freedom from the constraints facing most men of knowledge, and suffers from lack of guidelines and structure. Let us touch quickly on problems and criticisms facing the change agents.

Planned Change and Organizational Effectiveness

I can identify six dimensions of organizational effectiveness: legal, political, economic, technological, social, and personal. There is a good deal of fuzziness as to which of these change agents hope to affect, and the data are inconclusive. Argyris, who is the most explicit about the relationship between performance and interpersonal competence, is still hoping to develop good measures to establish a positive relationship. The connection has to be made, or the field will have to change its normative goal of constructing not only a *better* world but a more *effective* one.

A Question of Values

The values espoused indicate a way of *behaving and feeling*; for example, they emphasize openness rather than secrecy, collaboration rather than dependence or rebellion, cooperation rather than competition, consensus rather than individual rules, rewards based on self-control rather than externally induced rewards, team leadership rather than a one-to-one relationship with the boss, authentic relationships rather than those based on political maneuvering.

Are they natural? Desirable? Functional? What then happens to status or power drives? What about those individuals who have a low need for participation and/or a high need for structure and dependence? And what about those personal needs which seem to be incompatible with these images of man, such as a high need for aggression and a low need for affiliation? In short, what about those needs which can be best realized through bureaucratic systems? Or benevolent autocracies? Are these individuals to be changed or to yield and comply?

The problem of values deserves discussion. One of the obstacles is the emotional and value overtones which interfere with rational dialogue. More often than not, one is plunged into a polarized debate which converts ideas into ideology and inquiry into dogma. So we hear of "Theory X vs. Theory Y," personality vs. organization, democratic vs. autocratic, task vs. maintenance, human relations vs. scientific management, and on and on.

Surely life is more complicated than these dualities suggest, and surely they must imply a continuum—not simply extremes.

Lack of Systems Approach

Up to this point, I have used the term "organizational change" rather loosely. In Argyris' case, for example, organizational change refers to a change in values of 11 top executives, a change which was not necessarily of an enduring kind and apparently brought about some conflict with other interfaces. In most other cases of planned organizational change, the change induction was limited to a small, élite group. Only in the work of Blake and some others can we confidently talk about organizational change—in a systems way; his program includes the training of the entire management organization, and at several locations he has carried this step to include wage earners.

Sometimes the changes brought about simply "fade out" because there are no carefully worked out procedures to ensure coordination with other interacting parts of the system. In other cases, the changes have "backfired" and have had to be terminated because of their conflict with interface units. In any case, a good deal more has to be learned about the interlocking and stabilizing changes so that the total system is affected.

Some Generalizations

It may be useful, as peroration, to state in the most tentative manner some generalizations. They are derived, for the most part, from the foregoing discussion and anchored in experience and, wherever possible, in research and theory.

First, a forecast: I suspect that we will see an increase in the number of planned-change programs along the lines discussed here—toward *less* bureaucratic and *more* participative, "open system" and adaptive structures. Given the present pronounced rate of change, the growing reliance on science for the success of the industrial enterprise, the growing number of professionals joining these enterprises, and the "turbulent contextual environment" facing the firm, we can expect increasing demand for social inventions to revise traditional notions of organized effort.

As far as adopting and acceptance go, we already know a good deal.[6] *Adoption* requires that the type of change should be of proven quality, easily demonstrable in its effects, and with information easily available. Its cost and accessibility to control by the client system as well as its value accord have to be carefully considered.

Acceptance also depends on the relationship between the change agent and the client system: the more profound and anxiety-producing the change, the more collaborative and closer the relationship required. In addition, we can predict that an anticipated change will be resisted to the degree that the client system possesses little or incorrect

[6] See, in particular, Rogers, E. *The diffusion of innovations.* New York: The Free Press, 1962; and Miles, M. (Ed.) *Innovation in education.* New York: Bureau of Publications, Teachers College, Columbia Univer., 1964.

knowledge about the change, has relatively little trust in the source of the change, and has comparatively low influence in controlling the nature and direction of the change.

What we know least about is *implementation*—a process which includes the creation of understanding and commitment toward a particular change and devices whereby it can become integral to the client system's operations. I will try to summarize the necessary elements in implementation:

(a) The *client system* should have as much understanding of the change and its consequences, as much influence in developing and controlling the fate of the change, and as much trust in the initiator of the change as is possible.

(b) The *change effort* should be perceived as being as self-motivated and voluntary as possible. This can be effected through the legitimization and reinforcement of the change by the top management group and by the significant reference groups adjacent to the client system. It is also made possible by providing the utmost in true volition.

(c) The *change program* must include emotional and value as well as cognitive (informational) elements for successful implementation. It is doubtful that relying solely on rational persuasion (expert power) is sufficient. Most organizations possess the knowledge to cure their ills; the rub is utilization.

(d) The *change agent* can be crucial in reducing the resistance to change. As long as the change agent acts congruently with the principles of the program and as long as the client has a chance to test competence and motives (his own and the change agent's), the agent should be able to provide the psychological support so necessary during the risky phases of change. As I have stressed again and again, the quality of the client-agent relationship is pivotal to the success of the change program.

REFERENCES

1. Ackoff, R. L., & Rivett, P. *A manager's guide to operations research*. New York: John Wiley & Sons, Inc., 1963, p. 34.

2. Argyris, C. *Organization development: An inquiry into the Esso approach*. New Haven, Conn.: Yale University Press, 1960.

3. Argyris, C. *Interpersonal competence and organizational effectiveness*. Homewood, Ill.: Dorsey, 1962. P. 43.

4. Beckhard, R. An organization improvement program in a decentralized organization. In D. Zand (Ed.), *Organization development: Theory and practice*, in press.

5. Bennis, W. G., Benne, K. D., & Chin, R. (Eds.) *The planning of change*. New York: Holt, Rinehart and Winston, Inc., 1961.

6. Blake, R. R., Mouton, Jane S., Barnes, L. B., & Greiner, L. E. Breakthrough in Organization Development. *Harvard bus. Rev.*, 1964, **42** (6), 133–155.

7. Boskoff, A. Functional analysis as a source of a theoretical repertory and research tasks in the study of social change. In G. K. Zollschan & W. Hirsch, *Explorations in social change*. Boston: Houghton Mifflin Company, 1964.

8. Chin, R. The utility of system models and developmental models for practitioners. In W. G. Bennis, K. D. Benne, & R. Chin (Eds.), *The planning of change*. New York: Holt, Rinehart, and Winston, Inc., 1961. Pp. 201–214.

9. Chin, R. Models and ideas about changing. Paper read at Symposium on Acceptance of New Ideas, Univ. of Nebraska, November, 1963.

10. Coser, L. *The functions of social conflict*. New York: The Free Press, 1956.

11. Dahrendorf, R. Toward a theory of social conflict. In W. G. Bennis, K. D. Benne, & R. Chin (Eds.), *The planning of change*. New York, Holt, Rinehart and Winston, Inc., 1961. Pp. 445–451.

12. David, G. The Weldon study: An organization change program based upon change in management philosophy. In D. Zand (Ed.), *Organization development: Theory and practice*, in press.

13. Freeman, H. E. The strategy of social policy research. *The soc. welf. Forum*, 1963, 143–160.

14. Gibb, J. R., & Lippitt, R. (Eds.) Consulting with groups and organizations. *J. soc. Issues*, 1959, **15**.

15. Glock, C. Y., Lippitt, R., Flanagan, J. C., Wilson, E. C., Shartle, C. L., Wilson, M. L., Croker, G. W., & Page, H. E. *Case studies in bringing behavioral science into use*. Stanford, Calif.: Inst. Commun. Res., 1960.

16. Harrison, R. In C. Argyris, *Interpersonal competence and organizational effectiveness*. Homewood, Ill.: Dorsey, 1962. Chapter 11.

17. Leeds, R., & Smith, T. (Eds.) *Using social science knowledge in business and industry.* Homewood, Ill.: Richard D. Irwin, Inc., 1963.
18. Likert, R., & Hayes, S. P., Jr. (Eds.) *Some applications of behavioral research.* Paris: UNESCO, 1957.
19. Mann, F. Studying and creating change: A means to understanding social organization. *Research in industrial relations.* Ann Arbor: Industr. Relat. Res. Ass., 1957, Publication No. 17.
20. Merton, R. K., & Lerner, D. Social scientists and research policy. In D. Lerner & H. D. Lasswell (Eds.), *The policy sciences: Recent developments in scope and method.* Stanford, Calif.: Stanford University Press, 1951.
21. Myrdal, G. *Value in social theory.* New York: Harper & Row, Publishers, 1958. P. 29.
22. Parsons, R. T. Evolutionary universals in society. *Amer. sociol. Rev.*, 1964, 29, 339–357.
23. Salisbury, H. E. *To Moscow and beyond.* New York: Harper & Row, Publishers, 1960. P. 136.
24. Shepard, H. Three management programs and the theory behind them. In *An action research program for organization improvement.* Ann Arbor: Foundation for Research on Human Behavior, 1960.
25. Sofer, C. *The organization from within.* London: Tavistock, 1961.
26. Zetterberg, H. L. *Social theory and social practice.* Totowa, N. J.: Bedminster, 1962.

2.2   APPROACHES TO ORGANIZATIONAL CHANGE

Louis B. Barnes

Industrial managers are fond of noting that change is the only thing that remains constant in their work. They live from one upset to the next. They encounter a steady stream of new machines, processes, procedures, structures, and management faces. As education and technical knowledge have increased, so has the pressure within even conventional organizations for the introduction of new people, practices, and procedures.

Yet despite the common occurrence

From Louis B. Barnes, "Organizational Change and Field Experiment Methods," in Victor H. Vroom, *Methods of Organizational Research,* (Pittsburgh, Pa.: University of Pittsburgh Press, 1967).

of organizational change, its dynamics and underlying processes are understood in only rough, ill-defined ways. Managers and social scientists who create and study change situations find that organizational changes involve multiple sets of complex variables whose identity, interaction, and impact vary from situation to situation. Those involved in the serious study of organizational change face an even greater problem in describing change with a static language system when the very concept involves the shifting of dynamic variables in relation to each other. The situation can be illustrated by an example.

Before the orbiting of Russia's Sputnik I, most American aircraft manufacturers were in the airframe business. They designed, sold, and produced propeller or jet aircraft for military and commercial customers. Their interests were largely defined by the traditions of manned flight at subsonic speeds. The heroes of the industry were the men who designed and flew jets using knowledge of aerodynamics and engine performance. The great names of the industry were names that dominated it during and after World War II—Douglas, Martin, Grumman, Boeing, North American, Republic, Lockheed.

Since the advent of the Sputniks, the picture in and around these companies has changed considerably. Most of the airframe companies were subjected to severe internal shakeups and stresses as they tried to decide whether they were in the airframe, spacecraft, electronic systems, engine, or missile business. As technology and market possibilities expanded, so did the drain on financial resources and the entrance of new firms into the field.

As a project became not an aircraft but an entire space exploration system, new forms of coordination and cooperation developed. The single decision-maker found himself surrounded by a new breed of technical experts, hardware problems, and problem-solving processes. He ignored these at his peril. Yet more than one aircraft company almost disappeared in an attempt to adapt to space technology requirements.

This rough sketch describes a series of changes that drastically affected one industry. The changes involved more than technology, fuels, engines, and electronic systems. Along with the changing technology came changes in manpower, training, production facilities, personnel, scheduling, organizational structure, performance criteria, marketing strategies. In some cases, a new management was needed to introduce the new technologies. In other cases, an old management was able to adjust itself and alter an existing organization. Most important, the airframe–space age example shows that organizational change involves variable causes and effects not easily isolated from each other. A change in technology may result in management changes which may lead to new procedures and policies which may again result in new technologies, and so on. Under the circumstances, oversimplification becomes desirable and almost inevitable. An analyst almost *has* to choose a limited number of variables which are recognized as dynamically interdependent and then try to work from there toward a more accurate understanding of reality.

In an effort to do this, Leavitt (1965) selected four interacting variables which he called Task, People, Technology, and Structure. Task refers to the organization's production of goods and services and, while these sometimes change independently, according to Leavitt, they change more often in response to People, Technology and/or Structural approaches which influence the Task variable and each other.

Leavitt also notes that the People, Technology, and Structural approaches represent potential strategies for organizational change. Each attracts specialists who develop expertise in changing the strategic variable and then use this change strategy as their lever for improving organizational Task performance. The People specialists tend to focus on personnel placement, management development programs, job counseling, and human relationships within organizations. Technology specialists approach change as production engineers, computer experts, systems designers. Structural specialists work on organization planning, work flow procedures, and staff-line configurations, among other things.

Needless to say, each of the professional specialists may find himself overlapping into another's area from time to time. Despite these overlaps, each tends to develop strong biases for one variable being more "strategic" than another. The preferences probably reflect the skills and talents of the proponents more than they do any single "best" approach to change. Thus Chapple and Sayles (1961) argue for work flow and structural changes while attacking those People approaches that attempt to train and "convert." Golembiewski (1964) chooses Structure as the strategic approach whose dimensions either permit or frustrate human relationships. By contrast, industrial engineers introduce new work systems and Technology variables through the use of machine replacement, operations research, or simulation techniques. People strategists use training programs, placement procedures, and testing, as their major tools.

All of these efforts have led to many large scale organizational changes but few systematic studies. In order to correct this shortage, social scientists have recently become heavily involved in the study of organizational change both as participants and observers. They have even begun to design, plan, and implement changes that seemed exclusively within the manager's realm a generation ago. Behavioral scientists can be said to work with the same four variables mentioned above: Task, People, Technology, and Structure. However, their major contributions are in the area of People approaches to organization change. These approaches have involved what Leavitt (1965) calls "power equalization" and what some behavioral scientists like to call "planned change." As Bennis (1966, p. 82) describes the planned change approach, it involves "a *change agent* who is typically a behavioral scientist brought in to help a *client system* which refers to the target of change. The change agent, *in collaboration* with the client system attempts to apply *valid knowledge* to the client's problems."

The "planned change" approach may or may not apply more "valid" knowledge to the Task-People-Technology-Structure variables. It does, however, specify an outside change agent *collaborating* with a client system. But collaboration obviously is only one way of distributing power in a People approach to change. There are other ways which involve shifting attention from *what* is being changed (the variables) to *how* the changes are being introduced and implemented.

In this second vein, Bennis (1966) constructs a typology of seven other change styles in addition to "planned change." The eight approaches differ according to power distribution, goal setting, and change implementation. Briefly, the other seven approaches can be described as:

1. *Indoctrination Change.* Mutual and deliberate goal setting but under unilateral power.
2. *Coercive Change.* Unilateral goal

setting with deliberate intentions using unilateral power. Coercive change would be exemplified by Chinese "brainwashing" and thought control practices.

3. *Technocratic Change.* Unilateral goal setting but shared power. One party defines the goal; the other party helps to reach that goal without question as to the goal's value.

4. *Interactional Change.* Shared power under conditions where goals are not deliberately sought.

5. *Socialization Change.* Unilateral power but collaborative goal implementation; e.g., small children develop under the influence of parents who unilaterally define the goals.

6. *Emulative Change.* Unilateral power without deliberate goals. This is found in formal organizations where subordinates "emulate" their superiors.

7. *Natural Change.* A residual category. Shared power with nondeliberate goal setting; i.e., changes are due to accidents, unintended events, etc.

Bennis' typology, according to its author, is only a crude and overlapping approximation of approaches to change. But it does go one step beyond a consideration of the four change variables (Task, People, Technology, and Structure). It suggests that change can be initiated by using various power distributions which may be as important or more important than the variable itself in determining the outcomes.

In another study Greiner (1965) searched the literature on organizational change and identified the most commonly used approaches as:

1. *The Decree Approach.* A "one-way" announcement originating with a person with high formal authority and passed on to those in lower positions (e.g., Taylor, 1911; Gouldner, 1954).

2. *The Replacement Approach.* Individuals in one or more key organizational positions are replaced by other individuals. The basic assumption is that organizational changes are a function of personnel changes (e.g., Gouldner, 1954; Guest, 1962).

3. *The Structural Approach.* Instead of decreeing or injecting new blood into work relationships, management changes the required relationships of subordinates working in the situation. By changing the structure of organizational relationships, organizational behavior is also presumably affected (e.g., Burns and Stalker, 1962; Chapple and Sayles, 1961; Woodward, 1958; Dalton, Barnes, and Zaleznik [in press]).

4. *The Group Decision Approach.* Participation by group members in implementing alternatives specified by others. This approach involves neither problem identification nor problem solving, but emphasizes the obtaining of group agreement on a predetermined course (e.g., Coch and French, 1948; Lewin, 1958).

5. *The Data Discussion Approach.* Presentation and feedback of relevant data to the client system by either a change catalyst or by change agents within the company. Organizational members are encouraged to develop their own analyses of the data which has been

given to them in the form of case materials, survey findings or data reports (e.g., Mann, 1957; Andrews, 1953).

6. *The Group Problem Solving Approach.* Problem identification and problem solving through group discussion with the help of an outsider. This would be one type of "planned change" (e.g., Sofer, 1961).

7. *The T-Group Approach.* Training in sensitivity to the processes of individual and group behavior. Changes in work patterns and relationships are assumed to follow from changes in interpersonal relationships. T-Group approaches focus upon the interpersonal relationships first, then hope for, or work toward, improvements in work performance (e.g., Argyris, 1962; Foundation for Research on Human Behavior, 1960).

Not surprisingly, Greiner's seven approaches, like Bennis', tend to emphasize the power distribution style in each case. The approaches described above move in a roughly descending order from unilateral power to mutually-shared power; i.e., the Decree approach represents unilateral initiation by formal authority while the T-Group approach represents a highly collaborative attempt at shared influence. (At the same time, Greiner's Replacement and Structural approaches can be more generally classified as People and Structure approaches which can be implemented by any one of the other five power styles described by Greiner.) Without question, the Decree approach is more prevalent in industry than the other approaches. However, a survey of the literature shows increasing emphasis on Greiner's last four approaches and their greater uses of shared power. According to McGregor (1960) and Likert (1961) Problem Solving and T-Group approaches (with most shared power) are even supplanting the earlier (and more manipulative) Group Decision approaches.

Leavitt (1965) attributes the increase in shared control to the fact that power distribution is more directly confronted in organizations than it once was. Whereas power historically accompanied formal status positions, it no longer does to the same extent. In a modern industrial society, power conflicts can arise when formal status differs from status depending upon knowledge, informal social control, or professional reputation. Formal status no longer overshadows other sources of power to the extent that it once did. When other sources of power became more evident, says Leavitt (1965, p. 1153): "It was to be expected then that the next moves . . . would be toward working out the power variable. And it was obvious too that the direction would be toward power equalization rather than toward power differentiation. The theoretical underpinnings, the prevalent values, and the initial research results all pointed that way."

The importance of Leavitt's observation is shown in some further work by Greiner (1965) who sought to identify the conditions that differentiated "successful" from "less successful" large-scale change efforts. Greiner found that *all* of the nine published accounts that qualified for inclusion (on the basis of large-scale change effort and data adequacy) involved attempts at what Leavitt has called "power equalization." In these cases, the change approaches differed but power equilization seemed a common feature.

Our review of organizational change has ... described *what* is being changed and *how* it is being changed. Leavitt's four variables, Task, People, Technology, and Structure emphasize *what*

is being varied. The Bennis and Greiner descriptions show that differences in power distribution can affect how the changes will be initiated and implemented; change can be arbitrarily introduced by a single authority source, or the power can be more widely shared by the individuals concerned. ...

REFERENCES

1. Andrews, K. "Executive Training by the Case Method." in K. Andrews, ed., *Human Relations and Administration; The Case Method of Training*, Cambridge: Harvard University Press, 1953.

2. Argyris, C. *Interpersonal Competence and Organizational Effectiveness.* Homewood, Ill.: I-Dorsey, 1962.

3. Bennis, W. G., *Changing Organizations.* New York: McGraw-Hill, Inc., 1966.

4. Burns, T., and Stalker, G. M. *The Management of Innovation*, London: Tavistock Publications, 1961.

5. Chapple, E. D. and Sayles, L. R. *The Measure of Management.* New York: Crowell-Collier and Macmillan, Inc., 1961.

6. Coch, L. and French, J. R. P., Jr. "Overcoming Resistance to Change." *HR*, 1948, 1, 512–532.

7. Dalton, G. W., Barnes, L. B., and Zaleznik, A. *The Authority Structure as a Change Variable* (in press) .

8. Foundation for Research on Human Behavior. *An Action Research Program for Organizational Improvement (in Esso Standard Oil Co.).* Ann Arbor, Mich., 1960.

9. Golembiewski, R. "Authority as a Problem in Overlays." *Administrative Science Qtly., 9* (1) June 1964, 22–49.

10. Gouldner, A. *Patterns of Industrial Bureaucracy*, New York: The Free Press, 1954.

11. Greiner, L. E. "Organizational Change and Development." Unpublished Ph.D. dissertation, Harvard University, 1965.

12. Guest, R. *Organizational Change, The Effect of Successful Leadership.* Homewood, Ill.: Dorsey, 1962.

13. Leavitt, H. J. "Applied Organizational Change in Industry: Structural, Technological, and Humanistic Approaches." In James G. March, ed., *Handbook of Organizations.* Skokie, Illinois: Rand McNally & Company, 1965, 1144–1170.

14. Lewin, K. "Group Decision and Social Change." In E. E. Maccoby, T. M. Newcomb, and E. L. Hartley, eds., *Readings in Social Psychology.* 3d ed. New York: Holt, Rinehart and Winston, Inc., 1958, 197–211.

15. Likert, R. L. *New Patterns of Management.* New York: McGraw-Hill, 1961.

16. Mann, F. C. "Studying and Creating Change: A Means to Social Organization." In C. M. Arensberg, et al., eds., *Research in Industrial Human Relations.* New York: Harper & Row, Publishers, 1957.

17. McGregor, D. *The Human Side of Enterprise.* New York: McGraw-Hill, Inc., 1961.

18. Sofer, C. *Organization from Within.* London: Tavistock Publications, 1961.

19. Taylor, F. W. *The Principles and Methods of Scientific Management.* New York: Harper & Row, Publishers, 1911.
20. Woodward, J. *Management and Technology.* London: Her Majesty's Stationery Office, 1958.

2.3   THEORETICAL REQUIREMENTS OF THE APPLIED SOCIAL SCIENCES

Alvin W. Gouldner

It seems reasonable to assume that the applied social sciences develop more rapidly under some conditions than others. The aim of this paper is to take this simple assumption seriously, and to identify the theoretic and conceptual tools most conducive to the maturation of the applied social sciences. The ultimate objective is to codify these, so that they can constitute a paradigm useful for the systematic inspection of the different applied fields. Such a paradigm could provide a working model of what is "par" for the course. At the same time, it could also indicate those areas in pure social science where further work might bridge the gap between it and applied efforts.

Applied social science has distinctive intellectual requirements largely because it is éxposed to special exigencies and tensions. Its theories and concepts not only have to pass inspection before the bar of science, but they must also prove serviceable in coping with this specific set of social tensions. It is not

From Alvin W. Gouldner, "Theoretical Requirements of the Applied Social Sciences," *American Sociological Review,* published by the American Sociological Association, XXII, No. 1 (February 1957), 92–102. Some footnotes omitted. Abridged and used by permission.

enough, therefore, to examine the intellectual tools of applied social science in terms of their manifest scientific functions as technical instruments. They must also be considered in the light of their latent social functions for the peculiar system of human relations in which they are implicated. In this way, it may be seen that certain of the devices of applied social science, which sometimes seem scientifically senseless, are at least sociologically sensible.

Attention is directed to two historically different planes of work in applied social science. One of these is the ongoing work in such areas as race relations, housing, industrial sociology, criminology, or mass communications research. The second plane involves inspection of the work of such classic contributors to the applied social sciences as Karl Marx, Emile Durkheim, and Sigmund Freud.

The Model Outlined

Unlike pure science, the applied social sciences are not oriented solely to values intrinsic to science—such as increased information, objectivity, prediction, parsimony, replication, and the like. Applied social science is characterized by an orientation to the values of laymen, as well as of scientists. These lay values, extrinsic to science as such, are regarded by the applied social scientist as legitimate points of orientation for his professional and scientific work.

There seem to be four such value-foci on which the work of applied social scientists centers:

1. The reduction of various forms of social deviancy, as exemplified in efforts to rehabilitate criminals or juvenile delinquents
2. Improvement of the efficiency or effectiveness with which diverse lay goals are pursued, as exemplified in the work of some industrial sociologists or applied anthropologists
3. The reduction of tensions or conflicts, such as the work of some race relations specialists
4. The reduction of tensions that a group experiences in relation to its "environment," such as those found in personnel testing, market research, and public relations surveys.

Applied social scientists are more likely to use laymen as a reference group in organizing their professional work, and their work is more likely to occur in the context of, and be influenced by, their relationship with laymen.[1] For these reasons the applied social scientist is constrained to include among his dependent variables certain lay "social problems." As part of his work the applied social scientist is ultimately concerned with identifying those independent variables which can not only account for, but which can remedy, these "social problems." Preliminary though the model is at this point, it may yet be sufficient to permit discussion of why Marx, Durkheim, and Freud have been characterized as applied social scientists.

Freud, Marx, and Durkheim

It is easy to accept Freud as an applied scientist, and, indeed he is widely regarded as the twentieth century's master clinician. However, in viewing Marx as an applied social scientist the stance needed is that of a Machiavellian operationalism. The objective is neither to bury nor to praise him. The assumption is simply that he is better understood for being understood as an applied sociologist. This is in part the clear implication of Marx's *Theses on Feurbach*, which culminate in the resounding 11th thesis: "The philosophers have only interpreted the world in different ways; the point, however, is to change it." This would seem to be the tacit creed of applied scientists everywhere.

Marx is no Faustian, concerned solely with understanding society, but a Promethean who sought to understand it well enough to influence and to change it. He was centrally concerned with the

[1] It should be emphasized that the focus in this paper is on those characteristics common to various efforts at applied social science. There is no intention to suggest that there is but one kind of applied social science, or only one model of its social system. In a companion piece ["Explorations in Applied Social Science," *Social Problems*, 3 (January, 1956), pp. 169–181] attention was directed to variations in applied social science, and an effort was made to delineate two sub-models of its social system, the "clinical" and the "engineering."

social problems of a lay group, the proletariat, and there can be little doubt that his work is motivated by an effort to reduce their suffering, as he saw it. His diagnosis was that their increasing misery and alienation engendered endemic class struggle; his prognosis claimed that this would culminate in revolution; his therapeutic prescription was class consciousness and active struggle.

Here, as in assessing Durkheim or Freud, the issue is not in whether this analysis is empirically correct or scientifically adequate. Furthermore, whether or not this formulation seems to eviscerate Marx's revolutionary core, as critics on the left may charge, or whether the formulation provides Marx with a new veneer of academic respectability, as critics on the right may allege, is entirely irrelevant from the present standpoint. Insofar as Marx's or any other social scientist's work conforms to a generalized model of applied social science, insofar as it is professionally oriented to the values and social problems of laymen in his society, he may be treated as an applied social scientist.

Despite Durkheim's intellectualistic proclivities and rationalistic pathos, he was too much the product of European turbulence to turn his back on the travail of his culture. "Why strive for knowledge of reality, if this knowledge cannot aid us in life," he asked. "Social science," he said, "can provide us with rules of action for the future."[2] Durkheim, like Marx, conceived of science as an agency of social action, and like him was professionally oriented

[2] Emile Durkheim, *The Rules of Sociological Method*, Chicago: University of Chicago Press, 1938, pp. 47 and xxxix.

to the values and problem of laymen in his society. Unless one sees that Durkheim was in some part an applied social scientist, it is impossible to understand why he concludes his monumental study of *Suicide* with a chapter on "Practical Consequences," and why, in the *Division of Labor*, he proposes a specific remedy for anomie.

Durkheim is today widely regarded as a model of theoretic and methodologic sophistication, and is thus usually seen only in his capacity as a pure social scientist. Surely this is an incomplete view of the man who regarded the *practical* effectiveness of a science as its principal justification. To be more fully understood, Durkheim also needs to be seen as an applied sociologist. His interest in religious beliefs and organization, in crime and penology, in educational methods and organization, in suicide and anomie, are not casually chosen problem areas. Nor did he select them only because they provided occasions for the development of his theoretical orientation. These areas were in his time, as they are today, problems of indigenous interest to applied sociologists in Western society, precisely because of their practical significance.

Whatever their many differences, Marx, Durkheim, and Freud share the applied social scientist's concern with bringing social science to bear on the problems and values of laymen with a view to remedying their disturbances. In characterizing them as applied social scientists, reference is made to only one of many roles they played. An applied social scientist is a role, and the person playing this role can and does play others, and he may, therefore, also be a pure social scientist as well.

It is in such role-playing terms that these men are regarded as applied social scientists. It is to be expected that their work will bear the impress of the problems and needs of applied social science and may also contain some clues concerning the ways in which these needs can be variously satisfied, even by the applied social sciences today.

Laymen's Hypotheses

In dealing with lay "social problems," the applied social scientist is confronting questions for which laymen often believe they have answers. Laymen usually have some explanation or favored hypotheses concerning the source of their problems. However inadequate the applied social scientist may judge these to be, he cannot blithely ignore them. He must take some of the laymen's favored hypotheses into account if he is to establish or maintain a relationship with them. Thus Marx had to consider whether "love" or Christian Ethics could be regarded as an adequate lever of social change. Durkheim had to consider whether economic poverty could account for suicide, and Freud had to examine whether the prevailing biologistic explanations of mental disturbance were adequate. All of these men had to consider lay hypotheses, even if only to discredit them.

All social scientists, pure or applied, are of course obliged to test competing hypotheses in analyzing a problem. Applied social science, however, necessarily draws some of its competing hypotheses from a distinctive source, namely laymen. The applied social scientist may systematically examine a hypothesis, even if he puts little credence in it, because the resultant research may cement his rapport with a lay group.

The Western Electric studies thus began with experiments testing the effects of improved illumination or rest periods on industrial productivity, for these involved hypotheses then favored by industrial personnel.[3] Recent studies of jury behavior have sought to test hypotheses, favored by the legal profession, which had assumed that "hung juries" could be eliminated by relaxing the unanimity rule. The manifest function of testing independent variables favored by laymen is to provide compliances with lay expectations that strengthen the acceptance of social scientists. The latent function of such tests, however, is to document the inadequacy and breakdown of lay hypotheses, thus enlarging the area of intellectual discretion allowable to applied social scientists, and easing their introduction of independent variables that are novel to laymen.

Pure and Applied Science

If the applied social scientist is to find the theories of pure social science useful to him, there need to be in the pure theory some conceptual elements that can be reconceptualized into lay concepts, or vice versa. Unfortunately, however, this is not always the case.

[3] These are referred to as the "customary" statement of the human problems of management in F. J. Roethlisberger and W. J. Dickson, *Management and the Workers*, Cambridge, Mass.: Harvard University Press, 1939, p. 590.

An example may be found in the kind of phenomenon disaster specialists have been studying. Some of the difficulties encountered in the development of disaster research may occur because present pure theory in sociology does not allow for ready reconceptualization of the layman's notion of disaster. What after all is the common meaning of disaster? Webster defines it as "an unforeseen and ruinous mischance or misadventure which happens, often suddenly, either through culpable lack of foresight or through adverse external agency." Among other things, it commonly involves a sudden destruction of the material props of human action—homes, means of transportation, stores, furniture, food supplies, clothing—often, though not always, by the intrusion of sudden changes in the natural environment, such as floods, fires, blizzards, tornadoes, hurricanes, etc.

There are at least three counts on which pure sociological theory today fails to aid in the analysis of this problem: (1) It has very little to say about, and does not systematically deal with, the role of material props. Even the concept of "culture," which at one time involved reference to material traits, is increasingly defined in terms of normative elements alone. The theoretical location of material props, therefore, becomes steadily obscured as it gets thrust into a residual limbo. (2) Present pure sociological theory has given little thought to the relationship between social or cultural systems, and the so-called natural environment. Anthropologists like Meggers and Steward continue to confront this problem, but sociologists apparently find little of

interest in it.[4] (3) A disaster involves not only a change, but usually a fairly sudden one. Pure sociological theory, however, has only begun to develop models adequate to cope with the analysis of change, and is even more removed from the analysis of change tempo involving questions of sudden transition. The problem of change tempo is important to almost all applied social scientists, as the controversy over "gradualistic" desegregation in the South presently dramatizes.[5]

Unless applied social scientists can find existent pure theories containing concepts that can be reconceptualized into independent and dependent variables significant to laymen, they are under pressure to design their own formal theories, into which they can build the necessary bridging concepts. Perhaps the best example of this is Freud's work, which deliberately incorporated such lay concepts as "sexuality" in its formal theory, in a sense at least partially convergent with the manner in which it is used in everyday thinking.

The applied social scientist not only focuses on social problems perceivable to laymen but also requires knowledge to remedy them. Applied social science, therefore, is greatly concerned with

[4] See Betty J. Meggers, "Environmental Limitations on the Development of Culture," *American Anthropologist*, 56 (October, 1954), pp. 801–824; and the collection of essays by Julian H. Steward, *Theory of Culture Change*, Urbana, Ill.: University of Illinois Press, 1955.

[5] The problem of change tempo and desegregation is cogently examined in Kenneth Clark, "Desegregation: An Appraisal of the Evidence," *Journal of Social Issues*, 9 (1953), pp. 1–76.

facilitating the prediction and production of social and cultural change. Regardless of whether the applied social scientist wishes to make workers more efficient, or to transform alcoholics into mild-mannered tea-drinkers, or to re-shape ethnic bigots into tolerant democratic citizens, he requires knowledge, theories, and concepts, which bear upon the processes of *change*, to help him analyze and facilitate it.

The applied sociologist seeks knowledge that will shed light upon the problems of men in his society and will facilitate their solution. Unlike the pure scientist, who delights in maximizing knowledge either for its own sake or to test hypotheses and extend theories, the applied social scientist will sometimes forgo sources of knowledge, however rich in data they may be, if he fears their use will impede the intended change. For example, psychoanalysts might better verify and extend data derived from their patients by enlisting the aid of the patient's family and friends, but they ordinarily and voluntarily forgo use of such channels. One finds a similar refusal to maximize sources of information in the work of the Tavistock group, the staff of which discourages respondents from communicating information in confidence.[6] The impulse toward change dominates and may be at variance with the impulse to know.[7]

[6] Elliott Jaques, *The Changing Culture of a Factory*, New York: Holt, Rinehart and Winston, Inc., 1952, p. 3.

[7] This classic tension was early recognized by Freud who commented, "It is indeed one of the distinctions of psychoanalysis that research and treatment proceed hand in hand, but still the technique required for the one begins, at a certain point, to di-

Criteria for Concept Selection

If it is to be useful for change purposes, the applied social scientist's knowledge must have certain characteristics, which distinguish it from that of the pure social scientist's. The latter, for example, aims at identifying variables with predictive power, and the more powerful and reliable the prediction, the better. The applied social scientist's criteria for assessing the adequacy of an independent variable include predictive potency but go beyond this, adding certain standards not relevant to the pure scientist. For one, the applied social scientist inspects his independent variables to determine the extent to which they are accessible to control. Since his ultimate objective involves the furtherance of some kind of change, not all independent variables are equally suitable for this purpose, nor is the one with the highest correlation coefficient always the best.

For example, no matter how high an inverse correlation is found between the rate of urbanization and the birth rate, the applied demographer can do little to reduce the birth rate by manipulating the degree of urbanization. Demographers can, however, focus on an item, namely contraceptive materials and information, which they can control, at least in greater measure. Even if urbanization and industrialization are much more highly correlated with the birth rate than is the degree of available contraceptive material and information, the latter assumes strate-

verge from that of the other." Sigmund Freud, *Collected Papers*, Vol. II, London: Hogarth Press, 1949, p. 326.

gic significance because of its controllability. Thus the applied social scientist is concerned not merely with identifying predictively potent independent variables, but also with discovering some that are accessible to control.

There are a number of circumstances in which even a predictively potent independent variable will be of little use to the applied social scientist. One such is where there exists no technology by means of which it can be managed. Therefore, for instance, Huntington's sunspot theory of economic cycles had little appeal to New Deal statesmen. Contrariwise, because Keynesian theory identified a controllable element, the state, which could be used to restore economic equilibrium, it became the dominant economic theory of New Deal liberals. As one writer puts it:

The system of economic thought which has become regnant in the last generation is the keynesian. . . . Keynesian ideas have been accepted not because they explained more than others but because they provided a set of causal laws whose independent variables were accessible to action in the immediate present.[8]

For similar reasons, students of social disorganization have long been drawn to the hypothesis that there is a "casual linkage between 'bad' housing and social disorganization." This is so, not because they have regarded this hypothesis as possessing a shred of theoretical elegance, but rather because its independent variable was controllable and accessible. In this connection one might well inspect Loring's recent research, which appears to have found a correlation between certain indices of social disorganization and the amount of space occupied by a family, or a density factor. Loring's paper convincingly demonstrates that there is no inherent incompatibility between theoretical sophistication and a concern for controllable variables.[9]

Notice that the last two illustrations from demography and housing both invoke the forgotten man of sociological research, elements of so-called "material culture." It may be briefly indicated here that one meaning of Marx's materialism may be reappraised in this light. For while Marx was no crude materialist, there is a substantial sense in which he was impressed with the material props of human action, and stressed their importance. This, it may be guessed, was due as much to his commitment to an applied sociology as to his polemic against Hegel's idealism. For the material props of action are distinguished by their relative accessibility to control. Indeed, in one of its expressions "materialism" might almost be defined as an assertion, not of the ontological importance of "hard" matter, but of the strategic significance of any accessible variable, tangible or not. So-called material factors such as housing space, machines, or contraceptives are of interest to applied sociologists because they are open to control. It is likely that such concepts will continue to be required and highly regarded by applied sociologists.

[8] Lewis S. Feuer, "Causality in the Social Sciences," *Journal of Philosophy*, 51 (November, 1954), pp. 683–684.

[9] William C. Loring, "Housing and Social Disorganization," *Social Problems*, 3 (January, 1956), pp. 160–168.

In race relations research similar concerns with controllable variables are discernible. For reasons similar to those involved in Keynesian economics, the role of the state and of legal institutions continues to be given great stress by those seeking to modify patterns of ethnic discrimination. This despite the fact that, since Sumner's time, pure sociological theory has given scant analysis to legal institutions. The initial emphasis on the role of "stereotypes" involved a focus on the cognitive aspects of the prejudiced person's orientation to an ethnic minority, in part because these were regarded as the most controllable elements in his orientation. It was assumed that the beliefs bigots held about minorities could be more readily managed than could their affective feeling states, by directing accurate information at those holding the stereotypes. Even an excellent and recent volume on prejudice opens its section on methods of opposing prejudice with a discussion of ways of "eliminating false beliefs."[10] It is likely that the emergence of the concept of "stereotype," conceived of as a learned and not as a biologically given orientation to the minority group, and thus as relatively controllable, did much to foster modern race relations work.

There is a second circumstance in which even a predictively potent independent variable will provide little help to the applied social scientist. This involves situations in which, from the standpoint of the participating laymen, the instrumental management of a variable would violate their values.

[10] Gerhart Saenger, *The Social Psychology of Prejudice*, New York: Harper & Row, Publishers, 1953, p. 159.

For example, even though contraceptives are technologically controllable, they are not instrumentally manageable from the value standpoint of a believing Catholic population. Similarly, even though changes in informal organization are technologically feasible, they may violate values that stress that human beings should not be treated as means to an end, thus giving rise to charges of "manipulation." One reason that legal institutions and material props have played such a large part in the work of applied social scientists is that, in a culture such as our own, they are both instrumentally manageable and technologically controllable.

A third circumstance which may limit the value of an independent variable to an applied social scientist is the question of its cost. Utilization of a variable as a change agent always depends, in some measure, on whether or not there is some other variable available that can accomplish the same results with less cost. There is always a question of just how much change one is securing for a given expenditure of scarce resources. These are the kinds of problems that students of mass communication media frequently have to assess. Earlier, they sought to appraise whether it was most economical to use either the newspapers or the radio to communicate a given message. Presently, they may seek to assess how many minutes of radio time are worth a minute of television time. In like manner, Dodd's "Project Revere" seeks to determine the effectiveness of given amounts of a single type of communication stimulus, particularly leaflets, attempting to determine the proportion of a community that will be reached by varying amounts of leaflets.

Finally, it might be added that much of the interest in leadership in the applied social sciences functions to identify presumably efficient loci of intervention for purposes of group or mass persuasion. In Dean and Rosen's cogent *Manual of Intergroup Relations* for example, about a fourth of their 27 propositions, specifying ways and means of reducing discrimination, deal rather directly with the role of leadership.[11]

System Analysis

The applied social scientist's concern with the controllability and relative efficiency of different variables in producing given changes also has implications for the larger kinds of theoretical models he requires and utilizes. These distinctive contingencies dispose the applied social scientist to use models of system analysis, for several reasons: (1) System models forewarn the applied social scientist of the possibility that a change in one part of the system may yield unforeseen and undesirable consequences in another part of the system, due to the interdependence of its elements. (2) System models indicate that changes may be secured in one element, not only by a frontal attack upon it but also by a circumspect and indirect manipulation of more distantly removed variables. These, because of system interdependence, may ultimately produce the desired changes in the target variable.[12] (3) For this reason as well as others, system analysis therefore directs attention to the multiple possibilities of intervention with respect to a single problem.

Yet, insofar as such a model focuses only on the interdependence of elements within a system, it provides no clue, by itself, concerning preferential points of entry into that system. It fails to establish any generalized basis in terms of which the scarce resources available for change may be economically allocated among the diverse components of the system. It fails, in short, to satisfy the applied social scientist's interest in the comparative costs and efficiency of different variables.

Because the resources available for change-efforts are scarce, the applied social scientist requires some basis for assigning weights to different components in the systems with which he deals. He needs some basis for assessing their differential influence in determining various outcomes. If this need occurs in the absence of determinate methods of mathematical resolution, there is a tendency for the system model to break down in monistic, single-factor directions. Thus in both Marx and Freud's work there is, on the one hand, a focus on *systems* of social relations and personality, respectively. On the other hand, however, there is also a tendency monistically to focus on certain factors, such as economic or production relations in Marx's case, or

---

[11] John P. Dean and Alex Rosen, *A Manual of Intergroup Relations*, Chicago: University of Chicago Press, 1955. Similar implications of the studies of "opinion leaders" are found in Elihu Katz and Paul F. Lazarsfeld, *Personal Influence*, New York: The Free Press, 1955.

[12] Robin Williams, *The Reduction of Intergroup Tensions*, New York: The Social Science Research Council, 1947, has by far the most sophisticated discussion of these problems in the context of race relations analysis.

on sexual etiology in Freud's. Such monistic tendencies may be regarded as efforts to adapt to the economic exigencies of applied social science, and not merely as absolute expressions of theoretical preference. Tendencies toward monistic breakdown in the models of applied social science probably also derive, in some measure, from the scientist's relationship with a lay group who may find single-factor analysis more intelligible than system models.

A monistic resolution of the economic exigencies of applied social science seems to be manifested even in the analyses of a resolute system theorist such as Parsons. In his effort to develop a strategy for changing conquered Germany after World War II, Parsons identifies the economic-occupational structures as "much the most promising as a lever of institutional change . . . [because] it is a highly strategic point in the total structure . . . [and] through its close structural interdependence with kinship and the class structure, change there would have major repercussions in these neighboring areas."[13] Parson's stress here on the economic-occupational structure is surprisingly reminiscent of a Marxian analysis. If such a convergence between Parsons and Marx exists, it is certainly not because Parsons is a Marxist. Parsons converges with Marx because he confronts himself with a problem essentially similar to that to which Marx had persistently committed himself, namely, the introduction of planned change in a society. This necessarily involves questions of the economic allocation of scarce resources and thus requires the choice of efficient points of entry into a system of interdependent variables.

The Theory of Unanticipated Consequences

Still another expression of the applied social scientist's interest in the identification of controllable variables, is to be found in his persistent use of a theory of unanticipated consequences. It is noteworthy that Marx, Durkheim, and Freud, all, developed some version of a theory of unanticipated consequences.

Marx noted that the events that occur in a society governed by market institutions, and with only casually integrated economic enterprises, could not be predicted on the basis of knowing the actors' individual motives. For the things that happen, said Marx, are often sought by no man. Entrepreneurs seek profit and orient their production to this anticipation, yet their very actions have the unanticipated consequence of generating market gluts and economic depressions.

Durkheim's most prominent use of the theory of unanticipated consequences is in his analysis of suicide. Here he showed that events, which were seemingly understandable as acts of deliberate intention, could be understood as the unforeseen consequences of adherence to certain values. The higher suicide rate of Protestants, for example, is not regarded by Durkheim as due to their deliberate conformity with any cultural prescription concerning suicide, but as the unantici-

---

[13] Talcott Parsons, *Essays in Sociological Theory, Pure and Applied*, New York: The Free Press, 1949, p. 334.

pated consequence of conformity to other values that have no explicit implication for suicide.

Similarly, Freud was interested in the play of unanticipated consequences on a third level, the psychological. In his analysis of *The Psychopathology of Everyday Life,* he sought to show how language lapses and dreams derived from conflicts in individual motivation. Freud observed that human behavior was replete with unanticipated consequences because human personality contained unconscious motivations, which conflicted with the aims of which people were aware.

This convergence of Marx, Durkheim, and Freud in the identification and analysis of unanticipated consequences would seem to stem in part from their common participation in a system of applied social science, which exerts pressure to focus on the problematic concerns of laymen. The lay vocabulary is filled with terms indicating an interest in discriminating between foreseen and unforeseen occurrences. In the lay vocabulary, moreover, the unexpected is almost equivalent to the undesirable. Thus synonyms (in Roget's) for unexpected are: bolt from the blue, bewilderment, disappointment, disillusionment, miscalculation, to be caught unawares or off one's guard, stunned, staggered, and the like.

Unforeseen consequences are not, of course, always undesirable to the layman, as indicated by a term such as a "pleasant surprise." Nevertheless, other things equal, that is, given two identical events, one foreseen and the other unexpected, the former is usually preferential from the actor's standpoint.

One may have had to prepare even for *desired* events, but could not do so if they occurred unexpectedly. It is probably for this reason that the antonyms of unexpected, in lay terminology (again according to Roget), include words such as: preparation, provision, precaution, rehearsal, manufacture, arrange, and so forth. If not to the scientist, then to the layman, *prévoir* literally means *pouvoir.* The applied social scientist's interest in unforeseen events is, in important part, a focus on events that laymen find threatening. Stated differently, it is an interest in events over which layment have lost control and for which, therefore, their need for assistance in regaining it has become manifest. A concern with unanticipated consequences by the applied social scientist, therefore, locks onto the motivations and engages the profoundest interests of laymen.

The theory of unanticipated consequences has its closest links with the needs of both laymen and applied social scientists alike when it implicates the layman himself in the very difficulties of which he complains. Insofar as a theory of unanticipated consequences implies, as in Marx's case that the layman's own profit-seeking activities produce economic depressions, that his adherence to certain values elicits suicide as in the Durkheimian case, or that his difficulties stem from his own unconscious motivations as in the Freudian analysis, then the problems have been defined as having more directly controllable roots. For if it is the layman's own behavior that produces his own problems, at least in part, then a change in his own behavior can aid in remedying the problem. Thus the theory of unanticipated consequences is particularly suitable to the needs of applied social science, because it identifies independent variables more directly accessible to control.

Selznick's important contribution to the theory of unanticipated consequences is of interest precisely on this count, for it directly stresses the degree to which unanticipated consequences derive from the controllable actions of those who suffer from them.[14] Selznick conceives of the action from which unanticipated consequences stem as "commitments." In so doing he focuses on the ways in which these actions contain voluntaristic components of decision and therefore of choice.

By stressing that there are elements of decision and choice even in constraining situations, the notion of commitment identifies areas of intervention and control in them. The concept of commitment also indicates the ways in which present constraints are outcomes of earlier decisions and choices on the actors' part. This implies that the earlier choices were in some sense freer and possessed a greater variety of functional alternatives than did later ones. Different phases in the decision-making process are thus demarcated, distinguishing those phases having a greater area of controllability.

It is in part for these reasons that the work of present applied social scientists is replete with analyses of unanticipated consequences. In mass communications research, for example, an orientation to unanticipated consequences has been standardized in the notion of the "boomerang effect."[15] This concept directs the researcher to ascertain whether a given message has produced an audience response in conformity with the sender's intention, or whether it has yielded unforeseen consequences directly contrary to those intended. It has thus been discovered by students of race relations that certain communications intended to reduce ethnic intolerance have, in some measure, strengthened it, or have led the audience to an unexpected identification with the prejudiced person rather than the victim of prejudice. In criminology students of juvenile delinquency have indicated that arresting and booking juvenile delinquents may have the unforeseen consequence of crystallizing a criminal self-image.

In these and many other examples that can be drawn from current efforts in applied sociology, the problems of which laymen complain are analyzed as the unanticipated consequences of their own policies, actions, and commitments. Thus a theory of unanticipated consequences systematically directs the attention of laymen and applied social scientist alike to problem-generating forces most directly accessible to their control.

The theory of unanticipated consequences also has another, this time a rhetoric function, for the social system of applied social science. It systematically directs attention to factors most likely to be overlooked by laymen, that is, their own behavior and the ways in which it contributes to their own prob-

[14] Philip Selznick, *TVA and the Grass Roots*, Berkeley and Los Angeles: University of California Press, 1949, esp. pp. 253–259.

[15] See, for example: Paul F. Lazarsfeld and Robert K. Merton, "Studies in Radio and Film Propaganda," *Transactions of the New York Academy of Sciences*, Series II, 6, pp. 58–79.

lems. This is not likely to be regarded as common-sensical by laymen. On the contrary, it is frequently an important source of sudden "insight" that contributes so powerfully to the layman's validation of the applied social scientist's status.

One of the needs of applied social science, therefore, is for the full development of a generalized theory of unanticipated consequences. Consistent though not identical with this, is a need for a diversity of concepts, varying with the field of application, which direct laymen's attention to patterns of behavior and belief of which he was unaware. In short, an applied social science greatly needs a multiplicity of middle range concepts of both latent functions and latent structures.

The modern era in industrial sociology, for example, hinges on the introduction of a concept of latent structure, namely, "informal organization," in the Western Electric studies. This concept identified new areas of social organization that were utilizable for the realization of organizational objectives. It has been used precisely in this way, not only in factories, but in schools and mental hospitals as well, where it has literally brought into focus hitherto neglected social resources.

In this connection it is instructive to recall Merton's rationale for introducing the concept of latent functions.[16] He observes that there is an unfortunate tendency for some social scientists to confine themselves to the study of manifest functions, thus allowing the focus of their studies to be set by the

[16] Robert K. Merton, *Social Theory and Social Structure*, New York: The Free Press, 1949, esp. pp. 64 *et seq.*

interests of practical men of affairs. Pressures in the direction noted by Merton arise most compellingly when a social scientist has implicated himself in the social system of applied science. In effect, then, it may be said that Merton sees the concept of latent functions serving as a corrective for the applied proclivities of social scientists, facilitating their pursuit of the theoretic issues of pure science. The point here, however, is that not even the needs of applied social science are well served by dealing solely with manifest functions. The concepts of latent function and latent structure are equally useful to the applied social sciences.

Conclusion

An effort has been made to indicate some of the theoretical and conceptual needs of applied social sciences. It should be clear that some of these needs are not well met by the present development of pure theory. There is no intention, however, to suggest that the program of pure or basic theory ought to be organized, either in whole or part, around the discernible needs of the applied fields. It is likely, however, that even the most inveterate of pure theorists will profit from examining the hiatuses between the needs of applied fields and the accomplishments of the basic ones. For it may be that these gaps signalize, not only a handicap of the applied scientist, but also an unnecessary defect in pure theory itself.

If this paper has seemed to contain a curious juxtaposition of classical theorists and current empiricists, the implication is twofold. It is a mild suggestion to those presently involved in applied efforts that, even today, they may gain much from recognizing the continuity between their own efforts and those of the major and earlier sociologists. Current applied social scientists may see deeper significance in their work if they recognize that it is neither peripheral nor new foliage but that, on the contrary, it emerges from the deepest taproots of their disciplines and has the most venerable tradition. Finally, it is implied that the true office of the theorist is best performed when he exposes old theories to the current empirical tasks of his discipline.

2.4 THE MECHANISMS OF CHANGE

Edgar H. Schein

The conceptual scheme shown in Figure 1 was developed to encompass the kinds of changes in beliefs, attitudes, and values which we regard as fairly "central" or "deep"; changes which occur during socialization, therapy, and other processes involving the person's self or identity. The scheme also draws

Reprinted with permission from Bennis, Schein, Steele and Berlew (editors), *Interpersonal Dynamics* (Homewood, Ill.: The Dorsey Press) 1964, pp. 362–378. Abridged.

attention to a much neglected problem, that of having to unlearn something before something new can be learned. Most of the kinds of changes we are concerned with involve attitudes or behaviors which are integrated around the self, where change implies the giving up of something to which the person has previously become committed and which he values.

Any change in behavior or attitudes of this sort tends to be emotionally re-

Stage 1. **Unfreezing:** creating motivation to change
Mechanisms: a) Lack of confirmation or disconfirmation
b) Induction of guilt-anxiety
c) Creation of psychological safety by reduction of threat or removal of barriers

Stage 2. **Changing:** developing new responses based on new information
Mechanisms: a) Cognitive redefinition through
(1) Identification: information from a single source
(2) Scanning: information from multiple sources

Stage 3. **Refreezing:** stabilizing and integrating the changes
Mechanisms: a) Integrating new responses into personality
b) Integrating new responses into significant ongoing relationships through reconfirmation

FIGURE 1.   The Process of Influence and the Mechanisms Underlying Each Stage

sisted because even the possibility of change implies that previous behavior and attitudes were somehow wrong or inadequate, a conclusion which the change target would be motivated to reject. If change is to occur, therefore, it must be preceded by an alteration of the present stable equilibrium which supports the present behavior and attitudes. It is this step, difficult to pin down precisely, which we believe Lewin correctly saw as akin to "unfreezing"— making something solid into a fluid state. Any viable conceptual scheme of the influence process must begin with the process of unfreezing and thereby take account of the inherent threat which change represents. For any change to occur, the defenses which tend to be aroused in the change target must be made less operative, circumvented, or used directly as change levers.

Once the change target's present equilibrium has been upset, once he has become motivated to change, he will seek information relevant to his dilemma. That is, he will seek cues as to the kind of changes to make in his behavior or attitudes which will reestablish a comfortable equilibrium for him. Such information may come from personal or impersonal sources, from a single other person or an array of others, from a single communication or a prolonged search. It is this process, the seeking out, processing, and utilization of information for the purpose of achieving new perceptions, attitudes, and behaviors, which we have called "changing."

There remains the problem of whether the new behavior and attitudes fit well with the person's other behavior and attitudes, and whether they will be acceptable to his significant others. The process of integrating new responses into the ongoing personality and into key emotional relationships leads ultimately to changes which may be considered to be stable. If the new responses do not fit or are unacceptable to important others, a new process of unfreezing is initiated and a new cycle of influence is thereby set up. *Stable* change thus implies a reintegration or a stage of "refreezing," to continue with Lewin's terminology. Just as unfreezing is necessary for change to begin, refreezing is necessary for change to endure.

Let us next examine some of the key mechanisms which can be identified in each stage of the influence process.

1. Mechanisms of Unfreezing

LACK OF CONFIRMATION OR DISCONFIRMATION. The assumption which underlies a conceptual scheme such as the one proposed is that the change target's significant behavior, beliefs, attitudes, and values are organized around and supported by his self-image. It is further assumed that the person presents himself differently in different social situations. Therefore, it is his "operating self-image" which is relevant in any given situation.[1] This operating self-image does not exist in isolation but is usually integrated with the person's definition of the situation and his image of the other people in the situation. For example, when a young man enters a classroom and adopts the appropriate self-image of "student," this image is

[1] The articles by Erving Goffman, on "Face Work" and on "Cooling," pages 226–49 and pages 417–30, cited in *Interpersonal Dynamics* (eds. Bennis-Schein), are excellent analyses of the process of constructing "operating self-images."

integrated with his view of the larger situation as a school in which certain kinds of learning are supposed to take place, and with his image of others who are defined as teachers and fellow students.

Because of the interdependence of self-image, definition of the situation, and image of others in the situation, the process of unfreezing can begin by a failure of confirmation or actual disconfirmation in any one of the three aspects of the total situation.[2] The change target can be confronted with the information: (1) that his self-image is out of line with what others and the situation will grant him or be able to sustain; (2) that his definition of the situation is out of line with "reality" as defined by others in the situation; (3) that his image of the others is out of line with their image of themselves or of each other; and (4) one or more of the above in combination.

For example, the student entering the classroom may have seen himself as a passive listener only to discover suddenly that the teacher has called upon him; he may have defined the classroom as primarily a place to meet girls and relax, but discover that the course is, in fact, "hard" and that the instructor defines the classroom as a place for active participation by students; he may have perceived the instructor as a *laissezfaire* type of "good fellow," only to discover the instructor sees himself as a tough taskmaster determined to make his classroom into a real learning environment. Each of these types of information can be thought of as *disconfirmatory* of some assumption which the student had made about himself, the situation, and/or the others in the situation.

By contrast, *lack of confirmation* occurs when relevant information is lacking. Thus, if the student placed high value on himself as a ladies' man and defined classrooms as places to meet coeds, he would experience lack of confirmation if he discovered that there were no girls among his fellow students. Another example might be the case of two students who initially reinforce in each other a self-image of indifference to learning and engage in horseplay during class meetings. If the teacher asks them to sit far apart, and if little opportunity to interact outside of class exists, one could say that these aspects of their self-image would subsequently be lacking in confirmation. In a situation where aspects of the self fail to be confirmed, one may predict that a *gradual* atrophy or unlearning of those aspects will occur.[3] In a situation where

---

[2] In the fairly common situation where information conflicts, where both confirming and disconfirming cues are available, the person probably tends to pay attention only to the confirming cues. As long as confirmation occurs, therefore, there are no real unfreezing forces present.

[3] The best examples of lack of confirmation occurred in Communist controlled POW camps in which prisoners were systematically segregated from each other and their social structure undermined to such a degree that mutual mistrust led to virtually no meaningful communication. See E. H. Schein, "The Chinese Indoctrination Program for Prisoners of War," *Psychiatry*, Vol. 19 (1956), pp. 149–72. For a more extensive discussion of Communist indoctrination methods, see E. H. Schein with I. Schneier and C. H. Barker, *Coercive Persuasion* (New York: W. W. Norton & Company, Inc., 1961), and R. J. Lifton, " 'Thought Reform' of Western Civilians in Chinese Communist Prisons," *Psychiatry*, Vol. 19 (1956), pp. 173–95.

aspects of the self are actually discon-firmed, the person confronts a more immediate disequilibrium which requires some immediate change or new learning.

THE INDUCTION OF GUILT ANXIETY. The induction of guilt-anxiety refers to the process wherein the person reacts to lack of confirmation or disconfirmation, not by rejecting the information or its source, but by feeling some sense of inadequacy or failure in himself. The sense of inadequacy may (1) be felt in reference to a failure in living up to some ideal self-image; (2) result from a feeling of disappointing others whose reactions are valued; or (3) result from a failure to honor some obligation that has been assumed. Such feelings may be summarized by the concept of "guilt-anxiety." Change will occur in the attempt to reduce or, more commonly, to *avoid* guilt anxiety.

CREATION OF PSYCHOLOGICAL SAFETY BY REDUCTION OF THREAT OR REMOVAL OF BARRIERS. Unfreezing can also occur through the reduction of threat or the removal of barriers to change. In these instances, one must assume that the change target already has some motive or desire to change but experiences a conflict which prevents the actual change from occurring. Either the change is inherently anxiety provoking because it brings with it the unknown, or else, it is perceived by the person to have consequences which he is unwilling or unable to bear. The change agent may in these instances (1) try to reassure the change target; or (2) try to help him bear the anxiety attendant upon change; or (3) attempt to show the target that the outcome is more palatable than he may have assumed.

2. Mechanisms of Changing

COGNITIVE REDEFINITION. The problem of learning a *new* response or changing an attitude can be thought of as a problem of seeking out *reliable* and *valid* information from a plethora of sources which may or may not be credible to the target. In making this assertion, we are limiting the learning or change situation to those situations which are governed by *social reality* as contrasted with *physical reality*,[4] that is, we are only considering situations in which validity is *consensually* judged in terms of the beliefs and attitudes of others.

How does the change target choose and make up his mind from the welter of sources available? In the typical, stable social situation, the person pays attention to those sources of information (other people) who confirm his present behavior and attitudes. If others fail to provide confirmation or actually disconfirm present attitudes, yet the person must continue to interact with them (e.g., because the job demands it), we have a typical unfreezing situation with respect to those attitudes. The person knows something is wrong and that some kind of change is demanded of him, but he does not automatically know what is wrong or how to correct the situation.

In order to determine what is wrong or how to change, the person must first re-examine certain assumptions or beliefs he has about himself, others, and his definition of the situation. He must then decide if these assumptions are unwarranted or inconsistent with feel-

[4] L. Festinger, "Informal Social Communication," *Psychological Review*, Vol. 57 (1950), pp. 271–82.

ings and evaluations which the others in the situation hold about themselves, him, and the situation. *The first step in the change process, then, is to develop alternate assumptions and beliefs through a process of cognitive redefinition of the situation.*

This process involves (1) *new definitions* of terms in the semantic sense, (2) a *broadening of perceptions* or expanded consciousness which changes the frame of reference from which objects are judged, and/or (3) *new standards of evaluation and judgment.* The new attitudes and behavior which are the eventual outcome of the influence process result from this intermediate step of cognitive re-definition.

From this perspective, the process of unfreezing can be viewed as *becoming open* to certain kinds of information which are actually or potentially available in the environment. The process of changing is the *actual assimilation* of new information resulting in comnitive redefinition and new personal constructs.[5] These, in turn form the basis for new attitudes and new behavior.[6]

In making cognitive redefinition pivotal to the change process, we have clearly allied ourselves with Gestalt theories of learning and have rejected reinforcement theories of learning. We would like to point out, however, that the reinforcement principle is very much relevant to the process of unfreezing and refreezing. The process of influence *begins* with the failure to obtain certain social reinforcements (lack of confirmation or disconfirmation); the process of influence *ends* with the reinforcement (confirmation) of new attitudes and behavior. The reinforcement principle cannot conveniently explain the actual mechanisms by which new assumptions, beliefs, or constructs develop and in turn lead to new attitudes and behaviors. We reject the notion of blind trial and error learning in the realm of social reality, favoring instead a position which makes the assimilation of information from the social environment the central process. The person does experiment in the process of change, but each experiment is based on some new definition of himself, others, and the situation and has, therefore, already been preceded by some cognitive redefinition.

The question arises whether this mechanism of change is always conscious or not. The answer is clearly negative. We have dramatic examples of cognitive redefinition in the realm of physical perceptions which occur

---

[5] We are using constructs here in the sense that G. A. Kelly, *The Psychology of Personal Constructs* [New York: W. W. Norton & Company, Inc., 1955] defined them, as the beliefs, assumptions, and evaluations a person has about some object in his social world.

[6] The best examples of this process were provided to us by the Chinese Communists. The prisoner changed his attitudes only after a prolonged process of unfreezing, the end result of which was a readiness to pay attention to the cues which cell mates were providing all along. Once he was paying attention to this category of information, the prisoner discovered that his meanings for words such as "crime" were different from theirs, and his standards of judgment

based on his frame of reference were different from their standards because of their different frame of reference. Once he had redefined his own semantics and attempted to view the world from the cell-mates' frame of reference by applying their standards, he could accept himself as a guilty criminal and make a sincere confession.

entirely without awareness. There is no reason to doubt the existence of a similar process in the realm of social reality. The best examples come from psychophysical studies of judgments of weight or brightness. The entire frame of reference and pattern of judgments of the same stimuli can be altered simply by introducing an anchoring stimulus at either extreme of the scale.[7] The subject does not realize that his judgments have changed, yet clearly, cognitive redefinition has taken place. In the realm of social perception and rumor transmission, we have similar effects. Once certain key stimuli are introduced as anchors (e.g., identifying a certain person in the story as a Negro), the scale of judgment of other stimuli shifts, though the person may be completely unaware of the process.[8]

Let us turn now to the next problem, that of the *source of information* which the person utilizes in redefining his cognitions about himself, others, and his situation. At one extreme, we have the acquisition of new information through a single source via some process of *identification*. The cues to which the person responds are those that come from a model to whom the person has chosen to relate himself emotionally. At the other extreme, we have the acquisition of new information through *scanning* a multiple array of sources, which may vary in salience and credibility but which do not elicit the kind of emotional focusing implied by identi-

fication. The sources are usually other people, but they need not be physically present to exert an influence. Their information may have just as much potency in written or broadcasted form.

We have labeled these two extreme forms of information acquisition by the terms *identification* and *scanning*, recognizing that there are many forms, like imitation, which fall in between. Let us now examine each of these processes in greater detail.[9]

COGNITIVE REDEFINITION THROUGH IDENTIFICATION. We can distinguish two basically different kinds of identification which have major consequences for the kind of influence or change produced in a change target. We have labeled these as *Type I* or *defensive* identification and *Type II* or *positive* identification. The conditions for, psychological processes of, and outcomes of these two types are shown in Figure 2.[10]

Looking first at the *conditions* for

[7] H. Helson, "Adaptation-Level as a Basis for a Quantitative Theory of Frames of Reference," *Psychological Review*, Vol. 55 (1948), pp. 297–313.

[8] G. W. Allport and L. Postman, *The Psychology of Rumor* (New York: Holt, Rinehart and Winston, Inc., 1947).

[9] This analysis has been influenced by Kelman's excellent work on mechanisms of attitude change (H. C. Kelman, "Compliance, Identification, and Internalization: Three Processes of Attitude Change," *Conflict Resolution*, Vol. 2 [1958], pp. 51–60). We have not used his concepts of *compliance, identification,* and *internalization* because of our emphasis on deeper levels of change than those he deals with in his experiments. Kelman's concepts have greatly aided, however, in achieving some conceptual clarity in this area.

[10] The analysis of identification follows closely Slater's analysis of personal and positional identification. Our analysis, however, deals more with adult processes whereas his focuses on childhood socialization. For an excellent analysis see P. E. Slater, "Toward a Dualistic Theory of Identification" *Merrill-Palmer Quarterly*, Behavior and Development, Vol. 7, No. 2. (1961), pp. 113–26.

	Type I Defensive Identification	Type II Positive Identification
Conditions for the Processes	Target is captive in the change situation	Target is free to leave situation
	Target role nonvoluntarily acquired	Target takes role voluntarily
	Agent in formal change agent position	Agent does not necessarily occupy formal role
	Target feels helpless, impotent, fearful, and threatened	Target experiences autonomy, sense of power, and choice
	Target must change	Target experiences trust and faith in agent
		Target can terminate change process
Psychological Processes Involved	Agent is primary source of unfreezing	Agent is usually not the source of unfreezing
	Target becomes position oriented to acquire the agent's perceived power	Target becomes person oriented because agent's power is seen to reside in his personality, not his position
	Target has limited and distorted view of agent, and lacks empathy for agent	Agent will be chosen on the basis of trust, clarity, and potency
	Target tends to imitate limited portions of target's behavior	Target sees richness and complexity of agent as a person
		Target tends to assimilate what he learns from the model
Outcomes	New behavior in target is stilted, ritualized, restrictive, and narrowing	New behavior in target is enlarging, differentiated, spontaneous, and enabling of further growth
	New behavior is more likely to be acceptable to the influencing institution	New behavior is personally more meaningful but may be less acceptable to influencing institution

FIGURE 2. Analysis of Two Types of Identification

identification, we note that *defensive identification* tends to occur in settings which the target has entered involuntarily and from which he cannot escape. He usually experiences a sense of helplessness, relative impotence, fear, and threat. The relationship to the change agent is an imbalanced one in that the agent has most of the power. The agent usually occupies a formal position supported by institutionalized sanctions. The target's role is to change or learn and not to ask too many questions. The prototype of this relationship is the child *vis-à-vis* the powerful parent or the concentration camp prisoner *vis-à-vis* his captor.

Positive identification, by contrast, tends to occur in situations which the target has entered voluntarily and from which he feels free to leave. He experiences a sense of autonomy and feels he can make choices. Instead of fear and threat *vis-à-vis* the change agent, he experiences trust and faith. The power relationship is less tilted and is generally not supported by formal positions or institutional sanctions, though they may be present, as in the case of the psychotherapist. The prototype of this relationship is the mutual identification of husband and wife or close friends.

In terms of the *psychological processes* involved in the two types of identification, *defensive identification* generally implies a relationship in which the change agent operates as the primary source of unfreezing (i.e., he provides the bulk of the disconfirming cues). The target responds to this situation by becoming preoccupied with the change agent's position or status which is perceived to be the primary source of the change agent's power. This preoccupation with the position, in turn, implies a limited and often distorted view of the identification model. The change target tends to pay attention only to the power-relevant cues, tends to have little or no empathy for the person actually occupying the position, and tends to imitate blindly and often unconsciously only certain limited portions of the model's behavior. Or, to put it another way, if existing attitudes and parts of the target's

self are chronically and consistently disconfirmed in a coercive way, one solution for the target is to abandon them completely and to substitute those attitudes and values perceived to be a property of the powerful disconfirmer. . . .

Positive identification, by contrast, tends to be *person*—rather than *position*—oriented. The potential model is rarely the source of unfreezing and hence is less threatening. The model's power or salience is perceived to lie in some personal attributes rather than in some formal position. Because the change target feels free to leave the situation, he will use the criteria of trust and clarity to choose a model which, in turn, will lead to a fuller richer view of the personality of the model. He will tend to have empathy for the model and genuinely to assimilate the new information obtained from seeing the world through the model's eyes rather than directly imitating his behavior. Thus the target's new behavior and attitudes may not actually resemble the model's too closely. The whole process of identification will be more spontaneous, differentiated, and will enable further growth, rather than be compulsive and limiting.

Looking now at the *outcome*, we see that *defensive identification* leads to a more restricted, ritualized, and stilted set of responses and attitudes. On the other hand, *positive identification* leads to an enlarged, more differentiated, and fluid set of responses and attitudes. There is a greater likelihood of the latter process leading to psychological growth than is true of the former. However, the likelihood that the changes will be acceptable to the institution which has initiated the change process may be greater if defensive identification has taken place.

In both types of identification, the basic mechanism of change is the utilization of interpersonal cues which come from a change agent with whom the target identifies himself. These cues serve as the basis for redefining the cognitions the target holds about himself, others, and the situations in which he finds himself. But, it is obvious that a great deal of change occurs through processes other than these two types of identification. Even in the most coercive institutions, defensive identification may account for only a small portion of the total change in the target. To gain a more balanced picture of change mechanisms, we must look at the other end of the information acquisition scale, to the process we have called *scanning*.

COGNITIVE REDEFINITION THROUGH SCANNING. The process of *scanning* can best be differentiated from the process of *identification* by the degree to which the change target or learner focuses on multiple models as contrasted with a single model in his social environment. Scanning thus involves a "cafeteria" approach to the utilization of interpersonal information, and the absence of strong emotional relationships between the change target and his sources of relevant information. At the extreme, *scanning* implies attention to the *content* of the message regardless of the person, whereas *identification* implies attention to the *person* regardless of the content. In both cases, other people tend to be the primary source of information, but in scanning, others become

salient only in terms of their perceived relevance or expertness in solving the particular problem which is bothering the change target.

The contrast between *scanning* and *identification* can best be exemplified in a group engaged in group therapy or in human relations training. Let us assume that each member of the group is unfrozen with respect to some areas of himself and is seeking information which will permit him to redefine his situation so as to reach a more comfortable equilibrium. An example of *defensive identification* would be the case of the group member who, because of his great fear of the authority of the therapist or staff member in the group, attempts to change by mimicking and imitating what he perceives to be the staff member's behavior and attitudes. An example of *positive identification* would be the case of the group member who establishes a close emotional relationship with another group member or the staff member, and attempts to view his own problems from the perspective of this other person. An example of *scanning* would be the case of the group member who looks to any source in the group for reactions which bear upon the particular problem he perceives, and attempts to integrate *all* the reactions he obtains. To reiterate, when a person scans, he relates himself primarily to the information he receives, not to the particular source from which the information comes.

How does scanning compare with identification in the change outcome? In the case of scanning, the target may have a more difficult time locating reliable and useful information, but the solution he eventually finds is likely to fit better into his personality because of his power to accept or reject information voluntarily. If the change goal is personal growth, the change agent should attempt to produce a setting conducive to scanning or positive identification, and avoid a setting conducive to defensive identification. If the change goal is the acceptance of a particular set of behaviors and attitudes, the change agent should attempt to produce a setting conducive to positive identification and provide the target with a good representative of the point of view to be learned. To achieve the latter change goal, defensive identification would be next best and scanning would appear to be least likely to succeed.

PART TWO

Elements
of Planned Change

Chapter 3

THE UTILIZATION
OF SCIENTIFIC KNOWLEDGE

As George Kelly has made clear in his "The Expert as Historical Actor" in Chapter 1, the problems of utilizing men of knowledge effectively in the life of action and practice are by no means new problems. The ancient and continuing problems have been refocused in recent history by the advent of a new breed of men of knowledge upon the historical scene. The new men of knowledge are, of course, the scientists—men devoted to the building of knowledge by rational-empirical and, where possible, by experimental means. Research, laboratory, instrumentation, data collection and processing are as much trademarks of these men of knowledge as scholarship, texts, reflection, cloister, contemplation, and similar terms are trademarks of prescientific men of knowledge and of the contemporary exponents and professors of nonscientific knowledge. Modern intellectual history may be read in some large part as an effort to integrate scientific knowledge and scientific men of knowledge within the frameworks of prescientific knowledge and within the associations of men of nonscientific knowledge. That this integration is far from mutual or complete is confirmed by C. P. Snow's observations concerning the persistence of "two cultures" within Western academic and intellectual life and the storm of acrimonious debate which followed the publication of his observations.

Scientists have not yet been integrated with sages, literati, artists, priests, and philosophers within our institutions of higher learning or in the wider associations of our intellectual culture. And social and behavioral scientists, relative latecomers among men of knowledge, have not achieved stable integration with either "scientists" or "humanists."

Yet scientific experts have steadily grown in the favor of political and industrial elites as advisers in informing and empowering policy decisions and in implementing decisions as they are taken, despite the tensions and segregations which persist within the academic and intellectual community. Science has become an establishment or part of the establishment in industrialized nations. And social and behavioral science has gained an uneasy foothold within this scientific establishment. The proper place of nonscientific knowledge and men of knowledge in the advisement of policy making, in the formation of public opinion, and in the education of contemporary men and women—and we believe that this place should be more important than many in the scientific establishment might grant—is still in debate.

It is in such a context that discussions and analyses of the utilization of scientific knowledge should be undertaken today. Processes of utilizing knowledge must bridge between enterprises of knowledge discovery and building on the one hand, and enterprises of need meeting on the part of persons, groups, and organizations on the other. What intermediary processes, roles, persons, and institutions do and should bridge between and link pure knowledge and consumer and client needs constitutes the subject matter for studies and experiments in the utilization of scientific knowledge. Part of the growth in the power and prestige of science stems from the development of engineering disciplines and roles as part of the bridging mechanism between science and human need. The engineer looks on the one side to scientists for knowledge on which to base the technology he designs and tests, and on the other side to inadequately met consumer or client needs and/or to difficulties and inadequacies in the arts of practice. He undertakes applied and developmental research in finding answers to questions about the application of new knowledge and/or to questions about the improvement of action and practice.

The engineering mentality, partaking at once of the mentality of scientist and the mentality of practitioner, has spread widely among practitioner populations which are highly dependent upon thing technology in their practice— among managers of industrial production, military leaders, some medical and public health practitioners, and agriculturists (leaders, some say today, in the food and fiber industries). It has spread less widely in areas of social practice where the person and interpersonal relationships of the practitioner are major elements in the technology of practice—in teaching, psychotherapy, religious ministries, social work, salesmanship, and political leadership. Whether this relative lack of extension is due to the primitive state of knowledge development in the social and behavioral sciences, to prevailing antiscientific and nonscientific indoctrination of practitioners and clients in these latter areas, to the inherent character and complexity of inner-outer changes in human behavior and relationship, or to some combination of these defines an area of investigation important in achieving better understanding of the utilization of scientific knowledge.

At any rate, change agents, as we have defined the role, work as engineers in areas of social practice where, we have claimed, the spread of the engineering mentality has been least evident. The change agent is often concerned with helping clients to diagnose and deal with the human dimensions of changes in thing technology. But in such pursuits, and in other change projects as well, he wants to help clients learn to use person-and-relationship technologies in improving their human environments. He is thus concerned with gaining a better understanding of processes of utilizing nonbehavioral knowledge, but his mission requires a central focus upon the utilization of knowledge from the behavioral and social sciences in the improvement of various situations of practice.

One approach to understanding the utilization of scientific knowledge in practice is to analyze the contrasts and overlaps between science and art, between nomothetic and idiographic approaches to knowledge building and utilization, and between science and common sense. Benne, Bennis, and Chin offer such an analysis in the first reading of this chapter.

Another approach to an analysis of knowledge utilization is to study cases where planful attempts have been made to link people in knowledge-building centers, people in intermediary roles of engineering development and dissemination of new knowledge and technology, and people as ultimate consumers and clients into one social system of interrelationships. Havelock and Benne have used this approach in "An Exploratory Study of Knowledge Utilization" and have attempted to extrapolate a more general framework in which problems of knowledge utilization may be located and diagnosed.

Lippitt suggests in "The Process of Utilization of Social Research to Improve Social Practice" that utilization agents, drawn both from behavioral science disciplines and from various schools of professional practice, must be educated for the role of bridging between social research and social practice, if the present gap between nonutilized social research and social practice in need of new knowledge and technology is to be effectively bridged. He draws upon a wide range of experiences in which successful bridging between social research and social practice has been accomplished.

3.1   SCIENCE AND PRACTICE

Kenneth D. Benne
Robert Chin
Warren G. Bennis

The change-agent cannot afford to enjoy the intellectual luxury of the

Reprinted from the first edition of *The Planning of Change: Readings in the Applied Behavioral Sciences*, edited by Warren G. Bennis, Kenneth D. Benne, and Robert Chin. Copyright © 1961 by Holt, Rinehart and Winston, Inc.

historian or archeologist who focuses upon understanding and delineating changes that are manifest only in the relics of completed events. Nor can he be satisfied with the stance of the detached observer who interprets changes, while they are going on, from some calculated vantage point of noninvolvement. Those who undertake the functions of a change-agent must not only diagnose the ongoing events in which they are involved but must also find ways to intervene in these events to maximize the valid human values implicit in the events. Ideally, the change-agent should combine in some measure the wisdom and sense of perspective of the historian and the penetrating acumen of the scientific observer, while putting into practice the skills and arts of appropriate and resolute action.

Can such paragons be produced among social scientists and social practitioners? The question cannot be fully answered before the event. But we consider it no less realistic to seek to fulfill hopes than to succumb to fears when both are realistically justified by an examination of the human situation. The answer to the question depends in part upon the type of "realism" men embrace in confronting their condition. We are voting here for the brand of "realism" that accepts the uncertainties and ambivalences of the contemporary situation, while trying to maximize the hopes inherent in it. The notion of "change-agent" seems to us consistent with this brand of realism. It points to a prospect and program, in only the early stages of achievement, not to a finished fact. In this sense it is "realistic." It calls for a reorientation and reorganization in the patterns of thought, practice, and association widely prevalent among social scientists and social practitioners.

Such a call for reorientation and reorganization is disturbing both to social scientists and to social practitioners. The disturbance arises in part from the "realistic" difficulties always involved in effecting changes of any magnitude in existing patterns of thought and relationship. But the sense of disturbance may also reflect valuatively and attitudinally tinged issues concerning the place of "science" in human affairs and certain "conceptions" of behavioral science that we consider to be misconceptions. What are some of these issues and misconceptions?

Science versus Art in Practice

A practitioner who shapes and forms —or better, re-shapes and re-forms— materials of a certain sort must be something of an artist. He must have a "feel" for the materials with which he works. His knowledge of these materials must go beyond "knowledge about" them to "knowledge by acquaintance with" them. The latter knowledge does not come to him by detached observation and theorizing primarily or alone but by direct "handling" of his materials, by learning to appreciate their reluctances and readinesses, learning to guide his "handling" by the qualitative reactions of his materials to the "handling." Learning the arts of practice comes through a process of apprenticeship, preferably under the guidance of an experienced practitioner who has mastered the art, not through academic tutelage in theories and hypotheses "about" the materials handled by his craft.

This "art" dimension in practice is clearly evident in the functioning and the education of skilled artisans of various sorts. It is equally evident in the functioning and education of "helping professionals," whom we seek to characterize collectively as "change-agents." In seeking for conceptual tools to guide the functioning of change-agents, are we denying the "art" dimension in their work or selling it short? Are we, more pointedly, seeking to substitute scientific knowledge about people and their conduct in stability (structures) and change (processes), in sickness and in health, for knowledge by acquaintance with people as particular persons or kinds of persons, as particular groups, particular organizations, etc.?

This is not what we are aiming to do, of course. What we are rather doing is to deny a logical gulf between the knowledge of the artist and the knowledge of the scientist, which, by assumption, frequently separates the functioning and education of social scientists and of social practitioners. This gulf, we believe, is widened by the conventions of traditionally institutionalized practice—conventions that masquerade as inherent logical contradictions in the thinking of many social practitioners and of many social scientists as well. The gulf has been institutionally bridged in some areas of practice more than in others. It is least bridged in the arts of practice where people are the "materials" practiced upon and best bridged in areas of practice where physical things and processes are the "materials" to be altered, re-shaped, and re-formed through practice.

What can we learn by analogy, from historical experience in the latter areas of practice? Unfortunately, confidence in such analogies is undermined by a historical circumstance that probably reflects the unbridged gulf in thinking about "science" and "practice" previously mentioned. We have thriving scholarly disciplines in the history and philosophy of the "sciences" and in the history and philosophy of the "arts." Scholarly studies in the philosophy and history of "engineering" have been relatively neglected. Yet the growth of "engineering" disciplines has been the cultural response to the bridging of the gulf between the "physical sciences" on the one hand and the "practical arts" of altering, re-shaping, and re-forming physical things and processes on the other.

Despite the lack of adequate studies in the history and philosophy of engineering disciplines, two analogies between the place of "science" and "art" in "physical engineering" and the place of these in "human engineering" may be suggestive.

1. Engineering uses scientific knowledge of physical things and processes to exploit "new" possibilities and potentialities in the practices of handling and developing these things and processes. It continually passes beyond conventional views of "natural potentialities" in things and processes that are actually rationalizations of present techniques of practice. It is doubtful if artisans working with coal tar, for example, would or could ever have developed the flood of colors, old and new, locked up in coal tar, a substance so qualitatively different from the dyes that may be made to issue from it. Physiochemical knowledge derived from basic research about dyes and pigmentation and about the chemical composition of coal tar opened up for engineering diagnosis hitherto closed "natural potentialities" and led to the construction of "human artifacts" for actualizing these potentialities. In doing so, engineers transformed "nature" as conventionally seen by an addition to the arts of human culture. And

"common sense" has generally absorbed this transformation of "nature," at least in cultures with a highly developed chemical technology. Newly invented concepts in basic research led to engineering concepts of practical utility.

Are the possibilities so different within the processes of human engineering? Are we limited in our current view of the possibilities and potentialities of human nature by our present arts of handling, managing, and developing human beings? Can basic scientific concepts and knowledge of processes of human conduct be introduced into practitioners' diagnoses of human potentialities and can the creation of social artifacts to elicit and stabilize hitherto unrealized possibilities in "human nature" be thus stimulated and facilitated? Can new arts of guiding human growth and development become a part of our culture through building bridges of "engineering" between our present arts of education, organization, and policy-making and the beginnings of basic scientific knowledge about human beings in their personal and collective behavior?

We see no logical reasons why analogous "engineering" developments in social practice are impossible. And we see the best hope of directing and managing processes of technological change toward humane ends in thus extending our conceptions of the possibilities of human nature and in building cultural and institutional artifacts to elicit and stabilize these new possibilities. One barrier to realizing this hope lies in the fear that "human nature," as we know it now, will be destroyed in deliberately devising new technologies for its renovation. Is this fear groundless?

2.   This question brings us to a sec-

ond analogue. Our fears about the dehumanizing effects of engineering practice stem from our experiences with past decisions about the uses of engineering competence that have involved neglect of or insensitivity to important moral and esthetic values. Competences in physical engineering have frequently been employed (or misemployed) by industrial and governmental bureaucracies to serve limited values, for example, maximization of economic advantages in the case of the former and maximization of "defense" advantages in the case of the latter. The effect has frequently been "selective inattention" by those with engineering competence to other human values at stake in the changes they have exercised their ingenuity to produce. Men fear that a similar "selective inattention" will work in the use of competences in social engineering as these develop. In fact, men can point to such "selective inattention" in "engineering" approaches to influence that have been widely publicized, for example, in manipulation of mass media by "hidden persuaders" or by votaries of "motivational research," and by the practitioners of "brainwashing."

The grounds for fear are evident enough. Where are the grounds for hope? We believe that they lie in the very fact that "values" have been served in the massing and utilization of engineering resources in the past. We need to unmask the pose of amorality that has, wittingly or unwittingly, been assumed by engineers, physical and social. A similar pose has been assumed widely by scientists and artists as well. Competitive economic advantage is a value and its disciplined pursuit a morality, albeit a limiting one. Similarly, competitive "defense" advantage in the cold war represents a value and its disciplined pursuit a morality, although again it is limited and constricting and probably eventually self-defeating, if exclusively employed in decisions about the development and utilization of engineering talent. No practitioner operates without the guidance of moral and/or esthetic norms, however unexamined, inarticulate, and uncriticized these may be. Our hope lies in this fact and in the possibility of stimulating examination, articulation, and criticism of the values that engineering competence does and should serve on the part of engineers themselves and those who employ their talents.

There is a morality inherent in the human enterprise of engineering itself (just as we have argued previously that there is a morality inherent in the human enterprise of science). Scholars like Veblen and Ayres have made this fact abundantly clear, however we may choose to criticize their particular articulations of its content.[1] As this inherent morality becomes clear to engineers and as they assume responsibility for extending and maintaining it in their work, it is doubtful to us that they will be able to collaborate wholeheartedly in inhumane utilizations of their talents. Since their role is increasingly necessary to the maintenance of both economic and political structures in "developed" countries, their moral voice will be heard. This is now true for engineers concerned with the de-

[1] Thorstein Veblen, *The Instinct of Workmanship* (New York: Crowell-Collier and Macmillan, Inc., 1914), and C. E. Ayres, *The Theory of Human Progress* (Chapel Hill: The University of North Carolina Press, 1944).

velopment of things. It will become increasingly true of engineers concerned with the development of human beings as well. Meanwhile, for many, the articulation of their moral voice remains an unfinished task.

Generalizations and Cases

As we have seen . . . , practitioners are certainly concerned with particular "cases," with their diagnosis and with planning treatments to effect improvements in them. Scientists, on the other hand, are concerned with particular "cases" primarily to verify or disprove generalizations about the relationships between variables that are somehow exemplified in the "cases." Claims for the utility of scientific findings for practitioners must take account of this important distinction between the two orientations. This valid distinction may be used to lend plausibility to the sharp conceptual cleavage between "knowledge about" and "knowledge by acquaintance with"—a cleavage already noted.

How do generalizations function in the thinking of practitioners about "cases" with which they are concerned? It is easy for practitioners who are focused on the "unique" character of case-situations to forget the "deductive" aspects of their diagnostic processes. Yet these "deductive" aspects are always present, however inarticulately. Previous experiences with other cases would have no meaning for this case if there were not some generalizations carried over from previous experiences and brought to bear upon the present one. An organizational consultant may have learned that some pattern of symptoms observed or revealed in the present instance connotes difficulties in communication upward in the hierarchy of the organization. Another pattern of symptoms may indicate unacknowledged competition between department heads. The practitioner thus develops "diagnostic orientations" in the course of his practice. And he deduces from these orientations meanings for observable symptoms and syndromes in the case he is diagnosing. Frequently these diagnostic orientations have not been well articulated by the practitioners themselves. The process of deduction of meanings from them may operate implicitly and the end-product of diagnosis may emerge into his consciousness as an "insight" that illuminates the complexities of the confronting case with a meaning and a direction for intervention in treatment of the case. Insight and intuition are then opposed sharply to logical operations from preformed theories or hypotheses. The value of stressing the uniqueness of the case is to reduce the prevalence of mechanical or nonorganic diagnoses accomplished only by derivations from previous knowledge. The disvalue may lie in producing the same effect through failure to examine and articulate the diagnostic orientations that are actually at work, wittingly or not, in the processes of diagnosis.

It is at the point of formulating, criticizing, or revising diagnostic orientations toward the cases with which he works that the practitioner finds the most direct use for scientific generalizations. For these generalizations are designed to point to meaningful connections between variables *possibly* at work within any situation being analyzed. A perfect science of human behavior, if one were available to prac-

titioners, would still point to structures of *possibility* within the cases with which he deals. It would not obviate the necessity for reconnaissance of particular situations to find which variables are at work there, for judgment of which variables are crucial in explaining the difficulty in the case, for measurement of the magnitudes of these variables as they combine to contribute to the difficulty. The arts of diagnosis are thus still necessary to the practitioner, but they can be validly informed by scientific generalizations that have been integrated into the diagnostic orientations he brings to the cases with which he deals.

Concepts versus Feelings in Practice

The gulf between the artist and the scientist divides them, often deeply, in their approaches to the emotions and feelings of men. First of all, there is an ideologically created distinction between concepts about knowledge, information, and other cognitive processes and those about emotions, feelings, and interpersonal relations. Philosophers and scientists long ago organized separately the terms and concepts for talking about and interpreting the cognitive and the affective aspects of man's behavior. Due to the process of abstracting, necessary for the creation of terms and concepts, a gulf between the two omnipresent aspects of man's behavior is made and widened. And we are then constrained to talk about separate and polarized entities: ideas versus emotions, rational versus nonrational, perceptions and cognitions as affected by emotions, rational task structures versus the structure of interpersonal relations in groups, and so on. What has been conceptually put asunder in the past by the use of separate terms has to be put back together again. The scientist takes his time in relating these polarized terms in his conceptual framework; the practitioner artist does it "on the fly" while working with a case. In so doing, the practitioner is led to another problem of his relationship to the scientist's concepts.

The gulf is widened when practitioners insist that the states of feelings or nonverbal emotional communications or the personal vocabularies of the emotions are destroyed or made trivial by the arid "scientific" concepts that are intended to capture, reflect, and analyze an emotional experience. The client's feelings, it is argued, can be understood primarily by the change-agent's apprehending the wholeness of the feelings, or some symbolic facsimile of them, and not through concepts intended to provide knowledge about the experiences of the client. It is as if the change-agent cannot know by conceptual and intellectual analysis, but can only comprehend by making use of his own feelings and reactions as a resonating instrument.

The impact of depth psychology upon man's view of man has both intensified and alleviated the struggle over the best way of apprehending man's feelings and emotions. Freud, on the one hand, stretched our horizons by redefining the range and explorable depths of the emotions, and thereby increased man's sense of awe and mystery about emotional manifestations and their role in man's behavior. In more recent times, Rogerian theory and therapy, existential psychology, and the widespread use of differentiated and complicated artistic mediums of emotional expression have strengthened assumptions about the fragile untranslatability of feelings and emotions into conceptual language. Further reinforcement for safeguarding the sanctity of the feelings and emotions comes from various defensive moves against the invasion of human affairs by "scientism" and from the poignant search of contemporary men for the wholeness and immediacy of experience that individual alienation and social fragmentation often deny him. Many seem to say "if you can talk about your feelings directly and conceptually, then they are not real, or have disappeared."

Yet, at the same time, Freud was using terms, concepts and constructions, metaphors and analogical language to provide a vehicle by which these very feelings and emotions could be organized and examined both by those who have them and by the analyst trained to recognize them and to make them accessible to scrutiny and analysis by the person with troubling or immobilizing feelings. By putting into concepts the very stuff of the irrational and nonrational feelings and emotions, he advanced immeasurably the use of concepts to describe and analyze the emotions and also to bring them under self-control.

This dilemma of the change-agent cannot be brushed away lightly. He must acknowledge the polarization of "feeling" and "rationality" that operates in many situations, he must recognize the limitations of present attempts to bridge the gulf between "knowledge" and "emotion," and he must supplement his diagnostic orientations with acknowledgement of the reality of his own personal feelings and those of others. In brief, the change-agent can and must learn to use his own feelings and emotional apparatus, along with his conceptual paraphernalia, to achieve the best understanding he can of his client's feelings and emotions. Balancing these modes of understanding is part of the artistic skill required of the change-agent. Sharpening his conceptual tools is a necessary step in the controlled use of his own feelings and emotional reactions.

Selection of Conceptual Tools

Contributing to the difficulty of the change-agent in making use of the knowledge of man contributed by social scientists is the sheer volume of clamorous and conflicting claims to primacy issuing from those in various scientific specializations. Shall he diagnose "role" difficulties? Or are personality mechanisms of the individuals concerned at the root of human difficulties? Or should the change agent concentrate upon the power structure of the organization? How does the practitioner guide his selection from among the competing wares offered by various social sciences?

Two interrelated ideas are useful in sorting out and evaluating the conceptual tools that are of use to the change-agent. First, he needs to look at the functions and limitations of a "concept," "conceptual framework," or "model"; second, he must examine the size of human units and the level of analysis which are of central relevance to a particular change-agent.

Change-agents, accustomed to dealing with "facts," often find hard sledding in dealing with "theory." But, we reiterate, facts are always, in truth, observations made within some conceptual framework. Concepts are invented in order to fix a particular slant on reality and to guide the production of new facts. The preoccupation of behavioral scientists with new concepts unintelligible to present common sense is based on this supposition. The resistance by practitioners to "jargon" may be understandable but if pushed to the extreme would deny the cornerstone of the scientist's contributions to knowledge.

Change-agents themselves make use of concepts and conceptual schemas, even while they are most vociferously attacking unfamiliar concepts in the name of naïve realism or common sense. Common sense itself is a loose collection of conceptual schemas, and is the end product of cultural accretions, of folk wisdom, habitual modes of thought and hidden assumptions about human nature, and the social arrangements of man. An explicit formulation of concepts into a conceptual schema to be used by the change-agent allows him to reveal, examine, and refine his "common-sense" diagnostic orientations. Conceding the fact that there are very many possible conceptual schemas, what underlying unity operates among all of them? Unity can be sought, and at the same time, valid groupings of particular conceptual schemas can be found by examining the thought model lying behind assorted conceptual schemas. The thought models of "system" and of "development" can, we believe, fulfill the function of sorting out and evaluating various concepts for use by change-agents.

But which is the correct model, the most useful conceptual schema, the most relevant and powerful concept for a particular change-agent? Again, as we have insisted in preceding sections, the artistic skills of the change-agent must be used in making such selective judgments. No cook book can tell him exactly what idea to use. He must select and combine from the available tools at hand and must create new tools when the existing stock is shown to be inadequate. He must in the last analysis create his own role and role relationships. But valid knowledge *will* be useful both in the process of creation and in evaluating its products.

Another assumption made by contemporary behavioral scientists is that when change-agents are dealing with an individual, a small group, an organization, or a community or nation, there are some similarities and some differences among these clients, regardless of size. All client-systems are assumed to be like all others in some ways, like some others in certain other ways, and like no others in still other ways. For example, an individual, a small group, an organization, or a community or nation all are analyzable in terms of the interdependent nature of a social system.

The discussion of *levels* of analysis may best be approached by an anecdotal illustration. A group of spectators sat watching a football game. They saw two groups of eleven men facing each other, heard a whistle blow, then suddenly action erupted, followed by another blast of the whistle, whereupon everyone stopped. One of the spectators said, "That was a good draw play, we gained eight yards." When questioned about his jargon, he said, "Well, the quarterback handed the ball to the fullback, who counted off several seconds, waiting for the opposition to be drawn in, and then crashed into the

middle of the line and advanced eight yards before being tackled and stopped. That's what is called a 'draw play.'" Someone asked a second spectator, "What did you see?" "Well," he replied, "I saw the acting out in different degrees of the needs for aggression and achievement in the players and the effects of how each views himself in relation to the other twenty-one men." A third spectator said, "I saw eleven men on either side engage in a pattern of coordinated behavior with very well worked out expectations of action for each position in regard to other positions, until these patterns were disrupted by the other side." A fourth spectator said, "I also saw your role relationship and integrations. But additionally, I saw a leadership structure, which included a man in one position calling signals during the play and a captain exercising some limited authority. I saw a social system of eleven men opposing another social system, each of which was composed of many subsystems and structures like leadership, conflict, plus a coach attached to each system." A fifth spectator said, "I saw two kinds of traditions: the ritualistic and emotional meaning of a game of this sort and the heightened excitement and tension of this particular game due to the traditional rivalry between these two teams. Both traditions reflect the competitive and peer values of our young adult culture."

Here we have a football fan's description and analysis of his "jargon." He has learned the concepts and conceptual schemas of football, and finds that it is a useful shorthand for describing a set of events. Also, we find an analysis of motives and self by the second spectator (perhaps an individual psychologist); a role analysis of expectations in a small task group by the third spectator (perhaps a small-group man); a portrayal of social structures and social systems by the fourth (no doubt a sociologist); and a statement of how the traditions and values of the culture affect behavior by the fifth (a cultural anthropologist). The statements and analyses are pitched at different levels of analysis, each using a different set of concepts and terms. The point is that no one level of analysis is the "real" one. Each is applicable for pointing up a different aspect of the behavior being observed and analyzed. It is conceivable that a football coach or a football player might find interpretations from any of these levels of analysis useful, depending upon the difficulty his team is encountering and the goals of improvement that have been agreed upon by coach and team.

Change-agents may not, in relation to the confronting case, be able to select their conceptual tools of diagnosis at one level alone. They may be forced to become multidisciplinary. Furthermore, the change-agent must select his tools of analysis on the basis of his preferred intervention strategy, his diagnosis of what he has power to do, the degree of accessibility of various variables to his influence, and the nature of his influence on and relationship to various parts of the client-system.

Pitfalls for the Unwary

In any hasty rapprochement between behavioral science and the arts of practice, we find some pitfalls.

1. One of these we may call the "etiological" pitfall. A major concern of many behavioral scientists is to find out how a given state of affairs came about; they are interested in "causes." In his eagerness to use scientific knowledge, the practitioner of planned change frequently has been boobytrapped into using a theory of origins of the problem as a basis for his intervening in helping to solve the here-and-now problem. We consider this search for "basic causes" by practitioners as a pitfall because identification of the "causes" of a state of disorganization in a social system does not mean that the change-agent can or should work at undoing or remedying these original "causes." The strategic intervention to help restore an organization to effective functioning may well require an entirely different action from that of trying to affect the "basic causes" of the problem, which are frequently located earlier in its history. In short, etiology, the "science of causes," may uncover both states and, in Allport's term, the functional autonomy of the present. One way of avoiding this pitfall of extreme dependence upon "etiology" is for the change-agent to start with scientific formulations of a strategy of action and intervention and then test the relevance of the diagnosis of origins or causes against the proposed plan. The consequence of this procedure is that we limit the amount and kind of diagnosis performed to those diagnoses that reveal future consequences of presently alterable factors. A preventive program of action, compared to a corrective one, does frequently require more etiological knowledge.

2. Another issue revolves around predictability and control. The behav-

ioral scientist seeks to unravel the complex causal connections in personal and social change processes, often under artificially controlled conditions, and to report his results as proven or disproven hypotheses. His example has sometimes lured the practitioner into thinking that a predictable specificity of consequences will follow if he but learns to act in the correct manner. But, as Merton and others have pointed out, unforeseen consequences are always built into any social action. A change-agent always encounters varying degrees of low predictability and lack of control. Therefore the despair of the change-agent over the limits of his ability to act "scientifically" must be converted to an acceptance of incomplete predictability as a condition of his work. We propose that a midpoint between unrealistic demands for predictability and control and defeatist acceptance of the all-too-true realities of unanticipatable consequences is the position for the change-agent to occupy. He must become a "probability expert." He should be a gambling man, who eschews "sure bets" and "long shots" simultaneously. But, like a professional gambler, he should seek the bets that give him a probability edge over pure chance. This is the best he can do in the immediately confronting problem, hoping in the long run he will come out ahead. The position suggested is actually in line with much current thinking in the natural and behavioral sciences; namely, to substitute probability calculations for oversimple cause and effect thinking.

3.   Another issue of paramount concern is the approach of the scientist and of the practitioner to the working contexts of "comprehension" and "verification." Using a simplified procedure, we suggest examining these two contexts as if they were separate dimensions. "Comprehension" and "understanding" are concerned with the exploration, formulation, and grasp of some phenomenon. "Verification" attempts to prove or disprove the "truth" of some hypothesis. It involves the cautious skepticism that demands more explicitly stated bases of demonstrating whether or not some diagnosis is "actually" so. The methods of the scientist typically emphasize the latter context through more and more rigorous procedures of demonstrating whether or not something is so. On the other hand, "comprehension" uses more personal, less elaborately codified procedures. The immersion in their materials on the part of historians, anthropologists, and practitioners such as psychiatrists, social workers, and consultants is reminiscent of the German sociological term for understanding, *Verstehen*. The "proof" of their conclusions by verification is not so easily obtained, at least within the predominant value system of the scientist. The point of this discussion is to suggest that we examine the issues surrounding our methods of diagnosing to assess the relative emphases to be placed on "understanding" and on "verification." Hopefully, we can maximize both; practically we may need to sacrifice some "comprehension" in achieving a high degree of "verification," and vice versa (and more typically), accept some lower degree of "verification" in order to achieve maximum "comprehension."

3.2 AN EXPLORATORY STUDY OF KNOWLEDGE UTILIZATION[1]

Ronald G. Havelock
Kenneth D. Benne

A. The Need To Study Utilization

In contemporary America, "science" is fast becoming an "establishment" in the political and industrial life of our society.[2] We use this term non-invidiously to indicate a social institution which is accorded continuing support and secure status apart from shifting and changing political and industrial

From Ronald G. Havelock and Kenneth D. Benne, "An Exploratory Study of Knowledge Utilization," Goodwin Watson, (ed.), *Concepts for Social Change*, Cooperative Project for Educational Development Series, (Washington, D.C.: National Training Laboratories, 1966).

[1] Credit for many of the ideas and insights contained herein should be given the members of a consultative seminar on knowledge utilization problems which was held at the University of Michigan between December, 1962 and May, 1963. Senior researchers at the Institute for Social Research on different occasions interviewed representatives from agriculture, economics, medicine, public health, and other fields. The resulting transcripts provided the raw material from which the authors developed the conceptual model which follows. The seminar and the subsequent analysis were supported by a grant from the Ford Foundation. Unless otherwise specified, quotations in this text are direct extracts from the transcripts of these seminar sessions. A much more extensive and detailed report on the seminar is to be published subsequently.

[2] See Don K. Price, *The Scientific Estate* for a full development of this theme.

leadership. This newly won estate raises serious questions about the organization of scientific effort and about the social responsibilities of the scientific enterprise. The scientists demand autonomy in developing their basic research and their abstract theoretical structures. The scientific rhetoric used in claiming support from society is based on the claim that accumulation of scientific knowledge is good in itself or on the promise that social investment in basic science will repay society by augmented, practical usefulness at some future time, but only in ways that cannot be defined in advance.

We are not concerned at this point to question the validity of the scientists' claim to support and status. The fact is that the scientific rhetoric has been generally "successful" with political and industrial leadership. Scientists have received a degree of political and administrative autonomy, along with financial support, which is without precedent among men of knowledge in American public life. Yet it seems clear to us that the establishment of science within our political and economic life has stemmed from a widespread faith among our political and industrial elites that the cultivation of science will lead to more powerful, more realistic, more effective public policies and modes of practice. The hope of those who maintain scientists in their position of heightened support and esteem is a new version of the old hope of Francis Bacon, Benjamin Franklin, and Thomas Jefferson that science will provide men with great new powers to meet human needs. Jefferson and Franklin believed that science would fulfill this hope primarily through dissipation of ignorance and superstition as scientific knowledge is learned by people generally. A contemporary view is that this hope can be fulfilled by the effective utilization of scientific knowledge and scientific methodology for the improvement of policy and practice in many particular social settings where specialized expertise strongly influences decisions taken—in medicine, industry, agriculture, education, and even politics. This historic shift in the human hope invested in scientific research deserves further explanation.

While utilization is a hope for some and even a firm expectation for others, it remains, for most of us, a poorly defined and poorly articulated concept. On the one hand, we are aware of an enormous and ever-increasing body of specialized scientific knowledge and, on the other hand, we have a vague vision of this knowledge being used by people to make better washing machines, safer automobiles, better schools, more healthful and productive organizations or happier community relations. Yet there is no clear picture of how we get from one end of the utilization chain to the other. We know, or at least we feel, that science has been and will be useful, but we do not know much about the transition from science to improved action and practice.

Many have previously concerned themselves with this problem, and here and there within our society we find highly developed and sophisticated systems of knowledge utilization. Systems such as those operating in the American Telephone and Telegraph Company and in the Agricultural Extension Service show evidence of many years of self-conscious effort to build and improve linkages between basic science and use. Such organizations are pathfinders and exemplars and are worthy of careful study. But they are not likely to answer all of the important questions about effective utilization. Many questions will remain. Can the same processes be introduced into other areas of action and practice where quality and quantity of information differ, where goals are less specified, and where vastly differing organizational patterns prevail? Can utilization in these exemplary systems be improved? Are the criteria and the long-range goals explicit and implicit in these systems adequate for general use?

Questions like these cannot be answered easily. And they cannot be answered in a vacuum. We need to make comparisons; comparisons not only with other fields and other instances, but also with ideal conceptual models of utilization processes as well. In short, a body of knowledge and theory about the processes of utilization is necessary before fully meaningful and accurate commentary can be made with respect to particular systems.

This paper will offer one general model of factors involved in knowledge utilization. This model is derived in part from an informal study of existing utilization systems. So in a rough sense it could be termed inductive or empirical. The intent, however, was to provide as *complete* a picture as possible of the *whole* problem, so that in much of our labors we were compelled to go far beyond the limited data available to us. As a result it should be viewed primarily as a theoretical offering. It is hoped that it will be of some use to researchers and practitioners in mapping out this complex and poorly understood domain.

There seem to be two ways to conceptualize utilization. One way is as a *system* and the other is as a *process*. A system model of utilization uses concepts such as "organization," "group," "person," "agent," "position," "role," "channel," and "link." A process model includes such concepts as "relationship," "linkage," "transfer," "exchange," "translation," "diffusion," and "communication." Some of the materials from the sessions seemed to fit most naturally into a system model, while other materials fell nicely into a process model. This fact helped us to realize that knowledge utilization cannot be properly understood without using *both* models. It was obvious, on the one hand, that utilization comes about through the conveyance of information along a complex series of pathways which connect groups and individuals fulfilling many different roles. These roles are associated roughly with such areas of activity as "basic research," "applied research and development," "practice" and "consumption" or "clienthood." Yet, in each interchange, each connection between one person or group and another, a *process* of communication (and influence) was going on, a process which could be understood and studied without regard to the specific groups or persons involved in the interchange. In other words, the interchange between a basic scientist and an applied scientist, or between a practitioner and a consumer or client, are both acts of communication and influence and they have many common properties which can be grouped together when utilization is viewed as a process.

B. Utilization as a System: The Structure of Utilization

A utilization system may be thought of as analogous to the human body. First of all, there is a chain or a network of relationships which has the function of carrying information and producing need-fulfilling behaviors. This information-carrying system, the counterpart of the human nervous system, we have designated "the flow structure" of utilization. The basic research "establishment" functions in this flow structure like the new brain (cerebrum), abstracting, generalizing, and ruminating, while at the other end the consumer functions like the old brain (thalamus, hypothalamus), needing, demanding, willing.

But the flow structure, like the nervous system, does not exist and cannot exist by itself. The nervous system is supported, supplied, built and rebuilt, protected, and to some extent controlled by other organs and subsystems within the total body system. In the same way the flow structure is supported and controlled by many groups and individuals in the greater society who are not primarily or necessarily information carriers. Such groups and individuals, and the subsystems of which they are a part, we have designated collectively as the "administrative" structure of utilization. Although there are probably more, we have isolated five aspects of this administrative backup to utilization. These are (1) education, (2) financial support, (3) legal or administrative control, (4) protection, and (5) growth or change maintenance. In the next few pages we will present what seem to be the important features, first of the flow structure and then of the administrative structures of utilization.

1. FLOW STRUCTURE. Two concepts are essential for the understanding of the flow structure of utilization. These are "barrier" and "unit of information." "Barriers" are the defining and identifying limits of any group or any individual and they are the *differences* between the frame of reference of the sender and the frame of reference of the receiver. "Units of information" refers to the substance of knowledge which is being transmitted, whether it be in the form of an idea, an observation, working model, finished manufactured product, advertising copy, or professional service. "Units of information" also refers to requests, questions, demands, payments, agreements, and OK and distress signals of every variety, these latter being units typically employed in "feedback" or "control."

A complete utilization chain is a need-fulfillment cycle in which a "consumer" expresses a need to a "resource person," who in turn finds the resources for satisfying the need and transmits these back to the "consumer" in a form in which the consumer can use them to satisfy the need.

Figure 1 might represent the relationship between a mother (practitioner) and her crying infant (consumer or client). The infant has a problem (let's say hunger) which can *not* be solved within its own system. Therefore, it must somehow or other convey awareness of this need to the mother, which it does by translating the need into a cry. This substitution of a noise for a felt need may be thought of as necessitated by the *barrier* between the infant's own body and the outside world. Once transmitted, however, the message must be heard and correctly interpreted by the mother, i.e., it must enter her system, thereby crossing a second barrier. The solution, once arrived at, must once again somehow leave her system and re-enter the system of the infant.

To complete any cycle, units of information must flow in both directions. Information which flows in the direction of the "consumer" may be termed "utilization flow." Information which flows in a direction away from the consumer may be termed "feedback."

When the practitioner is unable to fulfill the need by himself, he may have

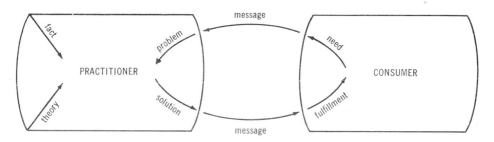

FIGURE 1.   A Simple Utilization System

to rely on other more specialized resource persons for assistance. The cycle is thereby extended over three persons and it may be further extended to include any number of persons and/or groups. Typically, a chain member is identified by a specific role designation, which refers to his position relative to the consumer. Most immediately related to the consumer is the "practitioner," followed by "applied researcher" or "developer," and ending with the "basic researcher."

The significance of barriers to the understanding of utilization may be better understood as we progress to more complex utilization systems.

Barriers do not exist only between individuals. They also exist between groups of individuals, and it is perhaps a tautology or definitional statement that communication among members of a group is more easily attained than communication with others outside the group. If we return to the mother who hears the persistent cry, her first resource may likely be her husband. Even though the pediatrician is much more likely to help her solve her problem than is her husband, the latter is far more easily accessible. She can tell him when the first twinge of doubt about what she should do arises, without fear of rebuke for presenting him with trivia

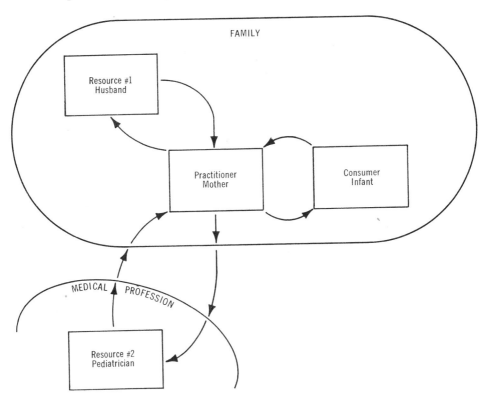

FIGURE 2.   Group Membership Barriers. The above diagram illustrates the practitioner's resource access problem. The most qualified and appropriate resource may be relatively inaccessible because of group membership barriers.

and without incurring a fee. Both of these factors represent barriers between the family and the outside group represented by the pediatrician. The fear of triviality may well be a barrier between herself and her husband, but it will be considerably less with members of her own family group, since the more formal barriers of fees, geographical distance, and restricted access are relatively absent within the family. The situation is presented diagrammatically in Figure 2.

A special advantage of the system approach to utilization lies in the great ease with which systems can be represented pictorially. The authors were able to build pictorial representations of the flow structure within each of the seven systems covered in the seminar sessions. These diagrams are especially helpful in highlighting organizational and psychological barriers and bonds at a gross level, and they are a most significant feature of the content analysis. It is to be hoped that with experience we will be able to refine our techniques of representation to include more features of a system and to show them with greater accuracy and clarity. Figure 3 is offered as an example of how a fully developed flow structure within a utilization system might look. As this diagram shows, the American Telephone and Telegraph Company contains within it a formal utilization scheme made up of several well-defined roles and subsystems.

The left hand side of this diagram, representing the academic community, is not actually tied into this utilization chain in any formal sense, but is shown here to suggest what the *orientation* of "basic" scientists employed by Bell Labs might be. Since these scientists are trained in universities, they thereby have status within various scientific disciplines, and membership in the learned societies.

In the total A.T.&T. scheme, division of labor has been carried out to a very high degree. As expected, at one end we have the basic research function, and at the other we have the practitioner function (the telephone companies) and the consumers of telephone service. But in between we have several separate phases of application. The "applied" and "development" research wings which exist within Bell Labs are concerned with general applications and the development of new devices, working models, etc. The phase which is concerned with development for actual production and distribution of the products which derive from research is carried on in a separate subsidiary of A.T.&T., Western Electric.

Utilization chains are beset by two principal kinds of difficulties, the impermeability of barriers and the overloading of resource persons. The extent of each tends to vary inversely with the extent of the other: the simplest chains which involve only a few resource persons and hence few barriers are continuously in danger of overloading, particularly where complex messages requiring many units of information are involved. Complex chains which contain many resource persons in separately defined roles tend to reduce the pressure on any one member, thereby reducing the danger of overloading. However, the addition of each new member means that the information must flow through additional barriers.

The problem of the proliferation of barriers is somewhat alleviated when the system makes effective use of the

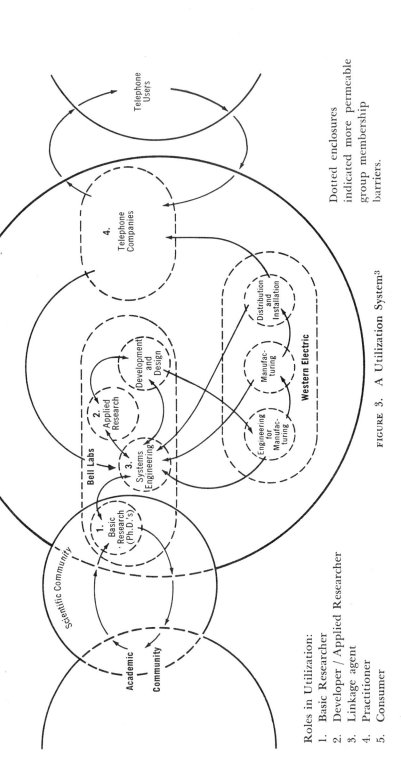

Roles in Utilization:

1. Basic Researcher
2. Developer / Applied Researcher
3. Linkage agent
4. Practitioner
5. Consumer

The above diagram outlines the knowledge utilization chain in a large corporation. Note especially the *linkage* role represented in this system by "systems engineering." Systems engineers are especially adept at deriving implications from basic research while leaving the basic researchers to pursue purely scientific interests without fear of company constraint.

FIGURE 3. A Utilization System[3]

Dotted enclosures indicated more permeable group membership barriers.

[3] Constructed from information supplied by a participant in the utilization seminar and supplemented by material from Morton, J. A. "From Research to Technology," *International Science and Technology*, May, 1964.

principle of *inclusion*. When division of labor occurs it is important to include the newly created roles within the pre-existing inclusive organization. It is especially important to maintain primary group ties which are so helpful in facilitating the free flow of information. The system depicted in the diagram just presented (Figure 3) utilizes this principle of inclusion to the maximum. Not only are all the major roles included in one company organization, but each suborganization includes a wide range of roles. Development and design engineers in Bell Labs have professional and functional ties with engineers employed by Western Electric, but organizationally they are tied to the basic researchers in Bell Labs. Likewise, by granting considerable autonomy and prestige to their basic researchers, Bell Labs attracts individuals who are respected members of the scientific establishment and who remain so. To facilitate permeability and at the same time to reduce overloading, some utilization chains contain one or more "linkage agents" whose roles are defined exclusively in terms of facilitating and controlling flow. For example, Bell Labs have introduced a special type of linkage agent whom they call the "systems engineer." The systems engineer must first and foremost have an overall "field view," a knowledge of the needs and resources of the entire organization and its relationships to the consumer. In addition, he must be conversant with the ongoing research efforts of Bell's basic scientists so that he can draw from these efforts information which can be utilized by the development branch of the organization. Actually, the systems engineer serves in several linkage capacities. He not only links basic research to development research, but he also links Bell Labs with other subdivisions of A.T.&T., and, most importantly, he provides a feedback link from each subdivision to every other subdivision.

Up to this point we have focused our discussion on those aspects of the flow structure which are formally laid down or institutionalized in a system of utilization. However, it has been universally observed by social scientists that there are certain informal channels which may carry a major traffic of communication within a system. These informal channels may serve to complement or buttress the formal structure, they may tend to undermine it, or they may render it utterly functionless by taking on all significant communicative tasks. An especially troublesome example of informal flow is what we have called the "by-pass." This occurs when certain consumers or practitioners, through their special knowledge of resources, are able to go directly to researchers for new knowledge useful to themselves, by-passing formally constituted linkage or application agents. For example, in agricultural extension it appears that the wealthiest and most knowledgeable farmers often by-pass the county extension agents and get new information directly from experiment stations and other scientific sources further up the chain.

Another reason for studying these informal channels is that they tend to be used to provide feedback where the formal system makes little provision for it. There is often a tendency to think of utilization as only a one-way process in which information flows from basic to applied levels and finally to the consumer, but the full utilization cycle requires information to flow also in the other direction. Thus, when the formal system ignores feedback, we may expect to find it occurring informally.

2. ADMINISTRATIVE STRUCTURES. As mentioned previously, the administrative backup to utilization may be divided into five areas: (a) education, (b) financial support, (c) control, (d) protection, and (e) change. Let us look briefly at each of these in turn.

a. The educational structure provides for the replenishment of the professionals, the maintenance of standards, and, above all, the preparation of consumers for the use of knowledge. However, the educational system as a whole seems to lay greater emphasis on training for *basic* and for *practice* roles at the expense of the equally important roles of *development* and *consumption*. There has also been a tendency to concentrate on recruitment and training of *new members* at the expense of the equally important educational functions of continuing education and consumer information.

b. How financial support is administered may determine the fate of a utilization effort. The *amount* of money available for various projects may be a major factor in their success, but there are other aspects of support which may be of equal importance. *Reliable* and *stable* support makes possible long-range, well-planned projects. In addition, many sources of financial support have strings attached such as "for pure science only" or "for application only, not research" which tend to break up some of the vital linkages. However, the experience of certain creative funding agencies suggests that it is possible, through the careful and thoughtful allocation of financial support, to promote effective utilization of knowledge.

c. Utilization systems also need control structures. Successful utilization requires that goals be specified and that people coordinate their activities toward the fulfillment of these goals. Certain persons are therefore endowed with the powers to see to it that this is the case. An important question to be asked is, "Who should be so endowed?" Persons directly involved in some aspect of the *flow* structure of utilization ("on-line") were seen as being more conversant with the details of knowledge and practice in a given area; but such persons might be unable to take an objective view, a view which would reckon with every aspect of the process without any concern for self-interest or the special prejudices of one's own professional group. Other topics considered under control structure are the desirable degree of centralization, the aspects of behavior to be controlled, and the means of control.

d. A fourth administrative function which overlaps somewhat with both the educational and the control structures is the protection structure of utilization. What gate-keeping functions are necessary to keep one group from encroaching on another? What kind of licensing is necessary to protect the consumer from improper or premature utilization? What kind of patenting or copyrighting procedures are necessary to protect the creative researcher from exploitation? When we answer all these questions, we will have built up a coherent picture of what the protection structure of utilization systems is and might be.

e. Somewhat tentatively, we have proposed that there is a fifth administrative function which is served by what might be called a "change" or "growth" structure. Preparing for new developments, expected or unexpected, is an administrative function which is, only recently beginning to receive major recognition. Within any utilization system provisions should be made to ensure adaptability to new knowledge and new circumstances, and to keep abreast of the changing needs of the consumer. It seems probable that utilization systems have to be open systems, flexible enough to gear themselves to changes in knowledge and in the technology of knowledge utilization and communication. The mechanisms which are employed in some fields and organizations to ensure this kind of flexibility—including training and development programs—can properly be called the "change structure" of these fields and organizations.

With the discussion of these five administrative structures, we round out our presentation of utilization as a system. To recapitulate, the system analysis of utilization was broken down into two parts which were called the flow structure and the administrative structure. Basic elements considered under flow structure were "barriers" and "units of information." Using these elements it is possible to construct diagrams which more or less faithfully depict the formal flow of information from basic science to the consumer. Such diagrams are helpful in diagnosing various problems in a system such as inadequate linkage, too many or too few barriers, overloading, and inadequacy of feedback or two-way flow. There are many activities necessary for the maintenance of a utilization system which do not fall properly within the flow structure itself, because they do not primarily involve information-carrying. These have been designated the administrative structures of utilization, and five have been identified: education, support, control, protection, and change.

C. Utilization as a Process

The systems approach gives us a good overview of utilization. It shows us the number and variety of roles and subsystems involved in a utilization chain, and it gives some idea of how utilization fits into the structure of the society as a whole. But the system approach becomes more cumbersome when we want to get a more detailed picture of what is going on at each of the exchange points or "linkages" in the flow structure. A utilization chain involves countless communicative acts, exchanges of information, contacts between persons and between groups. To study each of these linkages as a discrete phenomenon occurring at one and only one point in the system would be excessively redundant and more confusing than enlightening. All these separate linkages have many features in common, and they may all be considered as separate instances of one overall *process*.

What kind of process is this process of utilization? We think of it as a unique process which shares many aspects of processes of communication and economic exchange without being precisely either of these. It is like *communication* in that a message of some sort is transmitted from a source to a receiver, but the message may not contain information in the usual sense. What is transmitted may be a service or a product or it may be a payment or a word of thanks. Moreover, the relationship of the sender to the receiver is likely to be of a special sort. If the sender is nearer the "basic" end of the utilization chain, he may be more likely to deal with information abstractly and theoretically, and he may share to some degree the common prejudices and value orientations of the scientific "establishment." If the receiver is nearer the "applied" end of the chain, he may only be tuned to receive information which is practical, concrete, and of clear relevance to consumer need. He may also share the common prejudices and values of any one of the many practitioner "establishments." The problem of utilization is not simply to get a given piece of information across from a sender to a receiver, but to change it, transform it, so that it can be recognized and accepted as something of value in a system which views information differently.

Utilization is like *economic exchange*, on the other hand, in that the cash value or need fulfilling value of the message is always of primary relevance. One of the shortcomings of the traditional communication model is the inadequate emphasis it places on the motivational context of any exchange process. People don't just send messages automatically. They do so because they want to or because they feel they have to, and the same applies to the receiving of messages. When we think of utilization as a process, this becomes especially clear. Utilization means gaining information and ordering it so that it can be put to *use* to fill needs. Of course, the exchange may not be economic in the narrow sense, as we can see from the example of the mother and her infant, but the sender must be paid off in some way, whether this payoff be in the form of cessation of an annoying cry, an expression of gratitude, a sum of money, or merely some sign that the message has been received accurately, with respect, and with good intent.

It seemed, then, that in analyzing the utilization process, we had to give major emphasis to this motivational aspect. Other features of the process could be broken down into two major categories. The first of these we have called "interpersonal and group membership issues"; these deal essentially with the permeability problem, the problem of how individuals with different normative orientations can trust one another enough to share their knowledge. The second we have called "technical issues"; these deal with the content of the message itself, the manner in which it is prepared and transmitted, and the medium through which it is transmitted. There are, then, three features to the process of utilization: first, the motivational; second, the interpersonal; and third, the technical. Let us briefly consider some of the subcategories under each.

1. MOTIVATIONAL ASPECTS. When we discuss motivation, we should distinguish between motives which are based directly on consumer or client need and those which are not. Naturally, motivation comes from the consumer first and foremost. His needs are the *raison d'etre* of utilization. Yet it would be too much to expect that every role on the utilization chain is filled by someone who has the consumer's need always in mind. In fact, people fill these roles for a variety of reasons, all related to their own needs.

With respect to consumer needs, there are two questions of special interest: first, how needs come into being; and second, how needs get communicated. With regard to the first, we feel it would not be profitable to present a catalogue of all human needs which can be satisfied by knowledge utilization. But we do feel that some appreciation should be extended to the range, flexibility, complexity and variability of such needs. In view of these facts, it would seem undesirable to assess prematurely the "use-value" of a given piece of knowledge as "good" or "bad." The assumption that *all* knowledge has various potential *use values* is supported by what we know about human motivation.

With regard to the communication of human needs, the seminar sessions brought to light some fascinating and paradoxical findings. One might have thought that the effective communication of a need bears a direct relation to its urgency, but there seems to be no obvious formula for determining *psychological urgency*. Mortal needs, for example, are not always viewed by the public as most pressing:

Sometimes there is more concern with disfigurements than there is with fatal things. In the public health area, for example, work on polio, which has a relatively low fatality rate, received tremendous support. This is a crippling disease, and people are afraid of being crippled.[4]

Another example:

How did we learn about fluoridation? We learned about this because there was a dis-figuring coloring of the teeth which resulted from excess fluoride in water, and the time between the first adequate clinical description of this disease and the discovery of its cause—not cure, but prevention—was exactly sixteen years. This is an extraordinarily rapid development in the history of medicine.

Perhaps this all boils down to the fact that some needs are more visible than others, literally and figuratively. However, what is visible may not be most important for either the short-run or long-run welfare of the individual. This is a real problem in utilization. Some of the consumer's most desperate needs, like the need to overcome loneliness or the need to express feelings, have such a low visibility that chains of utilization do not readily work their way towards them.

Sometimes, urgency itself becomes a problem. Seminar participants discussed at least three circumstances in which the pressing nature of the need prevented effective utilization. First, there is the "too hot to handle" situation, where anxiety inhibits appropriate action. Another is the impulse to say "don't stand there, *do something*" when the most rational course is hands-off. And lastly, the tendency to use applied researchers to "put out fires," i.e. to find ad hoc solutions without regard to long-range needs or wide-range uses.

Among the second group of motives, those not based on consumer needs, the most salient are a) ego involvement, b) the need to know, and c) the need to tell. We have a general impression that there is a cacophony of motives involved in the utilization process, some good, some bad, some helping utilization, some hurting. Many of the

---

[4] The quotations used in this paper were taken from the interviews with the informants representing the various fields previously mentioned.

motives that lead to good utilization have no direct relevance to it. They are means to *other* ends, and utilization fruits are an incidental by product. This could be said of the need to know and the need to tell, and there are others: financial gain, status seeking, possibly even the need to control others. In each case, we might ask ourselves, "Does our end (good utilization) justify this means?"

Beyond these considerations is another. How are all these motives fitted together in the economy of the individual consumer or client to produce a good utilizer? The best way to answer this question and to conclude our motivation section is to quote an excerpt from one of the interviews.

I agree with what you've said, with the suggestion that you sort of look both to security and unrest. And it's the combination of security and unrest that makes for change, creative change. It's not revolution, but it results in some kind of improved condition.

A combination of security and unrest and uneasiness.

Confidence—security means a sense of confidence?

That's right, you have to be confident that you can be insecure.

The best college course I ever had was called 'Planning for the Unplanned Program,' and the main topic of the course was creating divine discontent, which is discontent with security.

2.   INTERPERSONAL AND GROUP MEMBERSHIP ISSUES. The process of communication is a matter of language, transmission, and having something to say, but this is only part of it. Communication is also contact and nonverbal exchange between persons and between groups. To be heard, a message must be received without suspicion. The sender must be trusted and believed. The receiver must be interested and receptive. There must be a rapport, a feeling of commonness of purpose or of spirit, or, at the very least, an implicit contract that what is said will be listened to.

In order to get a message through to another party, it is necessary to penetrate one or more interpersonal or intergroup barriers. There are innumerable individual and group differences which divide us from one another. Some of these differences are potential seeds of conflict, and can create noise and blockage in the communications between people.

We begin our outline of interpersonal and group membership issues by presenting a theoretical analysis of the concept of "permeability," reasoning that all barriers have common features regardless of their specific content. For example, all barriers may be characterized as having a greater or lesser degree of rigidity, durability, interconnectedness, and visibility; and the overall permeability of barriers is some function of these various properties. Among factors which seem to *cause* boundries to be more or less permeable, we found references to age and education levels, geographical separation, cohesiveness (psychological distance), and perceived external threat (self-preservation).

Discussion in the seminar sessions focused more concretely on the various kinds of boundary conditions that create problems for utilization. Among these, *status differences* and *value differences* were by far the most frequently mentioned.

The comments dealing with status

problems were divided into three categories: first, factors making for low status; second, factors making for high status; and third, observations on how status can be used as a vehicle of utilization. Factors making for low status included being young, being old, having too little education, imitating the practices of others, being associated with an applied discipline, and being associated with a young discipline. Factors making for high status included having a doctor's degree, belonging to an older profession, bypassing the practitioner, living in an "ivory tower," and being a specialist. Status barriers can be overcome or turned to the advantage of utilization in certain ways. There are certain persons in a group who have been identified by social scientists as opinion leaders, individuals whose ideas and practices are followed by other group members primarily because they hold high status. When dissemination efforts are aimed primarily at these opinion leaders, they have a greater chance of acceptance by the group as a whole. Interestingly enough, however, extremely low status persons may also be useful lead-ins to a target group because such persons present very little threat to high status professionals.

The influence of values and value orientations in the process of research utilization was given considerable attention in the interviews. Value orientations may be thought of as the results of crucial decisions which have been standardized and established in the life history of a person and/or group and which function as determinants of future decisions. The value orientations operate not only to shape future choices but also to maintain identity and continuity in the life and history of associations of which persons are members. They help to define and to maintain the self-image of the individual chooser, the limits of his influenceability. Where value orientations are linked to particular roles or memberships, they operate also to maintain the collective image, the normative boundaries of the group or organization. The resistive character of the value orientations of practitioners or consumers to changes in their customary modes of operation, when new knowledge or technology is made available to them, cannot be understood fully unless the self-maintenance and group maintenance functions of these orientations are taken into account. Similarly, the resistive character of the value orientations of basic researchers to changes in their mode of operation in response to knowledge of social or practitioner need cannot be understood until the self-maintenance and group-maintenance functions of these orientations are reckoned with. The differential rates of diffusion of various kinds of knowledge may well be illuminated by clarifying the kinds of knowledge and technology which, if chosen, would threaten central values of the potential adopters and so release self- and group-maintenance operations against this new knowledge or technology. Alternatively, certain kinds of knowledge or technology do not threaten central value-orientations and are readily adopted and rationalized within the existing value framework.

Although there are undoubtedly many more, we were able to identity fourteen issues with respect to value orientation which are likely to create conflicts among potential senders and receivers in the utilization process. Among these issues were: general vs. unique; orientation to past, present or future; unitary vs. pluralistic; man vs. nature; elegance vs. practicality; handwork vs. brain work; autonomy vs. dependence; and value cherishing stances vs. value rejecting stances.

We may illustrate the operation of some of these different value orientations by comparing and contrasting the orientations of a health practitioner with those of a basic researcher in a health-related discipline.

The value orientation of the knowledge builder coaches him to choose activities which will maximize knowledge production. The individual cases which he studies are viewed and evaluated from a "general" rather than a "unique" perspective, as instances which will confirm or not confirm some generalization which he is seeking to test as a candidate for knowledge status. His value orientation tends further to be "unitary" rather than "pluralistic" —he assumes that there are lawful relationships which will reduce the apparent plurality of qualitatively perceived objects and events. His time orientation tends to be toward the future— he emphasizes the need for time to perform all the research operations necessary to support confident statements about the subject matter he is studying. He tends to delay practical decisions in the interest of "accuracy" and "truth."

On the other hand, according to the analysis, the practitioner tends to operate with a "unique" rather than a "general" orientation to his cases and clients. His primary objective is to help improve the particular case, to abolish the difficulties or symptoms that in-

itially brought him into a relationship with it, whether the difficulty was one of pain, distress, inefficiency, ignorance, or uneconomic operation. Knowledge and technology are seen by the practitioner as important, but his criteria for judging primary importance are derived from difficulties in the case situations he is committed to help, not in terms of their fruitfulness in generating more knowledge. His world of cases tends to be "pluralistically" organized rather than seen and evaluated in a "unitary" perspective. His time perspective is oriented to the present and the immediate future—rewards that matter tend to come as immediate payoff rather than hopes for some long-range and ideal solution of *types* or *classes* of difficulty for *all* clients and cases.

This example illustrates how differing value orientations in various roles and subsystems within a utilization chain can result in a lack of communication and exchange between subsystems. The problem remains of how to develop trust and exchange between persons with different value orientations while respecting the "functionality" and "reality" of these differences. This is an important area for further investigation.

Whether they are caused by values, by status discrepancies, or by other aspects of group identity, the differences between groups create special problems for persons who attempt to serve as linkage agents. Some of the key functions in utilization are served by persons who are in intermediate positions between one professional ingroup and another. Unfortunately, persons who occupy such positions are beset by many woes peculiar to this "in between" status. In short, they are "marginal" men. They exist on the periphery of one discipline because of their connections with another.

Yet these are the men who pass on information, who get it applied, who create the linkage. Therefore, it is of the utmost importance for us to understand their problems, and ultimately we must come up with solutions to their problems of marginality which will not only allow these people to carry on in security and esteem, but which will also attract ever-increasing numbers to take on similar roles in our society.

There are a number of ways in which linkage roles can be secured so that marginality does not undermine the persons who occupy them. It is of the utmost importance that linkage persons have a secure institutional base. Most efficient and desirable from the point of view of rapid and effective utilization would be the securing of a firm base for linkage persons in both basic and practice fields. This can only be achieved if genuine dual membership is possible and if the linking person is able to deal constructively with problems of dual membership. Another solution to the marginality problem might be the establishment, perhaps in a university, of a separate base such as an institute for research application. However, such a separate institutional base could not be an island unto itself. It would need to be organizationally tied to and overlap with basic research and practice fields. A third possibility discussed in the seminar would be the achievement of linkage through the periodic rotation of certain members from basic to applied research settings or from practice to research settings. Viewing interpersonal and group

membership issues as a whole, we can see certain broad themes appearing. Effective linkage requires that the giver and receiver both have a sense of *security* or *trust in themselves.* Beyond that, and building on that, they must have a sense of *trust in each other.* These conditions can be brought about when there is full recognition of the importance of *self-esteem, self-identity maintenance, group-identity maintenance, and group esteem.*

3. TECHNICAL ISSUES. The task of communication is not completed when interpersonal problems are solved. Even when there is an atmosphere of acceptance and mutual understanding, the message must be composed, transcribed, translated, transmitted, received, and checked back for errors. Although these operations may become entangled in *interpersonal* or *intersystem* "noise," they should also be considered separately from interpersonal issues as additional ways in which problems in the utilization chain may arise. We are now concerned, then, with the mechanics of the flow of information, or the *technical* issues of utilization.

The technical aspect of the utilization process has two phases. The first phase is the *preparation* of the message, including the gathering of information, coding in suitable discourse, screening, and possibly labelling or titling. The second phase is the *transmission* of the message, the process of actually getting the message to the receiver.

Preparation of a message involves four steps. The first of these is assembly, bringing together the relevant facts which are to become the "content" of the message. The effectiveness of this step will depend in part on the extent to which the sender's field is a rationalized and systematized body of knowledge. Thorough cataloguing and indexing in a field makes the task of assembly much easier.

The second step in the preparation of the message is recoding the information so that it is understandable and acceptable to the receiver. This may involve organizing it in the receiver's categories, using the receiver's special language, summarizing and simplifying, and possibly incorporating a latent or explicit value message which would make the information more acceptable to the receiver's value orientation.

The third step is screening. The message should be reviewed and re-evaluated with respect to a number of criteria including safety, reliability, validity, error, relevancy and redundancy.

Finally, when the utilization message has been assembled, recoded, and screened, it should be carefully packaged and labelled. The all-important first impression of a message is given by its title, or its label, or the container in which it comes. The receiver should have a reasonably accurate expectation of the contents of the message and more especially the value the message may have for him.

Transmission of the message involves another set of considerations somewhat different from those involved in preparation. The most serious problems encountered in transmission have been discussed previously under the headings of lag, overload, feedback, and static. These difficulties vary, to a great extent, with the properties of the medium which is chosen as the vehicle of transmission. Writing is the primary carrier of information in a complex technological culture and it has the advantages of accuracy and volume transmission with a minimum of static. On the other hand, it is often slow, tends to be overloaded, and is ineffective for feedback. The mass media of television, radio, and lectures to large audiences have advantages over writing in that they provide speed in presentation and distribution, but, like writing, they provide poor feedback channels and are highly prone to static. Face-to-face transmission within small groups of people provides the best feedback opportunity, but may be inefficient for mass dissemination. An ideal vehicle for transmission of new knowledge of a complex nature would appear to be comprehensive in-residence learning sessions. Most important and most effective of all is to provide the receiver the opportunity to *experience* the new information, either through observing a demonstration or by trying it out himself.

Under "technical issues" we should also consider certain broad strategic questions when information is transmitted. Among these are: What is the most effective way to approach a known barrier? What is the most effective way to present evidence or "proof" of the validity of findings? How can we best insure that new knowledge, once absorbed and tested, will be retained and kept in use? And finally, how can we instill in the receiver the desire to pass on his newly acquired knowledge to others who are similarly in need?

D. Building a Program of Research on Utilization

Having laid down the basic dimensions of this schema, we would like to ask how such an outline may be used.

Does such a schema bring us any closer to a science of utilization? Does it further the study of utilization? How do we use such a schema? In the remainder of this paper we shall attempt to respond to these questions.

What use can be made of the schema? First of all, the schema helps to clarify the problem and to show its magnitude. It is an attempt to define utilization as completely and as precisely as possible. We know that we have not covered every angle; we are sure that omissions and errors will be found by others and by ourselves; but we have *tried* to be exhaustive, and in so trying we have often gone beyond the data of the seminars and have offered additional categories, or steps, or levels, where these seemed to be called for by the logic of the schema.

We hope, moreover, that this will not be the end of this undertaking. We are not offering a finished or a closed system. The building of a schema to cover such a vast and complex phenomenon as utilization should be a continuous undertaking. We should continue to argue and discuss, amend and add, so that the schema can more and more correspond to reality. But the present schema gives us something with which to start and on which to build, a working model which should be of help in giving guidance and coherence to our future efforts.

The schema may also be useful as a source for hypotheses about utilization processes and structures and their interrelationship. This would be a step beyond the mere definition and description of a problem area. We might ask, for example, how the availability of linkage agents improves utilization or how the presence of certain value conflicts is facilitating or inhibitory. It is recognized also that we will have to do more than delineate the important concepts if we want to test such hypotheses. The concepts need to be transformed into scalar variables, and measuring instruments must be developed so that the scales can be used meaningfully.

However, we cannot begin to test such hypotheses before we have a clear picture of what we mean by "good" or "bad" utilization. We need to know what the criteria should be, or, putting it another way, we need to decide upon some appropriate dependent variables. The most important and relevant criterion would seem to be the fulfillment of some "significant" human need, but to define what we mean by "significant" is difficult. Tentatively, we put *life*-saving and life-preserving needs first in significance, followed by needs related to *freedom* of choice, followed finally by needs related to the general pursuit of *happiness*. Besides the significance of human needs, additional criteria might be the expansion of knowledge, the number benefited, the scope of the benefit, the speed of adoption, and the long-term significance. It would be improper to take any one of these singly as the ultimate criterion for success or failure of a utilization attempt. Rather, they should be viewed as factors to be included in the composition of multiple criteria.

Because we are confronted with the lack of any common value base in contemporary society, we need to approach the question of evaluation criteria with utmost care. It would seem that there are at least four alternative strategies open to the evaluation researcher in this area. The first would be to accept as a base the goals and orientations of those who authorize and finance our research. In so doing the social scientist defers to others for a determination of the ultimate worth of the utilization attempt. The researchers need only designate "success" or "failure" within the limits specified by his client or his patron.

A second alternative would be to accept our own values as valid without consideration of clients and patrons. Rarely would a social scientist admit to this strategy. Nevertheless, it seems that all too often we unsuspectingly fall into this pattern primarily because we don't *spell out* our value-based assumptions either for the inspection of our clients or of ourselves.

Still another alternative is to identify the common and discrepant interests represented in ourselves, our patrons and our various clients, inviting the persons identified with these varying interests to formulate their own evaluation criteria independently of each other. This amounts to using multiple sets of criteria, emerging with multiple evaluations of the same project. This approach has the advantage of providing for a confrontation of discrepant value orientations and inviting efforts to narrow the range of discrepancies wherever this is judged desirable and possible.

A more heroic alternative is to seek a common value base out of which some common evaluation criteria can be derived. Perhaps a formula such as "life," "freedom," and "happiness" offered above would provide a start in developing this kind of base. In any case such an effort would need to be forever provisional, revised as the result of continuing evaluations and continuing reconsideration by social scientists, social philosophers, clients, and concerned citizens.

3.3   THE PROCESS OF UTILIZATION OF SOCIAL RESEARCH TO IMPROVE SOCIAL PRACTICE

Ronald Lippitt

My observations in this paper are based on some brief, but varied experiences with problems of science utilization encountered at our Center for Research on the Utilization of Scien-

From Ronald Lippitt, "The Process of Utilization of Social Research to Improve Social Practice," *American Journal of Orthopsychiatry*, XXV, No. 4 (1965), 663–669. Copyright, the American Orthopsychiatric Association, Inc. Reproduced by permission.

tific Knowledge at the University of Michigan. Our staff teams of sociologists, psychologists, and others are involved with such social problems as delinquency, illegitimate pregnancy of teen-agers, the educational motivation of culturally deprived children, the lack of creative teaching practices, leisure time programs for central-city girls, the pathology of communication between parents and teen-agers, and the mental health and productivity problems of work groups in government and industry. In each project a special effort is made to focus on the process by which scientific knowledge and personnel can help develop and validate significant improvements in educational and social practice.

Patterns and Research Utilization Processes

I want especially in this paper to distinguish between three patterns of research utilization which bring into the "science consumer system" new knowledge and validated practice from outside, and three other patterns which develop scientific knowledge within the system and then utilize it as a basis for improvement of practice.

1. In the first pattern, the scientist consultant in collaboration with a practitioner or practice group identifies and defines a problem of practice. This definition is used in retrieving research knowledge helpful in deriving both action implications and the design for an improvement of practice or the invention of new practice.

For example, a recent one-day consultation conference focused on the problem of how the several million citizens of a metropolitan area could be involved in the development of plans for the metropolitan region. A team of professional and political leaders from the metropolitan area spent the first half of the day interviewing invited resource people. Some of the outside resources were familiar with research and theory in this field and three of the outsiders were leaders of similar projects in other metropoli-

tan areas. With a predeveloped schedule of research retrieval probes the host team conducted a guided conversation with the visiting resource people. All this retrieved information was tape-recorded. During the second phase of the day's activities the local leadership took active initiative in attempting to formulate implications of this inquiry for the development of a program for their own metropolitan situation, and they began to project the elements of a design for action that drew from the implications both of previous research and previous practice innovations. The next steps of developmental work were also clarified and agreed on.

A second example started from the definition by elementary school personnel of their problem of "the in-betweeners." These were defined as primarily older elementary school acting-out boys who were too disruptive to be acceptable in the classroom or other educational facilities of the school, but too young and not seriously delinquent enough to be appropriately in the hands of the police and the court. A "knowledge retrieval" session of school people and scientists from child development, educational psychology, social psychology, and sociology identified a variety of relevant research findings and then focused on producing a series of statements about the possible implication of the findings for "things that should happen to the clients" in order for a significant process of resocialization and education to be achieved. These statements of implications from research findings were used as a springboard for a brainstorming session with the practitioners about program design that might deal with the problem. An action design for reeducation emerged which was quite different from anything which either the researchers or the practitioners had visualized originally. This design was later tested for feasibility in two schools, evaluated as successful, and subsequently diffused to other schools.

2. The second pattern for importing knowledge from outside the system entails conducting an extra-system feasibility test of a design procedure to meet some social practice issue. This test is conducted by the applied science team under controlled conditions, and, if the test proves successful, the newly developed model for improved social practice is demonstrated and recommended for adoption by the target system.

An example here concerns the development by our staff of the so-called cross-age socialization design. From our previous research we hypothesized that one of the major potentials in most educational and socialization situations was going unused, namely, the potential influence of older peers on younger peers. We decided to test experimentally the feasibility of training ten-, eleven-, and twelve-year-olds to function as educational aids and socialization agents with five-, six-, and seven-year-olds. The experimental settings were a camp and an elementary school where teams of scientists and social engineers controlled the experimental programs. Results indicated it was feasible to train the older peers to assume creative teaching functions. There was very significant response on the part of the young, and the older children showed great personal growth in their own attitudes and achievement because of their experience of responsibility in collaboration with adults and their learning from the training seminars.

It was possible thereafter to present this evidence to a school system concerned about the problems of achievement and motivation in young pupils. The school system adopted our model on a tryout basis and later made several creative adaptations in the process of carrying out and evaluating the design.

3. The third pattern of importation is a very exciting one to me. This is the process of identifying creative innovations invented by practitioners someplace else and developing procedures for getting appropriate documentation about these social inventions so that their relevance to local needs can be considered and the essential features of the practice adopted or adapted. One of the great tragedies in American education and social practice is that a large proportion of the creative inventions which are in line with good research and theory never become visible and are never appropriately transmitted from one setting and one practitioner to another. What dissemination does take place is of such low quality that successful high-quality adoption is usually impossible.

An example of a model for coping with this problem is illustrated in a current Center project with a state teachers association. All teachers in a selected school system now have an opportunity to fill out a "Teaching Practice Nomination Sheet" identifying their invention of a teaching practice to cope with a particular type of educational problem (for example, stimulating more motivation to learn) or the invention of a colleague. These nomination sheets go to a screening committee which reviews the conceptual and research relevance, the practical significance, and the potential adoptability of each practice. This experiment seeks to discover the kinds of practices that can be communicated by this written form, the kinds that require additional steps of observation, and the types that require more intensive training and consultation. Above all, we have developed a procedure for identifying, describing, and importing new models into the system which have been developed by practitioners in other communities, agencies, or organizations.

Let us turn now to three patterns of utilization of scientific resources which differ from the foregoing in emphasizing the *local* development of the resource knowledge to be utilized.

1. The first pattern has the organization or agency contract with the scientist team to collect diagnostic data relevant to some problem, analyze the data, and feed the data back for the sponsor's use. A brief example will illustrate this pattern:

The Center's action research team recently conducted an intensive city-wide study of a sample of delinquents and matched nondelinquents to assess factors related to the development and maintenance of delinquent behavior. They also conducted an interview study of key educational and socialization policy leaders concerning their conceptions of delinquency and its prevention. These data were analyzed by the scientist team and were reported back to the community leaders in a series of community seminars to which the key community leaders were invited. Staff members were available during these seminars to provide interpretation of the findings and to react to the generalizations and implications formulated by the community leaders.

2. The second pattern has the outside applied researchers supervise a self-study process within the sponsoring organization or community or agency, training local staff members to collect information and to participate in the processing of data, interpretation of findings, and the spelling out of implications for the development of change.

Our classroom teaching study is an illustration of this pattern of science utilization. Thirty teachers from seven school systems volunteered to work with us on a diagnostic self-study of their classroom education climate and the possible implications for changes in their teaching practice. During the spring the action-research team provided the teachers with questionnaires to inquire into their own attitudes and orientations, and with rating and questionnaire tools to use in eliciting information from their classroom group concerning orientation toward learning, toward the teacher, toward each other, and many other aspects of classroom dynamics. During the summer the teachers met regularly with the staff to help tabulate and analyze the data, to develop the concepts needed to work on interpretation, and to think through the implications of the findings for possible changes in their own teaching role in the fall. Consultation was provided in this thinking-through process, and in clarifying the plans for the use of new teaching procedures.

3. The third and final pattern of internal mobilization is quite different from the other two. It focuses on the idea that the practitioner needs training in learning how to be a consumer of scientific resources before he can be a utilizer of scientific knowledge.

a. One of our activities in this connection is focused on training teachers in the techniques of social science problem-solving and providing them with a tool kit of diagnostic tools and conceptual orientations to assist them in collecting appropriate information and using it to solve their problems of classroom management.

b.   In another project we have developed a laboratory course in behavioral science for elementary-school children. The students have an opportunity to discover who the behavioral scientists are and how their resources can be used, as well as to learn to carry their own inquiry projects on various problems of human relations. (It seems clear that part of the current negative orientation toward scientific resources, in mental health, education, and social welfare, is because of a serious lack of any such education about the nature and the utility of social research and the social scientists.)

The Roles and Training of the Social Research Utilization Agent

From our studies we have come to conceive the research utilization function of our staff as requiring them to be *linking agents* at various points in the flow of research utilization. We have to develop new skills of retireving and organizing research-based knowledge so that it links up to the needs of the social practitioner or client population. Helping the practitioner to clarify his resource needs is, of course, another aspect of this linking responsibility. And there is a necessary linkage function in helping the practitioner work through the implications of new knowledge.

As I have noted in several examples, still another function of the research utilization agent is to serve as inquiry consultant or trainer, assisting the client population in carrying through its own diagnostic research and working through the meaning of the findings for changes of practice. We must also find effective and appropriate ways of linking creative innovations to their colleagues to facilitate the spread and successful adaptation of new practice.

Our own experience with graduate seminars and practicums has revealed that there are significant numbers of students, both in the behavioral science departments and in the professional schools, who are eager to explore these new roles. These students seek new skills quite different from the research production skills typically taught in behavioral science departments and from the skills of operating practice taught in the professional schools. Certainly the training of research utilization agents requires a grounding *both* in behavioral science discipline and in professional values and technology. This obviously puts a new strain on the fairly segregated curriculum designs and training sequences which still exist in most of our graduate programs. The challenge is great—*and* surmountable.

Chapter 4

COLLABORATION
AND CONFLICT

A collaborative relationship between the change agent and the client system is an essential component of planned change. We defined a collaborative relationship in the first edition of this book as a complex series of expectations and encounters which include:

1. a joint effort that involves mutual determination of goals;
2. a spirit of inquiry—a reliance on determinations based on data, publicly shared;
3. a relationship growing out of a concrete, here-and-now encounter;
4. a voluntary relationship between change agent and client with either party free to terminate the relationship after joint consultation;
5. a power distribution in which the client and change agent have equal or almost equal opportunity to influence one another;
6. an emphasis on methodological, rather than specific, substantive goals.

We laid great emphasis on this collaborative relationship then as we do now for several reasons. Two of these reasons are obvious. First, collaboration is the crux of a healthy, trusting relationship. Without trust, mutual trust between client and change agent, completely valid data relevant to their situation cannot be educed for intelligent management of the situation. Without adequate data, diagnosis is false and misleading. This reason is basically pragmatic: before the change agent can really help the client, valid data must be generated and made public, and this can occur only as mutual trust is developed. In fact, the very process of gaining access to new and relevant data, new to both the client and change agent, is by itself often the major part of a change effort.

The second reason has to do with resistance to change and working through the resistance. Max Frisch wrote in one of his plays that man tends to fear change more than disaster. We interpret him to mean that man's fantasies about the undesirable, possibly degrading aspects of prospective change, lead him to resist it without rational consideration. (Certainly, it is true that change can and does lead to indignities and misfortunes, but the same unrealistic fantasies occur when change may eventually prove to be humanly fulfilling and beneficial.) Even at the very best—when change is mutually desirable and rational—a basic risk factor remains. For clients to take risks, to take new, even radical steps, support, help, trust are required. A trusting, positive relationship is essential in order for the client to overcome at least some of its (or his) strong fears of and resistances to change.

There is a third, less obvious but still powerful, reason for our emphasis on collaboration. It grows out of our experience and reports from others conducting change programs in a wide variety of settings, from psychotherapy to changes in hierarchical relationships in organizations. This emphasis is related to our criteria of evaluation in assessing change efforts. If the change agent seeks his client's acceptance and ownership of and commitment to changes undertaken in contrast to blind obedience or grudging acceptance, then the client must have or develop a real stake in the change effort. These criteria can be met only through a collaborative strategy. This means that the change agent must be open to influence from the client; that is, a mutuality of influence must develop. All of this implies an important generalization: the extent to which a change agent is successful (that is, influential) is dependent on the degree to which he is perceived as susceptible to influence by the client. In other words, *the more transactional the influence, the more durable and genuine the change.*

It is remarkable to observe how this generalization is supported in a variety of contexts where influence is at work. The observations of Erikson (1964) in psychotherapy,[1] the influence process from the point of view of social communication (Bauer, 1964, reprinted in this volume, p. 507),[2] and the new tradition of organizational leadership enunciated by McGregor (1960)[3] and Likert (1961)[4] all confirm this generalization from divergent vantage points. No one makes a more compelling case for this position than Carl Rogers in his first article reprinted in this chapter. A collaborative relationship turns out to be an essen

[1] Erik Erikson, *Insight and Responsibility* (New York: W. W. Norton & Company, Inc. 1964).

[2] Raymond Bauer, *American Psychologist*, XIX, No. 5, (May 1964), 319–328.

[3] Douglas McGregor, *The Human Side of Enterprise* (New York: McGraw-Hill, Inc. 1960).

[4] Rensis Likert, *New Patterns of Management* (New York: McGraw-Hill, Inc., 1961)

tial ingredient in all those change endeavors which aspire to be healthful and growth producing.

We tried to make clear in our earlier volumes that our demanding (and pure) definition of collaboration was a goal—a commitment—and this is rarely found as a pre-existing empirical reality. We pointed out that a relationship could never be wholly democratic, voluntary, or equipowerful. It is clear now that our earlier notion of collaboration was paradoxically both overgeneralized and overly constricting. Some questions and doubts emerged: what kinds of relationships are necessary for a change agent to begin work in a system or intersystem where no commitment to an ethic of collaboration has been developed? Would the conditions for collaboration be the same for an individual as for a larger collectivity, such as a community? Are there other strategies, aside from collaboration which could and should be utilized by change agents?

A recent study of community action programs (Warren and Hyman, 1966)[5] helps to sharpen, but not to resolve, some of the issues surrounding collaborative strategies. After considering some thirty-five cases of community action programs across a wide spectrum of conditions (size of community, amount of conflict around issue, type of issue, auspices of action system, and so on), the authors concluded that where there was a large measure of agreement among the principal parties to a community issue, what they termed "consensus," the change agent can be expected to employ collaborative strategies. Where there is little basic agreement around the issue, and little likelihood of obtaining agreement through persuasion, in brief, "dissensus," the change agent must either renounce his goal or utilize conflict strategies.

We see, then, that conditions of "dissensus" may lead to the misuse of power —strategies which perpetuate and deepen barriers to collaboration. Consensus conditions make supportive and trusting relationships easier to establish. There seems to be an inescapable trade off between the two which Walton develops in his article in this chapter: the misuse of power is detrimental to the achievement of collaboration.

The first two articles in this chapter, one by Carl Rogers on the helping relationship and the other by Walton on two strategies of social change clarify these two styles of influencing or helping. Rogers assumes that there is a similarity of goals between change agent and client. Thus, given agreement on the goal to be achieved, the therapist develops a trusting, supportive relationship with the client. Walton argues that change, under conditions of polarized disagreement, may be realized only by the use of threat, power, hostility. Walton asserts that the change agent must learn to accept and utilize coercive as well as collaborative strategies in order to create effective change.

There is a fundamental dilemma here. For certainly change agents face conditions where collaborative strategies would be impossible to initiate or would be rejected as naïve and irrelevant by those in the situation. Does this mean

[5] Roland L. Warren and Herbert H. Hyman, "Purposive Community Change in Consensus and Dissensus Situations," mimeographed (Brandeis University, 1965).

that the change agent avoids all conflict situations? Or does he apply strategies for resolving conflict that contradict his value orientation? These questions are fundamental because we believe that collaboration is a major foundation of the planned change which we would extend more widely in and among contemporary societies.

Perhaps attention to the nature and functions of conflict in human affairs will provide an additional basis for throwing light upon this dilemma of the change agent. There is much misunderstanding concerning conflict and the proper goals of conflict resolution in contemporary society. And the misunderstanding has roots not only in cognitive differences with respect to conflict but in differing attitudes toward the propriety and goodness of conflict among people —attitudes connected with deep differences in the life orientations and life styles of persons and social groups.

These attitudes reveal themselves in the differing connotations people ascribe to conflict, even when they are agreed upon the same denotation for the term. Conflict may connote animality, violence, destruction, barbarization, loss of civilized control, irrationality. Alternatively, conflict may connote adventure, novelty, growth, clarification, creation, growth, dialectical rationality. We have spoken as if one person or one social group will invariably ascribe one set of connotations, let us say a negative set, to conflict while another person or social group will ascribe another set of connotations, for example, a positive set, toward the term and the conditions it denotes. Actually, the typical situation is more complex than this. Nearly every person, within his life orientation, shows ambivalence toward conflict, that is, ascribes different connotations to different kinds of conflict. A devout pacifist may dote on football and verbal jousting. And a committed dialectical materialist may insist on family harmony and deplore the brutality of contact sports. A similar ambivalence toward conflict characterizes the life orientation of most, if not all, social groups, whether explicitly or implicitly.

The upshot of this discussion for change agents is that they need to be markedly self-aware of their own attitudes toward conflict, including their ambivalences. And they need ways of helping their clients to grow in such self-awareness, even in the midst of struggle. A change agent moved by irrational and unknown fears of conflict may avoid conflict situations. Or he may not allow conflict, whether between himself and his client, or between parts of his client, to develop to the point where incompatibilities in interest and value may be clearly seen and realistic, though limited, bases of collaboration recognized, found, or created. On the other hand, a change agent who enjoys conflict for its own sake but is unaware of his propensities, may be blinded to negative consequences of conflict released and encouraged indiscriminately within a tense situation and may destroy unwittingly the grounds for limited collaboration which existed initially within the situation. And similar effects may follow when parts of a social system or parties to an intersystem exchange are unaware of their own attitudes toward conflict. We believe that self-fulfillment through change needs to be distinguished from self-indulgence through change, difficult as it may be to make and maintain the distinction in complex practical situations.

In stressing the attitudinal elements involved in the management of conflict situations, we do not discount the importance of cognitive understanding of types and levels of human conflict by change agents or by client systems. One kind of conflict stems from different and incompatible goals for change held by various parties (persons, roles, or groups) within the same situation. And these different goals may reflect different ultimate values and concerns held by the conflicting parties, whether these ultimates be grounded religiously, politically, or in some other way. Another kind of conflict reflects not different constructions on the goodness of outcomes to be achieved in action and practice, but rather struggles over the allocation of commonly prized but scarce goods—whether money, material goods, power, or prestige and status. A third kind of conflict stems from ③ perceived threat to their very identity as persons or groups between or among parties to a conflict. The changes which one party is seeking and the ways in which that party is pushing for their desired changes are seen as devoid of consideration or respect for the identity and dignity of the persons and/or groups in the other party to the conflict. Oversimply yet fundamentally, a person's identity is threatened when he is deprived of choice concerning the conditions and direction of his life. If others with whom his life is intertwined are not open to his influence in decisions which affect them, these others are seen as threats to his identity and dignity as a person. Others in such a situation become objects to be resisted and, in fantasy at least, to be made impotent and destroyed. Groups with some feeling of identity respond similarly to others (persons and groups) who would rob them of their power to choose or decide. The threat to identity may or may not be felt and seen reciprocally by both or all parties in the conflict situation. Such conflict situations are marked by deep hostility and resentment. Phenomena of displacement, prejudicial stereotypy, autistic and ethnocentric orientations are rampant. Parties to such conflicts tend to become things or devils to each other—things or devils to be eliminated, cast out, or suppressed. The situation of conflict becomes dehumanized.

Certainly, these different kinds of conflicts call for different strategies of management and resolution. And, since actual conflicts seldom present themselves as pure types, change agents require the ability to sort out the types of conflict which are entangled in the actual situations in which they find themselves or to which they consciously choose to relate themselves. And such ability requires that effective change agents become more than casual students of human conflict.

Labor-management conflicts and cleavages in a win-lose context may be converted into a problem-solving approach on both sides by the efforts of a change agent team. "The Union-Management Inter-Group Laboratory: Strategy for Resolving Inter-Group Conflict" by Blake, Mouton, and Sloma, presents a strategy for conflict management which combines the application of basic research findings and of a technology of face-to-face confrontation, in open conflict, of the images each party holds of the other and of himself. The role of the change agent in conducting such a program and the theory of changing implied in it are presented in detail.

We may now re-examine the dilemma of the change agent posed earlier. Must a change agent forsake his commitment to collaborative strategies of changing when he operates in situations of dissension? Our discussion of conflict leads to two further issues which may lend clarification to the dilemma.

Is collaboration antithetical to human conflict of every kind? The answer is clearly no. In the first two kinds of conflict situations outlined above, collaborative strategies are clearly possible, however practically difficult they may be to introduce where coercive strategies are familiar and traditional for all contestants. Collaboration is possible because reality orientation has not been lost by parties to such conflicts. Limited and realistic bases of collaboration can be sought, found, and built upon by all parties without denial of their different interests and orientations and with full expectation that differences of interest and orientation will persist beyond the time and place of particular collaborations.

Collaboration is always an achievement not a gift. It is usually attained through open and grueling confrontation of differences, through conflicts faced and resolved, through limited areas of collaboration growing into larger areas of collaboration as fuller trust develops. The ways of collaboration must be learned, and they typically call for achievement of more complex skills and understanding on the part of change agents and clients alike than coercive strategies typically demand. Change agents who expect collaborative ways of working to occur without mutual confrontation, effort, and learning have limited understanding of either collaboration or conflict.

What of the third kind of conflict, in which reality orientation tends to be lost by all parties to the conflict? Such situations are pathological and call for sociotherapeutic and psychotherapeutic instead of educational approaches to their handling. Here, as in all psychotherapeutic processes, the achievement of a collaborative relationship between a change agent and the pathological client system or intersystem seems to be a necessary condition for reducing irrational and destructive definitions of the situation and for restoring conditions which will make rational compromise or synthesis of realistic incompatibilities possible. Our methods of sociotherapy are woefully inadequate today. Energy needs to be focused upon their improvement. Energy will be diverted from this task by premature decisions that only coercive strategies will effect change in situations of "dissensus."

A second question is suggested by our discussion of conflict. What are justifiable goals for a conflict resolution? We do not believe that the elimination of conflict is invariably or even typically the desirable goal in wise management of conflict as many who identify consensus with agreement tend to do. Conflicts stem basically from differences among persons and groups. Elimination of conflict would mean the elimination of such differences. The goal of conflict management is, for us, better conceived as the acceptance and enhancement of differences among persons and groups, accompanied by enlarged respect for and appreciation of the value of differences within the social fabric and augmented commitment to and skill in consensual ways of using continuing conflicts to serve purposes of personal growth and social progress. We do not see consensus or collaboration as opposed to conflict but rather as conditions of its creative utilization.

It is apparent that we have no easy answer to the dilemma of the change agent. Nor do we believe that any easy answer is available. We do believe that a few principles give help toward wise handling of the dilemma.

1. Collaboration is an achievement not a given condition. The ways of effective collaboration must be learned.
2. Conflict is not to be avoided by a change agent. Rather, he faces conflicts in himself and in others and seeks ways to channel the energies of conflict toward the achievement of personal and social gain for all concerned.
3. Power is not a bad thing, though much behavioral science literature treats it as such through indifference or ignorance.
4. Social action depends on power just as physical movement depends on energy. Nothing changes in human affairs until new power is generated or until old power is redistributed.
5. The change agent strives to utilize power that is based on and guided by rationality, valid knowledge, and collaboration and to discount power based on and channeled by fear, irrationality, and coercion. The latter kind of power leads to augmented resistance to change, unstable changes, and dehumanized and irrational conflicts.

The basic issue, then, facing a change agent is this: How can he operate in situations of dissension and conflict to help people in those situations to discover and affirm the values of collaboration and commit themselves to its achievement?

4.1 THE CHARACTERISTICS OF A HELPING RELATIONSHIP

Carl R. Rogers

I have long had the strong conviction—some might say it was an obsession—that the therapeutic relationship is only a special instance of interpersonal relationships in general, and that the same lawfulness governs all such relationships. This was the theme I chose to work out for myself when I was asked to give an address to the convention of the American Personnel and Guidance Association at St. Louis, in 1958.

Evident in this paper is the dichotomy between the objective and the subjective which has been such an important part of my experience during recent

Excerpted from Carl R. Rogers, *On Becoming A Person* (Boston: Houghton Mifflin Company, 1961), Chap. 3, pp. 39–58, "The Characteristics of a Helping Relationship." Used by permission.

years. I find it very difficult to give a paper which is either wholly objective or wholly subjective. I like to bring the two worlds into close juxtaposition, even if I cannot fully reconcile them.

My interest in psychotherapy has brought about in me an interest in every kind of helping relationship. By this term I mean a relationship in which at least one of the parties has the intent of promoting the growth, development, maturity, improved functioning, improved coping with life of the other. The other, in this sense, may be one individual or a group. To put it another way, a helping relationship might be defined as one in which one of the participants intends that there should come about, in one or both parties, more appreciation of, more expression of, more functional use of the latent inner resources of the individual.

Now it is obvious that such a definition covers a wide range of relationships which usually are intended to facilitate growth. It would certainly include the relationship between mother and child, father and child. It would include the relationship between the physician and his patient. The relationship between teacher and pupil would often come under this definition, though some teachers would not have the promotion of growth as their intent. It includes almost all counselor-client relationships, whether we are speaking of educational counseling, vocational counseling, or personal counseling. In this last-mentioned area it would include the wide range of relationships between the psychotherapist and the hospitalized psychotic, the therapist and the troubled or neurotic individual, and the relationship between the therapist and the increasing number of so-called "normal" individuals who enter therapy to improve their own functioning or accelerate their personal growth.

These are largely one-to-one relationships. But we should also think of the large number of individual-group interactions which are intended as helping relationships. Some administrators intend that their relationship to their staff groups shall be of the sort which promotes growth, though other administrators would not have this purpose. The interaction between the group therapy leader and his group belongs here. So does the relationship of the community consultant to a community group. Increasingly the interaction between the industrial consultant and a management group is intended as a helping relationship. Perhaps this listing will point up the fact that a great many of the relationships in which we and others are involved fall within this category of interactions in which there is the purpose of promoting development and more mature and adequate functioning.

THE QUESTION

But what are the characteristics of those relationships which *do* help, which do facilitate growth? And at the other end of the scale is it possible to discern those characteristics which make a relationship unhelpful, even though it was the sincere intent to promote growth and development? It is to these questions, particularly the first, that I would like to take you with me over some of the paths I have explored, and to tell you where I am, as of now, in my thinking on these issues.

The Answers Given by Research

It is natural to ask first of all whether there is any empirical research which would give us an objective answer to these questions. There has not been a large amount of research in this area as yet, but what there is is stimulating and suggestive. I cannot report all of it but I would like to make a somewhat extensive sampling of the studies which have been done and state very briefly some of the findings. In so doing, oversimplification is necessary, and I am quite aware that I am not doing full justice to the researches I am mentioning, but it may give you the feeling that factual advances are being made and pique your curiosity enough to examine the studies themselves, if you have not already done so.

STUDIES OF ATTITUDES

Most of the studies throw light on the attitudes on the part of the helping person which make a relationship growth-promoting or growth-inhibiting. Let us look at some of these.

A careful study of parent-child relationships made some years ago by Baldwin[1] and others at the Fels Institute contains interesting evidence. Of the various clusters of parental attitudes toward children, the "acceptant-democratic" seemed most growth-facilitating. Children of these parents with

their warm and equalitarian attitudes showed an accelerated intellectual development (an increasing I.Q.), more originality, more emotional security and control, less excitability than children from other types of homes. Though somewhat slow initially in social development, they were, by the time they reached school age, popular, friendly, non-aggressive leaders.

Where parents' attitudes are classed as "actively rejectant" the children show a slightly decelerated intellectual development, relatively poor use of the abilities they do possess, and some lack of originality. They are emotionally unstable, rebellious, aggressive, and quarrelsome. The children of parents with other attitude syndromes tend in various respects to fall in between these extremes.

I am sure that these findings do not surprise us as related to child development. I would like to suggest that they probably apply to other relationships as well, and that the counselor or physician or administrator who is warmly emotional and expressive, respectful of the individuality of himself and of the other, and who exhibits a nonpossessive caring, probably facilitates self-realization much as does a parent with these attitudes.

Let me turn to another careful study in a very different area. Whitehorn and Betz[2] investigated the degree of success

---

[1] A. L. Baldwin, J. Kalhorn, and F. H. Breese, "Patterns of Parent Behavior," *Psychol. Monogr.*, Vol. 58, No. 268 (1945), pp. 1–75.

[2] B. J. Betz, and J. C. Whitehorn, "The Relationship of the Therapist to the Outcome of Therapy in Schizophrenia," *Psychiat. Research Reports #5. Research Techniques in Schizophrenia.* (Washington, D.C., American Psychiatric Association, 1956), pp. 89–117; also "A Study of Psychotherapeutic Relationships between Physicians and Schizophrenic Patients, *Amer. J. Psychiat.*, Vol. III (1954), pp. 321–31.

achieved by young resident physicians in working with schizophrenic patients on a psychiatric ward. They chose for special study the seven who had been outstandingly helpful, and seven whose patients had shown the least degree of improvement. Each group had treated about fifty patients. The investigators examined all the available evidence to discover in what ways the A group (the successful group) differed from the B group. Several significant differences were found. The physicians in the A group tended to see the schizophrenic in terms of the personal meaning which various behaviors had to the patient, rather than seeing him as a case history or a descriptive diagnosis. They also tended to work toward goals which were oriented to the personality of the patient, rather than such goals as reducing the symptoms or curing the disease. It was found that the helpful physicians, in their day by day interaction, primarily made use of active personal participation—a person-to-person relationship. They made less use of procedures which could be classed as "passive permissive." They were even less likely to use such procedures as interpretation, instruction or advice, or emphasis upon the practical care of the patient. Finally, they were much more likely than the B group to develop a relationship in which the patient felt trust and confidence in the physician.

Although the authors cautiously emphasize that these findings relate only to the treatment of schizophrenics, I am inclined to disagree. I suspect that similar facts would be found in a research study of almost any class of helping relationship.

Another interesting study focuses upon the way in which the person being helped perceives the relationship. Heine[3] studied individuals who had gone for psychotherapeutic help to psychoanalytic, client-centered, and Adlerian therapists. Regardless of the type of therapy, these clients report similar changes in themselves. But it is their perception of the relationship which is of particular interest to us here. When asked what accounted for the changes which had occurred, they expressed some differing explanations, depending on the orientation of the therapist. But their agreement on the major elements they had found helpful was even more significant. They indicated that these attitudinal elements in the relationship accounted for the changes which had taken place in themselves: the trust they had felt in the therapist; being understood by the therapist; the feeling of independence they had had in making choices and decisions. The therapist procedure which they had found most helpful was that the therapist clarified and openly stated feelings which the client had been approaching hazily and hesitantly.

There was also a high degree of agreement among these clients, regardless of the orientation of their therapists, as to what elements had been unhelpful in the relationship. Such therapist attitudes as lack of interest, remoteness or distance, and an over-degree of sympathy, were perceived as unhelpful. As to procedures, they had found it unhelpful when therapists had given direct specific advice regard-

[3] R. W. Heine, "A Comparison of Patients' Reports on Psychotherapeutic Experience with Psychoanalytic, nondirective, and Adlerian Therapists," unpublished doctoral dissertation, University of Chicago, 1950.

ing decisions or had emphasized past history rather than present problems. Guiding suggestions mildly given were perceived in an intermediate range—neither clearly helpful nor unhelpful.

Fiedler, in a much quoted study,[4] found that expert therapists of differing orientations formed similar relationships with their clients. Less well known are the elements which characterized these relationships, differentiating them from the relationships formed by less expert therapists. These elements are: an ability to understand the client's meanings and feelings; a sensitivity to the client's attitudes; a warm interest without any emotional over-involvement.

A study by Quinn[5] throws light on what is involved in understanding the client's meanings and feelings. His study is surprising in that it shows that "understanding" of the client's meanings is essentially an attitude of *desiring* to understand. Quinn presented his judges only with recorded therapist statements taken from interviews. The raters had no knowledge of what the therapist was responding to or how the client reacted to his response. Yet it was found that the degree of understanding could be judged about as well from this material as from listening to the response in context. This seems rather conclusive evidence that it is

an attitude of wanting to understand which is communicated.

As to the emotional quality of the relationship, Seeman[6] found that success in psychotherapy is closely associated with a strong and growing mutual liking and respect between client and therapist.

An interesting study by Dittes[7] indicates how delicate this relationship is. Using a physiological measure, the psychogalvanic reflex, to measure the anxious or threatened or alerted reactions of the client, Dittes correlated the deviations on this measure with judges' ratings of the degree of warm acceptance and permissiveness on the part of the therapist. It was found that whenever the therapist's attitudes changed even slightly in the direction of a lesser degree of acceptance, the number of abrupt GSR deviations significantly increased. Evidently when the relationship is experienced as less acceptant the organism organizes against threat, even at the physiological level.

Without trying fully to integrate the findings from these various studies, it can at least be noted that a few things stand out. One is the fact that it is the attitudes and feelings of the therapist, rather than his theoretical orientation, which is important. His procedures and techniques are less important than his attitudes. It is also worth noting that it is the way in which his attitudes and

[4] F. E. Fiedler, "Quantitative Studies on the role of Therapists Feelings toward Their Patients," in O. H. Mowrer (ed.), *Psychotherapy: Theory and Research* (New York: The Ronald Press Company, 1953), chap. 12.

[5] R. D. Quinn, "Psychotherapists' Expressions as an Index to the Quality of Early Therapeutic Relationships," unpublished doctoral dissertation, University of Chicago, 1950.

[6] J. Seeman, "Counselor Judgments of Therapeutic Process and Outcome," in C. R. Rogers, and R. F. Dymond (eds.), *Psychotherapy and Personality Change* (University of Chicago Press, 1954), chap. 7.

[7] J. E. Dittes, Galvanic Skin Response as a Measure of Patient's Reaction to Therapist's Permissiveness," *J. Abnorm. & Soc. Psychol.*, Vol. 55 (1957), pp. 295–303.

procedures are *perceived* which makes a difference to the client, and that it is this perpection which is crucial.

"Manufactured" Relationships

Let me turn to research of a very different sort, some of which you may find rather abhorrent, but which nevertheless has a bearing upon the nature of a facilitating relationship. These studies have to do with what we might think of as manufactured relationships.

Verplanck,[8] Greenspoon[9] and others have shown that operant conditioning of verbal behavior is possible in a relationship. Very briefly, if the experimenter says "Mhm," or "Good," or nods his head after certain types of words or statements, those classes of words tend to increase because of being reinforced. It has been shown that using such procedures one can bring about increases in such diverse verbal categories as plural nouns, hostile words, statements of opinion. The person is completely unaware that he is being influenced in any way by these reinforcers. The implication is that by such selective reinforcement we could bring it about that the other person in the relationship would be using whatever kinds of words and making whatever kinds of statements we had decided to reinforce.

Following still further the principles of operant conditioning as developed by Skinner and his group, Lindsley[10] has shown that a chronic schizophrenic can be placed in a "helping relationship" with a machine. The machine, somewhat like a vending machine, can be set to reward a variety of types of behaviors. Initially it simply rewards— with candy, a cigarette, or the display of a picture—the lever-pressing behavior of the patient. But it is possible to set it so that many pulls on the lever may supply a hungry kitten—visible in a separate enclosure—with a drop of milk. In this case the satisfaction is an altruistic one. Plans are being developed to reward similar social or altruistic behavior directed toward another patient, placed in the next room. The only limit to the kinds of behavior which might be rewarded lies in the degree of mechanical ingenuity of the experimenter.

Lindsley reports that in some patients there has been marked clinical improvement. Personally I cannot help but be impressed by the description of one patient who had gone from a deteriorated chronic state to being given free grounds privileges, this change being quite clearly associated with his interaction with the machine. Then the experimenter decided to study experimental extinction, which, put in more personal terms, means that no matter how many thousands of times the lever was pressed, no reward of any kind was forthcoming. The patient gradually regressed, grew untidy, un-

[8] W. S. Verplanck, "The Control of the Content of Conversation: Reinforcement of Statements of Opinion," *J. Abnorm. & Soc. Psychol.,* Vol. 51 (1955), pp. 668–76.

[9] J. Greenspoon, "The Reinforcing Effect of Two Spoken Sounds on the Frequency of Two Responses," *Amer. J. Psychol.,* Vol. 68 (1955), pp. 409–16.

[10] O. R. Lindsley, "Operant Conditioning Methods Applied to Research in Chronic Schizophrenia," *Psychiat. Research Reports # 5. Research Techniques in Schizophrenia* (Washington, D.C.: American Psychiatric Association, 1956) pp. 118–53.

communicative, and his grounds privilege had to be revoked. This (to me) pathetic incident would seem to indicate that even in a relationship to a machine, trustworthiness is important if the relationship is to be helpful.

Still another interesting study of a manufactured relationship is being carried on by Harlow and his associates,[11] this time with monkeys. Infant monkeys, removed from their mothers almost immediately after birth, are, in one phase of the experiment, presented with two objects. One might be termed the "hard mother," a sloping cylinder of wire netting with a nipple from which the baby may feed. The other is a "soft mother," a similar cylinder made of foam rubber and terry cloth. Even when an infant gets all his food from the "hard mother" he clearly and increasingly prefers the "soft mother." Motion pictures show that he definitely "relates" to this object, playing with it, enjoying it, finding security in clinging to it when strange objects are near, and using that security as a home base for venturing into the frightening world. Of the many interesting and challenging implications of this study, one seems reasonably clear. It is that no amount of direct food reward can take the place of certain perceived qualities which the infant appears to need and desire.

Two Recent Studies

Let me close this wide-ranging—and perhaps perplexing—sampling of research studies with an account of two very recent investigations. The first is an experiment conducted by Ends and Page.[12] Working with hardened chronic hospitalized alcoholics who had been committed to a state hospital for sixty days, they tried three different methods of group psychotherapy. The method which they believed would be most effective was therapy based on a two-factor theory of learning; a client-centered approach was expected to be second; a psychoanalytically oriented approach was expected to be least efficient. Their results showed that therapy based upon a learning theory approach was not only not helpful, but was somewhat deleterious. The outcomes were worse than those in the control group which had no therapy. The analytically oriented therapy produced some positive gain, and the client-centered group therapy was associated with the greatest amount of positive change. Follow-up data, extending over one and one-half years, confirmed the in-hospital findings, with the lasting improvement being greatest in the client-centered approach, next in the analytic, next the control group, and least in those handled by a learning theory approach.

As I have puzzled over this study, unusual in that the approach to which the authors were committed proved *least* effective, I find a clue, I believe, in the description of the therapy based on learning theory.[13] Essentially it con-

[11] H. F. Harlow, "The Nature of Love," *Amer. Psychol.*, Vol. 13 (1958), pp. 673–85.

[12] E. J. Ends, and C. W. Page. "A Study of Three Types of Group Psychotherapy with Hospitalized Male Inebriates," *Quar. J. Stud. Alcohol*, Vol. 18 (1957) pp. 263–77.

[13] C. W. Page, and E. J. Ends, "A Review and Synthesis of the Literature Suggesting a Psychotherapeutic Technique Based on Two-Factor Learning Theory," unpublished manuscript, loaned to the writer.

sisted (a) of pointing out and labeling the behaviors which had proved unsatisfying, (b) of exploring objectively with the client the reasons behind these behaviors, and (c) of establishing through re-education more effective problem-solving habits. But in all of this interaction the aim, as they formulated it, was to be impersonal. The therapist "permits as little of his own personality to intrude as is humanly possible." The "therapist stresses personal anonymity in his activities, i.e., he must studiously avoid impressing the patient with his own (therapist's) individual personality characteristics." To me this seems the most likely clue to the failure of this approach, as I try to interpret the facts in the light of the other research studies. To withhold one's self as a person and to deal with the other person as an object does not have a high probability of being helpful.

The final study I wish to report is one just being completed by Halkides.[14] She started from a theoretical formulation of mine regarding the necessary and sufficient conditions for therapeutic change.[15] She hypothesized that there would be a significant relationship between the extent of constructive personality change in the client and four counselor variables: (a) the degree of empathic understanding of the client manifested by the counselor; (b) the degree of positive affective attitude (unconditional positive regard) manifested by the counselor toward the client; (c) the extent to which the counselor is genuine, his words matching his own internal feeling; and (d) the extent to which the counselor's response matches the client's expression in the intensity of affective expression.

To investigate these hypotheses she first selected, by multiple objective criteria, a group of ten cases which could be classed as "most successful" and a group of ten "least successful" cases. She then took an early and late recorded interview from each of these cases. On a random basis she picked nine client-counselor interaction units —a client statement and a counselor response—from each of these interviews. She thus had nine early interactions and nine later interactions from each case. This gave her several hundred units which were now placed in random order. The units from an early interview of an unsuccessful case might be followed by the units from a late interview of a successful case, etc.

Three judges, who did not know the cases of their degree of success, or the source of any given unit, now listened to this material four different times. They rated each unit on a seven point scale, first as to the degree of empathy, second as to the counselor's positive attitude toward the client, third as to the counselor's congruence or genuineness, and fourth as to the degree to which the counselor's response matched the emotional intensity of the client's expression.

I think all of us who knew of the study regarded it as a very bold venture. Could judges listening to single

[14] G. Halkides, "An Experimental Study of Four Conditions Necessary for Therapeutic Change," unpublished doctoral dissertation, University of Chicago, 1958.

[15] C. R. Rogers, "The Necessary and Sufficient Conditions of Psycho-Therapeutic Personality Change," *J. Consult. Psychol.*, Vol. 21 (1957), pp. 95–103.

units of interaction possibly make any reliable rating of such subtle qualities as I have mentioned? And even if suitable reliability could be obtained, could eighteen counselor-client interchanges from each case—a minute sampling of the hundreds or thousands of such interchanges which occurred in each case—possibly bear any relationship to the therapeutic outcome? The chance seemed slim.

The findings are surprising. It proved possible to achieve high reliability between the judges, most of the interjudge correlations being in the 0.80's or 0.90's, except on the last variable. It was found that a high degree of empathic understanding was significantly associated, at a .001 level, with the more successful cases. A high degree of unconditional positive regard was likewise associated with the more successful cases, at the .001 level. Even the rating of the counselor's genuineness or congruence—the extent to which his words matched his feelings—was associated with the successful outcome of the case, and again at the .001 level of significance. Only in the investigation of the matching intensity of affective expression were the results equivocal.

It is of interest too that high ratings of these variables were not associated more significantly with units from later interviews than with units from early interviews. This means that the counselor's attitudes were quite constant throughout the interviews. If he was highly empathic, he tended to be so from first to last. If he was lacking in genuineness, this tended to be true of both early and late interviews.

As with any study, this investigation has its limitations. It is concerned with a certain type of helping relationship, psychotherapy. It investigated only four variables thought to be significant. Perhaps there are many others. Nevertheless it represents a significant advance in the study of helping relationships. Let me try to state the findings in the simplest possible fashion. It seems to indicate that the quality of the counselor's interaction with a client can be satisfactorily judged on the basis of a very small sampling of his behavior. It also means that if the counselor is congruent or transparent, so that his words are in line with his feelings rather than the two being discrepant; if the counselor likes the client, unconditionally; and if the counselor understands the essential feelings of the client as they seem to the client—then there is a strong probability that this will be an effective helping relationship.

SOME COMMENTS

These then are some of the studies which throw at least a measure of light on the nature of the helping relationship. They have investigated different facets of the problem. They have approached it from very different theoretical contexts. They have used different methods. They are not directly comparable. Yet they seem to me to point to several statements which may be made with some assurance. It seems clear that relationships which are helpful have different characteristics from relationships which are unhelpful. These differential characteristics have to do primarily with the attitudes of the helping person on the one hand and with the perception of the relationship by the "helpee" on the other. It is equally clear that the studies thus far made do not give us any final answers as to what is a helping relationship, nor how it is to be formed.

How Can I Create a Helping Relationship?

I believe each of us working in the field of human relationships has a similar problem in knowing how to use such research knowledge. We cannot slavishly follow such findings in a mechanical way or we destroy the personal qualities which these very studies show to be valuable. It seems to me that we have to use these studies, testing them against our own experience and forming new and further personal hypotheses to use and test in our own further personal relationships.

So rather than try to tell you how you should use the findings I have presented I should like to tell you the kind of questions which these studies and my own clinical experience raise for me, and some of the tentative and changing hypotheses which guide my behavior as I enter into what I hope may be helping relationships, whether with students, staff, family, or clients. Let me list a number of these questions and considerations.

1. Can I *be* in some way which will be perceived by the other person as trustworthy, as dependable or consistent in some deep sense? Both research and experience indicate that this is very important, and over the years I have found what I believe are deeper and better ways of answering this question. I used to feel that if I fulfilled all the outer conditions of trustworthiness—keeping appointments, respecting the confidential nature of the interviews, etc.—and if I acted consistently the same during the interviews, then this condition would be fulfilled. But experience drove home the fact that to act consistently acceptant, for example, if in fact I was feeling annoyed or skeptical or some other non-acceptant feeling, was certain in the long run to be perceived as inconsistent or untrustworthy. I have come to recognize that being trustworthy does not demand that I be rigidly consistent but that I be dependably real. The term "congruent" is one I have used to describe the way I would like to be. By this I mean that whatever feeling or attitude I am experiencing would be matched by my awareness of that attitude. When this is true, then I am a unified or integrated person in that moment, and hence I can *be* whatever I deeply *am*. This is a reality which I find others experience as dependable.

2. A very closely related question is this: Can I be expressive enough as a person that what I am will be communicated unambiguously? I believe that most of my failures to achieve a helping relationship can be traced to unsatisfactory answers to these two questions. When I am experiencing an attitude of annoyance toward another person but am unaware of it, then my communication contains contradictory messages. My words are giving one message, but I am also in subtle ways communicating the annoyance I feel and this confuses the other person and makes him distrustful, though he too may be unaware of what is causing the difficulty. When as a parent or a therapist or a teacher or an administrator I fail to listen to what is going on in me, fail because of my own defensiveness to sense my own feelings, then this kind of failure seems to result. It has made it seem to me that the most basic learn-

ing for anyone who hopes to establish any kind of helping relationship is that it is safe to be transparently real. If in a given relationship I am reasonably congruent, if no feelings relevant to the relationship are hidden either to me or the other person, then I can be almost sure that the relationship will be a helpful one.

One way of putting this which may seem strange to you is that if I can form a helping relationship to myself —if I can be sensitively aware of and acceptant toward my own feelings— then the likelihood is great that I can form a helping relationship toward another.

Now, acceptantly to be what I am, in this sense, and to permit this to show through to the other person, is the most difficult task I know and one I never fully achieve. But to realize that this *is* my task has been most rewarding because it has helped me to find what has gone wrong with interpersonal relationships which have become snarled and to put them on a constructive track again. It has meant that if I am to facilitate the personal growth of others in relation to me, then I must grow, and while this is often painful it is also enriching.

3. A third question is: Can I let myself experience positive attitudes toward this other person—attitudes of warmth, caring, liking, interest, respect? It is not easy. I find in myself, and feel that I often see in others, a certain amount of fear of these feelings. We are afraid that if we let ourselves freely experience these positive feelings toward another we may be trapped by them. They may lead to demands on us or we may be disappointed in our trust, and these outcomes we fear. So

as a reaction we tend to build up distance between ourselves and others— aloofness, a "professional" attitude, an impersonal relationship.

I feel quite strongly that one of the important reasons for the professionalization of every field is that it helps to keep this distance. In the clinical areas we develop elaborate diagnostic formulations, seeing the person as an object. In teaching and in administration we develop all kinds of evaluative procedures, so that again the person is perceived as an object. In these ways, I believe, we can keep ourselves from experiencing the caring which would exist if we recognized the relationship as one between two persons. It is a real achievement when we can learn, even in certain relationships or at certain times in those relationships, that it is safe to care, that it is safe to relate to the other as a person for whom we have positive feelings.

4. Another question the importance of which I have learned in my own experience is: Can I be strong enough as a person to be separate from the other? Can I be a sturdy respecter of my own feelings, my own needs, as well as his? Can I own and, if need be, express my own feelings as something belonging to me and separate from his feelings? Am I strong enough in my own separateness that I will not be downcast by his depression, frightened by his fear, nor engulfed by his dependency? Is my inner self hardy enough to realize that I am not destroyed by his anger, taken over by his need for dependence, nor enslaved by his love, but that I exist separate from him with feelings and rights of my own? When I can freely feel this strength of being a separate person, then I find that

I can let myself go much more deeply in understanding and accepting him because I am not fearful of losing myself.

5. The next question is closely related. Am I secure enough within myself to permit him his separateness? Can I permit him to be what he is— honest or deceitful, infantile or adult, despairing or over-confident? Can I give him the freedom to be? Or do I feel that he should follow my advice, or remain somewhat dependent on me, or mold himself after me? In this connection I think of the interesting small study by Farson[16] which found that the less well adjusted and less competent counselor tends to induce conformity to himself, to have clients who model themselves after him. On the other hand, the better adjusted and more competent counselor can interact with a client through many interviews without interfering with the freedom of the client to develop a personality quite separate from that of his therapist. I should prefer to be in this latter class, whether as parent or supervisor or counselor.

6. Another question I ask myself is: Can I let myself enter fully into the world of his feelings and personal meanings and see these as he does? Can I step into his private world so completely that I lose all desire to evaluate or judge it? Can I enter it so sensitively that I can move about in it freely, without trampling on meanings which are precious to him? Can I sense it so accurately that I can catch not only the meanings of his experience

[16] R. E. Farson, "Introjection in the Psychotherapeutic Relationship," unpublished doctoral dissertation, University of Chicago, 1955.

which are obvious to him, but those meanings which are only implicit, which he sees only dimly or as confusion? Can I extend this understanding without limit? I think of the client who said, "Whenever I find someone who understands a *part* of me at the time, then it never fails that a point is reached where I know they're *not* understanding me again . . . What I've looked for so hard is for someone to understand."

For myself I find it easier to feel this kind of understanding, and to communicate it, to individual clients than to students in a class or staff members in a group in which I am involved. There is a strong temptation to set students "straight," or to point out to a staff member the errors in his thinking. Yet when I can permit myself to understand in these situations, it is mutually rewarding. And with clients in therapy, I am often impressed with the fact that even a minimal amount of empathic understanding—a bumbling and faulty attempt to catch the confused complexity of the client's meaning—is helpful, though there is no doubt that it is most helpful when I can see and formulate clearly the meanings in his experiencing which for him have been unclear and tangled.

7. Still another issue is whether I can be acceptant of each facet of this other person which he presents to me. Can I receive him as he is? Can I communicate this attitude? Or can I only receive him conditionally, acceptant of some aspects of his feelings and silently or openly disapproving of other aspects? It has been my experience that when my attitude is conditional, then he cannot change or grow in those respects in which I cannot fully receive him.

And when—afterward and sometimes too late—I try to discover why I have been unable to accept him in every respect, I usually discover that it is because I have been frightened or threatened in myself by some aspect of his feeling. If I am to be more helpful, then I must myself grow and accept myself in these respects.

8. A very practical issue is raised by the question: Can I act with sufficient sensitivity in the relationship that my behavior will not be perceived as a threat? The work we are beginning to do in studying the physiological concomitants of psychotherapy confirms the research by Dittes in indicating how easily individuals are threatened at a physiological level. The psychogalvanic reflex—the measure of skin conductance—takes a sharp dip when the therapist responds with some word which is just a little stronger than the client's feeling. And to a phrase such as, "My you *do* look upset," the needle swings almost off the paper. My desire to avoid even such minor threats is not due to a hypersensitivity about my client. It is simply due to the conviction based on experience that if I can free him as completely as possible from external threat, then he can begin to experience and to deal with the internal feelings and conflicts which he finds threatening within himself.

9. A specific aspect of the preceding question but an important one is: Can I free him from the threat of external evaluation? In almost every phase of our lives—at home, at school, at work—we find ourselves under the rewards and punishments of external judgments. "That's good"; "that's naughty." "That's worth an A"; "that's a failure." "That's good counseling";

"that's poor counseling." Such judgments are a part of our lives from infancy to old age. I believe they have a certain social usefulness to institutions and organizations such as schools and professions. Like everyone else I find myself all too often making such evaluations. But, in my experience, they do not make for personal growth and hence I do not believe that they are a part of a helping relationship. Curiously enough a positive evaluation is as threatening in the long run as a negative one, since to inform someone that he is good implies that you also have the right to tell him he is bad. So I have come to feel that the more I can keep a relationship free of judgment and evaluation, the more this will permit the other person to reach the point where he recognizes that the locus of evaluation, the center of responsibility, lies within himself. The meaning and value of his experience is in the last analysis something which is up to him, and no amount of external judgment can alter this. So I should like to work toward a relationship in which I am not, even in my own feelings, evaluating him. This I believe can set him free to be a self-responsible person.

10. One last question: Can I meet this other individual as a person who is in process of *becoming*, or will I be bound by his past and by my past? If, in my encounter with him, I am dealing with him as an immature child, an ignorant student, a neurotic personality, or a psychopath, each of these concepts of mine limits what he can be in the relationship. Martin Buber, the existentialist philosopher of the University of Jerusalem, has a phrase, "confirming the other," which has had

meaning for me. He says "Confirming means . . . accepting the whole potentiality of the other. . . . I can recognize in him, know in him, the person he has been . . . *created* to become. . . . I confirm him in myself, and then in him, in relation to this potentiality that . . . can now be developed, can evolve."[17] If I accept the other person as something fixed, already diagnosed and classified, already shaped by his past, then I am doing my part to confirm this limited hypothesis. If I accept him as a process of becoming, then I am doing what I can to confirm or make real his potentialities.

It is at this point that I see Verplanck, Lindsley, and Skinner, working in operant conditioning, coming together with Buber, the philosopher or mystic. At least they come together in principle, in an odd way. If I see a relationship as only an opportunity to reinforce certain types of words or opinions in the other, then I tend to confirm him as an object—a basically mechanical, manipulable object. And if I see this as his potentiality, he tends to act in ways which support this hypothesis. If, on the other hand, I see a relationship as an opportunity to "reinforce" *all* that he is, the person that he is with all his existent potentialities, then he tends to act in ways which support *this* hypothesis. I have then— to use Buber's term—confirmed him as

[17] M. Buber, and C. Rogers, "Transcription of Dialogue Held April 18, 1957, Ann Arbor, Mich.," unpublished manuscript.

a living person, capable of creative inner development. Personally I prefer this second type of hypothesis.

CONCLUSION

In the early portion of this paper I reviewed some of the contributions which research is making to our knowledge *about* relationships. Endeavoring to keep that knowledge in mind I then took up the kind of questions which arise from an inner and subjective point of view as I enter, as a person, into relationships. If I could, in myself, answer all the questions I have raised in the affirmative, then I believe that any relationships in which I was involved would be helping relationships, would involve growth. But I cannot give a positive answer to most of these questions. I can only work in the direction of the positive answer.

This has raised in my mind the strong suspicion that the optimal helping relationship is the kind of relationship created by a person who is psychologically mature. Or to put it in another way, the degree to which I can create relationships which facilitate the growth of others as separate persons is a measure of the growth I have achieved in myself. In some respects this is a disturbing thought, but it is also a promising or challenging one. It would indicate that if I am interested in creating helping relationships I have a fascinating lifetime job ahead of me, stretching and developing my potentialities in the direction of growth.

4.2 TWO STRATEGIES OF SOCIAL CHANGE AND THEIR DILEMMAS

Richard E. Walton

The type of intergroup setting which is of primary concern here is described by the following assumptions. First, assume a desire on the part of one group to change the allocation of scarce resources between two groups—these could be status, political power, economic advantage or opportunity, geographic occupancy, and so on. Alternately, assume incompatible preferences regarding social institutions—such as the Berlin Wall, racial segregation, union shop. Second, assume that although the leaders of the groups recognize these areas of conflict they also want to establish a more cooperative set of attitudes between the groups. Third, assume further that there is neither law nor a compulsory arbitration mechanism which can accomplish the desired change or settle the conflict of interest.

Some of our most pressing problems of social change fit these assumptions almost completely and others meet them to a lesser degree. In international relations, for instance, the important substantive conflicts between the United States and the Soviet Union are accompanied by a general desire for more favorable inter-nation attitudes. Moreover, in the present polarized world where the stakes of change

From Richard E. Walton, "Two Strategies of Social Change and Their Dilemmas," *The Journal of Applied Behavioral Science*, I, No. 2 (1965), 167–179. Used by permission.

can be enormously high, no international legal machinery is available to settle the important issues.

In race relations, the civil rights movement of the last decade has sought social change at times and in places where legal machinery could not be brought to bear to establish and enforce humane treatment for Negroes, to say nothing about equalizing their right to vote, to use public accommodations, to find housing, to apply for jobs, and so forth. At the same time, the majority of Negro and white leaders have commented upon the necessity for improved intergroup attitudes.

In labor-management relations, also, there are important substantive issues, such as hours, wages, and working conditions, which are neither specified by law nor amenable to resolution by appeal to a higher order of common values. Often these differences are accompanied by a genuine and mutual desire for harmonious intergroup relations.

How does the leadership of a group behave in these situations when they seek a change in the status quo? What actions are instrumental to the change effort?

Two groups of social scientists—viewing the same general situation—offer quite different explanations and advice. One change strategy is advanced by game theorists, diplomatic strategists, and students of revolutions. Their focus is on the building of a power base and the strategic manipulation of power. Another strategy is urged by many social psychologists and by many persons involved in human relations laboratory training. This approach involves overtures of love and trust and gestures of good will, all intended to result in attitude change and concomitant behavior change.

Tactics of the Power Strategy

In recent years there has been an attempt to explicate the rational tactics of power and strategic choice (Schelling, 1960; Rapoport, 1960; Boulding, 1962; Walton & McKersie, 1965). The work in this area suggests that the fixed sum games—those situations in which what one person gains the other loses—require the following tactical operations.

First, in order to establish a basis for negotiation with the other and improve the probable outcome for itself, a group must build its power vis-à-vis the other. Group A can increase its relative power by making group B more dependent upon it and by decreasing its own (A's) dependence upon B. Often the change is sought by groups with a relative power disadvantage. To command attention and establish a basis for a *quid pro quo*, they must threaten the other with harm, loss, inconvenience, or embarrassment. These threats in international relations range from nuclear war to unilateral cancellation of an official state visit. In civil rights they involve notoriety, demonstrations, consumer boycotts, and sit-ins, lie-ins, and the like. In labor relations they include wildcat strikes, authorized stoppages, unfavorable publicity campaigns. These tactics create a basis for negotiation only if the threats are credible. One important technique for increasing their credibility is to fulfill a given threat once or repeatedly, as required.

A second set of tactical operations is required in order for a group to make maximum use of its potential power. These include biasing the rival group's perceptions of the strength of the underlying preference functions. A leader of group A attempts to overstate his group's needs or preferences for various degrees of achievement of its stated objective. Also, leader A depreciates the importance to B of B's objectives. These operations require the skillful management of ambiguity and uncertainty. They involve manipulating communication opportunities such that B perceives A as being maximally (even if irrationally) committed to a course of action and that the leader of group B does not have a comparable opportunity to commit himself to a different set of actions.

An abundance of illustrative material from international relations is available for each of these tactical operations—for example, the Cuban missile episode, Berlin crises, and the crises over Suez, the Congo, and Viet Nam. Leaders of various civil rights groups have behaved in similar ways. Illustrative encounters are those in Montgomery (school-bus boycotts over public accommodations); Pittsburgh (consumer boycotts over employment); Chicago (lie-ins and demonstrations over de facto segregation in schools); Birmingham (demonstrations over public accommodations); Mississippi ("invading" the state in the interest of voter registration and freedom schools). Analyses of the negotiations in any of the major trade union strikes—such as those in steel in 1959, in rails in 1963, and in autos in 1964 —would reveal labor-management behavior which conformed to the tactical operations of the power strategy.

Tactics of the
Attitude Change Strategy

Theoretical and empirical work in recent years has identified the conditions and actions which result in change in intergroup relationships (Naess, 1957; Janis & Katz, 1959; Osgood, 1959; Kelman, 1962; Berkowitz, 1962; Sherif, 1962; Deutsch, 1962; Gibb, 1964; Walton & McKersie, 1965). The areas of agreement in these writings may be summarized in terms of the tactics of attitude change.

Increasing the level of attraction and trust between persons or groups involves the following types of operations, considering the leader of group A as the acting party: minimizing the perceived differences between the groups' goals and between characteristics of members of the two groups; communications to B advocating peace; refraining from any actions which might harm members of the rival group (inconvenience, harass, embarrass, or violate them in any way); minimizing or eliminating B's perception of potential threats from A; emphasizing the degree of mutual dependence between the groups, accepting or enhancing the status of the representative of the rival group; ensuring that contacts between groups are on the basis of equal status; attempting to involve many members in intergroup contact; attempting to achieve a high degree of empathy with respect to the motives, expectations, and attitudes of members of group B; adopting a consistent posture of trust toward the other group; being open about A's own plans and intentions; creating a network of social relations involving many mutual associations with third parties.

There is tension between the ideas which underlie the two change strategies outlined above. However, the two groups of social scientists who are associated with these respective change strategies tend to handle this tension either by ignoring it or by depreciating the assumptions, ideas, and tactics of the other. It is true that both systems of ideas treat certain realities of the total social field; and, admittedly, it is possible for one to center one's attention on those particular situations where his ideas by themselves are appropriate and upon those particular aspects of a more complex situation where his ideas apply. The practitioner himself cannot do this. He must deal with the total reality. The leader of a group who is advocating and seeking change directly experiences the tension between these two persuasive systems of ideas.

Social scientists can become more relevant and therefore more helpful to the practitioner if they, too, confront these tensions between ideas, these dilemmas in action programs.

It is important to identify still a third distinct process of change, namely, problem solving. This process can be used whenever the basic nature of the issue is one where there is the potential that arrangements can be invented or created allowing both parties to gain or where one party can gain without the other's sacrificing anything of value to himself. In other words, integrative solutions are logically possible (Blake, 1959). However, this alternative of problem solving is not applicable in the specific intergroup situations assumed here: The substantive conflicts are ones which by the nature of the issues and the parties' basic preferences can be resolved only by dominance-submission or some compromise outcome.

Leadership Dilemmas in Pursuing Both Power and Attitude Change Strategies

If—as we have assumed here—a leader of group A has the objective both of obtaining important concessions from B and of reducing intergroup hostility, he would prefer to pursue simultaneously both change strategies discussed above. But in many respects the strategies place contradictory tactical demands on a leader, forcing him to choose between these strategies or to find some basis on which to integrate the two in some broader strategy of change. Several of the contradictions, dilemmas, and choice points in the tactics of social change are discussed below.

OVERSTATEMENT OF OBJECTIVES VERSUS DEEMPHASIZING DIFFERENCES

On the one hand, it is often tactical to the power strategy to overstate one's ultimate goals or immediate objectives —in effect, exaggerating the differences between the two groups. The strategy of attitude change, on the other hand, would deemphasize differences. Thus, the U.S. references to the status of Berlin which overstate our pertinent preferences, needs, and requirements

may improve our position in bargaining for new terms there; but these statements run the risk of convincing the Soviet Union that our differences run even deeper than they do and that there is less basis for conciliation and trust than they had believed.

STEREOTYPING: INTERNAL COHESION VERSUS ACCURATE DIFFERENTIATION

Stereotyping members of the rival group, focusing on their faults, impugning their motives, questioning their rationality, challenging their competence—these are often employed by leaders and members of the first group to build internal cohesion and willingness to make necessary sacrifices. For example, these tendencies occurred in a moderate form as the Mississippi Summer Project prepared their field staff and student volunteers for their work in "hostile" Mississippi. The tendency to attribute negative attributes to members of the rival group may have aided in the implementation of the almost pure power strategy which characterized this particular project but this tendency would have been a clear liability in another civil right project where the objectives include achieving attitude change.

EMPHASIS ON POWER TO COERCE VERSUS TRUST

If group A increases B's dependence upon A, this may enhance A's power to obtain substantive concessions, but it will not elicit more positive feelings In fact, it can be argued that the trust building process requires that A would communicate about A's dependence upon B. A labor union may enhance its power position by making management more aware of the company's vulnerability to a strike. But the same union might elicit more trust if it were to indicate instead how much the union must count upon management.

INFORMATION:
AMBIGUITY VERSUS PREDICTABILITY

Whereas ambiguity and uncertainty are often tactical to the power strategy, openness and predictability are essential to the attitude change strategy. Similarly, the first strategy is facilitated when there is limited and disciplined interaction; the second, when there is a more extensive and more open contact pattern. Thus, the power strategy dictates that we restrict the flow of information and people between the Soviet Union and the United States and that the limited contacts be formal and structured and that the agenda of these contacts be quite guarded. Attitude change strategy on the other hand, calls for freedom of travel, a variety of settings for international contact, and spontaneity and openness in these interchanges.

THREAT VERSUS CONCILIATION

Review of the tactical operations of the two strategies reveals another important choice point in dual or mixed strategies, namely, What should be the role of threat or harm? When A is primarily pursuing an attitude change strategy, he communicates peaceful plans, he reduces perceived threat to B, and he refrains from actions that harm B. However, to pursue a power strategy in the interest of obtaining substantive gains, A engages in quite different tactics.

Even instances of uncontrolled aggression out of frustration can build bargaining power for the frustrated group and serve as an implicit threat of more aggression if substantive gains are not forthcoming. The Harlem riots in the summer of 1964 illustrate this point. Although it was generally said at the time that these outbursts hurt the civil rights movement (i.e., "had set the movement back several years"), many changes which accommodated the Negroes' demands and needs were soon made in the budgets, plans, and organization of several commissions and departments of New York City. One column headline in the *New York Times*, July 1964, the week following the riots, read "City Accelerates Fight on Poverty: $223,225 Grant Made Amid Reference to Racial Riots." A casual content analysis of items in the news after the riots in Harlem, Rochester, Philadelphia, and elsewhere suggests that there were both substantive gains and attitudinal losses. Notwithstanding the fact that all responsible civil rights leaders deplored the wanton destruction of property and the indiscriminate defiance of legal authorities, their bargaining power was nevertheless strengthened in certain respects.

HOSTILITY MANAGEMENT:
IMPACT VERSUS CATHARSIS

This dilemma is related to the preceding one but can present a somewhat more subtle problem for group leadership. Both change strategies involve the purposeful management of hostile feelings. In the power strategy the expression of hostile feelings is managed in a way which creates optimal impact on the other group, communicating strength of interest in the issue or making a threat credible.

The attitude change strategy also involves the expression of hostile feelings, but in a way which creates an optimal impact on the expressing group. Hostility expression is managed in a way which allows catharsis and the reevaluation of one's own group's feelings, but with minimum impact on the other group. Otherwise the hostility level will tend to be maintained or increased.

COALITION VERSUS INCLUSION

One final dilemma relates to the question of whether A tries to involve third parties or publics in a coalition *against* B or in a social group *with* B. Building bargaining power in the interest of substantive change may require A to isolate B and attempt to generate disapproval of B. This has been an important aspect of the strategy of the civil rights movement in the last decade. The movement has tried to identify and isolate those officials and power groups in the South who oppose integration and those national officials in the Republican Party who are unsympathetic with certain legislative and enforcement objectives. This has created a forced choice situation for the moderates and for the uncertain.

However, a strategy of attitude change involves creating a network of social relations among A, B, and others. Applied to the civil rights movement, an emphasis on attitude change would actively encourage dialogue, understanding, and mutual influence among (a) groups in the movement, (b) the middle-of-the-roaders, and (c) the segregationists and other right-wing groups.

Coping with the Dilemmas

How do those who seek both substantive changes opposed by another group and improvements in intergroup attitudes cope with these dilemmas?

If the group's leader sequences the emphasis placed upon these two objectives and their accompanying strategies, this does somewhat ameliorate the tension between the two sets of activities. In international negotiations between the East and the West, both sides have used a freeze-thaw approach. One may first engage in new initiatives intended to make substantive gains or to create a power base for the future, and then make peace overtures. As long as the cycle is not too short in duration and the initiatives and overtures are seen as genuine, a leader can engage in both sets of behaviors and still have them be credible. In race relations, a particular campaign may involve a street demonstration phase (power building) and a negotiation phase (a mixture of power bargaining and relationship building).

Another technique is to have the contradictory strategies implemented by different persons or subgroups. In international relations, power tactics occur in the confrontations between the United States and the Soviet Union in the United Nations General Assembly and Security Council, but their attitude change efforts are implemented by different groups involved in such activities as cultural exchange programs. In race relations, a similar distinction can be made between the programs of CORE and SNCC on the one hand and NAACP and the Urban League on the other. This technique makes it apparent that mixed or dual strategies can be pursued more readily by an organization than by a person, and more readily by a movement than by an organization.

Whether or not the activities are sequenced or assigned to different persons within a group, an important way of coping with these dilemmas is to choose actions which minimize them. Recognition of the tactical requirements of both strategies results in eliminating provocative acts which elicit negative attitudes and add nothing to the power strategy—for example, impeccable dress and demeanor in many civil rights demonstrations or the self-imposed norm of volunteers of the Mississippi Summer Project to avoid mixed racial couples' appearing in public even though eventual acceptance of such a pattern was one of the goals of the movement.

When the relationship between strategies is fully understood by the leader, he can select power tactics which have least negative impact on attitudes and choose attitudinal structuring activities which detract least from the power strategy.

Nonviolence is an attempt to meet the requirements of both strategies, but as a tactic it falls short of achieving an optimal integration. This is true in part because the distinction made between violence and nonviolence is more meaningful to the acting group than to the target group. The distinction usually refers to whether or not there is a physical violation of members of the rival group. In fact, other violations may be experienced by them as equally devastating—such as violation of their traditions and other social norms (inte-

grating schools), assaults on their power base (voting drives). In short, in some situations the only maneuvers which effectively increase bargaining power really do hurt.

Over-all Strategy Considerations

Although in many situations one must engage in the tactics of power only at some disadvantage in terms of achieving attitude change and vice versa, this is not always the case. Especially when one takes a longer-range viewpoint, one may discover that the substantive objectives of the power strategy are more likely to be realized at a later date if an improvement in intergroup attitudes is sought initially. The point is that attitude change may result in some lessening of the substantive conflict. If southern whites as a group were more accepting of Negroes (i.e., developed more favorable attitudes toward them for some independent reason), they would be less adamant on certain substantive issues—for example, segregated schools—and would, as a result, reduce the need for civil rights groups to utilize a power strategy. Moreover, in the case of many of the substantive gains which one may reach through the power strategy—an arms control agreement, a treaty on Berlin, an understanding reached regarding future employment practices affecting Negroes—the fulfillment of these arrangements is dependent upon the level of trust and confidence which exists in the relationship.

Similarly, a longer-range viewpoint may show that the objective of attitude change is more likely to be achieved at a later date if one engages in the power tactics initially. The substantive gains obtained by the power strategy almost always result in temporary setbacks in terms of the level of friendliness and trust between the groups; but in the somewhat longer run, the result may be better affective relations. Consider race relations. One reason why more positive attitudes may develop via the initial power strategy is that the commitment and self-respect which the Negroes usually demonstrate in pursuing the power strategy may engender respect on the part of the larger white community—after the initial heat of conflict has subsided.

Another indirect and eventual way that the power strategy can lead to more favorable attitudinal bonds is through the mechanism of dissonance reduction. If as a result of substantive gains a group must be treated differently (more equal), there is a tendency to regard them differently (more equal) in order to make one's beliefs and attitudes congruent with one's behavior.

There is a third reason why a power strategy designed to obtain substantive concessions may achieve attitude change as well, particularly for a group which is currently less privileged and exercises less power. This refers to an important precondition for achieving a stable and healthy intergroup relationship—equal status and power between groups. This suggests that as long as group A remains at a power disadvantage and there is a potential for achieving power parity, A's mix of power and attitude change tactics will include relatively more power tactics. Thus, the power strategy for the civil rights groups during the last decade has dominated the attitude change

strategy. This principle is also illustrated by the warlike actions of the Soviet Union during the period after World War II, when the United States alone possessed the atom bomb.

Whatever the existing balance of power, whenever B makes a move which would build his relative power, A will tend to act primarily in terms of the power strategy. This is illustrated by the United State's bargaining commitment moves when it discovered Soviet missiles in Cuba and when the Soviets attempted to make inroads in the Middle East and the Congo during the Suez and Congo crises respectively.

Implications

Recognition of these dilemmas is the first step toward developing a theory of social action which specifies the conditions under which one should conform to the tactical requirements of one strategy versus the other. But better theory is not enough. The agent of social change needs the behavioral skill required by simultaneously or sequentially mixed strategies. For example international officials and civil rights leaders should be flexible enough to employ strategies of attitude change when a particular campaign reaches the negotiation phase.

What are the implications for training of leaders of groups advocating major social change? Human relations training generally and laboratory learning in particular are geared to developing insights and skills central to the strategy of attitude change and are less relevant to the power strategy. I suggest that the conception of the problem of change should be broadened to incorporate—as necessary and legitimate—the power strategy.[1] We must understand what demands on leadership behavior are imposed by the power strategy of change both during the phase when power thinking necessarily dominates group leadership and the phase when preserving a power base is merely a consideration in designing an attitude change strategy. If these specialists deplore these power tactics simply because they violate their personal model of preferred social behavior, their advice which *is* appropriate and badly needed by the practitioner will be taken less seriously by him.

---

[1] In the interest of sharpening the issues about our conception of the problem, I offer the following assertions regarding the role of bargaining, power, and violence in social change:

First, bargaining and bargaining tactics (including tactical deception, bluff, commitment, promises, threats, and threat fulfillment) are often necessary in social change situations where there are basic conflicts of interest. Moreover, many of these tactical operations are amoral in such situations.

Second, attempts to create cooperative relations between parties are more effective if there is some parity in their power. Power of a party derives from its capacity to influence some aspect of the fate of the other —either rewards or punishments. Often the only avenue open to a party with less relative power is to increase its capacity to harm (embarrass or inconvenience) the other. Moreover, it may be necessary for the party to engage in a series of maneuvers which are increasingly persuasive in communicating to the other party both a capacity and a willingness to use the power.

Third, where they are used, tactics of nonviolence are effective at least in part because the other group perceives this method as an alternative to violence. The option of violence is indirectly suggested *by advocating nonviolence.*

Fourth, there is experimental evidence that a cooperative bid by A is more effective in eliciting a cooperative response from B when it occurs against a series of noncooperative moves by A. Maybe this paradox also operates in some social situations creating an incentive for initial noncooperation.

REFERENCES

1. Berkowitz, L. *Aggression: A social psychological analysis.* New York: McGraw-Hill, Inc., 1962.
2. Blake, R. R. Psychology and the crisis of statesmanship. *Amer. Psychologist,* 1959, **14,** 87–94.
3. Boulding, K. *Conflict and defense: A general theory.* New York: Harper & Row, Publishers, 1962.
4. City accelerates fight on poverty. *New York Times,* July 28, 1964, p. 15.
5. Deutsch, M. A psychological basis for peace. In Q. Wright, W. M. Evan, & M. Deutsch (Eds.), *Preventing World War III: Some proposals.* New York: Simon and Schuster, Inc., 1962.
6. Gibb, J. R. Climate for trust formation. In L. P. Bradford, J. R. Gibb, & K. D. Benne (Eds.), *T-Group theory and laboratory method: Innovation in re-education.* New York: John Wiley & Sons, Inc., 1964.
7. Janis, I. L., & Katz, D. The reduction of intergroup hostility: Research problems and hypotheses. *J. conflict Resolution,* 1959, **3,** 85–100.

8. Kelman, H. C. Changing attitudes through international activities. *J. soc. Issues*, 1962, **18**, 68–87.
9. Naess, A. A systematization of Gandhian ethics of conflict resolution. *J. conflict Resolution*, 1957, **1**, 140–155.
10. Osgood, C. E. Suggestions for winning the real war with Communism. *J. conflict Resolution*, 1959, **3**, 295–325.
11. Rapoport, A. *Fights, games, and debates*. Ann Arbor, Mich.: University of Michigan Press, 1960.
12. Schelling, T. *The strategy of conflict*. Cambridge, Mass.: Harvard University Press, 1960.
13. Sherif, M. (Ed.). *Intergroup relations and leadership*. New York: John Wiley & Sons, Inc., 1962.
14. Walton, R. E., & McKersie, R. B. *A behavioral theory of labor negotiations*. New York: McGraw-Hill, Inc., 1965.

4.3 THE UNION-MANAGEMENT INTERGROUP LABORATORY: STRATEGY FOR RESOLVING INTERGROUP CONFLICT

Robert R. Blake
Jane Srygley Mouton
Richard L. Sloma

The background against which this intergroup laboratory took place and certain events preceding it are described before presenting the actual events of the laboratory.

The plant employs nearly 1,000 managers and over 3,000 wage and salary personnel. It is one of several locations that make up the complex of a large publicly-owned corporation.

The wage membership is represented by four major unions. The international union involved in the present application is the bargaining agent for a highly specialized and skilled group, representing approximately 10 percent

From Robert R. Blake, Jane Srygley Mouton, and Richard L. Sloma, "The Union-Management Intergroup Laboratory: Strategy for Resolving Intergroup Conflict," *The Journal of Applied Behavioral Science*, I, No. 1 (1965), 25–57. Abridged and used by permission.

of the total wage force. Membership in this local is 95 percent of those eligible. It has been the certified bargaining unit for 25 years. At present, it is one of two international unions representing wage personnel. The other unions are independent.

Chronic long-term hostility typifies the relationship between management and this international local. No one seems to know clearly today how the conflict began. At the time just prior to the introduction of the union-management laboratory, there was no inclination to seek constructive solutions in either the union organization or among managerial personnel. Grievances had been on a steady rise. A rather large number of arbitration cases were pending. Only the financial expense involved in pushing issues through to arbitration had prevented many of the pending grievances from going all the way. Day-by-day frictions between representatives of both groups became sharper and more heated. The last round of contract negotiations had been characterized by accusation and counter-accusation. The eventual contract agreement represented a "no victory" result. Strike threats had become relatively commonplace. The union seemed to be moving in this direction as the basis for trying to achieve what it regarded as its inevitable right.

LOCAL PLANT IMPROVEMENT EFFORTS. For a period of three years, the management organization had been engaged in intensive study and application of a laboratory-seminar organization development effort. The significance in this connection is the fact that each member of management participated in such a laboratory-seminar. The curriculum of each laboratory-seminar included an experiment concerned with intergroup conflict and cooperation. Also included was the examination of behavioral science theory regarding the conditions for achieving sound relationships between two groups in conflict.[1]

In later organization improvement steps, management had applied the concepts and methods for conflict resolutions in the work situation. These application steps had brought about the restoration of problem solving between contending groups in a number of settings that involved friction between managerial components. In each of the applications substantial improvement was visible. These successes encouraged management to hope that the concepts and methods might find utility in the international union and management application.

A DECISION TO EXPERIMENT. Hardly a management meeting went by without the "question" of the international union coming up for discussion. Animosity toward the union was visible as management reacted to each new union "move."

An organization development specialist, who was auditing the development effort, was present at one such typical meeting. Following a review of the usual complaint, this specialist intervened with the following questions: "Why not experiment with the situation toward searching out a solution for it? Rather than continually complaining about the unsavory state of affairs, why not try to solve the basic problem rather than search for ways of defending against what you regard as inappropriate union behavior?

These questions took management by surprise. The intervention served as the basis for considering what the impact of such a union-management laboratory might be and how such consultation might be brought about.

Acting from the notion that such an

---

[1] Blake, R. R., Shepard, H. A., & Mouton, J. S. *Managing Intergroup Conflict in Industry*. Houston, Tex.: The Gulf Publishing Company, 1964; Blake, R. R., & Mouton, J. S. The intergroup dynamics of win-lose conflict and problem-solving collaboration in union-management relations. In M. Sherif (Ed.), *Intergroup Relations* *and Leadership*. New York: John Wiley & Sons, Inc., 1962, 94–140; Blake, R. R., & Mouton, J. S. Union-management relations: From conflict to collaboration. *Personnel*, 1961, **38**; and Blake, R. R. & Mouton, J. S. *Group Dynamics—Key to Decision Making*. Houston, Tex.: The Gulf Publishing Company, 1961.

effort could do no harm, though with low expectations that it would be of any substantial help, management personnel concluded that it would be worth a try.

AGREEMENT REACHED—WITH RESERVATIONS. The union's reluctance to meet with management stemmed from two sources. One was in the union's conviction that management's intention was "to get them, one way or another." Thus, the question was, How could such a meeting be of any real merit?

The other reluctance on the part of the union stemmed from fear that the proposal might involve some invisible gimmick. They suspected a management strategy that could result in the union's being caught in an even more difficult position. Other sources of reservation included the possibility that the methods involved would result in some kind of brainwashing and "softening up" of the union. Nonetheless, it was agreed that a two-day laboratory should be scheduled.

Those attending the union-management laboratory to represent the union included the international's business agent; Jones, the local president; Smith, the secretary; the vice-president; and others in the union hierarchy. In all, nine union members participated.

An equal number of plant management personnel participated. The nine included the assistant general manager, the head of administrative services, the employee relations manager and his field representative, a general foreman, two unit supervisors, and two first-line supervisors.

Two behavioral scientists conducted the laboratory. One met with the management group; the other with the union. Both attended all the joint sessions. The behavioral scientists familiarized themselves in advance with the situation of intergroup conflict that existed between the two participating groups.

The eight steps that were involved in the sequence, the content or activity involved in each step, and the amount of time allocated to it are shown in Table 1.

TABLE 1   Sequence of and Time Devoted to the Phases of the Two-Day Union-Management Intergroup Laboratory

Phase	Activity	Time (Hours)
1	Orientation	½
2	Intragroup development of own image and its image of the other	5
3	Exchange of images across groups	1
4	Clarification of images	2
5	Intragroup diagnosis of present relationship	4
6	Exchange of diagnosis across groups	3
7	Consolidation of key issues and sources of friction	2
8	Planning next steps	1

Phase 1—Orientation of Participants to the Laboratory (1/2 hr.)

At the outset, management and the union convened in one location for a brief orientation. The behavioral scientists in charge of the laboratory pictured the purpose, ground rules, and background considerations involved.

The senior behavioral scientist began by saying, "The last decade has seen some very important experiments in problem solving between groups that have become locked in an intergroup win-lose orientation. A great deal is now known about intergroup conflict and cooperation. The union-management situation, in particular, is very prone to becoming an intensely hostile, win-lose relationship; although its genuine purpose should be a problem-solving one.

"During these next two days, what we wish to explore are problems that are blocking the relationship—to identify them and, if possible, to plan constructive steps for their elimination.

"Therefore, we are not concerned with issues of bargaining, with specific problems of grievance handling, or with attitudes about problems that currently are under arbitration. Nor are we concerned with personalities, as such. Rather, the key concern will be with the *character* of the relationship between your two groups and with the strategies of the orientations that have characterized the two of you in the past."

It was further emphasized that this two-day intergroup laboratory might be regarded as a first activity in a sequence of events rather than as an interaction which was likely, in and of itself, to bring about a resolution of the differences.

Phase 2—Intergroup Development of Self-Image and Counter-Image (5 hrs.)

Following this orientation, the two groups received their initial two-part task assignment. First, each group, meeting separately, was asked to develop a written description—an image —of how it saw itself, particularly in its relationship with the other group. Second, management and the union were each asked to develop an image of how they saw the other group's behavior. As these images emerged, they were to be recorded on large newsprint sheets for use in reporting back when the two groups reconvened.

Organized groups do have characteristics of behavior and conduct that are visible sometimes only to members themselves. But more frequently, there are characteristics that are more clearly visible to outsiders who observe such groups. The review and exchange on an ingroup level of perceptions of how that group performs—how its behavior is motivated, what its conduct has been, what its intentions, purposes, and goals are—can do much to bring to an explicit level the assumptions, attitudes, and feelings that exist among members. It is likely that these will be areas of behavior which have never previously been exchanged and understood. The very process of doing so, indeed, frequently has been observed to result in ingroup members' coming to recognize that what they *thought* they had in common was not, in fact, widely agreed upon. Group members find it far easier to develop an image of the counter-group than to develop an image of themselves. The conduct, purposes, and so on of the counter-group are seen in the minds of ingroup members in a clearer and more vivid way than are similar aspects of their own group. The development of self-image versus the development of an image of the counter-group constitutes in itself a significant learning experience. Members on either side of the group cleavage are thus made more aware of themselves and of the fact that they, many times, are not clear regarding their own behavior, conduct, intentions, purposes, and goals.

Phase 3—Management and the International Exchange Images

RATIONALE

Each group presented its self-image for examination by the other group. It also presented its image of the counter-group as the basis for enabling the counter-group to compare its own self-image with its observed characteristics, as seen from the outside.

Each group quickly recognizes that the counter-group is more readily able to picture its opposing member than itself. Images evaluated from an ingroup point of view, and from an outgroup point of view, respectively, many times are grossly different. The sheer contradictions that they contain many times identify the hidden causes for much of the surface antagonism that makes problem solving difficult. The exchange results also in the identification of those areas of behavior and conduct, intentions, purposes, and goals where group members of the two groups do see themselves accurately. These correct perceptions may be intensely negative from the standpoint of establishing sounder intergroup relations. For example, one group may be dead set to maintain warfare. This perception from an outgroup point of view and valid recognition from an ingroup point of view, is sufficient to indicate that the approach to intergroup relationships therapy being involved here is without merit. In other words, where one or both parties are committed to continue fighting, there is then no basis for exploring how mutual problem solving might be achieved. If, on the other hand, the perceptions by the counter-group conform in many respects to those developed on the ingroup plane, and they are not of the kind that insures perpetuation of the conflict, then each group is substantially encouraged that the underpinnings of an improved relationship are present.

RESULTS. It was easier for both management and the union to discover and discuss negative aspects of the other's attitudes and behavior than of their own. On the other hand, the "goodness" of one's own intentions and the "rightness" of one's attitudes came out quite easily. Despite such unevenness, there were areas of agreement in the images and counter-images developed by the two. However, misinterpretations and misunderstandings were frequent and deep. The lists prepared by the two groups are shown in Table 2. Management's image of itself stressed especially:

1. We are running an aggressive, competitive, "hard-nosed," growing business.

2. We are competent at managing.
3. We are upgrading our supervision.
4. We are willing to be more fair in dealing with the international, to treat it as well as the (previously favored) independent union; we desire to get to the bottom of this running battle we have been having over the years.
5. We need to prevent loss of power to unions, to preserve our freedom to act, our right to manage things in the best interests of the business.
6. We are fair and honest in meeting our obligations. . . .

Contrasted with management's self-image, the union's image of management was short, crisp, and to the point. Even then, the major points the union made could have been summed up in one simple statement: "This company

TABLE 2 "Self" and "Other" Images Developed by Management and the International Union During Phase 2 of the Union-Management Laboratory

MANAGEMENT'S IMAGE

	Of Itself		By the Union
1.	Concerned with running the business effectively	1.	. . . . (an issue not considered)
2.	We show equal concern for production and people	2.	Management is concerned only with production
3.	Autonomous, decentralized decision-making body	3.	They follow all of headquarters' policies and dictates
4.	Want to learn to work better with international	4.	Opposed to all organized labor
5.	Prefer to deal with independent unions	5.	Prefer to deal with independent unions
6.	Strive continually to upgrade supervision	6.	. . . .
7.	Goal is to establish problem-solving relationship with the international	7.	Their goal is to drive us out of the plant
8.	Maintain flexibility in areas concerning our "rights to manage"	8.	Management wants power over every aspect of a worker's life—they are "fatherly dictators"
9.	We are inconsistent in how we treat independents and the international	9.	They treat the independents one way and us another
10.	Honest and aboveboard in our dealings	10.	They are underhanded and they lie

TABLE 2—*continued*

THE UNION'S IMAGE

By Management	Of Itself
1. Little concern shown for the profit picture of the company	1. Concerned primarily with *people*
2. They are skillful and have intense pride	2. Proud of our craft and skills
3. Controlled by a scheming professional leader and a minority clique	3. We are governed by the will of the total membership
4. Legalistic and rigid in interpreting contract	4. Approach problems and contract with open mind
5. The union pushes every grievance to the point of arbitration. When they want to establish a precedent, they want to arbitrate	5. Do not want to have to arbitrate every grievance. We want to work them out with management
6. They want to prove they can "win"—they don't care what, just so it is something	6. We want good relations and to solve our problems with management
7. They want to co-manage. They want a say in every decision we make	7. We want a voice in those areas that directly concern us
8. The union wants the training of their people back under their control	8. We want joint control of the training and apprenticeship program
9. The union does not communicate internally. Their people don't know what is going on	9. Our people always know what is going on and what important union business is coming up
10. Union is concerned only with seniority and job security. They are not concerned with our problems	10. We want greater consideration for our skills and what we can contribute to the plant

is opposed to organized labor in any form, shape, or manner!"

More specifically, the union charged:

1. Management, under pressure from headquarters to cut costs, would like nothing better than to throw out the international.

2. Management gives us a "run around" with every grievance case. You try to make the union look bad by failing to settle. You try to force

arbitration because you know we haven't the money to arbitrate every single case.

3. Management is a fatherly dictator. You think you are three stories taller than the worker who really makes this plant run. You want to tell us, as you do children, what is "best" for us.

4. Management took over the apprenticeship program and wrecked it.

5. Management has been chipping away at our membership for the past five years. Wherever possible, you have changed the class and scope of work that used to be under us. More and more work is contracted. You get people from the outside to do our work and pay them a dollar and a half less. You have already run one international out. We are the only sizable one left, and you are trying to starve us out.

6. Production and profits are Number One on your list. They have to be —that is your job, and headquarters won't let you forget it. That's why we have to take steps to keep you from running over our people. You're interested in a man for what you can get out of him.

7. Management is two-faced. In spite of everything headquarters and plant management have said and done, they deny publicly that they are against unions. You try to paint a different picture in the public's eye. From top to bottom, management talks out of both sides of its face at the same time.

Already it can be seen that deep differences have come to the surface. However, embedded in these differences are similarities neither party sees, particularly the union with respect to management's image. These differences and similarities will become sharper as we move through the images of the union. At this point, though, the union does not "see" or "hear" of management's interest in people. Yet, like the union, management says it *is* concerned with people. All the weight of the union's interpretation of management is given to management's *production* concerns. And the union sees much of this being "pushed" down from company headquarters. They do not see management as being autonomous—free to deal with the union in any way other than in an anti-union way. The international and management agree on management's past preference for independents. But the international sees this as meaning that management is openly against internationals.

1. We are people-oriented. That's our job—to see that our workers get a fair shake and everything that is coming to them.

2. We do our work; we are craftsmen; we do a job in the best and most skillful way it can be done; we return a fair day's work for a fair day's pay; we recognize our responsibility to the company and to the community.

3. We would like better relations with the company; that's why we are here today; but if you start to lean on us, we'll push back.

4. We are locally run; unlike management, we don't have to follow a "party line" from headquarters; we don't make decisions without going to our membership. (At this point, management objected that only

about 10 percent of members turn out for meetings.)

"I don't know out of what hat you pulled your figures," the union secretary returned, "but our regular attendance is well above that. At the last wage discussion, over 75 percent were there. Our people are always there when something important is going on."

The behavioral scientist suggested at this point, "Both of you are banging at each other and this could go on and on, but no real understanding will come from this. Let's move ahead."

5. The business agent continued: "The union wants more recognition. Management has never given us the recognition our skills and craftsmanship merit. To you, it's just another job. You wouldn't recognize a good piece of work if it were staring you in the face. We contribute a lot to the operations of this plant. And, much more could be contributed by us with half a chance. The international should have a voice in those things that affect our work and our livelihood. We don't want co-management. We want the recognition we deserve, and a chance to contribute."

1. The union is controlled by a small minority; it doesn't truly represent the membership; the business agent is a career man looking for a higher job in the international; he and a few rabble-rousers keep the membership stirred up; most members don't know what's going on and don't care; they are proud and skilled craftsmen, but are run by a small clique.

2. The union is a tough bargainer; you fight us every step of the way; all you really care about is winning; you don't care what is won, just so it's something; union leaders want to demonstrate to the membership that they are "successful"; you use more force and pressure on us in bargaining than any of the other unions; every point in the contract is given a rigid, legalistic interpretation; you never are willing to compromise.

3. Union rules on seniority hurt the business; we can't move up the men with the best skills.

The union spokesmen see themselves as democratic agents of the membership; management sees the membership as "sound" but misled by union leaders. The union is proud of skillful work but feels management fails to recognize this. The union wants to be more involved in the operations of the plant, and management has expressed the same desire; but neither sees this as a common interest at this point.

Phase 4—Clarification of Image (2 hrs.)

Each group asked questions of the other to insure understanding of what had been said. The aim was to clarify rather than to belittle or attack.

The purpose of this step is to insure that there is a complete and full understanding of the impressions, attitudes, feelings, and facts presented by each group. Less than full understanding can result in continued erroneous thinking concerning the goals, attitudes, and feelings of the other. At this point, interventions by the behavioral scientist can become critical. Frequently, without an outside observer to focus what is taking place, it is easy for the discussion to slip into one of charges and countercharges as each side seeks to defend itself against attack. Such actions and reactions, however, only tend to reinforce the beliefs each holds regarding the other's "intentions."

RESULTS. The next two hours were spent in a joint session over the images each had developed and presented. Neither side could believe the other could be so "wrong" about it. At times the discussion, designed to clarify, became heated and sharp. Each side quickly forgot its good intentions to work in a problem-solving manner. Renewed tensions and old sources of friction bubbled at the surface. Without interventions by the behavioral scientists to focus what was taking place, it is likely the discussion would have slipped onto the more typical win-lose exchange of vindictive accusations.

Phase 5—Intragroup Diagnosis: Self-Insight and Understanding (4 hrs.)

Although participants attempted to restrain themselves during the exchange of images, the clarification session ended on a note of "charges" and "countercharges." Each side sought to defend itself against the other. This only tended to reinforce the belief each held about the other's "intentions."

Phase 5, self-diagnosis, is a pivotal point in the union-management laboratory. The need at this point is for both sides to look "inside" themselves and underneath surface tensions to discover *why* the relationship has become what it is.

Both groups, meeting separately, spent the evening and part of the following morning in (1) self-analysis and (2) diagnosing the "why" of their own actions. Although still far from any real degree of mutual trust or understanding, the door at least was open for both management and the union to see what actions would need to be understood and shifted if a sound problem-solving relationship were to be achieved.

MANAGEMENT'S APPROACH TO THE DIAGNOSIS. Initially, upon returning to their meeting-room, the management group launched into berating the union's "gross misunderstanding" that they had just heard.

This line of self-justification continued for several minutes before the behavioral scientist who was meeting with management intervened with the following: "What you are doing now is not likely to move you toward better understanding of your relationship with the union. First, you are disregarding your initial commitment to work during the laboratory in a problem-solving manner. This will defeat why you are here and any progress that may have been made up to this point. Second, working through the present task, as it is intended, can help both you and the union to move toward the 'nub' of what it is that has brought about such wide differences between you."

At this, the employee relations manager made the following proposal. "Let's take their image of us as it is on the newsprint and just start listing everything we can think of under each one of their points that could possibly lie behind how they interpret us."

The proposal was picked up and management went to work.

THE UNION'S REACTION. Meanwhile, the union reacted in a similar fashion. Management, as far as they were concerned, had demonstrated to the union's satisfaction that they (the union) had been right all along.

Gradually union members began to get a feel for process examination. They moved more rapidly this time into digging into their attitudes and feelings and into their reactions to the images developed by management.

Under each item, management had listed contributions (past events and actions) that it felt it and the company had made to this image. This list was quite full—so full, in fact, that managment did not get to diagnosing the union's image of itself, except as it happened to relate to the management's image. The union, on the other hand, was more brief, but had studied both its own and management's images.

Both groups now were more openly exchanging their feelings and interpretations on a variety of events in their history. For this reason, the behavioral scientists did not intervene when the discussion slid into the union's picturing its analysis of management's counter-image. It was felt that, in this way, overlapping issues could be productively discussed as they were encountered. The interplay from this kind of interchange seemed to generate greater understanding for the moment than mechanically completing one group's presentation before moving to the next.

"While we have been talking all this time," the business agent said during a lull, "we have covered a number of the points we had to make with respect to your image of us. However, there are still a number of things we want to lay out on the table. So, unless there is more management has to add from their newsprints, I would like to summarize the remainder of our points now."

Management responded that they thought this would be good. They said, though, that they would like to keep it loose, the way it was. Management wanted to be able to interrupt and return to some point if something the union said triggered a thought in their minds.

This approach was agreeable to the union.

"There is one point," the business agent began, "that we think is a basic, fundamental, ideological breach in the thinking of our two groups. We are not sure this can ever be patched—that is, your overriding preference for independent unions. I don't want to get into, *again*, whether this means management is 'opposed' to internationals or not. But, I don't see how we can interpret so many arrows in this direction in any other way. Anyway, here is what we see. In many companies, and especially this one, *independent* unions are set up to *deny* workers the freedom to bargain. When people do not have the freedom to select between an international *or* an independent, then we feel that, actually, they do not have the freedom of choice they should have. And people in *this* plant *don't* have that choice."

The plant manager reacted to this one. "People in this plant have the right, 'freedom of choice' in your words, to be represented by either an independent or an international. I don't see why you say they don't. We can't keep an international out. Employees can join an international whenever they want. If that isn't freedom, I don't know what you mean by freedom."

"And what if they did?" the business agent asked. "You prefer an independent. Would you treat them in the same way? No! You wouldn't. That's my point. People have no choice but to stay with independents."

The assistant plant manager responded, "I don't think we would be that different. Maybe we would. But they still have freedom of choice."

"That's like asking a man whether he wants to be shot or hanged."

The question of "freedom of choice" was kicked around at greater length, with neither management nor the union able to agree on whether or not employees did have a "free choice." Management and the union seemed to be sparring, each testing for an opening.

"Decentralization is another anti-international strategy of the company," the business agent said as he shifted the topic somewhat. "It serves to spread us so thin that we can't be effective. That's the whole strategy behind scattering plants from one end of the country to the other. You say we misinterpret economic moves you make. And we say that headquarters' real motive is to get rid of international, not just to 'pinch' a few of the pennies they so dearly love."

THE UNION OPERATES DEMOCRATICALLY. "One of your points that we really can't understand is that 'the union is run by a clique.' Nothing could be further from the truth. We think management has this impression because they don't understand how we

operate. You have never been to a union meeting. Well, let me change that to say only Joe and Pete, who were once in the union, have been to union meetings. You guys ought to attend one to see what really happens. And you ought to read our by-laws to learn how we operate. Our organization is more democratic than yours."

The employee relations manager interrupted to say, "What the by-laws say and what really happens can be completely different. Didn't you just recently pass a dues rise when only a minority—the usual 10 percent—were present?"

"I don't know who your 'stool-pigeon' is," the union president shot back, "but he sure gave you some bum information."

"This is a good example of how little you know about how we operate," the business manager said. "Let us tell you the procedure we have. It's in our by-laws." He went on to describe how action must be taken. "If we take a position in bargaining, it is because we have discussed it with our people and that's what they want. And don't be too sure our people wouldn't strike if you pushed us into it."

The business agent went to his last point. "You also said we were not interested in production—that we were not concerned with your problems. The truth is, you don't want us to be interested; that is, not beyond the point of doing what management wants. This kills any incentive and any concern for management's viewpoint."

"You know what management's attitude is?" the union vice-president asked. "It is, 'Look, you are supposed to do *what* you are told *as* you are told to do it. We are not interested in your ideas.' With that kind of attitude, how can you expect us to act differently? Management at this plant still hasn't caught up with the idea that employees today want to be more autonomous and make a real work contribution. And that doesn't mean through some 'corny' coin-your-idea program."

The employee relations manager, who had been listening intently all this time, stood up with a look of disbelief on his face. He didn't seem to realize he was on his feet. "Do you mean to say you people are really interested in *production?*" He had listened to the union say this for two days, but he had just "heard" it for the first time. His next question was a simple one, but it triggered an hour-long discussion. He asked, "What could management do to use people more effectively?"

The earlier period of self-analysis and this exchange made it possible for both to "hear" better what the other was saying. In turn, being able to "hear" made it possible for both sides to communicate their attitudes and feelings more openly—more honestly. Some points of agreement and similarities in thinking came to the fore as differences were examined, put into perspective, and understood.

Progress was made and better understanding achieved during this latter exchange, yet under the surface underlying tensions still remained. Neither side was "owning up" any more than the other. Old "bargaining" habits still permeated the exchange between the two. On many points, one side was unable to see why the other felt or thought as it did. Often members yielded to the temptation to explain to the other side why they were "wrong."

Over-all, though, both sides were "listening" better to each other. Although not always agreeing, they were hearing each other out. As the session continued, questions and replies gained the quality of clarifying rather than of attacking or defending.

Phase 7—Consolidation of Key Issues (2 hrs.)

Although the two sides were far from having talked out their differences, the last part of the day was devoted to identifying those issues which seemed critical in the relationship between the union and management. Working with the behavioral scientists, union and management jointly identified, as barriers, those issues that would require more examination, discussion, and resolution if relations were to be improved. They were summarized as follows:

1. *Lack of Mutual Trust and Respect.* This was tagged as a key element in the relationship by both groups. The general feeling was that once genuine trust and respect between the two were achieved, many of the other things would fall into place. Management's preference for independents, despite its position that it wanted to learn to work with the international, was cited as an issue "that needed better understanding."

2. *Ideological Differences.* Both agreed there existed wide differences in matters of purposes and principles. Common purposes would need to be identified if joint problem solving were to become a reality.

3. *Inadequate Knowledge and Understanding.* During the exchanges it

became clear to both sides that many factual matters about each other were not known. Both the union and management felt that neither of them really understood how the other operated—how decisions, regulations governing their behavior, long-range plans, traditions, and so on, were handled at either level.

4. *Attitudinal Differences*. Differences in attitudes toward each other, plant operations, and the management of business affairs, existed between the union and management. Part of this was recognized as a difference in perspective—part was seen as due to different levels of knowledge and to past experiences and relations.

5. *Need for More Effective Use of People*. Both agreed there should be more participation and involvement of wage people in the operations of the plant. "We don't want to co-manage," the union said, for example, "but there are some areas where we have high stakes. In these matters we want to be consulted. We think we can contribute to the effectiveness of operations if management will involve us more."

6. *Better Understanding of Rights and Obligations*. Union and management, they felt, need to understand better and to respect the rights and obligations each has toward the other. There existed a need for better understanding and acceptance of each party's role in the bargaining process. Included here was the feeling that a better understanding of the mutual expectations each held for the other was needed.

7. *Better Communications*. It was also felt that management and the union need to communicate more openly, more freely, and more honestly with each other. Both felt that communication barriers precipitated many of their problems.

8. *Better Listening*. Along with a need for better communications, it was felt that both sides needed to listen more and "better" to the other. For example, the union pointed out that employees were concerned with and wanted their views heard on the economic health of the plant. One union member had remarked, "I know right now how to save the plant $10,000, but I haven't found anyone who will listen to me yet. I gave up trying a long time ago."

Phase 8—Planning Next Steps (1 hr.)

Based on the above summation, the final period of time was devoted to debating what follow-up steps, if any, should be taken to the two-day laboratory. It was agreed that many tensions and a residue of hostility still existed. Much remained to be talked out. It was felt that the two groups were not yet ready to tackle their operational problems. It was concluded that a lot of "air still needs to be cleared" before the two sides would be able to sit down together and work in an effective manner.

It was proposed and accepted that the two groups spend some time in considering what they had learned during the laboratory. Both wanted to talk among themselves about what had come out of the session and to consider what the next best step would be. Each wanted to report to its other group members the progress that had been made, to get their reactions, and then to make a tentative proposal of what they felt needed to be done next. With this, the union-management laboratory ended.

SUMMARY OF ISSUES. The union showed great concern for and tested, throughout the two days, the degree of local autonomy in management. There was a considerable amount of anxiety over what they saw as corporate ideology and implementation of an anti-international objective. The real question to the union, although they were not able to focus it, was not whether or not management had local autonomy, but the *degree* of autonomy management had.

The union was convinced that management was "dollar-oriented" all the way, without values with respect to people. Therefore, the union felt bound to counteract this "inhumanity" they saw in management.

Management again and again demonstrated extreme suspicion regarding the anti-democracy of the union and the "clique" qualities of the union leadership. Management genuinely felt that the union leaders did not represent the people.

Management's attitude was that the union was an institution with intrinsic goals of protecting and building itself. Management felt strongly on two points: (1) that the union had no concern for productivity and (2) that actually they had only an administrative concern for people, *i.e.*, wage rates, seniority, class and scope of work, security, and the like. In other words, management saw the union's concern for people to be an institutional one.

SIMILARITIES NOT SEEN. Several points of similarity were not observed by either management or the union because of their concern for the *differences* between them. For example, management saw itself as *production-oriented*. The union also saw this. But management also had a *human* interest which the union did not recognize.

On the other hand, the union saw itself as having a *people* obligation. This, in turn, management recognized in the union. The disparity here was that management did not see the same weight being attached to productivity by the union.

What the two groups shared in common, then, they were not able to recognize. More importantly, what they shared in common they saw as differences.

Conclusions

Intergroup conflict undergirds much of modern, complex organization life. More than ever, there is greater interdependence among the functions of groups. This interdependence can aid organizations to take giant strides forward toward the accomplishment of mutual goals. Or, this same interdependence can breed the most hostile and disruptive of conflicts. Once conflict erupts, it is difficult to bring it under control. It can consume everything and everyone it touches.

We have presented a view of the misunderstandings and misperceptions generated out of a long history of antagonism between an international union and the management of a large industrial plant. Both sides were weary from "battle," but neither knew how to alter the course of the conflict.

Based on behavioral sciences concepts, an educational-laboratory approach to the resolutions of the conflict was proposed. Leaders of the international and management met for a two-day period to confront the conflict between them. The differences between them, uncovered by the two groups, were presented in detail. These differences became the foundation on which the two groups began tediously to work toward a more healthy relationship. Through self-analysis and an exchange of views, management and the union moved slowly toward a better understanding of the relationship between them.

The greatest impact will become evident when *new* issues and different problems arise in the relationship. At that time, the parties will be able to apply themselves in a more problem-solving manner. In other words, the background of conflict does not dissolve. Rather, it remains to color and influence old issues born in that era. However, new issues, with no anchorage in the past, do not have the same "tug" in the directions of old norms and past practices. Members in both groups are not "bound" by old expectations. Instead, they are now free to explore jointly for new solutions with the other group under the more collaborative conditions produced by the laboratory sequence.

Correcting a situation of long-term, chronic hostility requires continuous and diligent follow-up efforts. As much as a five-year span may be needed before the root system that produced the original animosities can be replaced by a new and healthier root system— one that can cause the relationship to flourish.

Chapter 5

RELATED THEORIES OF
CHANGE AND INFLUENCE

ONLY verbal magic, if that, could convince the reader that the papers collected in this chapter fall neatly into any one logical rubric. On the face of it, they seem to (and do) represent widely divergent streams of research, discipline, and impact. Moreover, they are written for quite diverse subgroups within the behavioral sciences and with rather unique objectives. Ruth Leeds, for example, using an anachronistic (and welcome!) historic-sociological method, specifies the processes by which a nonconforming enclave within an organization can influence the total organization's objectives or values. David McClelland sets forth principles on how the need for achievement is taught and internalized. Elihu Katz attempts to bridge two research streams of sociology—mass communication and adoption practices—by analyzing their main charactistics and also by analyzing socialization which aims to demonstrate that reactions to social structures can explain almost all behaviors that are categorized as change or stability. Kelman focuses on various processes of influence, their antecedents and consequences.

Along as many dimensions as one could possibly detect, then, these articles are a mixed bag. There are theories which emphasize group and organizational factors (not necessarily by sociologists) and those that lay greater stress on individual-personality factors (not necessarily by psychologists.) There are some who view change as a deliberate planned process and others who either believe change is almost always adventitious or do not specify the deliberate (strategic) aspects of change.

192

The factors that separate the authors may overshadow their convergences. In any case, these must also be presented. In the first place, almost all of the authors are concerned with the processes of change. Secondly, they work to a greater or lesser extent in an interdisciplinary framework. In addition, they have drawn their theories from a confrontation with social problems rather than from a simplified application of traditional theory. Finally, they have almost all adopted a normative orientation. These basic similarities, of course, must be qualified, even more than their dissimilarities, a remark that certainly speaks for the current status of *a* theory of changing.

A convenient way to organize the articles in this chapter is a 2 × 2 table. (See below.) Along one axis, we place those articles that characterize the strategy of change as deliberate or adventitious. Along the other axis, we place those articles which identify the locus of change as either the individual or the group-organization.

| | | *Locus of Change* | |
		Individual	Group-Organization
Strategy of Change	Deliberate	McClelland Kelman	Katz
	Adventitious		Leeds Becker

We can spot an example in all but one cell. McClelland outlines a theory of change (achievement training) which focuses on the individual as the pivotal element in producing change. Becker views the social structure as the chief factor in socialization as well as in changes in individual behavior and in the stability of the behavior. He does not specify a strategy of how organizations can be contrived to create these changes. These two examples simply demonstrate how two crude dichotomies can account for currently prevalent orientations in developing strategic theories of change.

One final note. By and large, theories of change have tended to ignore strategic factors and emphasize the descriptive, nonmanipulative factors. This has led to an abundance of what we have referred to as "astronomer's" models of change. These theories describe accurately the mechanisms of change but do not allow for manipulation of the strategic variables. This is almost like observing the mechanism of a watch through a sealed glass case. More recently, we have seen the growth of engineering models, theories, and strategies that encompass variables that can be controlled and manipulated. But for the most part, even in the papers that we placed in the adventitious category—where the manipulatable variables were only implied—the articles in this chapter, disparate and unrelated as they might appear, are heading toward an engineering model of social change.

5.1 THE ABSORPTION OF PROTEST: A WORKING PAPER

Ruth Leeds

Introduction—The Nonconformist and the Enclave[1]

The usual fate of the nonconformist who occupies a position of some responsibility in a complex organization has been established: the cleric who waivers [sic] from the true path goes on retreat; the maverick army officer is appointed to an innocuous position; the recalcitrant political party deputy is temporarily suspended.[2] If temporary suspension or relegation to an insignificant position does not suffice to curb the nonconformist, he is gradually eased out of the organization. But what happens when an organization is faced with not just a single nonconformist but with several who form a cohesive enclave in its midst? The organization—specifically incumbents of positions superordinate to the nonconformists—must now check not just one individual but many who could potentially divert organization resources from their current commitments, undermine organizational effectiveness, or form a front capable of capturing control of the organization.

To control a nonconforming enclave, the organization has to employ techniques other than those typically used to check a single nonconformist. An individual's nonconformity often as not stems primarily from personality factors although structural determinants do contribute to it. The nonconformity of an enclave, which is shared by all its members, stems primarily from structural determinants rather than personality factors. Hence, different techniques are called for to check nonconforming enclaves.

There is one organizational technique—the subject of this chapter—that is particularly suited for controlling wayward groups. It consists of integrating the protest of the nonconforming enclave into the organization by converting it into a new legitimate subunit. Through conversion, the nonconforming enclave obtains a legitimate outlet for its nonconformity, and thereby contributes to the attainment of legitimate goals of the organization. The conversion from nonconforming enclave to legitimate subunit will be called the protest-absorbing process. Protest absorption might take as little

From Ruth Leeds, "The Absorption of Protest: A Working Paper," in William W. Cooper, Harold J. Leavitt, and Maynard W. Shelley II, *New Perspectives in Organization Research,* (New York: John Wiley & Sons, Inc., 1964), pp. 115–133.

[1] This paper is the theoretic part of a project initiated and directed by Amitai Etzioni. I very much appreciate the ideas, comments and time he gave to it. I am indebted to John C. Pock for reading critically several drafts of this paper. His many suggestions and willingness to argue with me over questionable points have been invaluable in adding clarity to it.

[2] Amitai Etzioni, pp. 241–244. This paper represents an expansion of an idea briefly discussed by Etzioni, pp. 245–248.

as a year or as long as a generation. Regardless, by the end of the process, the nonconforming enclave and the top authorities of the organization reach an accommodation such that the enclave is given some autonomy to pursue a specific activity (usually the activity which was the focus of the nonconformity), but, at the same time, it is expected to abide by the regulations and restrictions to which all legitimate subunits adhere.

Protest absorption is a structural "weapon" available to the organization. It is a weapon insofar as it is used to control nonconforming groups. It is a structural weapon insofar as its effectiveness rests on formal changes in the organizational structure, that is, on the formal positions of subunits vis-à-vis each other. As will be seen, the weapon is unleashed through the exercise of *authority*, although *power* is a variable in the protest-absorption process. Protest absorption should not be confused with co-optation which comes about through power differentials between the co-opters and the co-opted regardless of the authority structure.[3] Although reductionist concepts like power and charisma are variables in the protest-absorption process, they are not the major explanatory concepts. Structure and authority are the key concepts to an understanding of protest absorption, although these terms will be used only rarely to avoid awkward phrasing.

Organizational analyses which generate theories about the organization as if all structures were cut from the same cloth must be qualified when applied to specific organizations, e.g., a prison, an army, or a factory. The development of a comparative approach permits the enrichment of organizational theories by adding statements of regularities within one type of organization to statements of universal uniformities. Given this consideration, the first step is to delineate the type of organization in which protest absorption is expected to be an effective weapon. Then we can characterize the nonconforming enclave and the process by which it is converted into a legitimate and quiescent unit. The appendix presents an outline of cases which *illustrate* the protest-absorption model. Since this paper represents both an exploratory study and a preliminary report, we are not concerned here with the frequency with which the model is approximated.

Normative Organizations and the Distribution of Charisma[4]

Organizations can be characterized by the nature of the primary power that is used to control its lowest ranking participants. *Coercive* organizations, e.g., prisons, keep order through the use of physical force (or the threat of it); *utilitarian* organizations, e.g., factories, keep order primarily through monetary rewards; *normative* organizations, e.g., churches, elicit compliance through the allocation and manipulation of symbolic rewards. For reasons to be evident shortly, protest absorption is expected to occur most frequently in normative organizations.

Two other major characteristics distinguish the normative from the coercive and utilitarian organizations. First, a normative organization tends to demand a high degree of commit-

[3] Philip Selznick.

[4] Based on Etzioni.

ment and loyalty from its members, often to the point that members are expected to give their primary allegiance to the organization. The priest is symbolically wedded to the Church; in those organizations where secular marriage is permitted, the wife is drawn into the structure and is known by its name, e.g., a navy wife.[5] Voluntary exiting from the organization is perceived as a sign of insufficient loyalty; for example, resignation from academic departments tends to precipitate feelings of resentment and rejection among the professors who remain.[6] Criticism of the organization's institutionalized norms and methods is also taken as a sign of insufficient loyalty.

Second, most offices in normative organizations have charisma ascribed to them. The performances associated with the position of priest or military officer are charismatic and are symbolized by such devices as special dress, badges of office, and ritual courtesies. The charismatic elements of a particular office enrich the organization's symbols and rituals with additional meaning, and increase their reward value for the loyalty and discipline which lowest ranking members exhibit. Moreover, personal contact with an incumbent of a charismatic office is itself perceived as a reward by members. Thus charismatic power in its routinized form re-enforces the normative power of the organization.

At the same time that charisma helps to generate loyalty and discipline among the personnel, it also is a potential disrupter of discipline and loyalty to the organization itself. The problem

is present in latent form when the lower participants of the organization attribute the functionally specific charisma of office to a *particular* incumbent, and, in so doing, generalize the charisma so that it takes on diffuse characteristics. Where this occurs, the participants make personal commitments to the particular individual who occupies a charismatic office rather than to the office itself. If the charismatic officer uses these particularistic commitments for purposes that are functional to the organization as a whole (or for purposes that do not generate dysfunctions), then the problem remains latent. The case might be, however, that the charismatic employs these commitments to challenge organizational hegemony and integration, and to compete against regular subunits (sometimes laterally related) for resources, thereby undermining the organization's allocation and reward system. (That such a situation might occur indicates both the desirability and the apparent impossibility of routinizing charisma.)

The potential strain between charisma and discipline is greatest in those organizations where the gift of grace parallels the formal organizational chart, being characteristic of many offices as well as the top ones, and yet where formal authority is centralized. The Catholic Church and wartime military organizations are the major examples of organizations that have charisma distributed throughout their lines combined with a strong, centralized authority structure. Protest absorption is more likely to be used in these organizations to control nonconforming enclaves than in normative structures which have the potential for strain between charisma and discipline but lack

[5] Arthur K. Davis.

[6] Theodore Caplow and R. J. McGee, p. 66.

a strong central authority (e.g., Protestant denominations and the early Catholic Church).

The Process of Protest Absorption

The potential strain between charisma and discipline erupts into a tempest in a tepid teapot with the formation of a nonconforming enclave. More often than not, the enclave is led by a charismatic who is concerned with devising new ways for carrying out his responsibilities more effectively. The leadership of the enclave is strengthened by able lieutenants. The enclave itself is endowed with a militant spirit; its members are eager to undertake large-scale tasks and to execute them with novel strategies. The organization, grown weak internally in one or several respects, either cannot or prefers not to initiate change (although from some objective perspective change might be functionally required if the organization is to continue being effective). Protest absorption has two major consequences for the organization: it checks the nonconforming enclave by turning it into a legitimate subunit which remains loyal to the organization and it permits the introduction of change. The descriptive model

of protest absorption contains three parts: (1) The characteristics of the nonconforming enclave; (2) the state of the organization; and (3) the process of absorbing protest.

THE NONCONFORMING ENCLAVE

Two conditions are basic to the emergence of a nonconforming enclave. First, some members of a normative organization must attribute personal charisma to an official. This provides the official with an opportunity to lead a loyal following over which diffuse influence and control can be exercised. Second, the official must have tendencies toward nonconformity and unorthodoxy, and must disregard at least some traditional norms and strategies. Once the official has proved his capacity to acquire a personal following, he may be referred to as the enclave leader; once he leads in unorthodox directions, the enclave becomes a nonconforming group.

The leader's nonconformity stems in large measure from his position in the organization. Assume that the leader is in unit C_4 (Fig. 1). Assume further that C_4 is not functioning effectively with regard to its subunit goals. Lack of effectiveness could stem from one or several factors. For example, the unit

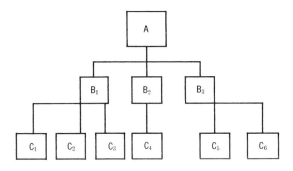

FIGURE 1. Boxes Denote Units in Organization

is functionally peripheral and so does not receive the optimum quantity and quality of inputs; or the unit is a long established one which has become more concerned with self-maintenance than with attainment of goals; or changes in the unit's environment have occurred which make present methods and procedures obsolete; or contingencies have emerged for which there is no formal provision. In short, the unit's responsibility for goals far exceeds its capacity for attainment of goals, thereby making it relatively ineffective.[7] One response to lack of effectiveness is to exercise trained incapacity, that is, to continue conforming to rules and procedures which have become inappropriate.[8] A second response is to search for new rules and procedures which would permit increased unit effectiveness. The first response is symptomatic of functional rationality and the second of substantive rationality.[9] The leader, either in his capacity as head of C_4 or as a member of it, exercises some degree of substantive rationality and assumes responsibility for devising methods which will make the unit more effective. Increased unit effectiveness would permit him to fulfill his own particular position more adequately.

In large measure, one's position determines whether one perceives the discrepancy between responsibility and control, and whether one chooses to respond functionally or substantively to it. The greater the responsibility for goal attainment or the greater the environmental contact associated with a given position, the more likely is the incumbent to respond substantively rather than functionally. In our simplified organization chart, the A level has over-all responsibility for organization goals; the C level is responsible for subunit goals. Moreover, both A and C levels have some contact with the environment. The B level serves internal coordination and communication functions. On a probability basis, then, the enclave leader is more likely to occupy a position in A or C rather than in B. To simplify presentation of our model, we assume that the enclave leader is located in C.

The leader's nonconformity is not to be confused with deviancy. Unlike a deviant, a nonconformist does not hide his dissent from the prevailing norms. He publicly challenges the efficacy of the existing norms and their applicability to specific situations in the hope of changing them without destroying the organization. The nonconformist justifies his challenge of the status quo by appealing to what the organization recognizes as its highest morality or its ultimate set of values.[10] The official

[7] See Etzioni, pp. 77–79 for a discussion of effectiveness.

[8] R. K. Merton, p. 198.

[9] Karl Mannheim, pp. 112–117.

[10] If the leader appeals to a morality or values not recognized by the organization, the likelihood of protest absorption is reduced and the organization will resort to other means to check him. Orde Wingate was able to organize and arm Jews to quell Arab raids on the British pipelines in Palestine in the late 1930's, despite British policy not to give arms to Jews. Wingate also hoped that his Special Night Squad would form the basis for a Jewish army which would help to pave the way for Palestine's independence. Wingate's advocacy of a cause which extended beyond military purlieus led to his recall from Palestine, and probably helps to account for the rapid deJudification of the Special Night Squad. See Christopher Sykes.

who emerges as a leader of a nonconforming enclave is justified in saying, in the area of his specific responsibility, "It is written . . . but I say unto you . . ." on two counts. First, because he has charisma attributed to him, and second, because as a nonconformist he is oriented to existing rules only in a negative sense—to challenge them.[11]

Concomitant with his personal charisma and tendency toward nonconformity, the leader also has a flair for originality which permits him to create new strategies, ideologies, and symbols to counter those of the organization.[12] The development and implementation of new strategies come to represent the goal of the enclave. The new ideology and symbols serve as extensions to the leader's charisma in welding the enclave into a cohesive, dynamic group.

The charismatic rarely leads the enclave by himself.[13] He is usually assisted by lieutenants who support his unorthodox tactics and innovations, and spearhead the enclave with their own missionary fire and ability to influence others. The leader, by granting his lieutenants some autonomy in a specialized area like procuring supplies, insures that they will remain subservient to him. Since the lieutenants are likely to promulgate their own ideas, a limited amount of autonomy may prevent rival ideas and methods from disrupting the unity of the enclave.

The energy and zeal of the nonconforming enclave are focused on innovations, which often assume the form of techniques intended to facilitate attainment of organizational goals. New techniques might be more effective in attaining existing goals by permitting higher output or they might revitalize goals which have grown fallow. (Later we shall have more to say about the enclave's objectives and their bearing on the protest absorption process.) In essence, the enclave maintains a high commitment to the basic goals of the organization, and desires to display this commitment through recognition of its innovations. The commitment inspiring the nonconformists is frequently viewed as higher than that possessed by others in the organization. The perceived or alleged discrepancy between the extremely high degree of loyalty to basic organizational values exhibited by the nonconforming enclave and the moderate degree of loyalty exhibited by other organization participants is likely to provoke conflict. Other participants have little tolerance for the enthusiasm of the enclave, for, by comparison, they appear less diligent and less loyal to the organization.

The nonconforming enclave is further distinguished by an unorthodox atmosphere which permeates many aspects of its life. This atmosphere varies from extreme austerity and asceticism to romance, adventure, and heroic sac-

---

[11] R. K. Merton, pp. 725–726, and Max Weber, p. 361.

[12] Dorothy Emmet, p. 258. The problem of what an administrator should do with the single nonconformist, the "creative genius," the person with a flair who is "beyond good and evil," receives excellent treatment by Professor Emmet. She feels that a solution might develop if the administrator has the capacity to comprehend different roles; with such understanding the administrator might create a special role in the organization for the nonconformist. In the present context, protest absorption would require the administrator to have some understanding of structure. Emmet does not deal with the problems presented by a group of nonconformists.

[13] See Weber, p. 360.

rifice. The unorthodox behavior of the enclave, whether reflected in the wearing of special clothing or in reckless courage, not only sets the enclave apart from the rest of the organization but also contributes to its cohesiveness and strength. A member can readily identify with a group symbolized by noticeable objects or mannerisms. If the group merits esteem from outsiders, it can be bestowed on easily recognized members. The symbols of unorthodoxy also facilitate recruitment in that they help publicize the group to potential members who share similar values and similar tendencies toward nonconformity.

In summary, the nonconforming enclave is characterized by a leader whose charisma of office has become personal. He pursues a course of action or cause which is perceived as unorthodox, and for which he creates symbols and an ideology. His immediate lieutenants are nonconformers in their own right, although less influential and original than the leader. The cause served is usually a means to revive allegedly neglected organizational goals or to achieve present organizational goals more effectively. Lastly, a peculiar aura, either of asceticism or of romance, envelops the enclave, contributing to its integration and highlighting its dedication to its cause.

The State of the Organization

Although nonconformity can erupt at all times, a cohesive nonconforming enclave is likely to emerge in a context in which one or a combination of the following variations of organizational weakness is prevalent. If, over time, the legitimacy of the organization procedures decreases generally or within any subunit, charisma tends to shift from office to person among those dedicated to the ultimate purposes of the organization. If an organization is insensitive to potential nonconformity (due to such factors as inadequacies of communication networks), control mechanisms might not be activated in time to forestall a nonconforming official before he gains a personal following.[14] If an organization's internal authority is weak, owing to the corruption of officers responsible for enforcing conformity or owing to the lack of (or limited) control over enforcement facilities, then whatever control mechanisms the organization might employ are ineffectual. Finally, resources diverted outside the organization to meet an external challenge, or stoppage of inputs, limit the availability of the means needed to combat nonconformity.

Once the enclave emerges, mild checks to contain the nonconformity are no longer adequate. If the organizational elite ousts the leader, his immediate lieutenants could assume control of the enclave, or members of the enclave might follow their leader and form the beginning of a competing structure. Such a possibility is particularly threatening when the organization

[14] In some instances the "following" emerges first and then casts about for a leader. According to Erle Wilson's less romantic account of the *Bounty* mutiny, the potential mutineers were ship's sailors, who, on becoming cognizant of each other's discontents, recruited Fletcher Christian to be their leader. Subsequent events indicated that the choice was not entirely fortunate, for Christian lacked the capacity to live up to the charisma which his followers attributed to him. See Erle Wilson.

enjoys a monopoly or duopoly position. If the organization is one of several of its kind, then one more similar structure in the environment makes little difference. Finally, if both the leader and the members of the enclave are dispersed throughout the organization, in an effort to disband the group, nonconformity might be spread rather than eliminated.

Given the inadequacy of control techniques which are typically applied to single nonconformists, the organizational elite must choose between several alternatives: condemnation, avoidance, expulsion, or protest absorption. The first three alternatives are not effective in containing the nonconformity unless the enclave itself is quite weak to begin with. Condemnation contains the danger of widening the rift between the enclave and the rest of the organization by forcing a polarization of issues.[15] Avoidance, which means consciously taking little account of the existence of the enclave, sidesteps the danger of polarization.[16] During the period that the organization elite ostensibly ignores the enclave, however, the enclave might grow in size and strength instead of dying out. Expulsion of the enclave represents a costly loss of resources which might yet be channeled to serve organizational goals.[17] Also, expulsion

could lead to the emergence of a rival structure (albeit it does permit tightening of organizational ranks). The negative consequences which might result from attempting to control the enclave through condemnation, avoidance, or expulsion are particularly dysfunctional to the organization when it displays one or more signs of weakness. Although protest absorption also entails some dangers, it is a more promising way of checking nonconformity on several counts.

If protest absorption is successful, it not only eliminates the pocket of nonconformity but also strengthens the organization by providing it with the services of an energetic, devoted group. Moreover, the process permits the legitimation of innovation which better equips the organization to face external challenges or to attain its own goals more effectively. Protest absorption can also lead to the elimination of nonconformity without the emergence of a devoted group or the introduction of innovation. This form results when the organization provides the enclave with an "opportunity to fail." When the enclave protests about matters beyond its ken or original bailiwick, and it is accorded legitimacy in the area of protest, it is likely to fail because it lacks the skills and knowledge to carry out the now legitimate activity. Any nonconformity which survives outright failure is expected to be sufficiently weakened so as to be eliminated easily. Should the enclave succeed despite its opportunity to fail, then the organization can reap the benefits. The risk accompanying protest absorption is that the nonconforming enclave may, during the time that the organization

[15] Z. Brzezinski, pp. 9–10.

[16] *Op. cit.*, pp. 11–12.

[17] A recent report of the AFL-CIO council stated:

It is obvious that expulsion as such does not cure the offending practices. And, what is more important, once outside the federation the membership of such an organization is no longer accessible to corrective influences from the parent body through education and persuasion. (Quoted in the *Reporter*, October 26, 1961, p. 18.)

attempts to check it, gain access to the key power positions and, subsequently, assume control of the total structure.

THE PROCESS OF PROTEST ABSORPTION

Once the nonconforming enclave has been converted into a new legitimate subunit, the organization is strengthened. During the protest-absorption process, however, the organization, especially that sector of it in which the enclave has erupted, faces a series of internal battles involving several levels of its hierarchy. The charismatic leader and his followers oppose those persons who formally are their immediate superiors. These shall be called the middle hierarchy and represent the enemy in the battles. Insofar as the organization has a centralized top hierarchy which can exercise authority over the middle hierarchy, these battles tend not to be fought to the death of one or the other set of combatants. Instead, the top hierarchy intercedes and more or less arbitrarily terminates the conflict. Protest absorption essentially is a process whereby the top hierarchy attempts to balance the two opposing forces—members of the nonconforming enclave against members of the middle hierarchy who are the immediate superiors of the former.

In some instances, units which are laterally related to the nonconforming enclave will also be aligned with the middle hierarchy in opposing the enclave. In other cases, the opposition will be made up only of heads of laterally related units and an opposing middle hierarchy will be absent. The varying composition of the "enemy" depends upon the location of the enclave in the organizational structure. The general pattern, however, might be diagrammed as shown in Fig. 2.

Assume that the enclave erupts in D_4. If the leader is the head of D_4, the enclave will encompass the entire unit. If the leader is only a member, the enclave will set itself up as D_4. In either case, the enclave will have to contend with C_2 who is responsible for D_1–D_4. Directly, or indirectly, the enclave will also have to contend with the other D units. The emergence of the nonconforming enclave creates increased com-

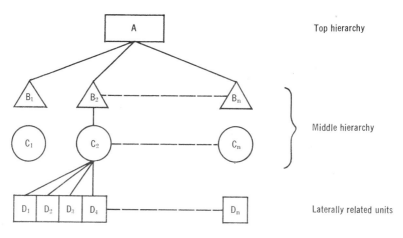

FIGURE 2

petition for resources among the D units. In addition, they perceive themselves as being cast in an unfavorable light by the enthusiasm and heightened activity of the enclave. Hence, the D units will pressure C_2 to suppress the enclave. The D units do not always form part of the opposition to the enclave; another variation is that C_2 might also be directly in charge of one D unit as well as having general responsibility for the entire D section. Such structural variations in the formation of the opposition to the nonconforming enclave do not affect the general pattern of protest absorption, although they help to explain slight variations from case to case. Hence, for simplicity's sake, in describing the process we shall limit the opposition to the middle hierarchy, although the reader should bear in mind that the opposition can vary in its composition.

Incumbents of positions constituting the middle hierarchy are more likely to exhibit "trained incapacity" than incumbents of other levels. Hence, they are usually incapable of comprehending the significance of the enclave's protest. Furthermore, their positions are threatened by the enclave, both because it reveals that their loyalty to basic values of the organization is not as strong as it could be and because it indicates that they cannot make use of the authority vested in them to maintain order in their own bailiwicks. Their response to the enclave is to attempt to suppress it through such means as closing the communication links between the charismatic leader and the top hierarchy, restricting the enclave members' freedom of movement, and reducing the resources available to them. From the perspective of the middle hierarchy,

the use of such techniques represent the full exercise of their rights of office.[18] From the perspective of the nonconforming enclave, such techniques are obstructions which indicate that the organization is against it, and hence, to carry out its cause, the enclave must try to be even more dynamic and more cohesive.

If the charismatic leader is to demonstrate his basic loyalty to organizational values and if he is to gain recognition and legitimation for his cause, he must have access to the top hierarchy. When such access via regular channels is barred, the leader develops his own routes to the top. Frequently this is done through an intermediary who is outside the organization but has legitimate access to the top echelon. Insofar as the charismatic leader is able to establish a particularistic relationship with such an intermediary which is beyond organizational control, he has relatively easy access to the top.

The particularistic communication line gives the nonconforming enclave some leverage in an attempt to have its cause recognized and legitimized. That the intermediary is willing to use his power over the top hierarchy in behalf of the enclave is regarded by its members as a significant step forward and a sign of incipient legitimation.

At the same time that a particularistic communication line gives the enclave hope that its cause will be successful, it also produces potential instability and unreliability. First, the

[18] When legitimate techniques fail to quell the enclave, the middle hierarchy might resort to illegitimate or nonlegitimate ones. Paradoxically, it is at such times that the middle hierarchy overcomes its "trained incapacity."

communication line is maintained at the will—or the whim—of the intermediary, which means that it can be opened and closed arbitrarily. Second, a particularistic request to the top hierarchy in behalf of the nonconforming enclave might elicit informal instructions to the middle hierarchy which it can easily overlook in its continued attempts to obstruct the enclave.

In some instances the charismatic leader need not resort to particularistic communication channels for he might be able to go to the top directly;[19] or the attention of the top hierarchy might be drawn to the nonconforming enclave as a result of the conflict between it and the middle hierarchy, especially if the conflict has affected task performance adversely.

Regardless of the means by which the attention of the top hierarchy is directed to the enclave, the leader who has gained this attention can demonstrate his basic loyalty to organizational values and communicate his ideas for their more effective realization in the hope of gaining official approval. Concerned with blocking such approval, the middle hierarchy urges the top to suppress the enclave. The top hierarchy is interested in enhancing general organizational effectiveness, and, by extension, is concerned with maintaining internal order. With its broader, more substantive, perspective, the top is more amenable to innovation than the middle hierarchy, especially when faced with internal weakness or external challenge. Hence, the top is more likely to accede to some demands of the nonconforming enclave, especially if its leader is backed by a powerful intermediary, than to the insistence of the middle hierarchy that the enclave be thoroughly curbed or eliminated.

The first round in the protest-absorption process is completed when the top hierarchy recognizes the nonconforming enclave and gives it a modicum of autonomy to pursue its advocated innovation. This is followed by several more rounds of obstruction by the middle hierarchy, unorthodox communication to the top by the nonconforming enclave, and a gradually increasing grant of resources, autonomy, and legitimacy to the enclave by the top hierarchy. With each round the enclave comes closer to approximating a new legitimate subunit.

In exchange for autonomy and legitimacy from the top hierarchy, the enclave must agree to accept certain stabilizers. The stabilizers are mechanisms to insure the loyalty of the new unit to the organization and its conformity to organization regulations. First, the protest-absorbing unit is expected to develop rules, subject to approval by the top echelon, to guide its conduct; any changes in these rules are also subject to approval by the top. Second, the unit must accept a regular source of finance through which it will acquire all or most of its inputs. In this way, unauthorized appropriations of resources and competition with existing units for available resources are minimized, and the frustrations of an irregular source of income, typical of a group during its nonconformist period, are avoided. Third, and most important, the unit's activity is limited to a particular sphere of operation,

[19] The leader's ability to communicate with the top hierarchy directly is determined in large part by other capacities, roles, and statuses which he might have within or outside of the organization.

usually that for which the leader and his followers advocated their innovation.[20]

With the introduction of stabilizers, the leader's personal charisma becomes attenuated. The personal charisma is reconverted to charisma of office as the leader (or his successor) assumes legitimate control of the protest-absorber unit. Furthermore, the most radical members of the former enclave perceive the leader as bowing to the dictates of the top hierarchy, thereby betraying the cause; they cease to accept the leader as a charismatic figure, leave the unit, and, where possible, even the organization. The more visible to his followers are the leader's negotiations with the top hierarchy, the more likely is this to be the case. In fact, the top hierarchy could reduce the leader's personal charisma considerably by sending a representative directly to the members of the enclave to grant it legitimacy. By circumventing the leader, the top hierarchy gives the impression that it had been wise enough to recognize the value of the enclave's cause of its own accord and so no credit need be given to the leader who has spearheaded the cause. Circumvention of the leader does present certain dangers, however. Such a procedure is most likely to be successful only if the representative has instructions to grant all or the most important of the enclave's demands. Otherwise, enclave members are likely to perceive the visitation of the representative as an attempt by the top hierarchy to sabotage the cause. Since, in most cases, the top is unlikely to grant major concessions in one fell swoop, this danger is almost always present and serves to strengthen the enclave. A second danger is that the representative himself might be affected by the leader's charisma and join the enclave rather than fulfill his orders.

Occasionally other stabilizers are also introduced, e.g., limiting the size of the protest-absorber unit, appointing a special supervisor to watch for and check any excessive enthusiasm which the unit might display, and restricting the use it may make of its particularistic communication channel. Generally, these particular stabilizers are instituted if the newly legitimized unit still remains somewhat recalcitrant in its adherence to organization rules.

The conformity of the unit is further enhanced through pressures arising within it to replace the instability of its charismatic nature with the stabilizing characteristics which accompany routinization. The nonconforming enclave, like the large-scale charismatic movement, faces "everyday" problems of economic and administrative organization. For example, the unit at some point must provide for the selection of a successor to replace its charismatic leader. (The criteria for selection may be established either by the enclave or by the organization.)

The external pressures toward protest absorption and the internal pressures toward routinization eventually tame the nonconforming enclave and convert it into a quiescent unit con-

[20] The nature of the task limitation imposed on the protest-absorber unit is in part determined by the form of the organization's division of labor, i.e., whether it is structured along geographic lines such that each unit engages in the same task but in a different locality, or around functionally specific lines where each unit engages in its own specialty, or is a combination of geography and functional specificity. See C. I. Barnard [44], p. 129 ff.

cerned with maintaining order in its own bailiwick.[21] The unit may show signs of quiescence simultaneously with its legitimation through protest absorption, or after a period of dynamism during which it expands and gives devoted service to the organization. Its concern with expansion and innovation is replaced by one of self-maintenance. The zeal and energy of the unit are dissipated in legitimized action without being replenished. Once the original members of the unit are gone, or have become concerned with preserving their newly legitimized positions within the organization, the verve that sparked the unit when it was a nonconforming enclave cannot be sustained. Successors to key positions in the unit most likely have been socialized by the organization, and tend to resemble the middle hierarchy more than the original members of the enclave.

The unit's agreement to restrict itself to a specialized sphere of operation is itself another contributing factor to the emerging quiescent period. The agreement helps to preclude the possibility that the unit will attempt innovation beyond its allotted sphere; and whatever success the unit has in its specialty also drains it of further nonconformity. Success is its own detriment when the question of new risks arises: members of the unit prefer to maintain rather than gamble their resources and status on a new venture.

Another factor in the elimination of nonconformity from the unit is time itself. Norms which the enclave had revitalized once again become eroded through increasing lack of strict adherence to them. Members of the unit remain committed to their once-new

[21] Robert Michels, pp. 174–175.

methods even though they have become outmoded and ineffectual. The unit as a whole is no longer dedicated to the ultimate values of the organization but rests content with the sinecure provided it through protest absorption.

The factors that contribute to quiescence—cessation of innovation, dissipation of zeal and energy, emergent conservative tendencies, modification of norms, and the obsolescence of methods —also set the stage for new protest and new forms of nonconformity, which are likely to erupt because the unit legitimized through protest absorption is more vulnerable to the strains between charisma and discipline than are other units. Its history of nonconformity remains unforgotten and lends it an aura of prestige, thereby distinguishing the former enclave from ordinary units. It is further distinguished by having institutionalized a more arduous socialization period for its recruits. Finally, its standards tend to be more strict and demanding than those of the organization as a whole, even with the corroding effects of time. These factors not only militate against the complete integration of the unit into the organization but also make it extremely attractive to recruits, particularly to those who tend to be strongly or rigidly committed to its original values. In short, the unit, limited to its own sphere of action, tamed by stabilizers, concerned with its own well-being, and yet, endowed with the aura of its unorthodox past which facilitates recruitment of potential nonconformers, nurtures a fertile field for the regeneration of a nonconforming enclave and another cycle of protest absorption.

In summary, the process of protest absorption follows several steps. A nonconforming enclave is able to gain some power within the organization because the latter is internally weak or faced with an external crisis. To check the internal threat without further weakening itself, the organization forms a new administrative unit to absorb the enclave, based on the institutionalization of new norms. The emergence of the unit represents a *Sturm und Drang* period: the enclave demands more autonomy and resources so that it can pursue its course of action while the organization reluctantly grants some autonomy and resources, and permits some innovation, in order to maintain peace and overcome the crisis confronting it. The *Sturm und Drang* begins to subside when the enclave achieves the status of a more or less legitimate unit within the organization, and is virtually quelled as the unit loses its initial *élan*, no longer taking on new ventures and becoming concerned with its own maintenance. From the perspective of the top hierarchy of the organization, protest absorption is a process of encapsulation. The nonconforming enclave becomes encased in a network of stabilizers which limits its freedom of action.

Implications of Protest Absorption for the Organization

In large measure, the significance of protest absorption for the organization as a whole depends upon the bearing which the enclave's cause has on the core policies and practices of the organization. From the standpoint of its proponents, the cause usually has a greater degree of significance for core policies than the top hierarchy is willing to acknowledge.

It is convenient to formalize what is generally involved here by means of a continuum in which the cause advocated by an enclave is scaled relative to the degree with which it is likely to affect core policies and practices. Then, as in Fig. 3, the enclave can be characterized as to where it *aspires to be* on the continuum, and where it is *willing to be placed*. The organization can be characterized as to where it would *like to* locate the enclave, and where it is *willing to place it*. The shaded area indicates the range of acceptability for an enclave and its organization; in this instance there is an overlap, although this is not necessarily always the case. Moreover, the ranges of acceptability can shift in the course of the protest-absorption process.

Once these ranges are known, further statements can be made about protest absorption. Where there is an overlap in ranges, protest absorption should prove more successful in controlling the enclave's nonconformity than where such an overlap does not exist. In the case where an overlap is absent (or in the case where the organization makes strong attempts to place the enclave below its minimum acceptable position —in Fig. 3 this would be below 4), the enclave will retain its zeal and unorthodoxy in order to attempt to achieve its cause in the face of control measures. For as the enclave is forced toward the lower end of the continuum, its cause becomes more attenuated, and its chances are lessened for realizing the goals which sparked it in the first place.

Furthermore, by locating the ranges of acceptability, we can predict approximately the number of rounds the protest-absorption process is likely to undergo. More rounds can be anticipated

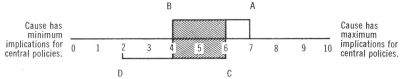

FIGURE 3. A. Enclave Desires Cause to Have Value of 7. B. Enclave Willing to Accept Value of 4. C. Organization Willing to Permit Value of 6. D. Organization Prefers Value of 2.

as the overlap between the two ranges is lessened. For the organization will usually try to check the enclave by locating it as low on the continuum as it can, while the enclave will continue its nonconformist activity until it is located as high on the continuum as it can be.

The more that protest absorption takes place at the higher end of the continuum, the more likely it is that an organization's central policies and practices will undergo a change. This is likely, if only for the reason that the more central the protest-absorber unit is to the organization, the more probable it is that its members will be promoted upward in the hierarchy until they reach the top.[22] The variables which determine where, on the continuum, the enclave will ultimately be absorbed, are those involved in the protest-absorption process itself: the degree

[22] The most cogent illustration of this process can probably be found in the history of the United States Air Force and of the submarine and aircraft carrier units in the United States Navy.

of weakness of the organization, the strength of the nonconforming enclave, the power of the intermediary, the nature of the stabilizers, etc. Thus the protest-absorption process can lead to a long-term chain reaction of major changes in the organization, as well as check nonconformity and introduce a particular innovation.

Finally, protest absorption can have implications for organizational policy for dealing with nonconformity. An organization which has had long experience with nonconformity, e.g., the Catholic Church, might institutionalize the rounds of protest absorption. This means that, as a nonconforming enclave emerges, it "automatically" will be converted into a new subunit over several stages, as it is able to meet criteria specified by the top hierarchy. If the adoption of protest absorption as a conscious organization policy is carried out effectively, an organization will strengthen its ability to cope with nonconformity and to implement changes flowing upward from the bottom.

REFERENCES

1. Barnard, C. I., *The Functions of the Executive* (Cambridge, Mass.: Harvard University Press, 1938).
2. Brzezinski, Z., "Deviation Control: A Study in the Dynamics of Doctrinal Conflict," *American Political Science Review*, 56, 1962, pp. 5–22.

3. Caplow, T., and R. J. McGee, *The Academic Marketplace* (New York: Basic Books, Inc., 1958), p. 66.

4. Davis, A. K., "Bureaucratic Patterns in the Navy Officer Corps."

5. Etzioni, Amitai, *A Comparative Analysis of Complex Organizations,* (New York: The Free Press, 1961).

6. Mannheim, Karl, *Ideology and Utopia* (New York: Harcourt, Brace & World, Inc., 1936).

7. Merton, R. K., *Social Theory and Social Structure*, rev. ed. (New York: The Free Press, 1957).

8. Michels, R., *Political Parties* (New York: Dover Publications, Inc., 1959).

9. Selznick, P., *TVA and the Grass Roots* (Berkeley, Calif.: University of California Press, 1949).

10. Weber, Max, *The Theory of Social and Economic Organization*, translated by A. M. Henderson and T. Parsons (New York: Oxford University Press, and New York: The Free Press, 1947).

11. Wilson, Erle, *Adams of the Bounty* (New York: Popular Library, 1959).

5.2   TOWARD A THEORY OF MOTIVE ACQUISITION[1]

David C. McClelland

The first step in a motive development program is to create confidence that it will work. Our initial efforts in this area were dictated by the simple practical consideration that we had to "sell" our course or nobody would take it. We were not in the position of an animal psychologist who can order a

From David C. McClelland, "Toward a Theory of Motive Acquisition," *American Psychologist,* XX, No 2 (1965), pp. 321–333. Abridged and used by permission.

[1] I am greatly indebted to the Carnegie Corporation of New York for its financial support of the research on which this paper is based, and to my collaborators who have helped plan and run the courses designed to develop the achievement motive—chiefly George Litwin, Elliott Danzig, David Kolb, Winthrop Adkins, David Winter, and John Andrews. The statements made and views expressed are solely the responsibility of the author.

dozen rats, or an academic psychologist who has captive subjects in his classes, or even a psychotherapist who has sick people knocking at his door every day. So we explained to all who would listen that we had every reason to believe from previous research that high n Achievement is related to effective entrepreneurship and that therefore business executives could expect to profit from taking a course designed to understand and develop this important human characteristic. What started as a necessity led to the first proposition dealing with how to bring about motive change.

Proposition 1. The more reasons an individual has in advance to believe that he can, will, or should develop a motive, the more educational attempts designed to develop that motive are likely to succeed. The empirical support for this proposition from other studies is quite impressive. It consists of (a) the prestige-suggestion studies showing that people will believe or do what prestigeful sources suggest (cf. Hovland et al., 1953); (b) the so-called "Hawthorne effect" showing that people who feel they are especially selected to show an effect will tend to show it (Roethlisberger & Dickson, 1947); (c) the "Hello-Goodbye" effect in psychotherapy showing that patients who merely have contact with a prestigeful medical authority improve significantly over waiting list controls and almost as much as those who get prolonged therapy (Frank, 1961); (d) the "experimenter bias" studies which show that subjects will often do what an experimenter wants them to do, even though neither he nor they know he is trying to influence them (Rosenthal, 1963); (e) the goal-setting studies which show that setting goals for a person particularly in the name of prestigeful authorities like "science" or "research" improves performance (Kausler, 1959; Mierke, 1955); (f) the parent-child interaction studies which show that parents who set higher standards of excellence for their sons are more likely to have sons with high n Achievement (Rosen & D'Andrade, 1959). The common factor in all these studies seems to be that goals are being set for the individual by sources he respects—goals which imply that his behavior should change for a variety of reasons and that it *can* change. In common-sense terms, belief in the possibility and desirability of change are tremendously influential in changing a person.

So we have used a variety of means to create this belief: the authority of research findings on the relationship of n Achievement to entrepreneurial success, the suggestive power of membership in an experimental group designed to show an effect, the prestige of a great university, our own genuine enthusiasm for the course and our conviction that it would work, as expressed privately and in public speeches. In short, we were trying to make every use possible of what is sometimes regarded as an "error" in such research—namely, the Hawthorne effect, experimenter bias, etc., because we believe it to be one of the most powerful sources of change.

Why? What is the effect on the person, theoretically speaking, of all this goal setting for him? Its primary function is probably to arouse what exists of an associative network in the achievement area for each person affected. That is, many studies have shown that talk of achievement or affiliation or power tends to increase the frequency with which individuals think about achievement or affiliation or power (cf. Atkinson, 1958). And the stronger the talk, the more the relevant associative networks are aroused (McClelland et al., 1953). Such an arousal has several possible effects which would facilitate learning: (a) It elicits what exists in the person of a "response" thus making it easier to strengthen that response in subsequent learning. (b) It creates a discrepancy between a goal (a "Soll-lage" in Heckhausen's—1963—theory of motivation) and a present state ("Ist-lage") which represents a cognitive dissonance the person tries to reduce (cf. Festinger, 1957); in common-sense terms he has an image clearly presented to him of something he is not but should be. (c) It tends to block out by simple interference other associations which would inhibit change—such as, "I'm too old to learn," "I never learned much from going to school anyway," "What do these academics know about everyday life?" or "I hope they don't get personal about all this."

After the course has been "sold" sufficiently to get a group together for training, the first step in the course itself is to present the research findings in some detail on exactly how n Achievement is related to certain types of successful entrepreneurial performance. That is, the argument of *The Achieving Society* (McClelland, 1961) is presented carefully with tables, charts, and diagrams, usually in lecture form at the outset and with the help of an educational TV film entitled the *Need to Achieve*. This is followed by discussion to clear up any ambiguities that remain in their minds as far as the central argument is concerned. It is especially necessary to stress that not all high achievement is caused by high n Achievement—that we have no evidence that high n Achievement is an essential ingredient in success as a research scientist, professional, accountant, office or personnel manager, etc.; that, on the contrary, it seems rather narrowly related to entrepreneurial, sales, or promotional success, and therefore should be of particular interest to them because they hold jobs which either have or could have an entrepreneurial component. We rationalize this activity in terms of the following proposition.

Proposition 2. The more an individual perceives that developing a motive is consistent with the demands of reality (and reason), the more educational attempts designed to develop that motive are likely to succeed. In

a century in which psychologists and social theorists have been impressed by the power of unreason, it is well to remember that research has shown that rational arguments do sway opinions, particularly among the doubtful or the uncommitted (cf. Hovland et al., 1953). Reality in the form of legal, military, or housing rules does modify white prejudice against Negroes (cf. Berelson & Steiner, 1964, p. 512). In being surprised at Asch's discovery that many people will go along with a group in calling a shorter line longer than it is, we sometimes forget that under most conditions their judgments conform with reality. The associative network which organizes "reality"—which places the person correctly in time, place, space, family, job, etc.—is one of the most dominant in the personality. It is the last to go in psychosis. It should be of great assistance to tie any proposed change in an associative network in with this dominant schema in such a way as to make the change consistent with reality demands or *"reasonable"* extensions of them. The word "reasonable" here simply means extensions arrived at by the thought processes of proof, logic, etc., which in adults have achieved a certain dominance of their own.

The next step in the course is to teach the participants the n Achievement coding system. By this time, they are a little confused anyway as to exactly what we mean by the term. So we tell them they can find out for themselves by learning to code stories written by others or by themselves. They take the test for n Achievement before this session and then find out what their own score is by scoring this record. However, we point out that if they think their score is too low, that can be easily remedied, since we teach them how to code and how to write stories saturated with n Achievement; in fact, that is one of the basic purposes of the course: to teach them to think constantly in n Achievement terms. Another aspect of the learning is discriminating achievement thinking from thinking in terms of power or affiliation. So usually the elements of these other two coding schemes are also taught.

Proposition 3. The more thoroughly an individual develops and clearly conceptualizes the associative network defining the motive, the more likely he is to develop the motive. The original empirical support for this proposition came from the radical behaviorist Skinnerian viewpoint: If the associative responses are the motive (by definition), to strengthen them one should elicit them and reinforce them, as one would shape up any response by reinforcement (cf. Skinner, 1953). But, support for this proposition also derives from other sources, particularly the "set" experiments. For decades laboratory psychologists have known that one of the easiest and most effective ways to change behavior is to change the subject's set. If he is responding to stimulus words with the names of animals, tell him to respond with the names of vegetables, or with words meaning the opposite, and he changes his behavior immediately and efficiently without a mistake. At a more complex level Orne (1962) had pointed out how powerful a set like "This is an experiment" can be. He points out that if you were to go up to a stranger and say something like "Lie down!" he would in all probability either laugh or escape as soon as possible. But, if you say "This is an experiment! Lie down!" more often than not, if there are other supporting cues, the person will do so. Orne has demonstrated how subjects will perform nonsensical and fatiguing tasks for very long periods of time under the set that "This is an experiment." At an even more complex level, sociologists have demonstrated often how quickly a person will change his behavior as he adopts a new role set (as a parent, a teacher, a public official, etc.). In all these cases an associative network exists usually with a label conveniently attached which we call set and which, when it is aroused or becomes salient, proceeds to control behavior very effectively. The purpose of this part of our course is to give the subjects a set or a carefully worked out associative network with appropriate words or labels to describe all its various aspects (the coding labels for parts of the n Achievement scoring system like Ga+, I+, etc.; cf. Atkinson, 1958). The power of words on controlling behavior has also been well documented (cf. Brown, 1958).

It is important to stress that it is not just the label (n Achievement) which is taught. The person must be able to produce easily and often the new associative network itself. It is here that our research comes closest to traditional therapy which could be understood as the prolonged and laborious formation of new associative networks to replace anxiety-laden ones. That is, the person over time comes to form a new associative network covering his relations, for example, to his father and mother, which still later he may label an "unresolved Oedipus complex." When cues arise that formerly would have produced anxiety-laden associations, they now evoke this new complex instead, blocking out the "bad" associations by associative interference. But all therapists, whether Freudian or Rogerian, insist that the person must learn to produce these associations in their new form, that teaching the label is not enough. In fact, this is probably why so-called directive therapy is ineffective: It tries to substitute new constructs ("You should become an achiever") for old neurotic or ineffective ones ("rather than being such a slob") without changing the associative networks which underlie these surface labels. A change in set such as "Respond with names of vegetables" will not work unless the person has a whole associative network which defines the meaning of the set. The relation of this argument is obvious both to Kelly's (1955) insistence on the importance of personal constructs and to the general semanticists' complaints about the neurotic effects of mislabeling or overabstraction (Korzybski, 1941).

But, theoretically speaking, why should a change in set as an associative network be so influential in controlling thought and action? The explanation lies in part in its symbolic character. Learned acts have limited influence because they often depend on reality supports (as in typewriting), but learned thoughts (symbolic acts) can occur any time, any place, in any connection, and be applied to whatever the person is doing. They are more generalizable. Acts can also be inhibited more easily than thoughts. Isak Dinesen tells the story of the oracle who told the king he would get his wish so long as he never thought of the left eye of a camel. Needless to say, the king did

not get his wish, but he could easily have obeyed her prohibition if it had been to avoid *looking* at the left eye of a camel. Thoughts once acquired gain more control over thoughts and actions than acquired acts do because they are harder to inhibit. But why do they gain control over actions? Are not thoughts substitutes for actions? Cannot a man learn to think achievement thoughts and still not act like an achiever in any way? The question is taken up again under the next proposition, but it is well to remember here that thoughts are symbolic acts and that practice of symbolic acts facilitates performing the real acts (cf. Hovland, 1951, p. 644).

The next step in the course is to tie thought to action. Research has shown that individuals high in n Achievement tend to act in certain ways. For example, they prefer work situations where there is a challenge (moderate risk), concrete feedback on how well they are doing, and opportunity to take personal responsibility for achieving the work goals. The participants in the course are therefore introduced to a "work" situation in the form of a business game in which they will have an opportunity to show these characteristics in action or more specifically to develop them through practice and through observing others play it. The game is designed to mimic real life: They must order parts to make certain objects (e.g., a Tinker Toy model bridge) after having estimated how many they think they can construct in the time allotted. They have a real chance to take over, plan the whole game, learn from how well they are doing (use of feedback), and show a paper profit or loss at the end. While they are surprised often that they should have to display their real action characteristics in this way in public, they usually get emotionally involved in observing how they behave under pressure of a more or less "real" work situation.

Proposition 4. The more an individual can link the newly developed network to related actions, the more the change in both thought and actions is likely to occur and endure. The evidence for the importance of action for producing change consists of such diverse findings as (*a*) the importance of recitation for human learning, (*b*) the repeated finding that overt commitment and participation in action changes attitudes effectively (cf. Berelson & Steiner, 1964, p. 576), and (*c*) early studies by Carr (cf. McGeoch & Irion, 1952) showing that simply to expose an organism to what is to be learned (e.g., trundling a rat through a maze) is nowhere near as effective as letting him explore it for himself in action.

Theoretically, the action is represented in the associative network by what associations precede, accompany, and follow it. So including the acts in what is learned *enlarges* the associative network or the achievement construct to include action. Thus, the number of cues likely to trip off the n Achievement network is increased. In commonsense terms, whenever he works he now evaluates what he is doing in achievement terms, and whenever he thinks about achievement he tends to think of its action consequences.

So far the course instruction has remained fairly abstract and removed from the everyday experiences of businessmen. So, the next step is to apply what has been learned to everyday business activities through the medium of the well-known case-study method popularized by the Harvard Business School. Actual examples of the development of the careers or firms of business leaders or entrepreneurs are written up in disguised form and assigned for discussion to the participants. Ordinarily, the instructor is not interested in illustrating "good" or "bad" managerial behavior—that is left to participants to discuss—but in our use of the material, we do try to label the various types of behavior as illustrating either n Achievement and various aspects of the achievement sequence (instrumental activity, blocks, etc.), or n Power, n Affiliation, etc. The participants are also encouraged to bring in examples of managerial behavior from their own experience to evaluate in motivational terms.

Proposition 5. The more an individual can link the newly conceptualized association-action complex (or motive) to events in his everyday life, the more likely the motive complex is to influence his thoughts and actions in situations outside the training experience. The transfer-of-training research literature is not very explicit on this point, though it seems self-evident. Certainly, this is the proposition that underlies the practice of most therapy when it involves working through or clarifying, usually in terms of a new, partially formed construct system, old memories, events from the last 24 hours, dreams, and hopes of the future. Again, theoretically, this should serve to enlarge and clarify the associative network and increase the number of cues in everyday life which will rearouse it. The principle of symbolic practice can also be invoked to support its effectiveness in promoting transfer outside the learning experience.

For some time most course participants have been wondering what all this has to do with them personally. That is to say, the material is introduced originally on a "take it or leave it" objective basis as something that ought to be of interest to them. But, sooner or later, they must confront the issue as to what meaning n Achievement has in their own personal lives. We do not force this choice on them nor do we think we are brainwashing them to believe in n Achievement. We believe and we tell them we believe in the "obstinate audience" (cf. Bauer, 1964), in the ultimate capacity of people to resist persuasion or to do in the end what they really want to do. In fact, we had one case in an early session of a man who at this point decided he was not an achievement-minded person and did not want to become one. He subsequently retired and became a chicken farmer to the relief of the business in which he had been an ineffective manager. We respected that decision and mention it in the course as a good example of honest self-evaluation. Nevertheless, we do provide them with all kinds of information as to their own achievement-related behavior in the fantasy tests, in the business game, in occasional group dynamics session—and ample opportunity and encouragement to think through what this information implies so far as their self-concept is concerned and their responsibilities to their jobs. Various devices such as the "Who am I?" test, silent group meditation, or individual counseling have been introduced to facilitate this self-confrontation.

Proposition 6. The more an individual can perceive and experience the newly conceptualized motive as an improvement in the self-image, the more the motive is likely to influence his future thoughts and actions. Evidence on the importance of the ego or the self-image on controlling behavior has been summarized by Allport (1943). In recent years, Rogers and his group (Rogers, 1961; Rogers & Dymond, 1954) have measured improvement in psychotherapy largely in terms of improvement of the self-concept in relation to the ideal self. Indirect evidence of the importance of the self-schema comes from the discussion over whether a person can be made to do things under hypnosis that are inconsistent with his self-concept or values. All investigators agree that the hypnotist can be most successful in getting the subject to do what might normally be a disapproved action if he makes the subject perceive the action as consistent with his self-image or values (cf. Berelson & Steiner, 1963, p. 124).

The same logic supports this proposition. It seems unlikely that a newly formed associative network like n Achievement could persist and influence behavior much unless it had somehow "come to terms" with the pervasive superordinate network of associations defining the self. The logic is the same as for Proposition 2 dealing with the reality construct system. The n Achievement associations must come to be experienced as related to or consistent with the ideal self-image; otherwise associations from the self-system will constantly block thoughts of achievement. The person might be thinking, for example: "I am not that kind of person; achievement means judging people in terms of how well they perform and I don't like to hurt people's feelings."

Closely allied to the self-system is a whole series of networks only half conscious (i.e., correctly labeled) summarizing the values by which the person lives which derive from his culture and social milieu. These values can also interfere if they are inconsistent with n Achievement as a newly acquired way of thinking. Therefore, it has been customary at this point in the course to introduce a value analysis of the participants' culture based on an analysis of children's stories, myths, popular religion, comparative attitude surveys, customs, etc., more or less in line with traditional, cultural anthropological practice (cf. Benedict, 1946; McClelland, 1964). For example, in America we have to work through the problem of how being achievement oriented seems to interfere with being popular or liked by others which is highly valued by Americans. In Mexico a central issue is the highly valued "male dominance" pattern reflected in the patriarchal family and in the *macho* complex (being extremely masculine). Since data show that dominant fathers have sons with low n Achievement and authoritarian bosses do not encourage n Achievement in their top executives (Andrews, 1965), there is obviously a problem here to be worked through if n Achievement is to survive among thoughts centered on dominance. The problem is not only rationally discussed. It is acted out in role-playing sessions where Mexicans try, and often to their own surprise fail, to act like the democratic father with high standards in the classic Rosen and D'Andrade (1959) study on parental be-

havior which develops high n Achievement. Any technique is used which will serve to draw attention to possible conflicts between n Achievement and popular or traditional cultural values. In the end it may come to discussing parts of the *Bhagavad Gita* in India, or the *Koran* in Arab countries, that seem to oppose achievement striving or entrepreneurial behavior.

Proposition 7. The more an individual can perceive and experience the newly conceptualized motive as an improvement on prevailing cultural values, the more the motive is likely to influence his future thoughts and actions. The cultural anthropologists for years have argued how important it is to understand one's own cultural values to overcome prejudices, adopt more flexible attitudes, etc., but there is little hard evidence that doing so changes a person's behavior. What exists comes indirectly from studies that show prejudice can be decreased a little by information about ethnic groups (Berelson & Steiner, 1963, p. 517), or that repeatedly show an unconscious link between attitudes and the reference group (or subculture to which one belongs)—a link which presumably can be broken more easily by full information about it, especially when coupled with role-playing new attitudes (cf. Berelson & Steiner, 1963, pp. 566 ff.).

The theoretical explanation of this presumed effect is the same as for Propositions 2 and 6. The newly learned associative complex to influence thought and action effectively must somehow be adjusted to three superordinate networks that may set off regularly interfering associations—namely, the networks associated with reality, the self, and the social reference group or subculture.

The course normally ends with each participant preparing a written document outlining his goals and life plans for the next 2 years. These plans may or may not include references to the achievement motive; they can be very tentative, but they are supposed to be quite specific and realistic; that is to say, they should represent moderate levels of aspiration following the practice established in learning about n Achievement of choosing the moderately risky or challenging alternative. The purpose of this document is in part to formulate for oneself the practical implications of the course before leaving it, but even more to provide a basis for the evaluation of their progress in the months after the course. For it is explained to the participants that they are to regard themselves as "in training" for the next 2 years, that 10–14 days is obviously too short a time to do more than conceive a new way of life: It represents the residential portion of the training only. Our role over the next 2 years will be to remind them every 6 months of the tasks they have set themselves by sending them a questionnaire to fill out which will serve to rearouse many of the issues discussed in the course and to give them information on how far they have progressed toward achieving their goals.

Proposition 8. The more an individual commits himself to achieving concrete goals in life related to the newly formed motive, the more the motive is likely to influence his future thoughts and actions.

Proposition 9. The more an individual keeps a record of his progress
toward achieving goals to which he is committed, the more the newly formed motive is likely to influence his future thoughts and actions. These propositions are both related to what was called "pacing" in early studies of the psychology of work. That is, committing oneself to a specific goal and then comparing one's performance to that goal has been found to facilitate learning (cf. Kausler, 1959), though most studies of levels of aspiration have dealt with goal setting as a result rather than as a "cause" of performance. At any rate, the beneficial effect of concrete feedback on learning has been amply demonstrated by psychologists from Thorndike to Skinner. Among humans the feedback on performance is especially effective if they have high n Achievement (French, 1958), a fact which makes the relevance of our request for feedback obvious to the course participants.

The theoretical justification for these propositions is that in this way we are managing to keep the newly acquired associative network salient over the next 2 years. We are providing cues that will regularly rearouse it since he knows he is still part of an experimental training group which is supposed to show a certain type of behavior (Proposition 1 again). If the complex is rearoused sufficiently often back in the real world, we believe it is more likely to influence thought and action than if it is not aroused.

As described so far the course appears to be devoted almost wholly to cognitive learning. Yet this is only part of the story. The "teachers" are all clinically oriented psychologists who also try to practice whatever has been learned about the type of human relationship that most facilitates emotional learning. Both for practical and theoretical reasons this relationship is structured as warm, honest, and nonevaluative, somewhat in the manner described by Rogers (1961) and recommended by distinguished therapists from St. Ignatius[2] to Freud. That is to say, we insist that the only kind of change that can last or mean anything is what the person decides on and works out by himself, that we are there not to criticize his past behavior or direct his future choices, but to provide him with all sorts of information and emotional support that will help him in his self-confrontation. Since we recognize that self-study may be quite difficult and unsettling, we try to create an optimistic relaxed atmosphere in which the person is warmly encouraged in his efforts and given the opportunity for personal counseling if he asks for it.

Proposition 10. Changes in motives are more likely to occur in an interpersonal atmosphere in which the individual feels warmly but honestly supported and respected by others as a person capable of guiding and directing his own future behavior. Despite the widespread belief in this proposition among therapists (except for operant

[2] In his famous spiritual exercises which have played a key role in producing and sustaining personality change in the Jesuit Order, St. Ignatius states: "The director of the Exercises ought not to urge the exercitant more to poverty or any promise than to the contrary, nor to one state of life or way of living more than another . . . [while it is proper to urge people outside the Exercises] the director of the Exercises . . . without leaning to one side or the other, should permit the Creator to deal directly with the creature, and the creature directly with his Creator and Lord."

conditioners), one of the few studies that directly supports it has been conducted by Ends and Page (1957) who found that an objective learning-theory approach was less successful in treating chronic alcoholics than a person-oriented, client-centered approach. Rogers (1961) also summarizes other evidence that therapists who are warmer, more empathic, and genuine are more successful in their work. Hovland et al. (1953) report that the less manipulative the intent of a communicator, the greater the tendency to accept his conclusions. There is also the direct evidence that parents of boys with high n Achievement are warmer, more encouraging and less directive (fathers only) than parents of boys with low n Achievement (Rosen & D'Andrade, 1959). We tried to model ourselves after those parents on the theory that what is associated with high n Achievement in children might be most likely to encourage its development in adulthood. This does not mean permissiveness or promiscuous reinforcement of all kinds of behavior; it also means setting high standards as the parents of the boys with high n Achievement did but having the relaxed faith that the participants can achieve them.

The theoretical justification for this proposition can take two lines: Either one argues that this degree of challenge to the self-schema produces anxiety which needs to be reduced by warm support of the person for effective learning to take place, or one interprets the warmth as a form of direct reinforcement for change following the operant-conditioning model. Perhaps both factors are operating. Certainly there is ample evidence to support the view that anxiety interferes with learning (cf. Sarason, 1960) and that reward shapes behavior (cf. Bandura & Walters, 1963, pp. 283 ff.).

One other characteristic of the course leads to two further propositions. Efforts are made so far as possible to define it as an "experience apart," "an opportunity for self-study," or even a "spiritual retreat" (though that term can be used more acceptably in India than in the United States). So far as possible it is held in an isolated resort hotel or a hostel where there will be few distractions from the outside world and few other guests. This permits an atmosphere of total concentration on the objectives of the course including much informal talk outside the sessions about Ga+, Ga−, I+, and other categories in the coding definition. It still comes as a surprise to us to hear these terms suddenly in an informal group of participants talking away in Spanish or Telugu. The effect of this retreat from everyday life into a special and specially labeled experience appears to be twofold: It dramatizes or increases the salience of the new associative network and it tends to create a new reference group.

Proposition 11. Changes in motives are more likely to occur the more the setting dramatizes the importance of self-study and lifts it out of the routine of everyday life. So far as we know there is no scientific evidence to support this proposition, though again if one regards Jesuits as successful examples of personality change, the Order has frequently followed the advice of St. Ignatius to the effect that "the progress made in the Exercises will be greater, the more the exercitant withdraws from all friends and acquaintances, and from all worldly cares." Theory supports the proposition in two respects: Removing the person from everyday routine (*a*) should decrease interfering associations (to say nothing of interfering appointments and social obligations), and (*b*) should heighten the salience of the experience by contrast with everyday life and make it harder to handle with the usual defenses ("just one more course," etc.). That is to say, the network of achievement-related associations can be more strongly and distinctly aroused in contrast to everyday life, making cognitive dissonance greater and therefore more in need of reduction by new learning. By the same token we have found that the dramatic quality of the experience cannot be sustained very long in a 12–18-hour-a-day schedule without a new routine attitude developing. Thus, we have found that a period somewhere between 6 to 14 days is optimal for this kind of "spiritual retreat." St. Ignatius sets an outside limit of 30 days, but this is when the schedule is less intensive (as ours has sometimes been), consisting of only a few hours a day over a longer period.

Proposition 12. Changes in motives are more likely to occur and persist if the new motive is a sign of membership in a new reference group. No principle of change has stronger empirical or historical support than this one. Endless studies have shown that people's opinions, attitudes, and beliefs are a function of their reference group and that different attitudes are likely to arise and be sustained primarily when the person moves into or affiliates with a new reference group (cf. Berelson & Steiner, 1963, pp. 580 ff.). Many theorists argue that the success of groups like Alcoholics Anonymous depends on the effectiveness with which the group is organized so that each person demonstrates his membership in it by "saving" another alcoholic. Political experience has demonstrated that membership in small groups like Communist or Nazi Party cells is one of the most effective ways to sustain changed attitudes and behavior.

Our course attempts to achieve this result (a) by the group experience in isolation—creating the feeling of alumni who all went through it together; (b) by certain signs of identification with the group, particularly the language of the coding system, but also including a certificate of membership; and (c) by arranging where possible to have participants come from the same community so that they can form a "cell" when they return that will serve as an immediate reference group to prevent gradual undermining of the new network by other pressures.

In theoretical terms a reference group should be effective because its members constantly provide cues to each other to rearouse the associative network, because they will also reward each other for achievement-related thoughts and acts, and because this constant mutual stimulation, and reinforcement, plus the labeling of the group, will prevent assimilation of the network to bigger, older, and stronger networks (such as those associated with traditional cultural values).

In summary, we have described an

TABLE 1   Variables Conceived as Entering into the Motive Change Process

A Input or independent variables	B Intervening variables	C Output or dependent variables
1. Goal setting for the person (P1*, P11)	Arousal of associative network (salience)	Duration and/or extensiveness of changes in:
2. Acquisition of n Achievement associative network (P2, P3, P4, P5)	Experiencing and labeling the associative network	1. n Achievement associative network
3. Relating new network to superordinate networks	Variety of cues to which network is linked	2. Related actions: use of feedback, moderate risk taking, etc.
reality (P2) the self (P6) cultural values (P7)	Interfering associations assimilated or bypassed by reproductive interference	3. Innovations (job improvements)
4. Personal goal setting (P8)		4. Use of time and money
5. Knowledge of progress (P3, P4, P9)		5. Entrepreneurial success as defined by nature of job held and its rewards
6. Personal warmth and support (P10)	Positive affect associated with network	
7. Support of reference group (P11, P12)		

* Note.—P1, P11, etc., refer to the numbered propositions in the text.

influence process which may be conceived in terms of "input," "intervening," and "output" variables as in Table 1. The propositions relate variables in Column A via their effect on the intervening variables in Column B to as yet loosely specified behavior in Column C, which may be taken as evidence that "development" of n Achievement has "really" taken place.

REFERENCES

1. Allport, G. W., "The Ego in Contemporary Psychology," *Psychological Review*, 50, 1943, pp. 451–478.
2. Andrews, J. D. W., "The Achievement Motive in Two Types of Organizations," *Journal of Personality and Social Psychology*, 1965.
3. Atkinson, J. W., (ed.), *Motives in Fantasy, Action and Society* (Princeton, N. J.: Van Nostrand, 1958).
4. Bandura, A., and Walters, R. H., *Social Learning and Personality Development* (New York: Holt, Rinehart & Winston, 1963).
5. Bauer, R. A., "The Obstinate Audience: The Influence Process from the Point of View of Social Communication," *American Psychologist*, 19, 1964, pp. 319–329.
6. Benedict, Ruth, *The Chrysanthemum and the Sword* (Boston: Houghton Mifflin, 1946).
7. Berelson, B., and Steiner, G. A., *Human Behavior: An Inventory of Scientific Findings* (New York: Harcourt, Brace & World, 1964).
8. Brown, R. W., *Words and Things* (New York: The Free Press, 1958).
9. Burris, R. W., "The Effect of Counseling on Achievement Motivation," Unpublished doctoral dissertation, University of Indiana, 1958.
10. Ends, E. J., and Page, C. W., "A Study of Three Types of Group Psychotherapy with Hospitalized Male Inebriates," *Quarterly Journal on Alcohol*, 18, 1957, pp. 263–277.
11. Eysenck, H. J., "The Effects of Psychotherapy: An Evaluation," *Journal of Consulting Psychology*, 16, 1952, pp. 319–324.
12. Festinger, L., *A Theory of Cognitive Dissonance* (New York: Harper & Row, 1957).
13. Frank, J., *Persuasion and Healing* (Baltimore: Johns Hopkins Press, 1961).
14. French, E. G., "Effects of the Interaction of Motivation and Feedback on Task Performance," In J. W. Atkinson (ed.), *Motives in Fantasy, Action and Society* (Princeton, N. J.: Van Nostrand, 1958), pp. 400–408.
15. Heckhausen, H., "Eine Rahmentheorie der Motivation in Zehn Thesen," *Zeitschrift für Experimentelle und Angewandte Psychologie*, X/4, 1963, pp. 604–626.
16. Hovland, C. I., "Human Learning and Retention," in S. S. Stevens (ed.), *Handbook of Experimental Psychology* (New York: John Wiley and Sons, 1951).
17. Hovland, C. I., Janis, I. L., and Kelley, H. H., *Communication and Persuasion: Psychological Studies of Opinion Change* (New Haven, Conn.: Yale University Press, 1953).
18. Kausler, D. H., "Aspiration Level as a Determinant of Performance," *Journal of Personality*, 27, 1959, pp. 346–351.
19. Kelly, G. A., *The Psychology of Personal Constructs* (New York; W. W. Norton, 1955).

20. Korzybski, A., *Science and Sanity* (Lancaster, Pa.: Science Press, 1941).
21. McClelland, D. C., *The Achieving Society* (Princeton, N. J.: Van Nostrand, 1961).
22. McClelland, D. C., *The Roots of Consciousness* (Princeton, N. J.: Van Nostrand, 1964).
23. McClelland, D. C., Atkinson, J. W., Clark, R. A., and Lowell, E. L., *The Achievement Motive* (New York: Appleton-Century and Crofts, 1953).
24. McGeoch, J. A., and Irion, A. L., *The Psychology of Human Learning.* (2d ed.) (New York: Longmans, Green & Co., 1952).
25. Mierke, K., *Wille und Leistung* (Göttingan: Verlag für Psychologie, 1955).
26. Orne, M., "On the Social Psychology of the Psychological Experiment: With Particular Reference to Demand Characteristics and their Implications," *American Psychologist*, 17, 1962, pp. 776–783.
27. Roethlisberger, F. J., and Dickson, W. J., *Management and the Worker.* (Cambridge, Mass.: Harvard University Press, 1947).
28. Rogers, C. R., *On Becoming a Person.* (Boston: Houghton Mifflin, 1961).
29. Rogers, C. R., and Dymond, R. F., (eds.) *Psychotherapy and Personality Change.* (Chicago: University of Chicago Press, 1954).
30. Rosen, B. C., and D'Andrade, R. G., "The Psychosocial Origins of Achievement Motivation," *Sociometry*, 22, 1959, pp. 185–218.
31. Rosenthal, R., "On the Social Psychology of the Psychological Experiment: The Experimenter's Hypothesis as Unintended Determinant of Experimental Results," *American Scientist*, 51, 1963, pp. 268–283.
32. Sarason, I., "Empirical Findings and Theoretical Problems in the Use of Anxiety Scales," *Psychological Bulletin*, 57, 1960, pp. 403–415.
33. Skinner, B. F., *Science and Human Behavior.* (New York: Crowell-Collier and Macmillan, 1953).

5.3 PROCESSES OF OPINION CHANGE*

Herbert C. Kelman

The Study of Social Influence

Social influence has been a central area of concern for experimental social psychology almost since its beginnings.

Excerpted from Herbert C. Kelman, "Processes of Opinion Change," *Public Opinion Quarterly*, XXV Spring 1961, 57–78. © Princeton University Press, 1961. Footnotes renumbered. Abridged and used by permission.

* This paper is based on a research program on social influence and behavior change, supported by grant M-2516 from the National Institute of Mental Health.

Three general research traditions in this area can be distinguished: (1) The study of social influences on judgments, stemming out of the earlier work on prestige suggestion;[1] (2) the study of social influences arising from small group interaction;[2] and (3) the study

[1] See, for example, S. E. Asch, *Social Psychology*, Englewood Cliffs, N.J., Prentice-Hall, Inc., 1952.

[2] See, for example, D. Cartwright and A. Zander, editors, *Group Dynamics*, New York, Harper & Row, Publishers, 1953.

of social influences arising from persuasive communications.[3] In recent years, there has been a considerable convergence between these three traditions, going hand in hand with an increased interest in developing general principles of social influence and socially induced behavior change.

One result of these developments has been that many investigators found it necessary to make qualitative distinctions between different types of influence. In some cases, these distinctions arose primarily out of the observation that social influence may have qualitatively different effects, that it may produce different kinds of change. For example, under some conditions it may result in mere public conformity—in superficial changes on a verbal or overt level without accompanying changes in belief; in other situations it may result in private acceptance—in a change that is more general, more durable, more integrated with the person's own values.[4] Other investigators found it necessary to make distinctions because they observed that influence may occur for different reasons, that it may arise out of different motivations and orientations. For example, under some conditions influence may be primarily informational—the subject may conform to the influencing person or group because he views him as a source of valid information; in other situations influence may be primarily normative —the subject may conform in order to meet the positive expectations of the influencing person or group.[5]

My own work can be viewed in the general context that I have outlined here. I started out with the distinction between public conformity and private acceptance, and tried to establish some of the distinct determinants of each. I became dissatisfied with this dichotomy as I began to look at important examples of social influence that could not be encompassed by it. I was especially impressed with the accounts of ideological conversion of the "true believer" variety, and with the recent accounts of "brain-washing," particularly the Chinese Communist methods of "thought reform."[6] It is apparent that these experiences do not simply involve public conformity, but that indeed they

[3] See, for example, C. I. Hovland, I. L. Janis, and H. H. Kelley, *Communication and Persuasion*, New Haven, Conn., Yale University Press, 1953.

[4] See, for example, L. Festinger, "An Analysis of Compliant Behavior," in M. Sherif and M. O. Wilson, editors, *Group Relations at the Crossroads*, New York, Harper & Row, Publishers, 1953, pp. 232–256; H. C. Kelman, "Attitude Change as a Function of Response Restriction," *Human Relations*, Vol. 6, 1953, pp. 185–214; J. R. P. French, Jr. and B. Raven, "The Bases of Social Power," in D. Cartwright, editor, *Studies in Social Power*, Ann Arbor, Mich., Institute for Social Research, 1959, pp. 150–167; and Marie Jahoda, "Conformity and Independence," *Human Relations*, Vol. 12, 1959, pp. 99–120.

[5] See, for example, M. Deutsch and H. B. Gerard, "A Study of Normative and Informational Social Influence upon Individual Judgment," *Journal of Abnormal and Social Psychology*, Vol. 51, 1955, pp. 629–636; J. W. Thibaut and L. Strickland, "Psychological Set and Social Conformity," *Journal of Personality*, Vol. 25, 1956, pp. 115–129; and J. M. Jackson and H. D. Saltzstein, "The Effect of Person-Group Relationships on Conformity Processes," *Journal of Abnormal and Social Psychology*, Vol. 57, 1958, pp. 17–24.

[6] For instance, R. J. Lifton, " 'Thought Reform' of Western Civilians in Chinese Communist Prisons," *Psychiatry*, Vol. 19, 1956, pp. 173–195.

produce a change in underlying beliefs. But it is equally apparent that they do not produce what we would usually consider private acceptance—changes that are in some sense integrated with the person's own value system and that have become independent of the external source. Rather, they seem to produce new beliefs that are isolated from the rest of the person's values and that are highly dependent on external support.

These considerations eventually led me to distinguish three processes of social influence, each characterized by a distinct set of antecedent and a distinct set of consequent conditions. I have called these processes *compliance, identification,* and *internalization.*[7]

Three Processes of Social Influence

Compliance can be said to occur when an individual accepts influence from another person or from a group because he hopes to achieve a favorable reaction from the other. He may be interested in attaining certain specific rewards or in avoiding certain specific punishments that the influencing agent controls. For example, an individual may make a special effort to express only "correct" opinions in order to gain admission into a particular group or social set; or in order to avoid being fired from his government job. Or, the individual may be concerned with gaining approval or avoiding disapproval

[7] A detailed description of these processes and the experimental work based on them will be contained in a forthcoming book, *Social Influence and Personal Belief: A Theoretical and Experimental Approach to the Study of Behavior Change,* to be published by John Wiley & Sons, Inc.

from the influencing agent in a more general way. For example, some individuals may compulsively try to say the expected thing in all situations and please everyone with whom they come in contact, out of a disproportionate need for favorable responses from others of a direct and immediate kind. In any event, when the individual complies, he does what the agent wants him to do—or what he thinks the agent wants him to do—because he sees this as a way of achieving a desired response from him. He does not adopt the induced behavior—for example, a particular opinion response—because he believes in its content, but because it is instrumental in the production of a satisfying social effect. What the individual learns, essentially, is to say or do the expected thing in special situations, regardless of what his private beliefs may be. Opinions adopted through compliance should be expressed only when the person's behavior is observable by the influencing agent.

Identification can be said to occur when an individual adopts behavior derived from another person or a group because this behavior is associated with a satisfying self-defining relationship to this person or group. By a self-defining relationship I mean a role relationship that forms a part of the person's self-image. Accepting influence through identification, then, is a way of establishing or maintaining the desired relationship to the other, and the self-definition that is anchored in this relationship.

The relationship that an individual tries to establish or maintain through identification may take different forms. It may take the form of classical identification, that is, of a relationship in which the individual takes over all or part of the role of the influencing agent. To the extent to which such a relationship exists, the individual defines his own role in terms of the role of the other. He attempts to be like or actually to *be* the other person. By saying what the other says, doing what he does, believing what he believes, the individual maintains this relationship and the satisfying self-definition that it provides him. An influencing agent who is likely to be an attractive object for such a relationship is one who occupies a role desired by the individual—who possesses those characteristics that the individual himself lacks—such as control in a situation in which the individual is helpless, direction in a situation in which he is disoriented, or belongingness in a situation in which he is isolated.

The behavior of the brain-washed prisoner in Communist China provides one example of this type of identification. By adopting the attitudes and beliefs of the prison authorities—including *their* evaluation of *him*—he attempts to regain his identity, which has been subjected to severe threats. But, this kind of identification does not only occur in such severe crisis situations. It can also be observed, for example, in the context of socialization of children, where the taking over of parental attitudes and actions is a normal, and probably essential part of personality development. The more or less conscious efforts involved when an individual learns to play a desired occupational role and imitates an appropriate role model would also exemplify this process. Here, of course, the individual is much more selective in the attitudes and actions he takes over from the other person. What is at stake is not his basic sense of identity or the stability of his self-concept, but rather his more limited "professional identity."

The self-defining relationship that an individual tries to establish or maintain through identification may also take the form of a reciprocal role relationship—that is, of a relationship in which the roles of the two parties are defined with reference to one another. An individual may be involved in a reciprocal relationship with another specific individual, as in a friendship relationship between two people. Or, he may occupy a social role which is defined with reference to another, reciprocal role, as in the relationship between patient and doctor. A reciprocal role relationship can only be maintained if the participants have mutually shared expectations of one another's behavior. Thus, if an individual finds a particular relationship satisfying, he will tend to behave in such a way as to meet the expectations of the other. In other words, he will tend to behave in line with the requirements of this particular relationship. This should be true regardless of whether the other is watching or not: quite apart from the reactions of the other, it is important to the individual's own self-concept to meet the expectations of his friendship role, for example, or those of his occupational role.

Thus, the acceptance of influence through identification should take place when the person sees the induced behavior as relevant to and required by a reciprocal role relationship in which he is a participant. Acceptance of influence based on a reciprocal role relationship is similar to that involved in classical identification in that it is a way of establishing or maintaining a satisfying self-defining relationship to another. The nature of the relationship differs, of course. In one case it is a relationship of identity; in the other one of reciprocity. In the case of reciprocal role relationships, the individual is not identifying with the other in the sense of taking over *his* identity, but in the sense of empathically reacting in terms of the other person's expectations, feelings or needs.

Identification may also serve to maintain an individual's relationship to a group in which his self-definition is anchored. Such a relationship may have elements of classical identification as well as of reciprocal roles: to maintain his self-definition as a group member an individual, typically, has to model his behavior along particular lines and has to meet the expectations of his fellow members. An example of identification with a group would be the member of the Communist Party who derives strength and a sense of identity from his self-definition as part of the vanguard of the proletarian revolution and as an agent of historical destiny. A similar process, but at a low degree of intensity, is probably involved in many of the conventions that people acquire as part of their socialization into a particular group.

Identification is similar to compliance in that the individual does not adopt the induced behavior because its content per se is intrinsically satisfying. Identification differs from compliance, however, in that the individual actually believes in the opinions and actions that he adopts. The behavior is accepted both publicly and privately, and its manifestation does not depend on observability by the influencing agent. It does depend, however, on the role that an individual takes at any given moment in time. Only when the appropriate role is activated—only when

the individual is acting within the relationship upon which the identification is based—will the induced opinions be expressed. The individual is not primarily concerned with pleasing the other, with giving him what he wants (as in compliance), but he is concerned with meeting the other's expectations for his own role performance. Thus, opinions adopted through identification do remain tied to the external source and dependent on social support. They are not integrated with the individual's value system, but rather tend to be isolated from the rest of his values—to remain encapsulated.

Finally, *internalization* can be said to occur when an individual accepts influence because the induced behavior is congruent with his value system. It is the content of the induced behavior that is intrinsically rewarding here. The individual adopts it because he finds it useful for the solution of a problem, or because it is congenial to his own orientation, or because it is demanded by his own values—in short, because he perceives it as inherently conducive to the maximization of his values. The characteristics of the influencing agent do play an important role in internalization, but the crucial dimension here—as we shall see below—is the agent's credibility, that is, his relation to the content.

The most obvious examples of internalization are those that involve the evaluation and acceptance of induced behavior on rational grounds. A person may adopt the recommendations of an expert, for example, because he finds them relevant to his own problems and congruent with his own values. Typically, when internalization is involved, he will not accept these recommendations *in toto*, but modify them to some degree so that they will fit his own unique situation. Or, a visitor to a foreign country may be challenged by the different patterns of behavior to which he is exposed, and he may decide to adopt them (again, selectively and in modified form) because he finds them more in keeping with his own values than the patterns in his home country. I am not implying, of course, that internalization is always involved in the situations mentioned. One would speak of internalization only if acceptance of influence took the particular form that I described.

Internalization, however, does not necessarily involve the adoption of induced behavior on rational grounds. I would not want to equate internalization with rationality, even though the description of the process has decidedly rationalist overtones. For example, I would characterize as internalization the adoption of beliefs because of their congruence with a value system that is basically *irrational*. Thus, an authoritarian individual may adopt certain racist attitudes because they fit into his paranoid, irrational view of the world. Presumably, what is involved here is internalization, since it is the content of the induced behavior and its relation to the person's value-system that is satisfying. Similarly, it should be noted that congruence with a person's value-system does not necessarily imply logical consistency. Behavior would be congruent if, in some way or other, it fit into the person's value-system, if it seemed to belong there and be demanded by it.

It follows from this conception that behavior adopted through internalization is, in some way—rational or otherwise—integrated with the individual's existing values. It becomes part of a personal system, as distinguished from a system of social role expectations. Such behavior gradually becomes independent of the external source. Its manifestation depends neither on observability by the influencing agent, nor on the activation of the relevant role, but on the extent to which the underlying values have been made relevant by the issues under consideration. This does not mean that the individual will invariably express internalized opinions, regardless of the social situation. In any specific situation, he has to choose among competing values in the face of a variety of situational requirements. It does mean, however, that these opinions will at least enter into competition with other alternatives whenever they are relevant in content.

It should be stressed that the three processes are not mutually exclusive. While they have been defined in terms of pure cases, they do not generally occur in pure form in real-life situations. The examples that have been given are, at best, situations in which a particular process predominates and determines the central features of the interaction.

Antecedents and Consequents of the Three Processes

For each of the three processes, a distinct set of antecedents and a distinct set of consequents have been proposed. These are summarized in Table 1. First, with respect to the antecedents of the three processes, it should be noted that no systematic quantitative differences between them are hypothesized. The probability of each process is presented as a function of the same three determinants: the importance of

TABLE 1   Summary of the Distinctions between the Three Processes

	Compliance	Identification	Internalization
ANTECEDENTS:			
1. *Basis for the importance of the induction*	Concern with social effect of behavior	Concern with social anchorage of behavior	Concern with value congruence of behavior
2. *Source of power of the influencing agent*	Means-control	Attractiveness	Credibility
3. *Manner of achieving prepotency of the induced response*	Limitation of choice behavior	Delineation of role requirements	Reorganization of means-ends framework
CONSEQUENTS:			
1. *Conditions of performance of induced response*	Surveillance by influencing agent	Salience of relationship to agent	Relevance of values to issue
2. *Conditions of change and extinction of induced response*	Changed perception of conditions for social rewards	Changed perception of conditions for satisfying self-defining relationships	Changed perceptions of conditions for value maximization
3. *Type of behavior system in which induced response is embedded*	External demands of a specific setting	Expectations defining a specific role	Person's value-system

the induction for the individual's goal achievement, the power of the influencing agent, and the prepotency of the induced response. For each process, the magnitude of these determinants may vary over the entire range: each may be based on an induction with varying degrees of importance, on an influencing agent, with varying degrees of power, and so on. The processes differ only in terms of the *qualitative* form that these determinants take. They differ, as can be seen in the table, in terms of the *basis* for the importance of the induction, the *source* of the influencing agent's power, and the *manner* of

achieving prepotency of the induced response.

1. The processes can be distinguished in terms of the basis of the importance of the induction, that is, in terms of the nature of the motivational system that is activated in the influence situation. What is it about the influence situation that makes it important, that makes it relevant to the individual's goals? What are the primary concerns that the individual brings to the situation or that are aroused by it? The differences between the three processes in this respect are implicit in the descriptions of the processes given above: (a)

To the extent that the individual is concerned—for whatever reason—with the *social effect* of his behavior, influence will tend to take the form of compliance. (b) To the extent that he is concerned with the *social anchorage* of his behavior, influence will tend to take the form of identification. (c) To the extend to which he is concerned with the *value congruence* of his behavior (rational or otherwise), influence will tend to take the form of internalization.

2. A difference between the three processes in terms of the source of the influencing agent's power is hypothesized. (a) To the extent to which the agent's power is based on his *means-control*, influence will tend to take the form of compliance. An agent possesses means-control if he is in a position to supply or withhold means needed by the individual for the achievement of his goals. The perception of means-control may depend on the agent's *actual* control over specific rewards and punishments, or on his *potential* control, which would be related to his position in the social structure (his status, authority, or general prestige). (b) To the extent to which the agent's power is based on his *attractiveness*, influence will tend to take the form of identification. An agent is attractive if he occupies a role which the individual himself desires[8] or if he occupies a role reciprocal to one the individual wants to establish or maintain. The term "attractiveness," as used here, does not refer to the possession of qualities that make a person likeable, but rather to the possession of qualities on the part of the agent that make a continued relationship to him particularly desirable. In other words, an agent is attractive when the individual is able to derive satisfaction from a self-definition with reference to him. (c) To the extent to which the agent's power is based on his *credibility*, influence will tend to take the form of internalization. An agent possesses credibility if his statements are considered truthful and valid, and hence worthy of serious consideration. Hovland, Janis and Kelley[9] distinguish two bases for credibility, expertness and trustworthiness. In other words, an agent may be perceived as possessing credibility because he is likely to *know* the truth, or because he is likely to *tell* the truth. Trustworthiness, in turn, may be related to over-all respect, like-mindedness, and lack of vested interest.

3. It is proposed that the three processes differ in terms of the way in which prepotency is achieved. (a) To the extent to which the induced response becomes prepotent—that is, becomes a "distinguished path" relative to alternative response possibilities—because the individual's choice behavior is limited, influence will tend to take the form of compliance. This may happen if the individual is pressured into the induced response, or if alternative responses are blocked. The induced response thus becomes prepotent because it is, essentially, the only response permitted: the individual sees himself as having no choice and as being restricted to this particular alternative. (b) To the extent to which the induced response becomes prepotent because the requirements of a particular role are delineated, influence

---

[8] This is similar to John Whiting's conception of "Status Envy" as a basis for identification. See J. W. M. Whiting, "Sorcery, Sin, and the Superego," in M. R. Jones, editor, *Nebraska Symposium on Motivation*, Lincoln, University of Nebraska Press, 1959, pp. 174–195.

[9] *Op. cit.*, p. 21.

will tend to take the form of identification. This may happen if the situation is defined in terms of a particular role relationship and the demands of that role are, more or less, clearly specified: for instance, this role is made especially salient and the expectations deriving from it dominate the field. Or, it may happen if alternative roles are made ineffective because the situation is ambiguous and consensual validation is lacking. The induced response thus becomes prepotent because it is one of the few alternatives available to the individual: his choice behavior may be unrestricted, but his opportunity for selecting alternative responses is limited by the fact that he is operating exclusively from the point of view of a particular role system. (c) Finally, to the extent to which the induced response becomes prepotent because there has been a reorganization in the individual's conception of means-ends relationships, influence will tend to take the form of internalization. This may happen if the implications of the induced response for certain important values—implications of which the individual had been unaware heretofore—are brought out, or if the advantages of the induced response as a path to the individual's goals, compared to the various alternatives that are available, are made apparent. The induced response thus becomes prepotent because it has taken on a new meaning: as the relationships between various means and ends become restructured, it emerges as the preferred course of action in terms of the person's own values.

Depending, then, on the nature of these three antecedents, the influence process will take the form of compliance, identification, or internalization. Each of these corresponds to a characteristic pattern of internal responses —thoughts and feelings—in which the individual engages as he accepts influence. The resulting changes will, in turn, be different for the three processes, as indicated in the second half of the table. Here, again, it is assumed that there are no systematic quantitative differences between the processes, but rather qualitative variations in the subsequent histories of behaviors adopted through each process.

5.4 THE SOCIAL ITINERARY OF TECHNICAL CHANGE: TWO STUDIES ON THE DIFFUSION OF INNOVATION

Elihu Katz

Rapid social and technical change is the hallmark of modern, urban society.

From Elihu Katz, "The Social Itinerary of Technical Change: Two Studies on the Diffusion of Innovation," *Human Organization,* published by the Society for Applied Anthropology, XX, No. 2 (Summer 1961), 70–82. Abridged and used by permission.

The last few years, for example, have seen an upturn in the birth rate; an invasion of small, foreign-made automobiles; the triumph of the hula hoop; the rise and fall of the sack dress; the widespread acceptance of antibiotics and tranquilizers; and so on. Despite all of this, there are surprisingly few studies of the diffusion of innovation in the sense of tracing the movement of: 1) a given new practice; 2) over time; 3) through specific channels of communication; 4) within a social structure. This is all the more remarkable given that one would be hard put even to define various fields of behavioral research without reference to the process of diffusion. Marketing, for example, obviously, has to do with the diffusion of products; anthropology has to do with the transmission and change of culture; sociology is concerned, among other things, with the consequences of technical change, or with the spread of fads and fashions. Yet, these additions have tended to ignore the itinerary of change in the sense in which the diffusion process is defined above.

The aim of what follows is to compare two studies which have made a start in this direction. The one, by Bryce Ryan and Neal Gross, is a study of how hybrid seed corn gained acceptance among farmers in two Iowa communities;[1] the other is a study of how doctors in four communities responded to the availability of a new "miracle" drug.[2] Despite the seeming difference between a new seed and a new drug,

and between farmers and doctors, the two studies will be seen to be comparable at many points, with respect both to research design and research results.

These studies also represent a noteworthy convergence of two traditions of social research which have had virtually no contact with each other. The hybrid-corn study is one of the earliest products of that branch of rural sociology which has concerned itself—for the last fifteen or so years—with the study of factors affecting the acceptance of new practices recommended to farmers for adoption. The drug study stems, ultimately, from the tradition of research into the effects of mass communication.[3] The two traditions have

_____

[1] Discussion of this study will be based on the journal article reporting some of the central findings and, particularly, on the later, more comprehensive report. These are, respectively, Bryce Ryan and Neal Gross, "The Diffusion of Hybrid Seed Corn in Two Iowa Communities," *Rural Sociology*, VIII (March, 1943), 15–24, and Ryan and Gross, *Acceptance and Diffusion of Hybrid Seed Corn in Two Iowa Communities*, Iowa State College of Agriculture and Mechanic Arts, Bulletin 372, 1950.

[2] A book by James Coleman, Elihu Katz, and Herbert Menzel, tentatively titled *Doctors and New Drugs*, The Free Press, New

York, is in preparation. Published reports on the study include: Menzel and Katz, "Social Relations and Innovation in the Medical Profession: The Epidemiology of a New Drug," *Public Opinion Quarterly*, XIX (Winter, 1955–56), 337–352, a report on the pilot study; Menzel, "Innovation, Integration and Marginality: Facts and Problems from a Survey of Physicians," *American Sociological Review*, forthcoming; Menzel, Coleman, and Katz, "Dimensions of Being 'Modern' in Medical Practice," *Journal of Chronic Diseases*, IX (January, 1959), 20–40; Coleman, Katz, and Menzel, "The Diffusion of an Innovation Among Physicians," *Sociometry*, XX (December, 1957), 253–270; and Coleman, Menzel, and Katz, "Social Processes in Physicians' Adoption of a New Drug," *Journal of Chronic Diseases*, IX (January, 1959), 1–19. An important part of the substantive material is contained in the latter two articles while other parts are available only in unpublished research reports of the Bureau of Applied Social Research, Columbia University.

[3] For a discussion of the sequence of studies which contributed to the formulation of the drug study, see Elihu Katz, "The Two-Step Flow of Communications: An Up-to-Date Report on an Hypothesis," *Pub-*

in common a concern with what has been called "campaigns"—attempts, in the short run, to change opinions, attitudes, and actions.[4] In this sense, a voting campaign, or a campaign to reduce prejudice, or a marketing campaign are similar to the campaign of an agricultural experiment agency to persuade farmers to adopt some innovation. Yet, despite this similarity, the two traditions have shown little interest in each other. The key to the vast gap which has separated them is, surely, the different images of society which they have held. Mass communications research has tended to envision society as an audience of isolated individuals, hooked-up to the mass media but not to each other. Indeed, the mass media are the very symbols of the atomized mass society. Rural sociology, on the other hand, conceives itself as being located near the opposite end of the "Gemeinschaft-Gesellschaft" continuum.

Very recently, however, mass communications research has begun to revise its images of the audience. A series of studies in the last few years has revealed not only that modern, urban society is not as individuated as had once been assumed but that the connections among family members, colleagues, and the like, have an important share in the communications process.[5]

It is this concern with interpersonal processes which is beginning to forge a link between the two traditions of communications research being considered here.[6] Nevertheless, the drug study was completed only a few years ago without any real awareness of its many similarities to the study which had been undertaken by Ryan and Gross almost fifteen years before.

This article has two parts. The first part is concerned with the *design* of the two studies. It is an attempt to illustrate the research strategies which are appropriate to research on the diffusion of innovation, and the main variables which must be taken into account. The second part of the article compares some of the *findings* of the two studies.

The Design of the Two Studies

The design of the two studies can be compared most usefully, perhaps, with respect to the basic elements already enumerated: 1) a given new practice; 2) time; 3) channels of communication; and 4) social structure. Each of these elements will be considered in turn.

A Given New Practice

Each study concentrated on a single new product. Hybrid corn seed emerged from its experimental stage in 1927 and had been almost universally adopted ten years later in the two communities

---

lic *Opinion Quarterly*, XXI (Spring, 1957), 61–78.

[4] This point is developed in Elihu Katz and Paul F. Lazarsfeld, *Personal Influence: The Part Played by People in the Flow of Mass Communication*, The Free Press, New York, 1956, pp. 15–25.

[5] Reviews of some of these studies may be found in Katz, "The Two-Step Flow . . .," *op. cit.* and in John W. and Matilda W. Riley, "Mass Communications and the So-

cial System," in Robert K. Merton *et al.* (eds.), *Sociology Today*, Basic Books, Inc., New York, 1959.

[6] See Elihu Katz, "Communication Research and the Image of Society: The Convergence of Two Traditions," *American Journal of Sociology*, LXV (March, 1960), 435–440.

studied. Gammanym, the newest member of a family of modern "miracle" drugs, became available to physicians in the early 1950's and achieved almost total acceptance in less than two years.[7]

The two products are far more comparable than they might appear to be. First of all, they both came *highly recommended* by competent scientific authority. They are both of *central importance* to the groups for whom they were intended. What is more, both seeds and drugs are the sorts of products whose effects can be measured with a rational yardstick which enables users to *see for themselves*, more or less, whether the innovation serves better than its predecessor. This is quite different from, say, fashion changes in clothing.

Another characteristic shared by hybrid corn and gammanym is that both could be accepted in *installments*. A farmer, for example, could experiment with the new hybrid seed in a small fraction of total corn acreage, just as a doctor could decide to try gammanym, initially, on only one or two patients. This is quite different, obviously, from take-it-or-leave-it innovations, like an air conditioner or a new car.

Still another important similarity between the two innovations is that both were essentially modifications of products with which farmers and doctors, respectively, had had considerable experience. Adoption of these innovations, then, required only relatively minor—but still not insignificant—changes in patterns of thought and action. Contrast these "substitute" products, for example, with the study of a "campaign" waged in a rural Peruvian community to gain acceptance of the

ostensibly simple practice of boiling water before drinking it, where acceptance required a radical change in the traditional concepts of health and illness as well as a change in the rhythms of food preparation and of work within, and outside, the household.[8]

The two innovations share still other similarities. One of the most important of these has to do with the fact that differentials in wealth, or in *economic profitability*, do not seem, *a priori*, to be of major relevance in determining response to the innovation. In the case of hybrid corn, Ryan and Gross explain that no farmer cited the price of seed as a reason for delaying adoption of the innovation, nor was there any reason to believe that the increased return from hybrid corn would be disproportionately greater for operators of larger farms than of smaller ones.[9] In the case

---

[7] The name gammanym is a pseudonym.

[8] Edward M. Wellin, "Water Boiling in a Peruvian Town," in Benjamin Paul (ed.), *Health, Culture, and Community*, Russell Sage Foundation, New York, 1955.

[9] "While it would be difficult to place a date at which the perfectly rational man would have adopted hybrid seed, under the assumptions of classical economic theory, the adoption date would have been practically the same for all operators. That is, variations in the rational desirability of the seed between farmers were at a minimum —the trait was economically advantageous to all, and to much the same degree." Ryan and Gross, *op. cit.*, 670. On the other hand, an economic analysis of time differentials in the diffusion of hybrid corn *between* different areas of the country (rather than *within* an area) shows that the "profitability" of the shift from open-pollinated to hybrid is highly associated with the rate of acceptance. See Zvi Griliches, "Hybrid Corn: An Exploration in the Economics of Technological Change," *Econometrica*, XXV (October, 1957), 501–522.

of gammanym, of course, it is the patient, not the doctor, who pays for the drug and thus doctors might all be expected to be equally likely to be the first to try the new drug.

This is not to say that there are no differences between the two products, or that the above enumeration necessarily catches up the most crucial dimensions. It can only be surmised that some of these dimensions—plus others like them—may well affect diffusion patterns. It is clear, at any rate, that any attempt to develop a comparative study of diffusion must incorporate a more systematic "content analysis" of the variable characteristics of innovations. Moreover, this must be done "functionally"; that is, the innovation must be characterized with respect to the patterns of thought and action of the people to whom it is directed.[10]

TIME

The second element of the diffusion process in terms of which the two studies may be compared is the element of time. In both studies, "acceptance" of the innovation was operationally defined as initial use of any amount of the product.

Notice that both studies *can assign a date* to initial acceptance and that

[10] Suggestive attempts to classify innovations in this way have been made by a number of authors. See, for example, Homer T. Barnett, *Innovation*, McGraw-Hill, Inc., New York, 1953; E. A. Wilkening, *Acceptance of Improved Farming Practices in Three Coastal Plains Communities*, North Carolina Extension Service Technical Bulletin No. 98, Raleigh, North Carolina, 1952; E. E. Emery and O. A. Oeser, *Information, Decision and Action*, University of Melbourne Press, Melbourne, Australia, 1958; and Herbert Menzel, "Innovation, Integration and Marginality," *op. cit.*

it is the element of time, perhaps more than any other, which makes the study of diffusion possible. In the case of the farmers, the year of first use of the new seed was determined by asking the farmer. In the case of the doctor, this was done by means of an audit of prescriptions on file in all pharmacies in the four communities which were studied. The month in which each doctor's earliest gammanym prescription appeared was counted as the date of his "acceptance" of the new drug. Thus the drug study had the unique opportunity of obtaining an *objective* measure of past performance by virtue of the availability of the written record of prescriptions, while the hybrid corn study relied on *subjective* recall.[11] But what is of fundamental importance that both studies devised a method of measuring time; this is the major key to their comparability.

[11] The drug study also asked doctors during the course of the interview, to recall the date of their first use of gammanym and the discrepancies between the objective and subjective information were analyzed. The data reveal that doctors erred in both directions, but the marked tendency most doctors was to report themselves having adopted the new drug considerably earlier than they actually did. Nevertheless despite the tendency to "update" themselves, there is a positive correlation between the adoption dates obtained from the doctors and from the prescription records. See Menzel, Coleman, and Katz, "Dimensions of Being 'Modern' . . ." *op. cit.* although it is probable that farmers also have faulty memories, given that corn is the most important crop and that they were asked to name the *year* of first use, it may be that their errors are smaller than those of the doctors. On the other hand, the farmers were interviewed long after many of them had begun using hybrid corn, thus increasing the chance of error.

Channels of Communication

Both studies rely, at least in part, on the respondent's own ability to "reconstruct" the sequence of factors which influenced his decision. Yet, it is by no means clear how much trust can be placed in this ability—particularly when it concerns a decision which was made months, sometimes years, before. Essentially, then, there are two methodological questions which both studies confront at this point: 1) Whether respondents are at all capable of reconstructing the elements which go into the making of their decisions; and if so, 2) whether there is not a time limit on this ability.

Again, the hybrid corn study places more faith in respondents' testimony than does the drug study. Ryan and Gross say only that:

. . . the channels through which farm operators first learned of the new seed were undoubtedly more complex than the farmers themselves realized.

But they deal with them at face value nevertheless. And, in fact, a number of their findings with respect to farmers' use of the channels of communication have been corroborated by other studies.

The drug study, on the other hand, is much more skeptical. More explicitly than the hybrid corn study, the drug study makes an attempt to use more objective means to uncover the relevant influences operating on the decision to adopt gammanym. Along with the respondents' own testimony as to what influenced them, that is, the drug study analyzes variations in time of adoption as a function of the channels of communication to which respondents are *generally* exposed. This is a step backwards, in one sense, since the correlation between, say, amount of journal reading and time of adoption raises problems of interpretation which need not be raised in the case of subjective retrospection. Similarly, it is impossible to get at the *sequence* of media-use by means of this method. On the other hand, however, despite the added risks of inference-making, there is reason to believe that this method produces results which would otherwise go undetected.[12]

Among the channels of communication are included such impersonal media as journals, direct mail advertising, and the like, and such personal ones as salesmen and colleagues. As has already been pointed out, both studies made special provision for taking account of the possible influence of neighbors and colleagues in the decision to adopt.

Social Structure

Social structure figures in a variety of different, although interrelated, ways in the sociological study of diffusion. Most basic, perhaps, is the fact that

[12] Ryan and Gross employ this kind of correlational analysis, too. For example, they inquire concerning reading habits in much the way the drug study does and they find, as the drug study does, that early and late adopters are noticeably different in their communications behavior. Their tendency, however, is to interpret such results as if they were part of the set of factors predisposing respondents to early or late adoption, rather than direct influences on the specific decision being studied. The drug study does this and more; it tries in certain instances, to establish a causal link between exposure to certain media and the specific decision to adopt—even though the respondent does not mention this medium in the "reconstruction" of his decision.

social structures serve as boundaries within which innovations spread. Thus, one can compare the extent or the speed or the sequence of penetration of a given innovation within different neighborhoods, or social classes, or adolescent gangs.[13] Differential rates of penetration can then be accounted for in the light of other elements which distinguish among social structures; social norms, for example, or different degrees of social integration, or status variations within some larger social structure.

Within a given structure, of course, individuals can be differentially "located" with respect to their statuses, relative integration, or the like. One can then examine the different responses to innovation characteristic of individuals in varying structural locations.[14]

Finally, social structures may also be seen as networks of interpersonal communication and, in this sense, obviously, the concern for channels of communication and for social structure coincides. Given this kind of social network, that is, one would want to trace the social itinerary of an innovation as it proceeds over time.[15] A child may not be able to "reconstruct" how he got the measles, but locating children with respect to their social structures— schools, friendship, community centers, etc.—will provide a good picture of the process of "social contagion," the relevant networks of communication within a structure and the comparative importance of different structures (school vs. community center, for example).

---

[13] For good examples, see Stuart C. Dodd, "Formulas for Spreading Opinions," *Public Opinion Quarterly*, XXII (Winter, 1958–1959), 537–554, and more impressionistically, William H. Whyte, Jr., "The Web of Word of Mouth," *Fortune* (November, 1954). The Swedish geographer Torsten Hagerstrand has mapped the spread of an innovation from urban centers to outlying districts, etc., emphasizing the role of social contacts within given localities. See, "The Propagation of Innovation Waves," *Land Studies in Geography*, No. 4, The Royal University of Lund, Sweden, 1952.

[14] See Public Administration Clearing House, "Experiences of Personnel of U.S. Voluntary Agencies," *Economic Development and Cultural Change*, II (June, 1954), 29–349. This presumes that group norms bind the more integrated members of a group more than the more marginal members and, hence, that group leaders are the most conformist members of their groups. For evidence concerning the relevance of this hypothesis for response to innovation,

see C. Paul Marsh and A. Lee Coleman, "Group Influences and Agricultural Innovations: Some Tentative Findings and Hypotheses," *American Journal of Sociology*, LXI (May, 1956), 588–594.

[15] Several studies have proceeded from a sociogram of friendship to map the flow of rumor. See Jacob L. Moreno, *Who Shall Survive*, Beacon House, Beacon, New York, 1953, pp. 440–450; Leon Festinger et al., *Social Pressures in Informal Groups*, Harper & Row, Publishers, New York, 1950, Chap. 7; Back et al., "A Method for Studying Rumor Transmission," in Leon Festinger et al., (eds.), *Theory and Experiment in Social Communication*, Research Center for Group Dynamics, University of Michigan, Ann Arbor, Mich., 1950. In the field of rural sociology, the most intensive analysis of the process of information diffusion within and between informal social structures has been the work of H. F. Lionberger. See, especially, Lionberger and Coughenor, *Social Structure and Diffusion of Farm Information*, Agricultural Experiment Station, College of Agriculture, Research Bulletin 631, University of Missouri, Columbia, Missouri, 1957, and the articles on this study in *Rural Sociology*, XIX (September and December, 1954), 233–344, 377–384.

Rather than interview a random sample of doctors, it was decided, in the drug study, to interview *all* doctors for whose practices the new drug was relevant. In addition to the usual questions concerning personal attributes, attitudes, communications behavior, etc., each doctor was also asked to name: 1) his three best physician friends; 2) the three or four physicians with whom he most often finds himself discussing cases or therapy; and 3) the colleagues on whom he most frequently calls when in need of special information or advice on questions of drug therapy. Thus, each doctor could be located with respect to the structures of friendship, case discussion, and advice, and within each of these structures, the doctor could be rated in terms of: 1) his relative integration or popularity—that is, *how many* of his colleagues designated him, and 2) his particular network of association—that is, *which* of his colleagues named him. Thus, sociometry provides one means for mapping the structure of interpersonal relations in order to determine their impact on individuals occupying different positions within them and to examine their role as potential paths for the flow of innovation.

The hybrid corn study also interviewed all the members of the two communities which were studied. But there is no sign that this aspect of the research design was put to use in determining the structure of social relations. Instead, information was simply collected from all community members as if they were unrelated respondents in a random sample. Attempts to map individual location within the social structure were made in more conventional ways. Respondents were asked

to indicate the organizations to which they belonged, the extent of their contacts outside the community, the number of neighbors whom they visited, etc. Nevertheless, the authors of the hybrid-corn study are keenly aware of the potential relevance of social relational variables and, indeed, explicitly regret not having designed adequate measures of social participation:

. . . due mainly to the great difficulty in devising them.[16]

The Findings of the Two Studies

Having noted the similarities in the design of the two studies, let us now compare some of the findings. This second section of the article will be concerned with the extent to which the empirical generalizations emerging from one study find support in the other. For, in a very real sense, these studies may be viewed as replications of each other.

We will proceed, point by point, to analyze their similarities and differences. But it will become apparent readily that there is a theoretical thread which connects these diverse points; it is a concern for the processes of interpersonal influence which figured so prominently in the diffusion of these two innovations.

1. THE RATE OF DIFFUSION

If the cumulative proportion of acceptors of hybrid seed is plotted over the ten-year period from its earliest adoption to the time when virtually all community members had tried it, the curve is S-shaped, indicating that: 1)

[16] Ryan and Gross, "Adoption and Diffusion . . .," *op. cit.*, 707, footnote 62.

there was an early period of adoption when a few pioneering farmers gradually tried the innovation; 2) a rapid middle period when many people adopted close upon each others' heels and 3) a late period when even the die-hards gradually accepted. The S-shaped curve has been associated traditionally with diffusion phenomena and has been assumed to imply not only that there are characteristic stages in the diffusion process but, more important, that there is intercommunication among the population of adapters. Such curves suggest, that is, that the fact that others have adopted is itself a source of

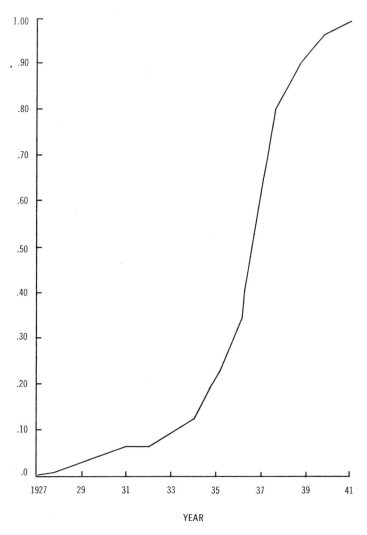

FIGURE 1. Cumulative Percentage of Farmers Accepting Hybrid Seed During Each Year of the Diffusion Process. (Adapted from Ryan and Gross, *Acceptance and Diffusion of Hybrid Seed Corn in Two Iowa Communities,* p. 672.) [Iowa State University].

influence making for further adoption. For example, if the "pioneers" who adopt an innovation immediately upon its appearance each tell their friends about it, and these friends subsequently tell their friends, and so on, the resulting curve of diffusion would look something like the curve in Figure 1.

Ostensibly, the curve of diffusion of gammanym (Figure 2) looks different. It shows that there was a rapid spurt of adoption in the months immediately following the release of the new drug which is described by the steep, nearly straight line reaching until the eighth month, during which period about two-thirds of the doctors wrote their earliest prescriptions. The curve tapers off

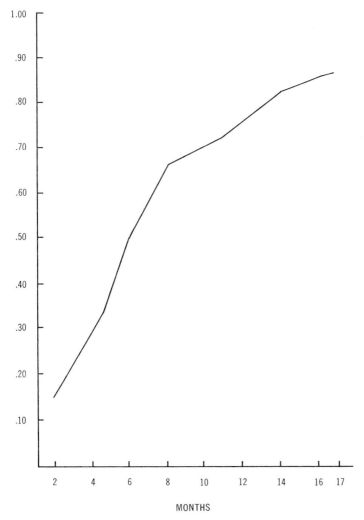

MONTHS

FIGURE 2. Cumulative Percentage of Doctors Accepting Gammanym into the Communities Studied over a 16-month Period (N = 125).

thereafter and in the remaining eighteen months another twenty percent of the doctors began using it, bringing the cumulative total of doctors who had tried the new drug to about ninety percent. It is fairly clear that this curve lacks the tentative phase characteristic of the early days of hybrid corn. Perhaps this difference between the two curves reflects the greater conservatism of Iowa farmers as compared with the doctors.

What is really important about these two curves is not at all accessible to the naked eye. For, despite manifest differences between them, the fact is that the drug study provides strong support for what the corn study could only hypothesize: that interpersonal networks of communication have an important share in the diffusion process. This can be seen in Figure 3 where the cumulative curve of gammanym diffusion is plotted *separately* for different groups of doctors, classified according to the number of choices they received as friends.

Compare the two extreme curves. The curve for the most "integrated" doctors continues steeply upward almost to reach its peak in the eighth month, while the curve for the "isolated" doctors rises at a constant rate. What is interesting about this is the fact that the curve for the "integrated" doctors can be closely approximated by a "chain reaction" model which grows as a function of the number of doctors who have already adopted. On the other hand, if one postulates a curve made up of a sequence of individual adoptions uninfluenced by interpersonal communication, one would approximate the curve actually obtained for the "isolated" doctors. This latter curve might

result, for example, from some constant stimulus—say, advertising—operating each month so as to influence a constant proportion of those who have not yet adopted. This would be the case, for example, if fifteen percent adopt during the first month, and fifteen percent of those remaining do so in the second month, and so on.[17] Unlike the social process of adoption, those who adopt in any given month are uninfluenced by those who adopted before they did.

In other words, the drug study argues that the curve of gammanym adoption is really made up of two quite different curves. One of these—that of the "integrated" doctors—resembles the S-curve of diffusion of hybrid corn in that both curves can be approximated by theoretical models based on the assumption that diffusion is a product of interpersonal influence. Thus, doctors who are close to their colleagues are, by the same token, also integrated into a powerful network of communication. Doctors who stand outside these relationships are apparently more individualistic (and slower) in their innovating behavior as well.

Diffusion curves are made possible by taking account, in the research design, of time-of-adoption and of social

[17] These matters are more fully, and somewhat more technically, discussed in Coleman, Katz, and Menzel, "The Diffusion of an Innovation . . .," *op cit.*, 256–262. This article also presents theoretical curves alluded to here. Note that only the factors associated with relative integration behave in this way. The curves which distinguish doctors who read many journals also distinguish between early and late adopters, but the slopes of the two curves are quite parallel. See the discussion in Coleman, Menzel, and Katz, "Social Pressures in Physicians' Adoption . . .," *op. cit.*, 13.

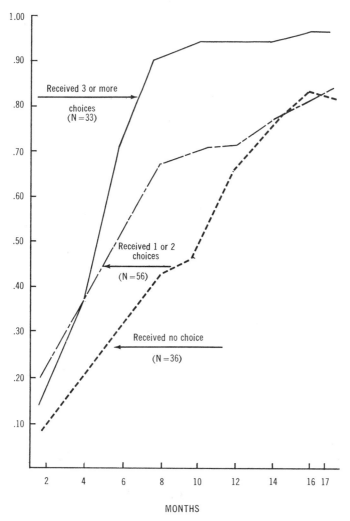

FIGURE 3. Cumulative Percentage of Doctors Accepting Gammanym over a 16-month Period by Number of Friendship Choices Received.[18]

structure (in the sense of setting social boundaries in terms of which diffusion is to be observed). The design of the drug study also called for classifying individuals in terms of relative integration in the social structure. Given these ingredients, it becomes possible to make *inferences* concerning the over-all importance of interpersonal influ-

ence in the diffusion process and its differential importance for individuals who are differentially "located."

[18] These figures have been corrected for seasonal variations in the general level of use of drugs of the gammanym type. The method employed to make these corrections will be discussed in the Appendix to the forthcoming volume by Coleman, Katz, and Menzel.

2. INNOVATION ON THE INSTALLMENT PLAN

Further evidence concerning the role of interpersonal influence can be inferred from a comparison of the degrees of caution exercised by early and late adopters in their initial trial of the innovation. It has already been noted that both hybrid seed corn and gammanym were not all-or-none innovations. You either purchase an air conditioner or you do not; you cannot begin with one part of an air conditioner, then slowly add more parts if it satisfies you. But farmers could do essentially just that with hybrid seed, and doctors could do it with gammanym. Planting hybrid in a certain percentage of his corn acreage or prescribing gammanym to a certain percentage of his patients, could constitute a sort of experimental trial for each innovator; then, if he were satisfied, he could add more.

This is, in fact, what happened. No farmer planted all of his corn acreage to hybrid in the year he began with the new seed. What is more, as Table 1

reveals, the earliest adapters were extremely conservative in the percent of their acreage planted to hybrid during the year of their initial adoption.

Something very similar seems evident among the doctors. By classifying doctors according to the date of their earliest prescription for gammanym and examining the number of gammanym prescriptions written by each doctor during the three-day period which includes his earliest prescription, it is possible to see whether the earliest doctor-innovators, like the farmer-innovators, are more conservative in the extent to which they adopt the innovation. The parallel is evident from Table 2.

Doctors whose initial prescriptions for gammanym appeared in the earliest prescription sampling period (one to two months following the release of the new drug) wrote an average of only 1.5 gammanym prescriptions during the three-day period while those who began in the following two months averaged 2.0 prescriptions, and so on. In other

TABLE 1   Median Percent of Total Corn Acreage in Hybrid by Year of First Use*

First Use	Percentage of Acreage in Hybrid during First Year
pre-1934	12
1934	20
1935	8
1936	20
1937	19
1938	25
1939	30
1940	69
1941	54

* Adapted from Ryan and Gross, *Acceptance and Diffusion of Hybrid Seed Corn in Two Iowa Communities*, Table 3, p. 680.

TABLE 2   Average Number of Earliest Gammanym Prescriptions by Month of First Use

Number of Months between Release of Gammanym and Month of First Use	Average Number of Earliest Prescriptions (3-day period)
1-2 months	1.5
3-4 "	2.0
5-6 "	2.7
7-8 "	2.6

words, the innovators, measured by *time* of adoption, seem to be conservative in the *degree* of their first use of the innovation, while those who are conservative in time of adoption appear to be bolder in their degree of first use.

This finding of the two studies suggests that later adopters could depend, in part, on the accumulated experience of the innovators. Ryan and Gross put it this way:

In a sense, the early acceptors provided a community laboratory from which neighbors could gain some vicarious experience with the new seed over a period of years.[19]

Thus, again—and from quite a different perspective—the empirical findings of the two studies appear to point to the relevance of interpersonal relations for the diffusion of innovation.

3. Information Is Not Enough

So far, we have been reporting essentially behavioral data relating to time-of-adoption, to relative integration, and to extent of first use of the two innovations. From these data, inferences have been drawn concerning the workings of interpersonal influence in the diffusion process. Now we turn to the respondents' own testimony concerning their

[19] Ryan and Gross, *op. cit.*, 681.

communications behavior. That part of the research design which is concerned with the channels of information and influence becomes relevant here.

One of the first questions which deserves to be asked in this connection is whether later adopters adopted late *for lack of knowledge* concerning the existence of the innovation. The evidence of both studies points to a negative answer to this question.

Ryan and Gross distinguished in their interviews between the diffusion of information and the diffusion of adoption. They asked farmers to indicate the year in which they first heard of the new seed along with the year in which they first adopted it. While they found that it took about thirteen years for news of the innovation to reach every single farmer, the spread of knowledge was, in fact, highly concentrated during a three-year period when sixty percent of the farmers learned about it. Perhaps the important fact, for the present purpose, is that while over ninety percent of the farmers had heard of the new seed by 1934, less than twenty percent had tried it by then.

The data from the drug study point in the same direction, although they are less vivid. The time gap between hearing and adopting was necessarily much smaller among the doctors, since the drug was almost completely accepted in the communities studied less than two years after it was announced. The curve of adoption follows the curve of hearing much more closely among the doctors than among the farmers. Nevertheless, particularly during the early months following the release of gammanym, there is a substantial difference between the proportion of doctors who had heard of it and the proportion who had tried it: About two-thirds of the doctors date their earliest knowledge of the drug to within four months of its initial availability, but only about one-third of the doctors actually adopted it during this period. In later months, however, the cumulative curve of adoption and the cumulative curve of hearing move much closer together and roughly parallel each other. In the case of the farmers, it appears that almost everybody knew before almost anybody had adopted, so that information does not even begin to explain the difference between early and late adopters. In the case of later-adopting doctors, however, adoption came relatively soon after obtaining information.[20]

[20] This is somewhat surprising in view of the fact that the drug company salesmen blanket a medical community quite early, and quite thoroughly, upon the appearance of a new drug. For this and other reasons, it seems likely that physicians knew about the drug earlier than they actually reported having heard about it. If this is true, it suggests that, whereas there is a tendency on the part of physicians to report an earlier date for actual use of the drug, there may be a tendency to report a later date for hearing about it so that the gap between hearing and action is shortened. This has not yet been looked into carefully and, of course, is difficult to check. For the

Nevertheless, there is a key of evidence which establishes that mere information did not constitute a sufficient basis upon which a doctor would decide to adopt, just as it was not sufficient for a farmer. The evidence is the fact that only about ten percent of the doctors reported that they had adopted gammanym after hearing about it from the source of information which brought them their first news of the new drug. In "reconstructing" the sequence of sources of information which had bearing on their decision to adopt, that is, doctors invariably named at least two, and usually three or four, such sources.

In other words, it seems reasonable to conclude that the availability of information that an innovation exists is not enough to make for its adoption. Additional factors must be sought, therefore, to explain the decision to adopt as well as differentials in time of adoption.

4.   THE IMPACT OF VARIOUS INFLUENCES ON THE DECISION TO ADOPT

Ryan and Gross report:

Throughout Iowa, the spread of information about hybrid seed became a major educational campaign in the thirties for both public and private enterprise. . . . Behind the hybrid movement lay not only the rational appeals and authority of research and governmental agencies, but also the initiative and ingenuity of private business interests.[21]

Almost one-half of the farmers indicated that a salesman brought them their first information about the new

moment, the data appear to imply that later adopters also heard about the drug later.

[21] *Op. cit.*, 682.

TABLE 3 Original Sources of Knowledge of Hybrid Seed and Most Influential Sources

| | Per Cent of Farm Operators Crediting Source with | |
	Original Knowledge	Most Influence
Salesmen	49%	32%
Neighbors and Relatives	18	50
Farm Journals	11	2
Radio Advertising	10	—
Extension Service	3	2
All Other Media	9	14
Total Farmers (100%)	(257)	(257)

Adapted from Ryan and Gross, *Acceptance and Diffusion of Hybrid Seed Corn in Two Iowa Communities*, Table 5, p. 682.

hybrid corn, as Table 3 indicates. The second sources of influence in degree of importance were farmer-friends and neighbors.

The drug company salesman was no less important for the doctor than the seed company salesman was for the farmer. Altogether, fifty-seven percent of the doctors indicated that the "detail man" had brought them their first information about gammanym. The only other source of any importance as a source of *first* news was direct mail from the drug company which accounts for eighteen percent of the doctors. Much less frequently did doctors name another physician (seven percent did so), or a professional journal (also seven percent) as a source of first information. (The picture is different for later sources of information, as will soon be seen.)

Both doctors and farmers typically went on to recount several other media as having been relevant—according to their recollections—for their decision to adopt the innovation. Although

neighbors were mentioned by farmer-respondents relatively late in the sequence of relevant media, when asked to evaluate the various sources in terms of their relative influence, neighbors were cited as more influential than any other medium (Table 3). Doctors, on the other hand, tended to evaluate salesmen as the single "most important" source followed by journal articles and colleagues (Table 4). But it is also clear that the commercial sources (salesmen and direct mail) lose in relative importance when source of first knowledge and most influential sources are compared, whereas sources inside the profession—journal articles and colleagues —gain.

The results of the drug study are comparable to the Ryan and Gross findings in another sense, too. This can be seen by examining the sequence of channels named by the doctors as having had a bearing on their decision, as is done in Table 5 for physicians (and they were in a majority) who named three sources or more.

TABLE 4   Original Sources of Knowledge of Gammanym and Most Influential Sources

| | Percent of Physicians Crediting Source with | |
	Original Knowledge	Most Influence
Salesmen	57%	38%
Colleagues	7	20
Direct Mail	18	8
Drug House Periodicals	4	5
Journal Articles	7	23
Meetings	3	—
All Other Media	4	6
Total Physicians (100%)	(141)	(141)

From Table 5 it appears that, while colleagues may not be important sources of *first information* about gammanym, they become increasingly important as *later sources* which come to *add* information and to exert influence. Thus, the table indicates that colleagues were, by far, the single most important "last source" of information prior to adopting the drug. Notice, too, that journal articles and drug house periodicals increase in importance over time, while salesmen and direct mail fall off. The suggestion of the table

TABLE 5   Sequence of Sources of Information Mentioned by Physicians in Connection with the Decision to Adopt Gammanym*

| | Percent of Physicians Crediting Source with | | |
	Original Knowledge	Additional Information	Last Information prior to Adoption
Salesmen	52%	27%	5%
Colleagues and Meetings	13	19	36
Direct Mail	22	16	14
Journal Articles	6	21	21
Drug House Periodicals	3	11	21
Other Media	4	7	3
Total Mentions*	(87)	(131)	(87)

* The modal physician named three or more sources of information and this table includes only the 87 who mentioned three or more sources. These 87 doctors named 131 sources intermediate to their first and last sources, and thus the middle column is percentaged so that 100% = 131 source mentions.

seems to be that the earliest source of information, the salesmen or direct mail, serves an *informational* role primarily but is not regarded as a sufficient basis for action. Before their decision to adopt is allowed to crystallize, physicians turn to less commercial and more professional sources such as colleagues, journal articles, and the quality publications of the drug companies. These appear to have a *legitimating* role; they indicate whether it is safe and right to go ahead. Ryan and Gross suggest exactly this:

Insofar as the farmers evaluations were accurate, it may be suggested that the diffusion agencies are divisible into two moderately distinct types: those important as *introductory* mechanisms, and those important as *activating* agents. Thus, salesmen were credited with informing the majority of the operators, but neighbors were credited with convincing them. . . . The spread of knowledge and the spread of conviction are, analytically at least, distinct processes, and in the diffusion of hybrid seed have appeared to operate through different although complementary channels.[22]

Recent work by other rural sociologists lends considerable support to this joint conclusion of the two studies. In general, it has been found that mass media serve to inform and that personal contacts are used to legitimate.[23] These findings seem to indicate that it is incorrect to view the media as essentially competitive. In fact, it may be that the search for the "most influential" medium is a fruitless one. It would seem that the focus should be the different uses of the media in varying social and psychological circumstances.[24]

Thus, the direct testimony of respondents in the two studies contributes further to a picture of the workings of interpersonal influence in the diffusion process. It adds to the inferences which were drawn earlier the notion that the diffusion process is rather more dependent on interpersonal communication as a source of legitimation than as a source of information. While the farmers' "reconstructions" of the channels of communication which figured in their decisions give major credit to interpersonal influence, the doctors mention this channel rather less prominently than the earlier data might have led one to expect. (The two sets of findings are not contradictory; but there is obvious need for research on the reconciliation of "objective" and "subjective" sources of data in diffusion research.)

5. COMMUNICATION BEHAVIOR OF EARLY AND LATE ADOPTERS— CONNECTIONS WITH THE WORLD OUTSIDE

The next question that needs to be asked is obvious: If informal interpersonal influence is so important, who influences the influentials? Assuming, for the moment, that it is the early adopters who influence later adopters, let us begin by determining who and what influences the early adopters.

---

[22] *Op. cit.*, 685.

[23] A good example is E. A. Wilkening, "Roles of Communicating Agents in Technological Change in Agriculture," *Social Forces*, XXXIV (May, 1956), 361–367.

[24] In this connection, see the new approach of George M. Beal and Joe Bohlen, *The Diffusion Process*, Iowa Agricultural Experiment Station, Special Reprint #18, Ames, Iowa, 1957; and James H. Copp, Maurice L. Sill, and Emory J. Brown, "The Function of Information Sources in the Farm Practice Adoption Process," *Rural Sociology*, XXIII (June, 1958), 146–157.

Since neither hybrid corn nor gammanym originated within the communities selected for study, an answer to this question will also help to locate the channels through which these innovations were "imported."

Turning again to the testimony of the respondents themselves, it is clear, from the hybrid corn study, that the innovators differed from those who adopted later by virtue of their greater reliance on salesmen. Later adopters mention colleagues far more frequently and more prominently and, hence, the picture of a "two-step flow" of diffusion suggests itself.[25] Hybrid corn was brought to the community by salesmen who were disproportionately influential for the early adopters, and the early adopters then were the primary sources of influence for those who followed them.

Again, the case of the doctors is less clear-cut. First of all, the channels mentioned by early and late adopters in their "reconstructions" fail to discriminate between them. From their subjective accounts, it appears that everybody, early or late, is exposed to much the same sequence of sources of influence. But then what explains the promptness of the innovators? The most persuasive evidence available tends to show that connections with the outside world do, indeed, influence the early adopters. In this case, however, the evidence is not based on the doctors' subjective accounts, but rather on the correlation of some of their known habits of communication and their early or late adoption. The innovator is more likely to subscribe to larger numbers of medical journals, for example, and this is so whether he is a specialist or not. The innovator is more often to be found in attendance at out-of-town meetings of medical groups; the specialty meetings, in particular, distinguish between early and late adopters. Moreover, early adopters of gammanym: 1) visit out-of-town medical institutions and teaching hospitals more frequently than non-innovators, especially institutions at which they themselves received their training, and 2) look to a greater number of out-of-town medical institutions as sources of their medical knowledge. In short, they are more "in touch" and, hence, more up-to-date than later adopters.

Looking at the matter in this way, of course, cannot establish conclusively that more extensive contacts with the medical world outside the local community "caused" the early adoption of gammanym. It might be that keeping "in touch" is but another reflection of the same underlying pre-disposition to be up-to-date professionally as is early adoption of a highly recommended new drug. Ryan and Gross, as a matter of fact, prefer this interpretation for their very similar findings.[26] They found that the earliest hybrid adopters (23 farmers prior to 1934) reported an average of 4.3 trips to Des Moines—the nearest urban center—in the year preceding the interview, whereas the latest group to adopt (17 farmers in 1940–41) visited Des Moines only 1.5 times during the same period. Trips to county fairs, too,

---

[25] The history of this concept is discussed in Katz, "The Two-Step Flow . . .," *op cit.* and its relevance for innovation in agriculture is discussed explicitly in Everett M. Rogers and George M. Beal, "The Importance of Personal Influence in the Adoption of Technical Changes," *Social Forces,* XXXVI (May, 1958), 329–340.

[26] Ryan and Gross, "Acceptance and Diffusion . . .," *op. cit.* 706–707.

differentiated among the adoption groups. And, like the doctor-innovators, farmer-innovators were disproportionately likely to be avid readers of agricultural experiment station bulletins and high consumers of mass media generally. But from these data for doctors and farmers it does not seem a very daring inference that during the course of these efforts to keep "in touch" one learns of many new developments. One gets "the word" concerning them. Contact with the outside world, then, seems to be characteristic of innovators in the two studies.

6. The Communications Behavior of Early and Late Adopters—Contacts with Colleagues

If the two studies are alike with respect to the differential contact of early and late adopters with the world *outside*, they appear irreconcilable with respect to contact *inside* the community. The hybrid corn study, as has already been indicated, finds that later adopters are more likely to indicate that neighbors had influenced them in their decisions to adopt. Furthermore, using the subjective testimony of the respondents concerning the extent of their "neighboring" as a measure of informal integration, Ryan and Gross find essentially no difference between early and late adopters in the extent of their *informal* community ties, although the early adopters are more likely to have been active in *formal* organizations of all kinds. Add to this the greater importance of outside connections for the innovator, and the resultant picture is one of a group of farmer-innovators who are oriented to connections outside their communities and who are proportionately more in-

tegrated in the formal organizational life than in the informal associational patterns.

At first glance, at least, this is not the case among doctors. The evidence of the drug study indicates that it was the *early* adopters who relied more heavily on their colleagues. In fact, the central finding of the study shows that integration in the medical community —measured sociometrically—is more closely related to time of adoption of gammanym than almost any other variable. And, unlike the relationship between outside connections and early adoption, in the present instance it can be shown that the fact of integration in the professional community "causes" early adoption via the intervening mechanism of interpersonal communication. Thus, it is evident from Figure 3 that the integrated doctors were the earlier adopters and, from the shape of the curve, one can infer that this is because they channeled the message through networks of interpersonal communication. Moreover, doctors who adopted early were likely to adopt the new drug "simultaneously" with a sociometric colleague. That is, if doctors are paired according to their sociometric partnerships, and if the date of adoption of each set of partners is compared, it is found that innovating doctors were more likely than later adopters to write their first gammanym prescription close on the heels of a sociometric partner who had already written one.[27] Later adopters, on the other hand, do not act simultaneously with their sociometric partners any more than would be expected by

[27] This matter is rather fully discussed in Coleman, Katz, and Menzel, "The Diffusion of an Innovation . . .," *op. cit.*, 262–268.

chance. The "togetherness" of the early adopters, it is argued, necessarily implies interpersonal influence.

Thus the two studies are hardly parallel at this point. The hybrid corn study finds that the channels mentioned by the farmers themselves distinguish early and late adopters; the drug study does not. The hybrid corn study concludes that neighbors are more important for later adopters than for early ones; the drug study comes to the opposite conclusion. The drug study finds that doctor-innovators are more integrated inside the community (just as they are more connected outside), while the farm study finds informal integration unrelated to innovating behavior. On the other hand, both studies find more formal affiliations—such as participation in hospital meetings, in the one study, and participation in organizations, in the other —to be positively associated with early adoption.

One possible approach to the understanding of these conflicting sets of findings emphasizes the special importance of interpersonal communication for early-adopting doctors as compared with early-adopting farmers. Innovation in medicine is risky business. A new drug represents a highly ambiguous stimulus to which the doctor is asked to respond without knowing all that he would like to know about it. In this kind of situation, communication among colleagues serves to spread, and thus to reduce, the individual risk. Talking over what has been learned about the drug through "outside" channels; evaluating it; deciding to adopt "together" and pooling early experiences—these are some of the functions of interpersonal communication among

integrated, innovating doctors. The data almost imply a kind of "group decision."[28] This is not to argue that colleagues were ineffective for later adopters among the doctors. Indeed, they are probably quite important for these groups—in much the way that Ryan and Gross found interpersonal communication important for later adopters among the farmers. The argument of the drug study, in fact, presumes that later adopters—particularly among the integrated doctors but to some extent, too, among the isolates— profited from the experiences of those who tried the drug earlier. The drug study, therefore, does not claim that interpersonal communication was unimportant for later adopters but only that it was unusually *important* for the innovators.

A second possible approach to an understanding of the two sets of findings focuses not on the different problems of innovating doctors, as compared with innovating farmers, but on the structure of *values* in the two communities. Ryan and Gross repeatedly emphasize that early adopters among the farmers were the vanguard of the secularization of rural life and:

... that farmers most emancipated from the traditional closely built neighborhood

[28] The role of interpersonal influence in ambiguous situations has been studied experimentally, notably by Muzafer Sherif, "Group Influences Upon the Formation of Norms and Attitudes," in Maccoby, Newcomb, and Hartley (eds.) *Readings in Social Psychology*, Holt, Rinehart and Winston, Inc., New York, 1958, pp. 219–233. The relevance of this formulation to other aspects of physicians' reactions to new drugs is discussed in Menzel and Katz, *op. cit.,* 344 and in Coleman, Katz, and Menzel, "Social Processes in Physicians' Adoptions . . .," *op. cit.,* 17–18.

life more easily emancipate themselves from a traditional technique. These innovators, with their far-reaching contacts, represent an antithesis to characteristic features of solidary primary-group living.[29]

This is not true for the doctors. Integration in the larger medical world and allegiance to the scientific values of that world are strongly consonant with informal integration in the local community of colleagues. Indeed, these two kinds of affiliations, although perhaps not wholly without conflict, are empirically correlated and tend to reinforce each other. The local-colleague group, that is, seems to be identified with the scientific ethic of the profession as a whole. Therefore, it is the doctors who are most integrated, both formally and informally, both inside the local community and outside, who are in the vanguard of medical innovation. There is no question for the doctor, as there is for the farmer, of emancipation from local primary groups as a prerequisite to the acceptance of innovation.[30] In a sense, there is a parallel in this approach to the finding, in another study, that informal leaders in farm communities which are

positively oriented toward innovation were ahead of the average community member in the number of recommended farm practices adopted, while the informal leaders of conservative-traditional communities were as far behind as the average member.[31] Where the norms of informal groups do not favor innovation, that is, innovators will not be found to be well-integrated members of such groups.

7. OTHER ATTRIBUTES AND ATTITUDES WHICH DISTINGUISH EARLY AND LATE ADOPTERS

A number of other factors distinguish early and late adopters and, although they do not bear directly on the role of interpersonal relations in the diffusion process, they are important for the comparative task undertaken here. One of the most interesting of these is the attitude of "secularism" which is invoked repeatedly in the hybrid corn study as a motivating factor in the behavior of innovators. It represents an openness to rationality rather than tradition as a criterion for decision making. The parallel among the doctors is the doctor with "scientific orientation," an attitude which also implies an openness to change. Thus, construction of an index of "scientific orientation" (based on doctors' concern with research, exchange of scientific information and scientific reliability of information) reveals that the more scientifically oriented doctors adopted gammanym earlier—this, despite the greater caution which one also associates with scientific orientation. Similarly, the innovating doctor is more "profession oriented" than "patient oriented." As

[29] Ryan and Gross, "Acceptance and Diffusion . . .," *op. cit.*, 707.

[30] Of course, there may well be types of innovation in medicine toward which the otherwise progressive norms of professional medical groups would be inhospitable. The history of medicine provides many examples such as those reported by Bernhard J. Stern in "Social Factors in Medical Progress," Faculty of Political Science of Columbia University (eds.), *Studies in History, Economics and Public Law*, No. 287, Columbia University Press, New York, 1927. See also Menzel, Coleman, and Katz, "Innovation, Integration and Marginality," *op. cit.*, for a discussion of different types of innovation in medicine.

[31] Marsh and Coleman, *op. cit.*

TABLE 6   A. The Design of the Two Studies

	Corn Study	Drug Study
A Specific Innovation	Hybrid corn	"Gammanym" (a "miracle" drug)
Time	Farmers classified according to own reports on year of first use	Doctors classified according to date of first prescription on file in pharmacies
Channels	Farmers' reports on the channels that influenced their decisions to adopt; farmers' reports on their general communications behavior	Doctors' reports on the channels that influenced their decisions to adopt; doctors' reports on their general communications behavior
Social Structure	All farmers in two Midwestern farming communities; individuals classified in terms of age, size of farm, etc., and in terms of their own reports concerning formal and informal integration	All doctors in four Midwestern communities; individuals classified in terms of age, type of practice, etc., and in terms of relative formal and informal integration measured sociometrically

B. The Findings of the Two Studies

Rate of Diffusion	Curve implies three stages in diffusion process; and operation of interpersonal influence	(Curve implies two stages?); curve for "integrated" doctors implies interpersonal influence; curve for "isolated" doctors implies individualistic adoption
Extent of First Use	Early adopters are conservative in extent of first use; later adopters, building on experience of their predecessors, give more acreage to hybrid in season of first use	Early adopters are conservative in extent of first use; later adopters, building on experience of their predecessors, write a larger number of gammanym prescriptions in month of first use
Channels of Information and Influence	Lack of information does not explain differentials in time of adoption implying that information alone is not enough to make for adoption	Only 10% of doctors adopt on basis of information brought by initial information source implying that information alone is not enough to make for adoption

TABLE 6   B.   The Findings of the Two Studies

	Corn Study	Drug Study
	Typical farmer heard first from a salesman, then talked it over with a neighbor. Neighbors were judged "most important" information source. Implication that commercial and formal sources "inform" while more informal sources "legitimate" decision to adopt	Typical doctor heard first from a salesman, then read about it in a journal and/or discussed it with a colleague. Salesmen were judged "most important" information source. Implication that commercial and formal sources "inform" while more informal sources "legitimate" decision to adopt
Communications Behavior of Early and Late Adopters	Early adopters read more farm bulletins	Early adopters read more medical journals
	Early adopters name salesmen as information sources more frequently than later adopters; latter name neighbors more frequently	No difference in recall of information sources by early and late adopters
	Early adopters make more trips to city, county fairs	Early adopters attend more out-of-town meetings
	Early adopters belong to more formal organizations; no difference in extent of informal neighboring	Early adopters more integrated than later adopters in informal friendship discussion and advice networks
Other Differences Between Early and Late Adopters	Early adopters more "secular" in attitudes; later adopters more "traditional"	Early adopters more "scientific" in attitudes; also more "profession-oriented" (rather than "patient-oriented")
	Early adopters have more corn acreage	Early adopters are heavier users of "miracle" drugs
	Early adopters have more income, more education	Early adopters have richer patients
	Early adopters are younger	Early adopters unlikely to come from oldest age group

compared with later adopters, he measures himself in the eyes of his colleagues rather than in those of his patients.

What personal attributes characterize the innovators? The early adopter of gammanym, first of all, was a heavy user of drugs in the gammanym family prior to the appearance of gammanym; the farmer-innovator, by the same token, had considerably more corn acreage than later adopters. Both farmers and doctors who adopted early tended to be of higher socioeconomic status than their fellows: the farmer-innovators had more education and higher incomes (although they were not significantly more likely to be owners of their own farms as compared with later adopters), while doctor-innovators were more likely to have patients of higher incomes (and, thus, presumably, to have higher incomes themselves). Nevertheless, as has already been pointed out, there is no *a priori* reason why economic status should have been associated with early acceptance of these innovations although new drugs, of course, are notoriously expensive and doctors with poorer patients cannot so readily confront their patients with drugs of this kind.

Farmer-innovators were young; doctor-innovators, while very unlikely to come from the oldest age group, were slightly more likely to be in the middle-age bracket than in the very youngest group.

A Summary of Similarities and Differences

Altogether, considering that farmers and corn seed were compared with physicians and drugs, the similarities in the findings of the two studies give strong support to a number of empirical generalizations.

The comparability of the two studies is made possible in the first place because both studies were designed to take account of the major components of the process of diffusion viewed sociologically. Thus, 1) both studies focus on a given innovation. 2) Both follow the spread of the innovation through time, by devising methods for assigning a date to each adopter's first use of the innovation. 3) Both studies are concerned with the channels of communication which carried news of the innovation as well as with the channels which carried word that it was all right to go ahead and try. And, finally, 4) both studies specify social structures within whose boundaries the innovation spreads and with respect to which individual adopters are differently "located."

Given this kind of research design, certain kinds of analysis follow directly. Thus, both studies plot curves of diffusion to map the spread of the innovation, over time, within the social structure or various parts of it. The authors of the corn study inferred from the curve that interpersonal influence would appear to account for the observed pattern of spread. The drug study went one step further and, by comparing the curves for "integrated" and "isolated" doctors, could show that interpersonal influence was operative precisely where it would most likely be expected—among the "integrated" doctors. Thus, the drug study was able to confirm and further to specify the conditions for the operation of interpersonal influence in the process of diffusion.

Similarly, employing the data on

channels of communication, both studies find that "information is not enough"—neither farmers nor doctors accepted the innovation upon first hearing. It was shown that there are media which typically inform a potential adopter about an innovation and that there are media which "activate" or "legitimate" the decision to adopt. The former tend to be more commercial and more formal; the latter more professional and more informal. The salesman is a key source of information in both studies; interpersonal influence among colleagues is a key source of legitimation. By cross-tabulating time-of-adoption and channels of communication, both studies find the innovators more closely connected to sources of information and influence outside the community. Innovating doctors make more trips to out-of-town meetings than do later adopters; innovating farmers make more trips to the city.

By cross-tabulating time-of-adoption and relative integration, the drug study finds that early adopters have relatively more contacts inside, as well as outside, their home communities; they are more integrated in informal social relations with colleagues. The corn study, however, finds the early adopters more "independent" of informal community ties. Two approaches to the reconciliation of the conflicting findings were proposed.

Whether these generalizations apply equally to the diffusion of other innovations remains to be seen, of course. Surely, the special characteristics of these innovations, the particular way in which they were marketed, the peculiar characteristics of the social structures into which they gained entry, must all have affected their social itineraries. Clearly, what is needed is a comparative study of innovation which will trace different innovations, variously classified, as they proceed through given social structures. Altogether, the aim of this article has been to contribute to the design of such research and to help sharpen the issues which must be confronted.

5.5 PERSONAL CHANGE IN ADULT LIFE

Howard S. Becker

People often exhibit marked change —in their attitudes, beliefs, behavior and style of interaction—as they move through youth and adulthood. Many social scientists, and others interested

From Howard S. Becker, "Personal Change in Adult Life," *Sociometry*, published by the American Sociological Association, XXVII (1964), 40–53. Used by permission.

in explaining human behavior, think that human beings are governed by deep and relatively unchanging components of the personality or self, so that important changes at late stages in the life cycle are viewed as anomalies that need to be explained away. They may trace the roots of behavior to personality components formed in early childhood—needs, defenses, identifications, and the like—and interpret change in adulthood as simply a variation on an already established theme. Or they may, more sociologically, see the sources of everyday behavior in values established in the society, inculcated in the young during childhood, and maintained thereafter by constraints built into major communal institutions. Like the personality theorists, those who use values as a major explanatory variable see change in adulthood as essentially superficial, a new expression of an unchanging underlying system of values. In either case, the scientist wishes to concern himself with basic processes that will explain lasting trends in individual behavior.

Both these approaches err by taking for granted that the only way we can arrive at generalized explanations of human behavior is by finding some unchanging components in the self or personality. They err as well in making the prior assumption that human beings are essentially unchanging, that changes which affect only such "superficial" phenomena as behavior without affecting deeper components of the person are trivial and unimportant.

There are good reasons to deny these assumptions. Brim, for instance, has persuasively argued that there are no "deep" personality characteristics, traits of character which persist across any and all situations and social roles.[1] In any case, it is clearly a useful strategy to explore the theoretical possibilities

opened up by considering what might be true if we look in other directions for generalizeable explanations of human behavior.

A good many studies are now available which suggest that an appropriate area in which further explanations might be sought is that of social structure and its patterned effects on human experience. Two of these seem of special importance, and I devote most of what I have to say to them. The process of *situational adjustment*, in which individuals take on the characteristics required by the situations they participate in, provides an entering wedge into the problem of change. It shows us one example of an explanation which can deal with superficial and immediate changes in behavior and at the same time allow us to make generalized theories about the processes involved. The process of *commitment*, in which externally unrelated interests of the person become linked in such a way as to constrain future behavior, suggests an approach to the problem of personal stability in the face of changing situations. Before dealing with these processes, however, I will consider a problem of definition which reveals a further influence of social structure, this time an influence on the very terms in which problems of socialization are cast.

The Eye of the Beholder

Many of the changes alleged to take place in adults do not take place at all. Or, rather, a change occurs but an optical illusion causes the outside observer to see it as a change quite different in kind and magnitude from what it really is. The observer (a lay-

[1] Orville G. Brim, Jr., "Personality as Role Learning," in Ira Iscoe and Harold Stevenson, editors, *Personality Development in Children*, Austin, Tex.: University of Texas Press, 1960, pp. 127–59.

man or a social scientist looking at the phenomenon from a layman's point of view), through a semantic transformation, turns an observable change into something quite different.

Take, for example, the commonly asserted proposition that the professional education of physicians stifles their native idealism and turns it into a profound professional cynicism.[2] Educated laymen believe this, and scientific studies have been carried out to test the proposition.[3] Observed changes in the behavior of fledgling physicians attest to its truth. Doctors are in fact inclined to speak with little reverence of the human body; they appear to be and probably are to a large extent unmoved in the emotional way a layman would be by human death; their standards are not as high as the layman thinks they ought to be, their desire for wealth stronger than it ought to be.

People describe these changes with reference to an unanalyzed conception of idealism and cynicism. It would not be unfair to describe the conception as the perspective of a disgruntled patient, who feels that the doctor he has to deal with is thinking about other things than the patient's welfare. The perspective of the disgruntled patient itself draws on some very general lay conceptions which suggest that those who deal with the unpleasant and the unclean—in this case, with death and disease—must of necessity be cynical, since "normal people" prefer what is pleasant and clean and find the unclean repulsive.

It is typically the case in service occupations, however, that the practitioners who perform the service have a perspective quite different from the clients, patients or customers for whom they perform it.[4] They understand the techniques used by professionals, the reasons for their use in one case and not in another, the contingencies of the work situation and of work careers which affect a man's judgment and behavior, and the occupational ethos and culture which guide him. The client understands nothing of this. In an effort to make sense of his experience with those who serve him, he may resort to the folk notions I have already mentioned, reasoning that people who constantly deal with what decent people avoid may be contaminated: some of the dirt rubs off. The client is never sure that the practitioner has his best interests at heart and tends to suspect the worst.

But why should we assess and evaluate the change that takes place in the doctor as he goes through professional school from the point of view of his

---

[2] This problem is discussed at greater length in Howard S. Becker and Blanche Geer, "The Fate of Idealism in Medical School," *American Sociological Review*, 23 (Feb., 1958), pp. 50–56, and in Howard S. Becker, Blanche Geer, Everett C. Hughes, and Anselm L. Strauss, *Boys in White: Student Culture in Medical School*, Chicago: University of Chicago Press, 1961, pp. 419–33.

[3] See Leonard D. Eron, "Effect of Medical Education on Medical Students," *Journal of Medical Education*, 10 (Oct., 1955), pp. 559–66; and Richard Christie and Robert K. Merton, "Procedures for the Sociological Study of the Values Climate of Medical Schools," *ibid.*, 33 (1958), Part II, pp. 125–53.

[4] See, for a discussion of this point, Howard S. Becker, *Outsiders: Studies in the Sociology of Deviance*, New York: The Free Press, 1963, pp. 82 ff.; and Everett C. Hughes, *Men and their Work*, New York: The Free Press, 1958, *passim*.

patient? Suppose we look at it instead from the characteristic perspective of the medical profession. If we do this, we find (as we would find if we studied the views of almost any occupation toward the institutions which train people for entrance into them) that medical schools are typically regarded as too idealistic. They train students to practice in ways that are not "practical," suited to an ideal world but not to the world we live in. They teach students to order more laboratory tests than patients will pay for, to ignore the patient's requests for "new" drugs or "popular" treatments,[5] but do not teach students what to do when the waiting room holds more patients than can be seen during one's office hours. Similarly, people often complain of schools of education that they train prospective teachers in techniques that are not adapted to the situation the teacher will really have to deal with; they idealistically assume that the teacher can accomplish ends which in fact cannot be gained in the situations she will face. They do not tell the teacher how to teach a fifteen-year-old fifth grader, nor do they tell her what to do when she discovers a pupil carrying a switchblade knife.

It is a paradox. In one view, professional training makes physicians less idealistic, in the other, more idealistic. Where does the truth lie? I have already noted that many of the changes seen as signs of increasing cynicism in the young physician do in fact take place. It can equally be demonstrated that the changes which make him seem too idealistic also take place. The medical

students we studied at the University of Kansas expected, when they graduated, to practice in ways that would be regarded as hopelessly idealistic by many, if not most, medical practitioners. They proposed to see no more than 20 patients a day; they proposed never to treat a disease without having first made a firm diagnosis. These beliefs, inculcated by a demanding faculty, are just the opposite of the cynicism supposed to afflict the new physician.[6]

The lesson we should learn from this is that personality changes are often present only in the eye of the beholder. Changes do take place in people, but the uninformed outsider interprets the change wrongly. Just as doctors acquire new perspectives and ideas as a result of their medical training, any adult may acquire new perspectives and ideas. But it would be a mistake to assume that these changes represent the kind of fundamental changes suggested by such polar terms as "idealism" and "cynicism." We learn less by studying the students who are alleged to have lost their idealism than we do by studying those who claim they have become cynical.

Even so, adults do change. But we must make sure, not only by our own observation but also by careful analysis of the terms we use to describe what we see, that the changes we try to explain do in fact take place. Parenthetically, an interesting possibility of transferring concepts from the study of adults to the study of socialization of children lies in defining the character of the changes that take place as children develop. Is it too farfetched to

[5] See Eliot Freidson, *Patients' Views of Medical Practice*, New York: Russell Sage Foundation, 1961, pp. 200–202.

[6] Becker, *et al.*, *Boys in White, op. cit.*, pp. 426–8.

say that the definitions ordinarily used are excessively parochial in that they are all arrived at from the adult point of view? What would our theories look like if we made a greater effort to capture the child's point of view? What does he think is happening to him? How does his conception of the process differ from that of the adults who bring him up and those who study his growing up?

Situational Adjustment

One of the most common mechanisms in the development of the person in adulthood is the process of situational adjustment. This is a very gross conception, which requires analytic elaboration it has not yet received. But the major outlines are clear. The person, as he moves in and out of a variety of social situations, learns the requirements of continuing in each situation and of success in it. If he has a strong desire to continue, the ability to assess accurately what is required, and can deliver the required performance, the individual turns himself into the kind of person the situation demands.

Broadly considered, this is much the same as Brim's notion of learning adult roles. One learns to be a doctor or a policeman, learns the definitions of the statuses involved and the appropriate behavior with respect to them. But the notion of situational adjustment is more flexible than that of adult role learning. It allows us to deal with smaller units and make a finer analysis. We construct the process of learning an adult role by analyzing sequences of smaller and more numerous situational adjustments. We should have in our minds the picture of a person trying to meet the expectations he encounters in immediate face-to-face situations: doing well in today's chemistry class, managing to be poised and mature on tonight's date, surmounting the small crises of the moment. Sequences and combinations of small units of adjustment produce the larger units of role learning.

If we view situational adjustment as a major process of personal development, we must look to the character of the situation for the explanation of why people change as they do. We ask what there is in the situation that requires the person to act in a certain way or to hold certain beliefs. We do not ask what there is in him that requires the action or belief. All we need to know of the person is that for some reason or another he desires to continue his participation in the situation or to do well in it. From this we can deduce that he will do what he can to do what is necessary in that situation. Our further analysis must adjust itself to the character of the situation.

Thus, for example, in our present study of college undergraduates,[7] we find that they typically share a strong desire to get high grades. Students work very hard to get grades and consider them very important, both for their immediate consequences and as indicators of their own personal ability and worth. We need not look very deeply into the student to see the reason for

[7] Statements about college students are based on preliminary analysis of the data collected in a study of undergraduates at the University of Kansas, in which I collaborated with Blanche Geer and Everett C. Hughes. A monograph reporting our findings is in preparation. The study was supported by the Carnegie Corporation of New York.

his emphasis on grades. The social structure of the campus coerces students to believe that grades are important because, in fact, they are important. You cannot join a fraternity or sorority if your grades do not meet a certain minimum standard. You cannot compete for high office in important campus organizations if your grades are not high enough. As many as one-fourth of the students may not be able to remain in school if they do not raise their grades in the next semester. For those who are failing, low grades do not simply mean blocked access to the highest campus honors. Low grades, for these unfortunates, mean that every available moment must be spent studying, that the time the average student spends dating, playing, drinking beer or generally goofing off must be given over to the constant effort to stay in school. Grades are the currency with which the economy of campus social life operates. Only the well-to-do can afford the luxuries; the poor work as hard as they can to eke out a marginal existence.

The perspectives a person acquires as a result of situational adjustments are no more stable than the situation itself or his participation in it. Situations occur in institutions: stable institutions provide stable situations in which little change takes place. When the institutions themselves change, the situations they provide for their participants shift and necessitate development of new patterns of belief and action. When, for instance, a university decides to up-grade its academic program and begins to require more and different kinds of work from its students, they must adjust to the new contingencies with which the change confronts them.

Similarly, if an individual moves in and out of given situations, is a transient rather than a long-term participant, his perspectives will shift with his movement. Wheeler has shown that prisoners become more "prisonized" the longer they are in prison; they are more likely to make decisions on the basis of criminal than of law-abiding values. But he has also shown that if you analyze prisoners' responses by time still to be served, they become more law-abiding the nearer they approach release.[8] This may be interpreted as a situational shift. The prisoner is frequently sorry that he has been caught and is in a mood to give up crime; he tends to respect law-abiding values. But when he enters prison he enters an institution which, in its lower reaches, is dominated by men wedded to criminal values. Studies of prisons have shown that the most influential prisoners tend to have stable criminal orientations and that inmate society is dominated by these perspectives.[9] In order to "make out" in the prison, the new inmate discovers that he must make his peace with this criminally oriented social structure, and he does. As he approaches release, however, he

[8] Stanton Wheeler, "Socialization in Correctional Communities," *American Sociological Review*, 26 (Oct., 1961), pp. 697–712.

[9] See Donald R. Cressey, editor, *The Prison: Studies in Institutional Organization and Change*, New York: Holt, Rinehart and Winston, Inc., 1961; and Richard A. Cloward, *et al.*, *Theoretical Studies in Social Organization of the Prison*, New York: Social Science Research Council, 1960.

realizes that he is going back into a world dominated by people who respect the law and that the criminal values which stand him in such good stead in prison society will not work as well outside. He thereupon begins to shed the criminal values appropriate to the prison and renew his attachment to the law-abiding values of the outside world.

We discovered the same process in the medical school, where students gave up a naive idealistic approach to the problems of medicine for an approach that was specifically oriented toward getting through school. As they approached the end of their schooling, they relinquished their attachment to these school-specific values and once more returned to their concern with problems that would arise in the outer world, albeit with a new and more professional approach than they would have been capable of before.

We find a similar change in college students, when we observe them in the Spring of their last college year. They look back over the four years of school and wonder why they have not spent their time better, wonder if college has been what they wanted. This concern reflects their preoccupation, while in school, with the pursuit of values that are valuable primarily within the confines of the collegiate community: grades, office in campus organizations, and the like. (Even though they justify their pursuit of these ends in part on the basis of their utility in the outside world, students are not sure that the pursuit of other ends, less valued on the campus, might not have even more usefulness for the future.) Now that they are leaving for the adult community, in which other things will be valuable, they find it hard to understand their past concerns as they try, retrospectively, to assess the experience they have just been through.

Situational adjustment is very frequently not an individual process at all, but a collective one. That is, we are not confronted with one person undergoing change, but with an entire cohort, a "class" of people, who enter the institution and go through its socializing program together. This is most clearly the case in those institutions which typically deal with "batches" of people.[10] Schools are perhaps the best example, taking in a class of students each year or semester who typically go through the entire training program as a unit, leaving together at the end of their training.

But situational adjustment may have a collective character even where people are not processed in groups. The individual enters the institution alone, or with a small group, but joins a larger group there already, who stand ready to tell him how it is and what he should do, and he will be followed by others for whom he will perform the same good turn.[11] In institutions where people are acted upon in groups by socializing agents, much of the change that takes place—the motivation for it

---

[10] See Erving Goffman's use of this idea in *Asylums: Essays on the Social Situation of Mental Patients and Other Inmates*, New York: Doubleday and Company, Inc., 1961, pp. 6 and *passim*.

[11] See Anselm L. Strauss, *Mirrors and Masks: The Search for Identity*, New York: The Free Press, 1959; and Howard S. Becker and Amselm L. Strauss, "Careers, Personality and Adult Socialization," *American Journal of Sociology*, 62 (Nov., 1956), pp. 253–63.

and the perceived desirability of different modes of change—cannot be traced to the predilections of the individual. It is, instead, a function of the interpretive response made by the entire group, the consensus the group reaches with respect to its problems.

The guidelines for our analysis can be found in Sumner's analysis of the development of folkways.[12] A group finds itself sharing a common situation and common problems. Various members of the group experiment with possible solutions to those problems and report their experiences to their fellows. In the course of their collective discussion, the members of the group arrive at a definition of the situation, its problems and possibilities, and develop consensus as to the most appropriate and efficient ways of behaving. This consensus thenceforth constrains the activities of individual members of the group, who will probably act on it, given the opportunity.

The collective character of socialization processes has a profound effect on their consequences. Because the solutions the group reaches have, for the individual being socialized, the character of "what everyone knows to be true," he tends to accept them. Random variation in responses that might arise from differences in prior experiences is drastically reduced. Medical students, for instance, began their training with a variety of perspectives on how one ought to approach academic assignments. The pressure generated by their inability to handle the tremendous amount of work given them in the first year anatomy course forced them to adopt collectively one of the many possible solutions to the problem, that of orienting their studying to learning what the faculty was likely to ask about on examinations. (Where the situation does not coerce a completely collective response, variation due to differences in background and experience remains. Irwin and Cressey[13] argue that the behavior of prisoners, both in prison and after release, varies depending on whether the convict was previously a member of the criminal underworld.)

In addition, where the response to problematic situations is collective, members of the group involved develop group loyalties that become part of the environment they must adjust to. Industrial workers are taught by their colleagues to restrict production in order that an entire work group may not be held to the higher production standard one or two people might be able to manage.[14] Medical students, similarly, find that they will only make it harder for others, and eventually for themselves, if they work too hard and "produce" too much.[15]

[12] William Graham Sumner, *Folkways*, Boston: Ginn and Company, 1907. See also Albert K. Cohen, *Delinquent Boys: The Culture of a Gang*, New York: The Free Press, 1955; and Richard A. Cloward and Lloyd E. Ohlin, *Delinquency and Opportunity: A Theory of Delinquent Gangs*, New York: The Free Press, 1960.

[13] John Irwin and Donald R. Cressey, "Thieves, Convicts and the Inmate Culture," *Social Problems*, 10 (Fall, 1962), pp. 142–55. See also Howard S. Becker and Blanche Geer, "Latent Culture: A Note on the Theory of Latent Social Roles," *Administrative Science Quarterly*, 5 (Sept., 1960), pp. 304–13.

[14] Donald Roy, "Quota Restriction and Goldbricking in a Machine Shop," *American Journal of Sociology*, 57 (Mar., 1952), pp. 427–42.

[15] Becker, *et al.*, *Boys in White*, pp. 297–312.

One major consequence of the collective character of situational adjustment, a result of the factors just mentioned, is that the group being socialized is able to deviate much more from the standards set by those doing the socializing than would be possible for an individual. Where an individual might feel that his deviant response was idiosyncratic, and thus be open to persuasion to change it, the member of a group knows that there are many who think and act just as he does and is therefore more resistant to pressure and propaganda. A person being socialized alone, likewise, is freer to change his ways than one who is constrained by his loyalties to fellow trainees.

If we use situational adjustment as an explanation for changes in persons during adulthood, the most interesting cases for analysis are the negative cases, those instances in which people do not adjust appropriately to the norms implicit or explicit in the situation. For not everyone adjusts to the kind of major situational forces I have been discussing. Some prison inmates never take on criminal values; some college students fail to adopt campus values and therefore do not put forth their full effort in the pursuit of grades. In large part, cases in which it appears that people are not adjusting to situational pressures are cases in which closer analysis reveals that the situation is actually not the same for everyone involved in the institution. A job in the library may effectively remove the prisoner from the control of more criminally oriented prisoners; *his* situation does not constrain him to adopt criminal values. The political rewards owed a student's living group may require a campus organization to give him an office his grade point average would otherwise make it difficult for him to attain.

More generally, it is often the case that subgroups in an institution will often have somewhat different life situations. College, for instance, is clearly one thing for men, another for women; one thing for members of fraternities and sororities, another for independents. We only rarely find an institution as monolithic as the medical school, in which the environment is, especially during the first two years, exactly alike for everyone. So we must make sure that we have discovered the effective environment of those whose personal development we want to understand.

Even after removing the variation in personal change due to variation in the situation, we will find a few cases in which people sturdily resist situational pressures. Here we can expect to find a corresponding weakness in the desire to remain in the situation or to do well in it, or a determination to remain in the situation only on one's terms or as long as one can get what one wants out of it. Many institutions have enough leeway built into them for a clever and determined operator to survive without much adjustment.

Commitment

The process of situational adjustment allows us to account for the changes people undergo as they move through various situations in their adult life. But we also know that people exhibit some consistency as they move from situation to situation. Their behavior is not infinitely mutable, they are not infinitely flexible. How can we account for the consistency we observe?

Social scientists have increasingly turned to the concept of commitment for an explanation of personal consistency in situations which offer conflicting directives. The term has been used to describe a great variety of social-psychological mechanisms, such a variety that it has no stable meaning. Nevertheless, I think we can isolate at least one process referred to by the term commitment, a process which will help explain a great deal of behavioral consistency.[16]

Briefly, we say a person is committed when we observe him pursuing a consistent line of activity in a sequence of varied situations. Consistent activity persists over time. Further, even though the actor may engage in a variety of disparate acts, he sees them as essentially consistent; from his point of view they serve him in pursuit of the same goal. Finally, it is a distinguishing mark of commitment that the actor rejects other situationally feasible alternatives, choosing from among the available courses of action that which best suits his purpose. In so doing, he often ignores the principle of situational adjustment, pursuing his consistent line of activity in the face of a short-term loss.

The process of commitment consists in the linking of previously extraneous and irrelevant lines of action and sets of rewards to a particular line of action under study. If, for instance, a person refuses to change jobs, even though the new job would offer him a higher salary and better working conditions, we should suspect that his decision is a result of commitment, that other sets of rewards than income and working conditions have become attached to his present job so that it would be too painful for him to change. He may have a large pension at stake, which he will lose if he moves; he may dread the cost of making new friends and learning to get along with new working associates; he may feel that he will get a reputation for being flighty and erratic if he leaves his present job. In each instance, formerly extraneous interests have become linked to keeping his present job. I have elsewhere described this process metaphorically as the making of side-bets.

The committed person has acted in such a way as to involve other interests of his, originally extraneous to the action he is engaged in, directly in that action. By his own actions . . . he has staked something of value to him, something originally unrelated to his present line of action, on being consistent in his present behavior. The consequences of inconsistency will be so expensive that inconsistency . . . is no longer a feasible alternative.[17]

A person may make side-bets producing commitments consciously and deliberately or he may acquire them or have them made for him almost without his knowledge, becoming aware that he is committed only when he faces a difficult decision. Side-bets and commitments of the latter type, made by default, arise from the operation of generalized cultural expectations, from the operation of impersonal bureaucratic arrangements, from the process of individual adjustment to social positions, and through the need to save face.

One way of looking at the process

[16] Howard S. Becker, "Notes on the Concept of Commitment," *American Journal of Sociology*, 66 (July, 1960), pp. 32–40.

[17] *Ibid.*, p. 35.

of becoming an adult is to view it as a process of gradually acquiring, through the operation of all these mechanisms, a variety of commitments which constrain one to follow a consistent pattern of behavior in many areas of life. Choosing an occupation, getting a job, starting a family—all these may be seen as events which produce lasting commitments and constrain the person's behavior. Careful study might show that the operation of the process of commitment accounts for the well-known fact that juvenile delinquents seldom become adult criminals, but rather turn into respectable, conventional, law-abiding lower-class citizens. It may be that the erratic behavior of the juvenile delinquent is erratic precisely because the boy has not yet taken any actions which commit him more or less permanently to a given line of endeavor.

Viewing commitment as a set of side-bets encourages us to inquire into the kind of currency with which bets are made in the situation under analysis. What things are valuable enough to make side-bets that matter with? What kinds of counters are used in the game under analysis? Very little research has been done on this problem, but I suspect that erratic behavior and "random" change in adult life result from situations which do not permit people to become committed because they deny to them the means, the chips, with which to make side-bets of any importance.

Members of medical faculties complain, for instance, that students' behavior toward patients is erratic. They do not exhibit the continued interest in or devotion to the patient's welfare supposed to characterize the practicing physician. They leave the hospital at five o'clock, even though a patient assigned to them is in critical condition. Their interest in a surgical patient disappears when the academic schedule sends them to a medical ward and a new set of student duties. The reason for students' lack of interest and devotion becomes clear when we consider their frequent complaint that they are not allowed to exercise medical responsibility, to make crucial decisions or carry out important procedures. Their behavior toward patients can be less constrained than that of a practicing physician precisely because they are never allowed to be in a position where they can make a mistake that matters. No patient's life or welfare depends on them; they need not persist in any particular pattern of activity since deviation costs nothing.[18]

The condition of being unable to make important side-bets and thus commit oneself may be more widespread than we think. Indeed, it may well be that the age at which it becomes possible to make lasting and important side-bets is gradually inching up. People cannot become committed to a consistent line of activity until later in life. As divorce becomes more frequent, for instance, the ability to make a lasting commitment by getting married becomes increasingly rare. In studying the possibilities of commitment afforded by social structures, we discover some of the limits to consistent behavior in adult life.

(It might be useful to apply similar concepts in studies of child socializa-

[18] Becker, et al., Boys in White, op. cit., pp. 254–73.

tion. It is likely, for instance, that children can seldom commit themselves. Our society, particularly, does not give them the means with which to make substantial side-bets, nor does it think it appropriate for children to make committing side-bets. We view childhood and youth as a time when a person can make mistakes that do not count. Therefore, we would expect children's behavior to be flexible and changeable, as in fact it seems to be.)

Situational adjustment and commitment are closely related, but by no means identical, processes. Situational adjustment produces change; the person shifts his behavior with each shift in the situation. Commitment produces stability; the person subordinates immediate situational interests to goals that lie outside the situation. But a stable situation can evoke a well-adjusted pattern of behavior which itself becomes valuable to the person, one of the counters that has meaning in the game he is playing. He can become committed to preserving the adjustment.

We find another such complementary relationship between the two when we consider the length of time one is conventionally expected to spend in a situation, either by oneself or by others, and the degree to which the present situation is seen as having definite connections to important situations anticipated at some later stage of development. If one sees that his present situation is temporary and that later situations will demand something different, the process of adjustment will promote change. If one thinks of the present situation as likely to go on for a long time, he may resist what appear to him temporary situational changes

because the strength of the adjustment has committed him to maintaining it. This relationship requires a fuller analysis than I have given it here.

Conclusion

The processes we have considered indicate that social structure creates the conditions for both change and stability in adult life. The structural characteristics of institutions and organizations provide the framework of the situations in which experience dictates the expediency of change. Similarly, they provide the counters with which side-bets can be made and the links between lines of activity out of which commitment grows. Together, they enable us to arrive at general explanations of personal development in adult life without requiring us to posit unvarying characteristics of the person, either elements of personality or of "value structure."

A structural explanation of personal change has important implications for attempts to deliberately mold human behavior. In particular, it suggests that we need not try to develop deep and lasting interests, be they values or personality traits, in order to produce the behavior we want. It is enough to create situations which will coerce people into behaving as we want them to and then to create the conditions under which other rewards will become linked to continuing this behavior. A final medical example will make the point. We can agree, perhaps, that surgeons ought not to operate unless there is a real need to do so; the problem of "unnecessary surgery" has received a great deal of attention both within and outside the medical profession. We might achieve our end by inculcating this rule as a basic value during medical training; or we might use personality tests to select as surgeons only those men whose own needs would lead them to exercise caution. In fact, this problem is approaching solution through a structural innovation: the hospital tissue committee, which examines all tissue removed at surgery and disciplines those surgeons who too frequently remove healthy tissue. Surgeons, whatever their values or personalities, soon learn to be careful when faced with the alternative of exposure or discipline.

Chapter 6

SYSTEMS IN CHANGE

THESE papers are threaded by a common notion of "system analysis." In system analysis, a high degree of interdependence of elements is assumed. In fact, even when the elements may not appear to be related, but do affect a phenomenologically different element, they may be treated as a system. Functional analysis in sociology and anthropology and analogous views in psychology share the same method of approach. In assuming or postulating that there must be some function for an observable element, and that the observer's job is to discover these functions at different levels, we open up new vistas for seeing how an organization operates.

E. L. Trist, in "Socio-Technical Systems," applies the model of "open system" to industrial enterprises in order to integrate the social human systems with the technical activity system and shows how spontaneous reorganization toward states of greater heterogeneity and complexity occurs while work goes on. Factors governing the "steady state" are located in both the internal and external environment. And, of course, the new state of the composite system acts back to affect its environment. The strategic reminder to be derived from this paper, a reminder necessary at least to behavioral scientists, is that major requirements in organization arise from the engineering and technical aspects of the enterprise. Another strategic consideration is that the process of organizational growth arises from system dynamics.

Clark continues the themes of organization and growth in his "Healthy Organizations." In exploring growth, he notes the operation of proactive forces in addition to the usally noted reactive forces. He defines as healthy any organization that takes into account and somehow integrates the equilibrium-seeking, reactive forces with the proactive growth forces at individual, group, intergroup, and organizational levels. His strategic contribution is his use of a multidimensional approach. This strategy is especially useful for those persons concerned with operating and managing an organization.

In "The Utility of System Models and Developmental Models for Prediction," Chin draws back from the observed behaviors of people in organizations to examine the mind-sets by which conceptualizations are organized, the models of thought. In skeletal fashion, the paper identifies the properties of a system model of analysis in contrast to a developmental model. In addition to presenting these well-known and often used models, he attempts to suggest some of the implications of each for the practitioner's conceptualization of changing. He goes on to examine the intersystem model of analysis as appropriate for planned change and for processes of changing where a change agent is related to a client system in helping to bring about change.

6.1 ON SOCIO-TECHNICAL SYSTEMS

E. L. Trist

My aim in this paper is to present a frame of reference within which industrial enterprises may be studied empirically—whether as wholes or as parts. This frame of reference has developed over a number of years between my colleagues and myself at the Tavistock Institute and has entailed a shift from looking at enterprises as closed social systems to looking at them as open socio-technical systems. That is to say, there has been a shifting on the one hand from thinking in terms of closed systems to thinking in terms of open systems; on the other there has been a change from a point of view in which enterprises were considered solely as social systems to one in which the technology is also taken into account and an attempt is made to relate the social and technological systems to each other. These relationships may of course be studied at any level: that of the individual, the primary work group, larger internal units involving various levels of management, and the enterprise as a whole. Several of us—my colleagues F. E. Emery and A. K. Rice, for example, and certainly I myself—have also come to believe that open system and socio-technical thinking imply each other in the study of the enterprise. If in this field of work one

From E. L. Trist, "On Socio-Technical Systems," an open university lecture jointly sponsored by the Departments of Engineering and Psychology at the University of Cambridge, 18th November, 1959. Used by permission.

starts on a piece of research socio-technically, sooner or later one finds one's self using open system theory, implicitly or explicitly. Similarly, if one's original approach to a problem is in terms of open system theory, our finding at any rate is that one ends up with a socio-technical rather than a purely social analysis. What I should like to see develop therefore is a general theory of the enterprise as an open socio-technical system—the present paper is offered as a contribution towards this end. The theoretical treatment follows closely that adopted in a joint paper by Emery and myself given to the Sixth International Congress of the Institute of Management Sciences last September, but much more research data will be presented than was possible on that occasion.

The analysis of the characteristics of enterprises as systems has, I would say, strategic significance for furthering our understanding of a great number of specific industrial problems. The more we know about these systems, the more we are able to identify what is relevant to a particular problem and to detect problems that tend to be missed by the conventional framework of problem analysis.

The value of studying enterprises as systems has been demonstrated in a series of empirical studies. Many of these studies have been informed by a broadly conceived concept of bureaucracy, derived from Weber and influenced by Parsons and Merton. These studies have of course conceived industrial organizations as social rather than socio-technical systems. The early Tavistock work is no exception to this.

Granted the importance of system analysis, and before considering social

v. socio-technical, there arises the prior question of whether an enterprise should be construed as a 'closed' or an 'open system', i.e. relatively 'closed' or 'open' with respect to its external environment. Von Bertalanffy first introduced this general distinction in contrasting biological and physical phenomena, one of the best accounts of his work from the standpoint of the social scientist being his 1950 paper on "The Theory of Open Systems in Physics and Biology", published in the journal *Science*. In the realm of social theory, however, there has been a strong tendency to continue thinking in terms of a 'closed' system, that is to regard the enterprise as sufficiently independent to allow most of its problems to be analysed with reference to its internal structure and without reference to its external environment. As a first step, closed system thinking has been fruitful, in psychology and industrial sociology, in directing attention to the existence of structural similarities, relational determination and subordination of part to whole. However, it has tended to be misleading on problems of growth and the conditions for maintaining a 'steady state'. The formal physical models of 'closed systems' postulate that, as in the second law of thermodynamics, the inherent tendency is to grow toward maximum homogeneity of the parts and that a steady state can only be achieved by the cessation of all activity. In practice system theorists in social science (and these include such key anthropologists as Radcliffe-Brown) have refused to recognize these implications. They have instead, but by the same token, tended to focus on the statics of social structure and to neglect the study of structural change. In an attempt to overcome this bias, Merton has suggested that "the concept of dysfunction—which implies strain, stress and tension on the structural level—provides an analytical approach to the study of dynamics and change". This concept has been widely accepted. But, while it draws attention to sources of imbalance within an organization, it does not conceptually reflect the mutual permeation of an organization and its environment that is the cause of such imbalance. It still retains the limiting perspective of 'closed system' theorizing.

The alternative conception of 'open systems' carries the implication that such systems may spontaneously re-organize towards states of greater heterogeneity and complexity, and that they achieve a 'steady state' at a level where they can still do work. Enterprises would appear to possess such 'open system' characteristics. They grow by processes of internal elaboration. They manage to achieve a steady state while doing work. They achieve a quasi-stationary, equilibrium in which the enterprise as a whole remains constant, with a continuous 'throughout', despite a considerable range of external changes.

The appropriateness of the concept of 'open system' can be settled, however, only by examining in some detail what is involved in an enterprise achieving a steady state. The continued existence of any enterprise presupposes some regular exchange in products or services with other enterprises, institutions and persons in its external social environment. If it is going to be useful to speak of steady states in an enterprise, they must be states in which this exchange is going on.

Now the conditions for regularizing this exchange lie both within and without the enterprise. Internally, this presupposes that an enterprise has at its immediate disposal the necessary material supports for its activities—a workplace, materials, tools and machines—and, no less, a work force able and willing to make the necessary modifications in the material 'throughout' or provide the requisite supports and to organize the actions of its human agents in a rational and predictable manner. Externally, the regularity of exchange or commerce with the environment may be influenced by a broad range of independent external changes affecting alike markets for products and inputs of labour, materials and technology.

If we examine the factors influencing the ability of an enterprise to maintain a steady state in the face of these broader environmental influences we find *first, with regard to outputs or exports* that the variation in the output markets that can be tolerated without structural change is a function of the flexibility of the technical productive apparatus—its ability to vary its rate, its end product or the mixture of its products. Variation in the output markets may itself be considerably reduced by a display of distinctive competence. Thus the output markets will be more attached to a given enterprise if it has, relative to other producers, a distinctive competence—a distinctive ability to deliver the right product to the right place at the right time. This idea of course has become classical in economics.

Next, with regard to inputs or imports, all may say that the tolerable variation in the 'input' markets is likewise dependent upon the technological component. Thus some enterprises are enabled by their particular technical organization to tolerate considerable variation in the type and amount of labour they can recruit. Others can tolerate little.

Two significant features of this state of affairs from the point of view of open system theory may be stated as follows.

The first point is this: that there is no simple one-to-one relation between variations in inputs and outputs. Different combinations of inputs may be handled to yield similar outputs and different 'product mixes' may be produced from similar inputs. An enterprise will tend to react in this way rather than make structural changes in its organization. One of the additional characteristics of 'open systems' is that while they are in constant commerce with their environment they are selective and, within limits, self-regulating.

The second, and no less important point, is that the technological component, in converting inputs into outputs, plays a major role in determining this self-regulating property. It functions as one of the major boundary conditions of the social system in mediating between the objectives of the enterprise and its external environment. Because of this the materials, machines and territory that go to making up the technological component are usually defined, in any modern society, as "belonging" to the enterprise and excluded from similar control by other enterprises. They represent, as it were, an 'internalized environment'.

Thus these—always, of course, from the social point of view—mediating boundary conditions of this internalized environment must be represented amongst "the open system constants" which, as von Bertelanffy suggests, de-

fine the conditions under which a steady state can be achieved. As the technological component plays a key mediating role, it follows that the open system concept must be referred to the *sociotechnical system*, not simply to the social system of an enterprise.

Study of a productive system therefore as an operating entity requires detailed attention to both the technological and the social components themselves both treated as systems. It is not possible to understand what is going on simply in terms of some arbitrarily selected single aspect of the technology such as the repetitive nature of the work, the coerciveness of the assembly conveyor or the piecemeal nature of the task. However, this is what is too often attempted. In the extreme case, of course, the technological component is entirely neglected. As Peter Drucker observes:—

It has been fashionable of late, particularly in the "human relations" school, to assume that the actual job, its technology and its mechanical and physical requirements are relatively unimportant compared to the social and psychological situation of men at work.

This is the inevitable end result of approaching the enterprise purely as a social system—and a closed system at that.

Even when there has been a detailed study of the technology this has not been systematically related to the social system but has been treated as background information.

In the earliest Tavistock study of production systems in coal mining it became apparent that so close was the relationship between these two aspects that the social and the psychological ould be understood only in terms of he detailed engineering facts and of he way in which the technological system as a whole behaved in the environment of the underground situation. We broke therefore with the earlier tradition of social research in his field and embarked on a systematic attempt to elucidate the relations between the social and technological systems, each taken as wholes, whatever he level at which the study was being made. We also related this level to at east the adjacent levels, above and below.

Though an analysis of a technological system in these terms can produce a systematic picture of the tasks and task interrelations required by a technological system, between these requirements and the social system there is not a strictly determined one-to-one relation but rather what is referred to as a correlative relation.

In a very simple operation such as manually moving and stacking railway sleepers ('ties') there may well be only a single suitable work relationship structure, namely, a co-operating pair with each man taking an end of the sleeper and lifting, supporting, walking and throwing in close co-ordination with the other man. The ordinary production process is, however, much more complex and there it is unusual to find that only one particular work relationship structure can be fitted to these tasks.

This element of choice, and the mutual influence of technology and social system, I will now illustrate from some of our more recent studies made over several years, of work organization in deep seam coal mining. The data which I have circulated are adapted from an unpublished monograph by Murray and myself.

Table 1 indicates the main features of two very different forms of organization that have both been operated economically within the same seam and with identical technology. [See Appendix at end of article for details of the composite mining system.]

The conventional system combines a complex formal structure with simple work roles: the composite system combines a simple formal structure with complex work roles. In the former the miner has a commitment to only a

TABLE 1   Same Technology, Same Coalseam, Different Social Systems

	A Conventional Cutting Long-wall Mining System.	A Composite Cutting Long-wall Mining System.
Number of Men	41	41
No. of completely segregated task groups	14	1
Mean job variation for members:		
—task groups worked with	1.0	5.5
—main tasks worked	1.0	3.6
—different shifts worked	2.0	2.9

single part task and enters into only a very limited number of unvarying social relations that are sharply divided between those within his particular task group and those who are outside. With those 'outside' he shares no sense of belongingness and he recognizes no responsibility to them for the consequences of his actions. In the composite system the miner has a commitment to the whole group task and consequently finds himself drawn into a variety of tasks in co-operation with different members of the total group; he may be drawn into any task on the coal-face with any member of the total group and do his share on any shift.

That two such contrasting social systems can effectively operate the same technology is clear enough evidence that there exists an element of choice in designing a work organization.

However, it is far from a matter of indifference which form of organization is selected. As has already been stated, the technological system and the effectiveness of the total production system will depend upon the adequacy with which the social system is able to cope with these requirements. Although alternative social systems may survive in

that they are both accepted as "goo enough" this does not preclude the po sibility that they may differ in effectiv ness.

Once the fact that there are altern: tives is grasped, the question natural arises of which will provide the opt mum conditions as distinct from thos which are just good enough. The desig and development of optimum soci technical systems becomes therefore field which is now open to systemati study by combined teams of engineer and social scientists.

In the present case the composit systems consistently showed a superio: ity over the conventional in terms c production and costs.

This superiority reflects, in the fir: instance, the more adequate coping i the composite system with the task r quirements. The constantly changin underground conditions require tha the already complex sequence of mir ing tasks undergo frequent changes i: the relative magnitudes and even th order of these tasks. These condition optimally require the internal flexibi: ity possessed in varying degrees by th composite systems. It is difficult to mee variable task requirements with any o:

TABLE 2　Production and Costs for Different Forms of Work Organization with Same Technology

	Conventional	Composit
Productive achievement*	78	95
Ancillary work at face (hrs. per man-shift)	1.32	0.03
Average reinforcement of labour (percent of total face force)	6	—
Percent of shifts with cycle lag	69	5
No. consecutive weeks without losing a cycle	12	65

* Average percent of coal won from each daily cut, corrected for differences in seam transpor:

ganization built on a rigid division of labour. The only justification for a rigid division of labour is a technology which demands specialized non-substitute skills and which is, moreover, sufficiently superior, as a technology, to offset the losses due to rigidity. The conventional longwall cutting system has no such technical superiority over the composite to offset its relative rigidity—its characteristic inability to cope with changing conditions other than by increasing the stress placed on its members, sacrificing smooth cycle progress or drawing heavily upon the negligible labour reserves of the pit.

The superiority of the composite system does not, however, rest alone in more adequate coping with the tasks. It also makes better provision to the personal requirements of the miners. Mutually supportive relations between task groups are the exception in the conventional system and the rule in the composite. In consequence, the conventional miner more frequently finds himself without support from his fellows when the strain or size of his task requires it. Crises are more likely to set him against his fellows and hence worsen the situation.

Similarly, the distribution of rewards and statuses in the conventional system reflects the relative bargaining power of different roles and task groups as much as any true differences in skill and effort. Under these conditions of disparity betwen effort and reward any demands for increased effort are likely to create undue stress. The undue stress created by conventional longwall conditions is in my view the major cause of the high absence rates commonly found among face-workers. Halliday, working on data collected in Scotland before the war, found the incidence of stress illnesses to be 2-1/2 times greater among miners than in any other occupational group in the insured population.

Table 3 indicates the difference in stress experienced by miners in the two systems. In a separate study made by Hill and myself in a steelworks, it was shown that once the role of stayer as distinct from leaver is accepted, the effects of work stress are reflected in temporary withdrawal of various kinds from the work situation and that all forms of absence are positively correlated. This gives the rationale for summing such figures in the present case.

I should like to pursue this question of stress effect a little further by commenting for a few moments on a special study carried out by Murray. . . .

The findings in mining were repli-

TABLE 3 Stress Indices for Different Social Systems

	Conventional	Composite
Absenteeism		
(Percent of possible shifts)		
Without reason	4.3	0.4
Sickness or other	8.9	4.6
Accidents	6.8	3.2
Total:	20.0	8.2

cated by experimental studies in textile mills in the radically different setting of Ahmedabad, India. In this case, the social scientist—my colleague A. K. Rice—had a role which enabled him to play a leading part with those concerned in designing the new socio-technical system. The idea I mentioned a little while back of system design teams including a social scientist is therefore already more than a mere aspiration.

However, two possible sources of misunderstanding need to be considered:

1   Our findings do not suggest that work group autonomy should be maximized in all productive settings. There is an optimum level of grouping which can be determined only by analysis of the requirements of the technological system. Neither does there appear to be any simple relation between level of mechanization and level of grouping. In one mining study we found that in moving from a hand-filling to a machine-filling technology, the appropriate organization shifted from an undifferentiated composite system to one based on a number of partially segregated task groups with more stable differences in internal statuses.

2   Nor does it appear that the basic psychological needs being met by grouping are workers' needs for friendship on the job, as is frequently postulated by advocates of better 'human relations' in industry. Grouping produces its main psychological effects when it leads to a system of work such that the workers are primarily related to each other by way of the requirements of task performance and task interdependence. When this task orientation is established the worker should find that he has an adequate range of mutually supportive roles (mutually supportive with respect to performance and to carrying stress that arises from the task). As the role system becomes more mature and integrated, it becomes easier for a worker to understand and appreciate his relation to the group. Thus in the comparison of different composite mining groups it was found that the differences in productivity and in coping with stress were not primarily related to differences in the level of friendship in the groups. The critical prerequisites for a composite system are an adequate supply of the required special skills among members of the group and conditions for developing an appropriate system of roles. Where these prerequisites have not been fully met, the composite system has broken down or established itself at a less than optimum level. The development of friendship and particularly of mutual respect occurs in the composite systems but the friendship tends to be limited by the requirements of the system and not to assume unlimited disruptive forms such as were observed in conventional systems and have been reported by Adams to occur in certain types of bomber crews.

The textile studies yielded the additional finding that *supervisory roles* are best designed on the basis of the same type of socio-technical analysis. It is not enough simply to allocate to the supervisor a list of responsibilities for specific tasks and perhaps insist upon a particular style of handling men. The supervisory roles arise from the need to control and co-ordinate an incomplete system of men-task relations. Supervisory responsibility for the specific parts of such a system is not easily reconcilable with responsibility for overall aspects. The supervisor who continually intervenes to do some part of the productive work may be proving his willingness to work, but is also likely to be neglecting his main task of controlling and co-ordinating the system so that the operators are able to get on with their jobs with the least possible disturbance.

Definition of a supervisory role presupposes analysis of the system's re-quirements for control and co-ordination and provision of conditions that will enable the supervisor readily to perceive what is needed of him and to take appropriate measures. As his control will in large measure rest on his control of the boundary conditions—those activities relating to a larger system—it will be desirable to create 'unified commands' so that the boundary conditions will be correspondingly easy to detect and manage. If the unified commands correspond to natural task groupings, it will also be possible to maximize the autonomous responsibility of the work group for internal control and co-ordination, thus freeing the supervisor for his primary task. A graphic illustration of the differences in a supervisory role following a socio-

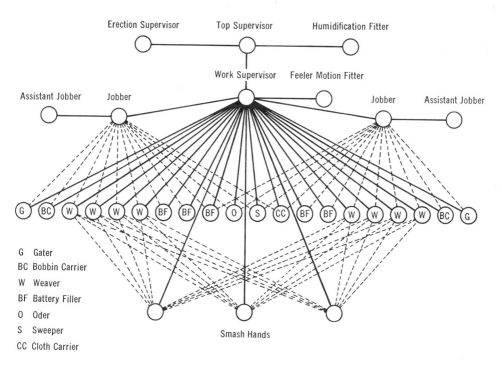

FIGURE 1. Management Hierarchy before Change

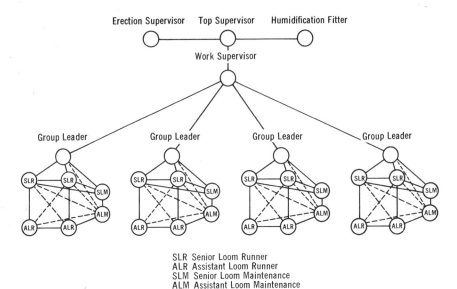

SLR Senior Loom Runner
ALR Assistant Loom Runner
SLM Senior Loom Maintenance
ALM Assistant Loom Maintenance

FIGURE 2.   Management Hierarchy after Change

technical re-organization of an automatic loom shed can be seen in the two figures attached: Figure 1 representing the situation before, and Figure 2 representing the situation after change.

This re-organization was reflected in a significant and sustained improvement in mean percentage efficiency and a decrease in mean percentage damage. . . . After certain setbacks which can be accounted for, the improvements were consistently maintained throughout a long period of follow-up.

The significance of the difference between the two organizational diagrams does not rest only in the relative simplicity of the latter (although this does reflect less confusion of responsibilities) but also in the emergence of clearly distinct areas of command which contain within themselves a relatively independent set of work roles together with the skills necessary to govern their task boundaries. In like manner the induction and training of new members was recognized as a boundary condition for the entire shed and located directly under shed management instead of being scattered throughout subordinate commands. Whereas the former organization had been maintained in a steady state only by the constant and arduous efforts of management, the new one proved to be inherently stable and self-correcting, and consequently freed management to give more time to their primary task and also to introduce a third shift, hitherto strongly resisted.

Similarly, the primary task in managing the enterprise as a whole is to relate the total system to its environment and is not in internal regulation *per se*. This does not mean that managers will not be involved in internal problems but that such involvement will be oriented consciously or unconsciously to certain assumptions about the external relations of the enterprise.

This contrasts with the common postulate of closed system structural-functional theories—namely that "the basic need of all empirical systems is the maintenance of the integrity and continuity of the system itself". It contrasts also with an important implication of this posulate, namely that the primary task of management is "continuous attention to the possibilities of encroachment and to the forestalling of threatened aggression or deleterious consequences from the actions of others". In industry this Maginot Line mentality represents the special and limiting case of a management that takes for granted a previously established definition of its primary task. Such managers assume that all they have to do, or can do, is sit tight and defend their market position. This is, however, the common case in statutorily established bodies and it is on such bodies that recent studies of bureaucracy have been largely carried out.

In general the leadership of an enterprise must be willing to break down an old integrity—even to create profound discontinuity—if such steps are required to take advantage of changes in technology and markets. The very survival of an enterprise may be threatened by its inability to face up to such demands, as for instance, switching the main effort from production of processed goods to marketing, or from production of heavy industrial goods to consumer goods. Similarly, the leadership may need to pay 'continuous' attention to the possibilities of making their own encroachments rather than be obsessed with the possible encroachments of others—on the Maginot principle.

Considering enterprises as 'open socio-technical systems' helps to provide a more realistic picture of how they are both influenced by and able to act back on their environment. It is a frame of reference which points in particular to the various ways in which enterprises are enabled by their structural and functional characteristics ('system constants') to cope with the 'lacks' and 'gluts' in their available environment. Unlike mechanical and other inanimate systems, they possess the property of 'equi-finality'; they may achieve a steady state from differing initial conditions and in differing ways. Thus in coping with internal change they are not limited to simple quantitative change and increased uniformity but may, and usually do, elaborate new structures and take on new functions. The cumulative effect of coping mainly by *internal* elaboration and differentiation is generally to make the system independent of an increasing range of the predictable fluctuations in its supplies and outlets. At the same time, however, this process ties down in specific ways more and more of its capital, skill and energies and renders it less able to cope with newly emergent and unpredicted change that challenge the primary ends of the enterprise. This process has been traced out in a great many empirical studies of bureaucracies.

However, there are available to an enterprise other aggressive strategies that seek to achieve a steady state by transforming the environment. Thus an enterprise has possibilities of moving into new markets or inducing changes in the old; of choosing differently than it has done from among the range of personnel, resources and technologies offered by its environment or of training and developing cadres and equipment. It can develop new consumer needs or stimulate old ones.

Thus, arising from the nature of the enterprise as an open system, management is concerned with 'managing' both an internal system and an external environment. To regard an enterprise as a closed system and concentrate upon management of the 'internal enterprise' is to expose the enterprise to the full impact of the vagaries of the environment. In several of the client organizations with which the Tavistock Institute has been concerned, we have encountered disastrous instances of this —some of them in firms which have made a specious hobby of good human relations as a defense against facing up to some of the more awkward problems of the business.

If management is to control internal growth and development, it must in the first instance control the 'boundary conditions'—the forms of exchange between the enterprise and its environment. As we have seen, mose enterprises are confronted with a multitude of actual and possible exchanges. If resources are not to be dissipated the management must select from the alternatives a course of action. The casual texture of competitive environment is such that it is extremely difficult to survive on a simple strategy of selecting the best from among the alternatives immediately offering. Some that offer immediate gain lead nowhere, others lead to greater loss; some alternatives that offer loss are avoidable, others are unavoidable, if long run gains are to be made. The relative size of the immediate loss or gain is no sure guide as to what follows. Since also the actions of an enterprise can improve the alternatives that are presented to it, the optimum course is more likely to rest in selecting a strategic objective to be achieved in the long run. The optimum strategic objective is one that will place the enterprise in a position in its environment where it has assured conditions for growth. Achieving this position is the *primary task* or overriding mission of the enterprise.

In selecting an overriding primary task of this kind, it needs to be borne in mind that the relations with the environment may vary with (a) the productive efforts of the enterprise in meeting environmental requirements; (b) changes in the environment that may be induced by the enterprise, and (c) changes independently taking place in the environment. These will be of differing importance for different enterprises and for the same enterprise at different times. Managerial control will usually be greatest if the primary task can be based on productive activity. If this is not possible, as in commerce, the primary task will give more control if it is based on marketing than simply on fore-knowledge of the independent environmental changes. Managerial control will be further enhanced if the primary task, at whatever level it is selected, is such as to enable the enterprise to achieve *vis-a-vis* its competitors, a *distinctive competence*. Conversely, in our experience, an enterprise which has long occupied a favoured position because of distinctive productive competence may have grave difficulty in recognizing when it is losing control owing to environmental changes beyond its control. Anyone in consulting industrial practice is only too familiar with instances of this kind.

As Selznick has pointed out, an appropriately defined primary task offers stability and direction to an enterprise, protecting it from adventurism on the one hand or costly drifting on the other. These advantages, however, as he illustrates, may be no more than potential unless the top management group of the organization achieves solidarity about the new primary task. If the vision of the task is locked up in a single man or is the subject of dissension in top management, it will be subject to great risk of distortion and susceptible to violent fluctuations. Similarly, the enterprise as a whole needs to be reoriented and reintegrated about this primary task. Thus, if the primary task shifts from heavy industrial goods to durable consumer goods, it would be necessary to ensure that there is a corresponding shift in values that are embodied in such sections as the sales force and design department.

A theory of enterprises as open sociotechnical systems must be prepared to look at these wide problems of top management just as much as at the more precise and restricted problems concerning primary work groups and departmental organizations. Though the bulk of this paper has been concerned with these narrower problems—because it is on these that most data is to hand—this survey would have been incomplete without at least a glimpse of the wider areas. It is into these areas especially, however, that social scientists must now seek to enter. From what experience I have so far had of them, I would say it is very difficult to get admitted, but, even more, once there, to understand what is going on.

APPENDIX

Characteristics of Composite System in the Seam

Work Method: The oncoming shift takes up the cycle at whatever point the previous shift left it and carries on with whatever jobs have next to be done.

Workmen: Multi-skilled miners, all qualified in filling, pulling, stonework and often also in drilling and cutting.

Work Groups: Self-selected autonomous teams responsible for allocating themselves to the various jobs that management required them to fill. Systems for the rotation of tasks and shifts among members used to regulate deployment.

Method of Payment: An 'all-in' flat rate plus a piece-rate bonus determined by cubic yards of coal produced. Common pay note divided equally among team.

Differences between Panels in Face Group Organization

NO. 1 PANEL	NO. 2 PANEL
'Face-wide'. Organized as two separate face teams.	'Panel-wide'. Organized as two main alternating shift groups over the whole panel.
'One-task' jobs: men tend to work at only one main task.	'Multi-task' jobs: men rotate tasks systematically and over time carry out a range of them.
Each work place and task 'tied' to a particular man.	Work places and tasks not tied to particular individuals.
Not customary for men to move from one work group to another.	Men move freely from one work group to another.

6.2 A HEALTHY ORGANIZATION

James V. Clark

What constitutes a "good" organization remains a matter of much debate. In this paper, I shall spell out my own current concept of organizational health and illustrate it by describing an organization I call healthy.

I consider an organization to be healthy if its members observe certain unstated but quite uniform codes of behavior which they accept as normal things to do, provided these codes produce behavior which allows all levels of the organization to meet two basic but diverse requirements—maintenance of the status quo, and growth.

Since man is a social being and business a group activity, the healthy organization must afford groups as well as individuals chances to fulfil their

Reprinted from the *California Management Review*, Volume IV, No. 4, Summer 1962. Copyright 1962 by The Regents of the University of California. Used by permission.

tendencies and capacities for equilibrium and growth. It must do this for the individual, for small groups, for inter-group relationships and for the total organization.

It goes without saying that each and all of these tendencies and capacities can never be completely and simultaneously maximized. That's not in the nature of things[1] but on balance and over time the healthy organization is one in which its component parts—group and individual—somehow manage to achieve an optimal resolution of their tendencies toward equilibrium (maintenance, homeostasis, status quo or call it what you will) and their capacities for growth (elaboration, complication, differentiation, negative entropy, or what not).

Before we go into particulars about the healthy organization, as I have just defined it, we must lay some groundwork. Let us, therefore, take a quick look at some of the different aspects of human behavior and some of the divergent ways in which these aspects have been studied. Then I shall illustrate these different aspects with common examples from business and everyday life. We will need, also, to examine what I mean by a norm which governs social behavior. After we have done all this, I will return to the subject of a healthy organization and try to show one in action.

Aspects of Behavioral Systems

For some time behavioral scientists have described individuals, small groups, intergroup complexes, total organizations and societies as systems, that is, "wholes," composed of interrelated, interdependent parts. Investigators have tended to concentrate on what could be called the "reactive" side of a system, which means that behavior which is analogous to a balloon returning to its original state after a finger has been inserted and withdrawn from its side.

More or less, these various investigators have played on some variation of Freud's "pleasure principle," that the primordial or initial principle of life is to reduce tension. Tension is said to be regarded as pain and absence of tension as pleasure. Individuals, small groups and bureaucracies have all been seen, in this light, as equilibrium-seeking, homeostatic, reacting, defensive, "closed" systems.

Recently, however, interest in so-called "open-ended" systems has intensified. Students regarding systems in such a light stress what might be called the "proactive" side of systems,

that behavior which is forward-pushing, growing, striving, learning, becoming. Such writers emphasize what are often called the "transactional" aspects of behavior—that as a system matures it enters into a more and more complex set of give-and-take relations with its environment, what Gordon Allport has described as "extensive transactional commerce."[2] Growth for a behavioral system, then, involves a greater complexity of relations with its environment, hence "open-ended" is an appropriate term.

While those who emphasize the "reactive" side of behavior often deny the "proactive" side and vice versa, many careful observers maintain that any system requires both aspects. A human being grows, but it also has a capacity to restore itself to health after an invasion of germs or injuries. A small group tends to perpetuate itself, but it also elaborates a complicated structure of power, interaction, beliefs, communication, and so on.

To me, any piece of organizational behavior tends to exhibit both aspects—reaction and proaction, maintenance and growth, even if one capacity is present only by virtue of its frustration. Hence, I will try to show that a healthy organization must somehow take account of both these tendencies. I have discussed briefly the attachment different students have had to these different tendencies so the reader may be on guard against any such parochial leanings in himself.[3]

Levels of Behavioral Systems

In addition to studying one or the other of these tendencies, investigators of behavior in formal organizations have often tended to concentrate on only one or two levels of investigation. This has usually been out of necessity, for one can't study everything. Nevertheless, the impression has sometimes been created that organizational well-being is arrived at only through satisfying individual needs, or small group needs, or by developing intergroup harmony, or by dealing rationally with only the formal organizational structure, or in some other partial manner.

As Koontz has illustrated, the "management theory jungle"[4] is peopled with schools of investigators which often center on aspects of administration and organizational behavior as if these aspects were the totality. It seems to me, however, that the different levels of organizational behavior are all in operation at any one time, and, in some sense, must all be taken into consideration. I cannot visualize a successful formal organization as one which attends only to individual needs for growth, or to small group needs for perpetuity, continuation and elabora-

tion, or to the total firm's needs for accomplishing its purpose to the exclusion of all else.

In summary, it can be said that, notwithstanding the historical preferences of different investigators, behavioral systems in formal organization can be seen on the different levels of individual, small group, inter-group and total organization, and exhibit both reactive and proactive tendencies and capacities at each level.

Behavioral Systems Illustrated

The different aspects and levels of organizational behavior are illustrated in Figure 1. In it I show a dotted line weaving back and forth between the two aspects of each different level, because it is almost always impossible to identify an instance of purely reactive or purely proactive behavior. As we shall show in succeeding paragraphs, what is apparently proactive behavior often has a hidden reactive meaning. I don't wish to claim or imply here, therefore, that a researcher or an ad-

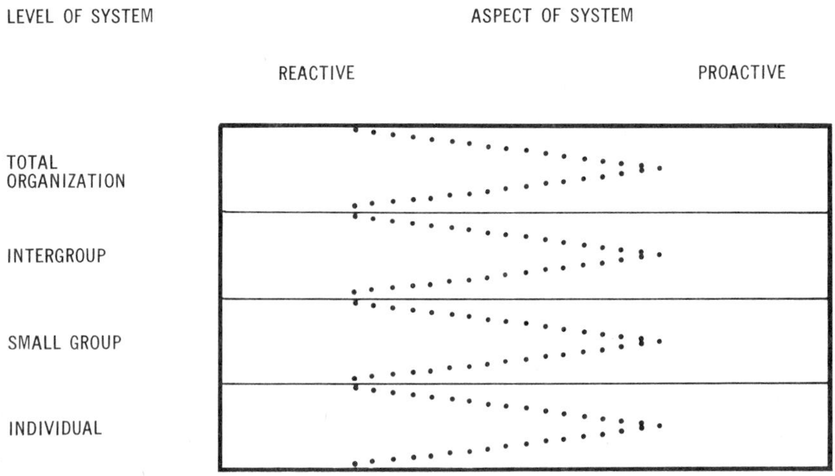

FIGURE 1.   Organizational Behavior

ministrator in an organization can categorically state what *the* meaning of a piece of behavior is. In fact, that's my point, one can't. Any piece of behavior always has a variety of meanings, and my thesis is that any organization to be healthy must recognize that variety.

To make these points clearer, I shall illustrate aspects of behavior that fit into the different boxes. Hidden meanings will not be alluded to in most instances since psychology and sociology have made us all generally familiar with them. I will, however, discuss such problems in relation to some of the boxes on our diagram, for these are places where we are not so accustomed to look for hidden meanings as we may be in individual behavior. Each of the areas in Figure 1 will be illustrated one at a time.

Individual Behavior

Instances of reactive behavior on the individual level are familiar to all of us. Typical examples are the student who defends his belief that he is an intelligent person by denigrating his professor's capacity to communicate, the professor who avoids examining his own capacity to teach by bemoaning the decline in student motivation over the past generation, the mother who maintains her self-concept as a loving person by decrying her inconsiderate children, etc. Such individuals are fending off new information which, if allowed to penetrate, would call for too radical a reorganization of the way in which they see themselves.

Proactive behavior on the part of an individual covers the whole range of human behavior designed to reorganize something in the self-world rela-

tionship. The ten-year-old boy struggling night and day to build something, the mother testing new ways of behaving with her children, the researcher trying to discover a new uniformity, the contemplative searching for a deeper understanding of man, nature, or God, the industrial worker designing a new tool bit for his lathe— all these show evidence of growthful, proactive behavior.

Of course, as any sensitive participant in human affairs knows, what looks like proactive behavior often turns out, on closer analysis, to have a strong reactive component, but such are the challenges and pitfalls confronted by those who choose to develop a science of human behavior— they simply cannot avoid the study of meaning. We will encounter this problem when I illustrate behavior at the total organizational level.

Small Group Behavior

On the level of the small group, an instance of reactive behavior is seen in the strengthening of shared beliefs and codes which occurs in a group when an outsider attempts to change it. Such behavior has been seen when industrial work groups face a methods man who has new ideas about how they should be organized, or when a branch plant management team receives new directions or a reorganization plan from headquarters, or when a group of high ranking military officers are visited by a critical congressman.

Outside of organizations, such behavior is encountered, for example, when an insensitive Easterner wears a suit and tie to a Los Angeles poolside party, or indeed when any representative of one culture encounters a group from another, and so on. Any group finds it difficult to assimilate such deviant people and behaviors and has an almost instantaneous reaction designed to restore its equilibrium roughly to where it was. At least the group members strive to establish equilibrium.

Proaction on the group level is seen in certain aspects of the behavior of a group of smelter workers recently observed by the author. One night this group sweated for an hour over 2000° molten metal to pull out a tool bit which would have left a trace impurity in the metal and for which they could not possibly have been held accountable nor received any credit for correcting.[5] This behavior was not called for either by their formal job requirements (technically, they were supposed to work alone) or their group norms to help one another with their work assignments, but represented a new pattern of behavior and beliefs not seen earlier in the structure of the group.

Something similar occurred in a freezing room group Louis B. Barnes and I studied in 1957.[6] This group of 5 or 6 workers in an ice cream plant spent nearly a year meeting at each other's homes to design and eventually execute a whole new methods handling system in their department. Their work went on unknown to management for months and involved new behavior patterns in the group and new effects on the group environment.

Such developmental behavior was also seen by Trist and his colleagues[7] among longwall method coal workers in Britain, when they were offered the chance to organize their own sociotechnological relationships. Similar de-

velopment was charted by Barnes[8] in an engineering group which was given comparatively high freedom to influence its own job structure.

Of course, groups, like other behavioral systems, will always tend to increase the differentiation of their parts through time. The rich rubric of social interaction which develops around betting, eating, coffee drinking, joking, and gaming rituals among so many white-and-blue-collar work groups in American organizations illustrates this. So one cannot say that group development always helps achieve management goals. In fact, it is only when certain specific variables are present that such activity will tend to become conscious and result in a group increasing its transactions with its environment.[9]

Intergroup Behavior

Reactive behavior on the intergroup level is seen when two groups increase their internal solidarity by facing each other, the "us" vs. "them" pattern. An individual member of one of these groups feels good to the extent he feels more securely identified with his group as it is different from the other group. As an example when a senator says to a large gathering of fearful and angry people in Los Angeles as he did, "Make no mistake about it, the Communists are black and all black. There are no greys among them," he is behaving in such a way as to facilitate the clearcut identification of one group against another. The bewildered and frightened people in his audience feel that they *are* something, and that something is "us" vs. "them." Much of what is called "bickering" between different departments of an organization—the classic disputes between sales and production, for example—can be viewed as serving this same function.

Professor Robert Blake of the University of Texas has illustrated reactive intergroup behavior dramatically in his laboratory simulations of intergroup conflict. Among other things, he has shown conclusively that groups in problem-solving competition situations inevitably pick their own solution as rationally superior to others, even in the absence of any rational criteria for making the judgment. Such phenomena are also encountered at the United Nations or around any labor-management negotiation table.

Proactive behavior between groups occurs when members break through their group boundaries and set up give-and-take relations between their group and another. Thus new patterns of behavior and beliefs emerge which change the relation between the groups. This was seen in R. L. Katz and J. A. Seiler's study[10] of the management organization in a 500-man firm, when individuals clearly emerged as linkers between groups. Of course, as expected, these linkers were almost never the people with the formal authority for relating the activities of the two groups. They emerged as the system matured, and they helped hold the total system together by relating its clearly differentiated subparts; and thus we are brought to the total organization.

Total Organizational Behavior

At the level of the total organization great complexity enters the picture. Reactive behavior of a certain kind is easy to identify. For instance, the fa-mous old Boston restaurant Durgin Park, will not serve its renowned Indian Pudding without ice cream, regardless of any customer's pleas to the contrary. The representatives of this organization feel rewarded when they perpetuate its age-old traditions, even in the face of customer derision, irritation, or withdrawal. The belief system of the organization thus reinforces itself against change from the outside.

The problem of analysis becomes complicated here, however, because much of what superficially looks like proactive behavior has a strong reactive component. That is, members of many organizations sense acceptance from their peers if they *talk* in terms of changing things through the use of stronger authority, firmer plans, clearer organization, an active anti-union program, or what not. On the face of it one can't tell whether such talk serves primarily the function of re-establishing cherished belief around which the organization is held together, or of describing actual proactive behavior.

Such questions often require careful research to answer. So much talk about "inner directedness," for example, or "rugged individualism" takes on a different cast when one realizes the extent to which certain individuals get social satisfaction from others by conforming to certain accepted codes. That is, an individual often gains membership in a management group or club to the extent he professes to value rugged individualism.

Here are some instances of behavior which have had the function of re-establishing and underscoring shared beliefs and values held by the powerful figures in an organization, but which were ostensibly proactive.

THE CASE OF THE TOO PRODUCTIVE CREW. In one electronics company recently investigated by Melvin Steckler at Harvard,[11] a small group of production girls was found to be contributing about 120 percent toward the profit of the firm. Because of an explicit action experiment by their foreman, these girls—most of whom had little formal education in general and none at all in electronics—were solving production and design problems which university professors and members of the company's engineering department couldn't cope with. Also productivity was constantly increasing in the group, some 300 percent in two years, and they were not on an incentive system.

As might be expected, these girls had considerable freedom in their jobs. They designed and operated their own testing equipment, their maintenance man made and supervised their expense and supplies budget which constantly showed a lower and lower percentage in relation to volume, they moved around a lot, traded jobs and so forth.

After this had been going on for over a year, higher-ups could stand it no longer, and instituted proceedings to break up the activity. The foreman was promoted away from the group, a new engineer was imported from Europe to "straighten up the confusion in the department," etc. What an engineering executive said to the researcher shortly before these proceedings were launched is instructive. As we listen to him talk, we are hearing strong reactive sentiments, sentiments so strong they even overlook making money—another variable sometimes seen as rewarding by organizational members. Said the engineer:

Dollarwise they're doing a pretty good job in here, as far as it goes, but they've got one overriding weakness in the way they are presently set up. Do you realize the girls do all their own testing in here? The same girls that make the tubes test them. It just isn't logical. Human nature isn't that way. You can't trust the same people who make something to also test it. It's not healthy.

. . . We've got plans in the works for taking on this place and really making it over. And when we do we'll see to it that the testing operations are carried on in a separate department. We'll really whip this operation into shape. . . . I'd like to make this a model showplace for the company. Right now its the worst in the company.

This place has never been under engineering control. That's the trouble with it. . . . Most of the product design changes that have been made have been developed and put into practice by the production people themselves. That's not good. . . . They design their own products, they alter and maintain their own production equipment and processes, and they are free to go off in all different directions at once. The first thing we would do if we could get hold of this room would be to put every operation under close engineering surveillance.

This engineer sounds proactive, but it is clear that the main underlying meaning of his behavior is to push back into shape a disequilibrium about which he feels deeply upset. Moreover, it is possible this disequilibrium is felt by him in many ways: as a threat to his knowledge and status, as a threat to the position of the engineering group in the company, as a violation of the status system in the company as a whole, and as a violation of the Western European culture's assumption about authority as appropriately flowing from "up" towards "down" through the vehicles of role incumbents.[12]

THE CASE OF THE SPEEDING ASSEMBLY LINE. Something similar was observed by Alex Bavelas in a toy factory on a paint line conveyor.[13] There, a group of girls were allowed to control the speed of the conveyor on which they were working. They sped it up when they felt like working, and they slowed it down when they didn't. Productivity and earnings soared, and soared higher by far than that which the engineers had believed to be normal output.

Consequently, the engineers took the control of the line's speed away from the workers, and restored it to a steady predictable pace. The girls, apparently, had established an equilibrium of their own, for they all quit in protest. So did their foreman. As with the engineer in the electronics company, the belief of the management group that control of technological process ought to move from the top down was reinforced, again to the exclusion of other beliefs such as the goodness of high productivity.

These are instances of one of the most commonly encountered findings of organizational research. Time and time again, management groups in business and elsewhere enforce procedures designed to keep behavior in line with beliefs about what "ought to be" under the guise that they are usefully effecting task accomplishment. In the instances above, for example, actual task efficiency was sacrificed for order and congruence with management beliefs.

In summary, it is no accident that the conditions under which groups achieve high job involvement, high productivity, high creativity, high satisfaction, low absenteeism and low turnover are among the best known findings in organizational behavior research and are perhaps those most ignored by managements. Of course this shouldn't surprise us, since the need of any behavioral system—individual, group, organizational or what not—to maintain itself through time is almost always stronger than mere new knowledge. Anyone knows this who has tried to change another's mind through what he believes is logic.

Having underscored in this way the extreme difficulty of assessing the meaning of behavior from the point of view of the total organization, we must realize that classifying behavior as proactive is just as difficult as pegging reactive tendencies.

However, consciously conceived and executed expansion is certainly an instance. Reorganization which introduces new differentiation into the system is another. Other examples can be seen in the increasing variety of special interests of the modern, large corporations. They are relating themselves to their community and wider cultural context in an array of ways hardly considered a few decades ago.

Art exhibits, gifts to colleges, community relations programs, educational aids and the like are all examples of the variety of transactions being sought and achieved by corporations. It is true that most of these activities are spoken of as having an economic base in good public relations, but the fact that the environment puts such pressure on growing organizations may indicate that the wider social context expects such increasing transactions from a growing sub-unit. Be that as it may, many activities of these kinds have only the vaguest connection to the often allegedly superordinate goal of profit. Indeed, as Robert N. Anthony[14] has pointed out, most corporations today have ceased maximizing profit, and have done so because of their other transactional relations with the wider society.

What Is a Norm?

Having thus illustrated the different aspects of organizational behavior, let us now examine what is meant by a norm.

What is meant by a norm, is a belief which a group of people act as if they hold, so that, if any person exhibits behavior which differs from the norm, the group will act to make the deviant person conform. By way of illustration, we might cite the situation of the Easterner who shows up at a Los Angeles swimming pool party dressed in a suit and tie. An elaboration of this event is instructive. Shortly after the Easterner's arrival the native members of this poolside group, both female and male, began to interact quite heavily with the deviant new member, making jokes about Easterners, expressing desires to someday see the new member in a sport shirt, making overtures of affection and welcome toward the new member, and even presenting him with the local costume, a sport shirt hastily borrowed from the oldest son of the host. The natives said that they wished to make the new member more comfortable this way.

The Easterner, remaining insensitive to the social meaning of the offering —to produce cohesion in the group— refused it, saying he was already comfortable, which was physically true. Thereafter, interaction dropped off sharply with the new member, an outcome predicted by S. Schachter's research on deviation.[15] (Subsequent research, by the way, indicates that in the future the Easterner and his mate are considering clothing themselves in native garments.)

The illustration chosen is perhaps trivial, but groups cannot exist without norms; human beings require affiliation for life, just as they require oxygen and water, and norm-breaking can be a serious thing. Anyone who doubts it might, to continue the illustration just cited, try going to an Eastern cocktail party dressed comfortably in a sport shirt.

One Healthy Organization

With this brief description of a norm and its function of maintaining a group, let us turn to some behavior in the Marshall Company, an organization studied by a group of field investigators from Harvard.[16] It is one which illustrates my definition of a healthy organization where members share norms such that they explicitly recognize the validity of the aspects of behavior in each of the areas shown in Figure 1. They also work to resolve the inevitable conflicts that arise between these different aspects.

As I state the Marshall Company norms and then illustrate them with behavior, we shall see the extent to which the different aspects of behavioral systems seen in our diagram are legitimatized by the norms we encounter.

The norms surrounding training, development, promotion and transfer in the Marshall Company were most interesting. Members of the organization behaved as if they believed that "Training occurs on the job and occurs when an individual asks questions and otherwise demonstrates a desire to know more about his work. Anyone in a superior position, including higher ranking production crew personnel, should give subordinates a chance to express their views on tasks and problems and allow them to help in areas of interest to them. A subordinate is not required to take initiative and to be eager to learn, though. It is acceptable in the Marshall Company for someone to stay on his present job until he decides he wants to retire."

A number of events were recorded by the field researchers which indicated the existence of such norms. For example, researchers observed the superintendent of the paper machines both training and being trained as he went about his business. Once, a new and very complicated paper machine was starting up, a process which took several hours. During this time, the superintendent's superior, the production manager, stood in the background and watched, along with a crowd of workers from other parts of the plant, as well as several men who had come in on an off day to observe. During the start-up period, the superintendent said to the researcher: "He [the production manager] doesn't often say much to me when I'm starting up a machine. Later on, he will tell me things he thought might have been

improved—even some of the little things. But now, he won't bother me."

The next day the men attempted to run paper through the machine. The superintendent observed a crew member—the "second hand"—climb up on the machine and try several times to thread new, wet paper into the press rolls. This was a difficult procedure and all gathered to watch. The man tried and failed a half dozen times, after which the superintendent placed his hand on the crewman's leg. The "second hand" immediately got down and the "first hand," who had been watching from a position near his own job, came over and climbed up. On his second try, he was successful. However, the paper started several times, but each time it broke within a few minutes. Once the superintendent himself fed the paper into the driers. Concerning the event with the "second hand," the superintendent said, "He's o.k. He just got a little nervous."

A few days after the machine had been operating, the researchers talked with a young foreman who was having a great deal of trouble with one part of the machine, although production was moving along steadily. The foreman could not solve the problem, and was often observed sitting by himself, staring at the floor. At one point he said, "I wish we had the old machinery back."

The researchers knew that the young foreman's progress in the company was well known to the production superintendent, who felt he had "brought him along" to be foreman. When the researcher, some days later, asked the superintendent about this particular technical problem, he learned that the superintendent had solved the problem mentally but hadn't yet told the young foreman about it. Grinning broadly, the superintendent said, "He's got enough to think about now, and there's no use trying to look too far ahead."

Why Training Really Worked

There were other instances of training practices among the men on the machines. For example, researchers observed a "second hand" on one of the paper machines helping a third hand temporarily perform the "second hand's" work. When asked about this, the "second hand" talked about how crewmen advanced at Marshall, saying, "You really just learn by doing. You master your own job, and then you watch the next fellow working, and do as much as you can. . . . A good man will keep you busy answering his questions; and when he does that, you bring him along. Of course, you've gotta keep learning so you know more than the other guys. . . . There's one fellow, he's no good. He came over from the other side [of the river dividing our plant here] during the war and worked up to be second hand. Now, guys are coming back from the service who know more than he does. Men under him are better than he is, but he gives orders and pretends to know more than anyone else. No one likes him."

In terms of my thesis, what are some of the significances of these various events? First of all, the ways in which individuals grow and learn are not violated by the norms that exist among the members of the Marshall Company. Men are rewarded by learning new tasks, but they are not pushed into

such new behavior, except when the organization's proaction requires it, as it would in the case of the necessity for a faster or better machine, for example. Moreover, a man can choose not to learn any new tasks at all, and he will not be punished for it, so long as he doesn't prevent others from satisfying their proactive needs. Thus an individual's needs for reactive behavior are legitimate in the Marshall Company system.

Notice, too, that the behavior which must surround an individual's proaction becomes the content for group norms in the Marshall Company. That is, behavior which does not support individual proaction is reacted against by the group. These were the instances of deviation observed in our examples: the crew member reporting the social ostracism of the man who gives orders to and doesn't help the people under him, for example, or the superintendent's punishing the young foreman by withholding help and assistance, because the foreman had given up on the problem and not asked for help.

The company-wide codes support requesting and giving help after an individual has tried on his own. Notice that such codes foster reciprocity between groups (superior-subordinate groups, for example), thus encouraging inter-group proactive behavior, and also are functional at the level of the total organization, which needs both to have problems solved and to have problem-solvers developed.

There is another manner in which these codes make legitimate the different aspects of organizational behavior. Notice that an individual must always ask for help, which places him in a subordinate position socially. But one of the basic aspects of elementary social behavior which holds groups together is the exchange of regard for help. At Marshall, the codes demand that not only should one ask for help from others whose knowledge is greater, but also one must give help to those who ask for it. Thus, this kind of social reciprocity, so vital to the continuation of social groups (as such authors as Alvin Gouldner[17] and George C. Homans[18] have pointed out) is institutionalized in such a way as to meet both the proactive and reactive needs of individuals, groups, and the total organization. A truly remarkable social invention.

Work Groups Cooperate

There are other instances of such multi-dimensionally useful behavior in Marshall, and all of them are not built around training. For example, the researchers noticed how any emergency was met by everyone in the area with the relevant skills jumping in to help. As those familiar with paper making know, the machines are rarely stopped. If a break occurs, a mountain of waste forms almost immediately.

The norm here was stated when a researcher said to a crew member, "I'm interested in the way you fellows jump to the breaks. . . . The first fellow on the spot goes ahead." "Oh, sure, you have to," the crew member replied. "The thing is, you all have to work together. You can't just do your own job, you have to pull with the crew."

Here we see an instance of a group norm which is clearly useful to the group because technological failure is so obviously the responsibility of a given crew at a given time. The Mar-shall Company technology is such that social relationships are congruent with an identifiable task and form the basis for what E. L. Trist has called an effective "socio-technical system."[19]

Although we cannot examine this extremely important point further here, there is evidence to suggest that when an organization designs a given technological task in such a way as to require an effective, separate social group for its performance, then the group responds by maintaining a high level of contribution to the organizational task.[20] For example, at Marshall, the crews rarely used a fancy resting room facility the company had built since it would take them away from their constant surveillance of their machines. Also, recall how several members of the crews came in on a holiday to watch the start up of the new machine.

Departments Work Together

Although we could continue examining instances of Marshall Company norms and behavior for some time, we shall conclude with one more type. As is well known, the typical company is plagued with conflicts between groups within it. The way the Marshall Company social practices deal with this is extremely interesting. First of all, a person develops his own area of competence in the company. No organization chart exists. The real organization of the company is an on-going creation of the members themselves.

People know who in the company is the person in charge of a given interest, for example, the quality of special coated papers, or the purchase of pulp, or customer relations with the printing industry. People grow into these positions as their interests and their developing competence allow, and no two "generations" of management personnel define these positions in quite the same way. That is, a person takes on a bundle of tasks in which he has interest and demonstrates competence.

There are several such people who interact frequently with the paper making crews and the norm of the organization is "When there are no conflicts between values or points of view, then an individual can contact a paper crew directly." No foreman, therefore, is offended when the quality control man lets his presence be known by his familiar red circle around some item on the "spec sheet" which is posted near a machine during any particular run. He knows that a visit has been made and that one or more of his men has likely been spoken to.

When there are interest conflicts in the company, the code is something like this: "Each of us has our special interest in one or another phase of our operation. We all know and respect the legitimacy of these special interests. We cannot force others to relinquish their interests to solve our problems. We must discuss and resolve conflicts with our peers."

An instance of this norm in operation occurred during the research when a machine was making paper too thick for a book publishing customer's specifications. Since paper was scarce, the customer was reluctantly continuing to accept it, but some people at the plant were worried. Two executives— both concerned with aspects of quality —were discussing the problem. They first discussed running the paper on other machines, which could produce

it correctly, but discovered that it would create almost insoluble problems for the scheduling office. They then thought of slowing the machine down, but rejected that since it would cut into the bonus of the production people and also because the tonnage for the month for the whole plant was a little behind projections. Next they considered changing the kind of pulp, but rejected that because other customers had already been promised paper requiring that sort of pulp. A decision was reached to let the situation alone for the time being—it was the lesser of several evils.

Notice the extent to which participants in this conversation considered the different legitimate interests in the organization. Is worker morale more important than total customer satisfaction? Is one customer's satisfaction more important than another's? Is better paper on one run worth slowing down production and consequent delivery of other orders, as would happen if machines were changed? These interests are all legitimate, of course, and somehow must be dealt with in any decision. Notice how this particular form of institutionally supported decision making explicitly dealt with intergroup reciprocity, as they discussed the consequences for the different groups of each possible decision.

Is It Good Business?

Because the Marshall Company sounds so unusual, it may well be asked whether such an organization of people also meets the reactive needs of the organization to make money and satisfy stockholders as well as the proactive needs of the organization to change and advance. Concerning the first of these questions, the Marshall Company, some 14 years after the investigation discussed here, had a production growth rate 33 percent higher than the industry, a sales growth rate 30 percent higher, and a net profit to sales ratio 30 percent above the industry average. Return on invested capital compared even more favorably with the rest of the industry. And market value of common stock was up 900 percent a share. Concerning the second question, Marshall was regarded by the foremost supplier of instruments and electronic control devices for paper making as "one of the most progressive firms in the paper industry."

Summary

Thus we can see that the Marshall Company has norms which make legitimate the behavior of its members addressed toward the satisfaction of needs at all levels of affiliation—individual, group, intergroup and total organizational, and not simply needs for proaction, but maintaining, equilibrium seeking, reactive needs as well.

Although space does not permit us to illustrate this further, it can be seen that I would not call any organization healthy which denied the legitimacy of any of these needs; which denied, for example, the needs of individuals to grow at their own pace, or the needs of small group social systems to develop and maintain themselves around tasks. I say around tasks, for without this important socio-technical qualification, such social systems could develop no transactions with their environment, and they would develop
only the internal differentiations seen so much in industrial research, betting, restriction of output, gaming, joking, excessive coffee breaks, etc.

Moreover, any organization which was set up only to meet the needs of individuals to grow, or to participate, or to be creative, or what not, and which did not consider the needs of people to form into groups, or of the total organization to engage in satisfactory transactions with outside groups such as stockholders or customers, cannot be considered healthy.

So many scientifically or humanistically oriented critics of large organization make an unfortunate mistake in regard to this last point which hinders the progress they so earnestly seek. Such critics make the double observation that (1) an organization is different from other social groupings in that it has a formal purpose, and in that its members seek to guide their own behavior rationally to accomplish that purpose and (2) that many organizations plan without knowledge of the needs of their various components. As a result, the critics maintain, we see the much deplored stunted creativity of individuals, the alienation or senseless social behavior of group members, inefficient intergroup competition and so forth.

But these are not necessary outcomes of planful activity. As Gilbert David[21] and Paul R. Lawrence[22] have pointed out, there is nothing humanistically wrong with planning per se. It is planning without awareness of the individual, small group and intergroup reactive and proactive needs that is scientifically and humanistically wrong, to say nothing of inefficient.

As I hope I have been able to demonstrate, one achieves the values of neither humanism nor efficiency if one maintains either value exclusively. It is my personal opinion that our capacity to understand and produce organizational health will develop only to the extent that we bring to it some kind of a multi-dimensional approach. Whether or not the present conception of the multi-dimensionality which is in the world appears fruitful is not important. What is important is that organizational investigators, management theorists, and administrators adopt some point of view large enough to include the other points of view which exist in any situation and which inevitably conflict with each other.

REFERENCES

(An earlier version of this paper was originally presented at a UCLA Graduate School of Business Administration faculty seminar. Discussants were Professor Richard Barthol, Psychology, and Professor Melvin Seeman, Sociology, for whose commentary the author is grateful. J.V.C.)

1. Paul R. Lawrence, *The Changing of Organizational Behavior Patterns: A Case Study of Decentralization* (Boston: Division of Research, Harvard Business School, 1958). See Chapter X.
2. Gordon Allport, "The Open System in Personality Theory," *Personality and Social Encounter* (Boston: The Beacon Press, 1960).
3. For a fuller treatment, see James V. Clark, "Businessmen vs. Behavioral Scientists: The Dynamics of Misunderstanding," unpublished paper.
4. Harold Koontz, "The Management Theory Jungle," *Journal of the Academy of Management*, Vol. 4, No. 3, December, 1961, pp. 174–188.
5. P. R. Lawrence et al., *Organizational Behavior and Administration: Cases, Concepts and Research Findings* (Homewood, Illinois: Irwin-Dorsey Press, 1961), Century Company (A) (B) (C), pp. 126–167.
6. Louis B. Barnes and James V. Clark, "Lakeview Diary," Harvard University, Unpublished Cases, 1957.
7. E. L. Trist, G. Murray, G. W. Higgin and A. B. Pollock, "Work Organization at the Coal Face" (London: Tavistock Institute of Human Relations, Doc. No. 506, 1959).
8. Louis B. Barnes, *Organizational Systems and Engineering Groups: A Comparative Study of Two Technical Systems in Industry* (Boston: Division of Research, Harvard Business School, 1960).
9. James V. Clark, "Motivation in Work Groups: A Tentative View," *Human Organization*, Vol. XIX, No. 4, Winter 1960–61, pp. 199–208. Also see the Barnes study, note 8.
10. R. L. Katz and J. A. Seiler, *Management Behavior: The Physiology of Organization* (Boston: Division of Research, Harvard Business School, to be published in 1962).
11. See note 5, American Radiatronics Corporation (A), pp. 266–302.
12. Walter B. Miller, "Two Concepts of Authority," *American Anthropologist*, Vol. LVII, No. 2 (April, 1955), pp. 271–89. (Condensed and reprinted in Lawrence, et al., *Organizational Behavior and Administration*, pp. 777–786.)

13. William F. Whyte *et al, Money and Motivation* (New York: Harper & Row, Publishers, 1955, Chapter X).

14. Robert N. Anthony, "The Trouble with Profit Maximization," *Harvard Business Review*, Vol. 38, No. 6, November–December 1960, pp. 126–134.

15. S. Schachter, "Deviation, Rejection and Communication," *Journal of Social and Abnormal Psychology*, Vol. 46 (1951), pp. 190–207.

16. See note 5, Marshall Company (A)–(1), pp. 634–692.

17. Alvin Gouldner, "The Norm of Reciprocity: A Preliminary Statement," *American Sociological Review*, Vol. XXV, No. 2, April, 1960, pp. 161–178.

18. George Caspar Homans, *Social Behavior: Its Elementary Forms* (New York: Harcourt, Brace & World, Inc., 1961), Chapters 3 and 4.

19. E. L. Trist, "Socio-Technical Systems" (London: Tavistock Institute of Human Relations, Doc. No. 572, 1960).

20. A. K. Rice, "Productivity and Social Organization in an Indian Weaving Shed," *Human Relations*, Vol. VI, No. 4, 1953. See also Eric J. Miller, "Technology, Territory, and Time," *Human Relations*, Vol. XII, No. 3 (1959), pp. 243–272. See also note 7.

21. Gilbert David, "Your Organization . . . In Sickness and in Health," Leader's Digest No. 2 (Chicago: Adult Education Association, 1955).

22. See note 1, Chapter X.

6.3 THE UTILITY OF SYSTEM MODELS AND DEVELOPMENTAL MODELS FOR PRACTITIONERS

Robert Chin

All practitioners have ways of thinking about and figuring out situations of change. These ways are embodied in the concepts with which they apprehend the dynamics of the client-system they are working with, their relationship to it, and their processes of helping with its change. For example, the change-agent encounters resistance, defense mechanisms, readiness to change, adaptation, adjustment, maladjustment,

Reprinted from the first edition of *The Planning of Change: Readings in the Applied Behavioral Sciences*, edited by Warren G. Bennis, Kenneth D. Benne, and Robert Chin. Copyright © 1961 by Holt, Rinehart and Winston, Inc.

integration, disintegration, growth, development, and maturation as well as deterioration. He uses concepts such as these to sort out the processes and mechanisms at work. And necessarily so. No practitioner can carry on thought processes without such concepts; indeed, no observations or diagnoses are ever made on "raw facts," because facts are really observations made within a set of concepts. But lurking behind concepts such as the ones stated above are assumptions about how the parts of the client-system fit together and how they change. For instance, "Let things alone, and natural laws (of economics, politics, personality, etc.) will work things out in the long run." "It is only human nature to resist change." "Every organization is always trying to improve its ways of working." Or, in more technical forms, we have assumptions such as: "The adjustment of the personality to its inner forces as well as adaptation to its environment is the sign of a healthy personality." "The coordination and integration of the departments of an organization is the task of the executive." "Conflict is an index of malintegration, or of change." "Inhibiting forces against growth must be removed."

It is clear that each of the above concepts conceals a different assumption about how events achieve stability and change, and how anyone can or cannot help change along. Can we make these assumptions explicit? Yes, we can and we must. The behavioral scientist does exactly this by constructing a simplified *model* of human events and of his tool concepts. By simplifying he can analyze his thoughts and concepts, and see in turn where the congruities and discrepancies occur between these and actual events. He becomes at once the observer, analyzer and modifier of the system[1] of concepts he is using.

The purpose of this paper is to present concepts relevant to, and the benefits to be gained from using, a "system" model and a "developmental" model in thinking about human events. These models provide "mind-holds" to the practitioner in his diagnosis. They are,

therefore, of practical significance to him. This suggests one essential meaning of the oft-quoted and rarely explained phrase that "nothing is so practical as a good theory." We will try to show how the "systems" and "developmental" approaches provide key tools for a diagnosis of persons, groups, organizations, and communities for purposes of change. In doing so, we shall state succinctly the central notions of each model, probably sacrificing some technical elegance and exactness in the process. We shall not overburden the reader with citations of the voluminous set of articles from which this paper is drawn.

We postulate that the same models can be used in diagnosing different sizes of the units of human interactions—the person, the group, the organization, and the community.

One further prefatory word. We need to keep in mind the difference between an "analytic" model and a model of concrete events or cases. For our purposes, *an analytic model* is a constructed simplification of some part of reality that retains only those features regarded as essential for relating similar processes whenever and wherever they occur. *A concrete model* is based on an analytic model, but uses more of the content of actual cases, though it is still a simplification designed to reveal the essential features of some range of cases. As Hagen[2] puts it: "An explicitly defined analytic model helps the theorist to recognize what factors are being taken into account and *what relationships among them are assumed* and hence to know the basis of his conclu-

---

[1] "System" is used here as any organized and coherent body of knowledge. Later we shall use the term in a more specific meaning.

[2] E. Hagen, chapter on "Theory of Social Change," unpublished manuscript.

sions. The advantages are ones of both exclusion and inclusion. A model lessens the danger of overlooking the indirect effects of a change of a relationship" (our italics). We mention this distinction since we find a dual usage that has plagued behavioral scientists, for they themselves keep getting their feet entangled. We get mixed up in analyzing "the small group as a system" (analytic) and a school committee as a small group (concrete) or a national social system (analytic) and the American social system (concrete) or an organizational system (analytic) and the organization of a glue factory (concrete). In this paper, we will move back and forth between the analytic usage of "model" and the "model" of the concrete case, hopefully with awareness of when we are involved in a semantic shift.

The "System" Model

Psychologists, sociologists, anthropologists, economists, and political scientists have been "discovering" and using the system model. In so doing, they find intimations of an exhilarating "unity" of science, because the system models used by biological and physical scientists seem to be exactly similar. Thus, the system model is regarded by some system theorists as universally applicable to physical and social events, and to human relationships in small or large units.

The terms or concepts that are a part of the system model are "boundary," "stress or tension," "equilibrium," and "feedback." All these terms are related to "open system," "closed system," and "intersystem" models. We shall first define these concepts, illustrate their meaning, and then point out how they can be used by the change-agent as aids in observing, analyzing, or diagnosing—and perhaps intervening in—concrete situations.

The Major Terms

system. Laymen sometimes say, "you can't beat the system" (economic or political), or "he is a product of the system" (juvenile delinquent or Soviet citizen). But readers of social science writings will find the term used in a rather more specific way. It is used as an abbreviated term for a longer phrase that the reader is asked to supply. The "economic system" might be read as: "we treat price indices, employment figures, etc., as if they were closely interdependent with each other and we temporarily leave out unusual or external events, such as the discovery of a new gold mine." Or in talking about juvenile delinquency in "system" terms, the sociologists choose to treat the lower-class values, lack of job opportunities, ragged parental images, as interrelated with each other, in back-and-forth cause-and-effect fashion, as determinants of delinquent behavior. Or the industrial sociologist may regard the factory as a "social system," as people working together in relative isolation from the outside, in order to examine what goes on in interactions and interdependencies of the people, their positions, and other variables. In our descriptions and analyses of a particular concrete system, we can recognize the shadowy figure of some such analytic model of "system."

The analytic model of system demands that we treat the phenomena and the concepts for organizing the phenomena as if there existed organization, interaction, interdependency, and integration of parts and elements. System analysis assumes structure and stability within some arbitrarily sliced and frozen time period.

It is helpful to visualize a system[3] by drawing a large circle. We place elements, parts, variables, inside the circle as the components, and draw lines among the components. The lines may be thought of as rubber bands or springs, which stretch or contract as the forces increase or decrease. Outside the circle is the environment, where we place all other factors which impinge upon the system.

BOUNDARY. In order to specify what is inside or outside the system, we need to define its "boundary" line. The boundary of a system may exist physically: a tightly corked vacuum bottle, the skin of a person, the number of people in a group, etc. But, in addition, we may delimit the system in a less tangible way, by placing our boundary according to what variables are being focused upon. We can construct a system consisting of the multiple roles of a person, or a system composed of varied roles among members in a small work group, or a system interrelating roles in a family. The components or variables used are roles, acts, expectations, communications, influence and power relationships, and so forth, and not necessarily persons.

[3] A useful visual aid for "system" can be constructed by using paper clips (elements) and rubber bands (tensions) mounted on a peg board. Shifting of the position of a clip demonstrates the interdependency of all the clips' positions, and their shifting relationships.

The operational definition of *boundary* is: the line forming a closed circle around selected variables, where there is less interchange of energy (or communication, etc.) *across* the line of the circle than *within* the delimiting circle. The multiple systems of a community may have boundaries that do or do not coincide. For example, treating the power relationships may require a boundary line different from that for the system of interpersonal likes or dislikes in a community. In small groups we tend to draw the same boundary line for the multiple systems of power, communications, leadership, and so on, a major advantage for purposes of study.

In diagnosing we tentatively assign a boundary, examine what is happening inside the system and then readjust the boundary, if necessary. We examine explicitly whether or not the "relevant" factors are accounted for within the system, an immensely practical way of deciding upon relevance. Also, we are free to limit ruthlessly, and neglect some factors temporarily, thus reducing the number of considerations necessary to be kept in mind at one time. The variables left outside the system, in the "environment" of the system, can be introduced one or more at a time to see the effects, if any, on the interrelationship of the variables within the system.

TENSION, STRESS, STRAIN, AND CONFLICT. Because the components within a system are different from each other, are not perfectly integrated, or are changing and reacting to change, or because outside disturbances occur, we need ways of dealing with these differences. The differences lead to varying degrees of tension within the system. *Examples:* males are not like females, foremen see things differently from workers and from executives, children in a family grow, a committee has to work with a new chairman, a change in the market condition requires a new sales response from a factory. To restate the above examples in conceptual terms: we find built-in differences, gaps of ignorance, misperceptions, or differential perceptions, internal changes in a component, reactive adjustments and defenses, and the requirements of system survival generating tensions. Tensions that are internal and arise out of the structural arrangements of the system may be called *stresses and strains* of the system. When tensions gang up and become more or less sharply opposed along the lines of two or more components, we have *conflict.*

A word of warning. The presence of tensions, stresses or strains, and conflict within the system often are reacted to by people in the system as if they were shameful and must be done away with. Tension reduction, relief of stress and strain, and conflict resolution become the working goals of practitioners but sometimes at the price of overlooking the possibility of increasing tensions and conflict in order to facilitate creativity, innovation, and social change. System analysts have been accused of being conservative and even reactionary in assuming that a social system always tends to reduce tension, resist innovation, abhor deviancy and change. It is obvious, however, that tension and conflict are "in" any system, and that no living system exists without tension. Whether these facts of life in a system are to be abhorred or welcomed is determined by attitudes or value judgments not derivable from system theory as such.

The identification of and analysis of how tensions operate in a system are by all odds *the* major utility of system analysis for practitioners of change. The dynamics of a living system are exposed for observation through utilizing the concepts of tension, stress and strain, and conflict. These tensions lead to activities of two kinds: those which do not affect the structure of the system (dynamics), and those which directly alter the structure itself (system change).

EQUILIBRIUM AND "STEADY STATE." A system is assumed to have a tendency to achieve a balance among the various forces operating within and upon it. Two terms have been used to denote two different ideas about balance. When the balance is thought of as a fixed point or level, it is called "equilibrium." "Steady state," on the other hand, is the term recently used to describe the balanced relationship of parts that is not dependent upon any fixed equilibrium point or level.

Our body temperature is the classic illustration of a fixed level (98.6° F.), while the functional relationship between work units in a factory, regardless of the level of production, represents a steady state. For the sake of simplicity, we shall henceforth stretch the term "equilibrium" to cover both types of balance, to include also the idea of "steady state."

There are many kinds of equilibria. A *stationary equilibrium* exists when there is a fixed point or level of balance to which the system returns after a disturbance. We rarely find such instances in human relationships. A *dy-*

namic equilibrium exists when the equilibrium shifts to a new position of balance after disturbance. Among examples of the latter, we can observe a *neutral* type of situation. *Example:* a ball on a flat plane. A small push moves it to a new position, and it again comes to rest. *Example:* a farming community. A new plow is introduced and is easily incorporated into its agricultural methods. A new level of agricultural production is placidly achieved. A *stable type of situation* exists where the forces that produced the initial equilibrium are so powerful that any new force must be extremely strong before any movement to a new position can be achieved. *Example:* a ball in the bottom of a goblet. *Example:* an organization encrusted with tradition or with clearly articulated and entrenched roles is not easily upset by minor events. An *unstable type of situation* is tense and precarious. A small disturbance produces large and rapid movements to a new position. *Example:* a ball balanced on the rims of two goblets placed side by side. *Example:* an organization with a precarious and tense balance between two modes of leadership style. A small disturbance can cause a large swing to one direction and a new position of equilibrium. *Example:* a community's balance of power between ethnic groups may be such that a "minor" disturbance can produce an upheaval and movement to a different balance of power.

A system in equilibrium reacts to outside impingements: (*1*) By resisting the influence of the disturbance, refusing to acknowledge its existence, or by building a protective wall against the intrusion, and by other defensive maneu-

vers. *Example:* a small group refuses to talk about a troublesome problem of unequal power distribution raised by a member. (*2*) By resisting the disturbance through bringing into operation the homeostatic forces that restore or re-create a balance. The small group talks about the troublesome problem of a member and convinces him that it is not "really" a problem. (*3*) By accommodating the disturbances through achieving a new equilibrium. Talking about the problem may result in a shift in power relationships among members of the group.

The concepts of equilibrium (and steady state) lead to some questions to guide a practitioner's diagnosis.

a. What are the conditions conducive to the achievement of an equilibrium in this case? Are there internal or external factors producing these forces? What is their quality and tempo?

b. Does the case of the client-system represent one of the typical situations of equilibrium? How does judgment on this point affect intervention strategy? If the practitioner feels the situation is tense and precarious, he should be more cautious in intervention than in a situation of stable type.

c. Can the practitioner identify the parts of the system that represent greatest readiness to change, and the greatest resistance to and defense against change? Can he understand the functions of any variable in relation to all other variables? Can he derive some sense of the direction in which the client system is moving, and separate those forces attempting to restore an old equilibrium and those pushing toward a new equilibrium state?

FEEDBACK. Concrete systems are never closed off completely. They have inputs and outputs across the boundary; they are affected by and in turn affect the environment. While affecting the environment, a process we call output, systems gather information about how they are doing. Such information is then fed back into the system as input to guide and steer its operations. This process is called feedback. The "discovery" of feedback has led to radical inventions in the physical world in designing self-guiding and self-correcting instruments. It has also become a major concept in the behavioral sciences, and a central tool in the practitioner's social technology. *Example:* in reaching for a cigarette we pick up tactile and visual cues that are used to guide our arm and finger movements. *Example:* our interpersonal communications are guided and corrected by our picking up of effect cues from the communicatees. *Example:* improving the feedback process of a client system will allow for self-steering or corrective action to be taken by him or it. In fact, the single most important improvement the change-agent can help a client system to achieve is to increase its diagnostic sensitivity to the effects of its own actions upon others. Programs in sensitivity training attempt to increase or unblock the feedback processes of persons; a methodological skill with wider applicability and longer-lasting significance than solving the immediate problem at hand. In diagnosing a client system, the practitioner asks: What are its feedback procedures? How adequate are they? What blocks their effective use? Is it lack of skill in gathering data, or in coding and utilizing the information?

OPEN AND CLOSED SYSTEMS

All living systems are open systems—systems in contact with their environment, with input and output across system boundaries. What then is the use of talking about a closed system? What *is* a closed system? It means that the system is temporarily assumed to have a leak-tight boundary—there is relatively little, if any, commerce across the boundary. We know that no such system can be found in reality, but it is sometimes essential to analyze a system as if it were closed so as to examine the operations of the system as affected "only by the conditions previously established by the environment and not changing at the time of analysis, plus the relationships among the internal elements of the system." The analyst then opens the system to a new impact from the environment, again closes the system, and observes and thinks out what would happen. It is, therefore, fruitless to debate the point; both open and closed system models are useful in diagnosis. Diagnosing the client as a system of variables, we have a way then of managing the complexity of "everything depends upon everything else" in an orderly way. Use of system analysis has these possibilities: (*a*) diagnosticians can avoid the error of simple cause-and-effect thinking; (*b*) they can justify what is included in observation and interpretation and what is temporarily excluded; (*c*) they can predict what will happen if no new or outside force is applied; (d) they are guided in categorizing what is relatively enduring and stable, or changing, in the situation; (e) they can distinguish between what is basic and what is merely symptomatic; (f) they can predict what will happen if they leave the events undisturbed and if they intervene; and (g) they are guided in selecting points of intervention.

INTERSYSTEM MODEL

We propose an extension of system analysis that looks to us to be useful for the problems confronting the change-agent. We urge the adoption of an intersystem model.

An intersystem model involves two open systems connected to each other.[4] The term we need to add here is *connectives*. Connectives represent the lines of relationships of the two systems. Connectives tie together parts (mechanics) or imbed in a web of tissue the separate organs (biology); connectives in an industrial establishment are the defined lines of communication, or the leadership hierarchy and authority for the branch plants; or they represent the social contract entered into by a therapist and patient; or mutual role expectations of consultant and client; or the affective ties between family members. These are conjunctive connectives. But we also have conflicts between labor and management, teenage gang wars, race conflicts, and negative emotional responses

to strangers. These are disjunctive connectives.

Why elaborate the system model into an intersystem model? Cannot we get the same effect by talking about "sub-systems" of a larger system? In part we can. Labor-management conflicts, or interpersonal relations, or change-agent and client relationship can each be treated as a new system with sub-systems. But we may lose the critical fact of the autonomy of the components, or the direct interactional or transactual consequences for the separate components when we treat the sub-systems as merely parts of a larger system. The intersystem model exaggerates the virtues of autonomy and the limited nature of interdependence of the interactions between the two connected systems.

What are some of the positive advantages of using intersystem analysis? First, the external change-agent, or the change-agent built into an organization as a helper with planned change does not completely become a part of the client-system. He must remain separate to some extent; he must create and maintain some distance between himself and the client, thus standing apart "in another system" from which he re-relates. This new system might be a referent group of fellow professionals, or a body of rational knowledge. But create one he does and must. Intersystem analysis of the change-agent's role leads to fruitful analysis of the connectives—their nature in the beginning, how they shift, and how they are cut off. Intersystem analysis also poses squarely an unexplored issue, namely the internal system of the change-agent, whether a single person,

[4] A visualization of an intersystem model would be two systems side by side, with separately identified links. Two rubber band–paper clip representatives can be connected with rubber bands of a different color, representing the connectives.

consultant group, or a nation. Helpers of change are prone at times not to see that their own systems as change-agents have boundaries, tensions, stresses and strains, equilibria, and feedback mechanisms which may be just as much parts of the problem as are similar aspects of the client-systems. Thus, relational issues are more available for diagnosis when we use an intersystem model.

More importantly, the intersystem model is applicable to problems of leadership, power, communication, and conflict in organizations, intergroup relations, and international relations. *Example:* Leadership in a work group with its liaison, negotiation, and representation functions is dependent upon connectives to another group and not solely upon the internal relationships within the work group. Negotiators, representatives, and leaders are parts of separate systems each with its own interdependence, tensions, stresses, and feedback, whether we are thinking of foreign ministers, Negro-white leaders, or student-faculty councils.

In brief, the intersystem model leads us to examine the interdependent dynamics of interaction both within and between the units. We object to the premature and unnecessary assumption that the units always form a single system. We can be misled into an utopian analysis of conflict, change-agent relations to client, and family relations if we neglect system differences. But an intersystem model provides a tool for diagnosis that retains the virtues of system analysis, adds the advantage of clarity, and furthers our diagnosis of the influence of various connectives, conjunctive and disjunctive, on the two systems. For change-

agents, the essence of collaborative planning is contained in an intersystem model.

Developmental Models

Practitioners have in general implicitly favored developmental models in thinking about human affairs, while social scientists have not paid as much attention to these as they have to system models. The "life sciences" of biology and psychology have not crystallized nor refined their common analytic model of the development of the organism, despite the heroic breakthroughs of Darwin. Thus, we are forced to present only broad and rough categories of alternative positions in this paper.

Since there is no standard vocabulary for a developmental model, we shall present five categories of terms that we deem essential to such models: direction, states, forces, form of progression, and potentiality.

The Major Terms

DEVELOPMENTAL MODELS. By developmental models, we mean those bodies of thought that center around growth and directional change. Developmental models assume change; they assume that there are noticeable differences between the states of a system at different times; that the succession of these states implies the system is heading somewhere; and that there are orderly processes which explain how the system gets from its present state to wherever it is going. In order to delimit the nature of change in developmental models we should perhaps add the idea of an increase in value accompanying the achievement of a new state. With this addition, developmental models focus on processes of growth and maturation. This addition might seem to rule out processes of decay, deterioration, and death from consideration. Logically, the developmental model should apply to either.

There are two kinds of "death" of concern to the practitioner. First, "death" or loss of some part or subvalue, as a constant concomitant of growth and development. Theories of life processes have used concepts such as katabolic (destructive) processes in biology, death instincts in Freud's psychology, or role loss upon promotion. On balance, the "loss" is made up by the "gains," and thus there is an increase in value. Second, "death" as planned change for a group or organization—the dissolution of a committee or community organization that has "outlived its purpose and function," and the termination of a helping relationship with deliberateness and collaboration of participants is properly included as part of a developmental model.

DIRECTION. Developmental models postulate that the system under scrutiny—a person, a small group, interpersonal interactions, an organization, a community or a society—is going "somewhere"; that the changes have some direction. The direction may be defined by (*a*) some *goal* or end state (developed, mature); (*b*) the *process* of becoming (developing, maturing) or (*c*) the degree of achievement *toward* some goal or end state (increased development, increase in maturity).

Change-agents find it necessary to believe that there is direction in change.

Example: self-actualization or fulfillment is a need of the client-system. When strong directional tendencies are present, we modify our diagnosis and intervention accordingly. A rough analogy may be helpful here. A change-agent using a developmental model may be thought of as a husbandman tending a plant, watching and helping it to grow in its own natural direction of producing flowers. He feeds, waters, and weeds. Though at times he may be ruthless in pinching off excess buds, or even in using "grafts," in general he encourages the plant to reach its "goal" of producing beautiful flowers.

IDENTIFIABLE STATE. As the system develops over time, the different states may be identified and differentiated from one another. Terms such as "stages," "levels," "phases," or "periods" are applied to these states. *Example:* psychosexual definition of oral, and anal stages, levels of evolution of species, or phases of group development.

No uniformity exists in the definition and operational identification of such successive states. But since change-agents do have to label the past, present, and future, they need some terms to describe successive states and to identify the turning points, transition areas, or critical events that characterize change. Here, system analysis is helpful in defining how parts are put together, along with the tensions and directions of the equilibrating processes. We have two polar types of the shifts of states: (*a*) small, nondiscernible steps or increments leading to a qualitative jump. (*Example:* black hair gradually turning gray, or a student evolving into a scholar); (*b*) a cataclysmic or critical event leading to a sudden change. (*Example:* a sickness resulting in gray hair overnight, or an inspirational lecture by a professor.) While the latter type seems more frequently to be externally induced, internal factors of the system can have the same consequence. In other words, the internal disequilibration of a balance may lead to a step-jump of the system to a new level. Personality stages, group stages, and societal phases are evolved and precipitated from internal and from external relations.

FORM OF PROGRESSION. Change-agents see in their models of development some form of progression or movement. Four such forms are typically assumed. First, it is often stated that once a stage is worked through, the client-system shows continued progression and normally never turns back. (Any recurrence of a previous state is viewed as an abnormality. Freudian stages are a good example: recurrence of a stage is viewed as regression, an abnormal event to be explained.) Teachers expect a steady growth of knowledge in students, either in a straight line (linear) or in an increasingly accelerating (curvilinear) form.

Second, it is assumed that change, growth, and development occur in a *spiral* form. *Example:* A small group might return to some previous "problem," such as its authority relations to the leader, but now might discuss the question at a "higher" level where irrational components are less dominant.

Third, another assumption more typically made is that the stages are really phases which occur and recur. There is an oscillation between various states, where no chronological priority is as-

signed to each state; there are cycles. *Example:* Phases of problem-solving or decision-making recur in different time periods as essential to progression. Cultures and societies go through phases of development in recurrent forms.

Fourth, still another assumption is that the form of progression is characterized by a branching out into *differentiated* forms and processes, each part increasing in its specialization, and at the same time acquiring its own autonomy and significance. *Example:* biological forms are differentiated into separate species. Organizations become more and more differentiated into special task and control structures.

FORCES. First, forces or causal factors producing development and growth are most frequently seen by practitioners as "natural," as part of human nature, suggesting the role of genetics and other in-born characteristics. At best, environmental factors act as "triggers" or "releases," where the presence of some stimulus sets off the system's inherent growth forces. For example, it is sometimes thought that the teacher's job is to trigger off the natural curiosity of the child, and that growth of knowledge will ensue. Or the leadership of an organization should act to release the self-actualizing and creative forces present in its members.

Second, a smaller number of practitioners and social scientists think that the response to new situations and environmental forces is a coping response which gives rise to growth and development. Third, at this point, it may be useful to remind ourselves of the earlier discussion of the internal tensions of the system, still another cause of change. When stresses and strains of a system become too great, a disruption occurs and a set of forces is released to create new structures and achieve a new equilibrium.

POTENTIALITY. Developmental models vary in their assumptions about potentialities of the system for development, growth, and change. That is, they vary in assumptions about the capabilities, overt or latent, that are built into the original or present state so that the necessary conditions for development may be typically present. Does the "seed"—and its genetic characteristics—represent potentialities? And are the supporting conditions of its environment available? Is the intelligence or emotional capability or skill-potential sufficient for development and change in a social and human process?

Change-agents typically assume a high degree of potentiality in the impetus toward development, and in the surrounding conditions that effectuate the potential.

UTILITY TO PRACTITIONERS

The developmental model has tremendous advantages for the practitioner. It provides a set of expectations about the future of the client-system. By clarifying his thoughts and refining his observations about direction, states in the developmental process, forms of progression, and forces causing these events to occur over a period of time, the practitioner develops a time perspective which goes far beyond that of the more here-and-now analysis of a system-model, which is bounded by time. By using a developmental model, he has a directional focus for his analysis and action and a temporal frame of reference. In addition, he is confronted with a number of questions to ask of himself and of his observations of the case: Do I assume an inherent end of the development? Do I impose a desired (by me) direction? How did I establish a collaboratively planned direction? What states in the development process may be expected? What form of progression do I foresee? What causes the development? His diagnoses and his interventions can become strategic rather than merely tactical.

The Change-Agent and Models

The primary concern of this paper has been to illustrate some of the major kinds of analytic models and conceptual schemas that have been devised by social scientists for the analysis of change and of changing human processes. But we need to keep in mind that the concern with diagnosis on the part of the social scientist is to achieve understanding, and to educe empirically researchable hypotheses amenable to his methods of study. The social scientist generally prefers not to change the system, but to study how it works and to predict what would happen if some new factor were introduced. So we find his attention focused on a "theory of change," of how the system achieves change. In contrast, the practitioner is concerned with diagnosis: how to achieve understanding in order to engage in change. The practitioner, therefore, has some additional interests; he wants to know how to change the system, he needs a "theory of changing" the system.

A theory of changing requires the selection, or the construction, by theoretically minded practitioners, of thought-models appropriate to their intended purpose. This has to be done according ⸱o explicit criteria. A change-agent may demand of any model answers to certain questions. The responses he receives may not be complete nor satisfactory since only piecemeal answers exist. At this period in the development of a theory of changing, we ask four questions as our guide lines for examining a conceptual model intended for the use of change-agents.

The first question is simply this: does the model account for the stability and continuity in the events studied at the same time that it accounts for changes in them? How do processes of change develop, given the interlocking factors in the situation that make for stability? Second, where does the model locate the "source" of change? What place among these sources do the deliberate and conscious efforts of the client-system and change-agent occupy? Third, what does the model assume about how goals and directions are determined? What or who sets the direction for movement of the processes of change? Fourth, does the model provide the change agent with levers or handles for affecting the direction, tempo, and quality of these processes of change?

A fifth question running through the other four is this: How does the model "place" the change-agent in the scheme of things? What is the shifting character of his relationship to the client-system, initially and at the termination of relationship, that affects his perceptions and actions? The questions of relationship of change-agent to others needs to be part and parcel of the model since the existential relationships of the change-agent engaged in processes of planned change become "part of the problem" to be investigated.

The application of these five questions to the models of systems and models of development crystallizes some of the formation of ingredients for a change-agent model for changing. We can now summarize each model as follows:

A "system" model emphasizes primarily the details of how stability is achieved, and only derivatively how change evolves out of the incompatibilities and conflicts in the system. A system model assumes that organization, interdependency, and integration exist among its parts and that change is a derived consequence of how well the parts of the system fit together, or how well the system fits in with other surrounding and interacting systems. The source of change lies primarily in the structural stress and strain externally induced or internally created. The process of change is a process of tension reduction. The goals and direction are emergent from the structures or from imposed sources. Goals are often analyzed as set by "vested interests" of one part of the system. The confronting symptoms of some trouble is a reflection of difficulties of adaptability (reaction to environment) or of the ability for adjustment (internal equilibration). The levers or handles available for manipulation are in the "inputs" to the system, especially the feedback mechanisms, and in the forces tending to restore a balance in the system. The change-agent is treated as separate from the client-system, the "target system."

The developmental model assumes constant change and development, and growth and decay of a system over time. Any existing stability is a snapshot of a living process—a stage that will give way to another stage. The supposition seems to be that it is "natural" that change should occur because change is rooted in the very nature of living organisms. The laws of the developmental process are not necessarily fixed, but some effects of the environment are presumably necessary to the developmental process. The direction of change is toward some goal, the fulfillment of its destiny, granting that no major blockage gets in the way. "Trouble" occurs when there is a gap between the system and its goal. Intervention is viewed as the removal of blockage by the change-agent, who then gets out of the way of the growth

Assumptions and Approaches of Three Analytic Models

MODELS OF CHANGE

Assumptions and Approaches to:	System Model	Developmental Model	Model for Changing: Intersystem
1. *Content*			
Stability	Structural integration	Phases, stages	Unfreezing parts
Change	Derived from structure	Constant and unique	Induced, controlled
2. *Causation*			
Source of change	Structural stress	Nature of organisms	Self and change-agent
Causal force	Tension reduction (creation?)		Rational choice
3. *Goals*			
Direction	Emergent	Ontological	Deliberate selection
Set by	"Vested interests"		Collaborative process
4. *Intervention*			
Confronting symptoms	Stresses, strains, and tensions	Discrepancy between actuality and potentiality	Perceived need
Goal of intervening	Adjustment, adaptation	Removal of blockages	Improvement
5. *Change-Agent*			
Place	Outside the "target" system	Outside	Part of situation
Role	External diagnoser and actor	External diagnoser and actor	Participant in here and now

forces. Developmental models are not very sharply analyzed by the pure theorist nor formally stated, usually, as an analytic model. In fact, very frequently the model is used for studying the unique case rather than for deriving "laws of growth"; it is for descriptive purposes.

The third model—a model for "changing" is a more recent creation. It incorporates some elements of analyses from system models, along with some ideas from the developmental model, in a framework where direct attention is paid to the induced forces producing change. It studies stability in order to unfreeze and move some parts of the system. The direction to be taken is not fixed or "determined," but remains in large measure a matter of "choice" for the client-system. The change-agent is a specialist in the technical processes of facilitating change, a helper to the client-system. The models for changing are as yet incompletely conceptualized. The intersystem model may provide a way of examining how the change-agent's relationships, as part of the model, affect the processes of change.

We can summarize and contrast the three models with a chart (page 310). We have varying degrees of confidence in our categories, but, as the quip says, we construct these in order to achieve the laudable state of "paradigm lost." It is the readers' responsibility to help achieve this goal!

The Limitations

It is obvious that we are proposing the use of systematically constructed and examined models of thought for the change-agent. The advantages are manifold and—we hope—apparent in our preceding discussion. Yet we must now point out some limitations and disutility of models.

Models are abstractions from the concreteness of events. Because of the high degree of selectivity of observations and focus, the "fit" between the model and the actual thought and diagnostic processes of the change-agent is not close. Furthermore, the thought and diagnostic processes of the change-agent are not fixed and rigid. And even worse, the "fit" between the diagnostic processes of the change-agent and the changing processes of the "actual" case, is not close. Abstract as the nature of a model is, as applied to the change-agent, students of the change-agent role may find the concepts of use. But change-agents' practices in diagnosing are not immediately affected by models' analyses.

Furthermore, there are modes of diagnosing by intervening, which do not fall neatly into models. The change agent frequently tries out an activity in order to see what happens and to see what is involved in the change. If successful, he does not need to diagnose any further, but proceeds to engage in further actions with the client. If unsuccessful, however, he may need to examine what is going on in more detail.

The patch work required for a theory and model of changing requires the suspension of acceptance of such available models. For this paper has argued for some elements from both the system models and the developmental models to be included in the model for practitioners, with the use of a format of the intersystem model so as to include the change-agent and his relationships as part of the problem. But can the change-agent wait for such a synthesis and emerging construction? Our personal feeling is that the planning of change cannot wait, but must proceed with the available diagnostic tools. Here is an intellectual challenge to the scientist-scholar of planned change that could affect the professions of practice.

PART THREE

Dynamics of Planned Change

Chapter 7

CHANGE STRATEGIES

CHANGE is an alteration of an existing field of forces. This remark sounds prosaic enough and yet all of the papers in this chapter and most of the change strategies are based on this idea. The implications are monumental. It means that stability is an illusion, the myopia of the rigid and/or the unimaginative. It means that there is an array of forces, not one or two, and that they are counterpoised in dynamic tension. It means that changes involve a force field with high tension or low tension. It means that we have choice in change, that we can control some forces and not others, and that we can increase tension or decrease it. Other more dramatic implications can be derived from the general formulation. For example, we can assert that an effective change program, however defined, comes about when there is general agreement about the wisdom of controlling one set of forces instead of another set. We can also assert that the effective change agent is one who helps a client to recognize the forces in his field, to understand the consequences of manipulating certain forces, and to provide whatever support is needed to take action.

All of the writers included in this chapter are Lewinians, whether or not they explicitly recognize it. Two of the papers are straightforwardly so in that they lean exclusively on a force-field model for diagnosing and implementing change. The other three papers focus on organizational change through variants of laboratory training and invoke Lewinian thinking in one way or another. To introduce the articles as well as to underline the change strategies, we will summarize their main themes.

1. Creating change is equivalent to solving problems. The good manager and the good change agent are interchangeable. Managing change, then, requires the ability to identify forces or variables surrounding a problem and to develop consensus about the relevant forces and a strategy of manipulating these forces.

2. Any change program involves a set of core values. The core values of the change strategies included here can be summarized crudely as the "Theory Y" values articulated by Douglas McGregor. These values are lucidly detailed in the appendix of Sheldon Davis' paper. Basically, they place emphasis on man as a proactive, growth-seeking, inquiring, confronting *person*. In addition, the value system features an influence process that is transactional, meaning that the influence is a two-way process and that, regardless of status differences, there must be reciprocity in any influence transaction if the decision is to be really owned by both parties.

3. All three of the papers dealing with organizational change (Bennis-Schein, Winn, and Davis) feature laboratory training as the main (though not exclusive) strategy of change. We do not mean that only residential labs are employed, but that educational methods which exemplify laboratory values are used. These values are: open and trusting communication, confronting conflict and managing it through rational means (which involves the recognition of irrationality), true collaboration, relying on here-and-now, publicly shared experiences, and so on.

4. Although the papers on organizational change were written from different vantage points and take into account different environmental and technological settings (for example, Winn writes about a heavy industry based on natural resources and Davis writes about the aero-space industry), both make two interesting strategic points. First, organization change must ultimately affect the *culture* of the organization and not only the *individuals* within the organization. This means that change agents must reckon with the value system, social structure, and technical system if important changes are to be accepted and implemented. This means further that off-site, residential training may be a necessary but insufficient basis for organizational change. Equal attention must be placed on the organization itself. This is the basic idea behind the article by Winn.

The second basic strategic principle is that change agents must be prepared to work with the healthy parts of the organizations. The rejected alternative here is to become overly obsessed with the sick elements of the system, the resisters. While resistance is an inescapable aspect of every change program and must be reckoned with—and even exploited as Klein suggests (p. 498)—we have to work with the parts of the system that desire to change. These are present in every organization. Sometimes these healthy parts are latent and hard to discern. In those cases, the first task of the change agent is to locate and mobilize this invisible strength. In other cases, they come through loud and clear. Douglas Bunker has noticed, for example, that adaptive organizations have incumbents who are dissatisfied with the way things are and want to change them. They are not the marginal or beatnik fringe, but esteemed and powerful people who sense discrepancy between what is and what might be. He calls them "variance sensors." Ruth Leeds (p. 194) has referred to the absorption of protest and how management can use these cabals of protestors as agents of change. The point that all three of the organizational change papers make is that an effective change program must start organically; that is, work with indigenous forces ready and willing to change.

The paper by Benne and Birnbaum outlines the method of Lewinian force-field analysis and enumerates certain change principles derived from it.

Returning to the theme we started with, we can reiterate that good management and good change agents start and end with the same assumptions:

1. Change is an alteration of an existing field of forces.
2. Effective change is bringing about an alteration of these forces so as to reduce tension and gain commitment to ("ownership" of) the change.
3. The effective change agent and manager accomplish this by understanding the total array of forces operating on a particular equilibrium and reach consensus on a change strategy.
4. Consensus is built through obtaining as much participation and commitment as possible in the diagnosis and manipulation of the relevant forces.
5. Organizational cultures must be changed to reinforce and maintain changes achieved by individuals.

7.1   SOCIAL CHANGE IN INDUSTRY: FROM INSIGHT TO IMPLEMENTATION

Alexander Winn

> *The self-sufficient man, with his peculiar property which concerns no one else, is a concept without any validity for modern civilization.*
>
> Alfred North Whitehead

In an address before the American Psychological Association, Bennis (1964) forecast the decline of bureaucracy and the emergence of an "organic-adaptive system" which will dominate the world of scientific and intellectual achievements. He views the future of human organizations as leading to increased problem-cathexis, to perpetual change and high frequency of temporary social systems. He adds, "Learning how to live and tolerate ambiguity will be the task of education and the goal of maturity."

Bennis predicts that the individuals in the new organizations will be permitted and encouraged to use their imagination, fantasy, and creativity to

Alexander Winn, "Social Change in Industry: From Insight to Implementation," *The Journal of Applied Behavioral Science*, II, No. 2 (1966), 170–183. Used by permission.

an extent unheard of at present. If we look at our social structures, he argues, as manifestations of repression and our suffering as derived from it, then, with time, civilization will learn to require less renunciation and will sanction play and individual freedom of expression through work. Our need for repression seems to decrease with the maturity of civilization (Marcuse, 1965).

Sublimation, the path which mankind has followed since it began to write its history, does not lead away from human neurosis but, on the contrary, leads to its aggravation. If ignorance of this human condition is by and large a matter of self-ignorance, then a greater opportunity of self-expression, of knowing oneself more intimately, of freeing oneself from an overwhelming repressive tendency, would move us closer to a fuller life— with its freedom to imagine and create and where the boundaries between work and play will become blurred— and away from destruction and death-in-life.

Our social structures today are somewhat distant from the organic-adaptive model which Bennis projects for the future. The present is a model of a mass impersonal society which has destroyed the fabric of communal life. It is an age of "overt-anxiety," as Camus calls it, of alienation, of "anticipated fear of punishment and disapproval, withdrawal of love, disruption of personal relationships, isolation or separation" (Fromm-Reichmann, 1955).

It is an age of "galloping variables" and "lightning chess games." It is an age where individual or organizational survival depends on the ability to adapt. Schein (1961) writes, "Our fundamental values, whether we think

of them in terms of super-ego, or moral conscience, or some other concept, probably depend to a great extent on the social support of individuals or institutions which operate as surrogate for the parents or significant others from whom we have learned . . . . The ongoing integrity of the individual . . . depends on adequate social integration."

Administrator as a Change Agent

Conscious of the extent of the cost in such terms as low motivation, blocks in communication, untapped human potential, interpersonal and intergroup conflict which the absence of integration produces, some administrators of industrial organizations are moving slowly into a role of active agents of social change. Their concern is with personnel development and education for "what is real." Conceivably on the preconscious level, the administrator may be somewhat frightened with the continually shifting environmental forces and with the fluidity and fuzziness around him. He senses the urgency to mobilize the human resources available to him to allay fears of his own isolation and loneliness. The administrator who uses himself as a tool in the same way a carpenter uses his equipment becomes increasingly aware that to affect administrative situations responsibly requires self-knowledge. He has to be "on speaking terms with himself" before he can communicate with others.

Some industrial organizations in Canada and the United States have come to the conclusion that leaving personnel development and training in human relations to chance is costly. For the past two decades a variety of training programs have sprung up in industry. The training goal has been to help the student to become more effective and responsible in working with and through people. The aim has been for him to acquire the capacity to respond effectively in human situations.

Schutz (1964) points out the similarity of the historical development of training programs in diverse fields such as industry, psychotherapy, and education. These fields initially employed a more traditional method (lecture or group discussion), but ended up facing the here-and-now, the immediate existential encounters of group members.

Company Program Initiated

The beginning of Alcan's company-wide sponsored program dates back to the late Forties. At that time, shortly after the end of World War II, the organization faced the problem of attracting and integrating more than 100 university graduates a year who, as a result of the shortage of reserve in managerial ranks and the attrition of its cadres during the war years, were to occupy administrative positions on joining the company. An initial program evolved around lectures covering such subjects as industrial sociology as well as the more traditional topics, including the history of the company and its corporate organization. It soon became evident, however, that these imposed lectures gave "answers" to no questions raised explicitly or implicitly by the group. The critical question which was then faced has been stated effectively by Kubie (1958):

. . . what is the effective value of knowledge of externals in the absence of equally deep personal insight? Can there be wisdom even about the objective world around us (considering how many distorted fantasies we project onto this outer world) in the absence of wisdom about the inner world from which these projections arise? It is my conviction that education without self-knowledge can never gain wisdom or maturity.

The Case Method

By the early Fifties the case method and, to a much lesser extent, role playing were adopted as ways of teaching administration and human relations. Concurrently the composition of the student group changed. Supervisory personnel with five, ten, or twenty years' experience replaced young university graduates in the class.[1] Cases reflected actual administrative situations involving people, their thoughts, assumptions, attitudes, and behavior.

Class discussions offered simulated business experiences. It was hoped that through discussions and confrontation of ideas, the participant became somewhat more aware of his own generalizations about human behavior and that this helped him to reexamine his own attitudes and assumptions. He was thus assisted to become a more effective and responsible member of his organization.

The case program was carried on for

[1] The "Elite" or "Crown Prince" approach to personnel development created some dissatisfaction among older employees. Management has also felt that offering the case program to people with experience and, assumedly, with greater involvement and commitment, will produce greater impact on the organization. Older employees, it was believed, had also more to contribute from their own experience to the discussion, analysis, and diagnosis of administrative situations.

several years in a residential setting. It included some 40 participants from the ranks of the company's middle management and lasted four to five weeks. An elaborate evaluation of classroom progress was carried out. Written analyses of cases, questionnaires, and Rogers' S.O. scale (1954) were administered before and after sessions. Invariably curricular, substantive knowledge increased and some indication of sharpened self-knowledge was found. However, no difference was noticed in the participant's behavior in his back-home situation, and no evidence was found of his attempting to experiment with a different style of behavior. Perhaps this should have been anticipated. When there is no group self-analysis, when all interaction is channeled through the instructor, when the discussion material is "out there," the opportunity for expansion in depth is rarely available to the student.

In the meantime, management became increasingly conscious of the possible impact of greater intra- and intergroup cooperation on the organization. "The human side of enterprise" became prominent in the minds of some top managers who began to express feelings about the necessity to offer a more intense personal growth experience to the staff.

Introduction of T Groups

So the T Groups were born.[2] From a slow beginning in 1961, the program expanded steadily. It now comprises

some six general two-week residential "cousin" laboratories,[3] several continuous human relations laboratories, and "family"[4] and "interface"[5] programs, the three last-mentioned of three to five days' duration. More than 300 supervisory personnel passed through these laboratories in 1965, with the levels ranging from shift foremen to vice-presidents and with personnel of both sexes included.

The case discussion offers the student a simulated business experience. The T Group is an analogue of life itself. Slater (in press) elaborates:

. . . what differentiates training groups from "natural" task groups is their mortality, their confusion, and their leadership structure. Most groups which are formed to accomplish some purpose are potentially immortal, have a more or less clear goal or at least a plan of action or an agenda, and a clearly defined leadership. Training groups are born knowing that they must die; do not know, except in the vaguest possible way, why they are there or what they are going to do; and struggle perpetually with the fact that the object, whom they fantasy to be powerful and omniscient, in fact does nothing, fails to protect them or tell them what to do, and hardly seems to be there at all. Is this unlife-like? Is the most persistent theme of the training group situation the plaintive, "What are we sup-

---

[2] The author owes a great measure of gratitude to James V. Clark for his contributions to the introduction of T Groups into the company. See his book, *Education for the use of behavioral science*. Los Angeles: Institute of Industrial Relations, University of California, 1962.

[3] The "cousin" group consists of a "diagonal slice" across the organizational chart. The people in a specific T Group are not from the same department and are not functionally related.

[4] The "family" laboratory involves two or three hierarchical levels of a division, department, or plant.

[5] The "interface" laboratory consists of an intergroup setup like staff-line or head office-plant personnel, functionally related.

posed to be doing? What is the purpose and meaning of it all?" a query that is never heard outside the esoteric confines of an unnatural "laboratory" setting? On the contrary, it issues from the central dilemma of life itself, that which human beings always have been most afraid to face, taking refuge instead in collective fantasies of a planned and preordained universe, or in the artificial imperative of the daily routine and personal and institutional obligation.

Basic T Groups

As I have indicated elsewhere (Winn, 1964), the setting of T Groups represents a complete change from learning situations the participants have been used to. The concern of the T Group is with the immediate existential confrontation, the here-and-now experience rather than a case "out there." One can no longer hide oneself behind characters in the case; one can no longer too easily hang somebody in effigy. One is involved and immersed in a "real" situation oneself.

A T Group may be seen as operating on two levels. The first is the evocative one, the level of emotions, feelings, and sentiments, a Dionysian model, somewhat nonrational and regressive; the second is the rational Apollonian model, which allows the participants to understand, rationalize and incorporate. Compared with case discussions, a T Group is considerably more engaging and involving. The T Group's members are both investigators and subjects of the learning experience; they are both participants and observers.

The participant is provided with an opportunity to reexamine his normative orientation and his self-image, and the group develops a climate of trust which permits this. We can never learn about our own self except through interaction with and feedback from others. Norbert Wiener once said, "I never knew what I said until I heard the response to it." The T Group is like a hall of mirrors reflecting back to us images of ourselves as seen by others. In existential terms, the T Group widens considerably the individual's range of choice and increases his awareness of freedom he may wish to enjoy. The final decision (and responsibility) for the choice he makes remains his own.

The T Group removes the external determinants which shape behavior so that the behavior becomes shaped by the internal and intrapsychic determinants. The absence of structure and familiar pattern of role, status, and authority, the withdrawal of help and direction which aggravates the dependency needs, coupled with the trainer's silence, facilitate regressive tendencies. The trainer's silence must be explained (or denied), and the relationship to authority and to peers must be to some extent resolved. These two problems, relationship to authority and relationship to peers, epitomize our historical ambivalence to power and love, dependency and interdependency, distance and intimacy.[6]

It would appear from the company's experiences that whatever orientation the trainer has—whether he is group dynamics orientated (when his interventions would tend to focus on the process of decision making, emergence

[6] In some ways, the participant's working through his ambivalences toward power and love is reminiscent of "corrective emotional experience." See Alexander, F. *Fundamentals of psychoanalysis.* New York: W. W. Norton & Company, Inc., 1963.

of norms, or differentiation of roles, and so on) or more oriented toward the individual's needs—T-Group processes remain by and large the same.[7]

Although no attempt has been made to quantify the effectiveness of the basic laboratories, their impact has begun to be felt.[8] To the members of the company's T Groups one could apply Slater's (in press) evaluation: ". . . they benefit in reverse proportion to their therapeutic needs, although their not uncommon decision to seek psychotherapy . . . following a group experience perhaps is an exception to this rule."

There is accumulated clinical evidence which supports continuation of basic laboratory training within the company. As might have been expected, the experience affects the individual where his relationships with others are most crucial, where he is most involved in a deep personal sense, where his ambivalent feeling has the strongest resonance: in his home, in his daily contact with his wife, children, or parents.

[7] Possibly owing to the fact that Alcan's basic laboratory usually consists of four T Groups under one roof in a residential setting, where the "training community" provides a ground for exchange of personal experiences across the T-Group composition, differences in trainer style tend to be cancelled out. This view is supported by Slater's (in press) observation that great stylistic variance in trainer patterns seems to produce minor differences in group structure and development.

[8] For an excellent and elaborate evaluation of laboratory training, see Blake, R. R., Mouton, Jane S., Barnes, L. B., & Greiner, L. E. Breakthrough in organization development. *Harvard Bus. Rev.*, November-December, 1964, *42* (6).

A Tentative Model for Planned Change

In many ways, the company's basic laboratory reflects the bias held by most clinical psychologists, i.e., that insight leads to more effective functioning. The experience tends to confirm Bennis' (1963) view that there is no immediate correlation between "insight" and organizational change. Although insight implies both intellectual and emotional components, it lacks "manipulability" of strategic variables. We may have "insight to spare" and still suffer from many organizational diseases. Bennis argues:

. . . It is not obvious that insight leads to sophistication in rearranging social systems or in making strategic organizational interventions. It seems therefore that the insight strategy . . . is a questionable strategy. If anything, applied social science depends on the policy makers controlling the relevant variables. Insight provides these as far as personal manipulation goes, but it is doubtful that it can lead directly to external manipulations of social systems.

The critical question here (the trainer's despair) is the question of transfer. How does one transfer one's insight, one's sharpened ability to communicate with oneself, the deeper understanding of group phenomena, the realization of how one's behavior affects others, even the acquisition of more adequate "cognitive maps" from a "microculture" of a laboratory into the outside world? It is true that the company has experienced some dramatic instances of successful transfer into the organizational system. But if one listens to the participants, weeks or months after their return from the laboratory, one is struck by their prevailing references to family life. They are quite articulate in their descriptions of how the laboratory experience affected their relationships with their sons or their wives; they talk about their feeling of greater freedom to experiment within their families, of making decisions, of the lessened feeling of guilt—in short, of the rediscovery of joy in their family relationships.[9] Frequent references to the application of T-Group training to the home situation are not limited to our experience. Bradford[10] and others[11] report similar findings.

It is obvious that transfer of skill to a new culture is a difficult undertaking for the participant. His organizational environment, more frequently than not,

[9] In some instances, individuals who had previously contemplated divorce decided to invest more in their relationships with their wives. There are indications of success. In other cases, a basic T-Group experience may have precipitated decisions to separate or to divorce. What is perhaps most important is that the mode of avoiding a deep interpersonal issue, of "sitting on the fence," is no longer acceptable.

[10] Bradford, L. P. Personal communication. Summer 1964.

[11] In a letter commenting on the first draft of this paper, E. James Anthony writes ". . . . Incidentally, one quite frequently meets a similar situation in child psychiatry, where a child undergoing psychotherapy will soon bring back glowing reports from family life, whilst the teacher still finds him, as a pupil among 30 other pupils, a 'pain in the neck.' Later on, there is a spread to school behaviour, but the child is less emotionally engaged in the school environment, and so the delayed effect is understandable. I am sure if one would give the individual a second or third T-Group experience, it would soon spread beyond family life into his work relationships."

shares different values, different beliefs, norms, and expectations. But above all else, the question we must ask ourselves is how can one transfer the climate of trust, of emotional support and acceptance for what one is, from a laboratory into a wider culture? Could it be that the relationship with one's son or with one's wife, to which one has an inherently greater emotional commitment in a culturally prescribed environment of lesser mobility and greater trust (the family), provides a more receptive ground for experimentation with one's own behavior? The impassive, impersonal industrial organization does not invite most T-Group participants to try to implement their new perception and skill. Even in a department from which most of the key people went to a "stranger" or "cousin" laboratory, the impact of newly acquired insight may not be felt too dramatically. Something more, then, is required to effect a change in the social system.

The "Family" Laboratory

For some time now, we have been moving beyond the basic "cousin" laboratory into organizational "family" and "interface" laboratories. Both of these new types of laboratories are of a weekend's or a week's duration, again in a residential setting away from the job environment. Family laboratories involve two or three hierarchical levels, more often than not an organic work or task group in a department or division. A family laboratory is quite different from a basic T Group. Quite frequently it is a variation of a work conference in which, in addition to the manifest topic or agenda, the process, or the here-and-now, is explored. Questions pertaining to the immediate, to the authenticity of relationships, and to openness are raised at the beginning by the trainer and by members of the group as the conference progresses. The purpose of the family laboratory is to identify and work through the intra-group problems, including such things as superior-subordinate and peer-group relationships. The real authority figure, not a surrogate, is present along with one's work partners. Usually most, if not all, the members of the family laboratory have had previous basic T-Group experience. The climate of inquiry and experimentation which the group endeavors to develop permits these relationships to be explored, and as a result they tend to become more authentic, more open and free.

The here-and-now in a family group is obviously not limited to the data which the group generates in its confrontation at the meeting. Their past experiences, their anxiety and frustration, their feelings of hostility as well as friendship are carried over to the family laboratory. By making explicit the many blocks to interpersonal and intragroup communication and by seeking to break through these, it tends to influence the social system quite powerfully. Its influence on deep intrapersonal dynamics is necessarily limited; a "stranger" group, with considerably more perceived freedom, encourages a deeper personal involvement. However, the immediate effects of the family laboratory on organizational effectiveness are most promising.

In many ways, a family laboratory promotes trust formation within the task group. Human needs for interdependence, love, and mutual support are strong. It becomes a new T Group, in which one discovers that one's basic T Group had no monopoly on understanding and support and that, to one's surprise, the "human condition" is ubiquitous. Having lost some "delusion of the uniqueness of one's personality" in the basic laboratory, one is ready to lose the delusion of the uniqueness of one's original T Group. And there is joy in the discovery that a more meaningful and authentic relationship with one's superior and peers or subordinates is equally possible.

The "Interface" Laboratory

The "interface," or the intergroup laboratory, is the third phase of the tentative model for planned organizational change. An interface laboratory is essentially a confrontation of two or more family laboratories. The intergroup laboratory seems to promise the greatest influence on organizational effectiveness. The complexity of the contemporary industrial organization, with the functional interrelatedness of its parts (staff-line, head office-local plants, and so on), is a fertile ground for costly duplication of efforts and struggle for influence. Enemy Number One frequently becomes a staff man from the technical, sales, or maintenance department, rather than any of one's competitors. Available resources outside one's own task group are ignored at a heavy organizational cost in both psychological and material currency.

Again, confrontation of these task groups in a work conference breaks through many of the barriers and creates a climate of a fuller and more open communication. Several exercises like "role reversal" are frequently introduced to encourage each of the individual task groups to look at the situation through the others' lenses. Potentially, the third stage, the intergroup laboratory, has the greatest, the most visible and measurable result in organizational effectiveness. It permits maximum influence of the pattern of relationships within a broad segment of the social system.[12]

Resistances

There is no problem with regard to securing as many as 200 or more participants from its managerial and professional ranks for the many basic two-week laboratories organized every year. The participants come voluntarily, and most of the personnel look forward with a great deal of anticipation to this experience. The situation changes drastically, however, when it comes to filling the places for a family or intergroup laboratory. Voluntarism decreases markedly, and resistances reappear in strength. It is all right to play "the behavior-change game" away from subordinates or peers or work companions, but it is not quite the same to play this "forbidden game" at one's work. It is too threatening.

It would appear that a great deal of preparation is required to create the necessary level of acceptance for a family or interface group. This preparation involves research, interviewing, identification of some of the crucial interpersonal and intergroup issues, and, in general, helping individuals to overcome some of their apprehension.

Conclusions

What is perhaps most important in Alcan's attempt to raise the level of organizational effectiveness—to make

[12] The author had a most fascinating experience (December, 1964) in organizing and participating in a laboratory for a class of some 50 third-year students of the Department of Business Administration, Faculty of Commerce, Laval University, Quebec City. The case method of instruction is used in the department. At the beginning of the year the class was divided "sociometrically" into five groups of ten students each. These groups are known as "seminar" groups and are constituted for the purpose of prediscussion of assigned readings and cases. They meet once a day for one and one-half hours. The laboratory was of four and one-half days' duration, immediately prior to the Christmas vacation. Its design initially included heavy concentration on T Groups, two general sessions, and one meeting of the seminar groups. (The composition of the T Groups was random and cut across the seminar groups.) What was fascinating in this experience was the determination of the students, halfway through the laboratory, for immediate transfer of their T-Group learnings into their seminars and into the general classroom setting. Their penetrating insight into their past behavior was astounding. They became conscious of and verbalized the dysfunctional norms which prevented them from learning: their misplaced "loyalty" to their seminar group's findings, whatever the evidence and analysis offered by others in the classroom; the taboo against offering anything beyond what was prediscussed in the seminar; and their "win-lose" attitude toward learning. The effectiveness of the class's total social system was appreciably influenced by this experience.

progress toward the organic-adaptive model of the social scientist—is the effect on the organizational culture of the introduction of basic T Groups on a scale perhaps unprecedented in large companies and the determination of some to pursue the laboratory method and laboratory training in all possible phases of organizational activity.[13] As a consequence, the company culture is gradually beginning to change. Its change model has become a complex one. If one uses Bennis' typology (1963), one finds several components in the model, ranging from the "élite corps" through the "socio-therapeutic" to the "organic" and "developmental" concepts. There is some evidence that the value system, the norms, beliefs, and expectations of the organization are changing. The authoritarian stance is giving way, in some instances, to more participation in decision making, to freer and more open communication with one's superior; the concept of "economic man" and "mechanical" views of the organization are being questioned; "the human side of enterprise" is being talked about; and perhaps what is most important, the expression of one's feelings has been by and large legitimized.

The effect of this changing culture varies. Some managers have rediscov-

ered meaning in personal relationships and are helping to build a new social system. They enjoy the support and accept expressions of affection (as well as hostility) from their personnel; some others find it difficult to reconcile the new values with beliefs deeply rooted in past organizational experience. Some cannot tolerate the ambiguity and find themselves in a sort of "double bind" of mixed signals from within and from without. Change for them is too frightening. Only their past systems can adequately ward off their anxiety. For them the newness is not a challenge but a forewarning of more anxiety to come. They cling ferociously to their past beliefs and past fantasies.

The "return of the suppressed," the way to "lost innocence," is a long and tedious process. Development for the individual, as Slater (in press) says, is simply a matter of rescuing more and more pieces of reality, like bits of dry land emerging from the sea. To paraphrase him, as the individual becomes more conscious, more realistic, more tension-free, and less predictable, it does not necessarily mean that the realm of fantasy will diminish—that the more light, the less darkness. On the contrary, the brighter the light, the deeper the darkness seems by contrast.

So it is with development and social change in industrial organizations. The rate of advance toward a more open and freer system varies within different parts of the organization. If one part moves toward greater self-realization, other subsystems, stubbornly clinging to their past, make further development of the total organization seem so much more difficult by contrast.

[13] Illustrative of the many applications of laboratory method at Alcan are the weekend laboratory for university recruiters (involving both employment personnel and line managers from local plants); the three-day laboratory for a selection committee interviewing candidates for the Aluminium Limited Management School, Centre d'Etudes Industrielles in Geneva; and other similar programs.

The individual, whether at home, in his organizational family, or in his relationships with other functional task groups, has the capacity to move forward. However hesitantly, he can cover some distance toward a more meaningful and fuller life. The rate of his advance seems to vary proportionately with his emotional commitment: from the greatest impact on his primary family life to the slowest rate of progress in the affectively neutral organizational environment. But the transfer does take place, however delayed and at times agonizingly slow and disappointing the impact on the total organization may seem. What is important, however, is that the impersonal and impassive bureaucratic organization can be affected and the human cost of work paid in hard psychological currency decreased through determined use of developmental programs. The organizational environment can become more tension-free, and the individual can enjoy a more adequate social integration.

Although the administrator may be encouraged by signs that social change may be induced in his organization, he is still left with the perplexing question of how fast and how far this process can go. In the world of inconsistency, uncertainty, and inperfection, he feels, however, that he is contributing his share in moving his organization somewhat closer to the full realization of its human potential.

REFERENCES

1. Bennis, W. G. A new role for the behavioral sciences: Effecting organizational change. *Administrative Sci. Quart.*, September, 1963, *8* (2).
2. Bennis, W. G. Organizational developments and the fate of bureaucracy. Paper read at a meeting of the Division of Industrial and Business Psychology, American Psychol. Assn., Los Angeles, September, 1964.
3. Fromm-Reichmann, F. *An outline of psychoanalysis.* New York: Random House, Inc., 1955.
4. Kubie, L. *Neurotic distortion of the creative processes.* New York: The Noonday Press, 1958.
5. Marcuse, H. *Eros and civilization.* Boston: The Beacon Press, 1965.
6. Rogers, C. R., & Dymond, R. F. (Eds.) *Psychotherapy and personality change.* Chicago: University of Chicago Press, 1954.
7. Schein, E. H. Interpersonal communication, group solidarity, and social influence. In W. G. Bennis, K. D. Benne, & R. Chin (Eds.) *The planning of change.* New York: Holt, Rinehart and Winston, Inc., 1961.
8. Schutz, W. C. A theoretical basis for training in group processes. Unpublished manuscript, 1964.
9. Slater, P. E. *Microcosm: The dynamics of structural change in small social systems,* in press.
10. Winn, A. Laboratory training in industry. *Personnel Administration*, May-June, 1964, *27* (3), 6–17.

7.2   PRINCIPLES OF CHANGING

Kenneth D. Benne
Max Birnbaum

No institution or organization is exempt from change. Today the student who returns to his alma mater ten years after graduation can expect to find changes, not only in personnel, but also in personnel policies and teaching practices. The executive returning to the firm where he once worked, the nurse going back to her old hospital, the social worker visiting his agency— all can expect to find sweeping changes.

It is fairly easy to identify changes in institutional patterns after they have occurred. It is more difficult to analyze changes while they are going on and still more difficult to predict changes or to influence significantly the direction and the tempo of changes already under way. Yet, more and more, those who have managerial functions in organizations must analyze and predict impending changes and take deliberate action to shape change according to some criteria of retrogression or progress. The planning of change has become part of the responsibility of management in all contemporary institutions, whether the task of the institution is defined in terms of health, education, social welfare, industrial production, or religious indoctrination.

Whatever other equipment managers

Kenneth D. Benne and Max Birnbaum, "Change Does Not Have To Be Haphazard," *The School Review*, published by the University of Chicago Press, LXVIII, No. 3. Used by permission.

require in analyzing potentialities for change and in planning and directing change in institutional settings, they need some conceptual schema for thinking about change. This need stems from the profusion and variety of behaviors that accompany any process of change.

One useful model for thinking about change has been proposed by Kurt Lewin, who saw behavior in an institutional setting, not as a static habit or pattern, but as a dynamic balance of forces working in opposite directions within the social-psychological space of the institution (1).

Take, for example, the production level of a work team in a factory. This level fluctuates within narrow limits above and below a certain number of units of production per day. Why does this pattern persist? Because, Lewin says, the forces that tend to raise the level of production are equal to the forces that tend to depress it. Among the forces tending to raise the level of production might be: (a) the pressures of supervisors on the work team to produce more; (b) the desire of at least some team members to attract favorable attention from supervisors in order to get ahead individually; (c) the desire of team members to earn more under the incentive plan of the plant. Such forces Lewin called "driving forces." Among the forces tending to lower the level of production might be: (a') a

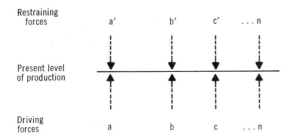

group standard in the production team against "rate busting" or "eager beavering" by individual workers; (b') resistance of team members to accepting training and supervision from management; (c') feelings by workers that the product they are producing is not important. Granted the goal of increased productivity, these forces are "restraining forces." The balance between the two sets of forces, which defines the established level of production, Lewin called a "quasi-stationary equilibrium." We may diagram this equilibrium . . . [in the figure above].

According to Lewin, this type of thinking about patterns of institutionalized behavior applies not only to levels of production in industry but also to such patterns as levels of discrimination in communities; atmosphere of democracy or autocracy in social agencies; supervisor-teacher-pupil relationships in school systems; and formal or informal working relationships among levels of a hospital organization.

According to this way of looking at patterned behavior, change takes place when an imbalance occurs between the sum of the restraining forces and the sum of the driving forces. Such imbalance unfreezes the pattern: the level then changes until the opposing forces are again brought into equilibrium. An imbalance may occur through a change in the magnitude of any one

force, through a change in the direction of a force, or through the addition of a new force.

For examples of each of these ways of unfreezing a situation, let us look again at our original illustration. Suppose that the members of the work team join a new union, which sets out to get pay raises. In pressing for shifts in over-all wage policy, the union increases the suspicion of workers toward the motives of all management, including supervisors. This change tends to increase the restraining force—let's say restraining force b'. As a result, the level of production moves down. As the level of production falls, supervisors increase their pressure toward greater production, and driving force a increases. This release of increased counterforce tends to bring the system into balance again at a level somewhere near the previous level. But the increase in magnitude of these opposed forces may also increase the tension under which people work. Under such conditions, even though the level of production does not go down very much, the situation becomes more psychologically explosive, less stable, and less predictable.

A war that demands more and more of the product that the work team is producing may convert the workers' feelings that they are not producing anything important—restraining force c'—to a feeling that their work is important and that they are not working hard enough. This response will occur provided, of course, that the workers are committed to the war effort. As the direction of force c' is reversed, the level of production will almost certainly rise to bring the behavior pattern back into a state of equilibrium at a higher level of productivity.

Suppose a new driving force is added in the shape of a supervisor who wins the trust and the respect of the work team. The new force results in a desire on the part of the work team to make the well-liked supervisor look good— or at least to keep him from looking bad—in relation to his colleagues and superiors. This force may operate to offset a generally unfavorable attitude toward management.

These examples suggest that in change there is an unfreezing of an existing equilibrium, a movement toward a new equilibrium, and the refreezing of the new equilibrium. Planned change must use situational forces to accomplish unfreezing, to influence the movement in generally desirable directions, and to rearrange the situation, not only to avoid return to the old level, but to stabilize the change or improvement.

This discussion suggests three major strategies for achieving change in any given pattern of behavior: the driving forces may be increased; the restraining forces may be decreased; these two strategies may be combined. In general, if the first strategy only is adopted, the tension in the system is likely to increase. More tension means more instability and more unpredictability and the likelihood of irrational rather than rational responses to attempts to induce change.

It is a well-known fact that change in an organization is often followed by a reaction toward the old pattern, a reaction that sets in when pressure for change is relaxed. After a curriculum survey, one school system put into effect several recommendations for improvement suggested by the survey. The action was taken under pressure from the board and the superintendent, but when they relaxed their vigilance, the old pattern crept back in.

This experience raises the problem of how to maintain a desirable change. Backsliding takes place for various reasons. Those affected by the changes may not have participated in the planning enough to internalize the changes that those in authority are seeking to induce; when the pressure of authority is relaxed, there is no pressure from those affected to maintain the change. Or, a change in one part of the social system may not have been accompanied by enough co-relative changes in overlapping parts and subsystems.

On the basis of this model of analysis, several principles of strategy for effecting institutional change may be formulated. We shall present the principles with illustrations of each.

To change a subsystem or any part of a subsystem, relevant aspects of the environment must also be changed.

The manager of the central office of a large school system wants to increase the efficiency of the secretarial forces by placing private secretaries in a pool. It is the manager's hope that the new arrangement will make for better utilization of the secretaries' time. In this situation at least two driving forces are obvious: fewer secretaries can serve a larger number of subexecutives; a substantial saving can be expected in office space and equipment. Among the restraining forces are the secretaries' resistance to a surrender of their personal relationship with a status person, a relationship implicit in the role of private secretary; the possible loss of the prestige implicit in the one-to-one secretary-boss relationship; the prospective dehumanization, as the secretaries see it, of their task; and a probable increase in work load. Acceptance of this change in role and relationship would require accompanying changes in other parts of the subsystem. Furthermore, before the private secretaries could wholeheartedly accept the change, their bosses as well as lower-status clerks and typists in the central office would have to accept the alteration in the secretarial role as one that did not necessarily imply an undesirable change in status. The secretaries' morale would surely be affected if secretaries in other parts of the school system, secretaries to principals in school buildings, for example, were not also assigned to a pool.

Thus to plan changes in one part of a subsystem, in this case in the central office of the school system, eventually involves consideration of changes in overlapping parts of the system—the clerical force, the people accustomed to private secretaries, and others as well. If these other changes are not effected, one can expect lowered morale, requests for transfers, and even resignations. Attempts to change any subsystem in a larger system must be preceded or accompanied by diagnosis of other subsystems that will be affected by the change.

To change behavior on any one level of a hierarchical organization, it is necessary to achieve complementary and reinforcing changes in organization levels above and below that level.

Shortly after World War II, commanders in the United States Army decided to attempt to change the role of the sergeancy. The sergeant was not to be the traditionally tough, driving leader of men but a supportive, counseling squad leader. The traditional view of the sergeant's role was held by enlisted men, below the rank of sergeant, as well as by second lieutenants, above the rank of sergeant.

Among the driving forces for change were the need to transform the prewar career army into a new peacetime military establishment composed largely of conscripts; the perceived need to reduce the gap between military life and civilian status; and the desire to avoid any excesses in the new army that might cause the electorate to urge a return to the prewar volunteer military establishment.

Among the immediate restraining forces were the traditional authoritarian role behaviors of the sergeancy, forged by wartime need and peacetime barracks service. These behaviors were in harmony with the needs of a military establishment that by its very nature is based on the notion of a clearly defined chain of command. Implicit in such a hierarchy are orders, not persuasion; unquestioning obedience, not critical questioning of decisions. Also serving as a powerful restraining force was the need for social distance between ranks in order to restrict friendly interaction between levels.

When attempts were made to change the sergeant's role, it was discovered that the second lieutenant's role, at the next higher level, also had to be altered. No longer could the second lieutenant use the authority of the chain-of-command system in precisely the same way as before. Just as the sergeant could no longer operate on the principle of unquestioning obedience to his orders, so the second lieutenant could no longer depend on the sergeant to pass orders downward unquestioningly. It was soon seen that, if the changed role of the sergeant was to be stabilized, the second lieutenant's role would have to be revised.

The role of the enlisted man also had to be altered significantly. Inculcated with the habit of responding unquestioningly to the commands of his superiors, especially the sergeant, the enlisted man found the new permissiveness somewhat disturbing. On the one hand, the enlisted man welcomed being treated more like a civilian and less like a soldier. On the other hand, he felt a need for an authoritative spokesman who represented the army unequivocally. The two needs created considerable conflict. An interesting side effect, which illustrates the need of the enlisted men for an authoritative spokesman for the army, was the development of greater authority in the rank of corporal, the rank between private and sergeant.

To recapitulate briefly, the attempts to change the role of the sergeancy led unavoidably to alterations in the roles of lieutenant, private, and corporal. Intelligent planning of change in the sergeancy would have required simultaneous planning for changes at the interrelated levels.

The place to begin change is at those points in the system where some stress and strain exist. Stress may give rise to dissatisfaction with the status quo and thus become a motivating factor for change in the system.

One school principal used the dissatisfaction expressed by teachers over noise in the corridors during passing periods to secure agreement to extra assignments to hall duty. But until the teachers felt this dissatisfaction, the principal could not secure their wholehearted agreement to the assignments.

Likewise, hospitals have recently witnessed a significant shift of functions from nurses to nurse's aides. A shortage of nurses and consequent overwork led the nurses to demand more assistance. For precisely the same reasons, teachers in Michigan schools were induced to experiment with teacher's aides.

The need for teachers to use the passing period as a rest period, the desire of the nurses to keep exclusive control over their professional relationships with the patient, and the resistance of teachers to sharing teaching functions with lay people—all these restraining forces gave way before dissatisfactions with the status quo. The dissatisfactions became driving forces sufficiently strong to overcome the restraining forces. Of course, the restraining forces do not disappear in the changed situation. They are still at work and will need to be handled as the changed arrangements become stabilized.

In diagnosing the possibility of change in a given institution, it is always necessary to assess the degree of stress and strain at points where change is sought. One should ordinarily avoid beginning change at the point of greatest stress.

Status relationships had become a major concern of staff members in a certain community agency. Because of lowered morale in the professional staff, the lay board decided to revamp lay-professional relationships. The observable form of behavior that led to the action of the board was the striving for recognition from the lay policy-making body by individual staff members. After a management survey, the channels of communication between the lay board and the professional staff were limited to communication between the staff head and the members of the lay board. The entire staff, except the chief executive, perceived this step as a personal rejection by the lay board and as a significant lowering of the status of staff members. The result was still lower morale. Because of faulty diagnosis the change created more problems than it solved.

The problem of status-striving and its adulteration of lay-professional relationships could have been approached more wisely. Definition of roles—lay and professional—could have been undertaken jointly by the executive and the staff in an effort to develop a more common perception of the situation and a higher professional *esprit de corps.* Lack of effective recognition symbols within the staff itself might have been dealt with first, and the touchy prestige symbol of staff communication with the lay board put aside for the time being.

If thoroughgoing changes in a hierarchical structure are desirable or necessary, change should ordinarily start with the policy-making body.

Desegregation has been facilitated in school systems where the school board first agreed to the change. The board's statement of policy supporting desegregation and its refusal to panic at the opposition have been crucial factors in acceptance of the change throughout the school system and eventually throughout the community. In localities where boards of education have not publicly agreed to the change, administrators' efforts to desegregate have been overcautious and halfhearted, and the slightest sign of opposition in the institution or the community has led to a strengthening rather than a weakening of resistance to desegregation. Sanction by the ruling body lends legitimacy to any institutional change, though, of course, "illegitimate" resistance must still be faced and dealt with as a reality in the situation.

Both the formal and the informal organization of an institution must be considered in planning any process of change.

Besides a formal structure, every social system has a network of cliques and informal groupings. These informal groupings often exert such strong restraining influences on institutional changes initiated by formal authority that, unless their power can be harnessed in support of a change, no enduring change is likely to occur. The informal groupings in a factory often have a strong influence on the members' rate of work, a stronger influence than the pressure by the foreman. Any worker who violates the production norms established by his peer group invites ostracism, a consequence few workers dare to face. Schools, too, have their informal groupings, membership in which is often more important to teachers than the approval of their supervisors. To involve these informal groups in the planning of changes requires ingenuity and sensitivity as well as flexibility on the part of an administrator.

The effectiveness of a planned change is often directly related to the degree to which members at all levels of an institutional hierarchy take part in the fact-finding and the diagnosing of needed changes and in the formulating and reality-testing of goals and programs of change.

Once the workers in an institution have agreed to share in investigating their work problems, a most significant state in overcoming restraining forces has been reached. This agreement should be followed by shared fact-finding by the group, usually with technical assistance from resources outside the particular social system. Participation by those affected by the change in fact-finding and interpretation increases the likelihood that new insights will be formed and that goals of change will be accepted. More accurate diagnosis results if the people to be changed are trained in fact-finding and fact-interpreting methods as part of the process of planning.

This article has been written from the standpoint that change in an institution or organization can be planned. Is this a reasonable view? Can change be deliberately planned in organizations and institutions as complex as school systems, hospitals, and armies? Do not many determinants of change operate without the awareness or knowledge of those involved?

It is true that most people are unaware of many factors that trigger processes of change in the situations in which they work. And most people are unaware of many factors that influence the direction of change. Many factors, even when known, are outside the power of people in an organization to control. For some forces that influence change in an organization stem from the wider society: new knowledge, new social requirements, new public demands force the management of a school system to alter the content and the methods of its instructional program. Some factors cannot be fully known in advance. Even when they are anticipated, the school cannot fully control them.

Some forces that work for change or resistance to change in an organization stem from the personalities of the leaders and the members of the organization. Some of these factors are unknown to the persons themselves and to those around them. Some personality factors, even when they are known, cannot be altered or reshaped, save perhaps by therapeutic processes beyond the resources of school teachers or administrators.

All this is true. Yet members and leaders of organizations, especially those whose positions call for planning and directing change, cannot evade responsibility for attempting to extend their awareness and their knowledge of what determines change. Nor can they evade responsibility for involving others in planning change. All concerned must learn to adjust to factors that cannot be altered or controlled, and to adapt and to alter those that can be. For as long as the dynamic forces of science, technology, and intercultural mixing are at work in the world, change in organizations is unavoidable. Freedom, in the sense of the extension of uncoerced and effective human choice, depends on the extension of man's power to bring processes of change, now often chaotic and unconsidered, under more planful and rational control (2).

REFERENCES

1. Kenneth D. Benne and Bozidar Muntyan, *Human Relations in Curriculum Change* (New York: Holt, Rinehart and Winston, Inc., 1951).
2. Ronald Lippitt, Jeanne Watson, and Bruce Westley, *Dynamics of Planned Change* (New York: Harcourt, Brace & World, Inc., 1958).

7.3 PRINCIPLES AND STRATEGIES IN THE USE OF LABORATORY TRAINING FOR IMPROVING SOCIAL SYSTEMS

Warren G. Bennis
Edgar H. Schein

. . . Introducing laboratory training into the climate of a formal organization (such as a hospital or factory or university or ship) brings about a set of strategic questions and raises certain issues of social change. We will discuss the background and perspectives on the use of laboratory training for changing social systems and consider the elements that make for its successful adoption by social systems: the state of the target system or subsystem, the role and competence of the change agent, and the strategies of implementation. After presenting the elements that lead to success, we will discuss three cases of failure. This article ends with some propositions about the uses of laboratory training in effecting social change.

Background and Perspectives on the Use of Laboratory Training for Changing Social Systems

WHY THIS RECENT IMPETUS TOWARD THE USE OF LABORATORY TRAINING FOR ORGANIZATIONAL IMPROVEMENT

. . . Labor supply, the professionalization of management, automation, the growing complexity of the enterprise, . . . with the need for better communication and decentralization, . . . [the] characteristics of our work force, the

Warren G. Bennis and Edgar H. Schein, "Principles and Strategies in the Use of Laboratory Training for Improving Social Systems," *Personal and Organizational Change Through Group Methods* (New York: John Wiley & Sons, Inc., 1965), pp. 201–233. Used by permission.

network of boundaries and transactions which clogs up the turbulent environment of the organization and a host of other factors must be included even in a superficial survey.[1] For us, the crucial factor is the inadequacy of present day organizations to cope with the complexity of rapid change and problems of human collaboration. Adaptation and collaboration are two of the main problems confronting contemporary society, and our organizations will fail or succeed depending upon their mastery of these two tasks.

This is only a part of the explanation. The inadequacies of bureaucracy have been examined in detail by many organizational theorists for a number of years. And they have produced countless thoughtful suggestions and ideas about a new vision of social architecture which would be more in keeping with what is known about human motivation. *The point is that laboratory training provides the instrument whereby the normative goals and improvements set forth by organization theorists and practitioners of organizations can be achieved.*

. . . Take the problem of *intergroup conflict.* There is an urgent need to understand the network of interdependencies which stems from the myriad of specialties and complexity of technologies. When we talk with managers of large-scale operations, they frequently mention intergroup conflict and collaboration as one of their main problems. From a theoretical viewpoint, Likert (1961) arrives at the same conclusion and suggests the importance of a "link-

[1] See Bennis (1963) for a more detailed discussion.

ing pin," a mechanism for integrating groups that are work related. *But how is this mechanism developed?*

USE OF LABORATORY TRAINING FOR IMPROVING SOCIAL SYSTEMS

Or take the problem of *authority and leadership* in organizations. McGregor (1960), in particular, has focused in his writings on the archaic workings of authority systems in bureaucratic structures. What is now needed, asserts McGregor, are systems of collaboration, of colleagueship between superiors and subordinates, not the blind use of controls and coercions. What we now need is increased autonomy, not dependencies and counterdependencies. *But how are systems created and people changed so that bosses trust enough to give their subordinates more autonomy, and how can subordinates learn to trust so that they can rely on self-control and collaboration?*

Lewin (1947), Allport (1945), and others have, for some time, produced evidence and arguments which show that as individuals participate directly in the decisions that are relevant to their work and life, they develop a higher state of morale and implement the decisions more effectively. *But how do organizations develop better and more responsive mechanisms for participative management?*

One final example: Argyris (1962) and others have insisted that *interpersonal competence* is a necessary ingredient in the role of a manager. He must be able to size up a situation, be aware of human factors impinging on a situation and develop a diagnostic sensitivity as well as behavioral flexibility in dealing with human problems.

But how do managers and other practitioners develop this interpersonal competence?

The point of these examples is this. Ever since the historic studies of Mayo and Roethlisberger at Western Electric, there have been many profitable revisions and suggestions developed to improve the operations of the human organization. We have mentioned some of these in the examples above: better systems of collaboration, of adaptation, of authority, greater interpersonal competence. There was no shortage of criticism or prescription. The problem was that there had been no organizational mechanism capable of implementing these suggestions. Laboratory training appeared at the time when formal organizations were most pressed for revision, for change. *It provided an instrument whereby these normative goals and revisions could be translated into practice.*

WHAT ARE THE CONCEPTUAL GOALS OF LABORATORY TRAINING WITH RESPECT TO ORGANIZATIONAL CHANGE

We have just been discussing the growth of laboratory training in terms of the needs and problems of the managers and practitioners, as they saw them. Now we want to shift our emphasis to the *change agents* who have collaborated with these target systems. What do they have in mind as change goals?

. . . We are using the term change agent to refer to a person or group, practitioners or social scientists, who are using the theory which underlies laboratory training in order to improve the functioning and effectiveness of organizations. Later on, we will go into

more detail about change agentry, but for the moment we will return to our original question: What do they have in mind as change goals?[2]

Although each change agent has in mind a set of unique goals, based on his own theoretical position and competencies as well as the needs of the target system, roughly speaking there are some general aims which most change agents would agree to.[3] Argyris provides a graphic model which can serve us as an example. In Figure 1 he shows (at the far left) the value system which dominates modern organizations. These values, basically impersonal and task-oriented and denying humanistic and democratic values, lead to nonauthentic relationships. These nonauthentic relationships tend to be coercive, phony, static, unhelpful, and basically incomplete; that is, they do not permit the natural and free expression of feelings which often must accompany task efforts. These nonauthentic relationships, then, lead to a state which Argyris calls "decreased interpersonal competence," a result of the shallow and threatening state of the relationships. Finally, without effective interpersonal competence among the managerial class, the organization is a breeding ground for mistrust, intergroup conflict, conformity, rigidity, and so forth, which in turn lead to a decrease in whatever criteria the organization is using to measure their effectiveness.

This is the basic paradigm: Bureaucratic values tend to stress the rational,

[2] For a full discussion of change agents, see Lippitt et al. (1958) and Bennis et al. (1961).

[3] For a more complete and detailed statement, see Bennis (1963).

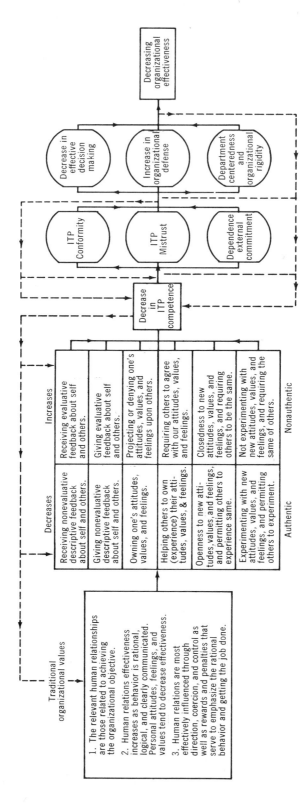

FIGURE 1. Model of Organizational Dynamics (Argyris, 1962, p. 43, ITP Stands for Interpersonal.) [Reprinted with permission from Chris Argyris, *Interpersonal Competence and Organizational Behavior* (Homewood, Ill.: Richard D. Irwin, Inc. and The Dorsey Press) p. 43.]

task aspects of the work and to ignore the basic human factors which relate to the task. Managers brought up in this system of values are badly cast to play the intricate human roles now required of them. Their ineptitude and anxieties lead to systems of discord and defense which interfere with the problem-solving capacity of the organization. The aims of change agents then, are (1) to effect a change in values so that *human factors and feelings come to be considered as legitimate* and (2) to assist in *developing skills among managers in order to increase interpersonal competence.*

There are variations to this paradigm, to be sure . . . : For example, changed attitudes toward own role, role of others, and organizational relationships, or increased adaptibility of the organization to external stress. But basically, the variations show up more sharply in the *strategic models* employed to induce the change than they do in the conceptual goals. Let us turn to that now.

WHAT STATEGIC MODELS FOR INDUCING CHANGE ARE USED

This question has to do with the problem of *how*: How are change agents selected? How do they achieve their goals? How do they gain their influence and power? In order to get a foothold on these issues, let us pose two central questions: (1) Are the change agents internal or external to the target system, i.e., are they regular employees of the target system or not? (2) What is the basis of the change agent's power or ability to exert influence on the target system?

1. Change agents: internal or external? Whether or not the change

agents are actual members of the target system is a crucial question to practitioners and students of organizational change. There are some who say that a significant change cannot occur without the impetus generated by the external agent (Lippitt et al., 1958; Seashore and Van Egmond, 1959). They argue that only a skilled outsider-consultant can provide the perspective, detachment, and energy so necessary to effect a true alteration of existing patterns. There are advocates of the internal model who take the opposite position. They argue that the insider possesses the intimate knowledge of the target system that the external change agent lacks. In addition, the internal change agent does not generate the suspicion and mistrust that the outsider often does. His acceptance and credibility are guaranteed, it is argued, by his organizational status.

2. The second question is: What is the source of the change agent's power? Generally speaking, he derives his power and influence from a combination of two sources: *expert* power and *line* power. As these terms suggest, the change agent is seen as possessing certain skills and competencies (expert power) or he is seen as occupying a certain office or holding status in an organization which legitimizes his influence (line power).[4]

In our experience, the most common model used is the *external* change agent

[4] We have ignored some of the more personal and intangible elements which enter into questions of strategy, such as the change agent's personality, charisma, etc. These personal factors are rarely written about explicity and only infrequently recognized. For these reasons, we do not feel confident in stressing anything but their *presence*.

employing *expert* power. We call this the *Consultant* model because outside change agents are employed as consultants to the organization (usually, but not always, to the Personnel division) and attempt to help the target system build adequate laboratory training programs. In some cases, the consultants actually conduct laboratory training; in other cases, they coordinate laboratory training activities along with other consulting functions.[5]

. . . Models implementing laboratory training for improving organizations can be viewed along two dimensions, internal vs. external and line vs. expert power. If the choice of change strategy is *internal*, then line or expert power can be utilized. The General Electric catalyst program is an example of the internal-expert model; the work of Alfred J. Marrow at Harwood is an example of the internal-line model. If the choice of the change strategy is *external*, then only one power alternative is open, that of expert, for line power must be drawn from sources internal to the target system. There are many examples of the external-expert model. We have already mentioned the work of Argyris, Beckhard, Blake, McGregor, Shepard, and others. It is probably the most widely used of the approaches we have singled out.

This classification we have developed for the uses of change strategies is crude, to be sure, and it ignores some of the more ingenious variations. But we would wager that over 90% of the change efforts utilizing laboratory training can be grouped in it. At the same

[5 See Sheldon Davis' article (p. 357) for an example of the Consultant model.]

time, however, new models are now being developed that may make this classification obsolete.

It seems increasingly clear to us that *combinations* and appropriate *sequencing* of these approaches may prove to be most useful. There are more and more signs, for example, that internal and external change agents, *in concert*, are more effective than either internal or external working alone. Moreover, all things being equal, a combination of line and expert power cannot help but be more effective than line or expert power working independently of each other. The evidence is far from conclusive at this point, but, from certain trends that we now see developing, new models for implementing organizational change will be used that rely on external *and* internal change agents in combination and using line *and* expert power. What this implies is a *team effort* involving a diverse set of skills, status, and roles in order to induce the organizational change. We believe this will prove to be the most useful strategy in the future.

Considerations for the Successful Adoption of Laboratory Training by Social Systems

In this section we will examine the conditions that facilitate the adoption of laboratory training by target systems. We will consider two: (1) the state of the target system or subsystem and (2) the role and competence of the change agent. Then we will discuss the interaction between the change agent and the target system in the strategy of implementation.

THE STATE OF THE TARGET SYSTEM OR SUBSYSTEM[6]

In considering the state of the target system, a number of questions must be asked:

1. Are the learning goals of laboratory training appropriate?
2. Is the cultural state of the target system ready for laboratory training?
3. Are the key people involved?
4. Are members of the target system adequately prepared and oriented to laboratory training?
5. Is voluntarism (regarding participation) insured?

1. *Are the learning goals of laboratory training appropriate?* To what extent do the goals and meta-goals relate to the effectiveness of the target system? We can think of many target systems where the answer to these questions may be negative, due to market, technological, and competitive conditions. Serious attention must be given, particularly in the early stages, to the appropriateness of laboratory training change goals for the particular target system. Later on we shall discuss some cases where laboratory training was obviously inappropriate in retrospect. A great deal of effort, at first, must be directed to diagnosing the target system's needs in relation to the anticipated outcomes of laboratory training. Are the outcomes relevant to the effectiveness of the target system? Is laboratory training timely, economical, congruent with the anticipated target system trends, and so forth? Later on, after discussing the cases where it failed, this question of appropriateness will again be raised.

2. *Is the cultural state of the target system ready for laboratory training?* What do we mean by "cultural readiness?" Each target system transmits and maintains a system of values that permeates the organization and is used as a basis for action and commitment. This does not mean that values are always adhered to, but it usually means that those who exemplify the values are rewarded and those who violate them are punished. Laboratory training also has a set of values . . . under the heading of meta-goals: we specified authenticity, choice, collaboration, and the expression of feelings among others. There is bound to be *some* value conflict between these values and the values of the target system, but situations should be avoided where the two sets of value systems clash extraordinarily.

The degree and range of value conflicts provide some of the best clues for diagnosing the cultural state of the target system. That is, if the discrepancy between laboratory training values and the target system's values can be realistically assessed, a fairly good idea about the target system's readiness can be obtained. Let us sample some of the most important dimensions of the cultural state.

The *legitimacy of interpersonal rela-*

[6] The boundaries of the target system which laboratory training affects may be a part (or subsystem) of the larger target system. For example, a target system like Aluminum Company of Canada has been directing the bulk of its laboratory training change program at one of its three main divisions. In the Esso change program, the refinery, a subsystem, became the chief target system. We will come back to this point later in our discussion of the strategy of implementation.

tionships, both in terms of its effects on the work and the degree to which members of the target system view it as susceptible to change, is an important aspect of the target system's culture. In many target systems, interpersonal phenomena are not considered appropriate to discuss, germane to the task, or legitimate as a focus of inquiry. As Henry Ford once said about his own philosophy of management: "You just set the work before the men and have them do it." While this view is becoming slowly outdated by modern techniques of management, there are still many situations where interpersonal influence is regarded as invalid, illegitimate, or an invasion of privacy.

Another cultural variable which must be taken into account is the *control and authority system presently employed by the target system.* If it is too rigid and authoritarian, it may be too much at variance with the values of laboratory training.

The presence and intensity of conflict within the target system represents still another cultural factor which must be considered. It is difficult to generalize about conflict in terms of its relationship to the adoption of laboratory training. The impression we gain, however, is that it is best not to introduce laboratory training under conditions of intense conflict. In this case, the organization is under stress and may be *too* plastic; laboratory training may then be only a temporary dodge, become a tool in a power play, or be used later on as a convenient scapegoat. This is not to say that it may not be strategically employed during periods of conflict. It is only to say that the type, causes, and intensity of conflict must

be examined in relationship to the laboratory training program.

The internal boundary system of the target system must be carefully examined in order to avoid situations where laboratory training values are internalized in one subpart of the system only to be rejected by and cause disruptions in an adjacent system.[7] In other words, the interdependence of the parts within the target system must be carefully scrutinized so that unanticipated changes in some parts of the system do not backfire or create negative repercussions in another part of the target system.

The last item to consider in assessing the cultural readiness of the target system is the most difficult to render in objective terms, and, yet, it is possibly the most important factor in estimating the probability of success. *It has to do with the change agent's relationship with the target system,* in particular, the quality and potentiality of the relationship.

If the change agent believes that it is possible to establish a relationship with the target system based on a

[7] George Strauss and Alex Bavelas (1955) report an interesting example of this when a subunit of girls on an assembly line developed an ingenious and new method which increased their job satisfaction and improved their performance significantly. The only trouble was that it had repercussions on interdependent parts of the organization. The program eventually had to be stopped. Though we know of no such case, it will be interesting to identify sources of strain that laboratory training might create with the target system's *external* boundary system: suppliers, customers, government, employee sources, etc. It is doubtful that it would generate the same degree of strain as internal interdependencies, but it still bears examination.

healthy, realistic understanding of his role and with realistic expectations regarding the change, then a change program may be indicated. But if the relationship is based on fantasy, on unrealistic hopes, on fear or worship or intimidation, then the change agent and/or the target system must seriously re-examine the basis for their joint work.[8]

We are suggesting that one of the best ways of diagnosing cultural readiness has to do with the way the target system reacts to and establishes a relationship with the change agent. The quality and vicissitudes of this encounter—insofar as it is a miniature replica of the intended change program —provide an important clue regarding the fate of the laboratory training change program.

What we mean by readiness is the degree of value conflict between laboratory training values and the target system's values in terms of: legitimacy of interpersonal phenomena, the range, depth, and intensity of conflicts and modes of conflict resolution, concepts of control and authority, the interdependence of parts of the target system, and the relationship between change agent and target system. Though they are difficult to measure precisely, thorough attention and rough

assessment must be made before laboratory training can be introduced. Assuming that the cultural readiness of the target system has been carefully assessed and found to be appropriate, we must ask:

3. *Are the key people in the target system involved in or informed of the laboratory training program?* It can be disastrous if the people most affected by laboratory training are not involved, informed, or even advised of the program. To guarantee success, a great deal of energy and time must be devoted to assessing the extent to which the laboratory training is supported by the key people and the attitudes individuals generally hold regarding laboratory training.

4. *Are members of the target system adequately prepared and oriented to laboratory training?* The usual forms of *preparation* and *orientation* do not seem too effective for laboratory training, primarily because the word rarely conveys the sense of the experience. Laboratory training, if anything, is experience-based, and words, without an experimental referent, often tend to confuse and, in some cases, cause more apprehension than necessary.

Some introductory *experiences* often prepare and orient future participants adequately. We have tried a miniature laboratory (waggishly called by one of the participants an "instant laboratory") to simulate as accurately as we could the laboratory environment. In this case, an entire laboratory was compressed into one full day of training. In other situations we have executed a specific training exercise with some prospective delegates in order to give them a feel for the learning environment. In any case, we advocate some

---

[8] Let us be clear about this. We mean that if the change agent can *foresee* a healthy relationship in the future, he might well consider the laboratory training program. We do not think it is possible for the relationship to be totally trusting and realistic during the beginning phases of work. In any case, the main point we want to stress is the diagnostic validity of the relationship; the problems that inhere in that relationship are probably symptomatic of the problems to be encountered.

experience-based orientation in order to provide a reasonable facsimile of laboratory life.

Another alternative frequently used is seeding. Selected members of the client system attend stranger laboratories on their own. In this way, the organization can successfully build up a significant number of personnel who are familiar with laboratory training.

5. *To what extent is laboratory training viewed as voluntary by the participants?* We feel this is an important, perhaps crucial factor for the successful adoption of laboratory training by target systems. We think it is crucial

TABLE 1   Five-Step Model for Diagnosing State of Target System

1. Are laboratory training change goals appropriate to target system? If yes, then:	If *not, stop* and reconsider appropriateness of laboratory training.

2. Is the cultural state of target system prepared for laboratory training:
  a. Degree and type of value conflict?
  b. Legitimacy of interpersonal phenomena?
  c. Degree, range, intensity, resolution of conflict?
  d. Concepts of control, authority?
  e. Interdependence of target system?
  f. Relationship of trust and confidence between change agent and target system?
If yes, then:
	If *not, stop* and examine areas where more preparation is needed or where value conflicts should be reduced.

3. Are key people involved and committed: If yes, then:	If *not, stop* and examine ways to develop more commitment to program.
4. Are members of the target system adequately prepared and oriented to laboratory training? If yes, then:	If *not, stop* and examine ways to develop more commitment to program.
5. Is voluntarism (regarding participation) insured?	If *not, stop* and examine attitudes toward laboratory training: why people go or do not want to go to laboratories. After diagnosis, attempt to accurately indicate the place of laboratory training in career development.

not only for the obvious ethical reasons but also for realistic learning considerations. In order for a participant to profit the most, he must not feel coerced or pushed into the experience.[9] Involuntary attendance is particularly hard to avoid in those cases where the entire organization undergoes laboratory training and where there is a tacit rejection of those who refuse to attend. Still it is important for target systems to provide as much choice and voluntarism as possible, by providing the individuals with as much orientation as possible so that choice is meaningful and by minimizing organizational pressure to attend. . . .

THE ROLE AND COMPETENCE OF THE CHANGE AGENT

We mentioned earlier that the idea of change agentry, as we are using the term here, is very new. Because of its novelty, its fundamental outline is still emerging. Thus the role of the change agent is protean, changing, difficult to grasp, and practically impossible to generalize. However, it may be useful to make some tentative remarks about it in this section.

There are a number of things we would like to call attention to about the role of the change agent. We shall discuss each of them in more detail. The change agent's role must be construed in the following way. It is: . . .

1. The change agent is a *professional*. He counts heavily on a body of

valid knowledge in order to realize his aims, under guidance of certain ethical principles, and with the client's interest, not his own, in mind. This last point should be emphasized; the change agent must defer his own personal gratification in his dealings with the target system, his client. Particularly in dealing with something as important as a large and complex organization—where the change agent's actions may affect thousands of individuals—he must continually check his own needs, motives, and wishes against the reality of the client's needs.[10]

2. The change agent is *marginal*. He does not have formal membership in the target system or with a band of colleagues working close by. Typically he works alone and his marginality can work to his advantage and to his discomfort. On the positive side, the marginality can enhance his detachment and perception; it can also create insecurity and an absence of mechanisms (like colleagues) for reality testing. In any case, both the target system and the change agent have to come to terms with the idea of marginality.[11]

[9] This often creates the dilemma of the people who most need the laboratory training experience resisting it and those who least need it volunteering for it. However unsatisfactory the resolution of this dilemma is, nothing would be gained and a lot possibly lost if people were captive to the experience.

[10] The change agent must be made painfully aware of some of the unconscious gratifications of his role too, so that these can be brought under control. We have in mind such fantasies as high-powered manipulation, an uncontrollable quest for power and omnipotence. . . .

[11] In a recent case which we heard about, a change agent reported to work for his first day on the job and the plant manager requested him to do some work which seemed to be inappropriate for a change agent. It was work that one of the managers should have been doing. The change agent refused to carry out functions which properly belonged to management. In this case the manager could not come to terms with the marginal role of the change agent.

3. The role of the change agent is *ambiguous*. Essentially this means that the basic concept of the change agent is not widely understood and evokes a wide range of meaning. If one responds to the question, "What do you do?" with the answer, "I am a psychologist," it does not evoke the same bewilderment as the response, "I am a change agent." (In fact, the responder might be well advised not to answer in that vein.) The ambiguity of the role betrays its lack of legitimacy as well as credibility. It also involves certain risks such as drawing suspicion and hostility *because* of its ambiguity. On the other side, it can be helpful in providing the necessary latitude and breadth which more precisely defined roles do not allow.

4. The role of the change agent is *insecure*. This stems from a variety of causes: the precarious employment basis of the change agent (the fact that he may be the most expendable person under certain conditions); the lack of guidelines and adequate knowledge to guide many of his actions; the profound resistances which develop in attempting to change an organization. All of these factors tend to make the role insecure.

5. Related to the insecure elements in the change agent's role is the *risky* quality inherent in it, the risk not only to the target system but to the agent's professional status. As we shall see in the next section, the complexity of organizational change and some of its unanticipated consequences can lead to totally undesirable outcomes.

The *competence* of the change agent must encompass a wide range of knowledge including: (1) conceptual diagnostic knowledge cutting across the entire sector of the behavioral sciences; (2) theories and methods of organizational change; (3) knowledge of sources of help; (4) orientation to the ethical and evaluative functions of the change agent's role.

In addition to this intellectual grasp, the change agent must also possess (5) operational and relational skills: of listening, observing, identifying, and reporting, of ability to form relationships and trust, of a high degree of behavioral flexibility. The change agent must be able (6) to use himself, to be in constant communication with himself and to recognize and come to terms with (as much as is humanly possible) his own motivations, . . . (7) act congruently (authentically), in accordance with the values (meta-goals) he is attempting to superimpose upon the target system's value system. The change agent must not impose democratic or humanistic values in an authoritarian or inhuman manner. If the change agent is concerned with creating more authenticity and collaboration, he must behave in ways that are in accord with these values. We say this not only for the obvious ethical reasons, but for deeper reasons as well. The fact of the matter is that so much of the change agent's influence grows out of his relationship with the target system and the extent to which he is emulated as a role model, that any significant discrepancies between the change agent's actions and his stated values cannot help but create resistance. . . .

STRATEGIES OF IMPLEMENTATION

1. First and perhaps the most important strategic question is: *Who is the client?* The organization? A particular T-group? The group or person

who appointed and pays the change agent? An individual in stress? This is a hard question to answer and we would guess that the *salient* client shifts and oscillates among a host of different clients throughout the course of a laboratory training program. But the question itself should never be too far from the change agent's mind.

2. *Where is the point of entry?* That is, at what level of the organization should laboratory training be directed first? The top management group? Middle levels? Lower levels? There are some change agents, like Argyris (1962) and Blansfield (1962) who believe that change can only succeed if it starts at the top and percolates down, that in order for a real change to take place, the highest command must be the primary initiating force.

Others disagree with this strategy. They claim that change programs utilizing laboratory training can start at lower levels of the target system and still be successful. Furthermore, they argue, it is sometimes *preferable* to start the change at lower levels because in some situations, due to a variety of organizational conditions, starting at the top may be too risky.

To some extent, the problem of point of entry can be decided on the basis of the kind of model of change employed. If it is a *line* model, then the consequences of starting at the lower levels may be different than in a *consultant* or *staff* model. The kind of model used also pertains to our third question.

3. *Which systems are involved?* Obviously everyone cannot be trained at once. This raises the question of priorities and choice. Can training be isolated in certain components of the organization, leaving other components without it? Or should attempts be made to include segments of all subsystems of the target system in the initial stages of the program? In any case, a careful diagnosis needs to be undertaken in order to trace the most strategic circulation of effects throughout the total target system. In our experience, some of the most critical unanticipated consequences arose when a diagnosis of the interdependencies of the subsystems within the target system was not carefully worked out. . . .

4. *To what extent can the change agent involve the target system in planning and executing laboratory training?* In order to act in accordance with the values of laboratory training, the change agent should attempt to involve the target system in planning and goal setting for the change program. Sometimes this is easier said than done because the target system may not have the experience or expertise to collaborate realistically with the change agent. In any case, the change agent must attempt to make an adequate diagnosis of the extent to which the target system should be involved in the planning, goal setting, and execution of laboratory training.[12]

---

[12] There is a dilemma here that is often commented upon by change agents and practitioners. How can systems of collaboration be established if one party to the encounter cannot adequately *choose* due to inexperience or lack of knowledge? Does coercion or faith have to be used during the very first phase of change? Can one start a democratic change program, for example, by ordering people to attend? Can a change agent insist that his client attend a laboratory so that collaboration, of a deep and enduring kind, can be achieved?

Three Cases of Failure

. . . . What we propose to do is this: We will present three brief anecdotes or actual cases that have come to our attention in one way or another. (We have doctored and disguised the cases sufficiently so that no confidences will be endangered.) The cases will be presented consecutively and without comment until the third and last one; then we will attempt to develop some principles from the case material.

CASE 1: A LETTER FROM A GOVERNMENT TRAINING CENTER

This is a letter which came to one of the authors from a government training officer (Dr. A) connected with a large government training center. Laboratory training was started at the center several months before and since that time the following things happened: (1) the Director (Mr. Z) went to a two-week laboratory at Bethel, (2) about 250 government officials underwent a five-day laboratory at the center under Dr. A's leadership with other staff drawn from officials Dr. A had personally trained, and (3) Dr. A with the support of Mr. B (a strong advocate of laboratory training and second in command of the center) planned to set up a laboratory training experience for all 2,000 officials stationed there. This letter arrived shortly after plans were laid out to train trainers in order to execute a massive design.

. . . I'm still behind on the reports on our lab training here, at least on the reports I'd like to get out.

Some of the little things that have cropped up. The Director who went to the *two* week lab away from here feels that those who have only gone through four or five days training here don't really have the capacity to talk to him.

Those members of the faculty who got the training late wonder why they were left to last. An "in" group and "out" group developed in the faculty. Some of the outs resented being trained by one of their peers. Some wanted to know: "How did you get to be a trainer?"

The head of our medical department told the Director that lab training type of training is dangerous.

The chief in Washington (over our Director!) asked someone in an aside: "What the hell is Dr. A doing giving that kind of training!"

A Grade 15 called in a Grade 12 scheduled to attend a five-day lab in April and said, not once but twice: "You don't have to go to this thing you know. I want you to understand it is entirely voluntary, you don't have to go unless you want to . . . What are you going to do if some younger official tells you he doesn't like the way you conduct yourself?"

One man comes up to me occasionally, looks around as if to make sure no one is watching, and then makes the sign of T with both hands.

The Director's deputy wrote a letter to Headquarters and asked for an evaluation of lab training. "If it's good for one, is it good for all?"

I received an informal request from a staff official in Headquarters asking me to answer about 12 objections commonly raised to lab training.

In short, a considerable number of anxieties have been raised. Some are intrigued, some are scared.

Two weeks elapsed and another letter arrived from Dr. A:

. . . We have unfortunately hit a snag. How serious it will be remains to be seen. Mr. B (Dr. A's main line support) has been transferred. This removed our chief advo-

:ate suddenly. Within a week the Director, Mr. Z, called in the Head of Curriculum and outlined how he wanted lab training out into the curriculum. A meeting was set up wth me, the Director, and the Head of Curriculum.

(Up until this time we had been planning, with Mr. B's approval and backing, to put the training into one department and start in September. We proposed, if we could get the money, to get two outside trainers in for three weeks in August, to train this Department's staff. Someone from National Training Laboratories had been down and talked this over with the staff and I had manage to find a friend in Washington who said he would underwrite the program. We had not gotten down to the nuts and bolts of actually drawing up detailed plans for September, but that was the large outline.)

In the May 3rd meeting, Mr. Z started out by saying NTL didn't have any final answers to lab training and that his trainers at Arden House were quick to admit they didn't know all the answers. Thus, he said, we had a chance to strike out on our own and did not have to be bound by the fixed two-weeks approach pioneered by NTL. (Up to this time he was the only one who had been insisting on two weeks; we had been talking in terms of four and five days.) Furthermore, we could not have officials foregoing their vacations in August, so any ideas about giving them three weeks of training couldn't be considered. Anyway, it didn't take much training because all his trainers did was sit there, they hardly opened their mouths during the two weeks. He would train the officials himself and he thought possibly one afternoon would be enough. What he proposed then was that after about six or seven weeks all the students be given one or two days to give each other feedback. This would be preceded by four or five lectures during the first week or so which would tell them what to be watching for. Keeping what they had observed in mind, they could then tell each other after the sixth week what they had observed. At the end of school, the students would be given another day or two days to give each other feedback. And so on. One or two of us tried to offer some comments or observations and were either cut off or ignored. As a consultant of sorts, I didn't feel quite up to exploring all the implications of his plan in front of the staff because I felt it was his prerogative to run the school as he wanted to.

Since that time various staff sections have been busy trying to pass on to other staff sections the job of trying to figure out what Mr. Z wants and making plans for his wishes. I've been invited to a meeting in the morning and will see what develops. I intend to talk to Mr. Z by himself after this if I can.

I'm curious to find out if he will tell me why he changed his mind, apparently, so suddenly and why he chose not to build on any of the data we had so painstakingly gathered. All this he just threw out of the window. And either just before or just after the May 3rd meeting he forwarded to Headquarters a report of the school activities in which he asked for funds for the August training I described.

We are unable to figure out whether Mr. B's leaving triggered the change, whether he is scared to try a four-day lab with students, whether he balks at paying the training price, whether he is irked at me, or just what the score is. But what makes it so hard to figure is that all the reports, letters, plans, etc., that he has seen and signed have nothing to do with what he has proposed. Some of what he says might be worked out into something quite useful, but in the meeting he brooked no comment—all he wanted was a rubber stamp.

I am not ready at this point to say the effort has failed because a lot of pressure has been building up in the past ten days. How much it will mean has yet to be disclosed. Certainly, at this moment the plans for the August training seem dead, although we may yet get the test in one Department rather than among 800 students. This really bugged me, trying something completely unknown and untested on 800 men.

Several weeks following this letter, Dr. A called to say that the Government Training Center had stopped its laboratory training and "had gone back to more traditional training methods."

CASE 2: A LETTER FROM MEDICAL SERVICES

This letter was sent as a confidential memorandum from the chief medical officer of a large manufacturing company to the Vice President of Personnel. A copy of this memo was sent to Dr. A, chief training officer for the company. Dr. A had been hiring consultants who use laboratory training quite regularly in their work for this company.

The medical division is concerned about the possibility of medical casualties from the T-group type of training program.

Dr. Jones says that T-group programs have greater likelihood of producing a higher percentage of disabling mental disturbances than do ordinary work situations.

The purpose of the Training Division is training.

The purpose of Medical Division is the prevention of illness and disability.

We feel the purpose of our Division warrants our scrutiny of any Company activity likely to be related to disabilities.

We recommended several months ago that the list of candidates for training sessions be passed before the local Company medical officer for his approval or comment regarding the names thereon. The suggestion is held impractical by some on the basis that the Company medical officers are not psychologically or psychiatrically

oriented, have little knowledge or comprehension concerning the nature of the sessions and are not qualified to determine who are high risk candidates. It is my conviction that something along the following lines should be required by the Company, if for no other reason than the doubt surrounding the advisability of having therapy for medical conditions unsupervised by medical people.

a) Collaboration should start immediately to arrange a long weekend session in a suitable place, to be attended by the senior medical representative from each of our plants. Dr. A should prepare a clear statement of the purpose of these T-sessions, a clear statement of the procedure used in attempting to achieve the purpose, a clear statement on what these procedures demand from the individual, and a clear statement of the signs which the trainers use as indicators of impending disability, no matter how temporary. In addition, this working session should provide a sample experience for the doctors attending. The purpose of this session would be to take away any feeling that the local doctor was completely "clueless" regarding what is appearing to take on the shadowy form of a mystic cult; . . .

This case had a reasonably successful outcome. The chief medical officer himself attended a two-week laboratory at Bethel and shortly after his return organized a long weekend session that was led by two laboratory trainers, for all of his doctors, other key personnel and line officials. This 3-day weekend session was designed as a modified laboratory, and, according to the participants and the trainers, it accomplished its purposes: a better understanding of laboratory training by the doctors, and an improvement in the collaboration between medical and training divisions.

Case 3: The Undercover Change Agent

The following anecdote is based on interviews conducted with members of an organization in which laboratory training was tried and failed. The training endeavor was almost totally disastrous: the staff member conducting the laboratory training was fired, his colleague transferred; the director of training was ordered to stop all training connected with management development and to provide only technical training; the Vice President of Personnel resigned.

The company itself is a large retailing combine operating about fifteen department stores in the Midwest. The headquarters are located in Milwaukee and many of the branch stores are located in the conservative, German farming centers throughout Wisconsin and Minnesota. The company is family-owned and operated by the son of the founder, Mr. Hess.

The company committed itself to a considerable amount of executive training through its personnel department. Each year most of its managerial staff attended a one week course at a small hotel in the lake country near Milwaukee. For the most part, the human relations training was based on cases very like those collected and used at the Harvard Business School. These case courses were deemed very successful by management and by the participants.

Last year the company hired a new trainer (Mr. Jones) for their one week human relations training program. Before taking the job, Jones attended a two week laboratory and was deeply impressed by the experience. After several weeks of conducting case study discussions Jones asked his boss, the director of training, if they could try some laboratory training. The director of training did not understand it completely but said he would take the matter up with his boss, the Vice President of Personnel. The latter had only an inkling of what laboratory training was all about but passed on whatever he knew to the President. It was not at all clear who "cleared what with whom" or how much anyone understood about the idea of laboratory training, but, in any case, nine weeks of laboratory training took place with nine different groups, all at the lower echelons of management. During the ninth week the President arrived unannounced at the training site and demanded to be given entry into the T-groups. Jones refused at first but finally gave in to the President's orders.

Shortly after the President's return to Milwaukee, the training ceased and Jones was fired, etc. What had happened?

Leading up to the President's visit to the laboratory, which culminated in his storming into the resort hotel during the breakfast hour demanding entrance into the T-group, was a whole series of events. First of all, the President had heard about some "interesting" training going on, quite unlike what he had come to expect from case study discussions. He knew nothing about this "group dynamics business" and was angry at not being told about it. Second, rumors had come to his attention that some "hanky panky" was going on there. In fact, the Vice President of Buying had overheard a conversation between two of his assistant buyers that was reported to the President. One of the buyers had just returned from a one week laboratory and the other buyer was quizzing her about it. The conversation the Vice President reported to the President went something like this:

Buyer A: Oh, you just came back from Marlboro? (the training site)
Buyer B: Yes.
Buyer A: How was it?
Buyer B: This course was the deepest experience I have had in my life so far . . . Can you imagine, there was one man who took off his clothes completely!
Buyer A: A strip tease?
Buyer B: Uh huh.

Apparently, Buyer B was attempting to indicate to A the depth of the experience, the emotional revelations. In fact, what Buyer A passed on to her boss was that a literal strip tease took place at Marlboro. To this day there are some places in the company where this story is still believed.

There had been an attempted suicide by one of the participants in the training shortly after his return from the week at Marlboro.

Finally, whenever the President asked his Vice President of Personnel whether he visited Marlboro and whether he was aware of what was going on there, the Vice President said he did not really know what was going on and that he was advised by Mr. Jones to stay away. These events led to the President's surprise visit to Marlboro.

He arrived at Marlboro at breakfast in the third day of a week's program and demanded his entrance in the T-group. According to Jones:

I tried to dissuade him but to no avail. He insisted that he had the right. "If you have nothing to hide," he said, "then let me in. If you have something to hide, then

I must find out." So he observed us for a two hour T-session. After the meeting I told him that it was hard to get a realistic picture of what goes on in T-groups. He noted this and smiled at my remarks and expressed astonishment about the lack of structure in the group.

After the meeting, while having coffee, he voiced a little surprise about my passive attitude and my not exercising leadership at all. I tried to explain to him how important this is, but I felt there was an enormous wall of prejudice I could not get behind.

Then I gave a lecture to the group on leadership drawing most of my material from McGregor's *The Human Side of Enterprise*. Then I asked the participants to organize the last day's training activities. . .

In the afternoon, right after their second T-group of the day, when people were on their feet, the President rose and told everyone to remain in their seats and then delivered a twenty minute speech. He first said that supervisory training was an important thing and that the company had already spent a lot of money on it. He thought the participants were getting something from the company which was not at all self-evident that a company would do for its people. Then he went on to say that these are critical times, that the competitive situation was worsening and that success would require the greatest effort of everybody. This could be achieved, he said, by working hard and by following the given orders without question—all the requisites, I thought, of a paternalistic management. He went on speaking then like a military leader. Then he referred to my short lecture on leadership and said that there was one point he did not agree with at all. (One of the participants asked if a subordinate always has to follow orders to the word. I gave a very qualified answer trying to show that there could be conditions for questioning a superior.) The President said that he most strongly wanted to emphasize that a subordinate had better follow orders—there was no question about that! Then he went into a monologue about leadership philosophy all of which ended up as a flat contradiction of the whole philosophy of the course. People were baffled by this sudden outbreak by the President and there was a certain amount of confusion about it. The participants realized that here were two exponents of two different philosophies. . . .

Here is the President's version of that fateful day!

They were discussing group relations, I guess. They were sitting in a circle and they would sit silently for awhile and they would ask: "What is your impression of me and what do others make of me? And I'd like to tell you what I think of you, Jane, or you, Jim." Then there would be silence, long silence and the pressure and tension would steadily mount and then it would explode and everyone would start talking at once about impressions people had of each other. They would "give feedback," they said. I don't know, I suppose that one can learn a lot about how one feels and sees, but I did not think that this kind of discussion was crucial for management training. Matter of fact, some of it seemed like communism to me; they've gone too far for me, too revolutionary!

Propositions about the Uses of Laboratory Training in Effecting Social Change

. . . What we would like to do now is consider both the successes and the failures and develop propositions about social change which are related to and clearly build upon the second section of this chapter concerning the considerations for the successful adoption of laboratory training by social systems.[13]

---

[13] These principles can encompass any planned social change, not only those directed by laboratory training.

In Undertaking Any Planned Social Change Using Laboratory Training, the Core of the Target System Values Must Not Be Too Discrepant with the Laboratory Training Values. Every target system has a core of values that characterizes it and determines a good deal of its decisions. Laboratory training, also, has a system of core values. We discussed these earlier in terms of legitimacy of interpersonal phenomena, concepts of control, and so forth. We stated then that the target system's values should be somewhat in accord with, or *potentially* congruent to, laboratory training values. Where the two systems of values are widely discrepant and rigid, and where the value system of the target cannot yield without vitally endangering the target system's core values, change induced by laboratory training will probably not succeed.

Let us be specific. In the case of the Government Training Center and the department store, it is obvious that the institutional base was perceived, by men in power, as seriously threatened. The values, the normative patterns, the set of shared expectations were all in flux due to the training endeavors of Dr. A and Mr. Jones. . . .

What we have been calling training is probably misnamed. For certainly a program that aims to change the very structure of the organization through modifying a role orientation[14] is not training in the usual sense of this word. This is not only a semantic issue. Training, in its dictionary sense and in the

---

[14] The meta-goals we outlined . . . signify certain orientations toward role, for example, openness, collaboration. Contrast these role expectations with President Hess's expectations.

way that most personnel managers use it and top management construes it, is viewed conservatively: fitting people to roles. Training in the sense that it was employed in these cases signifies a *fundamental* change, an alteration of the values, norms, and patterns of expectations. In this sense President Hess was completely correct in viewing laboratory training as "revolutionary" and General Z perfectly justified in going slowly on laboratory training at the military base. It is revolutionary to the extent that the core of institutional values that the leadership was striving to preserve was basically threatened by the laboratory training change programs.

Putting it a bit differently, most organizations agree to various training and development programs insofar as they strengthen the core of institutional values and insofar as they facilitate the functioning of the organization. When programs are seen as imperiling the institutional base, we can expect the strong resistance evinced in these cases.

But most social change programs, certainly laboratory training, attempt to alter institutional values. How, then, can the inevitable and powerful resistance be reduced?

In Undertaking Any Planned Social Change, Legitimacy for the Change Must Be Gained through Obtaining the Support of the Key People. This is not to say that laboratory training should start at the top; it does mean that a careful and deliberate effort must be made to gain acceptance by the top management group. Without this, the laboratory training is constantly in peril. Notice what happened when Mr. B (the top line official in the government center supporting laboratory training) was transferred: The program came apart at the seams. If Mr. B's successor had been well-briefed and oriented, and if Mr. Z were briefed and oriented, then the program might have had more resilience to shock. The same is true regarding the department store case: Nobody really seemed to know "what was up" except possibly Jones. And if the Vice President of Personnel had been able and competent to tell President Hess what was really going on at Marlboro, then it might not have been necessary for him to make the surprise trip.

In any case, efforts must be made to provide top management with as clear and realistic picture of laboratory training as possible. This is done not only as an acquaintance process but also as a test of top management's commitment toward the potential changes. If the commitment is weak at the top level, then a total re-evaluation of the strategy is required. It is far better to discover this early than late. In the case of the department store, partly out of fear and mostly from futility, the training staff worked surreptitiously, with the faint hope that the training effects would be accepted. The outcome produced an unstable situation where the lowest levels of management maintained values that were in conflict with top management. The tension created by this value conflict was reduced by removing its source, Jones, and restoring the old orientation.

Obtaining hierarchical acceptance, no matter how painstaking and difficult, provides at least some guarantee that management can understand, and hence, manage the change without undue tension.

In Undertaking Any Planned Social Change, the Process of Installing the Change Programs Must Be Congruent with the Process and Goals of Such Programs. We are talking here of a fairly simple, but crucial, matter. The change agent should know what he is doing and should act congruently and authentically. While we are not absolutely confident of this proposition holding in every situation (installing a totalitarian system, for example), we are sure that this is essential for a democratic change program. For reasons that appeared sensible at the time, Jones operated more as an undercover agent than as an agent of change. It is doubtful that he understood the consequences of his decisions: The fact that he viewed laboratory training as a simple substitute for the case method gives rise to this question. Were the goals and *meta-goals* of laboratory training clearly understood by the change agents?

It is not obvious that they were understood. Jones, in particular, violated to some degree the meta-goals: Authenticity was abandoned by the underground methods used to start the program. Action was taken without a spirit of inquiry, and the nature of the change program was far from a collaborative one. The way Dr. A dealt with Mr. Z and the way Mr. Jones dealt with President Hess were not examples of authentic and collaborative relationships.

Unanticipated consequences can jeopardize any change program. Only the omniscient can be blamed for those. But in the case of the department store, many of the consequences could have been foreseen and avoided—if Jones had used the processes of laboratory training in installing the change program. What we observed instead was the blind use of a tool in a way which contradicted its essence.

In Undertaking Any Planned Social Change, the Employment Security of the Change Agent Must Be Guaranteed. Blau (1961) points out that one of the prerequisites for adaptation in bureaucracy is the minimum employment security of the personnel. In terms of the brute reality of existence this means that most people would not risk their job in order to create change. Given the laboratory training approach to organizational change, minimum employment security is essential for the change agent, particularly if he is a member of the organization. The training staff must maintain their separateness from other company employees and must develop some discretion and autonomy insofar as training functions are concerned.

For Jones there was no real alternative but to let the President sit in; it was either that or dismissal. If a situation similar to that one occurred but the trainer had maximum employment security or was an outside consultant, employed temporarily by the company, possibly there would have been a different outcome.

In Undertaking Any Planned Social Change Utilizing Laboratory Training, the Voluntary Commitment of the Participants May Be a Crucial Factor in the Success of the Program. We have discussed this at some length earlier.

But for emphasis we repeat that the difficulty of describing laboratory training through verbal orientation, plus the problematical aspects of organizational legitimacy to influence interpersonal behavior, lead to only one conclusion with respect to participant attendance at laboratories. This is that all delegates must undertake laboratory training in a completely voluntary spirit. It is highly doubtful that they will learn if this condition does not prevail.

In Undertaking Any Planned Social Change Utilizing Laboratory Training, the Legitimacy of Interpersonal Influence Must Be Potentially Acceptable. The spread and belief of the "striptease" rumor shows the desirability of an orientation for prospective participants. But it shows more than that. We must ask: How much and in what way can (should) an organization influence the personalities of its employees? It is not exactly obvious that interpersonal competence is correlated with effective role functioning; in some specific situations, there may be no, or an inverse, correlation. Indeed, the theoretical foundations of bureaucracy are based on *impersonality*. And even with the modern role conception of the modern manager—which includes social system management and responsibility—the prevailing norms of legitimacy of organizational influence must be explored and understood fully by the target system.

In Undertaking Any Planned Social Change, the Effects on the Adjacent and Interdependent Subsystems Relating to the Target System Must Be Carefully Considered. All three cases demonstrate this principle, but perhaps none so dramatically as in the "Letter from Medical Division." Here we see so clearly how the reverberations and repercussions of laboratory training come back to haunt its creators unless the shock can be absorbed by their neighboring units. In this case, the company doctors could have easily absorbed the shock (as they later did after an orientation session) if they had been simply informed about and involved in laboratory training. They were irked because they were ignored and disturbed by perceived encroachment on their authority. But whether it is doctors or headquarters or colleagues or bosses, a complete diagnosis of the total effects on all relevant parts must be made before, not after, the training starts.

In Undertaking Any Planned Social Change, the State of Cultural Readiness Must Be Assessed. We emphasized this in the preceding section in terms of the internal state of the target system. Here we mean more. We have in mind the relationship between the organization and the wider society within which the target system is embedded. It would appear that Mr. Jones (and Dr. A, to some extent) failed to comprehend completely the normative structure they were attempting to alter. The values of President Hess were known well in advance of the training failure, and he reflected the German cultural values of the farming communities his stores prospered in. Cultural readiness depends to some degree on the normative structure of the wider society; a clear diagnosis cannot be made without understanding these forces. . . .

REFERENCES

1. Allport, G. (1945), "The Psychology of Participation," in G. Allport (1960), *Personality and Social Encounter*, Boston, The Beacon Press.
2. Argyris, C. (1962), *Interpersonal Competence and Organizational Effectiveness*, Homewood, Ill., Dorsey Press.
3. Bavelas, A., and Strauss G. (1955), "Group Dynamics and Intergroup Relations," in W. F. Whyte (Ed.), *Money and Motivation*, New York, Harper & Row, Publishers, pp. 90–96.
4. Bennis, W. G. (1963), "A New Role for the Behavioral Sciences: Effecting Organizational Change," *Administrative Science Quarterly*, Vol. 8, pp. 125–165.
5. Bennis, W. G., Benne K. D., and Chin R. (1961), *The Planning of Change*, New York, Holt, Rinehart and Winston, Inc.
6. Blansfield, M. G. (1962), "Depth Analysis of Organizational Life," *California Management Review*, Winter, pp. 29–42.
7. Blau, P. (1961), "The Dynamics of Bureaucracy," in A. Etzioni (Ed.), *Complex Organizations*, New York, Holt, Rinehart and Winston, Inc., pp. 343–355.
8. Lewin, K. (1947), "Group Decision and Social Change," in T. Newcomb, and E. Hartley (Eds.), *Readings in Social Psychology*, New York, Holt, Rinehart and Winston, Inc.
9. Likert, R. (1961), *New Patterns of Management*, New York, McGraw-Hill, Inc.
10. Lippitt, R., Watson, J., and Westley, B. (1958), *Dynamics of Planned Change*, New York, Harcourt, Brace and World, Inc.
11. McGregor, D. (1960), *The Human Side of Enterprise*, New York, McGraw-Hill, Inc.
12. Seashore, C., and Van Egmond, E. (1959), "The Consultant-Trainer Role in Working Directly with a Total Staff," *Journal of Social Issues*, Vol. 15, pp. 36–42.

7.4 AN ORGANIC PROBLEM-SOLVING METHOD OF ORGANIZATIONAL CHANGE

Sheldon A. Davis

A few weeks ago, I learned from a vice president of a large national corporation that two of the three top executives in his company had recently attended an NTL Presidents' Laboratory, and further, that before and after

Sheldon A. Davis, "An Organic Problem-Solving Method of Organizational Change," *The Journal of Applied Behavioral Science*, III, No. 1 (1967), 3–21. Used by permission.

attending the lab, these two were highly committed to "Theory Y" notions as described by Douglas McGregor in *The Human Side of Enterprise*. However, my acquaintance expressed concern with the form this commitment was taking. He mentioned that one of these two individuals was chairing a meeting during which he expressed his commitment to those assumptions stated by

McGregor. As a concrete example of this commitment, he said that a few days earlier a key subordinate presented some work for approval. The "boss" did not like the quality of the work and said so. The subordinate pointed out that his people had worked very hard in producing the work and were highly committed to it. The top executive said, "Okay, in that case, let's go ahead."

To me, this is *not* an example of what McGregor meant. It is an example of very soft human relationships that are not task oriented, and therefore, in my opinion, irrational. However, it does represent a problem presented in lab training. How can we eliminate some of the soft, mushy, "sweetness and light" impressions that some people feel are implicit in sensitivity training?

An example of a different approach recently took place within TRW Systems.

A section head, the lowest managerial level in the organization, discovered that a certain Quality Control procedure for Manufacturing hampered his effectiveness. He sought to get the procedure modified, only to be told that this was impossible because it covered all of the divisions and therefore couldn't be modified. He was further told that a change would raise the ire of at least one general manager of another division. The section head refused to accept the explanation and personally called a meeting of the general manager identified, the manager of Manufacturing—both vice presidents of the company, and four levels above the section head—and the director of Product Assurance. Within an hour the procedure was modified in the direction desired by the section head.

The foregoing vignettes dramatize the differences which can occur because of markedly different applications of behavioral science theories within an organization. In both instances, the individuals involved were convinced they were using the best of behavioral science techniques. The consequence of their interpretation and application had decidedly different payoffs.

Confrontation: The Missing Element in Behavioral Science Literature

The values that Doug McGregor stood for and articulated regarding organizational development have in them a very real toughness: in dealing with each other we will be open, direct, explicit. Our feelings will be available to each other, and we will try to problem-solve rather than be defensive. These values have in them a very tough way of living, not a soft way. But unfortunately, in much of the behavioral science literature, the messages come out sounding soft and easy, as if what we are trying to do is build happy teams of employees who feel "good" about things, rather than saying we're trying to build effective organizations with groups that function well and that can zero in quickly on their problems and deal with them rationally, in the very real sense of the word. An example of this kind of softness is that I do not remember reading in any book in the field that one of the alternatives in dealing with a problem person is the possibility of discharging him.

There is no real growth, there is no real development in the organization or in the individuals within it, if they do not confront and deal directly with their problems. They can get together and share feelings, but if that's all they do, it's merely a catharsis. While this is useful, it has a relatively minimum usefulness compared to what can happen if they start to relate differently within the organizational setting around task issues.

Labs Are Not Enough

I think one important theme of the nearly four-year organizational change effort at TRW Systems is that of using laboratory training (sensitivity training, T-grouping) clearly as a means to an end, of putting most of our energy into on-the-job situations, real life intergroup problems, real life job family situations, and dealing with them here-and-now. This effort has reached a point where sensitivity training, per se, represents only 10 to 15 percent of the effort in our own program. The rest of the effort, 85 to 90 percent, is in on-the-job situations, working real problems with the people who are really involved in them. This has led to some very important, profound and positive changes in the organization and the way it does many things, including decision making, problem solving and supervisory coaching of subordinates.

One generalization I would draw from this and other similar experiences is that laboratory training in and of itself is not enough to really make the kind of difference that might be made in an organization forcefully trying to become more rational in its processes of freeing up the untapped potential of its people and of dealing more sensibly with its own realities. Attending a stranger's lab, or in our case a cousins' lab (that is, being a T-group with people who are not necessarily from the same job family but who are from the

same company) is a very useful, important experience. Most people learn much in laboratory training as has been well documented and discussed. However, this is not enough.

We have felt that the laboratory experience (the sensitivity training experience itself) should not just be three days or a week or whatever is spent in the laboratory off-site. As a result, we have undertaken important laboratory pre-work as well as post-work. The pre-work typically consists of an orientation session where the staff very briefly presents some of the theoretical aspects of the program and an explanation of why we do labs. During this time, participants in the coming lab can ask any kind of question, such as: is this therapy? is the company going to evaluate my performance? and so on.

Also, we typically hand out a questionnaire to the participants for their own use. They are not asked to turn it in. This presents questions such as: "What are the three most pressing problems you feel you pose for those who have to work with you?" It is an attempt to get the person to become introspective about his own particular work situation; to begin his articulating this to himself.

Then there is the laboratory itself. This is followed up by on-site sessions several weeks apart, perhaps one evening every other week for three or four sessions. At this time a variety of actions are taken in an attempt to help phase into their work situation. There is continued working in the small training groups; there can be exercises such as intergroup competition.

The laboratory is a very intensive experience. Attitudes toward it can be very euphoric and people can experience tremendous letdowns when they return to the on-going culture—even a highly supportive one. Therefore, there is major emphasis on working in the on-going situation in real life job families as well as in intergroup situations and mergers, for example.

Recently, we have added to the follow-on work an opportunity for the wives of the participants to experience a micro-lab. This might be a 1:00 to 5:00 p.m. session on a Saturday for the wives with a staff available to give some feel for the laboratory experience.

One of the problems many people have as a result of laboratory training is returning to their continuing organizational culture and finding it quite hostile to the values learned and to the approaches they would like to try. The notion very early in the TRW Systems effort was to focus on changes in the on-going culture itself: the norms, values, rewards, systems and processes. If all we did was have a lot of people attend sensitivity training, this might indeed be useful to them as individuals, but its usefulness would be quite limited with respect to the total organization.

We have had other kinds of concerns with laboratory training. We have tried hard not to *send* people to a laboratory but to make it as voluntary as possible. People who are sent usually spend much of their time wondering why they were sent instead of working on relevant issues.

If we look at the processes of change itself, it is quite clear that it is not enough for an individual to gain enormous insight into his own situation, his own dynamics, and his own functioning. This will help him develop a better understanding of how groups work and of the complexity of communication processes. However, if he can't take his understanding and turn it into action in the on-the-job situation, if he can't find other people who are interested in trying some of the same ideas, if he can't make a difference in his real life, the value of the laboratory is very severely minimized. In real life, what do we find? We find organizations typically with very traditional methods of management and with very unrealistic assumptions about people (the kind of Theory X assumptions that Doug McGregor stated). There has to be an emphasis on changing the on-going organization. The direction has to be toward working in the organization on a day-to-day basis.

The Organizational Setting and Development of the Program

I would like to describe the program underway at TRW Systems as an example of this kind of an effort—of a non-mechanical, organic approach to career development—the development of the careers of the individuals in the organization and the career of the organization itself, both inextricably tied.

TRW Systems currently has about 12,500 people. About a third are professional engineers, and half of these have advanced degrees. It is an organization with products of tremendous innovation and change. It is an organization that is highly interdependent. We have a matrix organization: there are project offices and functional areas of technical capabilities such as structures, dynamics, guidance and control. A project office, to perform its task, must call upon capabilities and people throughout the organization. This is a very complicated matrix of interdependencies. No one can really get his job done in this kind of a system without working with others. As a result, problems of relationships, of communication, of people being effectively able to problem-solve with each other are extremely critical.

The program started at a time when the company was going through a significant change in its role—from an organization with essentially one Air Force contract for systems engineering on ballistic missile programs (Thor, Atlas, Titan and Minuteman) to a company that would be fully competitive in the aerospace market. This has indeed happened over the past six years. We now have many contracts, many customers. Most of our work is done under fixed-price and incentive contracts; we produce hardware such as unmanned scientific satellites, propulsion engines for the Apollo mission, as well as other types of hardware. The company has become exceedingly more complex in its product lines and its mix of business.

All through this growth and diversification there has been a concern about the careers of the people in the organization, about trying to maintain certain qualities within the organization. . . . [A] list of these qualities . . . was prepared in September of 1965—an attempt to list qualities which seem to have a direct bearing on the kind of success we have been having over the past six years (see page 369). That success has been quite striking—a tremendous increase in sales, in the number of contracts, a good record in competitions for programs in our industry, and a large increase in the number of employees.

In the middle of 1961, TRW Systems, then called Space Technology Laboratories, began to think about organizational development. At that time, Herb Shepard, then on the faculty at Case Institute of Technology, spent a portion of the summer at TRW, including some time with key executives. The following summer, 1962, he spent a month with the organization. Just prior to this visit, the director of Industrial Relations and his associate attended a laboratory conducted by UCLA.

Shepard's visit and discussions centering around it led to a growing articulation of what we might want to do with respect to career development. Several things happened in the next several months.

One was the preparation of a white paper on career development—a statement of how we might approach the subject. The paper discussed why a program was needed, assumptions to be made about employees (a paraphrase of McGregor's Theory Y), the type of organizational climate and training needed as well as some general indications of how we might proceed.

An assumption we made was that most of the people in the organization are highly competent, very bright, and very experimental. If they could be freed up enough to look at some of their behavior, to question some of their assumptions, to look at assumptions other people are making, to try new approaches, this group could pretty much develop their own specific management theory.

The white paper was circulated to a number of key people. Interviews were then conducted to determine possible next steps. A series of events led from this point.

One event was the first of many team development laboratories. By team development laboratory, I mean an activity which might, for example, be a three-day off-site meeting involving a supervisor and the people who immediately report to him. The agenda for the meeting is: "How can we improve our own effectiveness?" The first team meeting involved one of the program offices in the company. It turned out to be quite successful. With this experience under our belt, we had further discussions to formulate what we wanted to do as an organization with respect to the careers of the people comprising the organization.

Employees within the Personnel organization began attending sensitivity training labs such as the Arden House Laboratory conducted by NTL.

A very significant event in the total development of this change effort occurred in May of 1963 when a group of 12 key executives attended a laboratory. Their co-trainers were Herb Shepard and myself, an outside consultant and a member of the TRW Systems organization.*

* This has been one of the important notions in the approach at TRW Systems. We use at this point about nine consultants who are members of NTL, people like Mike Blansfield, Dick Beckhard, Chuck Ferguson, Jack Gibb, George Lehner, Bob Tannenbaum, Herb Shepard and others. These people, in their work either in T-group training or on-the-job consulting, are always coupled with someone inside the organization, typically a personnel manager in one of the line operating units.

The participants in this first laboratory were very positive in their feedback to the director of Industrial Relations and the president of the company, who was very interested in how people were reacting to the training. The president had given support for us to be experimental: "Let's try things, if they work, continue them; if they don't modify them, improve them or drop them."

A consulting team evolved over time. The consultants were not used in any one-shot way, but were asked to make a significant commitment of time over a long-term period. They have become involved with us. They have learned our culture and our problems. While our consultants are all qualified T-group trainers, most of their time is spent in on-the-job situations. There is a need to function as a team since we are all dealing with one organization, with one culture, one social system. The kind of cohesiveness that takes place during consulting team meetings has been a very critical part of the program here at TRW Systems.

In one sense we started at the top of the organization, and in another we didn't. In the beginning, there was a shared general understanding between the president and the key people in Industrial Relations about the type of program we wanted. There were some shared values about the organization we had and wanted to maintain and build and develop. So, in McGregor's term, this was not Theory X management and Theory Y training effort. Both had a Theory Y quality.

In another sense we did not start at the top: the president and a number of the top management team were relatively late in getting involved in laboratory training and applying this training to their own job families. The president of the company attended an NTL Presidents' Lab early in 1965. Directly after that experience, his top team had an off-site team development meeting in March of 1965. In April 1966, they had a follow-up meeting.

Prior to this top team activity many other things had happened with a number of other people in other job families. In fact, this other activity helped us get to the point where the top management team became interested in trying to apply some of these techniques.

Since the program started, more than 500 key people in the organization have attended sensitivity training laboratories, primarily laboratories conducted by the company. The staff of these laboratories is drawn from our consultants, the Personnel organization, and more recently, from skilled and interested personnel in line management.

We have also conducted more than 85 team development efforts. These vary in format, but a typical one involves interviews with each of the members of the team (a job family consisting of a supervisor and his immediate subordinates) and then perhaps a three-day off-site meeting where the interview data is fed back for the groups to work with. The team ends the meeting with explicit action items. Follow-on to the off-site meeting involves implementing the many action items.

We have been devoting much effort to intergroup problems: relationships between manufacturing and engineering, between Product Assurance and other parts of the organization, between various interfacing elements in the engineering organizations. We have found that these efforts have a great deal of leverage. We have done some work on facilitating mergers, and with key people on approaching satellite launches—the latter become very tense, tight operations where people can become very competitive and behave in ways which clearly get in the way of having an effective launch.

Characteristics of the Process

We ended up with a number of notions: that we did not want to have a program that was canned, but one that was experimental. We wanted it to have a voluntary characteristic on the part of the participants, rather than something that the company forced upon them. We did not want it to be a crash program (in our industry, there are many crash programs). We wanted the training to be very task oriented. If it was not relevant to making a difference on today's problems, it was not a successful program. We wanted to have the emphasis on experience-based learning, which implies, in a very general sense, the use of laboratory methods, of people really looking at how they were doing, examining the assumptions behind their management style, identifying alternate ways of problem solving, and making choices based on a wider range of possibilities. We wanted to be concerned with everyone's career, not just key people. We wanted to be concerned about company goals and the actual on-the-job work environment, since this has a profound effect on the careers of people. We wanted to place the emphasis on measuring ourselves against our potential, on being quite introspective on how we were doing. So, for example, if there were an either/or situation (and there usually is not), we would rather not have someone come in and lecture on how to conduct staff meetings, but have ourselves look introspectively at our own staff meetings as they are conducted. And we wanted to continuously do research on how we were doing so that it could be fed back into the program for further development.

I would like to describe what I think we have come to mean by an organic approach to organizational change within TRW Systems. There are a number of points which, at least for me, tend to describe what is meant by organic methods.

1. There is the notion that if you are interested in improving a particular culture, a particular social system, you must be able to step out of it in the sense of being very analytical about it, of understanding what is going on, by not being trapped within the culture and its own particular values. If you look at a culture from its own values, you are not going to come up with anything very startling and different for it to do. You have got to be able to step out of it and say, "What really would make sense here?" This ability to step out of the culture and yet not leave it, not become alienated to it, is a very important one. C. Wright Mills expressed this concept in *The Sociological Imagination.*

2. A bias toward optimism regarding the chances for meaningful organizational development to take place increases the psychological freedom for those trying to introduce the change. There is certainly a tremendous amount of evidence at this point that significant, even profound changes can occur in the behavior of individuals and organizations.

3. Taking a systems engineering approach to the effort (i.e., looking at the totality of the system, dealing with fundamentals within it, considering how a change in one part affects parts elsewhere) provides an analytical approach which increases the conceptual freedom.

4. The extensive use of third party facilitation is made with respect to interpersonal and organizational problems. A consultant who is not directly involved in an emotional sense in a situation can be useful just by that fact.

5. Direct confrontation of relevant situations in an organization is essential. If we do not confront each other, we keep the trouble within ourselves and we stay in trouble. With respect to confrontation, the whole notion of feedback is crucial. Giving persons feedback on how they are doing gives them a choice to do better. Caring is an important part. Confronting without caring can be a rather destructive process. (See "Who's Afraid of Virginia Woolf?") It does turn out that people in general can be very caring of each other.

6. Becoming the other is an important part of the organic method. This is the empathic notion that Carl Rogers and others have developed. To really have a meaningful exchange, one somehow

has to look at the situation as the other sees it. For a consultant to work effectively with an organization, he has to be perceptive and understanding about the organization and its people from their point of view.

7. Dealing with the here and now and increasing the ability of people within the organization to do the same has a great deal of leverage. It is important in an organizational development effort to start with what is going on now within the organization, and deal with those things effectively. One of our objectives is to help the organization build its own capability, to deal with its problems as they emerge. Problems are constantly emerging in any live organization, and so our objective is *not* to end up with an organization that has no problems: that would be a very fat, dumb and happy kind of place.

8. Multiplier planning is rather crucial in the early stages of introducing organizational change. What can we next do that will have the largest effect? There is always a wide range of alternatives and possibilities, there is never enough time, money and energy to do all the things you might do, so you are constantly picking and choosing.

9. Fanning out is coupled with the multiplier planning aspect. It is important in an effort of this kind, if it is not to be subversive, sub rosa, hidden, squashed out, to be something that does fan out; someone does something that leads to

others doing something that leads to still others.

10. A person can act and then act again and then act again, or he can act, critique what he just did, then act, then critique, then act. And, that is the whole notion of going back and forth between content and process, between doing the job and then looking at how we are doing it. Building that into the day-to-day culture is a major objective.

11. Finally, there is the notion of testing of choices. One always has choices, within any particular situation. However, it is typically true that we don't test the choices we have. So someone might say, "Well, I really can't do that because these fellows won't let me," or "Yes, I would very much like to do the following but I can't because of so and so." These limits, these choices, do not get tested. One of the efforts is to get people to be aware of the various possibilities they have and to test them, not to accept the stereotypes in the situation, the sacred cows, that exist in any kind of organization, but to really say, "Okay, this is what makes sense to me in working that problem, this is what I want to try to do."

Underpinnings to the Effort

The principles of confrontation, that laboratory training must be seen as a means to an end, that most of the effort has to be done after people have attended labs, and not in the laboratory itself, has been central to this effort.

This has affected the way we budget time, the way we spend money, the assumptions we make about what we are doing.

Another significant development in this large scale effort has been a deliberate, successful attempt to build up the internal resources to carry out the program. Two years ago in a sensitivity training laboratory put on by the company, there would be a staff or six, four or five of which would be outside consultants. This has completely reversed itself. Today, when a T-group cousins' lab is conducted, four or five of the people are from inside the organization and only one or two are external consultants.

Furthermore, in the on-the-job aspects of the program, the effort is carried on by people within the organization, primarily individuals in Personnel and, increasingly, managers from the line organization.

A very interesting aspect of the program has focused on the question of risk taking. In my opinion, those of us engaged in this kind of work are quite often too cautious, too constrained, and not experimental enough in trying things within the organization. We don't behave as though we fully believe the implications of McGregor's Theory Y formulation: that people are creative, that they are strong, that they are motivated, that they want to make a difference. We tend sometimes to approach them very gingerly and very tentatively. These are constraints more within ourselves than within others or within the situation.

Many times our consultants have reported that their experience at TRW Systems has been a very stretching one: they have been fully challenged, people at TRW Systems are experimental, want to try things, are saying: "Okay, that was useful, what should I do next?" Much of the effort in the consulting team meetings has been to push ourselves to be more developmental, more experimental in the approaches that we take within the effort.

For example, until relatively recently, many people in the field felt laboratory training was not something you could do within a job family. It seems to me the whole objective of sensitivity training is to develop an on-the-job culture within which we can relate to each other interpersonally just the way we do in a T-group. We at TRW want to make that transfer; we don't want the T-group to be a separate, special kind of experience. We prefer to say: "Okay, let's sit down and really level with each other. Let's do this on-the-job, day-to-day." That is the objective. It leads to a more effective, efficient, problem-solving organization.

Working with teams in real life situations is exactly what we are after. Otherwise the program can be ethereal, not particularly related to the company's real life situations. It cannot be gutty in that it doesn't get to some of the tougher issues and deal with them, lift them up, have people involved, working actively to solve problems.

In September of 1963, I put together a short paper which conceptualized several plateaux that we might be moving through as an organization in this change effort.

The first one is characterized as problem awareness—that point in time during which there is general recognition and awareness on the part of some people within the organization that there are crucial interdependencies which exist in order for us to function, and there are problems due to inappropriate means of dealing with these interdependencies.

The second plateau, the identification and freeing of key people within the organization, is seen as consisting of two parts. The first part is an effort to identify key people in the organization who seem to be perceptive about the problems the company is experiencing, and who have a desire to work these problems. They are key people in the sense that their efforts to deal with organizational problems could produce a multiplier effect leading others to similar action.

The second part of this particular phase of the program is characterized by an effort to provide a situation which would initiate the process of freeing up these potential multipliers from the organizational and personal constraints which in the past kept them from responding effectively to their awareness of the problems. Here, the strangers' laboratories, the cousins' laboratories conducted by the company, and the team development laboratories are seen as being very relevant.

The third phase or plateau involves action steps to follow-up: experimental steps stimulated by a participation in the various kinds of laboratories that are taking place. These action steps have taken many forms: a supervisor holding a team development lab within his own job family; a family group diagnosing the kinds of interaction problems it has with other parts of the organization and beginning to resolve these problems in an open,

direct manner, searching for a creative solution rather than an avoidance compromise; where a problem in relationship between two people exists, these people moving in on that problem and doing some work on it; new ways of looking at functions in the organization.

The fourth plateau occurs when the effort itself gains an independent status and becomes a self-supporting system. At this plateau, there are norms within the organization that support open, direct confrontation of conflict, resolution of conflict without resorting to the power structure unless there was somehow a failure in the process, and a shared commitment to objectives as a consequence of being interdependent. These organizational norms would support the giving and receiving of feedback, openness, experimentation and day-to-day problem-solving.

In this fourth phase we are trying to build procedures into the day-to-day situation which hopefully put into concrete terms some of the things we have learned in the earlier phases. For example, when a new project office is started, it is probably useful for some team building to be programmed early in the life of that project office. When there is a new merger within the organization, particular attention can be paid to the merger process. One of the things we have learned is that specific attention should continuously be paid to the processes within the organization: how we make decisions, how we fill key spots, how we communicate with each other, how we decide to reorganize, how we make other important decisions. There is a heavy people involvement in these processes, and typically they do not get enough legitimate attention. If I am concerned about the quality of staff meetings I attend, I tend to talk about them in the hallways or go home and kick the dog and tell my wife about them. I don't exert effort during the staff meetings to try to change their quality and improve them, because somehow that is not legitimate. "Let's keep personalities out of it, don't get emotional"— that kind of expression inhibits me from dealing with the problem.

Development through the four plateaux requires considerable invention, because the state of the art of organizational change is, in my opinion, one where you cannot program in advance everything you are going to do within the organization. There are some people who approach organizational change this way. I believe their efforts tend to be mechanical and relatively superficial.

Another important aspect of this effort which I think is very consistent with Theory Y formulation is that the direction and pace that the effort takes should be one that is meaningful to the members who are participating in it. The consultant in any particular situation has to get in touch with the needs and concerns of the people involved from their point of view, not from his.

I have tried to suggest that in many situations in which behavioral scientists are trying to apply their principles, the real serious limitations are not within the people or organizations they are working with, but within themselves, their own skills and ability and courage to act. Theory Y has deeply ingrained in it the very profound belief in the abilities, strengths and

motivation of people in general and in specific. Many times we do not act as if we fully believe or understand that set of formulations.

Next Steps

In TRW Systems, we are now moving in a number of directions, and I would like to describe some of these. We are moving more toward day-to-day coaching—on-the-job feedback, if you will, with or without consultants, without calling special meetings, but just as we work together. We are paying continued attention to process as a way of doing business. We are moving more and more toward using third party facilitation as a standard operating procedure.

So far there has not been a heavy involvement of the rank and file. The first several years in the effort were specifically biased toward working with key people. These are the ones who have a large effect upon the culture, upon the processes of the organization, upon the tone of the climate. But we are at a point where we want to get more and more involvement of all the employees within the organization.

I think that the experience of the past several years within TRW Systems has rather clearly demonstrated the potential high leverage of applying some of the behavioral science formulations of people like McGregor, Lewin and Likert. I think it has also demonstrated that there needs to be much more organizational theory development based upon experience, not upon someone sitting in a room by himself and thinking about the topic. Some of the statements written about organizational development are to me naive, impractical, unrealistic, and not really related to organizational problems as they really exist. Through experiences gained at TRW Systems and many other places, we should be able to develop a more sophisticated understanding of organizational development.

In my opinion, there is great potential in the development of this theory and in its application within organizations. That seems to me to be one of the leading edges within the field of behavioral science.

Qualities of TRW Systems Which Have a Direct Bearing on Its Success

In thinking about the problems associated with the very dramatic growth of TRW Systems, I attempted to identify those qualities which have had a great deal to do with our success in the past and which therefore ought to be maintained in the future:

1. The individual employee is important, and focus is on providing him the tools, etc., he needs for him to carry out his assignments.
2. The systems within the organization (policies, procedures, practices) have been designed to be a platform *from which* the individual operates, rather than a set of ground rules *within which* he must confine himself.
3. One objective of the organization has been: the work we do ought to be fun (personally rewarding, meaningful, enjoyable), and this has had a direct effect on assignments, etc.
4. There is a great deal of trust displayed in the individual person: minimum of rules, controls, forces outside the individual telling what to do and how to do it.
5. "Technical democracy": society of peers rather than rigid hierarchy. There is a relative lack of social distance between employees and managers and the various echelons of management. There has been a spontaneous willingness and interest in keeping social distance at a minimum, and while managers enjoy the accouterments of rank, they are not used as barriers between themselves and others at lower levels of the organization.
6. A great deal of emphasis on quality: attract best people, give them best working conditions, provide them with challenging assignments, demonstrate that paramount importance is placed on the professional, technical excellence of work assignments.
7. While within TRW Systems there has been continuous, rapid change, the organization as a whole has been relatively stable, providing long term career opportunities for a high percentage of our key people who are positive about the emphasis on internal, upward mobility and individual chance for many diversified job assignments. This is career development in a very literal sense.
8. In giving responsibility to individuals, we have had a bias toward giving "too much responsibility too soon" rather than being conservative. This has stretched the individual, and for those who are capable, has led to rapid growth and outstanding performance.
9. There is, in a relative sense, less

organization "politics" (e.g., people ruthlessly working at getting ahead, back-stabbing) and more focus on task. Part of the language is "working the problem."

10. On task issues, there is a great deal of direct confrontation rather than passing-the-buck, maneuvering, etc.

11. There is a great deal of delegation downward within the organization, so that a relatively large number of people end up with relatively highly responsible tasks.

12. The management group has been quite experimental in its approach to its task rather than generally traditional.

13. The individual employee enjoys the relative freedom to be personally responsible for oneself and the job. The job is generally seen as an important one, making a significant contribution to the important technological advances in our society.

14. People who will be importantly affected by decisions feel they will have the opportunity to a greater degree than is customary elsewhere to participate in the decision making process.

Chapter 8

INSTRUMENTATION

Agents of "planned change," as we have chosen to define this term, take a transactional view of the processes of change in which they participate. According to this view, the change agent uses his own person and the relationships that he jointly builds, adapts, and terminates with the client system he is seeking to help, as major tools in liberating, informing, and empowering the client to deal more aptly with itself (or himself) and its (or his) worlds. Simplistically, one might argue that self-knowledge and skill and capacity in establishing, maintaining, and terminating mutually helpful relationships with clients are the only instrumentation a change agent needs. And, although this is an oversimplified statement of the instrumentation required, it does point to a core element in any change agent's technology, whatever further specialized and sophisticated additions are needed to round out his technological equipment.

Change-agent technologies and instrumentations have grown up around the principal formats through which change agents work with clients and client systems. The literature developed around three such formats—training, consultation, and data collection and feedback—is sampled in this chapter. It is important to recognize that these three formats are not conceptually discrete forms of social practice. Rather, their discreteness is conventionally based. In actual practice, they are variously permuted and combined.

Though conventional, the differentiation between training, consultation, and data feedback is not without value. The three may be seen as representing distinguishable responses of a client or client system in quest of help from men of knowledge in relation to a felt difficulty or inadequacy in functioning. A client, feeling difficulty or inadequacy in the conduct or management of his or its affairs, may decide to go to school to learn better ways of doing or managing things or, in the case of an organization or community, may decide to send some of its people to school. Education or training is an attempt on the part of men of knowledge to meet this kind of client response.

Or a client in difficulty may seek the advice and help of men of knowledge addressed more directly and continuously to a perceived particular difficulty in functioning. Consultation is an attempt to meet this sort of client response.

A client in difficulty may attempt to use men of knowledge in yet a third way—to invite them in to study his situation and to tell and discuss with him what they have found out in the course of their study. Data collection and feedback is an attempt to meet this type of client response to difficulty in functioning.

Looked at in this way, it is not surprising that discussions of training by and for change agents should lead to comparisons of training with other forms and types of education and schooling. Harrison and Hopkins, in their study of the preparation of Peace Corps workers and others for work as change agents in foreign cultures, are led to a detailed analysis of the inadequacies of conventional American higher education for this task of preparation.

Since the target of *training* is behavioral change and re-education, the educational concern of trainers extends beyond the acquisition of new information and new ways of verbalizing about information to other inner determinants of behavior—attitudes, self-image, discrepancies between inner and outer functioning. Clark seeks to explain how personal growth occurs in a training group through the quests of members for congruent and authentic interaction with the trainer and with each other. In his discussion some of the false distinctions between group training and group psychotherapy are dissolved.

Since consultation grows out of a response to client needs for advice about particular difficulties in functioning, discussions of consultation involve a differentiation between various forms of advice giving prevalent among men of behavioral knowledge in our culture. One type of advice giving takes the form of recommendations to a particular client drawn primarily out of the expert knowledge of the advice giver about how other systems comparable to the one of the client have met similar difficulties. Another form of advice giving, more in keeping with the philosophy of the change agent as we have defined him, is for the outside helper to stimulate, assist, and support the client in developing, applying, and evaluating his own advice for himself and his confronting situation. Ferguson provides a generalized description and analysis of the consultant role and of the process of consultation. Caplan, out of his long and varied experiences in mental health work, identifies four types of consultation and illustrates the problems and processes of consultant functioning in each with examples drawn from the mental health field. Argyris, out of a study of the work of internal consultants in large organizations, analyzes the difficulties of such consultants which grow out of their marginal position in the organization in which they work and offers general suggestions to organizations and con- *evaluates* sultants about ways to overcome these difficulties.

The third format in which change agents are seeking and developing instrumentation for their work grows out of the client system's need for experts to study the client situation and to feed back the results of their study as a basis for finding improved ways of functioning. This way of working calls upon the resources of the change agent for research expertise and for effective ways of communicating research results to the subjects of research in the interest of client change and improvement. Miles describes and evaluates an effort to use the feedback of survey research results to administrators in a school system as a way of inducing organizational change. Lorsch and Lawrence propose the joint involvement of outside researchers and inside managers in diagnostic research on an organization in order to lay the groundwork for action plans by the managers to improve their organization. They contrast this approach to data collection and feedback with other approaches which sometimes use feedback to convince organizational leadership of the wisdom of an action plan for improvement which the outsiders had in mind from the beginning of their work with the organization.

The issues in these latter discussions have to do with proper and effective relations between outside researchers and client systems in change projects—the degree to which researcher-subject relationships can be integrated with helper-client relationships and some of the ways in which such integration can be effected.

Beckhard has invented and tested a feedback system which is immediately informative of the climate of the organization after an internal change has occurred and which is designed to accomplish planning for change in a matter of hours. Representatives from all levels of organization management meet together and exchange with each other the problems caused by the change made within the organization. Planning for action is done in smaller subgroups which are concerned with a particular area. Plans are then presented to the total group, some are selected, and the proper resources are made available to put these plans into effect. This is accomplished in four and one-half to five hours.

8.1   THE DESIGN OF CROSS-CULTURAL TRAINING: AN ALTERNATIVE TO THE UNIVERSITY MODEL

Roger Harrison
Richard Hopkins

The inapplicability of traditional, university-based training has become a

Roger Harrison and Richard Hopkins, "The Design of Cross-Cultural Training: An Alternative to the University Model." *Journal of Applied Behavioral Science*, III, No. 4 (1967), 431–460. Used by permission.

chronic complaint in organizations which must prepare large numbers of persons for service overseas. In the Peace Corps, for example, which in 5½ years has trained more persons for overseas work than any civilian government agency, complaints about the irrelevance of traditional classroom training have been growing steadily since the first Volunteers entered training. (The Peace Corps continues to train most of its Volunteers at universities, for a variety of reasons not having to do with the quality of training; but a vigorous effort is made to influence the training institutions to design programs that differ sharply from the standard curriculum design.)

The complaints are not directed toward the content of the traditional academic disciplines that bear on overseas work. The content can be relevant to performance in an alien culture. Moreover, the acknowledged experts in the subject matter fields appropriate to overseas work are found in universities and colleges for the most part. The dissatisfaction is with the ways in which such subject matter is taught.

When returned Peace Corps Volunteers talk about their training, they don't complain about incompetent professors; they complain about the sense in which their experiences in training, however interesting or well presented they may have been, simply did not prepare them for the total life they had to lead overseas. Despite the overall success of the Peace Corps, it has not been uncommon for even a "good" Volunteer to take five or six months, or one-fourth of his tour overseas, to become fully operational in an overseas environment.

Now prospective Peace Corps Volunteers are highly-motivated students, keenly aware that their success in a strange and alien environment will depend in large measure on their ability to deal with the dynamics of the culture in which they will be working. Above average in commitment to their work, energetic, imaginative and intelligent, they exhibit a happy blend of attitudes and motives. Yet, primed for a really stirring training experience as they were, many of those who have completed their two years abroad seem unusually dissatisfied with the training that preceded their overseas tour. Somehow training had little more bearing on what actually happened to them overseas than the rest of their middle-class life experiences, including their experiences in college prior to the Peace Corps.

The purpose of this paper is to examine the basis for such discontent by dissecting the relationships between the ends and means of training for cross-cultural performance. The conclusion to which the analysis leads is that the traditional methods of higher education simply won't get the job done. Nor are they well suited to training for any application situation that requires the ability to adapt to or to act in unfamiliar and ambiguous social situations. (Included in this category would be all types of community development or community action work, at home or abroad, especially when such work is with the disadvantaged, as well as work in institutional sub-cultures that differ basically from the "outside world.")

Further objectives of this paper are to present a conception of some learning processes that can lead to the ability to cope with ambiguity and to take action under stress, to present some design principles for such training, and to specify the kinds of skills and competence needed to design and operate effective cross-cultural training programs. Finally, we will discuss a Peace Corps training program in which some of these design principles were tested.

Diagnosis of the Problem

With few exceptions, formal systems of higher education in the United States provide training in the manipulation of symbols rather than things; reliance on thinking rather than feeling and intuition; and commitment to understanding rather than to action. These systems were designed originally for the training of scholars, researchers and professionals, for whom rationality, abstract knowledge, emotional detachment and verbal skills are primary values. These systems, however, are applied across the board to almost all students, regardless of their occupational goals.

The criteria of performance used to evaluate the effectiveness of the traditional educational experience are familiar to all of us. They consist of tests, papers, reports, and the evaluation of performance on laboratory problems. With few exceptions, these methods of evaluation are verbal and intellectual.

There are attempts to provide action-oriented and experience-based learning models in many institutions of higher learning, but these less intellectual and more emotionally-involving learning settings tend to be peripheral and ancillary to the main work of the college or university. Student governments and student organizations, for example, have an ambiguous, unintegrated relationship to the faculty and the classroom. The status of Deans of Students and Directors of Student Activities is

cloudy when it is not second-class. The classroom remains a stronghold of rationality.

When colleges or universities are approached to design or conduct training for work overseas, the resources made available to work on the problem are often those of the traditional part of the organization. Training design is usually based upon the university model.

Until quite recently, for example, the typical Peace Corps university training program was chopped up into components which conformed, by and large, to university departmental lines, and time was assigned to each component on an hourly-bloc basis: so much to language, so much to technical studies, so much to area studies, etc. Such a program was more than likely conducted in an environment that differed little from the one the trainee had just escaped, with all or most of its *in loco parentis* rules and regulations, its classrooms and blackboards, its textbooks and reading lists, its blue-book examinations, its air-conditioned dormitories and student-union atmosphere.

In many of these programs the environment was restrictive and authoritarian, a kind of exhausting endurance contest, which the trainee survived by a sort of game-playing designed to get him through the Peace Corps' selection process as painlessly as possible. Recognizing that *something* ought to be different in a Peace Corps program, university project directors typically designed programs that ran from dawn to dark—and beyond—up to as much as 65 or 70 hours a week of intensive instruction, for 11 to 15 weeks.

Thus, although one of the prime

objectives of training was to convince the prospective Volunteer that he was no longer a college student, he was placed in a training environment where he could be nothing else.

In any case, the goals and methods of this model focus upon the development of the students' intellectual capacity and on a certain kind of gamesmanship that enables him to *cope* with the training program. There is no manifest concern with his feelings, with an ideal behavior model or with the interpersonal aspects of the work he may be doing. Students in a typical university setting spend most of their time reading and writing; more time talking about ideas than acting on them; and their professors are much more interested in students' ideas than in their feelings. To be emotional as opposed to being rational and objective, at least in the classroom, is to transgress the bounds of appropriate student or professorial behavior.

Universities and colleges do succeed in influencing students to move toward the traditional goals. Students do become more rational, more critical, more detached and more adept at the manipulation of words, symbols and abstractions. In terms of the desired outcome of training for cross-cultural work, the university model can provide an *intellectual* understanding of cultural diversity, of values and assumptions that differ from their own.

Nothing in this paper should be construed as suggesting that this kind of understanding is of *no* value, or that it is totally irrelevant to overseas work. It does not, however, provide a trainee with all he needs overseas. Its weakness is that in those aspects of overseas performance having to do with interpersonal effectiveness the traditional model offers little help. This is a serious weakness, indeed. The experiences of all our overseas agencies, private, governmental, religious, have demonstrated that the human elements of overseas work are at least as important as the technical ones in the success of a job or mission, and that overseas personnel are much more likely to be deficient in these human aspects of work performance than in technical skills. The gravest problems of Peace Corps Volunteers, said David Reisman in a recent seminar on the Peace Corps as an educative experience, are "emotional and interpersonal."

By interpersonal effectiveness we mean such functions as establishing and maintaining trust and communication, motivating and influencing, consulting and advising—all that complex of activities designed to inculcate change. In overseas jobs, the performance of these relationship activities must take place across differences in values, in ways of perceiving and thinking, and in cultural norms and expectations.

These requirements suggest a very different set of goals from those of the university model. To sharpen the contrast, here are some important and divergent goals of the two educational enterprises.

Even though the goals on the left are not universally honored in American colleges and universities, they do represent a spirit or ideal of academic excellence. They have a pervasive influence on the values and behavior of educators. They are important goals that have contributed much to our civilization. The transfer of these goals from generation to generation is not the least important function of higher

Some Major Goals
of University Education

Communication: to communicate fluently via the written word and, to a lesser extent, to speak well. To master the languages of abstraction and generalization, e.g., mathematics and science. To understand readily the reasoning, the ideas and the knowledge of other persons through verbal exchange.

Decision-making: to develop critical judgment: the ability to test assertions, assumptions and opinions against the hard facts and the criteria of logic. To reduce susceptibility to specious argument and to be skeptical of intuition and emotion. To search for the best, most rational, most economical and elegant solution.

Commitment: commitment is to the truth. It requires an ability to stand back from on-going events in order to understand and analyze them, and to maintain objectivity in the face of emotionally involving situations. Difficult situations are handled by explanations, theories, reports.

Ideals: to value the great principles and ideals of western society: social justice, economic progress, scientific truth. To value the sacrifice of present rewards and satisfactions for future advancement of these ideals and to find self-esteem and satisfaction from one's contribution towards distant social goals.

Some Divergent Goals
of Overseas Education

Communication: to understand and communicate directly and often non-verbally through movement, facial expression, person-to-person actions. To listen with sensitivity to the hidden concerns, values, motives of the other. To be at home in the exchange of feelings, attitudes, desires, fears. To have a sympathetic, *empathic* understanding of the feelings of the other.

Decision-making: to develop ability to come to conclusions and take action on inadequate, unreliable and conflicting information. To be able to trust feelings, attitudes and beliefs as well as facts. To search for the *possible* course, the viable alternative, the durable though inelegant solution.

Commitment: commitment is to people and to relationships. It requires an ability to become involved: to be able to give and inspire trust and confidence, to care and to take action in accordance with one's concern. Difficult situations are dealt with by staying in emotional contact with them, trying to take constructive action.

Ideals: to value causes and objectives embedded in the here-and-now and embodied in the groups and persons in the immediate social environment. To find satisfaction, enjoyment and self-esteem from the impact one has directly on the lives of others. To be able to empathize with others who live mostly in the present and to work with them toward the limited, concrete goals which are important to them.

Some Major Goals
of University Education

Problem solving: a problem is solved when the true, correct, reasonable answer has been discovered and verified. Problem solving is a search for knowledge and truth. It is a largely rational process, involving intelligence, creativity, insight and a respect for facts.

Some Divergent Goals
of Overseas Education

Problem solving: a problem is solved when decisions are made and carried out which effectively apply people's energies to overcoming some barrier to a common goal. Problem solving is a social process involving communication, interpersonal influence, consensus and commitment.

---

education. The trouble is that they are often not relevant in an action situation.

The goals on the right above are typical of the aims of Americans working closely with counterparts in overseas situations. They are not universal, but they represent the reach and thrust of many persons who are concerned and active in the improvement of overseas effectiveness. (These goals are also operative in a number of domestic programs, especially in community development activities.)

University education and cross-cultural training are sharply different, too, in what Schein and Bennis[1] have called the "meta-goals" of training. Meta-goals are approaches to learning and personal development which the learner acquires in the *process* of being educated in a particular system. In other words, meta-goals represent what the learner learns, in addition to the *content* of instruction, about how to approach and solve subsequent problems outside the classroom.

[1] Schein, Edgar H. and Bennis, Warren G., *Personal and Organizational Change through Group Methods.* New York, John Wiley & Sons, Inc., 1965.

They represent the problem solving processes, the learning styles, which the trainee or student becomes committed to in the course of his educational experience. Meta-goals have to do with "learning how to learn." In some learning settings, for example, an authoritative person acts as the source of solutions to problems, while in others the learner must look to peers or to himself for information and suggestions. Such differences can be critical in overseas work.

Below are listed some meta-goals of university education, contrasted with meta-goals which seem appropriate for the cross-cultural situation.

At the level of meta-goals, university education and cross-cultural training diverge significantly. The sources, settings and approaches of the former tend to be formal, bookish, rational, dependent on authority and lacking in opportunities to gain competence in learning through interpersonal contact.

They differ profoundly along the dimension of freedom. It is here that the inappropriateness of traditional educational system for overseas work is most evident. The high degree of control and dependence upon authority common in

Meta-Goals of Traditional College and University Classrooms

Source of Information: information comes from experts and authoritative sources through the media of books, lectures, audio-visual presentations. "If you have a question look it up."

Learning Settings: learning takes place in settings designated for the purpose, e.g., classrooms and libraries.

Problem Solving Approaches: problems are defined and posed to the learner by experts and authorities. The correct problem solving methods are specified, and the student's work is checked for application of the proper method and for accuracy, or at least reasonableness of results. The emphasis is on solutions to known problems.

Role of Emotions and Values: problems are largely dealt with at an ideational level. Questions of reason and of fact are paramount. Feelings and values may be discussed but are rarely acted upon.

Criteria of Successful Learning: favorable evaluation by experts and authorities of the quality of the individual's intellectual productions, primarily written work.

Appropriate Meta-Goals For Cross-Cultural Training

Source of Information: information sources must be developed by the learner from the social environment. Information gathering methods include observation and questioning of associates, other learners and chance acquaintances.

Learning Settings: the entire social environment is the setting for learning. Every human encounter provides relevant information.

Problem Solving Approaches: the learner is on his own to define problems, generate hypotheses and collect information from the social environment. The emphasis is on discovering problems and developing problem solving approaches on the spot.

Role of Emotions and Values: problems are usually value- and emotion-laden. Facts are often less relevant than the perceptions and attitudes which people hold. Values and feelings have action consequences, and action must be taken.

Criteria of Successful Learning: the establishment and maintenance of effective and satisfying relationships with others in the work setting. This includes the ability to communicate with and influence others. Often there are no criteria available other than the attitudes of the parties involved in the relationship.

the college classroom does not lead to the development of a learning style facilitative of success in an overseas environment. This is not just because freedom is a good thing and everyone ought to have a lot of it. It is because so much external control implies a dependency on experts and authorities for direction, information and validation. When the learner is deprived of these sources of support, as he is almost certain to be in the overseas environment, he is in an uncomfortable and sometimes emotionally crippling situation. He not only must solve new problems in a new setting, but he must develop a new learning style, quite on his own. This experience—not knowing how to learn without traditional supports—may be productive of a good deal of the anxiety and depression grouped under the rubric, "culture shock." It is certainly responsible for much individual failure, even when it does not lead to chronic depression and anomie.

Education for cross-cultural applications should train the individual in a system of learning operations that is independent of settings, persons and other information sources not found in the overseas environment. If the trainee can be educated to be an effective and independent learner, he need not be filled with all the information he can contain before going into his new job. He will have the capacity to generate his own learning as needed. Indeed, he will have to generate his own learning in any case, whether he is trained to do this or not, for the simple reason that no training agency can train for every exotic contingency, for every aspect of life and work in another culture.

The other dimension on which the two learning models described above differ is that of encounter—the extent to which the emotions, values and deeper aspects of the self are actively involved, touched and changed in the learning process. The intellectuality and the formality, the emphasis on ideas and on the written word, the appeals to logic and reason implicit in university education, all combine to encourage an emotional distance from the learning material and a relativism about values.

But it is not possible to maintain such emotional distance from the sights, the smells, the sounds and the customs of an alien culture. (And for one who is attempting to effect change or to act as an advisor in another culture, it is certainly not desirable, either.) Those aspects of life which in one's own culture are familiar and which would be supportive if they were present overseas (eating habits, standards of hygiene and cleanliness, language, social systems, subliminally-perceived signals of all kinds) are *not* present, and their absence is emotionally disruptive. One's assumptions and values are called into question again and again by the most trivial kinds of events. The interpersonal competencies that work well in one's own culture suddenly don't work anymore. The cues are different. One can avoid the encounter only by retreating into some kind of physical or emotional enclave, into the kinds of American compounds that wall off Yankees from "natives" all over the world.

Education in the classroom teaches one to deal with emotionally loaded questions of value and attitude by analyzing and talking about them in an atmosphere of emotional detachment. Such a scholarly, scientific attitude is appropriate to the task of *understanding*, but by side-stepping direct, feeling level involvement with issues and persons, one fails to develop the "emotional muscle" needed to handle effectively a high degree of emotional impact and stress. Lacking "emotional muscle," the individual under stress tends to withdraw as much as possible from exposure of his self-esteem, or at the other extreme he impulsively risks too much in an effort to get the anxiety and suspense over with. Either of these reactions to stress can, and often does, lead to failure overseas. Thus an important objective in training for overseas work should be the development in the trainee of the ability and willingness to take moderate emotional risks in situations where his sense of self-esteem is involved.

The concept of moderate risk-taking can be illustrated by examining the alternatives one faces when a friend or colleague has become noticeably unapproachable, cold and unresponsive. The alternative actions one may take may be classified as low, moderate or high risk, according to how emotionally impactful the likely outcomes are for one's self-esteem. Low risk alternatives might include withdrawal from the relationship, or resort to written rather than oral communication. High risk alternatives might include retaliation with some kind of personal attack on the colleague, reproaches for his unfriendliness, or demands to his face that he change his behavior.

The low and high risk approaches allow the causes of the situation to remain unknown and undealt with. They are more designed to get rid of the tension and uncertainty than to solve the problem.

In contrast, the moderate-risk approach is characterized by a willingness to increase tension somewhat in order to obtain information about the difficulty. Such an approach might take the form of asking the other person if there were anything the matter; indicating that one was puzzled about the behavior of the other; trying to arrange increased interaction in non-work settings to see whether a relationship could be built on some more personal foundation; and so on. The important thing is not that these attempts be successful in resolving the problem but that they develop more information about it with low risk of further damage to the relationship. They also all involve some increase in tension for the subject, since failure might be painful. Moderate-risk approaches require more ability to stand emotional tension over a period of time than do the others.

The ability to deal directly with a high degree of emotional impact is not likely to be developed in the university classroom. The kinds of problems dealt with in the classroom neither require nor reward attempts to turn the learning situation into an opportunity for interpersonal encounter.

In summary, then, the classroom approach is poorly adapted to training persons to operate in settings, overseas or anywhere else, where they must define and attack problems without the aid of authoritative or expert assistance (freedom), and where the degree of emotional, attitudinal and value involvement is so high as to require dealing directly and continually with emotionally laden issues (encounter).

Toward an Alternative Model: Design Principles

Design principles for cross-cultural training differ from those of the university classroom. The purposes of the former are to: (1) develop in the student more independence of external sources of decision, information, problem definition and motivation; (2) develop in the student the "emotional muscle" he needs to deal constructively with the strong feelings which are created by conflict and confrontation of values and attitudes; (3) enable him to make choices and commitments to action in situations of stress and uncertainty; and (4) encourage him to use his own and others' feelings, attitudes and values as *information* in defining and solving human problems.

There are a number of design principles which follow directly from these aims and goals.

PROBLEM SOLVING. The individual should be continually exposed to situations that require him to diagnose what is going on, define a problem to solve, devise a solution and take action upon it. Because information and theory which are not used in the problem solving process will not be readily available to the learner when he must solve problems under stress, *information is not presented which is irrelevant to the solution of real problems which the learner is asked to solve in the here and now.*

IMMEDIATE DATA ORIENTATION. Immediate data is information gathered by observation of the physical environment and experience with persons involved in some problem, as distinguished from second hand and abstract information obtained from experts and authorities. Learning to use immediate data, particularly from the social environment, frees the learner from dependence on authoritative sources of information. In cross-cultural training designs, problems should be constructed so that their definition and solution require the problem solver to develop information from the persons who are present with him in the problem situation.

VALUE ORIENTATION. Almost any action a person takes in a culture other than his own involves a confrontation between his values and those of the host country. In the marketplace, in work situations, in businesses, in social relations of all kinds, the visitor abroad must confront and cope with unfamiliar values and customs. Thus, the problems which the learner deals with in training should also require a confrontation of opposing values. Furthermore, it is not enough that the learner examine these value conflicts with interest and detachment. In the cross-cultural application situation he will not be able to escape choices among conflicting values. The choices he makes will have important consequences. Therefore, in the training situation the learner should be confronted with problem solving situations forcing him to *make choices among competing values which have consequences for his relationships with others in the training situation.*

EXPERIENCE-ACTION ORIENTATION. A basic problem in cross-cultural training design may be stated inelegantly as "connecting head and guts." This means that training designs which lead only to understanding are never good enough. Training problems must require that the person *experience* the emotional impact of the phenomena with which he is dealing, as well as understand them. He must be able to translate ideas and values into direct action, with all the attendant risks and difficulties. This requires that the learner influence others to action.

The principle, then, is that training situations should require that discussion and analysis lead to decision and action on the part of the trainee. This would imply, for example, that even the best led "discussion group" is only half a training situation, because it does not lead to action.

USE OF AUTHORITY. The authority of the educator or trainer should not be used to diagnose situations, define problems, provide information, or select alternative courses of action for the learner. If these functions are performed for the learner, he learns through dependency on expert or authoritative help.

On the other hand, plunges into anarchy and laissez-faire may so traumatize the learner that he must spend most of his energy in defending himself emotionally from the learning situation. If he is allowed to, he may defend himself by sidestepping confrontation with problems and the hard work on their definition and solution which is the heart of the learning process as we have prescribed it. A delicate and unusual use of authority is thus called for.

It is clear that authority must not be used to deprive the learner of the opportunity to have his own experience. In general he is not provided with information, but encouraged to seek it; he is not given solutions, but asked to come to conclusions on his own; he is not told what action to take or how to take it, only that action is expected of him.

Authority is used to support the learner in his first steps in an unfamiliar learning environment. At the same time, he is not left completely without sources of help. He is encouraged to experiment, to try and fail and try again, to take risks, to express himself and his values in words and action. He is rewarded by those in authority, not for succeeding or getting the right answer or expressing the right opinion, but for engaging actively and wholeheartedly in the learning process.

The restrictive side of this use of authority is that the learner *is* to some extent "fenced in" to keep him in contact with the problems he is expected to solve. Sanctions or punishments are applied, not for goofing up but for goofing off; not for making mistakes but for failing to act; not for taking an illogical or unreasonable position but for failure to take a stand.

USE OF EXPERTISE. A premise of this model is that a person does not learn to exist effectively in another culture simply by being provided with information about that culture. Although we can predict to some extent the general types of difficulties the learner will have to face in the cross-cultural situation, we cannot predict with any certainty the exact information which he will need to solve the particular difficulties he gets into.

We can, however, specify the conceptual framework which the learner needs to make sense of an alien and ambiguous social situation, and to take action in that situation. The learner's need for expert help is less to provide information about the *content* of the other culture than to teach the problem solving *processes* and to develop the feeling-thinking linkages which are primary goals of our proposed training designs.

The expert interacts with the learner first through designing situations constructed so that if the learner follows his own natural adaptive styles, he will be confronted with the processes and problems which it is desired for him to learn about. These are "free movement" situations in that the learner's specific actions and activities are only loosely prescribed; he is free to solve the problem in almost any way he wants.

Further, the educator should help the learner reflect about his experience. The process of linking thought and feeling is as difficult when one begins with a concrete problem and moves toward conceptualization of the experience, as it is when one starts with ideas and facts and tries to move toward action based upon an intellectual analysis. The educator does not simply construct problems and then sit back while the learner runs through a maze like a rat. At the very least, the educator should ask the learner what meaning the experience had for him and what, if any, connections and generalizations he can make between this particular experience and what he knows about himself, his goals in the cross-cultural situation, his own culture and the alien culture. His role is that of any teacher working intuitively—to ask the right questions at the right time.

Without this kind of guidance, it is just as possible for a person to have an experience-packed and emotionally laden but conceptually meaningless learning experience as it is for him to have an intellectualized and detached but emotionally bland one.

It is not unusual, for example, for returned Peace Corps Volunteers working as staff in a Peace Corps training program to see in their overseas experiences a kind of kaleidoscope of impactful, difficult, rewarding but essentially unconnected experiences. The returned Volunteer often does not have a clear conception of the processes which he used to adapt himself to the culture, to develop sources of information, or to formulate and test hypotheses about problems. When he communicates to trainees he often communicates at the level of "war stories." These anecdotes usually have as their implied message, "it's no use to prepare for much of anything, because whatever you expect, it is not going to come out as you anticipated."

Many of these veterans of the real world seem not to have been able to turn their own experience into real learning or to make it available as training for others. They have been through an experience-based learning situation in their overseas assignment without learning anything which they see as clearly transferable to other social situations. They have not been able to conceptualize their experiences, partly because they were not taught how to do so in their training. But of course learning has occurred; it is latent, waiting for some structured, conceptual framework into which it may be fitted in a coherent way. The purpose of experience-based cross-cultural training is to inculcate in the learner the ability somehow to see and know what he is learning and has learned, so that he can articulate it afterwards and act on his learning consciously.

The role prescribed for the teacher, the educator, in such a learning system is one of aiding in an inductive rather than the traditional deductive learning process. He helps the learner to verbalize his feelings, perceptions and experiences and to draw conclusions and generalizations from them.

If the teacher succeeds, the trainee will not only be more successful in the field situation; the entire experience will have been a richer and more rewarding one for him. He will, to one degree or another, have learned something about how to learn.

Toward an Alternative Model: Training Settings

The principles of training enunciated here have been applied in an actual training situation. During the summer and fall of 1965 the authors collaborated—one as project director, the other as consultant—in the design and implementation of two community development training programs at the Peace Corps Training Center in Puerto Rico. The two programs will be referred to as one program; they were planned together, operated under the same design, and ran concurrently.

The Peace Corps Training Center consists of two camps located in a semi-rain forest area of central Puerto Rico about 15 miles from the coastal city of Arecibo. Each camp has a capacity of about 110 trainees. Trainees live in simple wooden cabins. There is no indoor plumbing for trainees, or hot water. Nature is kind (despite 140 inches of rain a year), but life is primitive.

The camps were utilized until the fall of 1964 as so-called Outward Bound camps, where trainees were received before or after university training for three or four weeks of rigorous, graduated physical activities designed to confront trainees with challenges which stretched their capacity to deal with stress.

In September, 1964, however, after a small pilot project, the camps were converted into a full-scale training center for Latin America. Since that time, only full-length (10–12 week) training programs have been conducted there.

In the summer of 1965, the staff of the Training Center consisted of: a director; five assistant directors, four psychologists responsible for trainee assessment; an administrative officer; an associate administrative officer and 30 maintenance workers and cooks; two nurses; about 15 native-speaking language informants; and finally, approximately 30 former PCV's from Latin America (average age 25), who comprised the core instructional and coordinating staff. The resident staff was supplemented in each cycle by from 12 to 20 academicians and technicians who come to the Training Center for stays of from three to ten days each.

The training that is discussed in this paper took place only at one camp. Two projects were involved:

The Ecuador RCA/Colonization Project included 40 trainees—two recent-graduate engineers, eight nurses and 30 so-called B.A. generalists. They were to work in newly colonized areas of the Oriente region of Ecuador as elementary teachers or technicians and, what is most important, as community development workers.

The Latin American Regional Arts and Crafts Project included 42 trainees, all artisans (weavers, potters, metal workers, painters, etc.), several of them graduates of art schools or technical institutes. They were to be divided among three countries—Ecuador, Chile and Bolivia—where they would work with native artisans in developing exportable handicraft items through the organization and administration of producer cooperatives.

As in all Peace Corps training programs, these trainees were subject to the Peace Corps' selection process. Eighty-two trainees reported for training; fifty-seven were sent overseas; twenty-five trainees, in other words, either resigned or were, as the Peace Corps euphemism goes, "selected out."

The remainder of this paper will draw heavily on this program. But it should be understood that it was not conducted under rigorous laboratory conditions. No systematic effort was made to collect objective data while it was going on.

In previous programs at the Puerto Rico Center, the director's authority role had been that of a traditional academic administrator. He designed the curriculum, scheduled all training activities, and left the subject matter to the faculty. For the most part, material was presented in the standard way: the instructors talked, the trainees listened, took notes and asked questions.

In this case, though, the young staff was offered autonomy, and the chance to design and conduct its own program. The director and consultant would be on hand to participate as they were

wanted; they would advise and make comments; but they wouldn't run things. Responsibility lay in the staff itself.

Ultimately only about a third of the staff accepted this offer of autonomy. They planned the experimental program over a period of about six weeks, meeting for several hours daily seven days a week. At the end, they were ready to take the risks involved in a model that differed significantly from the training they had received before *their* Peace Corps tours, and which also differed from that previously conducted at the Training Center.

The training program, as it was designed, was to have these general characteristics:

1. From their arrival, the trainees would be encouraged to participate actively in the planning of their program. In fact, in a sense, there wouldn't be a program unless they planned it through determining what kind of a training program they needed in order to reach the objectives they had formulated.

2. Formal classroom lectures would be played down; small-group interaction would be played up, as would informal interaction of all kinds.

3. Except for Spanish (four hours a day) and weekly evaluation sessions (of which more later), attendance at the "happenings" of the program would *not* be compulsory.

4. An effort would be made to do away with component labels and thus to "integrate" the elements of the program.

5. The program would be "experience-based." There would be ample

opportunities furnished for "doing things," such as organizing and operating co-ops, raising chickens and pigs, planting and tending gardens, approaching "academic" subjects through research projects, etc. Trainees with needed skills would be urged to teach them to others, formally or informally. The emphasis, in short, was to be on trainee activity, not passivity.

6. Emphasis would be placed throughout on awareness of the environment of the training program, of what was going on and how the trainees were reacting to it (and to each other). This was to be achieved through weekly small-group "evaluation sessions." The personnel of these core groups, including the leaders, would remain more-or-less constant throughout the program.

It didn't turn out as neatly as all this, of course. Some trainees took to this kind of design; some didn't. Several staff members demonstrated anxieties under the inevitable pressures of the program. There were many pressures to revert to the standard model. But somehow this never happened. Trainee morale was extraordinarily high; the trainees did in large measure take responsibility for their own training, and especially for defining the goals of training.

Four major elements seem to us to have combined to make this a unique educational experiment:

Staff Preparation:

First was the degree and intensity of planning that occurred before the trainees arrived. The kind of design we advocate here cannot be conducted by an unprepared staff, or by a staff that has not confronted, grappled with and in some measure dealt beforehand with most of the issues such training raises. When using traditional classroom models, one can assume that the other educators are using roughly similar designs. Much more communication among the training staff is needed to develop commitment to a new model, to test whether proposed training designs do in fact exemplify the model and to resolve inconsistencies between different parts of the program.

It is not necessary to build a seamless united front in the planning phase, but in a program designed to shift the orientation of the trainees away from a dependence on authority to reliance on their own abilities to diagnose, gather data and develop independent solutions, it is important that all the learning activities work toward this meta-goal. While there is room for the application of a number of personal teaching styles among staff members in such a program, it is important that there be basic consensus on the importance of giving trainees as much responsibility as they can manage, on the desirability of trainee activity-initiation as opposed to passivity-receptivity in all learning settings, and on the responsibility of staff members continually to help trainees build connections and bridges between their training experiences and the situations for which they are preparing in the field.

It is easy to provide trainees with experiences and problems to solve. It is more difficult to think through the learning and adaptation processes that must take place in this experience, to help trainees devise ways of collecting data on them and to aid trainees in conceptualizing the processes so that they may be applied in overseas situations which on the surface may seem to be radically different from the projects assigned during training. This form of elaboration requires the trainee to take account of the training experience, to dig into it rather than float on its surface, to formulate hypotheses and questions. Without such elaboration, experiences are not converted into learning. Trainees should receive assistance in conceptualizing and generalizing their experience. It is impossible to reproduce or simulate or even to know precisely what conditions will be faced by trainees in an overseas situation. Crude simulations may be the best available. The *processes* of diagnosing and taking action on a problem are similar in the training and application situations, but the content of the problems are different. Unless the trainee has help in abstracting the process from the particular events he experiences, he will face difficulty in translating what he has learned into usable form.

He will not receive this help from staff members who have not been deeply involved in planning the program and who do not manifest the commitment that can only result from involvement. Involvement of this depth and intensity cannot be developed in a traditional administrative situation. The teacher must write his own job description, through interaction with his colleagues. The planning phase must constitute a training phase for the staff.

It is important, too, that much of the planning bear on process issues— that is, the interpersonal and behavioral patterns that can be expected to develop in the course of training. There is a very real sense in which the planning phase can be a kind of mock-up of the training program that is to come, with the staff members experiencing similar conflicts and anxieties which they must work through before they are ready for the innumerable interpersonal transactions that will make up the actual training program. In planning for this program much of the focus of the work of the consultant was on staff process issues and their relevance to training. By the time the participant arrived, staff members could empathize with the confusion, hostility and anxiety which this program would create for the trainees: the staff had experienced and examined similar feelings as they sought to relinquish the security of traditional classroom models and plan a venture into the ambiguous and unstable world of experience-based training.

Since small group activities were a critical design characteristic in this model, the staff needed well-developed skills in managing group discussions. The need for skill was especially acute where trainees were being asked to reflect on their own performance and experiences in the more stressful parts of the program. Trainees understandably resisted connecting their behavior in the training situation with how they were likely to function in the overseas situation. When trainees sought to withdraw from the ambiguity and stress of being responsible for their own learning they had to be confronted with this avoidance pattern. All of these problems in learning require sensitivity, skill and compassion on the part of the staff. The consultant spent considerable time with the staff working on these skills of discussion leadership. This involved both theory and practice during the planning phase, and observation and consulting with individual staff members after the program was under way.

Use of Authority:

The non-traditional use of authority was of first importance in this program. First, a studied effort was made throughout the program and in the basic design to wean the trainees (and the staff) away from a traditional reliance on authority in learning settings. Second, the staff sincerely tried not to use authority arbitrarily, and especially not to use it in defining the goals of the training program for the trainees or in playing any kind of role *in loco parentis*. The trainees were treated like responsible people capable of making their own decisions about the vital issues of training. Throughout the training program, the staff attempted to level with the trainees, to keep them informed and to avoid manipulation of trainee behavior by explicit or implied reference to the threat of deselection. As a result, the trainee tended to trust the staff, despite occasional difficulties.

The earliest manifestation of the non-traditional use of authority in the program came with the orientation—the prelude to the subsequent activities of the program. The trainees arrived in Puerto Rico with expectations of receiving more or less traditional classroom training, with perhaps a dash of exposure to Puerto Rican life thrown in for seasoning. The orientation was the first opportunity to break this set

and to begin the staff-trainee dialogue which would, hopefully, lead to new attitudes and assumptions about the learning process. The trainees were told (although they did not fully understand at the outset) how the staff would and would not use its authority; what kinds of information, direction and help the staff would provide; and against what criteria their performance would be evaluated.

The staff made it clear that the trainees were responsible not only for the maintenance of the training camp, but also for the organization of their own governing bodies, the parcelling out of work, disciplinary action against slackers, and for the formulation of camp rules and regulations. The freedom to create social structures was so different from the attitudes of college administrators (most of these trainees were just a few weeks out of college) that it set them back on their heels.

They were further shocked to learn that the training program was unplanned, at least in the conventional sense, and that attendance at most activities was not compulsory. Instead, they were given written information about the countries and work situations into which they would go in some four months, and were asked to meet in small groups with staff members to discuss what kind of a training experience this information implied would be useful.

Thus, the orientation began to build a conceptual framework for the training. It illustrated how authority would be applied in the program, and it began activities in support of this framework. In a design of this sort, authority is not absent. It is used differently and with lesser intensity than is customary, but it *is* used. It must be. Trainees must know that there are people around who know what they're doing. Many of them need support in beginning to use their own resources for learning. They are well adapted, most of them, to the passive-receptive learning role. They do not abandon it easily. Why should they when it has worked for them in the past? They profit from authoritative encouragement, even when authority is used to prescribe the use of resources rather than to assure continued dependence.

As it happened, in the Puerto Rico programs there were wide variations in the ability of the staff to work with trainees in helping them to get the most out of their experiences. Those who were least committed to the experience-based model vacillated between excessive and inadequate control over trainee activities. On the one hand, they were concerned lest the trainees "get out of hand" and the staff lose control over the community. On the other, they tended to see the alternatives to rigid control as being no staff influence over trainees at all. It seemed to be particularly difficult for them to conceptualize and practice the supportive authority discussed above, possibly because they had never been on the receiving end of it. This was a continuing concern throughout the training and was the subject of much discussion among both trainees and staff. It was also another major focus of the consultant's work with the staff.

Emphasis on Process:

The third distinctive element in the program was the emphasis placed on process issues, and on developing awareness of the total emotional, interpersonal, and organizational environment in which trainees and staff were living and working.

Throughout the training period trainees were urged to consider the camp and the training program as a community—to be charted, researched, understood, and if need be, changed. In the weekly evaluation sessions trainees were urged to review the organizational climate of the program, their relations with each other, and to comment on such phenomena as the power structure in the Training Center, and the formation of trainee subgroups. The first group of trainees to arrive at the Center was encouraged to consider and deal with its feelings of intergroup competition arising from arrival of a second group a week later, and *vice versa*. When crises occurred, those affected by them were urged to analyze what had really happened and why the principals had acted as they did.

The "Project" Approach:

The training program consisted of large and small problem-solving projects, planned for the most part by the trainees themselves, who related to the staff through a complex of formal and informal interpersonal and intergroup transactions.

The term project is used here to describe an activity requiring a learner to:

1. Obtain information from the social environment (communication);
2. Formulate and test hypotheses about forces and processes present in the environment (diagnosis);
3. Select and describe some part of the

situation which is to be changed or altered (problem definition);

4. Plan action to solve the problem (commitment, risk-taking);
5. Carry out the action, enlisting the help and cooperation of others (influencing and organizing);
6. Verbalize attitudes, perceptions and tentative learnings from the experience (cognition and generalization).

Projects should be the heart of an experience-based training program. They may take almost any form; they may be short or long; they may overlap with other training activities; they may involve activity inside or outside the training location.

In the programs described here trainees established cooperatives; they planted gardens and raised chickens and pigs; and they organized mutual teacher-learning activities for the sharing of specialized skills such as accounting, welding and arts and crafts. They participated in such staff-designed projects as rock-climbing, trekking, survival experiences, construction tasks and field training in Puerto Rican villages.

The emphasis on trainee-developed projects reinforced the staff's initial message regarding autonomy, responsibility and initiative. The more aggressive trainees responded eagerly to the message; the less independent trainees tended to substitute the leadership of other trainees for the authority they found missing in the staff. Often, not being required to do anything specific, they did nothing. Some trainees were capable of accepting autonomy with regard to both the ends of a project and the means; the less creative, the less able, the less independent, the less

trusting required the specification of ends before they could proceed to devise the means of getting there. In no case, however, were both the ends and the means specified. Tasks were designed to require trainees to diagnose a situation, develop a variety of possible approaches and select one, and to take initiative to produce the end result desired.

In the training-center-as-a-community project trainees set goals as homely as influencing the dining room to serve a wider variety of food, and bringing other trainees to a higher level of sanitation and neatness in their living quarters. A principal activity was the trainees' persistent efforts to influence the staff to provide learning resources (reading, lectures, discussions, etc.). This hunger for learning was in sharp contrast to the avoidance games many of the trainees had shared with their college classmates only a few short weeks earlier.

The critical factor in a project-focussed program is the manner in which staff members support and assist the trainees in elaborating their projects. At one extreme, a project may be presented to a group of trainees to solve as best they can, with the learning falling where it may. No special effort is made to organize comparisons between experiences, to examine value issues or conflicts, or to influence conceptualization of the influence styles and interaction patterns used by different individuals in planning and executing the action.

At the other extreme, an effort may be made to force learning from each part of the experience. Trainees may be convened in small groups and urged to formulate the problem of diagnosis, conflict, influence and organization implicit in their project. Staff members participate in work and planning sessions as process consultants whose role is to help participants to observe and become aware of the social forces with which they are dealing in the here and now.

It is the elaboration of an experience-based training design which requires most skill on the part of staff. It is much easier to provide trainees with problems to solve than it is to think through the social and individual processes which will be going on; devise means of bringing them to light; and aid trainees in conceptualizing the experience so that their learning may be applied in later overseas situations which are on the surface quite different.

It is here that the discussion leadership skills of the staff become critical, for they must be used to draw out of the trainee the principles and generalizations which are latent in the experience. If this does not occur, much of the potential learning will be lost.

Most of the staff worked hard at performing this function. They found it among the most difficult of the responsibilities they had accepted in designing an experience-based program. Many of the trainees were adept at avoiding examining the implications of this experience, particularly when the experience was stressful and anxiety-provoking. The staff were understandably reluctant to push such confrontation. Considerable learning was undoubtedly lost through caution and lack of skill, but during the course of the program the staff's effectiveness as inductive teachers increased steadily with practice.

Field Training:

The trainees in this program spent a total of almost a month in small Puerto Rican villages, where they faced problems of adaptation similar to those they would confront in Latin America. Here, too, efforts were made to assist the trainees in designing projects around their field living and to convert them into real learning afterward.

Puerto Rico, of course, offers an almost ideal transitional environment for trainees bound for Latin America. But if adequate help in conceptualizing and generalizing is available, almost any alien situation can become a meaningful field training assignment in preparation for cross-cultural work. For urban dwellers, rural living may be alien; for members of the middle class, experience with the poor, angry and the disadvantaged provides real confrontation. It is *desirable* to conduct field training in a culture similar to that for which a trainee is being prepared, but this is by no means essential. The important thing is to create as much "cultural distance" as possible from the life the trainee has been living, so that the values and attitudes that have worked for him before are no longer adequate. The cultural *content* may differ from that of the area for which the trainee is bound, but the process problems that grow out of confrontation are similar.

Integration of Content and Process:

A persistent problem was how to make fact, theory and opinion about the cultures to which the trainees were going and the jobs they were to do relevant to the problem solving environment of the training program. On the one hand, lectures and books seemed to provide an escape from involvement and confrontation for those trainees who needed to defend themselves against the personal exposure of the program. On the other hand, for those trainees who did become heavily involved, the lectures and readings often seemed dry, abstract and unreal. Trainees were given responsibility for organizing the use of visiting lecturers, which may have increased their feeling of responsibility, but it did little to connect the content to problem-solving processes.

Martin Tarcher[2] has recently described a feasible approach to the integration of content and process. In a program for community leaders he created project teams as the central learning units. The teams were responsible for using data from an exhaustive community survey to diagnose and plan action for development of the community. Outside lecturers were asked to familiarize themselves with the same data and to introduce only material directly relevant to the solution of the problems revealed in the data. Thus, content input was directly tied to the problem-solving process.

There is strong reason to believe that only content which can be used and practiced in the training situation is usefully learned in an experience-based training program. Tarcher's design meets this criterion.

[2] Tarcher, M., *Leadership and the Power of Ideas*, New York, Harper & Row, Publishers, 1966.

Behind the Design: The Teacher

Even those who are attracted to the approaches to learning we have described here may well ask where the teachers will come from to carry them out. Clearly, the desired skill mix is sharply divergent from the blend of intellectual competence and verbal facility found in good classroom teachers.

The teacher in an experience-based program is involved with people, not books; with real situations, not abstractions. He must collaborate closely with his colleagues. In his work with students, he will do little presenting and much listening. Instead of organizing content material, he will seek patterns, principles and generalizations in the reactions of trainees.

Subject matter competence is useful, of course; but it will not get the job done without true competence in the facilitation of learning through focus on process. All of us are trained to cooperate comfortably in traditional systems of teaching and learning. The traditional systems in which most of us were formed do not value the subtle and sophisticated teaching skills described here.

There are, however, incompletely-exploited sources of the competence which is needed. Industry, government and the military all have had to develop methods of education that will pay off in immediately transferable skills. Educational innovation and change have been much more rapid in these applied settings than in colleges and universities. Industrial trainers in particular must be open to innovation and experimentation, or they don't survive.

For the overseas agencies, such as the Peace Corps and the Agency for International Development, a ready source of *potential* educators exists in returnees from the field. The Peace Corps program discussed here was conducted largely by former Volunteers, few of whom had previous teaching experience. As our strictures about staff planning and preparation imply, though, it cannot be assumed that persons with practical experience are necessarily qualified to teach and communicate it. This is a particularly unjustified assumption when the proposed training is highly inductive. The "practical man" has at his disposal a fund of "war stories" which purport to illustrate how to handle various concrete and specifi situations abroad. But concrete and often-undigested experiences such as these are of limited value. The "practical" man, if he is to become an effective trainer, must learn to conceptualize the cross-cultural learning experience in terms applicable to experience-based learning. For example, if a practical community developer can come to see working with trainees as "another kind of community development," then he is well on his way to translating his cross-cultural experience into training design. He will have begun to understand the learning process in which he participated overseas, and to consider how such experiences might be simulated for trainees in process, if not in content.

Many cross-cultural workers, however, are so practical and concrete in their thinking that they learn only those aspects of a culture which they directly encounter. They find it difficult to generalize beyond their own experiences. They may have learned, but they have not learned *how* they learned.

Among those who have taken part in cross-cultural experiences, however, there will be those who *have* learned how to learn and who can, with further training, build experiences which will transmit what they know to others. To do this requires a clear understanding of such principles of learning as those described in this paper. The conceptual framework for experience-based training is *not* implicit in our educational background. We operate comfortably within a traditional learning system both as pupils or teachers, but this does not mean that we *understand* the conditions which facilitate learning and the transfer of learning to an application situation.

When, therefore, an individual is asked to participate in the design and conduct of training of a radically different form from traditional models, he needs a basic education himself in the teaching and learning process. He needs supervised and assisted experience in designing training, conducting it and evaluating the results. He needs to work with others who are also struggling with the tasks of putting together and operating experience-based training designs.

The plans proposed in this paper have no fail-safe ingredients to protect them from failure. The launching of educational innovation requires more than a blue-print for success.

Fortunately, there are some resources and forces towards innovation of the kind we have proposed. Our culture is highly pragmatic. Americans are receptive to ideas that work. Supporting this pragmatism are the experiences of those who have lived in the cross-cultural situation, who have been open to their experience and have been able to generalize from it.

In addition, there is a small body of experience-based pedagogy which provides crude models of what this training may look like and accomplish. Practitioners of sensitivity training have been using experience-based pedagogy for some time. The same is true of much industrial and military training. The models are available, but they must be refined and adapted to the purposes at hand.

Lastly, the climate for educational innovation has never been better than it is now. For the first time in recent years students (and some of their professors) in institutions of higher educa-

tion are beginning to question the goals and procedures of their education. There is a hunger for educational experiences which involve the whole person, which get to the "heart of the matter," which seem to have a more direct connection with life as it is lived in our relativist, kinetic, peripatetic, crisis-ridden society. Perhaps this questioning is the prelude to changes in our diverse but tradition-bound institutions of higher learning. In the hope of influencing that change this paper has been written. For we cannot escape the conclusion that the design principles we have enunciated here might have validity in preparing people for the ambiguities of life at home, as well as for life abroad.

8.2   AUTHENTIC INTERACTION AND PERSONAL GROWTH IN SENSITIVITY TRAINING GROUPS[1]

James V. Clark

This paper is an attempt to state a recurring order of events I see in sensitivity training groups, events that have to do with the improvement of significant self-learning.

Throughout the paper I will use the first person as a way of underscoring that at the present stage of its development this theory is largely a personal attempt to state the uniformities I have

seen as a trainer in approximately fifty of these groups. I will, however, frequently use the language of some of those who have done research in psychotherapy.[2] I do this because I see no

James V. Clark, "Authentic Interaction and Personal Growth in Sensitivity Training Groups," *Journal of Humanistic Psychology* (Spring 1963). Used by permission.

[1] The author is grateful to Dr. Charles Ferguson of U.C.L.A. for helpful discussion and clarification.

[2] It is sometimes debated whether sensitivity training "should" or "should not" be psychotherapy. I personally share Maslow's point that "therapy should be taken out of the office and spread to many other areas of life. Furthermore, it should not only be more broadly used, but also *more ambitiously defined* to include the growth-fostering techniques." (Italics mine.) Abraham Maslow, Toward a Humanistic Psychology, *ETC*, Vol. 14, No. 1 (Autumn, 1956).

advantage in introducing new language to point to previously observed phenomena occurring in a new setting.

Reports in the literature of both impressions[3] and analytic measurements of changes[4] during small-group human-relations training programs for business and professional people often suggest substantial personal growth resembling that seen in psychotherapy. This paper is a beginning effort to explain these results by stating—in potentially testable "if-then" terms—the dynamic of events in such groups which lead to these kinds of personal learnings.

The series of events on which this paper will focus, then, has to do with self-learning as it occurs in the interpersonal context. By self-learning I mean the development of one's awareness of his self, including its hidden and denied aspects and its relationship to the here-and-now environment.

Of course, other kinds of learning must take place in training groups—certainly at the same time and probably earlier. As Bion[5] and others[6] have stated, much early behavior in training

groups has a group-wide avoidance component to it. Members, while typically denying they are a group at all, are usually engaged in a silent pact to avoid confronting their here-and-now present, which is so frightening. At such times, little if any deep, real individual learning is likely to take place until the basic issues of dependency on the trainer and intimacy within the whole group are somehow grappled with and tentatively worked through by the group as a whole. Stated differently, group members grapple first with their social selves, and later with their individuality. As a trainer, however, I do believe that learning about and taking more responsibility for the self-in-here-and-now-interpersonal settings is the main task or goal of the so-called T-group. Therefore, when such a group is "working," in the sense that Bion used that term, or is "at a high level," in the sense that Thelen[7] and his colleagues meant it, it is engaging in the kinds of activities I will attempt to describe.

The sequence of activities listed below occurs uniformly in groups I call "successful." I will first present the list without elaboration, and will then discuss each stage in the sequence as well as draw attention to work in other fields which relates to the dynamics going on at that stage.

---

[3] See, e.g., I. R. Weschler, F. Massarik, and R. Tannenbaum. The Self in Process: A Sensitivity Training Emphasis, in I. Weschler and E. Schein (eds.), *Issues in Sensitivity Training* (Washington: National Training Laboratories, 1962), pp. 34–46.

[4] See, e.g., William C. Schutz, and Vernon L. Allen, On T-Groups, mimeo., University of California, Berkeley, 1961, and Richard L. Burke and Warren G. Bennis, Changes in Perception of Self and Others During Human Relations Training, *Human Relations*, Vol. 14, No. 2, May, 1961, pp. 165–182.

[5] W. R. Bion, *Experiences in Groups*, London: Tavistock Publications, 1961.

[6] Warren Bennis, and Herbert Shepard, A Theory of Group Development, *Human*

Relations, Vol. 9, No. 4 (1956), pp. 415–457. See also Felicidad Sycip, The Silent Language of Sensitivity Training, prepared for inclusion in Jerome Reisel (ed.), *Explorations in Sensitivity Training* (in process).

[7] Saul Ben-Zeev, Ida Gradolph, Phillip Gradolph, William Hill, Dorothy Stock, and Herbert Thelen, *Methods for Studying Work and Emotionality in Group Action* (Chicago: Human Dynamics Laboratory, University of Chicago, 1954).

The Sequence of Authentic Interaction and Personal Growth

1. In a training group there exists some persistent, incongruous behavior by member A. A is said to be incongruous if others see him as not being fully aware of his own feelings and reactions, or as not communicating those feelings of which he is aware.[8]

2. To the extent A's incongruous behavior is neither too trivial nor too gross, it is explicitly and persistently reflected back to A by some of the other members, B . . . $_n$.

3. To the extent such reflection causes A to perceive those aspects of his own behavior which are at variance with his self-concept, he is in a psychological crisis.

4. To the extent such persistent reflection comes from members who are perceived by A as congruent and to the extent A perceives the group as having some degree of empathy and positive regard for him, there is a new integration by A—his self-concept enlarges to include the reality with which he has been confronted.

5. A's behavior tends to change in line with his new integration, and he therefore tends to be more congruent. At this point, the sequence begins again (see step 9 for a description of the improving nature of this recurrence).

Steps 6 through 8 describe a special form of this developing sequence, a form which does not occur nearly so often as that seen in steps one through 5.

6. For some members, B . . . $_n$, A's behavior change precipitates in them a psychological crisis;[9] they now have negative feelings about the new behavior of A, which they had helped bring about either by their active confrontation or passive acquiescence while it was going on.

7. Members B . . . $_n$ either deny A's change or act aggressively toward it, thereby behaving incongruously in regard to their earlier (step 2) behavior.

8. Member A (and/or the trainer or other members) communicates this new incongruity to the members B . . . $_n$.

9. The sequence repeats itself, at one time or another involving all members. Each time the sequence recurs, it involves more people who are becoming more congruent and, hence, tends to improve. As people are thus helped more, deeper feelings are experienced, and the amount of time spent in the present increases. The longer the group lasts, the more helpfully and authentically do the members interact.

Interaction is difficult to perceive, even for one who has been so trained. I started in groups expecting to use either group-wide or individual concepts for dealing with my experiences. It began to dawn on me, however, that the significant units to which I was attending as a trainer were not so much

---

[8] See Carl Rogers, A Tentative Formulation of a General Law of Interpersonal Relationships, in *On Becoming a Person* (Boston: Houghton Mifflin Company, 1961).

[9] Such a reaction is whimsically alluded to in Bud Freeman's song, "I Can't Get Adjusted to the You Who Got Adjusted to Me," *Songs of Couch and Consultation* (Hollywood: Commentary Records).

the total group nor any one individual in it, but rather *dyads*. As I thought about my behavior as a trainer, it seemed that what I frequently attended to and commented on was a set of shifting polarities, some of which involved me directly, many of which did not. If one pictures a group as a circle, my mental image often was of a set of shifting diameters. Of course, these polarities were occurring within a group context, and one of the participants was often visibly supported by other group members. But I am fairly sure that the participants were primarily *experiencing* these "public dyads," even when one or the other member was a group surrogate. I also get the distinct impression that early in a group's life, members address it as a conglomerate other. That is, they deal with the whole complex as if it were a dyad.

This realization opened a new vista for me. For some time I had been impressed with the research of Rogers and his group on the necessary and sufficient conditions for therapeutic personality change. Rogers points out more than once that these conditions are attitudinal and behavioral in nature and not primarily theoretical or "professional"; clients improved when they saw their therapist as congruent, empathic, and having positive regard for them.[10] More recently, an associate of Rogers has shown that the presence or absence of these characteristics in a group therapist significantly relates to remission rates in therapy groups with hospitalized patients.[11] In training groups, however, it seemed to me that *members* participating in these shifting dyads were behaving "therapeutically" toward one another. By therapeutically, here, I mean that they were doing something which seemed to encourage significant growth in others, and this "something" seemed to be the same "something" Rogers had discovered—behavior which the recipient saw as congruent, empathic, and full of positive regard. Moreover, it seemed that they were *improving* such *therapeutic* behavior the longer their group lasted. Whether or not this sequence can be described and predicted must wait for subsequent research, which is currently under way.

It is clear that the above list and the following discussion have as their central focus the dyad. The implicit assumption is that one individual can act therapeutically toward another. In short, however, I am attempting to state as clearly as I can what happens in some one of these relationships as it occurs in a T-group.

Something like what I have described in the list happens in every group I have participated in, and it may be helpful if I present a few typical case examples before I attempt to delineate the process analytically. These cases, by the way, are instances of therapeutic *events*; no explicit or implicit claim is being made that these persons entered their groups as "neurotics" and left them as "cured."

Case 1.—A vivacious and bright young girl participated actively in the group ac-

[10] Carl Rogers, The Necessary and Sufficient Conditions of Psychotherapeutic Personality Change, *Journal of Consulting Psychology, Vol. 21* (1957), pp. 95–103.

[11] Charles B. Truax, The Process of Group Psychotherapy, *Psychological Monographs*, Vol. 75, No. 7 (1961).

tivities throughout the first 40-odd hours of its life. Infrequently during this period, though, two members tried to tell her that she seemed aloof and withdrawn from anything "human" or emotional. They tried, politely, to tell her that she seemed more interested in other people's insights and involvement than her own. One of these two members, a young man, finally forced the issue by calling the girl a "phony" and helping the other member, an older woman, clarify and specify similar feelings. He did this slowly, methodically, and apparently without rancor or hostility, but more in the spirit of honesty. A week later the young girl made a long speech to the group, saying over and over again how much she wanted to be in the group and receive people's real feelings about her. The trainer intervened, asking her how come she kept filibustering, then? She reacted with a flood of tears and anger. She pleaded that she was really trying, and berated the trainer for not appreciating her. After this outburst had spent itself, she began to have several deep insights. She talked of how parents and friends had always put her on a pedestal and how she was realizing that she could not respect them for this. She then realized, almost with awe, how afraid she had been to step down off that pedestal. She seemed excited and relieved over these insights. During the remaining 30 hours of the group's life, she was highly involved in the emotional side of the group, often playing a central role in it. Her voice and gestures changed, too, from being over-polite and restrained to more expansive and spontaneous.

Case 2.—A group member in another group, an executive in his middle forties, wore solemn clothes, rarely smiled, and talked in a confusing fashion. He expressed dislike of his confused speech, also. Once when another member was silent and withdrawn, however, the "solemn" one reached out for him, asking him clearly and warmly if he didn't really want to be himself in the

group and be liked for it. The remaining group members were delighted with this behavior and confronted him with the fact that he had in fact exhibited warm, emotional, and completely clear speech and behavior. He denied the reality of this, but tape recorder evidence and strong expressions of contrary opinion continued to be directed at him. The next meeting he appeared in a red vest, checked shirt, and carrying a miniature blank pistol. The latter he discharged into the group's midst, saying he had always wanted to dress this way and shoot off a pistol. His behavior continued to be somewhat eccentric during the day, and was marked by a kind of euphoria. During the remaining meetings of the group, however, he was not at all bizarre, and played a warm and supportive role toward other members. He was particularly helpful in clarifying feelings people were trying to express.

Case 3.—A nurse in her middle forties was in a group which contained a number of college-age members. One of these, Henry, a young man in his early twenties, expressed in an early meeting his trouble in feeling a part of the group, as well as his strong desire to become a real member. Several times during subsequent meetings, when he would start to come in and participate, the nurse would interrupt, saying, "Isn't it *nice* that Henry is talking finally?" Over a period of two or three meetings Henry, another group member, and the trainer expressed strong feelings that she was dominating and mothering Henry. The group member said the nurse's actions were not at all supportive, but *hateful*, and once when the nurse made this kind of a remark the trainer doubled up as if he had been hit in the stomach. The nurse looked shocked, and fell absolutely silent for two meetings. When someone finally asked her about the silence, she refused to answer, but the trainer commented that if he were she, he would be keeping quiet so he wouldn't appear to be a hateful person.

The next day she sought out the trainer, almost bubbling over with enthusiasm. She said that after all these remarks, she had suddenly seen that all her life, being tall, she had simply *hated* short and unassertive men, which was how she saw Henry. She had never realized her hatred before, and felt exhilarated at this insight. She had always seen herself as motherly and "nursely" and now thought this to be a cover-up for much angry and hostile behavior, in her home life and at work. She returned to the group, after dramatically changing her hair style, putting on make-up and wearing younger and more feminine clothes. She no longer "mothered" Henry.

Having shown some examples, I will now turn back to an attempt to analyze the important steps in this process. I will repeat each of the steps in the list and expand on it.

1. *In a training group there exists some persistent, incongruous behavior by member A. A is said to be incongruous if others see him as not being fully aware of his own real feelings and reactions, or as not communicating those feelings of which he is aware.*

The event which inaugurates this whole sequence is behavior on the part of a member which is perceived by other members as being incongruous. That is, some other members either believe that A is experiencing something of which he is not aware, or they believe that he is aware of something which he is not communicating. They, therefore, are in some doubt as to how to behave toward A in such a way that their interpersonal needs will be met. In the three examples cited above, this doubt was generated in Case 1 by the vivacious, withdrawn young girl; in Case 2 by the warm, clear-speaking executive who regarded himself as somber and confused; and in Case 3 by the dominating, hostile nurse who saw herself as supportive and motherly.

Warren Bennis[12] draws attention to this dynamic in one of its forms when he points out that regardless of what A may communicate overtly, there is an aspect of himself of which he is not aware and of which others are aware. Such others are also aware that A is not aware of it and, therefore, they are thrown into doubt and confusion as to how to respond to A and still get what they need from him. They know, of course, that typically A does not want to be responded to along the dimensions of his self of which he is not aware. In most social systems, as Goffman[13] has pointed out, this results in a ritual interaction in which all participants of a social group agree to respond to one another only along those dimensions of which they are aware and which are more or less socially expected.

In a T-group, however, a different atmosphere is created, either by the expectations of the participants when they come and which they gain from former participants, by public announcements, through theory sessions during the course of the training period, through trainer intervention, or through the influence of those members who advocate "honest" relationships toward one another in the group. Regardless of the causes, the whole "cul-

[12] Warren Bennis, Interpersonal Communication, in Warren Bennis, Kenneth Benne, and Robert Chin, *The Planning of Change* (New York: Holt, Rinehart, and Winston, Inc., 1961).
[13] Erving Goffman, On Face-Work, *Psychiatry*, Vol. 18, No. 3 (Aug., 1955).

ture" surrounding a T-group supports atypical social behavior and tends to allow for the genuine reactions people have toward incongruity (or, more accurately, toward their own perceptions of incongruity).

2. *To the extent A's incongruous behavior is neither too trivial nor too gross, it is explicitly and persistently reflected back to A by some of the other members, B . . . ₙ.*

Some members of the group notice the incongruity in A and they respond to it. This was seen in the three examples, where the girl's behavior was called "phony," the executive's self-image was denied by others, and the nurse's behavior was called "hateful." Charles Ferguson and I have noticed in a group we shared and in recalling our experiences with other groups that there is a tendency to discuss neither trivial incongruities nor incongruities that are too great. Rather, group members tend to operate continually in a middle ground. We have been referring to this behavior as a kind of "innate social wisdom." In a recent volume, Fiske and Maddi[14] have brought together and conceptualized a growing body of research on varied experience in animals and in humans which tends to explain this behavior. This research suggests that organisms tend to seek an optimal level of excitation. That is, experiments with humans have shown they have a stronger tendency to notice and move toward incongruent stimuli rather than congruent, redundant ones. Similar experiments have been conducted among animals. On the other

hand, Hebb's work[15] has shown that stimuli which are *too* incongruent (for example, the model of a human head which was clearly without a body when it was exhibited to chimpanzees) produce fear and flight. He noticed that mildly incongruous stimuli (such as the head of a man standing behind a partition) do not produce fear and flight, but rather investigation and approach behavior. These findings, while by no means conclusive, do suggest that it is people's general tendency toward *optimal* exploration and variety which determines both their confronting someone whom they perceive as incongruous and their apparent "wisdom" in avoiding someone with too gross incongruities.[16] An instance of avoidance was seen in a group of businessmen, among whom was one man who was seen by the others as having homosexual behavioral characterisics of which he was seemingly not aware. The group included him in their activities

[14] Donald W. Fiske and Salvadore R. Maddi, *Functions of Varied Experience* (Homewood, Ill.: Dorsey Press, 1961).

[15] See, for example, D. O. Hebb, *A Textbook of Psychology* (Philadelphia: W. B. Saunders Company, 1958), p. 114.

[16] It is interesting to speculate that this tendency to seek out and advance toward optimal incongruity, to resolve it, and then to continue to advance toward new incongruities may constitute a part of the "drive toward growth" so often postulated by Rogers and others in psychotherapy. The process of clarifying feelings is the process of stating a client's feeling at a level slightly ahead of what the client has symbolized. This slight difference between therapist and client can be consistently measured. (See Carl R. Rogers and Richard A. Rablen, A Scale of Process in Psychotherapy, mimeo., University of Wisconsin, 1958.) As successful clients proceed through psychotherapy, they consistently move toward and incorporate into their self-image these confrontations of aspects of themselves they had previously not admitted to awareness.

and, indeed, gave him a great deal of feedback about certain aspects of his behavior (his tendency to dominate others by fooling around, telling jokes, etc.), but the whole area of his suspected homosexuality—so threatening and "out of line" in this group of business executives—was never discussed.

When A's recurring incongruous behavior is neither too trivial nor too gross, some members persistently point it out. In the early stages of this process A tends to ignore or deny the reflection that is being held up to him. With or without the trainer's aid, however, the confrontations become more and more and more specific: "You say you just want to be one of the boys, but here are specific instances today where you dominated and suppressed others. How come?"

3. *To the extent such reflection causes A to perceive those aspects of his own behavior which are at variance with his self-concept, he is in a psychological crisis.*

A, like every other member of the training group, is seeking to present himself and his behavior in such a way as to gratify his own needs and to gain satisfaction in interpersonal relationships in his usual manner. But when he discovers the fact that people are persistently responding to him with confusion and hostility, it means to him that he is embedded in a situation in which his usual behavior is not meeting his needs. The more he realizes this, the more frightened and anxious he becomes. He is in what Gerald Caplan has called a *psychological crisis*. Recall that in each case, crisis behavior was evident: the young girl's angry crying, the executive's bizarre dress and be-

havior for several meetings, and the nurse's withdrawal and silence for more than a week. Caplan's discussion of these kinds of phenomena is relevant to the point we are discussing, and so I will quote it at length:

When we talk about someone being mentally healthy or unhealthy, we are making a rating of an equilibrium of his functioning in his relationship with his environment . . . This equilibrium is kept stable by a complicated series of re-equilibrating or homeostatic mechanisms operating both within his personality and in the social system of his network of close interpersonal relationships. Changes in the type of equilibrium and in the person's state of mental health may occur during crisis periods. A crisis is a period of disequilibrium which overpowers the homeostatic mechanisms when the person is faced by a problem, which on the one hand is of basic importance to him because it is linked with his fundamental instinctual drives, and on the other hand is such that he is not able to solve it quickly by means of his normal range of problem-solving mechanisms. Although any individual will have idiosyncratic reactions to specific life events which will constitute crisis problems to him, we may build a list of hazardous life events which will be likely to throw many people into crisis as defined by the above criteria, for example, pregnancy, birth, death, important role transitions, such as starting school, a new job, or getting married, adaptation to incapacitating illness, etc.

During the period of disorganization of a crisis old conflicts, which are symbolically linked with the present problem, are revived and the pattern of their previous solution may influence the present adaptation, but by the same token, adaptive responses in the present may repair former damage. As the tension in a crisis mounts to a peak, there is a preliminary period of ineffectual functioning as the individual faces the fact that he is not able to solve the problem in one of his usual ways. This may be followed by the mobilization of latent strengths both inside an individual and in his relationships with others.

A critical factor in determining the outcome will be the support which is mobilized on his behalf from significant people in his environment and from the traditional helping practices of his culture . . .

During the relatively short period of a crisis, and especially at its peak, when the emotional forces inside the individual and in his interpersonal network are off balance, a relatively minor effort in operation for a short time will weigh the equilibrium down in a positive or negative direction as regards mental health. Help at this time produces long lasting effects quite out of proportion to the effort expended.[17]

As a trainer, I find myself playing a watchful and rather active role around these kinds of events in group life. In general, I have a careful eye out for the extent to which the incongruity is communicated only with hostility or the extent to which it is communicated in such a way that member A is likely to feel understood and positively regarded by members B . . . ₙ who are doing the communicating. As I said earlier, recent researches by Rogers and his colleagues have shown that these three attitudinal characteristics on the part of one person —the capacity to communicate congruently, the capacity for communicating empathy, and the capacity to regard another with unconditional and positive regard[18]—are central determinants of the other person's psychotherapeutic growth. If the attitudes of empathy and

positive regard are missing in the group (which they are rarely in a heterogeneous group), it is extremely important for the trainer to fill them in or to help the members fill them in.

Caplan's formulation helps me to understand the number of rather positive dramatic attitudinal and behavioral shifts I have seen in training groups. The individual thrown into a crisis is both helped to face it and given support for that activity by the rest of the group. Under these conditions, both Caplan and Rogers maintain that strong internal tendencies in member A tend to take over and determine the success of his search for a new and more adequate way of dealing with this situation. My own experience suggests that the T-group is another environment in which these same tendencies can operate.

4. *To the extent such persistent reflection comes from members who are perceived by A as congruent and to the extent A perceives the group as having some degree of empathy and positive regard for him, there is a new integration by A—his self-concept enlarges to include the reality with which he has been confronted.*

In most instances, this stage consists of A admitting to awareness aspects of his self of which in the past he had not been aware. Usually these include feelings which he had behaved as if he did not experience. Rogers' "Process Conception of Psychotherapy"[19] shows the new kinds of communication which tend to emerge at this point or throughout this process and which illustrate

[17] Gerald Caplan, An Approach to the Study of Family Mental Health, in *The Family*, ed. Galdston (New York: International Universities Press, 1961) , p. 52.

[18] See note 9.

[19] In his *On Becoming a Person*.

the admitting of previously denied parts of the self.

In training groups some illustrative events are the silent member who doesn't talk because he "doesn't want to be a blabbermouth" and who begins to experience the hostility and fear which underlie his reluctance and starts to assert himself; or the person who wants "to help everyone grow" and who begins to recognize the feelings of mastery or insecurity which underlie this behavior, and starts to become less aggressive; and so on. More specifically, the case examples showed the young girl becoming more warm and "present," the executive becoming more outgoing and clear, and the nurse becoming less hostile and more feminine.

5. *A's behavior tends to change in line with his new integration, and he therefore tends to be more congruent. At this point, the sequence begins again (see step 9 for a description of the improving nature of this recurrence).*

As the above illustrations suggest, A's new integrations are usually accompanied by some new behavior. These new behaviors are often dramatic, exhibiting what seem, as suggested above, to be opposite tendencies from the way the member previously behaved: a dominating member tends to fall relatively silent, a retiring member tends to speak up and initiate certain subjects of conversation, a cold and distant person exhibits some warm and more human behavior, and so on.

Schutz's research[20] at the 1959 Western Training Laboratory suggested that these kinds of changes do occur, both

[20] Schutz and Allen, *op. cit.*

during and after membership in a sensitivity training group. He found significantly lower correlations between before and after sensitivity training FIRO-B tests for sensitivity-training-group members than for a control group of nonmembers. The nonmembers showed stable FIRO-B scores; the members changed. Since the correlation between actual behavior and Schutz's instrument is not known, the research is not conclusive; these results were predicted and statistically significant, though, and thereby gain credence.

The next few phases tend to occur three or four times in every group, but not to as many members as do the first five. This may be largely a function of the short amount of time that is available in most groups. I believe, although this has not yet been demonstrated, that steps 6 through 8 occur more often in those groups where the people live or work together ordinarily when they are not in training—so-called "family groups."

6. *For some members, B ... ₙ, A's behavior change precipitates in them a psychological crisis; they now have negative feelings about the new behavior of A, which they had helped bring about either by their active confrontation or passive aquiescence while it was going on.*

A's new behavior (which is frequently perceived by A as being more congruent) is perhaps by its very newness frequently perceived as incongruous by B. Perhaps this is because B was originally responding to those aspects of A's behavior about which B had ambivalent feelings—perhaps toward similar behavior in himself. But, whatever the reason, if A actually now no longer engages in those kinds of behavior, it tends to produce a whole new situation for B; the traditional ways of having his interpersonal needs satisfied with A are now no longer effective for him; certain needs of his of which he is not aware are not being met by the new A.

An illustration occurred in a recent group. A pretty, retiring young coed was encouraged to notice that the comments she mumbled half to herself actually were intellectually sound and offered needed direction to the group. After several meetings she finally announced that she now knew there was a "me" and that she could *act*, not just be acted *upon*. As she changed to a more genuine, forceful, and mature participant of the group, three other members became upset. One fell silent for several meetings and the other two started skipping classes. Such a dynamic did not occur in cases 1 and 2 above, nor was it discussed in case 3. But in case 3, some other members of the group were shocked at the nurse's change in appearance and behavior. They wondered why she didn't talk more and why she had altered her hair style so dramatically.

7. *Members B...ₙ either deny A's change or act aggressively toward it, thereby behaving incongruously in regard to their earlier (step 2) behavior.*

The typical behaviors of people at this stage are denial and aggression. Often member A will appear, to a relatively uninvolved person such as the trainer or an observer, as quite changed, yet B...ₙ may continue in their criticism of A, much as if A were still behaving in the same fashion that he used to. Or B...ₙ may respond to A's changed behavior by criticising A for the very fact of change; A may be told that he is no longer acting his "natural self," or that he is "succumbing to group pressures to conform," and so on. When it is clear that B...ₙ are responding to needs which they did not previously appear to possess, they will be perceived by A (and perhaps also the trainer as well as other members of the group) as incongruous. That is, they will be seeking to deny or eliminate behavior in A which they so vigorously attempted to bring about in the past. At this stage, of course, they are quite like A was in his original incongruity. In the illustration cited in step 6, for example, two of the three other members, when they did start to talk to the girl, called her "unreal" and "Betty Coed" (labels which more accurately applied to her old behavior and which showed they were denying that she had changed). The other member called her "unfeminine"—an aggressive attempt to get her to return to her earlier, more docile role. In the case 3 example, those who disapproved of the nurse's new appearance and less active behavior tended to avoid and exclude her.

8. *Member A (and/or the trainer or other members) communicates this new incongruity to the members B...ₙ.*

Member A is often perceptive in reflecting back to B...ₙ this new incongruity. Since he now denies less of the reality within himself, he becomes a better perceiver of the reality outside himself. Moreover, he often becomes able to communicate congruently, but without the loss of empathy and positive regard often seen in early confrontation in a group. Again continuing the above illustration, the young coed was able to express her deep disappointment that these members did not understand her, without trying to force them to do so. This communication helped some of the resisting members to confront their own incongruity.

9. *The sequence repeats itself, at one time or another involving all members. Each time the sequence recurs, it involves more people who are becoming more congruent and, hence, tends to improve. As people are thus helped more, deeper feelings are experienced, and the amount of time spent in the present increases. The longer the group lasts, the more helpfully and authentically do the members interact.*

Every time incongruity is understood by someone, it is integrated into his self-in-the-world concept. This new awareness means that the individual is now more congruent and hence, by that very fact, more capable of helping others achieve greater congruence, as Rogers has suggested.[21] Therefore, the dynamics of authentic interaction and personal growth have a potentially self-improving quality since as more people become more congruent, the group's capacity to help increases.

A major purpose of training groups is to increase members' capacity to understand others. There has been some debate as to whether the goals of human-relations training groups should be for trainees primarily to learn about them-

selves or others.[22] This dichotomous discussion does not seem useful to me. It can be seen that, as the above sequence occurs, group members become increasingly able to communicate with one another in the here-and-now.

Consequently, their knowledge of one another's phenomenological realities increases. Thus understanding of self and others must and does increase simultaneously; one does not incorporate another's confrontation of one's own incongruities unless one perceives the other's congruence, and perceiving and accepting one's own incongruence increases one's capacities to understand another's. And so these dual capacities go on in a group, reinforcing one another when they occur, hampering one another when they do not occur. It thus seems evident that neither increased understanding of self nor increased understanding of others can occur in isolation.

A critic—a psychotherapist—has described my step 9 as "Panglossian." His own experience as a practicing therapist has suggested for him that this development "tops off" someplace, owing either to anxiety or to the patient's desire to test his new capacities outside the therapist's office. However, the sensitivity training group almost always has a fixed termination point known to all the members—the end of a semester, the end of a residential training program, or something. This is an important difference between the structure of psychotherapy and sensitivity training. How this experience would top off in

[21] Carl Rogers, The Characteristics of a Helping Relationship, *op. cit.*

[22] For a discussion of this see James V. Clark, Some Troublesome Dichotomies in Human Relations Training, *Human Relations Training News*, Vol. 6, No. 1 (Spring, 1962), pp. 3–6.

an open-ended training group is simply not known.

What is known is that this kind of growth does not by any means always occur in sensitivity training. Occasionally, whole groups never really get started, and almost always one or two members withdraw or never get very far. In psychotherapy, unpublished research by Rogers and his group suggests that those clients least likely to be successful are those who come to therapy with the least capacity to perceive accurately the therapist's attitudes toward them. Is this true in sensitivity training, also? In another few months, we hope to have some data on this, but for the present, we don't know.

It is clear that the above paragraph points to only one among several facets of this formulation which need to be validated by careful research. As I have already said, research is currently under way in the behavioral science laboratory at the Graduate School of Business Administration, U.C.L.A., in an attempt to learn more about how this whole sequence operates in sensitivity training groups. It will be reported on in subsequent papers.

8.3 CONCERNING THE NATURE OF HUMAN SYSTEMS AND THE CONSULTANT'S ROLE

Charles K. Ferguson

In the vast wonderful physical world of mass and matter everything is apparently divisible. Finer and finer discriminations of differentiated parts become possible as our tools and sophistication increase. The smallest of differentiated parts seems in turn to yield to the discovery of differentiated sub parts on ad possibly infinitum. An atom is now a relatively large unit. The page from which you are reading not only has such gross sub parts as type face, color and texture, but a highly complex molecular structure divided in turn into atoms, electrons, neutrons, protons, etc.

Charles K. Ferguson, "Concerning the Nature of Human Systems and the Consultant's Role," *The Journal of Applied Behavioral Science.* Used by permission.

This page can be maintained as a unit of value under proper circumstances or its sub parts can fall out of relationship into a state of partial or total disintegration. It all depends upon the relationship of the sub parts of the page and in turn, of course, upon their relationship to their environment.

Basic to understanding physical systems is the understanding of their subsystems and the relationship between all of these and their environment. It is important in the physical world to seek to know about the parts, and the parts of the parts, and the parts of the parts of the parts, and their environment, so also in the world of man whether as a single animal, in small groups, in organizations of varying size, or in societies. Man individually or collectively is a synthesis of sub parts and subsystems.

The opportunity for service as a consultant to large organizations, to small groups, and to individuals has led the writer to observations concerning similarities in human systems regardless of size, in terms of the relationship between sub parts or subsystems that make for collaboration and health or for imbalance, stress and dysfunction. It is along interfaces between parts that human organization within one man or among nations is welded, bonded and linked or stressed, damaged and broken. These counter potentials produce serenity or anxiety in one man, collaboration or disruptive competition in a group and peace or war in the world. It is the management of interfaces, relationships between sub parts or subsystems, that is the key responsibility of an individual in his own life, of chairman or responsible members in a group, of a manager in an organization, and of politicians or statesmen in the affairs of nations. When a consultant is invited to assist it is to this area he must look to help.

A Single Man

The human mind can variously be described as a two part field with conscious and unconscious subsystems, as a three part field with id, ego and super ego or as a *figure-ground* field with a center of consciousness or figure, drawing upon the ground of a complex, differentiated set of ideas, perceptions, assumptions etc. The mind can also be thought of as a "theory bin" housing an assortment of attitudes toward the self and others, a set of values, impressions, expectations, notions of many

sorts. The assortment of theories in any given person was learned from a variety of sources usually including mother, father, siblings, peers, school, community and religious groups, reading, etc.

There are consequently multiple models, multiple examples or learnings, multiple parts symbolically present within each cranium. These parts are often inconsistent, at odds or incompatible with each other. Intracranial or intrapersonal conflict results from competitive impulses of conflicting formulations within the person resulting in tension or worry. The reader has certainly experienced this phenomenon. If you learned to fight from your father and learned from your mother that fighting was barbaric, you have within you the kinds of "fight" vs "don't fight" counter theories that can cause competitive striving between parts of a single mind. It is easier for an individual to manage competing counter theories within himself when all available options are conscious and clear to him, and much more difficult when some of his options, impulses or ideas are hazy or less conscious. A well integrated individual assesses his possible options or possible formulations with reference to any challenge and responsibly selects one or several from which his behavior flows. A less well integrated individual is bedeviled by competing formulations which are either partially unclear or among which he cannot select or accommodate.

A driver can turn left or right, his mind contains both models, both theories are available to him. He ordinarily has no trouble efficiently turning left or right, going forward or backing up in a manner consistent with his goals and knowledge of pathways. He vacillates when he cannot see his options or does not know where they lead.

A young man approaching marriage can develop considerable anxiety as he mobilizes assumptions that make the future seem positive and successful and alternates with assumptions that portend trial and trouble.

Human life is constantly confronted with the need for choice among parts, among ideas, among values and goals. The fact that there are differentiations creates the requirement for choice and the attendant problems of management that each person must exercise in his own life. When a counselor is consulted by an individual his function should be to assist in the illumination of alternatives, or formulations or options, and to help the individual make responsible choices among them.

A man is characterized not only by the differentiation of his mind, and the many physical subsystems of his body, but also by the sub parts of his emotional structure. We each come into the world with the potential for positive and negative feeling. Differentiated feelings are standard human equipment. Loud sharp noises cause a baby to be fearful. Sudden withdrawal of physical support does the same. Prolonged frustration resulting from lack of food or discomfort will evoke anger and rage. Feeding and cuddling will produce contentment and satisfaction. Play can produce happiness. These differing feelings continue all through life contributing their share to the amazingly intricate relationship pattern between tangible and intangible sub parts and subsystems of each human organism. Individual physical and psycho-

logical health is the result of overall harmony and balance in the relationship within and between subsystems. Ill health results from imbalance within any one subsystem or because of incompatibility or significant disharmony in the relationship between subsystems.

The mind and the body are inextricably interrelated. If the mind and body are at odds over the satisfaction of any appetite the human system has a problem. The possibilities for subsystem conflict within one person are many. Incompatibility can occur between two parts of the mind or between two parts of the body. Reasonable compatibility betwen all parts has to be maintained for reasonable health.

A man has two management requirements for his person—first to prevent ill health, or if ill health occurs to institute processes that will return the organism to health. A major consideration in man's management of himself has to be concern for the compatible relationship of parts. within and between his own subsystems.

A Small Group

My skin and your skin create an interface boundary separation no matter how harmonious we otherwise are. There are inevitable differences. There are no groups without differentiated parts or without subgroups. Friendly people come together in meeting and sooner or later, or sooner and later, subgroup over matters of goals, or status and power, or procedures and methods of operation, or values, standards and points of view, or simply over liking and disliking other members. The reasons for disagreement and subdivisions in groups are countless. Sometimes divisions and subgrouping are rigid, fierce and relatively unchanging, sometimes they are fluid, friendly and continually changing. Subgroups can be intensely competitive or they can be tolerant and mutually stimulating. The point is that groups all have subdivisions, subsystems, subgroups: it is the relationship among and between sub parts that is basic to understanding, let alone influencing, group dynamics.

Families are small groups. The well publicized battle of the sexes occurs within close quarters in a family. It is a battle based on subgroup differences that can work out across that particular interface to a rewarding integration in some families, to a smoldering guerilla warfare played out over years in other families, or to spectacular explosions that rip some families asunder. Differences of sex, of generation, of role, cause subgroupings in families. The management of a family is largely the management of relationship between these sub parts.

The Supreme Court is a small group. It divides and redivides on both substantive and procedural issues. It also expresses unanimous decisions from time to time although unanimity is not at all a steady state.

A Large Organization

Organizations of size when viewed from inside are characterized by a complexity of sub groups. Specialization is the dominant occupational characteristic of our time. Organizations require specialized sub groups to perform many required tasks.

An electronics science-engineering organization will need different groups for engineering, research, fabrication, quality control, marketing, public relations, administration, purchasing, contracts, legal, etc.

A major oil refinery will need chemists, engineers, process people to move oil, mechanical people to maintain equipment of such diverse types as electricians, carpenters, boilermakers, painters, machinists, etc.

A government laboratory may need military personnel, civilian personnel, staff and line groups, basic and applied research groups, development groups, security, job shops, production shops, transportation pools, divisions, departments, branches, sections, etc.

Organizations from the inside look like beehives with many cells. A modern matrix organization is a grid with specialized projects and efforts overlaid upon centralized functions, resources or talents. An engineer on a project often must call upon a central testing group to test a part. A nurse on a ward must rely upon central supply for linens and equipment. A teacher in a classroom calls upon an academic communication division to obtain and show a film. A policeman on a beat calls central receiving hospital for an ambulance. In our specialized world all of us depend upon many other parts. Certainly within a modern organization interdependence between specialized parts or groups is essential.

Each group in an organization is a human subsystem in turn divisible into smaller human subsystems. The engineers in one typical group identify in turn as mechanical engineers and electrical engineers, each working on different parts of the same product. College trained engineers are differentiated from blue collar workers and they in turn break down into all kinds of specialized subgroups. So it goes, an organization like building blocks attains stability through the mutual effective interdependence of its parts.

In the World

Similar analysis applies if you take the world as the unit of analysis. The world contains easily distinguishable human systems built around language, culture, and race, with a current major boundary between the east and the west. Among the eastern countries there is further division in the major subsystems represented by China on the one hand and Russia on the other. In the west France currently represents a major subsystem in relation to the United States and other NATO countries.

At the point of sharpest and most violent contention in Viet Nam each side in turn divides. On one side are American soldiers (marine, army, air force) and American civilians, Australians, Koreans, South Viet Nam military, South Viet Nam civilians, Catholics, Buddhists, Montangards, French speaking, non French speaking, students, peasants etc. On the other side are Viet Cong, Communists, non Communists, North Vietnamese regulars, various irregulars, Chinese, Russians, military, civilians, etc.

Scandinavians, Orientals, Europeans, Latin Americans, North Americans, Africans, Arabs, Jews etc. all in turn divisible into smaller subsystems; as are Scandinavians (Danes, Finns, Norwegians, Swedes) or Orientals, (Japanese, Chinese, Thais, etc.). And each in turn again divisible as are Japanese (socialists, communists, capitalists, shintoists, christians, traditionists, modernists, etc.).

Competitive-Collaborative Tendencies in Human Systems

Competition and collaboration are natural forces. Often competition stimulates. Controlled competition between athletic teams can provide a tonic. Competition in a free market conducted under civilized rules has released creativity, productivity and widespread benefits. Unrestrained competition can produce havoc. Certainly within an interdependent system much competition is destructive. It is fine for the football teams of Yale and Harvard to compete but another thing entirely for the Yale backfield to compete with the Yale line. It is one thing for Douglas Aircraft to compete with Boeing, but another thing for the engineering department at Douglas to be engaged in a competitive relationship with the manufacturing department of Douglas. Yet this happens over and over again. Interdependent subsystems compete. Nations compete in a nuclear arms race that can destroy much of the world. Cold wars and hot wars within organizations are everywhere present. Engineers and salesmen in the same organization often reciprocally distrust and suspect each other. There are some classic, frequently competitive, relationships in industry: design engineers / production engineers, central offices / field offices, planners / executors, control functions / line functions, product assurance / manufacturing, sales / contracts, etc.

In hospitals: central services / ward personnel, night shift / day shift, operating room / other services, paramedical / medical, volunteer / professional, registered nurses / licensed vocational nurses, etc.

In universities: students / faculty, faculty / administration, liberal arts / professional schools, campus administration / statewide administration, etc.

Organizations are like a faulted geological area characterized by fissures, cracks, divisions. An organization from a distance looking like a homogeneous whole presenting uniform products under one brand name is actually up close an amalgam of many differentiated human subsystems that need to be held together in collaborative relationship.

Every boundary offers opportunity for collaboration or competition, both tendencies are ever present and possible. Every interface can produce friction or fit. Whenever things are joined they can come apart. All things are joined in many ways in many places.

It is also true for systems in motion that the relationship between moving subsystems can maintain a balance of grace and beauty or fall into turbulence and disorder.

What can be done to evoke collaborative tendencies between human subsystems and/or what to reduce the tendency toward destructive competition between interdependent parts?

The Consultant's Role

In my experience a consultant does much the same thing whether he is working with one person, a small group or a large organization. He uses himself to help a client system to externalize, to explicate "nonfit" between interfaces or along boundaries. He uses himself to release forces that move toward balance or health in human systems of any size. He is always an aide or an instrument; he should not be a principal or an essential member party. He precipitates a process the substance of which comes from the members. Here follow things he can do:

CAPTURE DATA. As stories are told, the consultant listens and captures in his mind or in his notes the essence of the pictures presented. It all starts with listening. The consultant can serve as a rock over which varying organizational stories wash like waves leaving essential traces; he listens for cause and effect, for discrepancies between stories, for dissonance or turbulence or symptoms of stress along subsystem boundary lines. He also listens for respect, confidence, trust, openness and signs of health.

SCAN FOR TROUBLED INTERFACES. As a consultant takes soundings from representative members of different organizational subgroups he may hear stories that are out of synchronization. The view of Group A will be in conflict with the view of Group B. Or it may become evident that one group misunderstands another or suspects or distrusts another. If parts must work together distortion between them may present an obvious systemic problem. It does not take a genius to recognize most critical problems, they present themselves loudly and clearly if one looks and listens. The consultant is a radar device addressed at the organization picking up blips and cues and making tentative working assessments as to which are normal acceptable cues and which deserve further investigation or treatment.

PROMOTE PSYCHOLOGICAL BONDING. A human organization survives because subsystems or subparts are adequately bonded. An airplane is a combination of subsystems worthy of passengers only if the parts are adequately bonded or riveted. The equivalent bonding among humans comes through mutual identification, communication, concern, understanding, caring. Effective human organization requires psychological-attitudinal bonds; a consultant can encourage processes that develop cohesiveness within and between human groups; meetings, interchanges, conversations, sharing knowledge and problems, mutual endeavor in the right kind of psychological climate are pathways a consultant can stimulate and enhance.

BE A LINKING AGENT BETWEEN PEOPLE AND/OR GROUPS. As a consultant listens he will identify strain, misunderstandings, disrespect, in short trouble between people or groups who need a high degree of collaboration in their relationship. He will note distance or remoteness along an interface that calls for intimacy. The consultant can serve to link people or groups that need to be brought together. His good offices in arranging confrontations of people and issues, and his skill at promoting effective interpersonal communication, can assist the linking of essential parts without which the whole is handicapped.

SERVE AS COMMUNICATIONS CONVEYOR BELT. In Holland at Philips Electrical Industries Ltd. there exists the longest physical conveyor belt in the world moving TV parts past assemblers. A consultant can be a human conveyor belt moving critical attitudinal data in and between parts of an organization in discreet and helpful ways. As a bee gathers and redeposits pollen so a consultant can move information or awareness from one part to another, one person to another. Communications move the lymph and blood of organizational life. When the circulatory system is sluggish or clogged there is a price to pay. Attitudes are intangibles no less important to move. A consultant should not be constricted to the formal channels of communication flow and thus as an auxiliary communications medium can often convey data more freely and easily than normal channels. Some data can most effectively be conveyed by a trained consultant who is uniquely sensitive by virtue of his experience, or because he is outside the normal system.

SUSPEND ANIMATION AND ANALYZE PROCESS. A consultant enters an ongoing stream of events without authority except the respect accorded to or earned by him. Since he is outside the real power structure he can, if he will, call for suspense in the organization's animation in order to temporarily freeze interaction to study and analyze its process. He temporarily asserts his professional authority, in the interest of organizational self study and learning, to suspend for the time being the real power structure and ongoing events in which members are involved. He temporarily neutralizes real authority by asserting his authority as a consultant so that the cause and effect relationship between the uses and consequences of real authority can be studied and learned from here and now in the moment; it is like stopping a film to examine a frame for greater detail, clarity and understanding. The consultant has a teaching-learning purpose, he asserts himself to require attention to experience from which analysis may yield insight, foresight, knowledge, increased awareness and interpersonal competence.

ASSIST IN DIAGNOSTIC FORMULATION AND REFORMULATION OF ISSUES. Often a problem is that the problem at issue is not very clear. Incidence of people fighting without knowing quite why they are fighting is very high. Thinking about complex issues is not a highly precise process. Often many successive formulations are required before interpersonal issues can be adequately stated. A consultant can help in the diagnostic process by searching for greater clarity of the issue surrounded, as it often is, by emotional smoke, and tentatively stating his understanding of it. Even if his understanding is incorrect a tentative statement of his understanding will likely lead to closer reformulation and so on until the issue is stated with sufficient clarity and understanding, so that proposals for solution can follow. It is likely to be wasted effort to try solving an obscure problem. A consultant can help in shaping formulations that are mutually understood by the parties, agreed to, and that can lead to solution. A consultant can keep his eye on the issues because he is not so caught in the emotionality more directly interested parties frequently feel.

LIFT UP RELATIONSHIP PROBLEMS AND FEELING DATA FOR CONSIDERATION. Some issues are more delicate than others.

Often issues between individuals involving negative feeling are sensitive ones. A consultant with understanding of the emotions can make a significant contribution by skillfully raising significant issues of this kind to a level where they can be discerned, vented and worked. Psychological-surgical ability is sometimes required to gently open an issue, like a boil, in a manner that will release its pressure and foster and institute healing where infection had been. There are many such interpersonal situations in organizational life. Readiness, confidence and other positive ingredients must be assessed in making the judgment to raise an issue of this nature to a level where consideration and correction become possible.

An organization has an emotional life just as an individual does. Individuals generate feelings at work and carry them to and fro. Feelings are frequently critical elements in the life of an organization. They often need to be brought to light as part of the necessary data. Since people often are reluctant to discuss feeling, especially in a work situation, a consultant can serve to legitimatize discussion and consideration of feeling.

USE CLINICAL SKILLS TO HELP MAKE COMMUNICATION MORE CONGRUENT (EFFECTIVE). When a person pounds the table, his face flushes, his jaw tightens, his voice gets steely and he says "I am not mad," his communication is incongruent; cues from his non verbal behavior are not in harmony with his words. That makes communication difficult. A consultant with clinical skill can intervene to catch and reflect incongruities and thus assist more honest, authentic interchanges. Consultants can help people level with each other—be more honest—open—congruent. A consultant is an agent outside the essential interchange who can monitor communication to exercise a kind of quality control over it.

ENCOURAGE FEEDBACK. A one way communication system is designed for danger. One way communication is certain to produce distortion, loss, misinterpretation and misunderstanding. There is no way to correct for inevitable errors bound to develop due to individual differences of perception and imperfections of hearing, attention, etc. The only way to correct mistakes and insure clarity is to build a feedback loop into a communication system. The recipients of messages must be able to feedback their reception of them and reaction to them. They must in turn be able to initiate messages of their own. Thus organizations live on multichanneled dialogues which require feedback loops to function well. A consultant should observe for instances of inadequate dialogue and use himself to encourage communication along two way, or multichanneled, interchanges.

SERVE AS A PLUMBER AND/OR OBSTETRICIAN. In the process of observing a human system with reference to its communications flow (of ideas *and* feelings) a consultant will often identify blocks. In some of these cases he can function much as a plumber might in reaming out a passage without destroying the channel. Gentle assists, gentle nudges or pertinent data tentatively offered never substitute for the natural flow of the system itself but sometimes can aid the circulation of necessary ideas and feelings.

Similarly a consultant is often in position to sense the birth of developments and to assist in the delivery of significant events much as an obstetrician does. Events are neither produced nor essentially determined by an obstetrician or a consultant but natural process can sometimes be profitably assisted by the intervention of competent help. This kind of help can be offered a human system to express and actualize its own potential and not as a substitute for it.

PROMOTE SPIRIT OF INQUIRY. The proper study of man will always be man. Life is the primary textbook. A consultant can promote examination of ever present immediate human data in the constant interactions of men, To ask "what is happening?", "why?", "how?", "how better?". To turn up data (rational *and* emotional) for inspection, consideration, generalization, learning. A consultant can model a spirit of inquiry through his own behavior and example and help develop in others the ability to learn how to learn from the dynamic human data of life.

ANALYZE ONGOING PROBLEM SOLVING MEETINGS. A consultant is an applied scientist. His is not an ivory towered world. He works in an arena where life goes forward, frequently rapidly, decisions are made, things change. He deals with momentum and thrust that must be analyzed even as a navigator checks the route of an aircraft in motion or a pilot in flight monitors his instruments. Complex human interaction must be arrested long enough or scrutinized adequately to describe it, maintain it, correct it, learn from it. The consultant can be a temporary brake; not to stop the system's momentum but to slow it and cause its own intelligence to be directed at assessing its effectiveness, its operation and its course. To learn from one's own experience one must pause long enough to regard and analyze it. A consultant can help by acting as a spokesman for this need at appropriate times in actual problem solving meetings where the data of greatest consequence is most apt to be present.

SET UP OPPORTUNITIES FOR MUTUAL COACHING AND TEAM BUILDING. In our society we spend millions of dollars insuring via proper coaching that athletic teams will learn to work together for greatest effectiveness. We build procedures like spring training, chalk talks, huddles, time outs, half times, clinics, etc. to offer opportunities for coaching help and team building. Yet when adults work together in the vocational world we fairly well assume they should know how to work together effectively. They often do not, at a great cost to society. A consultant can set up opportunities for constructive, reciprocal coaching among members of teams for the development of greater effectiveness. He can sometimes provide some coaching suggestions himself but much more importantly he can release the capacity of those members of the same team who work and live together, who interact and observe each other intimately, to share their observations and constructive suggestions in the interest of raising the quality of an operation upon which they are mutually dependent.

ASSIST IN THE MANAGEMENT OF CONFLICT. Intraorganizational conflict is inevitable, not because people are malicious, rather because they are different. They perceive and value things differently. They will always disagree to some degree and their disagreements will require the continued management of conflict. A consultant can help by questioning the effectiveness of norms that smother disagreement and by arranging situations where important disagreements can come into clearly focused confrontation. Successful management of conflict comes not from disguising or ignoring it but from accepting it as natural, as a source of energy and potential creativity. The consultant's role is not to decide in situations of conflict but to help in the management of conflict by assisting the process of sharpening and clarifying the dimensions of conflict so that a search for a larger basis of cooperation can proceed.

HELP PROMOTE A PROPER PSYCHOLOGICAL CLIMATE. You can feel psychological climate in the air. One feels whether things are stilted and stiff, formal and courteous or free and open, easy and creative. You can feel the differences between various groups and organizations. Psychological climate is made of the attitudinal ingredients radiated by significant members of a group. A consultant is ordinarily a key figure in a group and the attitudes he expresses can have important influence upon the climate. It makes a difference what the climate is. Productivity does not long flourish in an atmosphere of distrust, suspicion, overtight control, disrespect, apathy, misunderstanding, etc. In contrast it is established that people do flourish in a psychological climate of respect, consistency, human warmth, understanding, trust, openness, clarity, etc. A consultant's attitudes can do much to create a favorable psychological climate. Attitudes radiate from the human spirit. They are crucial in determining effective or less effective conditions of man. A consultant can make a personal contribution to a positive psychological climate and in addition he can help develop awareness of the importance of psychological climate that envelops all else.

TAKE CALCULATED RISKS BECAUSE HE IS EXPENDABLE. A consultant is not married to an organization in the same way an employee is. He should not be dependent upon it. His relative freedom from the system is an asset that can be used to take some of the risks in stretching perception and creating awareness that those who are locked into a system may not be as prepared to take. A consultant should regard himself as expendable and thus be prepared to serve a system prudently but courageously without tenure but boldly in its own interest as long as the consulting relationship is sustained. It is relative freedom from dependence upon a system that gives a consultant a unique opportunity to help.

8.4   TYPES OF MENTAL HEALTH CONSULTATION

Gerald Caplan

The term "consultation" is used in many ways. By some, it is applied to almost any professional activity carried out by a specialist; in England the professional office of a specialist physician is known as his "consulting rooms," and, when he is interviewing a patient, his secretary says "he is in consultation." Others use the term to denote specialized professional activity between two persons in regard to a third; thus two physicians "consult" about a patient, or a physician "consults" with a mother about her child. Some restrict the term to professional activity carried out by a highly trained person—a "con-sultant"—but without delimiting the activity or differentiating "consultation" from other functions of the "consultant."

In this book, the term is used in a quite restricted sense to denote the interaction between two professional persons—the consultant, who is a specialist, and the consultee, who invokes his help in regard to a current work problem with which he is having some difficulty and which he has decided is within the consultant's area of competence. The work problem involves the management or treatment of one or more clients of the consultee or the planning of a program to cater to such clients.

An essential aspect of consultation, as defined here, is that the professional responsibility for the client remains with the consultee. The consultant may

Chapter VIII of *Principles of Preventive Psychiatry* by Gerald Caplan, © 1964 by Basic Books, Inc., Publishers, New York. This chapter was published in an abbreviated form in the *American Journal of Orthopsychiatry*, Volume 33, No. 3. Tavistock Publications, Ltd. are the British publishers.

offer helpful clarification, diagnostic interpretation, or advice on treatment, but the consultee is free to accept or reject all or part of this help. Action for the benefit of the client which emerges from the consultation is the responsibility of the consultee.

Another essential aspect of this type of consultation is that the consultant engages in the activity not only in order to help the consultee with his current professional problem in relation to a specific client or program, but to add to his knowledge and to lessen areas of misunderstanding, so that he may in the future be able to deal more effectively with this category of problem. This definition applies not only to a single consultant dealing with one consultee, but equally to one consultant and a group of consultees or a group of consultants and a single consultee or group of consultees.

In defining consultation in this narrow way, there is no implication that this is the correct usage of the term and that other authorities are wrong in their different use of it; on the contrary, there is a deliberate intention to recognize that confusion exists because workers legitimately use the term in so many ways. The purpose here is to single out one of the various categories of meaning for special study and evaluation. A specialist who is formally or informally designated a consultant may engage in many types of professional activity; these resemble one another to some extent in goals, methods, and techniques. They include inspection, administrative manipulation, coordination, supervision, teaching, case work, psychotherapy, counseling, negotiation, liaison, collaboration, media-

tion, and so forth. I believe that we will attain a higher level of professional functioning when the specialist is able to differentiate these various activities and employ each of them consistently in relation to his assignment, his professional goals, and his understanding of the demands of each situation.

What has been said so far refers to consultation as a generic form of specialist professional activity. By the term "mental health consultation," I designate the use of this method as part of a community program for the promotion of mental health and for the prevention, treatment, and rehabilitation of mental disorder. Much, if not most, of the work with actual or potential patients in such programs is currently being carried out by professional workers who have no specialized training in psychiatry, psychology, or psychiatric social work, namely, nurses, teachers, family doctors, pediatricians, clergymen, probation officers, policemen, welfare workers, and so forth. Recruitment and training possibilities in the mental health professions are such that this state of affairs is likely to continue indefinitely. It seems important, therefore, that a significant proportion of the time and energies of mental health specialists be focused on improving the operations of these other care-giving professionals in relation to mental health and mental disorder. Mental health consultation is one of the methods which have been developed to achieve this goal. It provides an opportunity for a relatively small number of consultants to exert a widespread effect in a community through the mediation of a large group of consultees. In order to be effective along these lines, the amount of time devoted by a consultant to helping a consultee deal with the mental health problems of a case must be relatively short, and there must be the maximum educational carry-over to the consultee's work with other cases. It is also worth emphasizing that, in a comprehensive program of community psychiatry, mental health consultation should be used in appropriate balance with such other community methods as education on mental health issues in the preprofessional and in-service training of care-giving agents and planning and co-ordinating of care-giving agencies.

Types of Mental Health Consultation

It is of value to differentiate four fundamental types of mental health consultation, each associated with characteristic technical demands on the consultant. A consultation may focus on the consultee's problems in handling a specific client, as contrasted with his administrative problems in initiating and maintaining a program; a consultant may have the immediate goal of improving the client or the program, as contrasted with improving the insights, skills, and professional objectivity of the consultees. The four types have become known as client-centered case consultation, program-centered administrative consultation, consultee-centered case consultation, and consultee-centered administrative consultation. The remainder of this chapter will be devoted to a brief description of these types of mental health consultation. Because of its special tech-

nical interest, consultee-centered case consultation will be discussed in greater detail than the others. . . .

CLIENT-CENTERED CASE CONSULTATION

In this type of consultation, the problems encountered by the consultee in a professional case are the focus of interest; the immediate goal is to help the consultee find the most effective treatment for his client. Educating the consultee so that he may in the future be better able to deal unaided with this client or class of clients is a subsidiary goal. Since the primary goal is to improve the client, the consultant's fundamental responsibility is to make a specialized assessment of the client's condition and to recommend an effective disposition or method of treatment to be undertaken by the consultee. The consultant's attention is centered on the client, whom he will probably examine with whatever methods of investigation his specialized judgment indicates are necessary in order to arrive at an adequate appraisal of his difficulty.

On the other hand, the consultant will pay attention to what the consultee says in order to ascertain what type of help he is requesting; sometimes, the consultee may ask for consultation when he really wishes to refer a patient for treatment by the specialist, and he will be angry when the patient is sent back with a diagnosis and a prescription for nonspecialist management. Sometimes, all he is requesting is help with screening so that he can decide to which specialized agency he should refer the patient. In that event, he is not interested in receiving a complicated diagnostic formulation, and the consultant might well spare himself the time and effort of working this out. Here, as elsewhere in community psychiatry, energy expended on diagnostic investigation should be no greater than that necessary to answer the questions which will meaningfully affect disposition or treatment.

The consultant will also pay attention to what the consultee says in order to learn how to communicate with him. The more the consultant knows about the consultee's language, conceptual framework, and ways of working, the better is his ability to formulate a diagnosis in comprehensible words and to suggest treatment which the consultee can carry out effectively in his professional setting. Too many consultants write reports in which they communicate only with themselves and with their specialist reference group. This would not affect the welfare of the client if the specialist were carrying out the treatment, but in consultation the treatment is carried out by the consultee; only messages which improve his operations will help the client. Needless to say, the consultant must make a correct diagnosis and must suggest effective treatment in order to improve the client's condition. The content as well as the manner of the communication is important for success.

A general practitioner asked for help from a psychiatrist for one of his patients, a twenty-eight-year-old woman. She was suffering from depression, insomnia, loss of appetite, frequent weeping spells, and loss of interest in her work. The symptoms began five weeks earlier, after a man, with whom she was in love, informed her that he was going to marry another woman. The psychiatrist interviewed the patient and then sent her back to the general practitioner, with whom he communicated both by letter and by telephone. He told the doctor that the patient was not suffering from a psychiatric illness, but from the symptoms of a bereavement crisis brought on by her disillusionment and the loss of her lover. He predicted that the symptoms would probably lessen in intensity over the next few weeks. He suggested that the doctor see the patient as often as she wished in order to give her emotional support and to encourage her to work through her feelings of mourning and deprivation, to resign herself to her loss, and only after that to begin to build a new life for herself. The psychiatrist offered to see the patient again if her symptoms did not clear up as predicted and made some suggestions about appropriate drugs to control the symptoms if they got too bad; but he advised that the drugs be used sparingly so as not to dull the pain to the extent of diverting the patient's attention from the psychological work she had to do in order to adjust in a healthy way to the frustration of her expectations.

PROGRAM-CENTERED ADMINISTRATIVE CONSULTATION

In this type of consultation, the consultant is called in by a consultee or, more often, by a group of consultees to help with current problems in the administration of programs for the prevention, treatment, or rehabilitation of mental disorder. The problems may relate to any aspect of the program, including the planning and administration of services and policies governing the recruitment, training, and effective utilization of personnel. In response to the needs expressed by the consultees, the focus of the consultant is a specialized assessment of the current program or policy predicament and recommendation of a plan of action to resolve the difficulty. As in the previous type of consultation, educating the consultees so that in the future they will be better able to deal on their own with such a difficulty is a subordinate goal.

In contrast to client-centered case consultation, the consultant may, in analyzing the problem, make use of the information about the institution which the consultees had collected. He will, however, take into account that the consultees will inevitably distort their reports. He will collect some of the essential data himself, using his own specialized methods. And he will cross-check the other data, since, in this type of consultation, the assessment of the problem is his responsibility alone, however actively he may enlist the consultees' cooperation in assembling the facts. His reason for enlisting their aid is that he will probably need many agents to collect the large amount of complicated data necessary to understand the problems of an institution. An important aspect of these problems may involve the interrelationships of the staff, which he can observe in action as he works with the staff members. Also, through his own interactions in this process, he can learn about the language, values, and traditions of the institution so that his recommendations for remedial action will be expressed comprehensibly and will be feasible within the current and future reality of the institution.

Administrative consultants will usu-ally be requested to present their analysis of the institutional problems and their recommendations for solution in a written report. This report will often deal with short-term solutions which are feasible in terms of the current staff and are in line with the current administrative framework. It will also contain long-term suggestions for an ideal solution, which may act as distant goals toward which the institution may strive. The long-term recommendations will be largely based on the consultant's general knowledge and his experience in a variety of other programs, as well as on his professional value system. They will, of course, be directed toward the local situation, but, in formulating them, the consultant will only be minimally influenced by the ideas of the consultees.

On the other hand, the short-term recommendations, in order to be acceptable and implemented, must fit closely within the expectations and the capacities of the consultee group. Experienced administrative consultants find that the best way of ensuring this is to communicate their developing judgments to the consultee group and progressively modify these recommendations in light of the reactions of the consultees. The responsibility for the recommendations is not shared with the consultees, and the fact that one or more of them may disagree with certain of the recommendations will not necessarily persuade the consultant to change them. However, the discussions will enable him to see how close the fit is between his plan and the culture of the group and will prepare the consultees for his eventual report. When the consultees read the consultant's report, they should find little in it that he has not already discussed with them and on which they have not been able to express an opinion.

An interesting variant of this type of mental health consultation deals not with programs for the promotion of mental health and the prevention and control of mental disorder, but with the mental health aspects of other programs. In this consultation, the mental health specialist is asked for help in those problems of administration which may influence the mental health or personal effectiveness of personnel or of recipients of the program. His specialized knowledge of personality dynamics and personal relationships in social systems is exploited in order to help administrators behave more effectively and, at the same time, with a greater regard for the human needs of their colleagues, subordinates, and clients. Operational efficiency in an institution, such as a hospital or a factory, can be achieved in various ways. Some of these may frustrate fundamental needs of the participants and may lead to an increased risk of mental disorder. The mental health specialist may be able to help the administrators maintain or raise the productivity of their institution while improving the mental health potential of the workers.

The director of a city health department called in a psychiatrist to advise on the establishment of a mental health program. The consultant discussed the terms of his assignment with the health officer and learned from him of previous abortive attempts to establish a mental health program in the department. He interviewed individually and in group meetings the relevant division and bureau chiefs in charge of nursing, sanitation, regional health services, maternal and child health, health education, and so forth and explored their opinions on the need for a mental health service and their suggestions for its operation. He also set the biostatistics unit working to assemble data on the magnitude of mental disorder in the jurisdiction of the health department. He interviewed such relevant key people from other community agencies and institutions as the state commissioners of mental health and public health, the director of the council of social agencies, and the executive director of the local voluntary mental health association.

On the basis of these explorations, the psychiatrist suggested a tentative plan to restrict the proposed program to the health department, since extension to the community would encroach on existing and proposed services of other agencies. He suggested that the budget be initially derived from the federal grant-in-aid to the state and later become a city responsibility. He solicited reactions from health department personnel, and, during a series of meetings, it became clear to him that the unit most eager to avail itself of the proposed program was the nursing division.

He then suggested that the program initially take the form of an inservice training program for the public health nurses, to be followed later by a consultation program on a case basis and be implemented by hiring the part-time services of a psychiatrist currently working in the local university teaching hospital. This man was known and liked by the nurses, having in the past occasionally taken part in their inservice training programs. The health officer suggested that this psychiatrist also see cases in the prenatal and well-baby clinics. The consultant discovered that the latter suggestion was not welcomed by the physicians of the bureau of maternal and child health, who were old, conservative and not on good terms with the health officer, whom they suspected of being critical of their standards of professional work. Three years earlier, a psychologist had been employed to begin a mental health program in the well-baby clinics and had seen mothers on referral by the pediatricians. His program had proved a failure, since hardly any cases were referred to him and since those he did handle turned out to be of poor prognosis.

In his final report, the consultant restricted his short-term recommendations to a program of in-service training and consultation with nurses to be carried out by the psychiatrist. He also advised, as a long-term goal, that eventually the consultation program be extended to the other units in the health department when their staff members felt the need for such assistance. He advised against a psychiatric treatment program for patients in the department, but recommended that a collaborative relationship and an active referral system for this purpose be arranged with the local university psychiatric clinic. This report was approved by the health officer and the staff of the health department and was implemented.

CONSULTEE-CENTERED CASE CONSULTATION

The focus of the consultant in this type of consultation is on the consultee, rather than on the particular client with whom the consultee is currently having difficulties. True, the problems of this client were the direct stimulus for the consultation request and will form the main content area of the consultation discussion, and a successful consultation will usually lead to an improvement in the consultee's handling of the current case, with consequent benefit for the client. But, in contrast to client-centered case consultation, in which the consultant's main interest is diagnosing the difficulties of the client, his primary endeavor in the present instance is to assess the nature of the consultee's work difficulty and to help him overcome it.

Most or all of the consultant's time will be spent talking to the consultee about the client, and little or no time spent in specialist examination of the client. The consultant realizes that, because the consultee is having difficulties with the client, his perceptions and understanding of the case are probably distorted and that a correct diagnosis of the client by the consultant is unlikely if his data are restricted to the consultee's information; but, since his goal is to improve the consultee's functioning and not to make a diagnosis of the client, this is not important. In fact, in this type of consultation, the distortions and omissions in the consultee's report on the client provide the consultant with his basic material. He need not learn the objective reality of the client in order to identify these distortions and omissions. Instead, he appraises them by identifying internal inconsistencies in the consultee's story and verbal and nonverbal cues in the consultee's behavior and in that of others in the consultee institution. When the consultant has pinpointed the nature of the consultee's difficulty, he attempts to remedy this by helping the consultee master the significant issue by means of a discussion of the problems of the client and of the consultee's contribution to their solution.

There are four major categories of difficulty which interfere with a consultee's ability to deal adequately with the mental health problems of his client, stimulating him or his administrative superiors to seek consultation help. These are: lack of understanding of the psychological factors in the case, lack of skill or resources to deal with the problems, lack of professional objectivity, and lack of confidence and self-esteem.

LACK OF UNDERSTANDING. In this type of difficulty, the consultee has either not learned enough psychology and psychopathology to realize which factors are operating in this case, or he has learned the general laws of mental functioning but does not see how they apply to the idiosyncratic complexities of this client and his psychosocial milieu. The consultant will try to help the consultee by adding to his knowledge and by clarifying the data on the client in order to help the consultee see meaningful connections between parts of the psychosocial pattern. In doing this, it is important for the consultant to know a good deal about the professional subculture of the consultee so that the information he imparts will be consonant with the type and level of psychological understanding of the consultee's profession. Consultants should guard against trying to turn such consultees as nurses, clergymen, and pediatricians into proxy psychiatrists or junior psychologists. This im-

plies the need not only to use the terminology of the consultee profession or lay expressions, but to avoid dealing with such concepts as penis envy, castration fears, and pregenital fantasies, the proper understanding of which demands the conceptual framework and style of thinking of a mental health specialist.

Mental health consultation on an individual basis is an expensive way of teaching the facts of human behavior to professional workers. Consultants who find that, in a particular agency or community, many requests are made for this type of consultation would be well advised to consider organizing preprofessional or in-service training courses in mental health, in order to economically achieve comparable results through systematic group instruction.

A young teacher asked for consultation help with an eight-year-old boy, who she felt was becoming a juvenile delinquent. She described how he had recently begun to take things from other children. One day she saw him excluded by the other children from their game because of attention-getting behavior, after which he went to the children's coat locker and took some money from a pocket. The teacher described a visit to the boy's home and told how angry the mother was because of the child's recent hostile behavior, which was particularly upsetting to her because she was in the final stages of pregnancy and felt very tired.

The consultant discussed the possible meaning of stealing and behavior disturbance in young children as a symptom of unhappiness and deprivation and helped her see the connection between the mother's pregnancy and the boy's recent symptoms, as well as pointing out that his attention-getting behavior had led to further rejection. When she was able to understand the boy's stealing and misbehavior as a sign of pain and a symbolic cry for help as well as a childish way of making up for loss of love, rather than as a sign of some deep-seated character taint, the teacher's sympathy was aroused; she began to actively plan how to give him extra emotional supplies in school and how to mobilize sources of love and support in his family in order to tide him over the crisis.

LACK OF SKILL. The difficulty here is not lack of understanding of the client's problems, but either lack of professional skill on the part of the consultee, including how to make professional use of the self in dealing with the psychological complications of clients, or lack of knowledge of appropriate specialist resources in the community or of how to invoke their help for the benefit of the client. The consultant deals with this by assisting the consultee to choose a suitable plan of action. He will be sensitive to the consultee's level and rate of professional development, and, as in the previous category of consultation, he will ensure that the various action possibilities are drawn from a range of actions consonant with the consultee's professional subculture and not plans peculiar to mental health specialists. In order not to endanger the professional integrity of the consultee, a consultant who uses this technique must know a great deal about the details of role functioning in the consultee profession.

This type of consultation, which fosters the development of professional skills, is similar to technical supervision. Many categories of consultees, such as family doctors, clergymen, and pediatricians, have no institutionalized system of technical supervision, and mental health consultation may be the only way of getting help with skill development. (Group instruction should always be considered as a useful supplement to individual consultation.) Whenever an institution or a profession does provide supervisors, such as in schools, kindergartens, nursing agencies, and social agencies, the mental health specialist should avoid prescriptions for action by line workers and substitute suggestions for educating the supervisors. In this way, responsibility for action can remain undisturbed within the system of the consultee agency. In all the care-giving professions, the mental health specialist should attempt to influence preprofessional training so that these skills are learned effectively.

A clergyman asked for advice from a psychiatrist, with whom he had built up a consultation relationship, regarding a problem he was facing with a family in his congregation. The father had died two months earlier, and the problem involved his married daughter, who was in the middle of her first pregnancy. During his sick calls prior to the man's death, the clergyman had been impressed by the daughter's devotion to her father, and yet he was surprised that she had appeared calm at the funeral and during his subsequent condolence calls. The previous day, he had encountered her young husband in the street, and, in response to the clergyman's inquiries, the husband had said that his wife seemed to have adjusted well to her father's death but appeared apathetic in regard to her pregnancy. The clergyman, who had a keen interest in preventive psychiatry, felt that all was not well with this woman, that she had not mourned adequately for her father and might be moving toward an unhealthy relationship with her future baby. He wanted to know what he could do, if anything, to deal with this danger.

After obtaining further details on the case, the psychiatrist agreed with the clergyman's appraisal of the situation and in particular on the advisability of preventive intervention. The consultation then focused on the various ways in which the clergyman might help. These included discussing the issue with the girl's obstetrician and with an uncle who lived in the home and for whom the girl had much respect. How the clergyman might raise the matter directly with the girl and her husband was then discussed in some detail. He had doubts about whether such intervention was appropriate to his role as a clergyman or whether, in view of the girl's pregnancy, such an interview should be carried out by a physician. It became clear that she trusted him—he had known her for years and had officiated at her wedding—and that, unless he aroused her motivation to seek medical help, she would probably not do so, since she seemed to be suffering no discomfort at present. The psychiatrist reassured his colleague that, if he stimulated the girl to feel anxious about her situation, this would not have a bad effect on her—quite the contrary. The clergyman then decided that he would call the husband to his office for an interview, talk frankly with him

about the problem, and invoke his aid in bringing his wife for a joint interview. The pros and cons of having this interview at the church as compared to having it in the girl's home were discussed, and the strategy of the joint interview was considered.

All went as planned, and the clergyman reported that, at the interview, the girl had broken down and wept for the first time since her father's death. She had talked about her feelings of guilt that, because she was pregnant, she had not been able to give adequate care to her dying father. The clergyman planned to see her a few more times in order to supervise her mourning process and to watch out for the necessity to refer her to the psychiatrist if he felt that the situation was beyond his competence. At the psychiatrist's suggestion, he was going to suggest that she choose a pediatrician for her baby before the birth; he intended to talk with this pediatrician concerning the possibility that some unresolved conflicts about her father's death might introduce tensions into the future mother–child relationship.

LACK OF OBJECTIVITY. Experienced, well-trained, and well-supervised consultees will occasionally meet situations which are beyond their knowledge and skills and may necessitate one of the two previous categories of consultation, but more often, when such a person asks for consultation help, it is because he is unable for various reasons to exploit his knowledge and skills with the particular client. This is usually manifested by a disorder in his professional objectivity owing to subjective factors. His professional empathy with the client and other actors in the client's life may be replaced by identification and personal involvement leading to partisanship, or he may turn from the client's situation because it stimulates in him some personal sensitivity. In either case, there is likely to be a distortion of perception and judgment and a lowered effectiveness in utilizing professional knowledge and skills.

My colleagues and I at the Harvard School of Public Health have for some years been particularly interested in this category of consultation, and we have formulated the consultee's difficulty as being due to the intrusion into his professional functioning of an interfering problem theme. The latter is derived from some long-standing personality difficulty brought into focus by a symbolic trigger in the client's case, by a current situational conflict in the consultee's home life, or by some problem in work—either a role conflict of the consultee or a more general social-system disequilibrium, acute or chronic, involving the authority structure or communication pattern within the institution or between it and its surrounding community.

Whatever the proximate or ultimate causes, the final common path leading to the work difficulty and the request for consultation is usually a "theme interference," a symbolic inhibition of free perception and communication between consultee and client and a concomitant disorder of objectivity. This is usually accompanied by some degree of emotional upset in the consultee, ranging from relatively mild tension when he thinks about certain aspects of the client's case (which we call "segmental tension") to a marked crisis

response, in which the consultee's general professional functioning and emotional equilibrium are temporarily upset. The consultee usually ascribes his discomfort to his difficulties with the client, onto whose case he displaces feelings of anxiety, hostility, shame, and depression, which can be seen by the consultant to be partly or even primarily originating in his personal life or in his involvement with the social-system problems of his institution.

A teacher spoke hopelessly about a ten-year-old girl in his class, who he felt was mentally retarded. He had spent much time trying, in vain, to teach the child to read. He felt that, unless he succeeded, she would inevitably become an outcast in society and that others would exploit her weakness. The consultant realized that the teacher was identifying with the child, whom he was perceiving in a stereotyped way as a mental defective who must inevitably come to a bad end unless rescued by him through greatly augmenting her ability to achieve. The teacher was not perceiving the child's assets—she was quite popular among her peers and had nonverbal skills which might one day help her make a useful place for herself in society. He was also exaggerating the likelihood that more intelligent people would exploit her because of her backwardness; he felt that this was inevitable.

This teacher was currently worrying about his own ability to achieve in a new school to which he had come after an unsatisfactory experience elsewhere as a principal. He was particularly sensitive in his relationship with the headmaster, a driving man who demanded high standards from his teachers. The theme of mental retardation was also important in the teacher's past life, because he had been backward himself as a child and had only begun to improve at the age of ten.

This example illustrates a general characteristic of interfering themes— they can be formulated as preconscious syllogisms which mold the consultee's expectations. In this case, the parts of the syllogism are:

This girl is mentally retarded. Mentally retarded people inevitably fail in life and are exploited by more intelligent people. Therefore, this girl is doomed, despite everything I will do to rescue her.

The stereotyped expectation that all mentally retarded are doomed to exploitation and failure applies equally to himself and to the girl, both of whom are defined by him as fitting into this category.

Other examples of such syllogistic expectations in consultees include:

An inhibited teacher who sees a nine-year-old boy with poor control over aggressive impulses as inevitably destined to become a criminal, because, once a person loses control, he starts on a slippery path downward toward complete loss of restraint over instinctual drives.

A middle-aged married nurse who fears that a menopausal patient showing some depressive symptoms will inevitably become psychotic and injure her children.

A consultee who suggests: "This Negro family does not keep a clean house or take proper care of the children, who are dirty and untidy. Parents who behave this way do not love their children. Unloved children suffer personality distortions; therefore, these children will become mental cripples, and their present symptoms are the first sign of this."

This is the child of adultery. Adultery is sinful, and the punishment is visited upon the child. Therefore, this child is fated to a life of suffering, and it is useless to try to change this.

This man has aggressive outbursts, and he also drinks. People who lose control and who drink become alcoholics and eventually psychotic. Therefore, this man is headed for disaster, and nobody can save him.

In each of these instances, the consultee stereotypes the perception of the client into a symbol which has a personal meaning for the consultee; this leads to a fixed expectation of some sort of doom for the client which inhibits the consultee's professional efforts because of a feeling of hopelessness.

In handling this type of situation, our approach is to respect the separation of the consultee's personal life from his work difficulty and not investigate the causes of the theme interference, but to focus on defining the nature of the theme by a careful examination of its manifestations in the work context. The consultant then reduces the theme interference by influencing the consultee to adopt a reality-based expectation for the client.

In effect, the consultee is defending himself against direct confrontation of a personal problem by working with it vicariously in the client. Irrational fantasies which prevented his dealing directly with his own problem are also hampering him in helping the client. He communicates these to the consultant by the latent content of his descriptions of the client's predicament. The consultant attacks the irrational elements in these fantasies by in turn talking about the client in such a way that he conveys a corrective message through the use of the same symbolism as the consultee's. The result of this is that the consultant deals with the consultee's problems without interfering with his defenses and without arousing anxiety and resistance. Because of this and because he does not need to uncover the personal sources of the theme in the consultee's current or past life, this type of consultation is most economical. Successful cases usually need only two or three sessions. The effect on the consultee seems to depend on the degree of his personal involvement with his client. This is evidenced by the degree of interference with his customary professional objectivity and by the intensity of his emotional upset in handling the difficulties of his client.

As an example of the reduction of theme interference, let us return to the case of the teacher who asked for consultation with the mentally retarded girl. In this particular case the consultant, by chance, learned enough about the consultee to recognize the personal source of the theme interference. This knowledge was not necessary for his consultation, and consultants usually do their utmost to prevent such personal material entering the content of their discussions with the consultee. When the consultee nevertheless does bring such issues into the consultation, the consultant does not comment directly on them, but turns the discussion back to a consideration of some aspect of the client's problem. In this case, the consultant accepted the consultee's contention that the girl was backward, but attacked the inevitability of a bad end for her by involving the teacher in a joint examination of those aspects of her current life from which predic-

tions about her future might validly be made. This was not an entirely intellectual process, since the consultant delayed the discussion until he had encouraged the building of a supportive relationship between himself and the teacher. On the basis of this relationship, he was able to influence the teacher to pay attention to such items as the girl's nonverbal skills and her social poise and popularity, which introduced some hope that she might not be entirely useless and unhappy in her future life. The crux of the consultation, however, was a message which the consultant conveyed by implication— by the way he spoke about the girl and by the way he took it for granted that others would deal with her—that, even though it might be recognized that she was mentally dull, the intelligent people in her environment would not necessarily exploit her.

The invalidation of such a fixed expectation about a personally meaningful issue in the client has an effect not only on the consultee's feelings of hopelessness about this client, but also on similar feelings about himself. It also prepares him to be able to handle, with his customary professional objectivity and skill, other clients who may be correctly or incorrectly perceived as fitting the first part of the syllogistic proposition.

In this type of consultation, it is important not to unlink the client from the first statement of the syllogism—in this case, the perception, "this is a mentally retarded girl." Such an unlinking might be effected through the consultation relationship. For instance, the consultant might have pointed out that the girl's nonverbal skills indicated a higher level of intelligence and that she was not mentally retarded, just slow in the use of words or perhaps possessed of emotional blocks in reading because of certain experiences. Had the teacher accepted this possibility, his worry about the girl would have dissipated, but he would have left the consultation with no reduction in his theme problem, either in regard to himself as mentally retarded or in regard to future pupils who might appear mentally retarded. In fact, he would very likely search for some other child to take the place of the girl as a displacement object for his personal problem. It is of interest to point out that, had this case been misdiagnosed by the consultant as due to lack of understanding of the signs and meaning of mental retardation, the consultation might have been conducted in just such a manner.

LACK OF CONFIDENCE AND SELF-ESTEEM. This type of difficulty is usually easily identified. The consultee's functioning is interfered with in a non-specific way by illness, fatigue, infirmity, or by lack of confidence owing to inexperience or youth. What is demanded from the consultant is non-specific ego support. The only technical difficulty is that this should be tactfully given so that the consultee is not further weakened by the explicit recognition of his personal difficulties in a context which may lead to a further loss of self-esteem.

For instance, a young and inexperienced nurse asked for consultation about an unmarried Negro mother who refused to bring her baby to the well-baby clinic. The psychiatric consultant respectfully discussed the nurse's findings in the case, and, instead of sympathizing with her feelings of frustration at her impotence to influence the patient, he emphasized the value of the nurse's interest to the mother, pointing out that the patient needed to be assured that the health department workers respected her love for her baby and wished to cooperate with her in giving it the best possible care. In this case, there is a specific link between the nurse's situation and the patient about whom she chose to consult. Often, there is nothing in the content of the client's case which is linked in this way with the consultee's feeling of insecurity.

Professional workers who have the benefit of adequate technical and administrative supervision rarely need this type of consultation, but, for those who work on their own, mental health consultation may be a useful source of support.

CONSULTEE-CENTERED
ADMINISTRATIVE CONSULTATION

As the title implies, the primary goal of this category of consultation is to help consultees master problems in the planning and maintenance of programs for the prevention and control of mental disorder and in the interpersonal aspects of agency operation. As with program-centered administrative consultation, this method is often applied in group situations and is directed toward helping a group of administrators, but it is not infrequently invoked by an administrator on an individual basis. Since a specialist's assessment of the administrative problem is not demanded, it is quite feasible to operate with an individual administrator and restrict consultation help to his area of institutional life.

This type of consultation is similar to consultee-centered case consultation, with the major exception that few mental health consultants have as thorough a knowledge of administrative problems as they have of the psychosocial complications of an individual client; they must be careful to restrict their help to those factors of the administrative situation, such as the interpersonal and group dynamic aspects, in which they do have special competence. Most mental health specialists who act as administrative consultants make a serious study of administration and social science in order to augment the traditional knowledge of their own profession. In successful cases, the resulting amalgam leads to a clinical approach to administrative problems which many administrator consultees find peculiarly helpful and characteristically different from the kind of help they are accustomed to receiving from specialists in their own field.

As with case consultation, individual consultee-centered administrative consultation may be invoked *ad hoc* to deal with current problems necessitating a short block of sessions. Because of the great complexity of the administrative situation, consultees will almost always have some problem burdening them, and regular scheduled meetings with a consultant may be set up on a long-term basis in order to deal with whatever is uppermost at the moment. In this pattern of operation, consultants must guard against their role unintentionally altering to one of supervision, nonspecific emotional support, or psychotherapy.

Consultee-centered administrative consultation in a group setting is a more complicated operation, and its intricacies await adequate clarification. It is almost invariably conducted over a lengthy period and in the form of regularly scheduled meetings. At these meetings, the consultees raise any current administrative problem, which may be the central topic of one or several meetings. The simplest course of action is for the consultant to help the group clarify the complexities of the problem and to contribute to the discussion on the basis of his specialized knowledge of intrapersonal motivations and interpersonal relations, as well as of the human needs of personnel and clients. He may facilitate the consultees' acquisition of group-dynamic skills and help them explore new patterns of action in dealing with administrative complexities. The main technical difficulty is how he should handle theme interference when he identifies it in a group member or as a group manifestation.

The techniques of theme-interference reduction as practiced in case consultation are often hazardous in handling an individual member in the presence of the group. If the consultees are psychologically sophisticated, one of the individual's colleagues may realize his subjective involvement and make a defense-destroying interpretation before the consultant can stop it. Such a situation may rapidly slide into group psychotherapy, in which the separation of personal and work problems is set aside, with the usual arousal of anxiety and resistance. In order to avoid this, the group consultant must structure the ground rules to prevent the airing of personal problems and must maintain a tight control over the direction of the discussion, so that he can avoid a focus on theme interference in an individual member. Sometimes, this is relatively easy, because that member is acting as spokesman for the group and his individual theme interference is the presenting example of an issue which is common to the group. He may have been stimulated by other members to act as their mouthpiece. In this situation, the consultant can actively refocus the issue as a group problem and turn the spotlight from the individual member.

Such a maneuver raises the technical question of how to deal with theme interference at the group level. In other words, how does the consultant handle the discussion of a program or policy question when he identifies as a major source of difficulty unstated personal conflicts among group members or between the group and other people— usually administrative superiors or high-status figures in some other division of the organization? Are such issues to be opened up for explicit discussion, and, if so, how does the consultant differentiate such an approach from analytic group psychotherapy? The answer is not clear, but the differentiation appears to lie in restricting the content of consultation discussions to role conflicts and minimizing the discussion of personal factors. This is not easy, since personality idiosyncrasies and incompatibilities are frequent sources of role clashes. A rule of thumb which has proved useful is to avoid discussing the personality of any member of the consultee group, apart from alluding to fundamental aspects of human nature which are common to everyone, the consultant included.

A psychiatrist was invited by the nursing director of a general hospital to help deal with the interpersonal aspects of her administrative duties. The psychiatrist arranged to meet regularly on a continuing basis with her and eight assistant directors and to act as a specialist resource person during discussions of problems of administering the affairs of the nursing division. At these meetings, problems of current interest were raised by individual administrators either on the spur of the moment or by prior arrangement with their colleagues. The consultant helped to clarify certain aspects of the topics from the standpoint of his knowledge of personality dynamics, interpersonal relations, group dynamics, social-system theory, and community organization. Sometimes, his contributions added to the knowledge and understanding of the group and sometimes helped them work out new skills of problem solving. He was naturally sensitive to the emotional climate of the group and to the more-or-less clearly expressed attitudes on the content of the discussion. Occasionally, he would support the group in facing an uncomfortable topic, but he made no interpretations of the group process or of the feelings of individual group members.

He maintained a special orientation in relation to the group. He directed his efforts to satisfying the needs of the group and not his personal needs; his contributions aimed at facilitating the group's deeper insight into the administrative problems, and he took no stand himself on any of the action issues which emerged. His contributions carried a special weight because of attitudes of mutual liking and respect which developed in his relationship with the group and its members, but he made no attempt to persuade any-one to change an opinion. He did not direct the group or compete with its natural leaders—the director and associate director. Nor did he keep himself apart from the group as far as personal issues were concerned; in fact, he often illustrated his contributions with anecdotes about his own administrative or professional problems, and spoke quite openly about his own human feelings and failings in problem situations. He thus exhibited solidarity with the group in its struggles with complicated issues, acting in a more egalitarian way than is customary in psychotherapy, but in a way which is characteristic of the consultation approach as described in this chapter.

Choosing the Type of Consultation

In mental health consultation, the consultant has the responsibility of deciding which type of consultation is appropriate in a particular situation. He may decide to use one of the four main types in pure form or an appropriate mixture. This decision should be an explicit judgment, which takes into account the needs expressed by the consultees, the policies of the consultant's agency, and the sanction which has previously been obtained from the various authority figures in the consultee's agency.

These factors are often not congruent. The consultee may want explicit advice on a plan of action for his client, i.e., client-centered case consultation. The consultant agency, on the other hand, may wish to promote consultation which will improve the capacity of consultees, since this will have a wider spread in relation to the expenditure of consultant effort, i.e., may want to provide consultee-centered case consultation. The consultee agency may have agreed to this and may be particularly opposed to the consultant giving advice on action because this would be trespassing on the preserves of their supervisory staff. Finally, the consultant himself may recognize that the consultee's problem with the case is produced mainly by a social-system disequilibrium which prevents adequate use of the specialized resources of the institution because of internal communication blocks, and he would like to offer administrative consultation to deal with this. In any particular situation, the consultant will resolve such conflicts as a result of complicated judgments. But one thing is clear: whether or not a consultant manages to achieve goals in line with the policies of his own agency, he would be well advised not to utilize types of consultation which have not been sanctioned by the consultee agency. In our example, this means that he must handle the problem on a case-consultation basis and must not deal explicitly with the administrative difficulties, even though these may be obvious to him.

A consultant who does not bind himself to make an explicit decision between the various possibilities is likely not to define the conflicting expectations and sanctions and will wander in confusion between one set of goals and techniques and another. The reasons for his failures will then be as obscure to him as the reasons for his successes; this is a questionable basis for professional advance.

8.5 EXPLORATIONS IN CONSULTING-CLIENT RELATIONSHIPS

Chris Argyris

I should like to explore the role of the consultant based upon an analysis of two cases of a particular consultant group. Obviously one cannot generalize very much from such restricted data. This descriptive and exploratory report has as its objective the delineation of some issues and the generation of hypotheses. It marks the first stage of a long-range program whose ultimate goal is the development of appropriate models to understand the client-consultant relationship and its impact on organizational change and development.

The Nature of the Data Available

The consultants studied have had at least several years of experience as a team offering consulting advice to any unit within the corporation which requests it. Typically, they make notes of all their activities during each day in the field. These notes vary greatly in detail and scope. Although the policy followed is to record one's notes as soon as possible, there are times when there is a delay of several days.

I was given access to all the personal notes of all the consultants. Also, all the files were open for my use and

Chris Argyris, "Explorations in Consulting-Client Relationships," *Human Organization*, published by the Society for Applied Anthropology, XX, No. 3 (Fall 1961), 121–133. Used by permission.

study. According to my count, I read over three thousand pages of notes and research reports. I was given the freedom to interview anyone that I wished on the team or at the plants. Because of the exploratory nature of the study, I limited my interviews and discussions to the consultants. Although I had the complete cooperation of everyone, the nature of the data available does not permit us to reach any conclusions. The most that we can do is to raise questions for further research and indulge in some hypothesizing as to what might have happened if the consultants and the clients behaved differently.

I have selected two cases from the files which I believe best illustrate the problems which I wish to discuss. The selection is, therefore, *not* a random one. It is specifically loaded in the direction of cases that illustrate the difficulties which consultants face. Consequently, the reader should not infer that the material accurately represents the competence, activities, and successes of the consultants.

The Values of the Consultant Group

If we are to ascertain the effectiveness of the consultants, it is important to learn their objectives. What are they offering the client. Once having ascertained their objectives, then we may explore the degree to which they are able to achieve them. We may hypothesize that the consultants' effectiveness will tend to increase as the degree to which they achieve their objective increases.

The consultants studied offered professional assistance in the field of human relations. They view their overall objective as helping an organization solve its problems in such a way that it becomes more competent in solving the same or a similar class of problems without the continued help of the consultants. Thus we can ask at the end of the paper if the clients have resolved their problems in such a way that they no longer need the consultants.

There is another dimension along which insights can be obtained regarding the effectiveness of the consultants. They believe that there is a hierarchy of values whose fulfillment will tend to enhance the effectiveness of human relationships within organizations. These values are particularly relevant to our study. They may be outlined as follows.

1. Two important and interrelated components of administrative competence may be described as technical, intellective competence and interpersonal competence. Both levels of competence are important. If either or both is low, or if either is significantly higher than the other, administrative difficulties will tend to arise.[1]

2. Interpersonal competence, the consultants believe tends to increase as the executive:

[1] Empirical research will be required to define the point at which interpersonal competence is low or the point where the gap between the two is too large.

   a. becomes more aware of himself and of his impact upon others.

   b. solves human problems in such a way that the same or a similar class of problems do not recur.

3. These two components of interpersonal competence will tend to increase as executives are able in their relationships to:

   a. give and receive feedback about self and others so as to create minimal defensiveness in self and others.

   b. own, and to help others own their feelings, values, and attitudes.

   c. remain open to new values and attitudes and help others to experience the same.

   d. experiment with new values and attitudes and help others to do the same.[2]

From the above we may hypothesize that the consultants will perceive that they are achieving their objective as the clients begin to give and receive feedback with minimal defensiveness, to own their feelings, etc. But, as we shall see in a moment, in order for the consultants to be of help to the client along these dimensions they (the consultants) must behave according to these values. The consultants must behave *genu-*

[2] The major activities of the consultant group reside in the area of increasing interpersonal effectiveness within the organization. Because the consultants focus in this area it should not be interpreted to mean that the consultants do not feel that there are other areas which are as relevant to administrative competence and organizational development. The consultants recognize the importance of environmental and organizational factors and do include these in their studies whenever they feel they are relevant to the solution of the problem.

inely which we may define as behaving in accordance with one's values.[3] But to behave genuinely is not enough. It is important to behave genuinely in such a way that others (in this case the clients) have freedom to behave genuinely. Whenever human relationships are established where genuineness is possible on the part of *both* parties, they may be defined as *authentic*. Individuals cannot be authentic; authenticity is a property of interpersonal relationships. In our terms, the consultant hopes to influence his client to learn to establish more authentic relationships within the firm. In order to accomplish this, the consultant must also strive to establish authentic relationships in his relations with the client.

The Dilemma of the Consultant

Formal organizational strategy tends to reward communication, openness, experimentation on the rational level. It tends to penalize openness, levelling, and experimentation on the interpersonal and emotional levels.[4] This, in turn, tends to decrease the participants' interpersonal competence within the organization.[5]

The emphasis upon rationality tends to create an organizational culture in which feelings are considered to be "bad," "immature," "irrational," and many times irrelevant. For example, in a recent study of a top management group ($N = 18$), all but one reported that:

. . . personal feelings should be kept out of group meetings.

. . . if people did become emotional it would be the leader's responsibility to bring them back to the facts being discussed.

. . . if the personal feelings continued the leader should call off the meeting and talk to the individuals involved separately.[6]

The point I am trying to make is that it is not possible for this type of consultant to help an organization deal with its interpersonal difficulties and with those organizational problems that have an interpersonal base without helping the clients to deal with feelings and emotions. Yet these are the very factors that the clients would tend to find painful, and which they have "learned" to consider as signs of "immaturity" and "incompetence."

A consultant therefore, who wishes to help an organization learn to solve its own interpersonal difficulties is faced with a serious dilemma. He believes that in order for him to be of help he may have to ask the client to consider values that are fundamentally different from those upon which the organization, its controls, and his leadership pattern are based. For example, instead of considering feelings and emotions as irrelevant in administration (as is the case of most of industry) he sees them as being central to the resolution of human problems and the enhancement of openness,

[3] The concept of genuineness is, I believe, similar to and most certainly stimulated by Dr. Carl Roger's concept of congruence.

[4] Chris Argyris, *Personality and Organization*, Harper & Row, Publishers, New York, 1957.

[5] The degree to which each of these generalizations holds in real life is a matter of empirical study. I am predicting, however, that the overall trend would be in the direction implied in the propositions.

[6] Chris Argyris, "Toward a Theory of Authentic Relationships," mimeographed report, Yale University, Fall, 1960.

accurate information flow, trust, and an attitude of experimentation and risk taking.[7]

As such, the consultant will probably be threatening to the members of the organization. Quite understandably, the members will tend to question seriously the necessity for the reduction of hostility, tension, interpersonal rivalries, etc. They may be even more skeptical about the consultant's assumption that openness, trust, feedback, experimentation, etc., if increased, will tend to alleviate significantly some of the problems that they have come to perceive as part of organizational life.

One of the best ways a client has to test the effectiveness of the consultant's ideas is to see if his "product" works. In most cases the client has to wait until the consultant is finished before he can make such a judgment. However, in the case of the consultant offering to increase the effectiveness of the human relationships, the client can actually begin to test the validity of the consultant's approach from the outset of the relationship. If the consultant's views of effective human relationship are valid and effective, the client reasons, I should be able to evaluate the consultant by seeing if he (the consultant) uses them while attempting to help the organization change and develop. If the consultant does not use his views to stimulate effective changes, why should the client adopt them in his relationships within the organization? Moreover, the client can increase the difficulty of the test which the consultant has to pass by simply increasing the forcefulness with which he apparently adheres to his ideas and "rejects" the consultant's. If, as the consultant attempts to help the client change, he does not behave consistently with his ideas and values then why should the client use these ideas and values?

The consultant is in a very difficult position. If he behaves according to his ideas and values, he stands a good chance of being a threat to the client. He could be asked to leave. If he decides to behave even temporarily in accordance with the client's values, he may be accepted but he runs a serious risk of failing to change and develop.

Case A

Let us begin with the consultants feeding back their results of a systematic interview-questionnaire diagnosis to the top management of plant A. The comments emphasized such findings as: 1) the employees report a barrier between themselves and the management, 2) the employees feel uninformed, and consequently 3) tend to feel confused and "left out" while at the same time, 4) they fear to communicate upward their feelings of mistrust. These findings were digested by the top management for several weeks before they invited the consultants to the plant for further consultations. A meeting was held where the results were again discussed.

Two of the consultants reported their impressions about the meeting:

Consultant A
This meeting was interesting in that the plant manager was neither outspoken nor defensive. We reviewed some of the highlights of the findings and certain members of the management committee discussed these in the meeting in his office. The meet-

[7] *Ibid.*

ing did not have too much spark until one of the young technical men started to express resentment in terms of being critical, partly of the accuracy of our findings, and partly of the fact that some of their employees were disloyal in the type of comments they made. Otherwise, most of the management committee seemed to be accepting the findings in the report, although admittedly they were not very vocal in expressing suggestions as to how to bring improvements.

Consultant B

At this meeting the newest department head was most angrily defensive about the report. His clear expression made it possible to focus the issues, openly face the fact that the report was a "hot potato," and also that necessity which fully justifies management actions could produce some unwanted results.

The meeting ended with the issue of what to do next up in the air. No one quite knew how the plant manager felt. There was an assumption that he would make a decision, but he did not make any.

The Consultants Do Not Behave According to Their Values

The consultants as well as many of the subordinates reported that they felt frustrated and had a sense of incompleteness as a result of the plant manager's silence. However, this frustration and concern was not communicated. They were not being open or leveling. Instead someone asked if the results should be fed back to the next lower level of management. The discussion was guarded and most looked toward the plant manager for his views. He decided, and the subordinates "agreed," that it would be best to give only a summary or "light" report of the findings.

This was done. The consultants attended the meeting where the data were fed back to the lower management in a summary form. They reported that,

. . . the reaction of the supervisors at this point is that the survey had not accomplished very much.

However, added the consultants, the supervisors were not too disappointed because,

. . . their expectations had not been too high that any public reporting of the data would be any more explicit than it was.

Here we see the consultants exposed to a situation where they chose not to behave according to their values. The plant manager, they reasoned, was not ready to discuss his feelings about the report, no less his interpersonal impact upon those at the meeting.

The Impact of the Consultants' Behavior

The immediate "payoff" for the consultants is that they are still in the "good graces" of the plant manager. But this is obtained at a cost. The first part of the cost is that the plant manager has living evidence that under stress the consultants do not tend to behave in accordance with their values. On the contrary, they use the values of the client-system. Why then should he change? A second part of the cost is that those present at the meeting also see that the consultants behave in accordance with the values of the client system. Understandably, they may also have questions about the validity and practicality of the consultants' values. Moreover, they can also interpret the consultants' actions as being submissive toward the plant manager. If this is the case, they may reason, the plant manager may have the consultants under hi control. Perhaps they had best be careful in "leveling" with the consultants. Finally we note from the consultants' reports that the subordinates who viewed the feedback at a separate meeting concluded that "nothing had changed or would come of the research." Therefore, as some suggested later on, they concluded that the consultants might be "on the top management side" or at least certainly associated with the status quo.

To summarize, the costs for the consultants of going along with the client-system values seem to be fourfold. All the members of the client-system may begin to have decreased confidence in the consultants and especially in the values that they represent. Second, the subordinates may begin to view the consultants as agents of the plant manager. Third, the consultants, unknowingly let themselves and their research create an administrative situation in which the client-system values and the status quo are reenforced. Fourth, the clients may have learned that if enough pressure is placed upon the consultants they can be manipulated to change their values. This conclusion may make the clients feel more secure in that they can "control" the consultants. However this "control" can also act to increase deeper fears and insecurities because it is not comforting to know that one's consultant can be as nongenuine as the client he is attempting to help.

Another alternative action for the consultants would have been to behave in accordance with their values. They could have told the plant manager during the meeting that they felt a sense of frustration and incompleteness. They might have asked the group if others felt as they did. Finally, they could have, again at the group meeting (or later in private if necessary) predicted for the plant manager some of the impacts outlined above. This could help him to see more clearly his impact upon the organization and prevent the reenforcement of the feelings of being left out, mistrusted, etc., reported in the diagnostic survey. More about this in the final section.

THE CLIENT-SYSTEM VALUES BECOME REENFORCED

Returning to the consultants, their notes suggest that they were aware of not behaving according to their values. However, they reported, this was necessary if they were to be asked to remain in the organization. They also reported that since they did not upset the plant manager they were in a better position to be of help to him.

The consultants held a meeting with the plant manager. They reported that they were able to convince the plant manager, "that a job lay ahead to develop the subordinates" especially in "leveling," "openness," "interpersonal impact," etc. Note that the plant manager was not told that he also may need such help. Moreover, the consultants suggested the establishment of a "steering committee" to help plan the laboratory.

The plant manager agreed. A Steering Committee was created whose task it was to examine the survey results to explore what ought to be done for organization improvement. As a result of the committee's meetings a decision was reached to hold a three-day workshop program where the survey results would be studied in detail by all the management to stimulate self-analysis.

The planning of the meetings was masterminded by one of the consultants. He wrote that he felt he had to engineer the programs since the committee lacked the concept of a "laboratory" program. He continued that he:

. . . is able to move them in the direction of the laboratory design.

The consultant being quite secure and extremely competent also noted,

. . . in this respect our meeting had been almost comic. I had insisted that the program was the Committee's or the management's and that my role was only to help them design it. However, I consistently felt that I should be designing the program since they didn't know how to. Of course, this eventually worked out into my doing so.

Thus we see that, in order to take some action, the consultants again had to behave in ways which reflect the values of the client system. They influenced the plant manager to approve training which he and few others in the client-system fully understood. Moreover, they created a Steering Committee to give the subordinates a greater feeling of participation. Yet they admittedly manipulated the members to go in the direction that they (the consultants) desired. All this was done in order "to get results."

This need, on the part of the consultants, to "get on with the job" is exactly what the clients desire. They can use it to manipulate the consultant to become responsible for planning and carrying out the change programs. The dependent relationship that the client has with the top management, he (the client) now creates with the consultant.

An example for the consultant's re-port that illustrates the points being made is:

Members of the Steering Committee made it clear [to the consultant] they felt some pressure to get going, the pressure coming partly from their own feelings of frustration about lack of decision, and in part because they thought management was breathing down their necks with respect to some proposals. The comment was made in a joking manner that we'd better get something going in order to have something to submit to the manager. The time of the next committee meeting was set up at this time and I was invited to attend.

In this example, the committee tries to communicate their sense of frustration and urgency to the consultant. However, they also imply to the consultant that, along with them, *he* is now responsible for the success or failure of the project. If the consultant accepts the responsibility, he has unwittingly placed himself in a traditional leadership position within the group. Under these conditions, the consultant soon begins to feel that he *is* responsible for doing the creative thinking about what the committee ought to discuss during the next meeting.

Apparently this is what happens. The consultant, after listening to the above, develops an excellent list of questions which, as he states,

It seems to me the committee should give attention to.

For example:

What is the plant manager's image of the desired direction which the company should go?

How are the goals used by the people at headquarters, to whom the plant manager reports, department heads and superintendents, operating management, and non management?

How much motivation is there to carry them out?

How about people's skills for carrying them out effectively?

What is required for movement toward these goals:

By the management group.

The work force?

What obstacles can be anticipated?

Action plans:

Communicating the committee's report and recommendations to the manager.

The manager cutting the rest of the management group in communicating the plan to the non-management group.

The first event in the improvement program.

These are important questions. However, in defining them as an agenda for the clients, the consultant becomes responsible for the group's diagnosis. In taking the initiative, the consultant again influences the clients to become dependent upon him. Such a requirement is congruent with the client's expectations and values, but not with the consultant's.

One wonders what would have happened if the consultant asked the group members why they were telling him about their failures and pressures. If, as he feels, this is an attempt by the clients to induce him to internalize their pressures and anxieties, he might profitably raise the issue. This would be an excellent opportunity for the committee to begin to become aware that they will seriously impair the consultant's potential contribution if they try to make him behave according to their values. If he is to be of help, he ought not to be controlled by the very values which are the cause of their problems. Assuming these problems are

worked through, then the consultant can help the group to develop its own list of questions. In doing so he places the emphasis upon the clients developing their own questions. He shows, by his actions, that he believes 1) clients can, through such activity, learn much about one another, their organizations, and the requirements of effective group problem solving, 2) that it is the group members who will have to take the action and thus should participate in the diagnosis, 3) which, in turn, would begin the process of decreasing the clients' dependence upon the consultant.

Returning to our case, the consultants actually planned and held several different types of short laboratories. The attendees reported positive feelings about the programs. Generally they reported that they had been helped to understand one another's job, as well as to set the ground work for some concrete changes to be made in the practices as well as the organization of work. The data available suggested that some of these changes were carried out and other changes were planned and also carried out.

Although the men reported new and enlarged awareness about the difficulties of their fellow managers in getting the job done, the data suggested that this behavior did not change very much. Also, there was evidence that the enthusiasm for change was highest when the consultants were present. This sign of dependence of the clients upon the consultants did not disturb the plant manager. Indeed, he reported satisfaction that concrete tasks of important value to the plant were being accomplished.

The plant manager had no reason

to be disappointed in the process by which these jobs were being done. It was the same one that he used in his relationships with the subordinates. The fact that the manager had established dependent relationships with the consultants did not displease him as long as actions were being taken. The consultants are now being perceived by the plant manager as resource people to be used by his subordinates in order to accomplish specific tasks. Little thought is being given to the original objective of helping the clients examine their basic values and interpersonal relationships. It is interesting to note that the consultants were lauded by the plant manager to their (the consultants') superior because:

... they were not forcing themselves upon the plant and letting themselves be used as the plant members saw fit.

One of the consultants was not content with the compliment. He wrote:

While this compliment sounds encouraging, I still have some feelings of uneasiness about the relationship. I think the main source of it now is that when I call the plant manager he is usually, in fact, almost always tied up at a meeting. Although I ask that he call me back he seldom does so. One day—I arranged an appointment with him to review how things were going. However, although I was there for a full half day, I was able to spend only approximately forty-five minutes with him, and this between telephone calls and other forms of interruption.

This is an excellent illustration of the human relationships which are typical of the client system. One possible reason is that the need for the consultant is now not as great. The plant manager may feel that he has received as much help as he can from the consultant. Another possibility is that, since the consultants have been incorporated and become so much a part of the client system, they no longer can put into use the skills and knowledge that they have regarding opening and facilitating effective change. Moreover, if the client can no longer see much difference between the consultants and the other members of the client system, there is no major reason to show any high interest in them. Finally, from research in clinical psychology and psychotherapy, we may hypothesize that a client can decrease his confidence in the consultant if he feels that he can manipulate the consultant to accept his (the client's) values and goals. A client, will probably not respect an individual who, in the face of stress, takes on the values and norms of the client culture. That is the very reason the client needs help.

We continue to describe other events. They would primarily illustrate that the consultants had achieved great success in helping the organization accomplish certain specific tasks. However, the success does not seem as great in the area of interpersonal effectiveness. The consultants began their relationships with a strategy to behave according to the values of the client system until they had achieved acceptance by the top management and helped the clients to accomplish specific work tasks. This did indeed win compliments. However, it also created a chain reaction where the plant manager and the other clients induced the consultants to behave according to the client-system values. The consultants were never able to break away from this chain reaction. Although they were able to help some of the clients to explore their values, the impact was never very great. In short, they became "accepted" by becoming *a part* of the client system. They were not accepted as consultants with a set of different values whose effectiveness the client-system ought to explore seriously.

Case B

The second case begins with the consultants' explorations at a particular plant. Upon conducting a reconnaissance, the consultants concluded that, since the management group was relatively free of suspicion of consultants, the latter might be able to create a program which would help "to free" the clients (management and employees) in such a way as to release their potential. Moreover, because the organization was relatively small, they might be able to offer a two-pronged tailor-made program which could help achieve the management's objectives. The first prong was an

. . . emphasis on organization improvement rather than crisis or criticism.

The consultants believed that such an emphasis would steer away from the plant's history of difficult problems and relations thereby decreasing the clients' defensiveness and simultaneously emphasizing progress to be made in the future. In the opinion of the consultants such a strategy would lead to minimal client resistance. In the consultants' opinion this would make it easier for the clients to accept the idea of an organization improvement project.

The second prong was the consult-

ants' desire to help the top management: 1) to

get [their] people to take a responsible lead in this work so that it is not just [top management's] program,

2) to prove that their objective is a desirable change, 3) that they had confidence in the organization, 4) that they are not criticising, that they are seeking consulting help to build for the future, and 5) that they are not trying to import "any packaged program."

It is interesting to note a contradiction in the consultant's behavior. On the one hand, there is the consultants' desire to help the plant manager make this *his* program so that *his* people would, in time, make it *their* program. On the other hand, is the fact that the consultants develop the prognosis with little or no participation from the clients. Assuming that the prognosis is valid, and assuming that it is accepted by the management, then one can predict that the plant manager will tend to develop a dependency relationship with the consultants. The plant manager will tend to feel that the program is not his but the consultants', to the extent that he accepts what they tell him they think he ought to do. One may also hypothesize that, if the above happens, it will decrease the probability that the subordinates will feel this is their program.

Another example of how the consultants tend to control the relationship with the client is when they decide unilaterally that the plant manager

. . . might consider improving upward communication; to signal ways he wants to operate.

Since the consultants believe the problems lay at the top, it would be necessary, they reason, to reassure the plant manager of his effectiveness and give him a chance to talk out his problems and ideas. Thus, once the top jobs are clarified as to scope and duties, it would be possible to reach out for new ideas.

If this strategy is valid, then the plant manager will be moved in the right direction *because of the consultants' prognostic* skills. But, the problem of the plant manager is to improve his own prognostic skills. A way for him to become more effective and simultaneously to decrease his need for the consultants would be for them to help him learn how to diagnose as effectively as they do.

The Projected Survey

The consultants recommended to the plant manager that a survey program be conducted to help the management people

... dig out and clarify their own goals and then find ways to attain them.

They also pointed out that,

... the consultants would act as if they were outside consultants. . . All data would be for the local plant only. None would be communicated to higher authorities without clearance with the authorities at the local level.

The plant manager accepted the project. He suggested that the consultants explain it to Mr. Brown, an "old timer," who, according to the plant manager, feels hurt because he expected to become a plant manager but never made it. The plant manager also suggested that the projected survey be discussed with the top management

Committee (hereafter known as the committee). The consultants agreed.

Mr. Brown apparently resisted the consultants and their program. He questioned if the people would tell the truth. The consultants decided not to help Mr. Brown explore his fears toward them, research, and the past. Rather they attempted to allay his fears by pointing out,

That they were not interested in looking backward, in studying the mistakes of previous managers or in studying the plant's morale, but rather that the focus would be on the future.

One may question the effectiveness of asking Mr. Brown to forget fears which are related to the past by assuring him that the consultants will do so. The consultants note, among themselves,

At the end of the meeting, Mr. Brown appeared to understand what the consultants were going to do from the point of view of the procedures involved in the survey. There is no evidence of support for the idea . . . the notion of organization improvement was not accepted or even understood by Mr. Brown.

Nor did they communicate to him their impression that in their opinion he is,

... an incessant talker, oblivious to listener reaction and very insensitive to his own needs and power.

This diagnosis may be correct. But is it not equally correct that one reason that the consultants did not "level" with Brown (a value which they hold) was because they were responding to their own needs? The consultants probably felt that it was best not to "level" with Mr. Brown lest this explode their projected survey.

The following day, the consultants held their meeting with the committee.

They were introduced by the plant manager who told his subordinates: 1) that he wanted the consultants to be of help,

2) emphasized that he believes there is potential gain in having an outside group observe and lend assistance, and 3) by being particularly careful to say that, in his opinion, there was not necessarily anything wrong at the plant, but under the best of circumstances one can look for ways to do a better job.

How helpful is this introduction of the plant manager to the consultants and to the clients? How is this project going to become the subordinates' if they come to a meeting where 1) they are told to accept the consultants, 2) they sense the plant manager's defensiveness when he says that the consultants are not looking for anything to criticize, and 3) that they are told the organization is not doing an effective job? How helpful is this approach if everyone concerned feels that there *is* something wrong? If there are not weaknesses why hold the survey? Will not this approach be perceived by the subordinates as more of the top management

. . diplomatic talk that is always going on?

If so, what will be their view of the consultants if this management nonauthenticity is sanctioned by them? Is this not an opportunity to test the consultants to see if they really mean that 'openness" is a good thing? If so, then the consultants tend to enhance the difficulties since they not only refrain from exploring the problem above but they sanction it by taking the same approach. They emphasize that they are not interested in the past, that they are not making a checkup of employee morale, and that they are interested in

the future, and how the consultants might help the management better to achieve their goals for the future.

If the consultants want the subordinates to make this their project, then why do they not find out if the subordinates want the same? Moreover, how will they be perceived by the subordinates when the findings are released and the majority of them deal with their morale? Is the consultants' strategy more of a response to the plant manager's anxieties about getting the project accepted, than a logically thought through plan which takes into account the total management group?

The consultants reported that the committee attitude appeared, on the surface, excellent, and that almost immediate joviality

. . . was used to mask feelings and keep conflict from becoming overt.

Here is an incisive hypothesis but the consultants do not explore its possible validity with the clients. The consultants also note that the committee does not function as a decision-making body. The consultants would not think of resisting the plant manager's proposal with the possible exception of Mr. Brown.

Why are these hypotheses not checked? One reason may be that the consultants want to refrain from doing anything which will upset the committee and doom the survey. Another may be that they believe that they ought not to begin to confront the committee until after the survey when the consultants will know much more about the clients. Finally, it may be that the consultants, temporarily acting as researchers, do not want to disturb the situation. However, subsequent data will show that the consultants continue this strategy after the survey is completed.

One interesting situation occurred during the survey. One manager reported to the plant manager that his people were worried over the possibility of holding a survey. Instead of helping the plant manager to resolve the issue, the consultants met with the reluctant group. They told them the same information that they gave the committee. Apparently (and we shall see later, only temporarily) the reluctant group "accepted" the survey. One wonders, for example, what might happen if, instead of doing the above, the consultant stated to the group.

I am told that you are concerned about the survey. It makes us feel good that you raise these concerns openly. What kinds of information do you wish from me? How can I be of help to you?

The consultant might also ask if the group could help him to understand the degree to which their concerns are shared by others. If so, what hunches they may have to deal with the problem.

The Results of the Survey

As in the previous case, a carefully planned systematic questionnaire and interview study was conducted. After feeding back the results to the plant manager the consultants suggested a series of courses of action that were indicated from the survey.

1. There is evidence of resignation if not a feeling of helplessness on the part of management.
2. Steps need to be taken to galvanize or stimulate the organization to new levels of spirit and enthusiasm.
3. Mr. Brown ought to be changed because the problems that his behavior cause could prevent the organization from carrying out any proposals that it evolves.
4. The number of levels of management need to be reexamined to see if they are all necessary.
5. To help the management look more creatively at what they can do both as individuals and as members of a team. Also to get them to feel that they *do* have the power, influence, and responsibility for getting it done.

In presenting the prognosis the consultants helped to focus the plant manager's attention on the steps that they felt were necessary if the organization was to improve. They were apparently most anxious to induce the plant manager to do something with Mr. Brown, who they felt was a thorn in the organization's as well as the consultants side.

A meeting was then held with the committee to feed back the results With the exception of Mr. Brown, the committee did not resist the results Mr. Brown raised questions about the validity of the study and according to the consultant made a bit of a nuisance of himself. One of the consultants

. . . purposely took a seat next to Mr Brown in order to restrain him from talking a great deal by putting his hand on Mr. Brown's arm or otherwise diverting his attention.

Although there was no overt disagreement by other committee members the consultants left the meeting questioning the committee's probable degree of commitment to work through the results. Perhaps if the consultant would not view Mr. Brown's behavior as a thorn but as stemming from a person who is so anxious that he breaks the barriers of secrecy and tells the consultants how he (and perhaps others) feel, the consultants might have utilized his charges about the research to learn more about the other members' feelings. Such a step would also help the consultants begin to reach one of the objectives that they define as crucial; namely, to help the committee work through their reluctance to be open.

Upon the return to the organization for further discussion with the committee the consultants explored plans which the plant manager might consider to cope with Mr. Brown. The plans became quite detailed to the point where the consultants considered suggesting a new organizational position for Mr. Brown; one which would, in effect, greatly decrease his power and control. From the consultants' viewpoint, this action was necessary if the plant was to progress.

Perhaps this was the case. However, if the plant manager accepted the plans, the consultants would make the plant manager more dependent upon them because one of the plant manager's basic problems was that he needed to become an effective diagnostician of such difficult situations. In filtering out the alternatives and presenting those with greatest merit, the consultants were preventing the plant manager from learning more about these crucial steps in the decision-making process. If the plant manager agreed with the consultants, then he would surely tend to increase his dependence upon them. Yet, the consultants believed that they must help the plant manager overcome his de-

pendence upon them. Moreover, the consultants wished that the committee be less dependent on the plant manager. But, why should the committee believe the consultants' view that dependence is bad when they see that their boss is being made dependent upon the consultants?

Returning to Mr. Brown, the plant manager accepted the consultants' recommendations. As soon as Mr. Brown left for a vacation the plant manager announced to the management the realignment of duties which radically changed Mr. Brown's duties. Exactly why this decision was made after Mr. Brown left is not clear. One can only hypothesize that the plant manager must have felt quite uncomfortable in making the decision and thus waited until Mr. Brown left. Whatever the reason, it seems that the consultants should have helped the plant manager to explore the impact of the decision. To be sure, the survey results suggest that the management group is not particularly in favor of Mr. Brown. But to demote a man in this way is to provide living evidence to the management that the plant manager and the consultants are not able to be open when making difficult decisions. What guarantee do any of the managers have that their jobs might not be changed in the same way someday when they are on vacation?

As one might predict, upon his return to the plant Mr. Brown was astounded to hear the news of the change. He became depressed and hostile. From then on Mr. Brown evidenced increased hostility toward the plant manager. Mr. Brown became more withdrawn but made one final attempt to be open with his hostile feelings. He refused to listen and resisted. The consultants dealt with this defensiveness by suggesting if Mr. Brown did not cooperate, the consultants might be forced to leave the organization. Mr. Brown reacted with "violent hostility." No other comments exist about the meeting. The consultants noted, however, that since that meeting Mr. Brown promised the plant manager to cooperate until his retirement.

Thus Mr. Brown was neutralized and the consultants felt an important obstacle was removed.

The Decrease in Management Interest

However, it was not long before a new problem seemed to arise. The committees created to work through the survey results and suggest concrete action were, for the most part, ineffective. At the same time, the plant manager reported to the consultants that

. . . plant people are looking upon [them] as spies.

One employee even asked

. . . is it a good idea to have them around so much?

Apparently, the consultants did not take any action to explore these rumors. About a month later, the plant manager visited the consultants and reported "discouragement with the program." He said it has slowed down for various reasons: a main one being that less time was being spent by the consultants at the plant. He stated that he was looking for some new ideas because of the loss of momentum in the program.

The consultants diagnosed the decrease in interest as

. . . caused by the fact that these [management] groups could not come up with any more problems and did not see any responsibility beyond problem definition.

The consultants apparently do not believe that they might be partially responsible for the lack of responsibility. After all, *they do* condone behavior on the part of the plant manager which is unilateral and punitive (Mr. Brown's case). Also, it *is* the consultants and the plant manager who want the study. Why should the shop feel responsible for something that they never really accepted?

According to the consultants, the few departments which needed help least were holding the more effective meetings. The poorer departments did not seem to be motivated to hold further meetings. After some visits by the consultants, the meetings were begun again. However, the consultants reported that there was not as much openness as they had hoped for.

After one meeting, a member told one of the consultants that the group wondered why he attended the meetings and wished they knew what they planned to do with his observations. They feared he might report upwards. The consultant reported that he was

. . . too confused after this meeting, because he was beginning to question whether his own behavior, as practiced in the meetings, was appropriate.

This is not an easy conclusion to contemplate and it illustrates the internal security of the consultant. One wishes that he would consider discussing his feelings with the management group. If he is able to be open with them about their relationship, would not this provide the clients with a rich living experience of how useful it is to explore one's inadequacies with a group of peers which provides a supportive climate? How is it possible for the consultants to expect the clients "to level" if they find it difficult to do so?

A New Change Program

Apparently, the consultants decided not to discuss their problems with their clients (e.g., being perceived as spies, etc.). Instead they decided that the next step should be a new workshop program.

In the meantime the plant manager again told the consultants that he was discouraged in the way the departmental meetings were dwindling. Perhaps, this would be an ideal moment for the consultants to invite the plant manager to become more aware of his dependency upon the consultants. It may also help the consultants to become more aware of their role in the problem. Moreover, if the plant manager experiences "the experts" raising questions about their effectiveness, he may begin to feel less anxiety about discussing his own difficulties.

Instead the consultants suggested that the plant manager might raise the question with the department heads as to whether or not they wished to continue. The plant manager replied that although he wished them to continue, he did not wish to legislate the group meetings.

The consultants reported that their impression was that the plant manager was attempting to get them to return to the plant and rejuvenate the program. For reasons not mentioned, the consultants do not use this ideal opportunity to explore their views of the plant manager's dependence upon them. Instead they suggest that they meet with some of the plant people to design a new program.

The consultants decided that a new training program might be useful because:

The consultants after this meeting discussed between themselves the merits of continuing versus discontinuing the group meetings. It appeared that most groups were by now under a good deal of tension. They could not seem to see clearly any responsibility beyond problem definition and felt they had exhausted problem defining. If they could not move to the next phase of exploring solutions and taking action, it might be well to discontinue the meetings. After several days of consideration, the consultants decided that the two problems that were a contribution to the problem of group movement were: 1) Inadequate understanding of the objectives of the program (the objectives had been becoming clearer since the survey) and 2) Lack of skilled leadership in meetings (group functions were not being performed). The notion at this point was that if the groups could be helped to continue meeting, a number of desirable consequences could be achieved. First, plant problems would continue to get worked on a lower level; second, groups and individuals would get greater sensitivity to problems of group functioning, and third, the desire of top management, especially the manager, to move groups toward a better understanding of the goal of greater self-determination at lower levels would be pursued.

A program was evolved by the consultants with the overall objective of developing within the plant an atmosphere in which all members 1) feel a greater responsibility for influencing the future of the organization, and 2) feel they can influence this future constructively.

In a way the program is ironic. The men are going to be induced to become more responsible yet they never really have been offered an opportunity to truly develop any program to enhance the clients' feelings of self-responsibility if the clients have almost nothing to say regarding their perceived need for the program, and the program, and the kind of human experience it shall be?

One can predict that if the program is composed of many experiences that involve the clients, and if these experiences are deeply meaningful to them, then they may increase their motivation. If this happens, one can predict further, however, that the "charge" given to them by the program will tend to wear off and a new program will be needed. If such is the case, then the consulting relationship has succeeded in shifting the dependence of the clients from their boss to the consultants.

Discussion and Conclusions

First, we must emphasize that the study is limited to those consulting relationships designed to increase the effectiveness of human interpersonal relationships within the organization. A consultant operating at this level tends to find himself in a major dilemma. It appears that if he tends to go along with the traditional values implicit in the formal organizational structure, he tends to set off a chain of events that have varying consequences. On the one hand, he does not tend to be very threatening to the client system. He is usually liked and accepted as "being one of the boys" and "part of the culture."

It also appears that the unintended consequences of this strategy are that the consultant soon finds that he has worked himself into the role of planning, creating, and implementing change. Moreover, he behaves toward the clients in the same way as the clients tend to behave toward their subordinates, i.e., in a directing, controlling manner. This relationship is usually well known by the subordinates. They, in fact, tend to use and go along with, the consultant in this relationship because they can control him and protect themselves. For example, they gladly take on the reciprocal role of being dependent upon the consultant. This leads to the consultant becoming primarily responsible for change that may occur. Under these conditions changes *are* made in the organization. However, the quality and usefulness of these changes is largely a result of the consultants' ingenuity. Thus, the organization has become dependent upon the consultants.

In traditional consulting practice, consultants who permitted themselves to get into such a position would probably be evaluated quite highly. After all, they have been able to get the organization to make progress in clearly defined and observable ways. Moreover, management acknowledges their value in helping to achieve certain crucial objectives. It may be argued that, given the realities of organizational life and the "human encounter" in which the consultants are immersed, this is probably as well as one can expect the consultants to perform. However, as we have seen, the success tends to be short lived and relegated primarily to certain non-human changes in interpersonal relationships and basic values which were originally planned never materialize.

A. THE MARGINAL ROLE OF THE CONSULTANTS

In an attempt to help us to begin to understand the complexity of the consulting role it might be useful to explore it more systematically. What follows is an attempt to relate aspects of the consultative process to certain basic psycho-social concepts. However, appropriate examples will be used from the data available.

To the extent that the client's present value system is different from the one the consultants represent, the consultant places himself in a marginal position because he will work in a system whose values and norms are different from those of his own team. To make matters more difficult, most client systems are usually composed of two sub-systems. On the one hand, is the group which desires to see their organization change. In most cases this sub-system is composed of those in management who invited the consultants. On the other hand, are all those who are either not aware of a necessity for change, or disagree as to the proper direction for change, or resist any attempt at change. To the extent that any one or a combination of these factors exists, the consultant will find himself confronted with another set of factors that will tend to reinforce and magnify the role of a "marginal man."

From the research on the role of "marginal man" it is possible to infer that the consultant will tend to experience the following kinds of problems.

1. Although he accepts the management's request to conduct diagnoses of the employees' world, the employees may choose not to inform him about the very problems he is supposed to help resolve.

In the cases above, no lower-level employees are included in the study. However, there are numerous examples where the lower-level supervisors tend to withhold information. For example, in Case A the lower-level supervisors were not willing to discuss the difficulties which they felt with the leadership pattern of the top management echelons. They also resisted talking about the question, "How am I doing?" which was a question in which top management was most interested. Similarly, in Case B the supervisors had some serious questions about the role of the home office in the life of their organization. However, they did not feel free to discuss them openly with the top management. (They did discuss them, however, with the consultants.)

2. Although the consultant is asked by management to help them, they may not inform him of their informal activities, especially those that they keep from one another. Usually, these are the activities that are the sources of many organizational problems.

It is difficult to cite examples of this condition because our raw data came primarily from the consultants' reports. However, there are a few examples that can be used where the top management withheld important information from the consultants. In Case A the management group met informally for four hours to discuss one of the consultants' questionnaires without inviting him to participate. Later the consultant learned that the management group never accepted phase X of his plan although for many months they acted as if they accepted it. In Case B the plant manager communicated confidential survey data about an employee to people outside the organization.

3. The consultant could experience frustration and conflict if he is asked by members in either sub-culture to participate in activities that the other does not sanction. To the extent that he feels "required" to comply the consultant will tend to increase the probabilities of jeopardizing his position in the organization.

According to the consultants they experienced conflict numerous times when top management asked them to make evaluations of subordinates. They felt the subordinates would not approve these discussions. Equally conflicting, but not as numerous, were times when the subordinates attempt "to pump" the consultants as to what they were learning from the "Top Brass."

4. The consultant will tend to experience conflict and frustration to the extent that the two — sub — cultures fluctuate in their decisons, norms, etc. For example, he might feel that management ought to make up its mind on a particular policy so that he can provide consistent replies when asked by the employees. He may also feel that the employee attitudes about certain things do keep vacillating, and he is therefore unable to make a valid report to the management (which may be the employee's objective).

5. The consultant will tend to experience conflict and frustration to the extent that his values are incongruent with the clients'.

The major portion of the paper is taken up with examples of the differences in values between the consultant and the clients. Whereas the former emphasizes openness, self-awareness, self-acceptance, and emotionality, the latter emphasized diplomacy, subordination, dependence and rationality. These basic differences forced the consultant into continual conflict choice situations. In most cases, we have seen, the consultant's values were subordinated to the clients'. The former became increasingly nonauthentic which pleased the clients but prevented the consultant from providing the degree of help which he is capable.

To summarize, the consulting relationship is influenced greatly by several complex factors. They are: 1) the discrepancy between the consultant's values and those of the clients, 2) the division of the organization into those who are aware of and/or wish, and those who are unaware of and/or do not wish, to bring about effective change, and 3) the division between those who invited the consultant "to straddle" a series of overlapping, conflicting, and at times antagonistic, sub-cultures.

This marginal status can lead to many difficulties for the consultant. If he attempts to behave simultaneously in accordance with the requirements of both sub-cultures, he will find himself in constant conflict since the demands are antagonistic. Moreover, he will tend to be perceived by those in the sub-culture, at best, as being ambivalent and unsure. At worst, the consultant will be perceived as a hypocrite and a man "playing both sides against one another." If he values one sub-culture over the other, then his behavior will be perceived as "management-dominated," or "employee-dominated," depending upon which subculture he values most and who is doing the judging.

Finally, each situation will tend to be

new for the consultant. Consequently even with a high degree of training and experience his behavior will not tend to be efficient (e.g., follow the shortest path to the goal). There will be much exploratory, trial-and-error behavior. Errors and false steps will be made at the very time that he is being most cautious. Frustration and conflict will occur as well as feelings of ambivalence. These, in turn, will tend to lead the consultant to vacillate, to shift his ground, his strategy. He may be easily influenced and easily led especially by those representatives of the subculture that he values. His resistance to suggestion from the same group will tend to be low.[8]

B. The Emphasis upon the Process of Development

The consultants upon whom we are focusing have an additional problem that confronts them continually. In many consulting relationships, the ends are considered more important than the means. If a marketing consultant comes up with a bright idea or an organization specialist suggests a more effective organizational structure, either not much attention is paid to the interpersonal processes involved in achieving these ends or strategies are developed and executed that "sell," "persuade," "pressure," "motivate," the employees to accept these changes.

A consultant who is interested in helping the organization achieve its needs in such a way that it can continue

to do so with decreasing "outside" aid must give attention to the processes by which the new plans are developed, introduced, and made part of the organization. He will tend to invite a much greater degree of participation on the part of the clients in all the phases of the program. Such participation, if it is not to become bogged down, will have to be based on effective interpersonal and group relationships. At the core of such relationships are such factors as openness, the capacity to create minimal defensiveness in oneself and in others, listening with minimum distortion, etc. In order to succeed in their work these consultants must therefore be interested in the *processes* or means for development as well as the ends. For example, it is not very worthwhile to use covert or diplomatic approaches to get the clients to see that they are not open or that they are diplomatic in their relationships. It does not seem effective to help the clients become aware of their defenses if, in the process, the consultants behave defensively. Thus we find that the consultant strives to create a process for change which requires the very values that he is supposed to help the organization to overcome.

It is extremely difficult, however, for the consultant, to be open when he is operating under the difficulties and ambiguities of a new situation compounded by being in a marginal role. All this is doubly compounded by the fact that his job depends upon not upsetting the clients whose basic problems are that they work in a system that sanctions non-authenticity and deplores authenticity. How is the consultant expected to behave according to his values and, at the same time, survive in a

---

[8] The analysis of the impact of a new situation on behavior is drawn from Roger Barker, Beatrice A. Wright, and Mollie R. Gonick, *Adjustment to Physical Handicap and Illness*, Social Science Research Council, Bulletin 55, 1946, pp. 1–44.

world in which these values may lead to failure. To make matters more difficult, he is on the client's payroll. Thus his job could be placed in jeopardy if he risks confronting the clients by questioning their values.

One implication is that management may need to learn to create a climate where the consultant can feel free and encouraged to express his beliefs, especially different ideas about the process of effective organizational change. Unless this is done, the consultant, quite understandably, out of fear of his own position and in need for acceptance, soon takes on the values already held by the organization that he is trying to help. At this point, he tends to lose the very qualities that would make him valuable to the organization.

Along with line management's helping to develop a climate where the consultants are helped to express their uniqueness, certain organizational changes might be considered organizationally to reinforce the consultants in their effective assistance. Specific recommendations for defining the nature of such a relationship go beyond the scope of this study. However, in other organizations, consultants have developed effective relationships where the following kinds of conditions existed. The consultants:

1. May never become part of line management.
2. Have their own professional salary scale as do medical directors.
3. May never be fired for focussing on such processes as openness and authenticity but,
4. May be dismissed if they are judged by their professional colleagues to be incompetent, and

5. May be dismissed as a part of the organization to the extent that it is coercing their behavior against their better judgment.

In addition, line management could optimize its return on the investment of the kind of consulting assistance discussed in this report if it would change its policy from asking for such assistance only when trouble is imminent or has already erupted to a more preventative philosophy of conducting their organizational diagnoses when the pressure "to put out a fire" is not at its peak. Under pressure of resolving a "hot issue," individuals tend to become more anxious, feel greater tension, see fewer alternatives, manifest less patience, become less effective at problem solving. Their organizational defensiveness becomes more pronounced, and they demand more urgent solutions. Under these conditions it is difficult indeed to solve effectively important long-range organizational issues. One can imagine the difficulty if these issues are rooted in human relations, human actions, and human effectiveness. Under these conditions, the consultants, who would be the first to admit the infancy of their profession, cannot be expected to do the effective job the management desires.

At this point some readers have asked, why is it dysfunctional for the consultant to accept temporarily the values of the client system? For example, is it not advisable for a consultant to suppress his feelings if he believes that the client is "not ready" to explore his interpersonal relationships. Why should not the consultant continue providing help to achieve the tasks with the hope that he will return to the interpersonal relationships later on? There are several reasons that might be worth exploring.

1. The two cases suggest that it is difficult for the consultants to help the clients to behave more openly if the consultants do not do so. The more the consultant is willing not to be open and to level, the more reason he gives the client to continue to lack genuineness. Every human interaction between client and consultant that is not authentic helps to build a norm of non-authenticness. If most of the clients' interactions initially are non-authentic, then the norm of the non-authenticness (which already exists in the organization) becomes embedded in the client-consultant relationship. As these norms are reinforced it will tend to be difficult for the consultant to switch values and it will place the client in a strong conflict situation.

2. There are limits to the consultant's openness. If he believes that the members of the client system are psychologically too disturbed to deal with interpersonal relationship (and if some of the organization's problems are related to these interpersonal relationships) then the consultant may find it appropriate to recommend that the executives consider some form of therapy. If the client, after careful explanation and exploration, decides against therapy, the consultant may wish seriously to consider leaving. Otherwise, these interpersonal relationships will eventually embroil him, the executives, and others in the organization in great difficulties which he will be unable to cope with since the client has said they were "off limits." If, however, the consultant believes that the client is not that defensive and that he can accept help in this area, even though at first it may be painful to the client, he should strive to provide help.

Some ask if the consultant does not run the risk of terminating the relationship if he upsets the client. The answer is yes he does run that risk. But, if he succumbs to this fear, then the client has control over the consultant. It is this fear of breaking off the relationship which probably makes the subordinates suppress their feelings. If the consultant can communicate that he does not fear terminating the relationship, then he helps the client to face up to his impact and responsibilities.

I do not, therefore, mean to imply that openness is an all-or-nothing phenomenon. Needless to say, the consultant will have to be cautious in his feedback until he ascertains the degree of receptivity of the client. I am suggesting, however, that, in an organization, the consultant may not have available to him as much time as he would wish to make a proper diagnosis, nor as much freedom to postpone being open. For example, in an individual therapeutic session, the therapist may be able to judge his openness primarily by the patient's response. In an organization, however, it is not so easy. If the key executive, for example, was more defensive and less aware than the subordinates then the consultant's "patient waiting" for the opportune moment may be perceived by the subordinates as the executive controlling the consultant. The reader may recall that this is what occurred in Case A during the first feedback session.

In several instances where I have sensed that the defensiveness of the key executive is significantly greater than the others, I have found it helpful to work with him personally before the relationship expands to the remainder of the organization. Under these conditions, I was able to move more slowly without developing the problems discussed above.

The defensiveness of the clients, however, is not the only relevant factor. The consultant's defensiveness is equally crucial. If he tends to be easily threatened by the hostility that understandably would flow from the confrontation of the client with his feelings, then he will not tend to see the appropriate moment for intervention, nor will he intervene in a way to optimize the possibilities for learning. He should strive to utilize his own values when he gives feedback. His feedback should be, as much as possible, descriptive of the situation as he sees it. He should minimize making evaluations. For example, the reader may recall that the consultants felt that Mr. Brown talked too much. There are several alternatives open to them for intervention. One is for the consultants to describe to Mr. Brown the impact he is having upon the group without evaluating it as good or bad. More important, however, they could hypothesize that Mr. Brown's talkativeness was not "too much." Rather they could view it diagnostically as Mr. Brown's attempt to deal with anxiousness about what the consultants were doing to him and to the others. If they could have raised this question (e.g., "Perhaps you feel we are meddling and not very helpful") this might have released the others to support that part of Mr. Brown's position which most of them felt was valid. The group support might have influenced Mr. Brown to

reduce the intensity of his need to fight the consultants.

In short, the appropriate time for the consultant to focus on interpersonal issues is when they become a problem. More specifically, the consultant should focus on interpersonal issues when he believes 1) that these are operating to block the client from achieving his stated objectives and 2) that the client, by not being genuine is beginning to prevent the consultant from providing the skills and assistance for which he was hired.

It should be evident by now that there are many factors operating on the consultant, influencing him away from being effective. This leads to the final recommendation. Client systems may have to recognize that they have certain responsibilities which they must fulfill if the consultant is to optimize his—and therefore eventually help the client's—genuineness. A consultant is first a human being. Although he has much knowledge about human behavior he too can be influenced by pressures, conflicts, frustrations, and non-authenticity in an organization. This suggests that the clients should strive to minimize these, or at least to encourage the consultant continually to raise the questions even though in doing so the clients should strive to minimize those situations where they are knowingly being non-authentic with the consultant.

Typically many consultants hide these responsibilities from the clients. Indeed, some even prevent them from coming to the client's awareness. As long as the client (unknowingly or knowingly) turns over his responsibility to the consultant, then a strong dependency relationship is established between the client and the consultant. In my own experience, many consultants prefer the dependency relationship not only for the increased "billing time." Less discussed, and perhaps equally important, is the consultant's deep anx-iety to face himself and to see what he is *really* doing to the client system. Perhaps, the best sign of the strength in these consultants is their willingness to face themselves and their practice and to learn from this experience.

8.6 THE CONSEQUENCE OF SURVEY FEEDBACK: THEORY AND EVALUATION

Matthew B. Miles
Harvey A. Hornstein
Daniel M. Callahan
Paul H. Calder
R. Steven Schiavo

The Project on Organizational Development in School Systems, based at Teachers College, Columbia University, grew out of two lines of work: the study of educational innovation processes (Miles, 1964), and applied organizational change in industrial settings (Bennis, 1963; Leavitt, 1965; Shepard, 1965). Work in educational innovation suggested that innovativeness should be conceived of as an organization property, rather than a personality characteristic of heroic "innovators." For example, school superintendents who succeeded to their jobs from outside the system are far more innovative than those appointed from within (Carlson, 1961). Personality explanations for this finding are possible, but it seems far more likely that the out-

M. B. Miles, P. H. Calder, H. A. Hornstein, D. M. Callahan, and R. Steven Schiavo, "Data Feedback and Organizational Change in a School System," a paper read at the American Sociological Association meetings, 1966. Abridged and used by permission.

sider is (a) more fully legitimated by the Board as a change agent; (b) less subject to internal sanctions applied if he deviates from collegial norms held by the teacher group. Some very thorough recent work by Reynolds (1965) shows a similar pattern.

If organization properties condition innovation rates, then two questions arise: (a) what are the crucial properties? (b) how can they be changed? The answer is of interest both scientifically (following the Lewinian notion that understanding of a system appears most rapidly when efforts are made to change it) and melioristically, given the current climate of popular and professional interest in school improvement. Much recent work in the industrial organizational improvement area has stressed technologies for planned change designed to increase the accuracy of internal communication, increase upward influence of subordinates ("power equalization"), aid the problem-solving adequacy of administrative "teams," and the like. This work has also involved the changing of organizational culture (i.e., the normative structure) toward more openness, trust, and collaborativeness.

Such work implies a conception of organizations—and their optimal functioning. We have conceived of the school system as existing in an immediate environment from which it receives various *inputs* (money, personnel, etc.) and to which it releases *outputs* (primarily children's academic learning and socialization). Internally, the system consists of four basic components: (1) *goal perceptions*, to which are connected a series of (2) *role specifications and performances* (workflow, communication, decision-making informal relationships, etc.). In order that role performance effectively contribute to desired outputs, problems of co-ordination and control (as Bidwell, 1965, has pointed out) become central. Regulation of role performance, we believe, occurs primarily through systems of (3) *reward and sanction*, and via (4) *norms* controlling the style with which interactions take place (for example, open, innovative, trusting styles as vs. closed, traditional, suspicious ones).

At a meta-level above these components of organization, we conceived of ten second-order properties, seen as "system health characteristics." A healthy organization, we felt, would not only survive, but continue to cope adequately over time, while continuously developing and extending its surviving and coping abilities.

These dimensions of "organization health"[1] can be divided [following

[1] See Miles (1965a) for more detailed discussion.

Argyris (1964), Bennis (1966) and Parsons (1955)] into three broad areas: those concerned with task accomplishment, those concerned with internal integration, and those involving mutual adaptation of the organization and its environment.

Survey Feedback

Survey feedback is a process in which outside staff and members of the organization collaboratively gather, analyze and interpret data that deal with various aspects of the organization's functioning and its members' work lives, and using the data as a base, begin to correctively alter the organizational structure and the members' work relationships.

From the beginning, the client system is usually involved in data collection activities; members are often asked explicitly to develop questions for the survey, and to plan with the outside staff for data collection (Neff, 1965). In addition, there may be individual interviews of a sample of clients to collect data upon which the final questionnaires and interviews will be based. These data collection instruments may deal with such issues as employee satisfaction, concern of individuals and role groups about particular problems, perceived influence of self and/or superior in decision-making, and perceptions of norms and goals.

After analyzing the data and summarizing them in a way that is clear and useful to the particular audience, they are fed back to the organization. Both Mann (1961) and Neff (1965) suggest that feedback is most effective when carried out through "work families"; that is, through groups which report to a common superior, with jobs related in some meaningful fashion. Decisions about the composition of these groups are made collaboratively with members of the client system.

Often, though not always, the data are shown first to the "head" of the family group, at which point his presentation of the data to the rest of the group may be discussed or rehearsed. Then the data are presented to the rest of the group, who are, in fact, "heads" of other family groups. Subsequently, they will examine the data with their groups. Thus, the survey feedback takes place through an interlocking set of conferences. Typically, outside staff members are present at each of the conferences.

Ordinarily, examination of the data leads to action planning in response to problems made salient by the data. Consequently, these feedback conferences provide clients the opportunity to engage in problem-solving activities in the presence of outside staff members, who attempt to use their training skills to help members of the groups improve their work relationship.

Survey Feedback: A Rationale

Survey feedback has three operationally verifiable components (see Fig. 1): First, *data* are presented; second, *meetings* of various family groups occur; third, in the course of these meetings, staff and eventually clients begin to *analyze the process* of their interaction. Some of these analyses refer to "here and now" interactions occurring just as the data are discussed and analyzed; others are more historically-oriented, involving analysis of events and processes occurring during the immediate past in the organization.

DATA. As we suggested earlier, in survey feedback the client system examines data about itself. Psychotherapy and the laboratory method of human relations training (Schein & Bennis, 1965) are analogous in this respect. But they differ from survey feedback in two ways. First, in psychotherapy and human relations training the process of feeding back *subjective* data is mediated by the therapist and/or other group members, respectively. In survey feedback, however, the process is mediated by *objective* data which group members have helped to collect, analyze, and interpret. Second, in therapy and training the analysis of data occurs mostly at the intrapersonal, interpersonal or group level; survey feedback usually focuses more centrally on the role, inter-group and organizational levels.

Presenting the data may have any combination of the following three effects. The data may *corroborate* the client's feelings ("Yes, that is just how things are."). Or, the data may have a *disconfirming* effect if they contradict beliefs ("I never would have expected that people could see things that way."). In addition, the data have *inquiry-encouraging* effects; clients begin to wonder *why* people responded as they did, what the underlying causes were, and how they might be altered. Examination of the data usually also leads to discussion of related problems not directly dealt with by the data.

Two or more people or role groups may, of course, have simultaneous and conflicting reactions to the same set of data. These reactions are in themselves useful for interpreting the data; making such reaction differences salient is part of the staff's process analysis task.

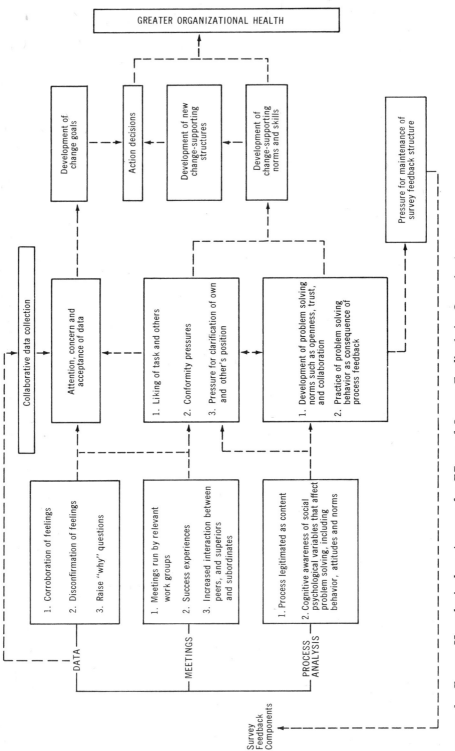

FIGURE 1. Factors Hypothesized to Account for Effects of Survey Feedback in Organizations

To the extent that these three effects occur, the data become increasingly meaningful for the clients. They see the data as reflecting their work-day needs and concerns, and not as abstract, irrelevant acts of statistics. Hence, attention to, concern with, and acceptance of data increases.

Their involvement with the data is intensified still further because of earlier participation in data collection activities, which enabled them to influence decisions concerning the kinds of data to be collected. Consequently, the data which are finally collected are as much theirs as they are the staff's.

One further note regarding acceptance of the data: Neff (1965) suggests that the meaningfulness of the data may be increased if one produces work-efficiency or other basic output data from the various subunits. When such data are available, feelings about what conditions lead to success and failure can be checked against these objective criteria.

The point we have been making is that the data corroborate or disconfirm feelings and raise "why" questions. These effects tend to encourage acceptance of the data. This is more likely to be true when the client group has collaborated in data collection. This acceptance, however, is also affected by events that occur during the course of survey feedback meetings. And it is to this second component of survey feedback meetings, that we now turn.

MEETINGS. We assume that insofar as meetings result in success experiences with work on problems, the data and the meetings themselves will be increasingly attractive to the participants. Conversely, if the meetings lead to failure experiences and frustration, we can expect the data and the meetings to be less attractive to the participants.

We further assume that regardless of how much work is actually accomplished at these meetings, the group members are more likely to evaluate their work positively when they feel that they are responsible for the work done at the meeting. Survey feedback insures the group's responsibility for work output by having these meetings organized around the existing work structures, and by having each family group conduct its own meeting. Thus, the client group becomes its own change agent. Group members have responsibility for interpreting the data; they have responsibility for conducting and scheduling meetings, and, they have responsibility for making and implementing action decisions.

All this requires increasing interaction within family-work groups composed of peers as well as superiors and subordinates. This increased interaction, which is probably fundamental to the success of survey feedback, has three effects which are of interest here: increased liking among the parties who interact; increased pressure for clarifying one's position on relevant issues; and increased pressure for conformity to group norms.

The increased liking for others, we believe, stems basically from the increased interaction in a positively-valued setting. (Cf. Riecken & Homans, 1954.) The positive sentiments are probably also a consequence of the novelty of the situation, of the opportunity to work on lingering problems, and of the success that one experiences in working on these problems.

As the data are presented and work

on problems begins, staff interventions as well as the group's own efforts make the need for individual reactions to data increasingly apparent. That is, as problem-solving efforts begin, if the group has developed a data-using, process-analytic orientation, they will feel hampered to the extent that members of the work group are seen as withholding their feelings. In addition, the increased visibility of *all* members of the "family group" will increase pressures to clarify one's own position.

Finally, as individual views on issues become clearer, it becomes increasingly difficult to hold a minority position. When this heightened visibility is combined with the pressures toward conformity which ordinarily accompany the formation of norms, uniformity in viewpoints increased.

Such uniformity is useful in some respects (e.g., when it encourages a common view of the urgency of a problem, the nature of the immediate goal in front of the group, and so on). However, it can also tend to impoverish solution-generation and eliminate creative conflict. The major corrective to such consequences of conformity pressure lies in efforts to help the group become steadily and reflexively aware of their existing norms, and to alter them when they prove barriers to productive work. Such efforts are part of the third component of survey feedback: process analysis.

PROCESS ANALYSIS. As groups work, they develop implicit and explicit normative notions of right and wrong, as well as characteristic ways of goal-setting, problem-solving, and decision-making. These social-psychological vari-ables affect the group's work; but, all too often, groups focus on the content of their regular tasks, and do not explicitly or publicly attend to these aspects of their life together. As a result, process problems which arise are frequently unresolved, and problem-solving on crucial issues is adversely affected.

In the beginning, staff members are the primary source for process analysis. They make comments on such things as interpersonal interactions, norms, and problem-solving procedures. Attention to these phenomena by staff (who are perceived as externally-based authorities) legitimates this area of work. Consequently, other members of the group begin to think reflexively, and to comment explicitly on the group's process and the behavior of others, from time to time.

As the group's process is focussed upon and diagnosed, we suggest that two things occur: First, members of the group inhibit old, less useful, behaviors and attempt to practice new behaviors in response to the feedback they are receiving about their current behavior. The second consequence is that the group develops norms (including the second-order process-analytic norm itself) which facilitate productive work by enabling direct expression of feeling, and self-corrective behavior when group problem-solving is effective.[2]

---

[2] Process analysis is, of course, the central feature of the human relations training group or T-group (Bradford, Benne, & Gibb, 1964); more and more it has also been applied to intact "work family groups," with or without survey data available (Clark, 1966).

Two sets of norms are most critical. One set, which is in operation as soon as the group accepts process feedback as legitimate, facilitates the *communication of information*. These can be thought of as norms centering around openness and trust. The implicit assumption is that open, two-way channels of communication facilitate the amount and accuracy of information which, in turn, improves problem-solving. The second set of norms, those which reward *collaborative activity*, affects not only communication (particularly by opening two-way channels) but also determination of goals, group cohesiveness, and group pressures for conformity.

Up to this point, we have suggested that the three primary components of survey feedback, (namely, data, meetings, and process-analysis), lead to attention to and acceptance of the data, liking of the family group and its activities, clarification of own and other's position, practice of new behaviors, and development of norms which support open, collaborative problem-solving. To the extent that these effects do occur, we can expect group members to see their work in the survey feedback meetings as both pleasant and productive. Hence, there will be some pressure for the maintenance of survey feedback as an organizational structure.

So far, effects have been limited to the "family" group immediately at hand. If these effects are strong, we hypothesize that developmental, organization-changing effects will follow. Working with the data, for example, leads groups to develop *new change goals* whenever they perceive problems

to exist. These change goals, in combination with the newly-developed *change-supporting norms and problem-solving skills* will lead to increasingly effective work on problems. This work may take the form of *action decisions* about solutions to resolve the problems, or the design of new, change-oriented, problem-solving *structures*. Thus, survey feedback not only tends to perpetuate itself as a method of planned organizational change, but also gives birth to other adaptive structural changes as well.

The norms and skills which are developed, the organization's ability to more effectively solve its problems, and its ability to develop new change-supportive structures where necessary can all be seen as connected to the notions of organizational health presented earlier.

Research on Survey Feedback

The remainder of this article describes the manner in which a particular survey feedback program was studied. The detailed events of the program have been described elsewhere (Miles et al, 1966; McElvaney, 1966); our intent here is to indicate the methodological approach used.

A survey feedback program was developed for a small school system. Summarized data displays were fed back first to the top administrative group which engaged in diagnosis and problem-solving. Then each building principal repeated this process with his faculty in a series of meetings. Following this, cross-building "task forces" were set up to work on problems noted in the feedback sessions; their proposals were considered for action by the administrative group.

FIT BETWEEN THEORY AND EVENTS

The congruence between the events in our survey feedback program and the theoretical components of survey feedback indicates roughly the extent to which we were able to meet the initial conditions that should result in organizational improvement.

To summarize briefly (see Fig. 1): The actual events in our survey feedback program were generally in accord with the major components of the survey feedback process. The client system was involved with our staff prior to the data collection. The data themselves were fed back at a work family session which was led by the head of that family group. At this session some of our staff members acted as consultants to guide interpretation of the data and to initiate process analysis.

Observer records of the feedback session indicate that the responses of the system members to the data were indeed those of corroboration and disconfirmation of feelings. In addition, the group members began to question why the respondents answered as they did. The observer records also show that from discussion of these data there evolved vigorous interaction, responsibility-taking by the group, problem-solving efforts, and action plans—all accompanied by increased process analysis among the participants. Rating scales collected during the sessions suggested that success experiences had occurred: satisfaction with the group's decisions increased significantly from the first to the last day (p < .05), and

optimism regarding the effects of the meeting changed as predicted, though not significantly. Own rated activity (interaction) also increased but not to a statistically significant degree. It should be pointed out that the sheer *amount* of interaction (as a group) was probably equal to that occurring in six months' work on the job.

Moving further to the right in Fig. 1, it did seem clear that attention to and concern with the data were high—and that the administrative group's decision to discuss the data with the teachers indicated the existence of pressure for the maintenance of the survey feedback structure.[3]

We do not have direct data on liking during the feedback sessions (though observers noted increased warmth and less interpersonal distance), nor on pressures for position clarification and conformity. (Ratings of group acceptance of own ideas increased, but nonsignificantly.) It does seem that norms supporting open, collaborative problem-solving did develop during the meetings: participant ratings of own openness, and of how well the group worked together both increased significantly (p < .05).

Looking at system change aspects of Fig. 1 (far right on the chart), change goals were being formulated (through the replies to the teacher "task force" committees), but few action decisions were made. Two new structures were developed: the task force committees; and the addition of a catalytic change-agent (the school psychologist who had

[3] The administrative group also strongly hoped to have another feedback session a year after the first one, but sufficient funds for this were not available.

helped to initiate the program) to meetings of the administrative group.

In general, then, many of the initial events and subsequent processes proposed as occurring in survey feedback designs did take place, though not decisively in some cases. And in other cases we had no direct measures.

There are some deviations from the model. Action decisions flowing from the feedback were absent, and new change-supporting structures few. Earlier, it was also true that the client system was minimally involved in data planning, since the instruments (except for a tailor-made one) had originally been developed for use in another system. Also, not all of the data were fed back to the client, as will be explained in the following section on data collection.

DATA COLLECTION

Quantitative data were collected at three different points in time prior to the data feedback program. The fourth, and final, data collection took place approximately 9 months following the first feedback of data (which were drawn from the third data collection).

(See Table 1 for an overview of the research design)

As indicated in Table 1, the sample size at both the 0_1 and 0_2 test periods was 33%. This included a random sampling of teachers and associated roles, and all central office administrators and principals. At test periods 0_3 and 0_4 all (100%) of the school system staff were sent instruments.

The purposes of this multiple-time series design have been explained fully elsewhere. (See Campbell & Stanley, 1963, and Benedict et al., 1966.) First, the design allowed us to account for seasonal and maturational effects—widely assumed to occur in school systems—by making comparisons of the 0_1, 0_2, and 0_3 data. Another problem in valid assessment occurs because testing itself might focus the individual's attention on the critical variables, and such increased sensitivity might result in change. This kind of change must be distinguished from the change which might result from the introduction of the independent variable—the data feedback program. The comparison of the new sample members to the old sample members at 0_3 allowed us to

TABLE 1   Overview of the Research Design

Season	Year	Event	Sample Size
Early Fall	1964	0_1	33%[a]
Midwinter	1964–5	0_2	33%[a]
Late Spring	1965	0_3	100%
June	1965	X[b]	
Midwinter	1965–6	0_4	100%

[a] This included a random sample of teachers, and all administrators and principals.

[b] The data feedback meetings took place at this time. All central office administrators and principals participated; a selection of the 0_3 data was used.

ascertain if test-sensitization effects had taken place. Finally, the effects of the data feedback program itself were established by comparing O_2 to O_4. Since two of the instruments were not given at O_2, some O_3 to O_4 comparisons were also made in order to test hypotheses. The former comparisons were preferred as tests of hypotheses, since the O_2 and O_4 data were collected at the same time of year. The latter, O_3 to O_4, were less preferred because they may have been influenced by seasonal fluctuations.

One further aspect of our design is important. To the best of our knowledge, in previous studies involving data feedback, *all* data collected have been fed back. Under these circumstances the measurement of change is contaminated, because considerable attention has in fact been focused on these data during the meetings. Change could either be explained as a true attitude or behavior change resulting from the introduction of the independent variable, or as a test sensitization response. To aid in determining which of these occurred, we followed two strategies: (1) wherever possible, withholding some items from an instrument measuring a particular variable, while feeding back others; (2) wherever possible, having alternate measures of the same variable, using a different measurement mode, and not feeding these back. These procedures could, we hoped, help us demonstrate that change on these two types of non-fed-back items could be assigned with more confidence to the effects of the data feedback program—as reviewed in the rationale above—and not simply to "test-wiseness" as a result of heavy exposure to the instruments.

FINDINGS

In brief, examination of a portion of the quantitative data (focusing on power equalization, communication, and norms) did not show more than chance fluctuation in the 36 indicators studied for the administrative group, and the 43 examined for teachers. There is some indication that the measures used were somewhat insensitive to change: a study of ratings at a single point in time showed that those principals who were highly satisfied with the feedback program did apparently induce similar satisfaction in their teachers, who also had higher morale in general.

Interviews with the administrators provided clear evidence that there was an improvement in communication, and interpersonal relationships, at least among the 11 top administrators. The interviews indicate that power equalization did not take place within the administrative group; if anything, the superintendent was exerting more decisive leadership, but without a corresponding increase in influence from his subordinates. An attempt had been made to include teachers in decision-making to a greater extent than previously but at the end of the school year, the final outcome of this attempt was still uncertain, since no final active decisions had been made on the "task force" reports.

CONCLUDING COMMENTS

Without trying to speculate on the relative sensitivity of interviews and quantitative questionnaires, the most sanguine conclusion would be that the survey feedback program did begin a process of organizational change at the top of the school system, which then showed some regression following the initial active involvement of lower-echelon people, with the net effect that no durable changes were found. The relative absence of action decisions by the time of the post-measurement, and of a durable change-supporting structure for continuing the work are also undoubtedly important.

The most pessimistic conclusion would be that the survey feedback program represented a momentary perturbation in the functioning of a stable system, and that no fundamental shifts in information flow, power handling or normative structure had occurred.

The morals to be drawn from this account by researcher and change agents alike will undoubtedly vary according to their predilections.[4] Those impressed with the equilibrium-seeking aspects of social systems can find confirmation in this account; those preoccupied with change and development can, if they wish, be stimulated to further speculation and investigation. For ourselves (since disconfirmation usually leads to heightened attention and increased exploratory behavior), we intend to keep examining deliberate change efforts of this sort in school systems, and invite the active entry of others into this area of inquiry.

[4] For further comment on the activities of this project, as seen from the perspective of the school psychologist who served as the local catalyst of the secondary phase, see McElvaney (1966).

REFERENCES

1. Argyris, C. *Integrating the individual and the organization.* New York: John Wiley & Sons, Inc., 1964.
2. Benedict, B. A., Calder, P. M., Callahan, D. M., Hornstein, H. A., and Miles, M. B. The clinical-experimental approach to assessing organizational change efforts. New York: Bureau of Publications, Teachers College, Columbia University. Horace Mann-Lincoln Institute of School Experimentation, 1966. Mimeographed.
3. Bennis, W. G. A new role for the behavioral sciences: effecting organizational change. *Admin. Sci. Quart.,* 1963, *8* (2), 125–165.
4. Bennis, W. G. *Changing organizations.* New York: McGraw-Hill, Inc., 1966.
5. Bidwell, C. E. The school as a formal organization. In J. G. March (Ed.) *Handbook of organizations.* Skokie, Illinois: Rand McNally & Company, 1965. Pp. 972–1022.
6. Bradford, L. P., Benne, K. D., and Gibb, J. R. *T-Group theory and laboratory method.* New York: John Wiley & Sons, Inc., 1964.
7. Campbell, D. T., and Stanley, J. Experimental and quasi-experimental designs for research on teaching. In N. L. Gage (Ed.) *Handbook of research on teaching.* Skokie, Illinois: Rand McNally & Company, 1963. Pp. 171–246.
8. Carlson, R. O. *Executive succession and organizational change.* Chicago: Midwest Admission Center, University of Chicago, 1961.
9. Clark, J. V. Task group therapy. Los Angeles: Institute of Industrial Relations, University of California, 1966. Mimeographed.
10. Leavitt, H. A. Applied organizational change in industry: structural, technological,

and humanistic approaches. In March, M. G. *Handbook of organizations*. Skokie, Illinois: Rand McNally & Company, 1965. Pp. 1144–1170.

11. Mann, F. C. Studying and creating change. In W. G. Bennis, K. D. Benne, and R. Chin. *The planning of change*. New York: Holt, Rinehart and Winston, Inc., 1961. Pp. 605–615.

12. McElvaney, C. T. The school psychologist's role in school improvement. Paper read at Amer. Psychol. Assn. meetings, 1966.

13. Miles, M. B. (Ed.) *Innovation in education*. New York: Bureau of Publications, Teachers College, Columbia University, 1954.

14. Miles, M. B. Planned change and organizational health. In R. O. Carlson *et al.*, *Change processes in the public schools*. Eugene, Oregon: Center for the Advanced Study of Educational Administration, 1965 (a). Pp. 11–34.

15. Miles, M. B., Calder, P. H., Hornstein, H. A., Callahan, D. M., and Schiavo, R. Steven. Data feedback and organizational change in a school system. Paper read at Amer. Sociol. Assn. meetings, 1966.

16. Neff, F. W. Survey research: a tool for problem diagnosis and improvement in organizations. In A. W. Gouldner & S. M. Miller (Eds.) *Applied sociology*. Pp. 23–38, 1966.

17. Parsons, T. A sociological approach to the theory of organizations. *Admin. Sci. Quart.*, 1955, *1*, 63–85 & 225–239.

18. Reynolds, J. Innovation related to administrative tenure succession and orientation. Ph.D. Dissertation. Washington University, Graduate Institute of Education, St. Louis, Mo. August 1965.

19. Riecken, H. W., and Homans, G. Psychological aspects of social structure. In G. Lindzey (Ed.) *Handbook of social psychology*, Vol. II. Reading, Mass.: Addison-Wesley Publishing Company, Inc., 1954. Pp. 768–832.

20. Schein, E. H., and Bennis, W. G. *Personal and organizational change through group methods: the laboratory approach*. New York: John Wiley & Sons, Inc., 1965.

21. Shepard, H. A. Changing interpersonal and intergroup relationships in organizations. In *Handbook of organizations*. Skokie, Illinois: Rand McNally & Company, 1965. Pp. 1115–1143.

8.7 THE DIAGNOSIS OF ORGANIZATIONAL PROBLEMS[1]

Jay W. Lorsch
Paul Lawrence

The Need for Diagnostic Models

In this paper we would like to discuss an approach to organizational change, which puts considerable weight on the diagnosis of organizational problems prior to the change effort. As a first step in this discussion, it is necessary to examine the need for diagnosis of organizational problems and some of the current thinking about diagnosis.

Jay W. Lorsch and Paul Lawrence, "The Diagnosis of Organizational Problems." Used by permission.

There is no doubt that change agents have various analytic models of organizations and of how to alter behavior in them. Their analytic schemes are both implicit and explicit, but it seems that there has been an increasing attempt to make them more explicit and particularly to gain an increased understanding of the change process. An interesting example of this trend is the recent *Harvard Business Review* article by Blake and Mouton, Barnes and Greiner.[2] The authors describe an attempt to systematically investigate and evaluate one of the "Managerial Grid" organizational development programs. While it is possible to be critical or skeptical on specific grounds, about this and other attempts to describe and understand organizational change, the fact remains that these attempts are being made with the best methods currently available and the eventual payout should be improved understanding of the dynamics of the change process.[3] These studies are mentioned, not as a prelude to discussing their particular strengths and weaknesses, but rather to indicate that the focus of much of the current work in the area of organizational change is toward an understanding of the change process itself. Much less attention is being devoted to the development of analytic models which could be useful in diagnosing organizational problems prior to the change effort.

This is not to suggest that change agents do not have some implicit analytic model in mind. Nor are we suggesting that they do not undertake a diagnosis, before beginning a development or a change program. In fact, as Greiner has pointed out, one characteristic of effective change efforts is the fact that some attempt, even though limited, had been made to gather data about organizational problems before the change effort was attempted.[4] Apparently, this helps to create an awareness of the need for change and often provides the motivation to begin the effort. It therefore seems to us that there is a need for some diagnosis and we now want to examine in more detail what these diagnostic steps usually entail and how the approach we have been using may differ from other attempts at diagnosis.

There are two aspects to the diagnosis of organizational problems: first the question of what data is gathered and second the manner in which the data is interpreted and presented to members of the organization. The diagnostic data gathering preceding change efforts seems to be typically carried out through interviews with a few significant managers at various levels of the organization. Less frequently, more systematic and thorough attempts have been made to gather data through the use of surveys.[5] One limitation of these diagnostic attempts as usually practiced, is, that they tend to be somewhat cursory and often tend to be conducted in spite of the fact that the action program has already been well planned in advance by the change agent. A second problem is that the change agent during the diagnostic phase is often more concerned with understanding and improving his relationship to the client organization than he is in understanding specific organizational problems. For example Seashore and Bowers indicate that the reason they decided to conduct their diagnostic survey was "to introduce a note of calmness and realism, while still advancing the intended work."[6] They decided on this diagnostic step to signal to the organization's membership what the project was all about and thus to strengthen their relationship with the client. While this is important it tends to support the view that insufficient attention is given to gathering data about organizational problems, prior to planning the change program.

Turning to the second aspect of diagnosis—the manner in which the data are presented and interpreted to members of the organization—this is generally accomplished in one of two ways. First, the raw data are discussed with top management, who are asked to make the diagnosis within their own framework; or second the change agent may present his own diagnosis without making his model for analyzing organizational behavior explicit. The problem with the first approach is that management is limited by its own framework and it tends to see each problem separately, failing at times to recognize the interrelationship between problems and what may lie behind them. The second approach has inherent in it the problems of communication in getting management to see why the change agent sees the problems the way he does. One example of this problem is cited by A. K. Rice when he describes the difficulties in getting management to understand his diagnosis and the necessity for making his conceptual scheme more explicit.[7]

A more general difficulty with either of these approaches derives from the close relationship between diagnosis and action. The action which is taken cannot be separated from the diagnosis made. Yet in many of the current change efforts, the emphasis seems to be on action and there tends to be a general action program which the change agent will apply to any organization regardless of its specific problems. For example, Blake has his well conceived action program based on the management grid which he is applying to many organizations, and Seashore and Bowers and their associates at Michigan had designed an action program for the Banner organization based on participative management prior to the diagnosis of any specific problems.[8] In thinking about these matters, we have concluded that if more weight were given to prior diagnosis before planning a change program, the action program could be better designed for the specific needs of the particular situation.

It is sometimes argued that diagnostic analysis is overdone. It is undoubtedly true that the request for "further study" can be a dodge to delay needed action in organizational problems. This is most apt to happen, however, when the diagnostic effort is, in effect, a general fishing expedition guided neither by a well developed conceptual framework or by a clear problem focus. The fact that diagnostic work is sometimes done in a weak and ineffective manner should not lead to a general short-circuiting of this step. Quality diagnostic work leads toward action and not away from it.

Recognizing the limitations of current diagnostic efforts and the relative absence of change attempts made on the basis of analytic models which were outlined to members of the organization, we have in a recent change effort placed much more weight on a careful diagnostic study and then have discussed in considerable detail both our analytic framework and the data collected.

Our general approach, then, has been to spend considerable time and effort through the use of questionnaires and a systematic interviewing program in gathering data to be analyzed in terms of a conceptual framework developed in our research efforts.[9] Having collected and analyzed this data we have then educated management to our conceptual scheme and have fed the data back to them, working through with them the meanings and the limitations of the data. The managers themselves have worked out whatever structural changes seemed required and have collaborated with us in the formulation of specific development programs to alleviate specific reorganizational problems. In the balance of this paper we will describe briefly the analytic framework we have used, some of the problems identified in this particular organization and some of the resulting change steps.

The Differentiation and Integration Model

At the outset of describing this analytic scheme, it is important to stress that it has been developed primarily for the study and understanding of intergroup or interdepartmental issues in organizations and it is in designing change programs aimed at this general class of problem that it has been useful. It is based on a set of ideas in the social sciences which go back to Herbert Spencer and probably beyond, differentiation and integration.[10] It is not either of these concepts, by themselves, but the intriguing interrelationship between them that is important. Any complex social system, which is the basic way we conceive of an organization, is made up of differentiated parts, the activities of which must be integrated into a unified effort if the organization is to cope effectively with its environment. In the case of business firms, the differentiated parts are the major departments. In the specific case of the organizations in this change effort, they consisted of the sales, production, research and development units involved in the innovation of products, which was the major external issue confronting these particular organizations. (The change program we shall describe here actually involved two unrelated product organizations and we shall treat each of these as a separate entity.)

The functional units in these organizations were each required to cope with quite distinct segments of the organization's environment—sales with the market, research with the scientific environment, etc. They each performed different tasks and in relation to these tasks the units developed distinct attributes. The conceptual scheme which we have been developing identifies four of these characteristics, the time orientation of members, the interpersonal orientation of members, and the unit's internal formal structure. As the organizational units engage in their separate tasks they become differentiated along these four dimensions. For example, our scheme hypothesizes and our findings confirm that a research laboratory has a low degree of structure (few rules, broad spans of control, few levels in the hierarchy, long time spans of reviews, and very general reviews). It has members whose primary goal orientation is toward science, whose primary time orientation is toward longer term matters and who mildly prefer a task oriented interpersonal style over a relationship oriented style. On the other hand a production unit has high structure, and personnel whose goal orientation is toward production costs and processing problems; whose time orientation is toward immediate problems; and whose interpersonal orientation is more strongly task oriented.

Basically what this way of looking at organizations suggests is that each of these units is different along these (and perhaps other dimensions) but they are differentiated from each other for good and proper reasons—because they are working on quite different tasks. For them to perform their individual tasks, they must be differentiated. The fly in the ointment, however, is the fact that these differences between units tend to be related to the problems of achieving effective integration. Our data indicate that the more different any pair of units in an organization are along these dimensions, the more problems are experienced in achieving collaboration between them. Thus two units which are quite similar in these organizations and in structure will achieve effective integration with each other while units which have quite different orientations and structures will have difficulty in achieving collaboration with each other. Differentiation is thus a two-edged sword—it is important for individual unit performance, but can be costly in achieving coordinated total performance.

While the processes of differentiation and integration seem to be basically antagonistic between pairs of units within one organization, we have found in comparing several organizations that an organization can achieve both the high differentiation required for individual unit performance and the effective integration required for effective total organizational performance. The key to the achievement of both high differentiation and integration seems to reside in the development of what we have conceptually identified as integrative devices, which function effectively. These integrative devices can be managers in linking roles, a separate departmental entity which has a coordinating function, or cross functional committees which are intended to facilitate the resolution of conflict and decision making between functional units.

In studying the processes of differentiation and integration in organizations we have identified some variables which seem to be related to the effectiveness of these integrative devices. For example integrating departments, whether they be called new products, development, marketing, etc., seem to be effective when their members have task, time, and interpersonal orientations as well as structures which are at some intermediate point between the units they are linking. If an integrative department is linking a sales and a research unit we have found that it will be most effective if its members do not have either a long-term orientation, as in research, or a short-term orientation, as in sales, but instead have a balanced time orientation. The same factor seems to hold for goals and interpersonal orientations and for structure. Similarly, we have identified some factors which seem to be related to the effectiveness of integrating committees. The most important of these seems to be the presence of norms for resolving conflict which sanction what Blake would call a 9.9 approach, that is, a problem solving confrontation of conflict rather than a win-lose or avoidance mode.[11]

This brief description of some of the factors influencing the performance of integrative devices and of the complex interrelationship between the processes of differentiation and integration should give some understanding of the conceptual framework we are using and perhaps a crude idea of the type of data we attempt to collect. It can be concluded by pointing out that our work suggests that effective organizational performance is related to the presence of both the differentiation and integration that are required by the characteristics of their immediate environment. In the particular industry in which we have been conducting our activities, the nature of the external environment dictates that high differentiation and high integration are required for effective performance. What this pattern will look like in other industries is something we have also investigated and on which we will subsequently report.

Some Problems Identified and Action Steps Taken

Having quickly laid out the concepts we have utilized in our diagnostic work, it may now be useful to add some life to them by demonstrating briefly how we have identified some specific problems in the organizations with which we have been consulting, and what action steps have been taken. The problems upon which we will focus are representative of an interrelated set of differentiation and integration issues identified in each of the two organizations, and were presented to the managers involved by comparing these two organizations with each other and with a third more effective organization in the same corporate structure which we had studied earlier.

In one of the organizations there were two research sub-units, one of which theoretically was supposed to be engaged in fundamental long-range research and the other of which was supposed to be an applied shorter range operation. The data which we collected indicated two things. First, that the research units were achieving extremely poor integration as compared to the effective organization. There were frequent conflicts between them and according to members of the organization their ability to achieve unity of effort with each other was limited. Second, we found that while these laboratories were highly differentiated in their structural and interpersonal attributes, they were quite similar in time and task orientations. In effect both laboratories seemed to be trying to perform essentially the same tasks with quite different structures and interpersonal orientations. Our interviewing also indicated to us that members of these laboratories often saw each other as competitors, rather than potential collaborators who were performing a different phase of the organization's total task.

Armed with this and similar data about other problems from questionnaires and interviews, we sat down with the teams of top managers responsible for all the functional activities related to this group of products. We first spent some time discussing our conceptual scheme and then relating these data to it. We explained that the high differentiation in interpersonal and structural attributes was related to the problems of achieving integration, but that the fact the units were occupying the same task and time space seemed to be intensifying the difficulties in achieving collaboration. In this discussion the managers recognized that two things were needed: first, a clearer differentiation of the role of the laboratories and second the development of improved integrative devices.

Management's reaction to this presentation and discussion was fairly typical of what we found in both organizations. The data supported their intuitive hunches but also clarified the factors underlying the problem. After considerable discussion about potential action steps, in which we took a minor role, the managers decided as a first step to begin a series of discussions with laboratory personnel and among themselves to clarify the tasks they wanted each unit to perform. Once these discussions have been concluded we will work with them in developing a tailored training program to sharpen the integrative process.

A problem which appeared similar on the surface can be used as an example from the second organization with which we were working. Here the two laboratory units were finding great difficulty in working with the coordinating unit. They complained that the coordinating unit was a "filter" which closed up and inhibited the flow of ideas. The data collected indicated that the coordinating unit was overly concerned with immediate customer problems rather than having the balanced outlook that effective coordinating units developed. In discussing this with the team of managers responsible for this product group, it became apparent

that the short-term customer orientation of the coordinating unit was the result of environmental pressure it felt to provide frequent and detailed service to customers. The managers in this instance also saw the data as supporting their hunches about their problems, but also saw that there was no way, given the competitive situation, to redesign the task of the coordinating unit. After considerable discussion of this issue both the managers and we saw the need for a training program which would have as its objective a greater awareness on the part of researchers and coordinators of the differences in their ways of thinking, so they would appreciate these differences and develop a greater tolerance for them and greater skill at resolving conflict caused by their different ways of thinking. On the basis of this plans were made for a training program.

As a first step in this brief training effort we fed back the same data to the participants as we had to the managers. Again, as with the managers, the data were received as being congruent with the experience of the scientists and coordinators in the session. But we had designed the training to move beyond this and to give the participants some appreciation of the way their concrete actions and behavior patterns affected persons in other departments and also to provide each group with some understanding of the task realities which were influencing the other group to have a differentiated behavior pattern. To accomplish this we divided the participants into three-way teams with representatives from each of the laboratories and the coordinating department. Each of these groups then met for four sessions. The first session was devoted to each man describing his own work activities and the factors that gave him the most satisfaction and the most dissatisfaction with his job. The second and third sessions were used for the participants to discuss the activities and behavior of other units which most facilitated and most blocked performance in their own groups. Out of these discussions the long-range researchers began to see what pressures the coordinators were operating under as they fought customer fires, and the coordinators literally blinked in disbelief as they realized that the scientists actually worked for months or years on a single project without any concrete feedback. Thus researchers became aware of why the coordinators were not able to drop everything and discuss their problems and the coordinators recognized that some of the decisions which they made in a very few minutes with little forethought could influence the work of an individual researcher for several months or years.

At this stage of the program an awareness of the differences between these groups had been created and hopefully some appreciation of the importance of these differences had developed. The fourth, and final, session was devoted to a discussion of how these differences were characteristically resolved and some of the factors underlying these modes of resolving conflicts. The fundamental researchers, for example, began to recognize that they had characteristically resolved conflict by smoothing it over. When they saw a problem they retired to their laboratories and waited. The coordinators, on the other hand, tended to be more aggressive, often forcing the more compliant researchers to alter courses.

The immediate response to this session was gratifying, since the participants recognized its relevance to their jobs and felt it had altered their perception of members of other units. While it is much too soon to make any final claims of success, a preliminary survey taken six months after the training indicates that in general the training and feedback sessions had many of the intended consequences. Members reported to an in-house behavioral scientist, who was not involved in the change program, that they are able to work more effectively together on interdepartmental teams.

One interesting exception to these generally positive results is the case of the fundamental research scientists. They reported a general worsening of relations with other units, particularly with the coordinators. The reason for this, which was developed in interviews, was that as a result of these training sessions these scientists felt that the coordinating personnel were going to take some concrete steps to improve collaboration with them. When this did not happen, apparently because of continuing time pressures with the coordinators, the researchers became further antagonized. This suggests that one danger of any such change effort is the raising of expectations which cannot be satisfied. In any case, these additional data have been fed back to the coordinating group and further efforts are being made to work through this problem.

This brief report of progress is not presented as a final evaluation of this change effort, but rather to indicate our continuing concern throughout the change effort of gathering data about the state of the organization as a guide to future change steps. It is consistent with our thesis that a change effort will be most successful if it is based on a careful diagnosis of the organization's problem.

Conclusions

We would now like to step back to look at what we have been trying to accomplish—first by using this particular conceptual scheme, and second by generally placing more emphasis on diagnosis. In doing this, it is most important to recognize that our evidence about whether we have succeeded while encouraging is still tentative and only suggestive.

First, looking at the value of this particular scheme, it enables us to focus not on just the problems of developing more effective integration, but also on the relationship between integration and differentiation, and the necessity for differentiation in achieving effective task performance. The change attempts described by Blake, Argyris and others place emphasis on the development of mutual trust, openness, and problem solving, all of which are important to facilitate organizational integration, but these change efforts may not be directed at the important problems of achieving clear differentiation so that units can work at their separate primary tasks.[12] The use of this conceptual scheme has enabled us to focus on both of these problems and to help in the development of an action program aimed at both issues.

Turning to the more general value of placing greater emphasis on diagnosis, it has permitted us to develop a more "tailored" approach to organi-

zational change and development. As the examples cited demonstrated, we have attempted to design interventions which fit the particular problems of the organization, rather than relying on a general program aimed at influencing behavior throughout the organization. Obviously this has cost less in time and money for the organization, but more important it provides strong guidance as to whether an educational or a structural intervention is more appropriate as a first step in the change process. Regardless of which of these intervention steps is taken first, it can, and in most instances probably should, be followed up with the other. If the first step is to be an educational one, the data can guide the design of a program that can present the participants with an educational experience which hopefully has some immediate relevance to problems they are encountering in their daily experience, and this provides them with more rewards for altering their existing behavior patterns. This is especially likely if the development program is followed or preceded by appropriate attention to task and structural redesign that grows out of the same diagnosis.

The emphasis on prior diagnosis also presents managers with some hard data which confirms or challenges their hunches. Based on these interpreted data, they can take charge of their own programs of actions. We have so far avoided making detailed recommendations to the management about either structural changes or educational change programs. Instead we have made ourselves available as resource people as the management group discussed the problem. Our limited experience seems to suggest that this enabled managers to engage these problems, become involved with them and to attempt to solve them. This experience is supported by Floyd Mann's view that, "Change processes organized around objective new social facts about one's own organizational situation have more force for change than those organized around general principles about human behavior."[13]

In this particular case we have been fortunate that we had made a comparative diagnosis of three separate organizational elements, one of which was outstanding in performance. The presence of this example provided the managers with a concrete comparison, which they could examine in relation to our conceptual scheme and our data. It presented a model of the desirable which was not an abstraction, but a real going concern. Our experience coupled with Dunnington's report of a similar experience in changing behavior in several IBM plants suggests that this is an important leverage point to be utilized whenever possible.[14] But the use of these real organizational models is not possible unless a thorough diagnostic study has been conducted.

By emphasizing diagnosis and data feedback, we have also left the management group with a new kit of tools which they can continue to apply to similar problems in the future. Too often, the change agent takes his conceptual scheme with him when he leaves and the organization must seek help for each new set of problems. It is our hope that by making our conceptual scheme explicit and by helping the managers to work with it, that we have given them a new cognitive map to think about future organizational issues.

REFERENCES

1. This paper is taken from a talk given before the Second Annual Conference of the Eastern Academy of Management, May 8, 1965.
2. Blake, R., Mouton, J., Barnes, L., and Greiner, L., "Breakthrough in Organization Development," *Harvard Business Review*, November-December, 1964.
3. For example, Seashore, S., and Bowers, D., *Changing the Structure and Functioning of an Organization: Report of a Field Experiment*, Ann Arbor; monograph # 33, Survey Research Center, Institute for Social Research, 1963.
4. Greiner, L., *Organization Change and Development*, unpublished doctoral thesis, Harvard Business School.
5. Seashore and Bowers, *op. cit.*
6. *Ibid.*
7. Rice, A., *Productivity and Social Organization*, London: Tavistock Publications, Ltd., 1958.
8. Seashore and Bowers, *op. cit.*
9. For a detailed explanation of this conceptual scheme see Lawrence, Paul, and Lorsch, Jay, "Differentiation and Integration in Complex Organizations," *Administrative Science Quarterly*, in press.
10. Spencer, H., *Autobiography*, New York, 1904, II, 56.

11. Blake, R., and Mouton, J., *The Managerial Grid*, Houston, Tex., The Gulf Publishing Company, 1964.

12. Blake, Mouton, Barnes, and Greiner, *op. cit.* and Argyris, C., *Integrating the Individual and the Organization*, New York: John Wiley & Sons, Inc., 1964.

13. Mann, F., "Studying and Creating Change" in *The Planning of Change*, Bennis, W., Benne, K., and Chin, R., editors, New York: Holt, Rinehart and Winston, Inc., 1962.

14. Dunnington, R. in a talk before MBA students at the Harvard Business School.

8.8   THE CONFRONTATION MEETING

Richard Beckhard

One of the continuing problems facing the top management team of any organization in times of stress or major change is how to assess accurately the state of the organization's health. How are people reacting to the change? How committed are subordinate managers to the new conditions? Where are the most pressing organization problems?

In the period following a major change—such as that brought about by a change in leadership or organization structure, a merger, or the introduction of a new technology—there tends to be much confusion and an expenditure of dysfunctional energy that negatively affects both productivity and morale.

At such times, the top management group usually spends many hours together working on the business problems and finding ways of coping with the new conditions. Frequently, the process of working together under this pressure also has the effect of making the top team more cohesive.

Concurrently, these same managers

Richard Beckhard, "The Confrontation Meeting," *Harvard Business Review* XLV, No. 2 (1967), 149–153. Abridged and used by permission.

tend to spend less and less time with their subordinates and with the rest of the organization. Communications decrease between the top and middle levels of management. People at the lower levels often complain that they are less in touch with what is going on than they were before the change. They feel left out. They report having less influence than before, being more unsure of their own decision-making authority, and feeling less sense of ownership in the organization. As a result of this, they tend to make fewer decisions, take fewer risks, and wait until the "smoke clears."

When this unrest comes to the attention of top management, the response is usually to take some action such as—

. . . having each member of the top team hold team meetings with his subordinates to communicate the state of affairs, and following this procedure down through the organization;

. . . holding some general communication improvement meetings;

. . . conducting an attitude survey to determine priority problems.

Any of these actions will probably be helpful, but each requires a considerable investment of time which is competitive with the time needed to work on the change problem itself.

Action Plans

Recently I have experimented with an activity that allows a total management group, drawn from all levels of the organization, to take a quick reading on its own health, and—*within a matter of hours*—to set action plans for improving it. I call this a "confrontation meeting."

The activity is based on my previous experience with an action-oriented method of planned change in which information on problems and attitudes is collected and fed back to those who produced it, and steps are taken to start action plans for improvement of the condition.

Sometimes, following situations of organizational stress, the elapsed time in moving from identification of the problem to collaborative action planning must be extremely brief. The confrontation meeting can be carried out in 4-1/2 to 5 hours' working time, and it is designed to include the entire management of a large system in a joint action-planning program.

I have found this approach to be particularly practical in organization situations where there are large numbers in the management group and/or where it is difficult to take the entire group off the job for any length of time. The activity has been conducted several times with a one evening and one morning session—taking only 2-1/2 hours out of a regular working day.

The confrontation meeting discussed in this article has been used in a number of different organization situations.

Experience shows that it is appropriate where:

There is a need for the total management group to examine its own workings.

Very limited time is available for the activity.

Top management wishes to improve the conditions quickly.

There is enough cohesion in the top team to ensure follow-up.

There is real commitment to resolving the issues on the part of top management.

The organization is experiencing, or has recently experienced, some major change.

In order to show how this technique can speed the process of getting the information and acting on it, let us first look at three actual company situations where this approach has been successfully applied. Then we will examine both the positive results and the possible problems that could occur through the use and misuse of this technique. Finally, after a brief summary there are appendixes for the reader interested in a more elaborate description of the phasing and scheduling of such a meeting.

Case Example A

The initial application of the confrontation meeting technique occurred in 1965 in a large food products company. Into this long-time family-owned and closely controlled company, there was introduced for the first time a non-family professional general manager. He had been promoted from the ranks of the group that had previously reported to the family-member general manager.

This change in the "management culture," which had been carefully and thoroughly prepared by the family executives, was carried out with a minimum number of problems. The new general manager and his operating heads spent may hours together and developed a quite open problem-solving climate and an effective, cohesive team. Day-to-day operations were left pretty much in the hands of their immediate subordinates, while the top group focused on planning.

A few months after the change, however, the general manager began getting some information that indicated all was not well further down in the organization. On investigation, he discovered that many middle-level managers were feeling isolated from what was going on. Many were unclear about the authority and functions of the "management committee" (his top team); some were finding it very difficult to see and consult with their bosses (his operating heads); others were not being informed of decisions made at his management committee meetings; still others were apprehensive that a new power elite was developing which in many ways was much worse than the former family managers.

In discussing this feedback information with his operating heads, the general manager found one or two who felt these issues required immediate management committee attention. But most of the members of the top team tended to minimize the information as "the usual griping," or "people needing too many decisions made for them," or "everybody always wanting to be in on everything."

The general manager then began searching for some way to—

. . . bring the whole matter into the open;

. . . determine the magnitude and potency of the total problem;

. . . give his management committee and himself a true picture of the state of the organization's attitudes and concerns;

. . . collect information on employee needs, problems, and frustrations in some organized way so that corrective actions could be taken in priority order;

. . . get his management committee members in better tune with their subordinates feelings and attitudes, and put some pressure on the team members for continued two-way communication within their own special areas;

. . . make clear to the total organization that he—the top manager—was personally concerned;

. . . set up mechanisms by which all members of the total management group could feel that their individual needs were noticed;

. . . provide additional mechanisms for supervisors to influence the whole organization.

The confrontation meeting was created to satisfy these objectives and to minimize the time in which a large number of people would have to be away from the job.

Some 70 managers, representing the total management group, were brought together for a confrontation meeting starting at 9:00 in the morning and ending at 4:30 in the afternoon. The specific "design" for the day, . . . had the following components:

1. Climate setting—establishing willingness to participate.

2. Information collecting—getting the attitudes and feelings out in the open.

3. Information sharing—making total information available to all.
4. Priority setting and group action planning—holding work-unit sessions to set priority actions and to make timetable commitments.
5. Organization action planning—getting commitment by top management to the working of these priorities.
6. Immediate follow-up by the top management committee—planning first actions and commitments.

During the day-long affair, the group identified some 80 problems that were of concern to people throughout the organization; they selected priorities from among them; they began working on these priority issues in functional work units, and each unit produced action recommendations with timetables and targets; and they got a commitment from top management of actions on priorities that would be attended to. The top management team met immediately after the confrontation meeting to pin down the action steps and commitments.

(In subsequent applications of this confrontation meeting approach, a seventh component—a progress review —has been added, since experience has shown that it is important to reconvene the total group four to six weeks later for a progress review both from the functional units and from the top management team.)

CASE EXAMPLE B

A small company which makes products for the military had been operating at a stable sales volume of $3 million to $4 million. The invention of a new process and the advent of the war in Vietnam suddenly produced an explosion of business. Volume rose to the level of $6 million within six months and promised to redouble within another year.

Top management was desperately trying to (a) keep raw materials flowing through the line, (b) get material processed, (c) find people to hire, (d) discover quicker ways of job training, and (e) maintain quality under the enormously increased pressure.

There was constant interaction among the five members of the top management team. They were aware of the tension and fatigue that existed on the production line, but they were only vaguely aware of the unrest, fatigue, concern, and loneliness of the middle manager and foreman groups. However, enough signals *had* filtered up to the top team to cause concern and a decision that something needed to be done right away. But, because of the pressures of work, finding the time to tackle the problems was as difficult as the issues themselves.

The entire management group agreed to give up one night and one morning; the confrontation meeting was conducted according to the six component phases described earlier, with Phases 1, 2, and 3 being held in the evening and Phases 4, 5, and 6 taking place the following morning.

CASE EXAMPLE C

A management organization took over the operation of a hotel which was in a sorry state of affairs. Under previous absentee ownership, the property had been allowed to run down; individual departments were independent empires; many people in management positions were nonprofessional hotel people (i.e., friends of the owners); and there was very low competence in the top management team.

The general manager saw as his priority missions the need to:

Stop the downhill trend.

Overcome a poor public image.

Clean up the property.

Weed out the low-potential (old friends) management.

Bring in professional managers in key spots.

Build a management team.

Build effective operating teams, with the members of the top management team as links.

He followed his plan with considerable success. In a period of one year he had significantly cleaned up the property, improved the service, built a new dining room, produced an enviable food quality, and begun to build confidence in key buyers, such as convention managers. He had acquired and developed a very fine, professional, young management team that was both competent and highly motivated. This group had been working as a cohesive team on all the hotel's improvement goals; differences between them and their areas seemed to have been largely worked through.

At the level below the top group, the department and section heads, many of whom were also new, had been working under tremendous pressures for over a year to bring about improvements in the property and in the hotel's services. They felt very unappreciated by the top managers, who were described as "always being in meetings and unavailable," or "never rewarding us for good work," or "requiring approval on all decisions but we can't get to see them," or "developing a fine top management club but keeping the pressure on us and we're doing the work."

The problem finally was brought to the attention of the top managers by some of the department heads. Immediate action was indicated, and a confrontation meeting was decided on. It took place in two periods, an afternoon and the following morning. There was an immediate follow-up by the top management team in which many of the issues between departments and functions were identified as stemming back to the modus operandi of the top team. These issues were openly discussed and were worked through. Also in this application, a follow-up report and review session was scheduled for five weeks after the confrontation meeting.

Positive Results

The experience of the foregoing case examples, as well as that of other organizations in which the confrontation meeting technique has been applied, demonstrates that positive results—particularly, improved operational procedures and improved organization health—frequently occur.

OPERATIONAL ADVANTAGES

One of the outstanding plus factors is that procedures which have been confused are clarified. In addition, practices which have been nonexistent are initiated. Typical of these kinds of operational improvement, for example, are the reporting of financial information to operating units, the handling of the reservation system at a hotel, and the inspection procedures and responsibilities in a changing manufacturing process.

Another advantage is that task forces, and/or temporary systems, are set up as needed. These may be in the form of special teams to study the overlap in responsibilities between two departments and to write new statements and descriptions, or to work out a new system for handling order processing from sales to production planning, or to examine the kinds of information that should flow regularly from the management committee to middle management.

Still another improvement is in providing guidance to top management as to specific areas needing priority attention. For example, "the overtime policy set under other conditions is really impeding the achievement of organization requirements," or "the food in the employee's cafeteria is really creating morale problems," or "the lack of understanding of where the organization is going and what top management's goals are is producing apathy," or "what goes on in top management meetings does not get communicated to the middle managers."

Organization Health

In reviewing the experiences of companies where the confrontation meeting approach has been instituted, I have perceived a number of positive results in the area of organization health:

A high degree of open communication between various departments and organization levels is achieved very quickly. Because people are assigned to functional units and produce data together, it is possible to express the real feeling of one level or group toward another, particularly if the middle echelon believes the top wants to hear it.

The information collected is current, correct, and "checkable."

A real dialogue can exist between the top management team and the rest of the management organization, which personalizes the top manager to the total group.

Larger numbers of people get "ownership" of the problem, since everyone has some influence through his unit's guidance to the top management team; thus people feel they have made a real contribution. Even more, the requirement that each functional unit take personal responsibility for resolving some of the issues broadens the base of ownership.

Collaborative goal setting at several levels is demonstrated and practiced. The mechanism provides requirements for joint goal setting within each functional unit and between top and middle managers. People report that this helps them to understand "management by objectives" more clearly than before.

The top team can take corrective actions based on valid information. By making real commitments and establishing check or review points, there is a quick building of trust in management's intentions on the part of lower level managers.

There tends to be an increase in trust and confidence both toward the top management team and toward colleagues. A frequently appearing agenda item is the "need for better understanding of the job problems of other departments," and the output of these meetings is often the commitment to some "mechanism for systematic inter-departmental communication." People also report a change in their stereotypes of people in other areas.

This activity tends to be a "success experience" and thus increases total morale. The process itself, which requires interaction, contribution, and joint work on the problems and which rewards constructive criticism, tends to produce a high degree of enthusiasm and commitment. Because of this, the follow-up activities are crucial in ensuring continuation of this enthusiasm.

Potential Problems

The confrontation meeting technique produces, in a very short time, a great deal of commitment and desire for results on the part of a lot of people. Feelings tend to be more intense than in some other settings because of the concentration of time and manpower. As a result, problems can develop through misuse of the techniques.

If the top management team does not really use the information from its subordinates, or if there are great promises and little follow-up action, more harm can be caused to the organization's health than if the event were never held.

If the confrontation meeting is used as a manipulative device to give people the "feeling of participation," the act can boomerang. They will soon figure out management's intentions, and the reaction can be severe.

Another possible difficulty is that the functional units, full of enthusiasm at the meeting, set unrealistic or impractical goals and commitments. The behavior of the key man in each unit—usually a department manager or division head—is crucial in keeping suggestions in balance.

One more possible problem may appear when the functional units select a few priority issues to report out. While these issues may be the most *urgent*, they are not necessarily the most *important*. Mechanisms for working *all* of the information need to be developed within each functional unit. In one of the case examples cited earlier, the groups worked the few problems they identified very thoroughly and never touched the others. This necessitated a "replay" six months later.

In Summary

In periods of stress following major organization changes, . . . much confusion and energy [are] expended that negatively affect productivity and organization health.

The top management team needs quick, efficient ways of sensing the state of the organization's attitudes and feelings in order to plan appropriate actions and to devote its energy to the most important problems.

The usual methods of attitude surveys, extended staff meetings, and so forth demand extensive time and require a delay between getting the information and acting on it.

A short micromechanism called a confrontation meeting can provide the total management group with:

An accurate reading on the organization's health.

The opportunity for work units to set priorities for improvement.

The opportunity for top management to make appropriate action decisions based on appropriate information from the organization.

An increased involvement in the organization's goals.

A real commitment to action on the part of subgroups.

A basis for determining other mechanisms for communication between levels and groups, appropriate location of decisions, problem solving within subunits, as well as the machinery for upward influence.

Chapter 9

RESISTANCE

IN writing about the venerable topic, resistance to change, in the first edition of this book, we said (rather wistfully): "Finally, more attention needs to be given to the transactional basis of influence." Our wistfulness was based on the idea that most thinking and research on the problem of resistance implied certain assumptions about the "target audience" that were dubious, if not contradictory, to many of the findings of social science. For example, the major theoretical backbone of the influence studies was a model of social compliance. The object of an influence program was destined to yield to the influence effort because of "reference group" theory or other theories that stress tendencies toward conformity. The typical resister was regarded as a deviant or an error term, an artifact of research methodology. The typical formulation of a good deal of research on the effects of mass media was (and is) the famous: "Who says what, through what channels (media) of communication, to whom, with what results." As Bauer says:

This apparently self-evident formulation has one monumental built-in assumption: that the initiative is exclusively with the communicator, the effects being exclusively on the audience. (p. 508)

It is interesting to note in passing the similarity of assumptions of man held by early organization theorists and mass media specialists. Man was considered

486

in both cases as inert and passive, malleable, and reactive. The point is that the study of communication and influence has traditionally been conducted from the point of view of the effects intended by the communicator. As Bauer points out:

> The failure in research to this point has been that the audience has not been given full status in the exchange: The intentions of its members have not been given the same attention as those of the communicator. (p. 510)

To a large extent the early mistakes are being rectified. A good deal of research is reversing the model of a one-way exploitative process of communication and developing a transactional, problem-solving point of view which we discussed in the introduction to Chapter 4. Nowadays, we tend to remember the cartoon in which one experimental rat says to another: "Boy! Have I got this guy trained! Every time I push this bar he gives me a pellet of food."

Of course, transactional models of change are far from universally accepted in the minds of administrators, managers, teachers, and reformers. Older mechanical models, which don't take into account the intent and rationality of the resister and take the rationality and intention of the changer as given, magnify the irrationality of resistance and resisters. A recent resignation of a top Massachusetts State administrator illustrates the problem. "A major reason for the resignation," he explained, "was the resistance I . . . encountered . . . Almost anything we wanted to do with basic management procedures was resisted."

Still and all, the tide is turning, even in the most unexpected quarters: behavioral scientists are beginning to take account of their subjects as having responses, ideas, and even hypotheses that may affect the research results if they are not reckoned with.

The articles in this chapter reflect the turning tide; that is, toward viewing all social influence as transactional in nature. This means essentially that both parties to an influence relationship have a stake in it, and more specifically, the intentions and behavior of the target (audience) must be reckoned with.

We have already referred to and quoted the Bauer article. He summarizes the history of mass media research and traces its historical trajectory from one-way communication to a transactional model. Klein's interesting piece identifies and describes an important new role in any change program, that of the defender and asserts that he can play a crucial role in planning change at the social system level. Bauer says the target system is crucial because it has motives, desires, expectations, and so on, and Klein goes beyond this by giving the defender the possibility of improving the quality of the change program and ultimately preparing the ground for a more basic commitment.

The paper by Watson focuses, for the most part, on the individual's resistances to change efforts. It provides a framework for understanding the forces of resistance and how these forces are undermined.

Shepard's emphasis is unique in that it is directed to the kinds of organizations (rather than individual responses) that resist or produce innovations. His focus of convenience raises many questions about larger social systems and how they can be revitalized.

9.1 RESISTANCE TO CHANGE *— educaker*

Goodwin Watson

All of the forces which contribute to stability in personality or in social systems can be perceived as resisting change. From the standpoint of an ambitious and energetic change agent, these energies are seen as obstructions. From a broader and more inclusive perspective the tendencies to achieve, to preserve, and to return to equilibrium are most salutary. They permit the duration of character, intelligent action, institutions, civilization and culture.

Lewin's (1951) concept of apparently static systems as in "quasi-stationary equilibrium" has directed attention to the importance of reducing resistance if change is to be accomplished with minimal stress. The more usual strategies of increasing pressures by persuasion and dissuasion raise tensions within the system. If the opposite strategy—that of neutralizing or transforming resistance—be adopted, the forces for change already present in the system-in-situation will suffice to produce movement. For example, administrators may try by exhortation to get teachers to pay more attention to individual differences among pupils. Or, they may analyze the factors which now prevent such attention (e.g. large classes, single textbooks, standard tests) and by removing these pressures release a very natural tendency for teachers to adapt to the different individual pupils.

During the life of a typical innovation or change-enterprise, perceived resistance moves through a cycle. In the early stage, when only a few pioneer thinkers take the reform seriously, resistance appears massive and undifferentiated. "Everyone" knows better; "No one in his right mind" could advocate the change. Proponents are labelled crack-pots and visionaries. In the second stage, when the movement for change has begun to grow, the forces pro and con become identifiable. The position can be defined by its position in the social system and its power appraised. Direct conflict and a show-down mark the third stage, as resistance becomes mobilized to crush the upstart proposal. Enthusiastic supporters of a new idea have frequently underestimated the strength of their opponents. Those who see a favored change as good and needed, find it hard to believe the lengths to which opposition will go to squelch that innovation. This third

Goodwin Watson, "Resistance to Change," Goodwin Watson (ed.), *Concepts for Social Change*, Cooperative Project for Educational Development Series, Vol. I (Washington, D.C.: National Training Laboratories, 1966). Used by permission.

stage is likely to mean life or death to the proposed reform. Survival is seen as depending on building up power to overcome the enemy. Actually, as Lewin's force-field analysis indicates, an easier and more stable victory can be won by lowering the potency of the opposing forces. The fourth stage, after the decisive battles, finds supporters of the change in power. The persisting resistance is, at this stage, seen as a stubborn, hide-bound, cantankerous nuisance. For a time, the danger of a counter-swing of the pendulum remains real. Any conspicuous failure of the reform may mobilize latent opposition which, jointed with the manifest reactionaries, could prove sufficient to shift the balance of power. Strategy in this fourth stage demands wisdom in dealing, not only with the overt opponents, but with the still dissonant elements within the majority which appears, on the whole, to have accepted the innovation. Many teachers of a "new math" today may be less than whole-hearted about its value. In a fifth stage, the old adversaries are as few, and as alienated as were the advocates in the first stage. The strategic situation is now that new change-enterprises are appearing and the one-time fighters for the old innovation (e.g. junior high schools) are being seen as resisters of the emerging change. (Edwards, 1927.)

At each stage of the innovation, from its inception to its defense as status quo, wise strategy requires perceptive analysis of the nature of the resistance. For purposes of this study, we shall focus first on the forces of resistance as they operate within the individual personality. Then we shall inventory the forces most easily identified in the social system. This is, of course, an arbitrary separation, utilized to facilitate the recognition of factors. In reality, the forces of the social system operate within the individuals and those attributed to separate personalities combine to constitute systemic forces. The two work as one.

A. Resistance in Personality

1. HOMEOSTASIS

Some of the stabilizing forces within organisms have been described by Cannon (1932) as "homeostasis." The human body has built-in regulatory mechanisms for keeping fairly constant such physiological states as temperature or blood sugar. Exercise increases pulse rate, but "resistance" to this change presently brings the heart-beat back to normal. Appetites rise, are satisfied, and the organism returns to its steady state. Raup (1925) generalized the reversion to *complacency* as the most basic characteristic of the psychological as well as the physiological behavior of man.

The conception of organisms as naturally complacent unless disturbed by intrusive stimuli has had to be modified in recent years because of contradictory evidence showing a hunger for stimulation. Years ago, W. I. Thomas proposed the "desire for new experience" as one of the four most basic wishes underlying human behavior. (Thomas, Znaniecki, 1918–20). Observers of rats, dogs, and chimpanzees have noted an 'exploratory motive' strong enough to counterbalance fear of the unknown (Hebb, 1958 p. 171). Experiments with perceptual isolation of human subjects showed that lying quietly awake in a comfortable bed, free from disturbing stimuli, soon became intolerable. People need to interact with a changing environment (Lilly, 1956).

Frequently, educational changes prove temporary. For a time, after sensitivity training, a school principal may be more open and receptive to suggestions from teachers. But with time, the forces which made him behave as he did before training, return him to his own more brusque and arbitrary manner.

2. HABIT

Most learning theory has included the assumption that unless the situation changes noticably, organisms will continue to respond in their accustomed way. At least one psychologist (Stephens, 1965) has argued that the *repetition* of a response—often used as a criterion for having "learned" it—offers no conceptual problem. The model resembles a machine which, unless something significant is altered, will continue to operate in a fixed fashion. There should be no need for repeated exercise or for a satisfying effect to "stamp in" the learned response; once the circuit is connected it should operate until rearranged. Once a habit is established, its operation often becomes satisfying to the organism. Gordon Allport (1937) has introduced the term "functional autonomy" to refer to the fact that activities first undertaken as a means to some culminating satisfaction often become intrinsically gratifying. The man accustomed after dinner to his chair, pipe and newspaper may resist any change in the details of his routine. The term "bus man's holiday" reflects

the fact that men sometimes enjoy continuing in free time an activity which has been part of their required work. The concept of functional autonomy is probably too inclusive. Not all activities which are often repeated take on the character of drives. We have no wholly correct basis for predicting which habits will show most intrinsic resistance to change.

Sometimes a new educational practice—e.g. a changed form of teacher's class record book or report card arouses much resistance. After it has been established, perhaps with some persuasion and coercion, it becomes as resistant to change as was its predecessor. The familiar is preferred.

3. PRIMACY

The way in which the organism first successfully copes with a situation sets a pattern which is unusually persistent. Early habits of speech may be recognized despite much effort in later life to change. A child who has several times heard a story told in certain words is likely to be annoyed if the key phrases are not repeated exactly when the story is re-told. Part of the joy in familiar music is the accord between established expectations and the flow of melody and harmony. Dreams of adults are often located in the settings of childhood. Even in senility, the recent experiences fade first, and the earliest associations persist longest. All later concepts perforce build on some of the earliest generalizations.

It is often observed that teachers, despite in-service courses and supervisory efforts, continue to teach as they themselves were taught. Their image of a teacher was formed in childhood and whenever they hear or read anything about better teaching, this is assimilated to that early and persisting concept.

4. SELECTIVE PERCEPTION AND RETENTION

Once an attitude has been set up, a person responds to other suggestions within the framework of his established outlook. Situations may be perceived as reenforcing the original attitude when they actually are dissonant. Thus, in one famous experiment, a common stereotype associating Negroes with carrying razors, led observers of a cartoon to think they had seen the razor in the hands of the Negro rather than the white man (Allport, Postman, 1945). Experiments with materials designed to bring about changes in attitude revealed that subjects did not hear clearly, nor remember well, communications with which they disagreed (Watson, Hartmann, 1939; Levine, Murphy, 1943). It is a common observation that people usually prefer news sources, whether in print or broadcast, with which they are already in agreement. (Klapper, 1960). By reading or listening to what accords with their present views; by misunderstanding communications which, if correctly received, would not be consonant with pre-established attitudes; and by conveniently forgetting any learning which would lead to uncongenial conclusions, subjects successfully resist the possible impact of new evidence upon their earlier views. There are relatively few instances in which old prejudices have been changed by better information or persuasive arguments.

The thousands of teachers who are exposed in graduate courses to different philosophies of education from those the teachers are accustomed to employ, may do very well at answering test questions about the new approach, but they carefully segregate in their mind, the new as "theory which, of course, would not work in the practical situation."

5. DEPENDENCE

All human beings begin life dependent upon adults who incorporate ways of behaving that were established before the newcomer arrived on the scene. Parents sustain life in the helpless infant and provide major satisfactions. The inevitable outcome is conservative. Children tend to incorporate (imitate, introject) the values, attitudes and beliefs of those who care for them.

All teachers were once beginners in the lower grades. At that time, their teachers loomed large and influential, whether friendly or hostile. The little pupil had to conform. His later adoption of the kind of teaching he then experienced is as natural as his acceptance of a particular alphabet and number-system.

There may later, in adolescence, be outbursts of rebellion and moves toward independent thought. But the typical adult still agrees far more than he disagrees with his parents on such basic items as language, religion, politics, child-rearing, and what a school should do.

6. SUPEREGO

Freud (1922) conceived one of the basic personality functions as engaged in the enforcement of the moral standards acquired in childhood from authoritative adults. From the first "No! No!" said to the baby, on through all the socializing efforts of parents, a code of controls is internalized. When the Oedipus complex is resolved, the child sets standards for himself corresponding to his image of the perfect and omnipotent parent. Any violation of these demanding rules is punished with a severity, the energy of which is derived from the attachment to parents as this operated in the Oedipal period —age three to five.

Here, then, in the Superego, is a powerful agent serving tradition. The repressive constraints which operate— partly unconsciously—do not derive from the realities of life in the present or the preceding generation. The Superego of the child corresponds to the Superego of the parent, not to his rational conclusions based on experience. Each mother and father passes on a heritage of taboos which he, in his childhood, acquired from ages past. An individual needs considerable ego-strength to become able to cope realistically with changing life situations in disregard of the unrealistic, perfectionistic demands of his Superego.

There is reason to believe that people who choose occupations in which they try to inculcate higher standards in others (clergymen, teachers, law-enforcement) are persons with extra strong Superego components. They take pride in making severe demands on themselves and on others. They bitterly resist any change which they conceive to be a relaxation of the firmest discipline and the highest expectations of perfection in performance. The influx of less able students into secondary schools and colleges has created almost intolerable conflict in teachers who still require achievement at levels which few can attain.

7. SELF-DISTRUST

As a consequence of the dependence of childhood and the stern authority of the tradition-oriented voice of the Superego, children quickly learn to distrust their own impulses. Each says, in effect, "What I would really want is bad! I should not want it!"

John Dewey in *Human Nature and Conduct* (1922) saw the possibility of human betterment in the liberation of the creative impulses of youth. "The young are not as yet subject to the full impact of established customs. Their life of impulsive activity is vivid, flexible, experimenting, curious." What Dewey did not say is that within each young person there are powerful forces condemning and repressing any impulses which do not correspond to the established routines, standards and institutions of society as it is and has been. The Puritan view that the enjoyable is evil gets a firm hold on children. Every clash between their desires and what adults expect of them, adds an increment to each child's self-rejection: "They must be right; I must be naughty to have such terrible feelings." Thus guilt is mobilized to prevent action for change. Men conclude that they are not worthy of any better life. To be "good" is to accept the *status quo ante*. Agitators and rebels speak with the voice of the evil serpent and should not be heeded.

The author, during the depth of the economic depression, found that most of a sample of unemployed men did not lay the blame for their predicament on faulty social mechanisms. Rather, they internalized the responsibility. They said, "I ought to have stayed on in school"; or "It was my fault that I lost the job; I shouldn't have said what I did!"; or "I should have waited to get married and have a family." Only about one in five wanted to change the economic system; the majority blamed themselves only (Watson, 1941).

Innumerable pupils, parents, teachers and administrators have felt impulses to alter school procedures. Most of these have been stifled by a feeling which is suggested by the expression: "Who am I to suggest changes in what the wisdom of the past has established?"

8. INSECURITY AND
REGRESSION

A further obstacle to effective participation in social change is the tendency to seek security in the past. The golden age of childhood is a Paradise Lost. When life grows difficult and frustrating, individuals think with nostalgia about the happy days of the past.

The irony is that this frustration-regression sequence enters life at just the time when change would be most constructive. When old ways no longer produce the desired outcome, the sensible recourse would be to experiment with new approaches. But individuals are apt at such a time to cling even more desperately to the old and unproductive behavior patterns. They are dissatisfied with the situation, but the prospect of change arouses even more anxiety, so they seek somehow to find a road back to the old and (as they now see it) more peaceful way of life.

Demands for change in school organization and practice become acute as a result of such social changes as automation, rapid travel to other lands, or racial desegregation. The reaction of insecure teachers, administrators and parents, is, too often, to try to hold fast to the familiar or even to return to some tried-and-true fundamentals which typify the schools of the past. A candidate for State Superintendent of Schools in California based his successful campaign in the mid-1960's, on return to the old-fashioned. The fact that California had been changing more rapidly in population, occupations, etc. than had any other state, was one factor in the appeal of this program of reaction.

B. Resistance to Change in Social Systems

1. CONFORMITY TO NORMS

Norms in social systems correspond to habits in individuals. They are customary and expected ways of behaving. Members of the organization demand of themselves and of other members conformity to the institutional norms. This is the behavior described by Whyte in the *Organization Man* (1956). It includes time schedules; modes of dress; forms of address to colleagues, superiors and subordinates; indications of company loyalty; personal ambition to rise; appropriate consumption; and forms of approved participation in recreation and community life. Teachers, even more than businessmen, have been expected to exemplify certain proper behaviors.

Norms make it possible for members of a system to work together. Each knows what he may expect in the other. The abnormal or anomic is disruptive.

Because norms are shared by many participants, they cannot easily change. Above all, the usual individual cannot change them. He can get himself rejected, for deviate behavior, but the norm will persist. A laboratory experiment (Merei, 1949) showed that even a child with strong leadership qualities was required, nevertheless, to conform to the established play norms of a small group of kindergarten children. An excellent teacher who declined to submit the prescribed advance lesson plans for each week, did not alter the norm; he was fired.

When one person deviates noticeably from the group norm, a sequence of events may be expected. The group will direct an increasing amount of communication toward him, trying to alter his attitude. If this fails, one after another will abandon him as hopeless. Communication to him will decrease. He may be ignored or excluded. He no longer belongs (Festinger, Thibaut, 1951).

The famous experiments, led by Lewin during the war, on altering norms of eating, indicated that changes are better introduced by group-decision than by expecting individuals to pioneer a practice not being used by their associates (Lewin, 1952).

The evidence indicates that if norms are to be altered, this will have to occur throughout the entire operating system. The sad fate of experimental schools and colleges (Miles, 1964) indicates the power of the larger system to impose its norms even on units which have been set apart, for a time, to operate by different standards and expectations.

2. SYSTEMIC AND CULTURAL COHERENCE

The Gestalt principle that parts take on characteristics because of their relationship within the whole, implies that it is difficult to change one part without affecting others. Innovations which are helpful in one area may have side-effects which are destructive in related regions. For example, a technical change which increased the efficiency of piece-workers in a factory enabled them to earn more than supervisors were being paid, so the new technique had to be abandoned. Electronic data processing in another company altered the size and relative responsibilities of related departments, generating considerable resentment (Mann, Neff, 1961). Studying change in a city Y.M.C.A., Sorenson and Dimock (1955) concluded: "No part of institutional change is an 'island unto itself': changes in program call for changes in every other part of the institution. . . . and advance in one sector cannot proceed far ahead of change in other sectors. For example, program groups cannot be changed without officer training. . . . which in turn is contingent upon advisor training. . . . which in turn depends upon staff reeducation. Similarly, changes in staff goals and ways of working are dependent upon administrative procedures, policies and budgets which in turn require changes in Boards and Committees." A parallel statement for school systems might indicate that a change in teacher-pupil relationships is likely to have repercussions on teacher-principal interaction, on parent-principal contacts, on pressure groups operating on the superintendent, on Board member chances for re-election, and perhaps on the relationship of the local system to state or Federal agencies. Any estimate of resistance which takes account only of the persons primarily and centrally concerned will be inadequate; the repercussions elsewhere may be even more influential in the survival of the innovation.

3.   Vested Interests

The most obvious source of resistance is some threat to the economic or prestige interests of individuals. A school consolidation which eliminates some Board members and a principal is unlikely to receive their warm support, although such cases have occurred. The most common resistance to educational improvements which would cost money comes from organized or unorganized taxpayers. Mort (1941) found that desirable school innovations were most likely to be adopted by communities with high financial resources. Poverty has been—at least until the recent anti-poverty program—a block to educational experimenting. The writer (Watson, 1946) found likewise that Y.M.C.A.'s located in communities with high volume of retail sales per capita were more likely to adopt recommended new practices.

A "vested interest" may be in freedom to operate as one pleases, quite as truly as in money-income or title on the door. Centralizing control of school decisions is usually unwelcome to the persons who would otherwise be making decisions in local school neighborhoods or classrooms.

Concern for school taxes and for positions on school boards is likely to center in the upper classes of the community. They are the people who have most power and influence. Newspapers and broadcasting are more accessible to them than to the underprivileged. A few powerful political or financial interests can block programs desired by a large majority of ordinary citizens.

The influence of upperclass families on school policies is vividly portrayed in Hollinghead's *"Elmtown's Youth"* (1949).

4.   The Sacrosanct

Anthropologists have observed that, within any culture, some activities are easily changed; others are highly resistant to innovation. Generally, the technology is receptive to new ideas and procedures. The greatest resistance concerns matters which are connected with what is held to be sacred. Some women can become managers of business or presidents of colleges in our male-dominated society, but they find it almost impossible to become a priest, rabbi, a bishop or pope in a conservative denomination. Translations of Scriptures into the vernacular have met strong disapproval. The ritual reading of some verses from the Bible or the recitation of a prayer is held onto with far more fervor than is spent on retention of school texts or equipment. Traditional ceremonies are apt to persist despite doubts as to their educational impact. The closer any reform comes to touching some of the taboos or rituals in the community, the more likely it is to be resisted. Introduction of improved technology in underdeveloped countries runs into formidable obstacles if it seems to impinge on religious superstitions, beliefs or practices (Spicer, 1952).

Cultures resist almost as stubbornly, alterations which enter the realm of morals and ethics. Even when few live by the traditional code, it must still be defended as "ideal" (Linton, 1945). A well-recognized illustration is the expectation of sexual continence between puberty and marriage. Kinsey may find very few youths who practice it, but schools, churches and courts must operate as if the prescription were unquestionable.

There is a clear connection between the operation of the superego in individuals and the taboos persisting in the culture. Both uphold impossibly high standards and react punitively to recognized infractions of the excessive demands.

5. REJECTION OF "OUTSIDERS"

Most change comes into institutions from "outside". Griffiths studying change in school systems concluded, "The major impetus for change in organizations is from outside" (In Miles, 1964 p. 431).

Few psychological traits of human beings are so universal as that of suspicion and hostility toward strange outsiders. Kohler (1922) observed this kind of behavior among his chimpanzees on the Island of Tenerife many years ago. Wood (1934) has explored, across different cultures, the mixture of curiosity and antagonism toward foreigners. A typical attack on any new proposal is that it doesn't fit our local conditions. Struggles to improve labor and race relations have commonly been discounted as inspired by "outside agitators" or "atheistic Communists". Research, development and engineering units are familiar with the way in which a new project is hampered if it is seen as NIH (not invented here).

The history of experimental demonstration schools is that they were often abserved but seldom replicated. "This is fine, but it wouldn't work in our system." Differences in class of children, financial support, equipment and tradition helped to rationalize the resistance. The genius of agricultural

agents a century ago led them away from model farms run by state colleges and toward demonstration projects within the local neighborhood. Farmers accepted what was being done within their county when they could not import new practices from far away.

A major problem in introducing social change is to secure enough local initiative and participation so the enterprise will not be vulnerable as a foreign-importation.

Summary of Recommendations

Our observations on sources of resistance within persons and within institutions can be summarized in some concise principles. These are not absolute laws but are based on generalizations which are usually true and likely to be pertinent. The recommendations are here re-organized to fit three headings: (1) Who brings the change? (2) What kind of change succeeds? and (3) How is it best done?

A. *Who brings the change?*
   1. Resistance will be less if administrators, teachers, Board members and community leaders feel that the project is their own—not one devised and operated by outsiders.
   2. Resistance will be less if the project clearly has wholehearted support from top officials of the system.
B. *What kind of change?*
   3. Resistance will be less if participants see the change as reducing rather than increasing their present burdens.
   4. Resistance will be less if the project accords with values and ideals which have long

been acknowledged by participants.

5. Resistance will be less if the program offers the kind of *new* experience which interests participants.
6. Resistance will be less if participants feel that their autonomy and their security is not threatened.

C. *Procedures in instituting change*

7. Resistance will be less if participants have joined in diagnostic efforts leading them to agree on what the basic problem is and to feel its importance.
8. Resistance will be less if the project is adopted by consensual group decision.
9. Resistance will be reduced if proponents are able to empathize with opponents; to recognize valid objections; and to take steps to relieve unnecessary fears.
10. Resistance will be reduced if it is recognized that innovations are likely to be misunderstood and misinterpreted, and if provision is made for feedback of perceptions of the project and for further clarification as needed.
11. Resistance will be reduced if participants experience acceptance, support, trust, and confidence in their relations with one another.
12. Resistance will be reduced if the project is kept open to revision and reconsideration if experience indicates that changes would be desirable.

REFERENCES

1. Allport, G. W. *Personality: A Psychological Interpretation.* New York, Holt, Rinehart and Winston, Inc., 1937.
2. Allport, G. W. and L. J. Postman. The basic psychology of rumor. *Transactions of N. Y. Academy of Sciences*, Series II, 1945, 8:61–81.
3. Cannon, W. B. Wisdom of the Body. New York, W. W. Norton & Company, Inc., 1932.
4. Dewey, John. Human Nature and Conduct. New York, Holt, Rinehart and Winston, Inc., 1922.
5. Dimock, H. S. and Roy Sorenson. *Designing Education in Values: A Case Study in Institutional Change.* New York, Association Press, 1955.
6. Edwards, L. P. *The Natural History of Revolution.* Chicago; University of Chicago Press, 1927.
7. Festinger, Leon and John Thibaut. Interpersonal Communication in Small Groups. *J. Abn. Soc. Psychol.*, 1951, 46:92–99.
8. Freud, Sigmund. Beyond the pleasure principle. London: Hogarth Press, Ltd., 1922.
9. Hebb, D. O. *A Textbook of Psychology.* Philadelphia: W. B. Saunders Company, 1958.
10. Hollingshead, A. B. *Elmtown's Youth.* New York; John Wiley & Sons, Inc., 1949.
11. Klapper, Joseph T. *Effects of Mass Communication,* New York; The Free Press, 1960.
12. Kohler, Wolfgang. Zur Psychologie des Shimpanzen. *Psychol, Forsehung*, 1922, 1:1–45.

13. Levine, M. M., and G. Murphy. The learning and forgetting of controversial material. *J. Abn. Soc. Psychol.*, 1943, 38:507–517.

14. Lewin, Kurt. *Field Theory in Social Science.* New York, Harper & Row, Publishers, 1951.

15. Lewin, Kurt. Group decision and social change. In G. E. Swanson, T. M. Newcomb and E. L. Hartley, Readings in Social Psychology, New York, Holt, Rinehart and Winston, Inc., 1952, pp. 463–473.

16. Linton, Ralph. *The Cultural Background of Personality.* New York, Appleton-Century-Crofts, 1945.

17. Mann, F. C., and F. W. Neff. *Managing Major Change in Organizations*, Ann Arbor, Mich. Foundation for research on human behavior, 1961.

18. Merei, F. Group leadership and institutionalization. *Human Rela.* 1949, 2:23–39.

19. Miles, M. B. (Ed.) *Innovation in Education,* New York, Bureau of Publications, Teachers College, Columbia University, 1964.

20. Mort, Paul R., and F. G. Cornell. *American Schools in Transition.* New York, Bureau of Publications, Teachers College, Columbia University, 1941.

21. Raup, R. B. *Complacency: The Foundation of Human Behavior*, Crowell-Collier and Macmillan, Inc., 1925.

22. Spicer, E. H. *Human Problems in Technological Change.* New York, Russell Sage Foundation, 1952.

23. Stephens, J. A. *The Psychology of Classroom Learning*, New York, Holt, Rinehart and Winston, Inc., 1965.

24. Watson, Goodwin. A Comparison of "adaptable" versus "laggard" Y.M.C.A.'s New York, Association Press, 1946.

25. Watson, Goodwin. What Makes Radicals? *Common Sense*, 1941, 10:7–9.

26. Watson, W. S., Jr., and G. W. Hartman. The rigidity of a basic attitudinal frame. *J. Abn. Socl. Psychol.*, 1939, 34:314–335.

27. Whyte, William H. Jr. *The Organization Man.* New York, Simon and Schuster, Inc., 1956.

28. Wood, M. M. *The Stranger,* New York, Columbia University Press; 1934.

9.2 SOME NOTES ON THE DYNAMICS OF RESISTANCE TO CHANGE: THE DEFENDER ROLE

Donald Klein

The literature on change recognizes the tendencies of individuals, groups, organizations, and entire societies to act so as to ward off change. Though it is generally acknowledged that human beings have a predilection both to seek change and to reject it, much of the literature has isolated the latter tendency for special emphasis. In fact studies of change appear to be taken

Donald Klein, "Some Notes on the Dynamics of Resistance to Change: The Defender Role," from *Concepts for Social Change*, Goodwin Watson, Ed., Cooperative Project for Educational Development Series, Vol. I. National Training Laboratories, Washington, D.C., 1966. Used by permission.

from the perspective or bias of those who are the change agents seeking to bring about change rather than of the clients they are seeking to influence. It seems likely, therefore, that our notions of change dynamics are only partially descriptive. It is interesting that Freud used the term "resistance" to identify a phenomenon which from his point of view, had the effect of blocking the attainment of his therapeutic objectives. One wonders whether patients would use just this term to refer to the same sets of interactions between themselves and their therapists.

Freud, of course, emphasized that resistances were a necessary and even desirable aspect of the therapy. He pointed out that without resistance patients might be overwhelmed by the interventions of the therapist, with the result that inadequate defenses against catastrophe would be overthrown before more adaptive ways of coping with inner and outer stimuli had been erected.

Desirability of Opposition

It is the objective of this paper to suggest that, as in patient-therapist dyads, opposition to change is also desirable in more complex social systems. It is further suggested that what is often considered to be irrational resistance to change is, in most instances, more likely to be either an attempt to maintain the integrity of the target system to real threat, or opposition to the agents of change themselves.

OPPOSITION TO REAL THREAT

Change of the kind we are considering consists not of an event, but of a process or series of events occurring over a period of time, usually involving a more or less orderly and somewhat predictable sequence of interactions. Though it involves the reactions of individuals, it also entails reorganization of group, organizational, or even community behavior patterns and requires some alteration of social values, be they explicit or only implicitly held.

Few social changes of any magnitude can be accomplished without impairing the life situations of some individuals or groups. Elderly homeowners gain little and sometimes must spend more than they can afford for new public school buildings or for the adoption of kindergartens by their communities. Some administrators may lose their chances for advancement when school districts are consolidated to achieve more efficient use of materials and resources. Other examples of real threat could be cited from public health, urban renewal and other fields. There is no doubt that some resistance to change will occur when individuals' livelihoods are affected adversely or their social standings threatened.

However, there are more fundamental threats posed by major innovations. Sometimes the threat is to the welfare of whole social systems. Often the threat is not clearly recognized by anybody at the time the change occurs; it emerges only as the future that the change itself helped shape is finally attained.

For example, the community which taxes property heavily in order to support kindergartens or costly educational facilities may very well be committing itself to further homogenization of its population as it attracts young families wealthy enough to afford the best in education and drives out working class groups, elderly people, and those whose cultural values do not place so high a priority on education. The community which loses a small, poorly financed local school in order to gain a better equipped and perhaps more competently staffed district facility may also be committed to a future of declining vigor as its most able young people are as a result more readily and systematically siphoned off into geographically distant professional, industrial and other work settings

It is probably inevitable that any major change will be a mixed blessing to those undergoing it in those instances when the status quo or situation of gradual change has been acceptable to many or most people. The dynamic interplay of forces in social systems is such that any stable equilibrium must represent at least a partial accommodation to the varying needs and demands of those involved. Under such circumstances the major change must be desired by those affected if it is to be accepted.

MAINTENANCE OF INTEGRITY

Integrity is being used here to encompass the sense of self-esteem, competence, and autonomy enjoyed by those individuals, groups, or communities who feel that their power and resources are adequate to meet the usual challenges of living. Unfortunately such integrity sometimes is based on a view of reality that is no longer tenable. When changes occur under such circumstances they force us to confront the fact that our old preconceptions do not fit present reality, at least not completely. Dissonance exists between the truths from the past and current observations. In some cases relinquishing the eternal verities would resolve the dissonance but would also entail a reduction of integrity. However irrational, the resistance to change which occurs in such cases may have as its fundamental objective the defense of self-esteem, competence and autonomy.

In our complex, changing world the assaults on individual, group and community integrity are frequent and often severe. The field of public education is especially vulnerable to such assaults. So much so, in fact, that one sometimes wonders whether there are any truly respected educational spokesmen left who can maintain the self-esteem, sense of competence, and necessary autonomy of the schools against all the various changes which are being proposed and funded before they have been adequately tested.

RESISTANCE TO AGENTS OF CHANGE

The problem is further complicated by the growing capacity, indeed necessity, of our society to engage in massive programs of planned change and by the development of ever-growing cadres of expert planners capable of collecting and processing vast bodies of information, of organizing such information into designs for the future apparently grounded on the best available expertise, and of marshalling arguments capable of persuading great numbers of political, business, and other civic leaders that action should be taken. The difficulties which arise stem from the very magnitude of the changes being projected, from the rapidity with which such changes can occur, and from the troubling realization that these changes often are irreversible as well as far reaching, thus ensuring the prolongation of error as well as of accuracy.

Most important of all, however, as a generator of defense would appear to be the frequent alienation of the planners of change from the world of those for whom they are planning. The alienation is one of values as much as it is one of simple information. It exists in many fields but is perhaps most apparent in the field of urban renewal, where planners have yet to devise mechanisms whereby they can adequately involve their clients in the planning processes. Many examples can be cited. Health professionals feel that matters of the public health should be left in the hands of the experts most qualified to assess the facts and to take the necessary action. They often decry the involvement of the public in decisions about such matters as fluoridation through referenda or other means. Educators, too, are often loath to encourage the development of vigorous parent groups capable of moving into the arena of curriculum planning, building design, or other areas of decision making.

Few expert planners in any field are prepared to believe that their clients can be equipped to collaborate with them as equals. What can the lay person add to the knowledge and rationality of the technical expert? And is it not true that the process of involving the client would only serve to slow down if not derail the entire undertaking? The result is that each planning project proceeds without taking the time to involve those who will be affected by the planning until such

a point when it is necessary to gain the client's consent. And if decisions can be made and implementation secured without involving his public, the planner's job is greatly simplified.

It is little wonder, therefore, that planners typically do not engage in collaborative planning with clients on specific projects. It is costly, time consuming, irritating, frustrating, and even risky.

However, the failure of planners to work collaboratively with those for whom they plan contributes to the well known American mistrust of the highly trained, academically grounded expert. Under the most benign circumstances, the client may be skeptical of the planner's recommendations. Given any real threat to livelihood or position, or given any feared reduction in integrity, clients' skepticism may be replaced by mistrust of planners' motives and open hostility towards them.

The motives of innovators are especially apt to be suspect when the planning process has been kept secret up until the time of unveiling the plans and action recommendations. By this time the innovators usually have worked up a considerable investment in their plans, and are often far more committed to defending than to attempting to understand objections to them. They are not prepared to go through once again with newcomers the long process of planning which finally led them to their conclusions. And they are hardly in the most favorable position to entertain consideration of new social data or of alternative actions which might be recommended on the basis of such information. The result often is that opposition to the recommended change hardens and even grows as the ultimate clients sense that their reactions will not materially influence the outcome in any way short of defeating the plan in open conflict.

Defense as Part of the Process of Innovation

Studies in such fields as agriculture and medicine have helped clarify the sequence of processes involved in successful innovation of new practices. Even in such technical fields where results can be more or less objectively judged in terms of profit, recovery rates, and the like, successful innovation occurs only after initial resistances have been worked through.

Innovation in any area begins when one or more people perceive that a problem exists, that change is desirable and that it is possible. These people then must decide how best to go about enlisting others to get the information needed to assess the problem further and to develop the strategy leading to implementation of a plan of action. However, we know that those people who are prepared to initiate change within their own groups, organizations or communities are often in a very unfavorable position from which to do so. In stable groups especially it is the marginal or atypical person who is apt to be receptive to new ideas and practices or who is in a position where he can economically or socially afford to run the risk of failure.

Thus it has been found necessary to carry out sustained efforts at innovation in which experimentation with new ideas can be followed by efforts at adapting or modifying them to fit more smoothly into existing patterns until finally what was once an innovation is itself incorporated within an altered status quo.

THE IMPORTANCE OF DEFENSE IN SOCIAL CHANGE:

Up to this point, this paper has touched on some of the factors contributing to the inevitability of resistance to change and has presented but not developed the major thesis, which is that a necessary pre-requisite of successful change involves the mobilization of forces against it. It has suggested that just as individuals have their defenses to ward off threat, maintain integrity, and protect themselves against the unwarranted intrusions of other's demands, so do social systems seek ways in which to defend themselves against ill-considered and overly precipitous innovations.

The existence of political opposition virtually ensures such defense within local, state and national government to the extent that the party out of power is sufficiently vigorous. The British system of the loyal opposition perhaps even more aptly epitomizes the application of the concept of necessary defense in the area of political life.

In more implicit ways, non-governmental aspects of community life have their defenders. These latter individuals and groups constitute the spokesmen for the inner core of tradition and values. They uphold established procedures and are quick to doubt the value of new ideas. Their importance stems from several considerations:

First, they are the ones most apt to perceive and point out the real threats, if such exist, to the well-being of the system which may be the unanticipated consequences of projected changes;

Second, they are especially apt to react against any change that might reduce the integrity of the system;

Third, they are sensitive to any indication that those seeking to produce change fail to understand or identify with the core values of the system they seek to influence.

THE DEFENDER ROLE

The defender role is played out in a variety of ways depending on such factors as the nature of the setting itself, the kind of change contemplated, the characteristics of the group or individual seeking to institute change, and the change strategy employed. In a process of orderly and gradual change, the defender role may be taken by a well established, respected member of the system whose at least tacit sanction must be gained for a new undertaking to succeed. In a situation of open conflict where mistrust run high the defender role may be assumed by those able to become more openly and perhaps irrationally vitriolic in their opposition. These latter are often viewed by the proponents of change as impossibly intractable and are dismissed as "rabble rousers" or "crack pots." This was frequently the attitude on the part of pro-fluoridationists toward the anti's.

Though crack pots may emerge as defenders under certain circumstances, it is suggested here that, so long as they are given support by a substantial segment of the population even though it may be a minority, they are expressing a reaction by all or part of the target system against real threat of some kind. In one community, I observed a well educated group of residents vote overwhelmingly against fluoridation at town meeting even though (as I viewed it) the small body of antifluoridationists expressed themselves in a highly emotional, irrational way. In later conversations it appeared that many who voted against actually favored fluoridation. They were influenced not by the logic of the defenders but by other dynamics in the situation which presumably the defenders also were reflecting. Some of those who voted "no" were unprepared to force fluorides on a minority; others pointed out that those presenting the case for fluorides had neglected to involve the voters in a consideration of the true nature and extent of the problem of tooth decay; and a third group wondered why the health officer and others fighting for the change were so insistent on pushing their plan through immediately rather than asking the town through the more usual committee procedure to consider the problem at a more leisurely pace. The pro-fluoridationists, on the other hand, were discouraged by the vote, felt rejected by fellow townspeople, and had grave doubts about bringing the issue up again in view of the fact that "they don't want to protect their children's teeth."

In the instance of fluoridation the defenders usually have been drawn from the ranks of those who do not hold public office and who do not consider themselves to be members of the Establishment. This is not always the case, however. In civil rights controversies the change agents typically are the disenfranchised; the defenders occupy public office or appear to be close to the sources of existing power. But no matter whether the innovation comes from top down or bottom up, in each situation the defenders are representing value positions which have been important not only to themselves but to larger groups of constituents, and presumably to the maintenance of the culture itself.

In the Boston controversy over de facto school segregation the School Committee Chairman was elected by an overwhelming vote of those who, however bigoted many of them may be, believe they are defending their property values, the integrity of neighborhood schools, and their rights to stand up against those who are trying to push them around. If any of us were faced in our neighborhoods with the prospect of a state toll road sweeping away our homes, we, too, might convince ourselves that we could properly rise up in defense of the same values. The point is not whether the schools should remain segregated; they should not. Rather as change agents we must be concerned with the values held by the opposition and must recognize that, to a great extent, their values are ours as well. Moreover, it would help if we could grant that, in upholding these values, the defenders—however wrong we believe they are in the stands they take and the votes they cast—are raising questions which are important in our society and which we must answer with them. It is far too easy to dismiss neighborhood schools as a reactionary myth or to hold that they are unimportant in face of the larger objective of reducing intergroup barriers. The issues become far more complex, however, when we grant that neighborhood schools were established because in the judgment of many educators and citizens they had merits apart from the current controversy over segregation. Once having granted this, the problem becomes one of seeking solutions which can minimize the losses in respect to such merits and maximize the gains in respect to integration. I would predict that, if it were possible for the change agents to consider seriously the concerns of the defenders in the case of school integration, many of the latter would no longer feel so embattled and would no longer require the kind of leadership which in Boston has just been renominated overwhelmingly for the School Committee.

But what about the motives of those who lead the opposition to good causes? Are they not apt to seize on virtuous issues simply as ways to manipulate opinion and to rally more support? No doubt this is true. Nonetheless, I think the point still holds that the virtues are there to be manipulated. They can be used as a smoke screen by demagogues only so long as those who follow them are convinced that the agents of change are themselves unscrupulous, unprincipled, and unfeeling. Therefore, we add to the anxieties and opposition of those who are being rallied by the demagogues if we dismiss the latter and fail to come to grips with the concerns of those who uphold them.

Of course, demagogues and rabble rousers do more than articulate the values of their followers. They also dare to give voice to the frustrations and sense of helpless rage which these followers feel but usually cannot express. Those who are the targets of change usually do not feel it is safe to give vent to their true feelings. The man who is a demagogue in the eyes of his opponent is usually a courageous spokesman to the follower whom he is serving as a defender.

How the Change Agent Views the Defender:

Thus an important implication for the change agent is that the defender, whoever he may be and however unscrupulously or irrationally he may appear to present himself and his concerns, usually has something of great value to communicate about the nature of the system which the change agent is seeking to influence. Thus if the change agent can view the situation with a sympathetic understanding of what the defenders are seeking to protect, it may prove desirable either to modify the change itself or the strategy being used to achieve it. In certain situations the participation of defenders in the change process may even lead to the development of more adequate plans and to the avoidance of some hitherto unforeseen consequences of the projected change.

It is important, therefore, for those seeking change to consider the costs of ignoring, overriding, or dismissing as irrational those who emerge as their opponents. To ignore that which is being defended may mean that the planned change itself is flawed; it may also mean that the process of change becomes transformed into a conflict situation in which forces struggle in opposition and in which energies become increasingly devoted to winning rather than to solving the original problem.

Outcome of the Defender Role

What happens to the defender role during a period of change is no doubt a function of many factors, such as the nature of the issue, previous relationships between opposing sides, and the various constraints of time, urgency of the problem, and the like. We are all familiar with situations in which defenders and protagonists of change have become locked in fierce conflict until finally the defenders have either won out or been shattered and forced to succumb. Frequent examples can be found in the early history of urban renewal when entire urban neighborhoods, such as the West End of Boston, were destroyed and their defenders swept away as a consequence. It is also possible for conflict to continue indefinitely with neither side able to gain the advantage, to the extent that both sides contribute to the ultimate loss of whatever values each was seeking to uphold. Labor-management disputes which shatter entire communities are instances where the interplay between innovative and defensive forces ceases to be constructive.

Often in communities the defenders of values no longer widely held become boxed in and remain in positions of repeated but usually futile opposition to a series of new influences. The consensus of the community has shifted in such a way as to exclude those who may once have been influential. In their encapsulation these individuals and groups are no longer defenders in the sense the term is being used here; for they no longer participate meaningfully in the changes going on around them.

Finally, as has already been suggested, the defenders may in a sense be co-opted, by the change agents in such a way as to contribute to an orderly change process.

SCHOOL ADMINISTRATOR—
DEFENDER OR CHANGE AGENT

Within school systems the balance between innovation and defense must always be delicate, often precarious. The history of education in this country is full of examples of major innovations accomplished by an outstanding superintendent which, no matter what their success, were immediately eliminated by his successor. Sometimes disgruntled citizens who have been unsuccesul in opposing innovations are better able to mobilize their opposition when no longer faced with powerful professional leadership. Sometimes teachers and staff members who have conformed to but not accepted the changes feel more secure to express their opposition to the new superintendent.

It has been pointed out by Neal Gross and others that the superintendent of a public school system faces the almost impossible task of mediating between the conflicting demands of staff, community, and other groups. He is almost continuously confronted with the opposing influences of innovators and defenders, not to mention the many bystanders within the system who simply wish to be left alone when differences arise. Under the circumstances it may well be that one of the most important skills a superintendent can develop is his ability to create the conditions wherein the interplay between change agents and defenders can occur with a minimum of rancor and a maximum of mutual respect. As we have seen in New York City and elsewhere, however, controversies do arise—such as civil rights—wherein the superintendent seems unable to play a facilitating role.

In situations that are less dramatic and conflict laden, the superintendent and other school administrators are usually in a position where they can and indeed must be both change agents and defenders. In the face of rapid social change they face the challenge of learning how to foster innovation, while at the same time finding the most constructive ways in which to act in defense of the integrity of their systems. It is also important that they learn how to differentiate between change which may pose real threat and change which is resisted simply because it is new and feels alien. Perhaps most important of all, they have the opportunity of educating the change agents with whom they work, either those inside their systems or those who come from the outside, to the point where the change agents perceive, understand, and value the basic functions and purposes of the schools.

THE FORCE FIELD
OF THE DEFENDER

In human relations training we have frequently used Lewin's force field model as a way to introduce learners to the objective analysis of the forces driving towards and restraining against a desired change. Here, too, we have tended to view the change field through the eyes of the protagonists. I think it would be illuminating in any study of educational innovation to attempt to secure analysis of the force field from defenders as well as change agents at several stages of the innovative process. Comparative analysis of the views of protagonists and defenders might help illuminate the biases of the former and clarify more adequately the underlying origins within the target system of the opposition. It also should provide us with a better understanding of the dynamics of the defender rule and how it can be more adequately taken into account in programs of social innovation.

9.3 THE OBSTINATE AUDIENCE: THE INFLUENCE PROCESS FROM THE POINT OF VIEW OF SOCIAL COMMUNICATION

Raymond A. Bauer

Not long ago, Henry Murray (1962), in an address entitled, "The Personality and Career of Satan," gibed at psychologists for undertaking Satan's task of shattering man's faith in his own potentialities:

Man is a computer, an animal, or an infant. His destiny is completely determined by genes, instincts, accidents, early conditioning and reinforcements, cultural and social forces. Love is a secondary drive based on hunger and oral sensations or a reaction formation to an innate underlying hate. . . . If we psychologists were all the time, consciously or unconsciously, intending out of malice to reduce the concept of human nature to its lowest common denominators . . . then we might have to admit that to this extent the Satanic spirit was alive within us [p. 53].

Isidor Chein (1962), too, sides with the humanist against the scientist in psychology.

among psychologists whose careers are devoted to the advancement of the science,

Raymond A. Bauer, "The Obstinate Audience: The Influence Process From the Point of View of Social Communication," *American Psychologist*, XIX, No. 5 (May 1964), 319–328. Used by permission.

the prevailing image of Man is that of an impotent reactor. . . . He is implicitly viewed as robot. . . .

The opening sentence of *Ethical Standards of Psychologists* is that, "the psychologist is committed to a belief in the dignity and worth of the individual human being." . . .

But what kind of dignity can we attribute to a robot [p. 3]?

The issue is not, however, whether the *findings* of social science do and should have an influence on how we run our lives and think about ourselves, an influence to a certain extent inevitable and, to some, desirable. The real issue is whether our social model of man—the model we use for running society—and our scientific model or models—the ones we use for running our subjects—should be identical. That the general answer should be "No," I learned when working on my doctoral thesis (Bauer, 1952), which was a chronology of Soviet attempts to keep the social and scientific models of man in line with each other, for I became soberly aware then of the delicacy and complexity of the relationship of the social and the scientific models of man.

I shall here discuss the relationship of these two models in the area of social communication. I shall set up two stereotypes. First, the social model of communication: The model held by the general public, and by social scientists when they talk about advertising, and somebody else's propaganda, is one of the exploitation of man by man. It is a model of one-way influence: The communicator *does* something to the audience, while to the communicator is generally attributed considerable latitude and power to do what he pleases to the audience. This model is reflected —at its worst—in such popular phrases as "brainwashing," "hidden persuasion," and "subliminal advertising."

The second stereotype—the model which *ought* to be inferred from the data of research—is of communication as a transactional process in which two parties each expect to give and take from the deal approximately equitable values. This, although it *ought* to be the scientific model, is far from generally accepted as such.

Whether fortunately or unfortunately, social criticism has long been associated with the study of communication. The latter was largely stimulated by the succession of exposés of propaganda following World War I, particularly of the munitions-makers' lobby and of the extensive propaganda of the public utilities. There was also social concern over the new media, the movies and radio, and the increasingly monopolistic control of newspapers. Propaganda analysis, which is what research communication was called in those days, was occupied with three inquiries: the structure of the media (who owns and controls them, and what affects what gets into them); content analysis (what was said and printed); and propaganda techniques (which are the devil's devices to influence people). In this period, *effects* for the most part were not studied: They were taken for granted. Out of this tradition evolved Laswell's (Smith, Laswell, & Casey, 1946) formulation of the process of communication that is the most familiar one to this day: "Who says what, through what channels [media] of communication, to whom [with] what . . . results [p. 121]." This apparently self-evident formulation has one monumental built-in assumption: that the initiative is exclusively with the communicator, the effects being exclusively on the audience.

While the stimulus and the model of research on communication were developing out of the analysis of propaganda, survey research, relatively independently, was evolving its technology in the commercial world of market research and audience and leadership measurement. As is well known, Crossley, Gallup, and Roper each tried their hands at predicting the 1936 presidential election and whipped the defending champion, the *Literary Digest*. By 1940, Lazarsfeld was ready to try out the new technology on the old model with a full-scale panel study of the effects of the mass media on voting in a national election, having tested his strategy in the New Jersey gubernatorial race in 1938.

The results of this study, again, are well known. Virtually nobody in the panel changed his intention, and most of the few who did so attributed it to personal influence (Lazarsfeld, Berelson, & Gaudet, 1948). The mass media had had their big chance—and struck out. Negative results had been reached before but none which had been demonstrated by such solid research. A number of equally dramatic failures to detect effects of campaigns carried on in the mass media followed, and by the end of the decade Hyman and Sheatsley (1947) were attempting to explain why. No one could take the effects of communication for granted.

As a matter of fact a considerable number of the sociologists studying communication grew discouraged with inquiring into the immediate effects of the mass media, and went looking for "opinion leaders," "influentials," the "web of influence," and so on. At the same time, a few here and there began doing something we now call "functional studies." They were curious to know how the audience was behaving.

In the meantime, at just about the time that the students of the effect of communication in a natural setting were beginning to wonder if communication ever had effects, experimental studies were burgeoning under essentially laboratory conditions. Experiments had been conducted before, but the tradition of experimenting on the effects of communication was vastly enhanced by the War Department's Information and Education Division, and after the war by Hovland and his associates at Yale (Hovland, Lumsdaine, & Sheffield, 1949). The Yale group's output, and that of colleagues and students of Kurt Lewin, account for a very high proportion of the experimental work on the subject in the past 2 decades.

The experimenters generally had no trouble conveying information or changing attitudes. Of course nobody stopped to record very explicitly the main finding of all the experiments:

that communication, given a reasonably large audience, varies in its impact. It affects some one way, some in the opposite way, and some not at all. But nevertheless the experimenters got results.

By the end of the 'fifties it was quite clear that the two streams of investigation needed reconciling, and Carl Hovland (1959) did so. More recently, pursuing the same theme, I stated Hovland's major point as being that the audience exercises much more initiative outside the laboratory than it does in the experimental situation (Bauer, 1962). The audience selects what it will attend to. Since people generally listen to and read things they are interested in, these usually are topics on which they have a good deal of information and fixed opinions. Hence the very people most likely to attend to a message are those most difficult to change; those who can be converted do not look or listen. A variety of studies attribute to this circumstance alone: the fact that actual campaigns have often produced no measurable results, while quite marked effects could be produced in a laboratory.

Two favorite problems of the laboratory experimenters take on quite a different aspect when considered in a natural setting. One is the question of the order of presentation of arguments. Is it an advantage to have your argument stated first (the so-called law of primacy) or stated last (the so-called law of recency)? In a laboratory the answer is complex but it may be quite simple in a natural situation: He who presents his argument first may convert the audience and they in turn may exercise their oft-exercised prerogative of not listening to the opposing case.

Hence to have the first word rather than the last could be decisive in the real world, but for a reason which may seem irrelevant to the relative merits of primacy versus recency.

Of course, another important variable is the credibility of the source. By creating an impression of the credibility of the stooge or experimenter in the laboratory, it is often possible to convert a person to a position far removed from his original one. But in real life, the audience usually does its own evaluation of sources, and at a certain point sometimes arrives at a result quite the opposite of that reached experimentally. If the audience is confronted with a communicator trying to convert it to a position opposed to its own, it is likely to see him as "biased," and the like, and come away further strengthened in its own convictions.

It was quite clear from Hovland's piece, and should have been even earlier, that the characteristic behavior of the audience in its natural habitat is such as to bring about crucial modifications of the results seen in the laboratory. In general, these modifications are strongly in the direction of suppressing effect.

In a sense, Joseph Klapper's 1960 book, *The Effects of Mass Communication*, marks the end of an era. Twenty years earlier, a social scientist would have taken effects for granted and specified the devices the propagandist employed to achieve them. But Klapper (1960) makes statements like these: "[my position] is in essence a shift *away* from the tendency to regard mass communication as a necessary and sufficient cause of audience effects, toward a view of the media as influences, working amid other influences, in a total situation [p. 5]." He sees communications as operating through mediating factors—group membership, selective exposure, defense mechanisms—"such that they typically render mass communication a contributory agent, but not the sole cause in a process of reinforcing the existing conditions. (Regardless of the condition in question . . . the media are more likely to reinforce [it] than to change) [p. 8]." Change takes place, according to Klapper, in those rare circumstances when mediating forces are inoperative, when they are occasionally mobilized to facilitate change, or in certain residual situations. He reviews the literature on the effect of variation in content, mode of presentation, media, and so on, but rather than taking effects for granted, he searches for the exceptional case in which the mass media change rather than fortify and entrench.

Klapper recommends what he calls the "phenomenalistic" and others have called the functional approach. The study of communication has traditionally (although not exclusively) been conducted from the point of view of the *effects intended by the communicator*. From this perspective, the disparity between actual and intended results has often been puzzling. The answer has come increasingly to be seen in entering the phenomenal world of the audience and studying the functions which communication serves. The failure in research to this point has been that the audience has not been given full status in the exchange: The intentions of its members have not been given the same attention as those of the communicator.

Some will argue that these generalizations do not hold true of advertising

They do. But until now no one has undertaken to match the effects of communication in various areas according to comparable criteria and against realistic expectation.

Actually much more is expected of the campaigns with which academic psychologists are associated than is expected of commercial promotion. For example, a paper on governmental informational campaigns concluded with these words (Seidenfeld, 1961): "while people are willing to walk into a drug-store and buy low calorie preparations and contraceptives, they are not very anxious to take shots for protection against polio or attend a clinic dealing with sexual hygiene." By the author's own figures, 60% of the public had had one or more polio shots and 25% had had the full course of four. According to his expectations, and probably ours, these were hardly satisfactory accomplishments.

Yet, what about the highly advertised product, low in calories, with which he was comparing polio inoculations? Presumably he had heard that it was a smashing commercial success, or had seen some dollar volume figure on gross sales. Actually, it was being bought by 4% of the market—and 10% and even 25% are larger figures than 4%. Our unacknowledged expectations must be reckoned with.

These differences in expectation and criteria produce much confusion, usually on the side of convincing people that commercial campaigns are more successful than others. Yet, consistently successful commercial promotions convert only a very small percentage of people to action. No one cigarette now commands more than 14% of the cigarette market, but an increase of 1% is worth $60,000,000 in sales. This means influencing possibly .5% of all adults, and 1% of cigarette smokers. This also means that a successful commercial campaign can alienate many more than it wins, and still be highly profitable.

Equally misleading is the frequent reference to percentage increase on some small base. This device has been a particular favorite of both the promoters and the critics of motivation research: One party does it to sell its services, the other purportedly to warn the public; both exaggerate the effect. Thus, for example, the boast, "a 300% increase in market share," means that the product increased; but it may easily be from 1% of the market to 3%. Or we may have a 500% gain in preference for "the new package" over the old one. That there is that much consensus in the esthetic judgment of the American public is a matter of interest, but it tells nothing about the magnitude of consequences on any criterion in which we are interested. I have made some computations on the famous Kate Smith war-bond marathon, which elicited $39 million in pledges. Kate Smith moved apparently a maximum of 4% of her audience to pledge to buy bonds; the more realistic figure may be 2%! In the commercial world this is a rather small effect as judged by some expectations, but yet an effect which often adds up to millions of dollars.

But commercial promotions often do not pay their way. The word is currently being circulated that a mammoth corporation and a mammoth advertising agency have completed a well-designed experiment that proves the corporation has apparently wasted millions of dollars on promoting its corporate image. Some studies have shown that an increase in expenditures for advertising has, under controlled experimental conditions, produced a decrease in sales.

The truth is now out: that our social model of the process of communication is morally asymmetrical; it is concerned almost exclusively with inequities to the advantage of the initiators, the manipulators. From the social point of view this may be all to the good. The answer to the question whether our social and scientific models should be identical is that there is no reason why we should be equally concerned with inequities in either direction; most of us consider it more important to protect the weak from the powerful, than vice versa. However, no matter how firmly committed to a morally asymmetrical social model, investigators should note that inequities fall in either direction and in unknown proportions.

The combination of this asymmetry and the varying expectations and criteria mentioned earlier fortifies the model of a one-way exploitative process of communication. And it is probably further reinforced by the experimental design in which the subject is seen as *re*acting to conditions established by the experimenter. We forget the cartoon in which one rat says to another: "Boy, have I got this guy trained! Every time I push this bar he gives me a pellet of food." We all, it seems, believe that *we* train the *rats*. And while the meaning of "initiative" in an experimental situation may be semantically complicated, the experimenter is usually seen there as *acting* and the subjects as *reacting*. At the very least and to all appearances, the experimental design tends to entrench the model of influence flowing in one direction.

The tide is, in fact, turning, although as a matter of fact, it is difficult to say whether the final granting of initiative to the audience, which seems to be imminent, is a "turn" or a logical extension of the research work of the past 25 or 30 years.

Meanwhile, new trends have been developing in psychological research on communication. Until about a decade ago, the failure of experimental subjects to change their opinions was regarded as a residual phenomenon. Little systematic or sympathetic attention was paid to the persistence of opinion. The considerable volume of recent research using what the Maccobys (Maccoby & Maccoby, 1961) call a homeostatic model is dominated by theories based on the psychology of cognition, Heider's balance theory, Festinger's dissonance theory, Osgood and Tannenbaum's congruity theory, and Newcomb's strain for symmetry. While the proponents of each theory insist on adequate grounds on their distinctiveness, all agree that man acts so as to restore equilibrium in his system of belief. In any event, homeostatic studies do finally accord some initiative to the audience. Specifically, they reveal individuals as deliberately seeking out information on persons either to reinforce shaken convictions or consolidate those recently acquired. Festinger, for example, is interested in the reduction of dissonance following upon decisions—which means he views people as reacting to their own actions as well as to the actions of others. This influx of new ideas and new research is a valuable and welcome addition to both the theory and practice of social communication.

Restoring cognitive equilibrium is, however, only one of the tasks for which man seeks and uses information. Furthermore, the homeostatic theories, while according initiative to the audience, make it peculiarly defensive. They do little to counteract the notion of a one-way flow of influence—although it must be conceded that a scientific model is under no moral obligation to correct the defects, if any, of the social model.

Much is gained by looking upon the behavior of the audience as full-blown problem solving. Such a viewpoint requires the assumption that people have more problems to solve than simply relating to other people and reducing their psychic tension, among them being the allocation and conservation of resources.

The mass media have long been criticized because they facilitate escape from the responsibilities of the real world. But Katz and Foulkes (1962) point out that if man is to cope adequately with his environment, he must on occasion retreat to gather strength. Hence, escape per se is not a bad thing: It is socially approved to say, "Be quiet! Daddy is sleeping," although not yet approved to say, "Be quiet! Daddy is drinking." They take a generally irresponsibly handled problem of social criticism and convert it into one of the allocation and conservation of resources. It would take close calculation to decide whether an hour spent drinking beer in front of the TV set would, for a given individual, result in a net increase or decrease in his coping effectively with the environment. Yet, while the data they

require are manifestly unattainable, their very way of posing the problem raises the level of discourse.

The necessity for taking explicit cognizance of the audience's intention was forced on us when we were studying Soviet refugees. We knew that virtually every Soviet citizen was regularly exposed to meetings at which were conveyed a certain amount of news, the party line on various issues, and general political agitation and indoctrination. In free discussion our respondents complained endlessly of the meetings so we knew they were there. But when we asked them, "From what sources did you draw most of your information about what was happening?" only 19% specified them, in contrast to 87% citing newspapers, 50% citing radio, and another 50% word of mouth (Inkeles & Bauer, 1959, p. 163). Gradually the obvious dawned on us; our respondents were telling us where they learned what *they* wanted to know, not where they learned what the regime wanted them to know.

A similar perplexity arose with respect to the use of word-of-mouth sources of information. It was the least anti-Soviet of our respondents who claimed to make most use of this unofficial fountain of information. Rereading the interviews, and further analysis, unraveled the puzzle. It was the people most involved in the regime, at least in the upper social groups, who were using word-of-mouth sources the better to understand the official media, and the better to do their jobs (Inkeles and Bauer, 1959, p. 161)! As a result we had to conduct analysis on two levels, one where we took into account the intentions of the regime, the other, the intentions of the citizen. Thus, viewed from the vantage point of the regime's intention, the widespread dependence upon word of mouth was a failure in communication. From the point of view of the citizen and what he wanted, his own behavior made eminent sense.

At the next stage, we benefited from the looseness of our methods, the importance of the people we were studying, and from highly imaginative colleagues from other disciplines. We were studying the processes of decision, communication, and the like, in the business and political community. As we studied "influence" by wandering around and getting acquainted with the parties of both camps, and kept track of what was going on, the notion of a one-way flow became preposterous. A Congressman, for example, would snort: "Hell, pressure groups? I have to roust 'em off their fat rears to get them to come up here." It also became clear that men in influential positions did a great deal to determine what sort of communication was directed toward them (Bauer, Pool, & Dexter, 1963). At this juncture, Ithiel de Sola Pool crystallized the proposition that the audience in effect influences the communicator by the role it forces on him. This idea became the organizing hypothesis behind the Zimmerman and Bauer (1956—this experiment was replicated by Schramm & Danielson) demonstration that individuals process new information as a function of their perceived relationship to future audiences. Specifically, they are less likely to remember information that would conflict with the audience's views than they are to remember information to which the audience would be hospitable.

The final crystallization of my present views began several years ago when a decision theorist and I together reviewed the studies by motivation researchers of the marketing of ethical drugs to doctors. Surprisingly, I found the level of motivation discussed in these reports quite trivial, but the reports provided perceptive cognitive maps of the physician's world and the way he went about handling risk. The now well-known studies of the adoption of drugs by Coleman, Menzel, and Katz (1959) contributed data consistent with the following point: Physicians become increasingly selective in their choice of information as risk increases either because of the newness of the drug or difficulty in assessing its effects. Thereupon, a group of Harvard Business School students (in an unpublished manuscript) established by a questionnaire survey that as the seriousness of the disease increased, physicians were increasingly likely to prefer professional to commercial sources of information.

Parenthetically with respect to the Coleman, Menzel, and Katz (1959) studies whose data I said are "consistent with" the notion of risk handling: I am convinced that this way of thinking is wholly compatible to the authors. Yet their presentation is sufficiently dominated by the prevailing view of "social influence" as a matter of personal compliance that one cannot be entirely sure just where they do stand.

Why doesn't the physician always prefer professional to commercial sources of information? The physician is a busy man whose scarcest resources are time and energy, two things which commercial sources of information, on the whole, seem to help him conserve. Even so, he is selective. Let us assume two components in the choice of source of information: social compliance and the reduction of risk. Consider, then, that the doctor may be influenced by his liking either for the drug company's salesman who visits his office, or for the company itself. We may assume that, of these two components of influence, social compliance will be more associated with his sentiments toward the salesman and risk reduction with the company's reputation.

In a study conducted with the Schering Corporation (Bauer, 1961), I found that in the case of relatively riskless drugs, the correlation of preference for drugs with preference for salesman and for company was about equal. However, with more hazardous drugs—and with large numbers of subjects—preference for the company carried twice the weight of preference for the salesmen: The physicians selected the source closest associated with reduction of risk.

In the latest and fullest development of this point of view, Cox (1962) asked approximately 300 middle-class housewives to evaluate the relative merits of "two brands" of nylon stockings (Brand N & Brand R) as to over-all merits and as to each of 18 attributes. After each rating the subject was asked to indicate how confident she was in making it. The subjects then listened to a tape-recorded interview with a supposed salesgirl who stated that Brand R was better as to 6 attributes, whereupon they were asked to judge the stockings again and to evaluate the salesgirl and their confidence in rating her. Finally, they completed a questionnaire which included three batteries of questions on personality, one of which was a measure of self-confidence.

The findings of interest here bear upon personality and persuasibility. Male subjects low in generalized self-confidence are generally the more persuasible. Females are more persuasible in general but on the whole this is not correlated with self-confidence or self-esteem.

The reigning hypotheses on the relationship of self-confidence to persuasibility have been based either on the concept of ego defense (Cohen, 1959) or social approval (Janis, 1954), and Cox chose to add *perceived self-confidence in accomplishing a task*. He was dealing, then, with two measures of self-confidence: generalized self-confidence, presumably an attribute of "personality"; and specific self-confidence, that is, perceived confidence in judging stockings.

It has been suggested that the reason that in women personality has not been found correlated with persuasibility is that the issues used in experiments have not been important to them. And importance may account for the strong relationship Cox found when he gave them the task of rating stockings. That he was testing middle-class housewives may be why the relationship was curvilinear. (That is to say, his subjects may have covered a wider range of self-confidence than might be found in the usual experimental groups.) Women with *medium* scores on the test of self-confidence were the most likely to alter their rating of the stockings in the direction recommended by the salesgirl; those scoring *either* high or low were less likely to accept her suggestion. As a matter of fact, countersuggestibility apparently crept in among the women low in self-confidence; those who rated lowest were almost three times as likely as the others to change in the *opposite* direction. Since these findings were replicated in three independent samples, ranging from 62 to 144 subjects, there is little reason to question them for this type of person and situation. The differences were both significant and big.

The curvilinear relationship was not anticipated and any explanation must, of course, be ad hoc. One might be that, faced with the difficult task of judging between two identical stockings and the salesgirl's flat assertion that one was better than the other, the women tacitly had to ask themselves two questions: Do I need help? Am I secure enough to accept help? Accordingly, the subjects most likely to accept the salesgirl's suggestion would be those with little enough self-confidence to want help, but still with enough to accept it. As an explanation, this is at least consistent with the curvilinear data and with the apparent counter-suggestibility of the subjects with little self-confidence.

This explanation, however, should not apply to individuals confident of their ability to perform the task. And this turned out to be the case. Among the subjects confident they could perform the *specific* task, generalized self-confidence played little or no role. The usual notions of social compliance and ego defense were virtually entirely over-ridden by the subject's confidence in her handling of the task—a conclusion which is supported, no matter how the data are combined.

My intention in telling this is to present a promising experiment in regarding the audience as being involved in problem solving. As already suggested, theories of social communication are caught between two contrasting models of human behavior. One we may call the "influence" model: One person does something to another. We have partially escaped from the simplest version of it, and now regard the audience as

influenced only in part, and in the other part solving problems of ego defense or of interpersonal relations. Meanwhile, there is the always endemic model of economic rationality which in one or another of its forms sees man as maximizing some tangible value. This latter, very simple problem-solving model we spontaneously use when we *judge* behavior, particularly with respect to whether it is rational or sensible or dignified. Thus ironically, we use the influence model, or the modified influence model, to explain why people do what they do, but we use the economist's problem-solving model for evaluating the behavior. There is scarcely a surer way of making people look foolish!

There is no reason why the two models should not be seen as complementary rather than antagonistic. But the fusion has not taken place to any conspicuous degree in the mainstream of research, as can be seen most clearly in literature on informal communication and personal influence. There are two major traditions from which this literature has developed (Rogers, 1962): One, that of the heartland of social communication, stresses social compliance and/or social conformity. The other tradition, that of rural sociology, is concerned with how farmers acquire knowledge useful in their day-to-day problems. While the two have in certain respects become intermeshed after some decades of isolation, overtones of social compliance and conformity persist in the social-psychological literature. There is little reference to problem solving.

The students of one of my colleagues who had read a standard treatment of the role of reference groups in buying behavior discussed it entirely without reference to the fact that the consumers might want to eat the food they bought!

The virtue of Cox's data is that they enable us to relate the problem-solving dimensions of behavior to social relationships and ego defensive. It is interesting that—in this study—the more "psychological" processes come into play only at the point at which felt self-confidence in accomplishing the task falls below a critical point. Thus, tendency to accept the suggestions of the alleged salesgirl in Cox's experiment must be seen as a function of both ability to deal with the task and personality.

The difficulty of the task may either fortify or suppress the more "social-psychological" processes, depending on the specific circumstances. Thus, study of drug preference shows that as the task gets easier, the individual can indulge in the luxury of concurring with someone whom he likes, whereas when risk is great he has to concentrate on the risk-reducing potentialities of the source of information.

Thus the full-blown, problem-solving interpretation of the behavior of an audience in no sense rules out the problems with which students of communication have recently concerned themselves: ego defense and social adjustment. As a matter of fact, such problems seem explorable in a more profitable fashion if, simultaneously, attention is paid to the more overt tasks for which people use information. Yet, while there has been a consistent drift toward granting the audience more initiative, it cannot be said that the general literature on communication yet accords it a full range of intentions.

Of course, the audience is not wholly a free agent: It must select from what is offered. But even here, the audience has influence, since it is generally offered an array of communications to which it is believed it will be receptive. The process of social communication and of the flow of influence in general must be regarded as a transaction. "Transactionism," which has had a variety of meanings in psychology, is used here in the sense of an exchange of values between two or more parties; each gives in order to get.

The argument for using the transactional model for *scientific* purposes is that it opens the door more fully to exploring the intention and behavior of members of the audience and encourages inquiry into the influence of the audience on the communicator by specifically treating the process as a two-way passage. In addition to the influence of the audience on the communicator, there seems little doubt that influence also operates in the "reverse" direction. But the persistence of the one-way model of influence discourages the investigation of both directions of relationship. With amusing adroitness some writers have assimilated the original experiment of Zimmerman and Bauer to established concepts such as reference groups, thereby ignoring what we thought was the clear implication of a two-way flow of influence.

At our present state of knowledge there is much to be said for the transactional model's pragmatic effect on research, but at the same time it is the most plausible description of the process of communication as we know it. Yet there seems to be a tendency to assume that words such as "transaction," "reciprocity," and the like imply exact equality in each exchange, measured out precisely according to the value system and judgment of the observer. This is nonsense. Obviously there are inequities, and they will persist, whether we use our own value systems as observers or if we have perfect knowledge of the people we observe.

The rough balance of exchange is sufficiently equitable in the long run to keep *most* individuals in our society engaged in the transactional relations of communication and influence. But some "alienated" people absent themselves from the network of communication as do, also, many businessmen who have doubts about the money they spend on advertising. The alienation is by no means peculiar to one end of the chain of communication or influence.

This point of view may be taken as a defense of certain social institutions such as advertising and the mass media. There is a limited range of charges against which *impotence* may indeed be considered a defense. Once more, ironically, both the communicator and the critic have a vested interest in the exploitative model. From the point of view of the communicator, it is reassuring that he will receive *at least* a fair return for his efforts; to the critic, the exploitative model gratifies the sense of moral indignation.

REFERENCES

1. Bauer, R. A. *The new man in Soviet psychology.* Cambridge, Mass.: Harvard University Press, 1952.
2. Bauer, R. A. Risk handling in drug adoption: The role of company preference. Publ. Opin. Quart., 1961, 25, 546–559.
3. Bauer, R. A. The initiative of the audience. Paper read at New England Psychological Association, Boston, November, 1962.
4. Bauer, R. A., Pool, I. de Sola, & Dexter, L. A. *American business and public policy.* New York: Atherton Press, 1963.
5. Berelson, B. What missing the newspaper means. In P. F. Lazarsfeld & F. N. Stanton (Eds.), *Communications research, 1948–1949.* New York: Harper & Row, Publishers, 1949. Pp. 111–129.
6. Bogart, L. Adult talk about newspaper comics. *Amer. J. Sociol.,* 1955, 61, 26–30.
7. Chein, I. The image of man. *J. soc. Issues,* 1962, 18, 36–54.
8. Cohen, A. R. Some implications of self-esteem for social influence. In C. I. Hovland & I. L. Janis (Eds.), *Personality and persuasibility.* New Haven, Conn.: Yale University Press, 1959. Pp. 102–120.
9. Coleman, J., Menzel, H., & Katz, E. Social processes in physicians' adoption of a new drug. *J. chron. Dis.,* 1959, 9, 1–19.
10. Cox, D. F. Information and uncertainty: Their effects on consumers' product evaluations. Unpublished doctoral dissertation, Harvard University, Graduate School of Business Administration, 1962.
11. Davison, W. P. On the effects of communication. *Publ. Opin. Quart.,* 1959, 23, 343–360.
12. Dexter, L. A., & White, D. M. (Eds.) *People, society and mass communication.* (Tentative title) New York: The Free Press, in press.
13. Herzog, Herta. What do we really know about daytime serial listeners? In P. F. Lazarsfeld & F. N. Stanton (Eds.), *Radio research, 1942–1943.* New York: Duell, Sloan & Pearce-Meredith Press, 1944. Pp. 3–33.

14. Hovland, C. I. Reconciling conflicting results derived from experimental survey studies of attitude change. *Amer. Psychologist*, 1959, **14**, 8–17.
15. Hovland, C. I., Lumsdaine, A. A., & Sheffield, F. D. *Experiments in mass communication*. Princeton, N.J.: Princeton University Press, 1949.
16. Hyman, H. H., & Sheatsley, P. B. Some reasons why information campaigns fail. *Publ. Opin. Quart.*, 1947, **11**, 412–423.
17. Inkeles, A., & Bauer, R. A. *The Soviet citizen*. Cambridge, Mass.: Harvard University Press, 1959.
18. Janis, I. L. Personality correlates of susceptibility to persuasion. *J. Pers.*, 1954, **22**, 504–518.
19. Katz, E., & Foulkes, D. On the use of the mass media for "escape." *Publ. Opin. Quart.*, 1962, **26**, 377–388.
20. Kimball, P. People without papers. *Publ. Opin. Quart.*, 1959, **23**, 389–398.
21. Klapper, J. *The effects of mass communication*. New York: The Free Press, 1960.
22. Lazarsfeld, P. F., Berelson, B., & Gaudet, Hazel. *The people's choice*. New York: Columbia University Press, 1948.
23. Maccoby, Eleanor E. Why do children watch T.V.? *Publ. Opin. Quart.*, 1954, **18**, 239–244.
24. Maccoby, N., & Maccoby, Eleanor E. Homeostatic theory in attitude change. *Pub. Opin. Quart.*, 1961, **25**, 535–545.
25. Murray, H. A. The personality and career of Satan. *J. soc. Issues*, 1962, **18**, 1–35.
26. Rogers, E. M. *Diffusion of innovations*. New York: Free Press, 1962.
27. Seidenfeld, M. A. Consumer psychology in public service and government. In R. W. Seaton (Chm.), Consumer psychology: The growth of a movement. Symposium presented at American Psychological Association, New York, September 1961.
28. Smith, B. L., Laswell, H. D., & Casey, R. D. *Propaganda, communication and public opinion*. Princeton, N.J.: Princeton Univer. Press, 1946.
29. Warner, W. L., & Henry, W. E. The radio daytime serial: A symbolic analysis. *Genet. Psychol. Monogr.*, 1948, **37**, 3–71.
30. Winick, C. Teenagers, satire and *Mad. Merrill-Palmer Quart.*, 1962, **8**, 183–203.
31. Zimmerman, Claire, & Bauer, R. A. The effects of an audience on what is remembered. *Publ. Opin. Quart.*, 1956, **20**, 238–248.

9.4 INNOVATION-RESISTING AND INNOVATION-PRODUCING ORGANIZATIONS

Herbert A. Shephard

An organization is itself an innovation, but most organizations of the past have been designed to be innovation-resisting. Like fully automated factories, organizations which contain people have customarily been designed to do a narrowly prescribed assortment of things, and to do them reliably. To ensure reliable repetition of prescribed operations, the organization requires

Reprinted from "Innovation-Resisting and Innovation-Producing Organizations" by Herbert A. Shephard in the *Journal of Business* of the University of Chicago, Vol. 40, No. 4, October 1967 by permission of the University of Chicago Press. Copyright 1967 by the University of Chicago.

strong defenses against innovation. Efforts to innovate must be relegated to the categories of error, irresponsibility and insubordination, and appropriate corrective action taken to bring the would-be innovators "back in line." Any change is likely to run counter to certain vested interests, and to violate certain territorial rights. Sentiments of vested interest and territorial rights are sanctified as delegations of legitimate authority in traditional organizations, thus guaranteeing quick and effective counteraction against disturbances. In theory, the innovation-resisting organization is not resistant to innovations issuing from the top of its authority structure. In the preface to one of the first Operations Research books, the authors stressed the importance of having the Operations Research team report directly to the chief executive, in recognition that the military organization can learn only at the top—changes in operations at lower levels occur by instruction from higher levels. But even the power of command is not always equal to the power of resistance, especially as society puts ever greater limitations on the power of command in civilian life.

For these reasons, exploration of the innovative process in organizations can conveniently proceed along two paths: first, how innovation is induced in settings which are resistant to innovation, and second, how to design an organization which is productive of innovations rather than resistant to them. A third path emerges out of an examination of the first two; namely, the exploration of a particular class of innovations, those which change an innovation-resisting organization into an innovation-producing one, or vice versa.

The Process of Innovation in Innovation-Resisting Organizations

Innovative ideas are most likely to occur to persons who have some familiarity with the situation to which the ideas would apply. Hence most novel ideas are likely to be generated at some distance from the power center of the organization. Since new ideas are disturbances, they are efficiently screened out of the stream of upward communication. But because power is centralized at the top, top support for an idea is almost a necessity if it is to move towards becoming an innovation. What strategies are available for breaking out of this system?

One alternative is to conceal the innovation from the rest of the organization. Almost all policing systems have loopholes. Perhaps the commonest example of concealment is the machine operator who develops a device to simplify his work, but does not use it when the industrial engineers are setting standards for his job. Similarly, salesmen often use methods and procedures which increase their effectiveness, but are unknown to their superiors and even explicitly contrary to company rules. Most organizations possess an underworld of technique and technology some of which is simply used to gain some freedom from the impositions of higher levels of authority, and some of which contributes to the achievement of corporate goals. Within the underworld, the innovations may or may not be circulated.

Most concealed innovations must take the form of local conspiracies if they are to be of real significance. Perhaps the most general formula for effective innovation is: "An idea; initiative; and a few friends." Sometimes large segments of organization conspire in this way. One vice-president speaks of "holding an umbrella" over certain of his subordinate organizations so that they are free to innovate. Another speaks of "surrounding the president with a moving framework" so that new developments can occur in the organization. An important weapon system was developed by a small group in a government laboratory over a five-year period in continuous violation of directives from headquarters to discontinue work. The entire laboratory gave support to the innovators in concealing their assignments, and the costs of development. Two of our largest corporations now do over a third of their business in areas which the board of directors explicitly decided not to enter, only to find that the company was already obligated by contracts negotiated at lower levels. A manufacturing vice-president successfully concealed from his superiors an experiment in union-management cooperation in one of his plants.

Outside as well as inside sources of support are often used by the successful innovator in acquiring a critical mass of support. A group of staff engineers in one company designed a process plant containing a number of radical innovations, then arranged to have a distinguished chemical engineer employed as consultant to evaluate their work. A comparison of two approaches within a university, both by men whose motivation was that of successful innovators, is instructive. Each was given an opportunity to develop an interdisciplinary research institute. One concentrated on building collaborative relations with key members of the departments involved; the other concentrated on raising research funds from outside the university which required the collaboration of only a few other members of the staff. Deducing which institute succeeded is left as an exercise for the reader.

As some of the above examples imply, respectability is an innovator's best friend, and since innovation is not a respectable undertaking in innovation-resisting organizations, he should choose respectable friends to support him. If he can find none in the organization, then he may seek them outside and help them find ways they can help him. But highly respected executives inside the firm are in a better position to serve as promoters and protectors, midwives and nurses.

Although top management support is always necessary for the adoption of an innovative idea, it is by no means sufficient to ensure its implementation. *The skill with which the career civil service staff of a government agency can frustrate the innovative efforts of a newly appointed chief from industry is often dramatic.* Similarly, the university president who seeks to reform the college is met with resistance tactics that the use of the power of his office cannot thwart. In industry a new chief executive entering the organization from outside finds it easier to remove subordinate executives who stand in the way of his innovative efforts, and even a chief executive promoted from within is able to rearrange the power structure with greater ease than can be done in government or in a university.

Radical innovations are most readily adopted and implemented in times of organizational crisis. Earlier it was noted that the innovator must find a way of breaking out of the closed organizational system that is resistant to innovation. During a crisis there is an external threat to the survival of that system; for a moment it is open and searching for new solutions to the basic problem of survival.

A state of crisis does not itself generate good innovative ideas. But the uncertainty and anxiety generated by the crisis make organization members eager to adopt new structures that promise to *relieve the anxiety*. Thus in an early crisis in the automobile industry, a new leader brought into one corporation had a ready-made plan for reorganization that made it possible for the firm to recover quickly and take the lead. In another company in the same industry the crisis brought panic innovations—for example, most of the telephones were removed—instead of innovations rationally designed to solve the problems.

So much for innovation in innovation-resisting organizations. It requires an unusual combination of qualities: a creative but pragmatic imagination; psychological security and an autonomous nature; an ability to trust others and to earn the trust of others; great energy and determination; a sense of timing; skill in organizing; and a willingness and ability to be machiavellian where that is what the situation requires.

Innovation in Innovation-Producing Organizations

An innovation-producing organization is one which is continuously learning, adapting to changes within itself and in its environment, and successfully innovating in that environment. What can we say about the organizational form, values and norms, decision-making processes, rewards, punishments, structures of authority, power, influence and status, and the mentality and character structure of members in successful innovation-producing organizations?

The nature of the problem confronting modern organizations has been changing rapidly. In the past, the major problem has appeared to be how to get and coordinate reliable efficient repetitive responses from specialized individuals: how to do complex, programmable tasks with people as the doers. But the direction of modern technology is to eliminate people from the doing of programmable tasks. What must be done many times can, in general, be automated. Principles of human organization developed to serve that end are almost certain to be misleading when the major problem becomes finding ways in which people can organize for innovative, unprogrammable activities. Yet manufacturing, command, mechanistic, bureaucratic principles are so pervasive in our society that all activities tend to be forced into this mold even when it prevents the achievement of announced objectives. The schools stand in the way of learning; the research organization stands in the way of research; the sales and service organizations stand in the way of sales and service.

Yet there are some organizations and parts of organizations whose principles of operation are different from the bureaucratic norm, and whose output is innovative. From observations of such organizational inventions, some tentative principles can be inferred.

One of the most prominent of these is periodicity—or a number of kinds of alternation associated with innovating groups. One kind consists in adapting organizational form to suit the requirements of the task at a given phase of innovation. For the generation phase of an innovation, the organization needs a quality of openness, so that diverse and heterogeneous persons can contribute, and so that many alternatives can be explored. For implementation, a quite different quality may be needed: singleness of purpose, functional division of labor, responsibility and authority, discipline, the drawing of internal communication boundaries, and so on. For example, a military raiding unit in the Pacific War made use of alternating organizational forms. The planning before a raid was done jointly by the entire unit—the private having as much opportunity to contribute to the planning as the colonel. During the raid, the group operated under strict military command system. Following each raid, the unit returned to the open system used in planning for purposes of evaluating and maximizing learning from each raid.

Some industries are provided with natural periodicities, either seasonal or through such industrial traditions as an annual model change. These rhythms permit an opportunity for alternation of periods of action, involvement, experience, discipline with periods of evaluation, revitalization, reflection, and planning (though the opportunities may not be grasped). In industries not provided with natural alternation, opportunities for periods of evaluation, revitalization, reflection and planning have to be created. There is an increasing use of executive "retreats" for these purposes.

Other types of periodicity which seem to be stimulating to the innovative process have been noted. One is to have two groups working in parallel on the same problem, with periodic opportunities for intergroup communication. The use of special task forces or a modified project form* of organization provides another kind of periodicity, so that members are regrouped and provided with novel challenges periodically.

Returning to the example of the military raiding unit, it seems clear that the interpersonal relationships and group norms of this unit were at variance with those of an innovation-resisting organization, even though at times the unit operated as a command system in accord with military regulations. It was as though they chose to operate as a command system by consensus, rather than operating at other times as an open system by command. Presumably their close interdependence for physical survival helped to create a climate of sufficient mutual trust and respect that rank could be cast aside and the private could feel free to criticize his superiors. The same qualities of trust, mutual respect, openness, and ability to confront conflict appear to characterize innovative groups in other contexts. This was the quality of relationships in some of the ad hoc project teams of distinguished scientists and engineers created by the government shortly after World War II to appraise certain key issues in national defense. The same was true of "Blackett's Circus," the pioneering operational research team in England during World War II. The boundaries of each in-

---

* By a project form of organization is meant one in which a temporary organizational unit is created for each task containing all the skills necessary for performing the task.

dividual's scientific territory were freely crossed, and symbols of differential status in the scientific community were thrown aside in favor of joint problem-solving.

It is significant that the examples that come to mind are in temporary systems created by national emergencies. They are in fact only further examples of the point already made with respect to the readiness of innovation-resisting organizations for innovation during a period of survival crisis. At such times men are readier to give up their boring and petty struggles for status, scientific politics, to become less alienated from one another, and from themselves.

Yet we know that simply putting one group against another under win-lose conditions does not lead to the best use of its resources. It is more likely to lead to panic innovation, closing off of communication lines, closed system operation, and punishment of nonconformity. The common factor in the above examples is that the groups operated as open systems—the national emergency provided a common cause, challenge, or superordinate goal, rather than a source of panic.

Under these conditions then—superordinate goals held in common, and a temporary system in which status struggles can for the moment be set aside—the members of the system all evidence, to greater or lesser degree, the "unusual" qualities earlier attributed to the innovator: a creative but pragmatic imagination; psychological security and an autonomous nature; an ability to trust others and to earn the trust of others; great energy and determination; skill in organizing; and a willingness and ability to be machiavel-

lian (in these cases, the group's mission called for just that).

Can equivalent conditions be attained in an organization whose task is to produce innovations? The character structure of the innovator in innovation-resisting organizations corresponds to what the existential psychologists call the self-actualizing person. He is his own man rather than the organization's man; his behavior and sense of self-worth are not blindly determined by the organization's reward and punishment system (either in the form of submission to it or rebellion against it); if he cannot transform his situation into one in which he and others can be both autonomous and interdependent, he feels free to fight it or to leave it.

Such men are rare because the institutions of our society do not provide the conditions under which many persons are able to grow to this degree of human maturity. The innovation-producing organization must aim to provide an environment in which this kind of growth can occur. This means a climate in which members can view one another as resources rather than competitive threats or judges; a climate of openness and mutual support in which differences can be confronted and worked through, and in which feedback on performance is a mutual responsibility among members so that all can learn to contribute more. Such an environment is difficult to provide, since it is at variance with traditional management doctrine.

The innovator who fails is likely to be motivated by rebelliousness against authority. For him the risk is in not innovating—in having to confront feelings of inferiority or subordination.

For the successful innovator, too, the subjective risk lies in not innovating. He risks his sense of self-worth if he must settle for compromises, or for less than full personal effectiveness and contribution. The "objective" risk, in terms of organization logic is of his job security or chances for advancement, but this does not mean that he is subjectively taking the risk in the hope of a large payoff in terms of personal advancement. In this sense *successful innovators are often marginal to the organization: that is, their basis for self-esteem is somewhat independent of organizational values as expressed in its reward and punishment system.* They are also, perhaps for the same reason, often marginal in the sense that they are more able than others to cross some traditional boundaries in the organization.

Innovations Which Help an Innovation-Resisting Organization Become an Innovation-Producing Organization

There are many organizations attempting to become innovation-producers within a framework of managerial assumptions and practices which are appropriate for innovation-resisting organizations. For them, the innovative processes which should be of greatest interest are ones which would help them to adopt and implement a framework more appropriate for the task.

This movement requires something more basic than structural change: decentralization, the use of a project form of organization, or the creation of a class of senior scientists who have freedom of mobility in the organization. Such structural inventions can help, but if the major preoccupation of members of the organization is with status, with controlling others, and with getting a larger slice of an unexpanding pie, these devices will not produce the desired results. The adaptability and creative application which are sought require a different outlook on life, on oneself, and on others.

The impact of traditional methods of education, child-rearing, and organizational experience has been to develop rather complex skills for competing with others in a variety of games with a variety of first prizes and booby prizes, and requiring a variety of facades. Viewed from the standpoint of the lofty humanistic ideals that we from time to time proclaim, our practice is a theatre of the absurd. At the same time, our capacities for collaboration, confrontation of ourselves and others, or for developing in ourselves and one another our full human potential have received very little attention; the rules of our organizational games discourage the development and use of these capacities.

In sum, movement towards innovation-producing organization requires processes of personal and interpersonal re-education so that more of us develop the qualities of independence and capacity for autonomous interdependence earlier attributed to the ideal innovator.

PART FOUR

Values and Goals

Chapter 10

FINDING DIRECTION
IN PLANNED CHANGE

WHATEVER else planning may mean, it signifies an anticipation of some future state of affairs and the confirmation of a vision of that future in the present in order to motivate, guide, and direct present action. A planner's present situation always includes a time perspective forward—a future different from the present, yet populated with more or less clearly delineated agents and counteragents, objects to be avoided, objects to be embraced, means to empower avoidance or embracing, and some context of interrelated factors and forces, human and nonhuman, benign, hostile, or neutral. Man as planner must climb out of his involvement in present transactions to look beyond the horizon of the present and to bring back a vision of the future to modify the tempo, quality, and direction of his present transactions.

It is the fact of change in the internal and external conditions of human life that makes planning important and necessary to time-bound men, choosing and acting of necessity within the medium of history. And it is the fact of change that makes planning difficult for time-bound men. If the future were to be like the present, there would be no need to give thought to preparing for it. Yet, since the future will be different from the present, men do not know how far to trust their present anticipations of it in preparing to meet and cope with it. All human planning is planning for change and requires judgments about the proper balance between investment of energy and resources in the pursuit or avoidance of consequences we can now anticipate and the massing of free and uncommitted energy and resources for coping with unanticipated consequences.

Kenneth Boulding has illuminated the predicament of men in attempting to plan the future of the social systems in and through which they live in his distinction between "evolutionary systems" and "mechanical systems."

One thing we can say about man's future with a great deal of confidence is that it will be more or less surprising. This phenomenon of surprise is not something which arises merely out of man's ignorance, though ignorance can contribute to what might be called unnecessary surprises. There is, however, something fundamental in the nature of our evolutionary system which makes exact foreknowledge about it impossible, and as social systems are in a large measure evolutionary in character, they participate in the property of containing ineradicable surprises.[1]

Mechanical systems have no surprise in them since time as a significant variable has been eliminated from them in the sense that they have no past or future and the present is a purely arbitrary point. The traditional lure among scientific students and planners of human affairs toward interpreting social systems as mechanical systems may rest on some inherent preference for a world of no surprise among scientific men. Yet system breaks which result in more or less sudden changes in the defining characteristics of the system itself seem to characterize the temporal careers of all human systems. And human planners must plan with the possibilities of system breaks somewhere within their field of consciousness.

We have spoken so far of the predicament of human planning in general. Yet planning always occurs within some time-bounded historical situation. What characteristics of the present historical situation have given new point and poignancy to men's efforts to find confident direction in planning for the future?

A radical increase in the rate of change in the conditions of life has thrown the problem of direction finding and planning into new perspective. Concentration of energy and resources in basic and applied research has resulted in a continuing revolution in the means and conditions of work, play, education, and family and community living. Men have found the established institutions and wisdoms from the past less and less dependable as guides to the effective and humane management of new knowledges and technologies in the conduct of life. Men in a slowly changing culture could validly assume that the ecological contours of their future life would be substantially similar to those of their past. Changes to be planned for could be seen as confinable and manageable within the patterns of a viable tradition out of the past. Modern men have been betrayed by tradition direction. They face both the hopes and terrors of an unknown future more directly than past men did, bereft of security in the guidance of traditional forms and wisdoms.

Finding direction for the future by projecting the forms and values of a traditional culture upon that future has been further undermined by the

---

[1] Kenneth E. Boulding, "Expecting the Unexpected: The Uncertain Future of Knowledge and Technology," Edgar L. Morphet and Charles O. Ryan (eds.), *Prospective Changes in Society by 1980* (Denver, Colo.: July 1966).

omnipresent fact of intercultural contact, confrontation, and mixing within nations and between nations. The development of vast networks of interdependence, the spread of mass media of communication, reduced security in spatial and political boundaries between cultures, due to space-destroying means of transportation and other related factors, have brought about uneasy contact and confrontation between traditionally segregated nations, classes, races, and subcultures. As we seek new bases for an interdependent future across these cleavages of culture by projecting the traditions of any one cultural tradition, the futility of this way of defining the future for purposes of planning becomes more and more apparent to modern men. If there is to be a common future, it must be constructed and reconstructed by men in a way to lead beyond the present maze of disparate and conflicting traditions. The outlines of the task have become clearer than the means for achieving it.

A third feature of contemporary man's struggles to find viable directions into his future is a widespread decline of confidence in a presiding Providence which will automatically and without human attention bring the plural and conflicting plans and actions of individual men and groups of men into the service of commonly valuable purposes. Confidence in some pre-established ordering principle within history—a principle which men can depend upon to bring meaningful and moral order out of the confusion and chaos of diverse and conflicting individual and group decidings and strivings—has taken many forms in the history of human affairs. The principle has been conceived theistically and naturalistically, personally and impersonally, immanently and transcendentally, pessimistically and optimistically. And it has been given many names—the Will of God, Fate, the Nature of Stoics and Taoists, the "Unseen Hand" of Adam Smith and the free-market mechanism of the classical economists, the Idea of Progress in Western liberalism, the historical inevitability of socialism in Marxism. One may recognize the common function which these versions of a superhuman directing principle have played in the direction of human affairs and in setting limits to human responsibility in planning man's future, without denying the differences which adherence to one version or another has made in the organization and deployment of human energies and resources. The effect of this confidence has been to narrow the range of human responsibility for finding and giving direction to the course of human history. Decline of confidence means a widening of man's responsibility for designing and inventing his own future. If there is to be an ordering principle in human planning, a principle attentive to the conservation and augmentation of human values, men must find, or better construct and apply, the principle through their own collective intelligence and volition.

If men are to invent their own future, they must assess and improve their ways of predicting that future. Daniel Bell, apparently agreeing with Santayana that whatever rationality is possible to the human will lies not in its substance but in its method, has examined the methods used by social scientists in predicting the future and has found twelve modes of prediction now in use. He describes and assesses these modes and suggests three areas of investigation by which our human powers of prediction might be augmented. His interest in augmenting these powers stems from a value commitment to widening the areas of human choice as men confront their future, not to producing a vision of the future as predetermined for man by forces outside of man's power to add or detract.

Margaret Mead works out of a similar value commitment in "The Future as the Basis for Establishing a Shared Culture." She is impressed by the fragmentation, "the agglomeration of partly dissociated, historically divergent and conceptually incongruent patterns" of culture and subculture which now block men and women in their search for a better future for mankind. Imaginatively, Miss Mead envisions a focus upon a future to be jointly built as the basis for uniting young and old, men and women, people of various nationalities and religions, scholarly and nonscholarly, in going beyond the fragmentation of culture which now divides them into the construction of a shared culture. The future, unlike the past, is always newborn. To involve all living persons in constructing the future is to release and facilitate change and growth all around. Mead's method of grappling with the future is more prophetic than Bell's in the sense that she is concerned not primarily with predicting but rather with invoking and shaping the future in the service of an overarching value—"shared culture."

Bell and Mead have discussed modern man's valid approach to his future as a general problem. Bennis seeks to envision the forms of human organization lying beyond bureaucratic forms which are now proving inadequate to coordinate productive effort under twentieth-century conditions. His method for bringing the future of organizations into present deliberations is a combination of prediction and prophecy. He is concerned both to project and extrapolate present trends in organizational change and to shape his vision of organization toward basic human values to be conserved and more fully realized than at present in and through future organization.

10.1   TWELVE MODES OF PREDICTION— A PRELIMINARY SORTING OF APPROACHES IN THE SOCIAL SCIENCES

Daniel Bell

In the *Cours de Philosophie Positive* (1830–1842), perhaps the last individual attempt to write a synoptic account of human knowledge, Auguste Comte cited as an example of the inherently unknowable, the chemical composition of the distant stars and the questions of

Daniel Bell, "Twelve Modes of Prediction—A Preliminary Sorting of Approaches in the Social Sciences," *Daedalus*, published by the American Academy of Arts and Sciences, Boston, Massachusetts, XCIII, No. 3 (1964), 845–

873. Footnotes omitted here are available in the original appearance. Abridged and used by permission.

whether there were "organized beings living on their surface." Within two decades, Gustave Kirchoff applied spectrum analysis to the stars and provided that very knowledge which Comte had declared to be impossible. And, as space probes reach Mars and Venus, we shall be in a position to answer the second question of the nature of the forms of life, if any, on the solar planets.

Few persons today would declare with confidence that something is unknowable. So secure is the dominion of science that the obverse attitude rules: today we feel that there are no inherent secrets in the universe, and that all is open; and this is one of the significant changes in the modern moral temper. And yet, every generation now feels that the foundation of its knowledge is inadequate and that the social forms as we know them are bound to change. We expect that science and technology will rework the map of society and no one any longer challenges their claims. One of the hallmarks of "modernity" is the awareness of change and the struggling effort to control the direction and pace of change.

The problem of any science is to understand the sources of change. And in this respect social science is fairly recent. The great intellectual barrier was that men always thought they knew the sources of change, which were also the sources of power, namely the personal will of kings, lawgivers and prophets, those who governed states, drafted laws, and established or reinforced religious beliefs. But only gradually did men realize that behind these visible sets of acts were such intangible nets as customs, institutions, and cultures, which subtly constrained and set the boundaries of social action. At the same time came the slow realization that there were "social forces" which generated change, whether they be impersonal processes such as demographic pressures (increased size and density of populations), technology, and science, or conscious strivings such as the demands of disadvantaged groups for equality or social mobility.

It is the modern *hubris* that we can effect the conscious transformation of society. What stands in our favor is that knowledge is cumulative. And, within the open community of science, it is self-corrective. What is more important, perhaps, is that we have a better appreciation of method. For what method allows us to do is to reformulate insight into consistent explanation. In this emphasis on method, the function of conjecture is not prediction but explanation. Prediction can be derived from experience, such as a farmer's expectation of crop production, without knowledge of the reasons why. Only with adequate explanation—an understanding of the relevant variables—can one seek to control or transform a situation. Conjecture, in this sense, stipulates a set of future predicates whose appearance should be explainable from theory. Prediction without explanation is insight, experience, or luck.

In this sense, too, the function of prediction is to reduce uncertainty. By stipulating, and thus testing, a hypothesis, one is able to verify the relevant factors which account for a predicted or observed change. For this reason, in distinguishing different kinds of prediction in the social sciences, I am ruling out historical theories of rhythms, periodizations and cycles—in most instances, recurrence is not really identity but, at best, analogy—wherein the investigator seeks for the Pythagorean number which rules the wheel of history or imposes a diachronic pattern on the rise and fall of civilizations.

In sorting out the different modes of prediction, I shall not be concerned with the relevant methodological tests of adequacy. The sorting is an effort to illustrate the *range* of approaches in the art of conjecture. The different modes are not "equal" to each other in the level of generality or scope of comprehension. Inevitably there are some overlaps, and a stricter reading might show that one mode subsumes some of the others. But to the extent that one can sort out a distinct number of types, the next step would be to order them in some logical classification and specify which mode of conjecture would be appropriate to what kind of problem.

1. Social Physics

The Comtean quest for "social laws" in which some basic regularities of human behavior or some major variables such as mass, pressure, gravitational velocity could be synthesized into a set of formulas akin to Newtonian or the later statistical mechanics of Willard Gibbs finds few serious adherents in the social sciences today. Yet one such model, Marx's "laws of motion" of capitalism, has been one of the most influential ideological doctrines of the past century (in but three years we celebrate the centennial of *Das Kapital*), and to the extent that it is still an element in the Bolshevik belief-system, it is a factor in assessing Communist policy.

Questions of politics apart, the Marxian model is still one of the most comprehensive efforts to create a large-scale system of prediction based on the in-teraction of a few crucial variables. Granted that the model has not worked, its "logic" is worth explication. Marx began, one may recall, with the components of value as constant capital, variable capital, and surplus value $(c+v+s)$, and from these, two ratios become central. One is the rate of surplus value, $s/v = s'$, and the other is the organic composition of capital, the relationship of labor to materials and machinery, $c/c+v = q$. These two are the primary variables from which the crucial variable, the rate of profit, is derived: $p = s' (1-q)$.

The "law of the falling rate of profit," which Marx derives from these equations, is the key to the system. Each capitalist, trying to increase his own profit, substitutes more constant for variable capital and ends by killing off the total of profits. Out of this tendency, Marx derives the corollary social consequences: the reserve army of the unemployed, the impoverishment of labor, the centralization (trustification) of capital, a deepening series of crises, the intensification of exploitation, sharpening class struggle, etc.

One can point out, as Paul Samuelson has, that the model rests on the difficult assumption of fixed coefficients and single techniques, and that modern tools such as linear programming can allow the substitution, analytically, of many alternative techniques in working out adequate production functions (i.e. the combination of units of labor and capital). Or one can argue the empirical point, as Strachey and others have, that the economic system is not autonomous and that a regulating agency, the State, can readjust the "equations" in response to political pressures.

The crucial element in the Marxian

model, which defines it as "social physics," is that these actions took place independent of the will of any single individual or, in the long run, of any groups of individuals. The interesting question remains whether such comprehensive, dynamic models are possible, even in the simplified versions such as Marx employed, and what would be the central variables that one would select to describe social and political interaction.

A different kind of "law," which has attracted increasing attention in recent years, is that of "logistics curves," which various authors have fitted to different time-series. The most startling of these are the laws of "exponential growth" or the "doubling rates" of different social phenomena.

The late Louis Ridenour has pointed out that the holdings of university libraries have doubled every eleven years since 1870, that long-distance telephone calls have doubled every seven-and-a-half years, that since Nellie Bly went around the world in 1889 the time for circumventing the globe decreased exponentially between 1889 and 1928 by a factor of two every quarter-century, and since the introduction of aircraft the rate of change has markedly increased. Derek Price has shown that the number of journals in science has increased by a factor of ten every half-century since 1790, and the number of abstracting journals has followed precisely the same law, multiplying by a factor of ten every half-century. At a certain point in these growths, "critical magnitudes" are reached and logistic curves react to "ceiling conditions" in different ways.

Ridenour, in fitting a number of such curves, has argued that the process of growth and saturation in social change follows the so-called "autocatalytic" processes of chemistry and biology. Price has sought to identify more differentiated modes of "reaction." He writes: ". . . growths that have long been exponential seem not to relish the idea of being flattened. Before they reach a midpoint they begin to twist and turn, and, like impost spirits, change their shapes and definitions so as not to be exterminated against that terrible ceiling. Or in less anthropomorphic terms, the cybernetic phenomenon of hunting sets in and the curve begins to oscillate wildly. . . . [One] finds two variants of the traditional logistic curve that are more frequent than the plain S-shaped ogive." One variant is the phenomenon, first recognied by Gerald Holton, of "escalation," in which growth curves "pick up" from earlier, related curves in repeated sequence. The other variant is one of violent fluctuation with a logarithmic decline to a stable maximum or to zero. This leads Price to conclude: "All the apparently exponential laws of growth must ultimately be logistic, and this implies a period of crisis extending on either side of the date of midpoint for about a generation. The outcome of the battle at the point of no return is complete reorganization or violent fluctuation or death of the variable."

If Ridenour's equations hold true and Price's generalizations regarding the "midpoints" of exponential curves are valid, one has here a powerful means of identifying processes of social change and making predictions about the outcomes.

And yet, the history of earlier, similar efforts to find underlying "laws" of variegated social phenomena should give us pause. In the late 1930s, the Harvard philologist George Kingsley

Zipf reported remarkable regularities in such diverse phenomena as the distribution of cities by size, the relation of rank order to frequency of word occurrences, the distribution of the frequencies of publication of scientists, and many others. Zipf tried to bring all these under the roof of a single mathematical relationship, the harmonic law, and devised a pseudo-explanation which he dubbed the "law of least effort." Fifteen years or so later, Herbert Simon was able to show that the similarity of these statistical distributions was not due to any overriding law but was a consequence of the similarity in the structure of the underlying probability mechanisms.

Yet this corrective effort has given us an interesting tool of prediction. For in the construction of such probability models we encounter stochastic processes, where the sequences of outcomes are uncertain and where we are forced to build "conjecturing" into the structure of the model. The development of stochastic reasoning, using probabilistic models, should allow us to do better estimating in problems involving frequency distributions, as well as those involving future outcomes involving the choice of further information.

Some recent efforts to create a "social physics" devolve from the work of the mathematical biologist Nicholas Rashevsky. One of his students, Anatol Rapoport, has written a book, *Fights, Games, and Debates* which sets up mathematical models for mass action and descriptive models for conflict situations. One section of the book deals with arms races, and the equations that are developed seek to describe the development of actual arms races in the same way that the equations of thermodynamics are meant to describe the actual behavior of gases. One intention of the new social physics is to set up general probabilistic laws governing behavior in game-like situations.

2. Trends and Forecasts

The most familiar form of prediction involves some form of extrapolation from time-series either as straight-line projections, cyclical turns, or alternative models based on some definition of upper and lower limits. One can say that this mode of prediction differs from "social physics" in that the latter seeks some general principle, or attempts to create a closed system; trend analysis takes some selected area and seeks to make a more limited prediction, *ceteris paribus*.

The three major kinds of trend analysis have been economic forecasting, demography, and technological change. The assumptions of economic forecasting itself would require a long paper, so I restrict myself to the other two.

Demographic prediction, in the large, has always been under the long shadow of Thomas Malthus. While the exact relationship between the arithmetical growth rate of food supply and the geometrical tendency of population increase is now suspect, the neo-Malthusians still hold to the general view that the present is in some way an exceptional period and that at some point, either fifty or a hundred years from now, the world "will have begun to go back," as Sir Charles Darwin has put it, "into . . . its normal state, the state in which natural selection operates by producing too many people, so that the excess simply cannot survive.

Sir Charles has made some specific estimates. He feels that by A.D. 2000 the world population will be four billion. He cites the fact that between 1947 and 1953 agriculture production increased by 8 per cent but the world's population by 11 per cent, "so that the world was hungrier at the end than at the beginning. And in fifty years, the four billion will be hungrier than the two and a half billion in 1950."

Leaving aside the question of the definition of hunger, the basic assumptions are threefold: that human population has followed the availability of food supply so consistently that the human animal is responding to biological conditions in no different manner than other animals; that improvements in technology cannot keep pace with the rise of populations; that the voluntary limitations on birth cannot be accepted by the whole of humanity, so that those who limited births would be swallowed up by the others who did not. Each of these is open to question in some manner. As to the first, while this may be true of primitive societies, it is less so of modern industrial countries where the standard of living becomes more controlling of the number of births; the second is still an open question; the third raises vital political questions most notably today about the role of China and secondarily of India in the desires of their governments to control or expand population in these countries and the checks thereon.

What this does point up is that demographic prediction, involving individual and aggregate decisions, the role of custom and the adaptation to standard of living, the influence of education and new class styles, the relationship to economic development and the political role of government, is one of the areas where systematic scrutiny of the conditions of prediction would yield important results.

The area of "technological trends" could lead us very easily, and temptingly, into the alluring field of science fiction. Here one's imagination could quickly climb William James's "faith ladder" and turn possibilities into probabilities and probabilities into certainties. While one would assume that the prediction of invention should be fairly easy, since the antecedent conditions are highly structured, the interesting thing is that a review of such predictions finds them to be singularly inept. Reality, it seems, is more recalcitrant than the imagination.

As S. Lilley writes: "The moral for forecasters is: Do not predict individual inventions in detail—that is usually a waste of time." The correct method, he argues, is twofold: extrapolation of present trends, and predictions in the form possibilities. "The predictor need not be concerned with how a technical problem is to be solved, but only whether it will be solved or not." This is based on the principle of "equivalent invention" enunciated by S. L. Gilfallen. Gilfallen, writing in 1937, cites the problem of flying in fog. There were twenty-five means suggested of solving it. To predict which means would be the most successful was hazardous; but one could predict that the problem was solvable. "The point is that we are not concerned with the prediction of inventions, only with their effects. And the fact that there are almost always many possible inventions that could lead to the same desired effect enormously increases the chances of successful prediction," Lilley concludes.

The methods of political forecasting —the work of the Gallup organization, the University of Michigan surveys, the Columbia University studies under Paul Lazarsfeld, the work of *Demoskopie* in Germany and *Sondages* in France—would require a separate paper. Strictly speaking, this is not trend analysis, though past trends may be important in such crucial questions as how to allocate "undecided" voters. At bottom the success of the forecast is a function of the accuracy of the sample and the reduction of interviewer bias. Certain presumed disqualifying effects, such as the poll itself creating a "bandwagon," can be discounted. The success of *ex post facto* explanation is a function of the "process analysis" (i.e. the selection of relevant determinants such as the mass media, or personal influence) employed.

3. Structural Certainties

In his *Essai sur l'Art de la Conjecture*, Bertrand de Jouvenel describes an *order of events* that are legally prescribed and traditionally reinforced, which he calls "les certitudes structurelles." This type of ordering differs logically from trends, because it does not describe processes or time-series that are derivable from aggregate behavior, or which may be immanent, but which are based on custom and law.

M. de Jouvenel's example is an interesting one. He describes the problem of a Democrat in 1962 who might like to succeed President Kennedy. He knows that there will be a president of the United States, that elections will take place on the second Tuesday of November in 1964 and 1968, that unless he has a physical accident, John F. Kennedy will be the Democratic candidate, since the party customarily designates the existing office holder. But Kennedy will not be a candidate in 1968 (assuming his re-election in 1964) because a constitutional amendment forbids a third successive term.

Of course M. de Jouvenel, like all of us, had no way of knowing that a physical accident would prevent John F. Kennedy from filling out his term. Yet the "structural certainties" remain. In this instance it is now taken for granted that Lyndon Johnson will be renominated in 1964, and, because he filled out less than half of his predecessor's term, he might well be a candidate for re-election in 1968 as well.

M. de Jouvenel had taken this "prosaic" set of facts to illustrate that much of human behavior can be predicted because of such structural certainties. Yet the concept is useful because it is one of the ways of ranking the stability of different kinds of political and social systems. (What are the structural certainties in the Brazilian political system?) This concept is analogous to what sociologists call "institutionalized behavior," and in any established social system, the chief problem is to define the prescribed norms, the modes of conformity, and the limits of legitimate deviation from such institutional norms which are allowed by the system.

4. The Operational Code

Structural certainties (or institutionalized behavior) are based on a known or open mode of conduct, the rules of which are prescribed and reinforced by legal or moral sanction, and this allows one type of prediction. But there is another form of conduct which is usually implicit, rather than explicit, often unrealized even by the actors, and which has to be inferred and explicated by an analyst. This form is the "operational code" or what might be called the "do's and don't's" of conduct, the implicit rules of the game.

In some instances, such as Machiavelli's *The Prince*, these are normative prescriptions for a ruler. But in other cases these are efforts to discern an underlying pattern of behavior, which is either an adaptive mechanism (or rules of strategy) for a political group, or simply a series of adjustments which permit political survival.

One pioneer in this type of analysis, and prediction, is Nathan Leites. In several books on the Soviet Union and on France, he has sought to codify rules. In the case of the Soviet Union, Leites has sought to establish the basic mode of Bolshevik conduct, which he derives from various maxims and precepts of Communist patristic writings; but he roots this, equally, in some psychoanalytic hypotheses regarding Bolshevik character structure. In his study of France, he has sought to delineate the "rules of the game" as observed in parliamentary behavior.

In an analogous but broader fashion, there have been attempts to establish the "national style" of a country. The national style, or the characteristic way of response, is a compound of the values and national character of a country. It is the distinctive way of meeting the problems of order and adaptation, of conflict and consensus, of individual ends and communal welfare, that confront any country. It has been observed, for example, that the American "style" is one that stresses action and achievement, is fundamentally optimistic, believes that life is tractable, the environment manipulable, and that all political problems can be "solved." This does not assume a distribution of such traits among all the persons in the country in any mechanical notion of national character; but it does assume that there is a characteristic way of responding to problems, which is typified in the leadership; and to this extent it can serve as a rough guide to political action.

5. The Operational System

The "operational code" is an attempt to infer styles of conduct derived from psychological hypotheses or the value patterns of social groups or countries. The "operational system," an older form of analysis, is an effort to specify the underlying source of "renewable power" in a society regardless of the momentary fluctuations of office. Here, too, as in the case of "social physics," the most direct effort derives from Marx, and the classic analysis of this "model" in his *The Eighteenth Brumaire of Louis Bonaparte*.

Louis Bonaparte, in Marx's analysis, is an "adventurer" representing no class or social group, although basing himself on the Society of December 10th and the *Lumpenproletariat*. To maintain power, he has to play off one group against another, representing himself at first for the peasantry, and then against them, for the workers, and then against them. Industry and trade prosper in hothouse fashion under the strong government. But the Bonapartist *Lumpenproletariat* is to enrich itself. "This contradictory task of the man explains the contradictions of his government, the confused groping hither and thither which seeks now to win, now to humiliate first one class and then another and arrays all of them uniformly against him, whose practical uncertainty forms a highly comical contrast to the imperious categorical style of the government decrees, a style which is copied obsequiously from the Uncle."

The executive authority has made itself an independent power. But underneath there is still a class system. "Bonaparte feels it to be his mission to safeguard 'civil order.' But the strength of this civil order lies in the middle class. He looks on himself, therefore, as the representative of the middle class and issues decrees in this sense. Nevertheless, he is somebody solely due to the fact that he has broken the political power of this middle class and daily breaks it anew. Consequently, he looks on himself as the adversary of the political and literary power of the middle class. *But by protecting its material power, he generates its political power anew.*"

The point here is that a renewable means of power provides continuity for a social system. Whether the specific historical analysis is right or wrong, methodologically, it does sensitize us to look for the institutional sources of power and to specify levels of analysis. Where a system is established (say, property in land), it is "neutral" as to "who" has power. As Schumpeter has said, the rise and fall of social classes is the rise and fall of families, but the *mode of defining classes* may remain a constant. In specifying levels of analysis, we can try to see what kind of political efforts seek to change the system itself, and which are changes *within* a system.

One of the problems of modern political analysis is that *many* "operational systems" coexist as modes of power. In western democratic countries there is property, transferred through inheritance; technical skill, acquired by education; and political entrepreneurship, whose base is a mass mobilization; and each of these systems provides competing or overlapping routes to power. Yet the identification of such systems and the specification of the levels of analysis is a necessary condition for political prediction.

6. Structural Requisites

The idea of structural requisites focuses not on any underlying system but on the minimal set of concerns any government faces and it tries to identify "strains" or problems on the basis of the government's ability to manage those concerns. The list of what constitutes an invariant set of functions for any political system and the kinds of structures necessary to facilitate performance have varied with different authors. But what the approach does seek is a comprehensive typology which, in the words of one of these system-builders, Gabriel Almond, could allow the political analyst to "make precise comparisons relating the elements of the three sets—functions, structures, and styles—in the form of a series of probability statements."

In the formulation by Almond, the product of the three sets would yield a matrix with several hundred cells, and an effort to sample frequencies over time by performances of these three sets would create a stupendous problem. Yet the effort to create a typology is the first necessary step for distinguishing different kinds of political problems.

Au fond, what this approach suggests is what the anthropologist Alexander Goldenweiser once called "the principle of limited possibilities." Goldenweiser was trying to "mediate" the argument between anthropologists on the question of diffusion or independent invention of techniques. Methodologically, he argued that the "relatively fixed features which determined the conditions of effective use" of an object indicated a necessary convergence of forms. (One might say, analogously, that Pareto's *Tratto* of General Sociology is based on the same principle. In it, Pareto disregards the manifest political content of doctrines and seeks to establish a limited number of basic residues, derivations and sentiments, and in the combination of these to establish the basic political forms possible in society.)

Most of these theoretical efforts, if they ever come to fruition, would produce vast sociological "input-out" tables; but a rougher and readier use, implicitly, of the principle of limited possibilities indicates some of its predictive value. Thus, in 1954, Barrington Moore analyzed Soviet society in these terms. According to Moore, the recruitment to a ruling group could be handled through *traditional* (inheritance or nepotism), *rational-technical* (skill), or *political* (party loyalty) criteria. The use of any one criterion limits the range of workable alternatives for the solution of problems requisite to the system. Industrialization requires high technical criteria, but the nature of the power struggle dictates that top jobs should go to trusted individuals, while the traditional modes of clique groups serve to protect individuals from the competition of those selected by the other two criteria. By setting up these three "ideal types" Moore posited a number of alternative combinations as predictors of the future direction of Soviet society. One important consequence of this simplified model was the prediction that terror had gone too far and that some new means of rationalization had to be found.

In a different sense, the principle of limited possibilities, by concentrating on the constraints in a system, indicates the limits of change. Edward F. Denison has argued that the institutional economic arrangements in the United States make it difficult to achieve a 5 or even 4 per cent growth rate as hoped for by both President Kennedy and Governor Rockefeller. By analyzing patterns of investment, sources of capital, tax policies, habits of consumption, etc., Denison argues that an upper limit of 3 per cent a year can be reached. Any other efforts would require some drastic changes in the institutional structure of the society with losses of different kinds of economic choice.

7. The Overriding Problem

Leicester Webb's essay, "Political Future of Pakistan," provides an interesting illustration of political analysis and prediction which is pitched on the identification of a single overriding problem.

While pointing to the obvious problems of unifying a state whose territorial divisions are a thousand miles apart, whose two units speak different languages, whose population is 85 per cent illiterate and which lacks a viable political system, Webb finds that the chief problem which must be solved, before any efforts can be made to deal with the others, is the problem of a social solidarity which could be the foundation for a national identity.

The question of national identity has been singled out by Lucian Pye, for example, as the overriding problem in the creation of a viable political system in Burma. Where Pye, though, locates the Burmese problem in the general set of cultural ambiguities (e.g. the contradiction of gentleness and violence in the culture), the Webb essay is more focused in that it points to a fundamental dilemma in Pakistan: the effort to use religious sentiments to create a secular state.

The unity of Pakistan lies in its adherence to Islam, yet Islamic thought, and the retrograde attitudes of the sect leaders, hinders the creation of a meaningful political entity. The anomaly, says Webb, is that Pakistan is a "religiously-based state . . . at loggerheads with its religious leaders." From the first, President Ayub has been conscious of this dilemma. In his public addresses he returns again and again to the theme: Pakistan needs an ideology; that ideology must be Islamic. But his two roles are in conflict. As the restorer of order and political innovator, he is of necessity a secularizer; as a solidarity maker he must appeal to religious sentiments. The answer, says Webb, is that

there has to be a radical readjustment of Muslim religious thought to bring its precepts in line with new secular needs; and for this reason "Ayub is a religious as well as a political reformer."

In his paper, Webb indicates the steps that Ayub has to take to break the power of the local sect leaders and to create his own political institutions. There is a clear set of stipulations by which one can judge whether these steps can be taken, and to this extent the paper serves admirably as a means of predicting the course of Pakistan's political development.

The question whether in any society there is a single overriding problem is largely an empirical one. Yet methodologically it is useful to try and see if such a single problem might emerge, if not in the present, then in the future. In her book *New Nations*, Lucy Mair establishes a proposition that "the world of technology is one of large political units" and thus raises the question whether some of the new states "are big enough to stand on their own feet." In his absorbing study of the breakdown of the Weimar Republic, Professor Karl D. Bracher sets up a model (applicable, he feels, to the political breakdown of a number of democratic states) in which the turning point comes when the established regime confesses that some basic problem seems to be "insoluble." In Weimar Germany, Professor Bracher feels that the insoluble problem was unemployment, giving rise to a sense of despair in the regime and a loss of faith in the political system. One could argue that Algeria was one such problem for France in recent years. Or the failure of the Belgians to create an administrative machinery (as the British did in Pakistan, India, Nigeria, etc.) was the cardinal problem in the Congo.

8. The Prime Mover

In Marxian theory, again, the mode of production was the determinant, directly or indirectly, of the political, legal, and ideological forms of the society. There were always two difficulties with the theory. One was the difficulty of any monistic theory—that in explaining everything, it really explains nothing. The other was the ambiguity of the phrase "mode of production." At various times, Marx would talk of the forces of production, the techniques of production, the social relations, etc., but meanings shifted markedly. A number of writers felt that if the term had any meaning, it could only apply to technology. At one point, I identified fourteen different variables that could be included under "mode of production" if one wanted to use it analytically. Yet the general idea of the mode of production has had a powerful influence as the idea of a prime mover of history or prime determinant of social structure.

For analytical reasons, if not always for historical or empirical ones, there may be situations in which a single powerful force can be taken as the independent variable and a whole series of ancillary changes predicted as a consequence of changes in this independent variable. This is the method, for example, that Herman Kahn has adopted in his book *On Thermonuclear War* and in an unpublished study, "Deterrence and Defense in the Sixties and Seventies."

As Kahn writes: "In a sense we are adopting an almost Marxian view of the world, with military technology replacing the special role that Marx assigned to the means of production as the major determinant of behavior, and with conflicts between nations replacing the class struggle."

It is not, of course, that other elements do not enter; surely political decision is the most decisive and is relatively autonomous, though one can say, after Skybolt, that missile technology has replaced steel production as the indicator of a strength among nations. But for purposes of analysis of future changes in a society, one may want to take a major determinant or prime mover and trace out its effects. The chief point that Kahn is making is that since 1945 there have been three major revolutions in the art of war, with consequent effects on the economy and political strategies of the two major duelists and their allies. By a "revolution" Kahn means a big change, such as the introduction of new sources of energy or a quantum jump in destructive power from a kiloton to a megaton —changes significant enough to render a prevailing strategic doctrine obsolete. "The year 1951," he writes, "is typical of the new era in which there is the introduction, full procurement, obsolescence, and phasing out of complete weapons systems without their ever having been used in war."

In the "mobilized societies" of the West, military technology, in its impact on the economic budget, in its stimulus of research and development, in its absorption of scientists, in the way it constrains certain political decisions (e.g. the need for overseas bases as a consequence of a weapons system), is in many respects a prime mover and can be studied with profit. Kahn has provided one model by setting up three hypothetical technologies for 1965, 1969 and 1973 (he was writing in 1961), and seeking to assess the alternative strategies and problems created by these changes. It is conjecture as a high art.

9. Sequential Development

Few persons today believe in a theory of social evolution in which each society passes through defined stages in moving from a simple to a complex state. Yet the phrases "economic development," "political development," and even "social development" do suggest that societies go through some sequential phases as they confront greater tasks and have to create specialized mechanisms to handle them.

Are there some ordered steps that one can identify, at least as an ideal type? In the construction of the theory of industrial society one notices the lineaments of such a theory. One source, clearly, is Emile Durkheim's *The Division of Labor in Society*. In accounting for the change from "mechanical" to "organic" solidarity, Durkheim posited a number of steps. Population increases give rise to certain densities. This leads, under certain conditions, to increased interaction and thereby to competition. Social units in competition (e.g. cities, or occupational guilds) can either engage in a war to the death or begin to differentiate into specialized and complementary units. The distinguishing aspect of modern society for Durkheim is the role of the division of labor in creating a more differentiated society.

Talcott Parsons, the American sociologist, has taken Durkheim's theory and tried to account for western institutional development in terms of a theory of structural differentiation. Economic development is only possible when there is a separation of the household and the firm. Within the firm there goes on a renewed process of differentiation, separating planning from operations, later ownership from control, etc. In the society, functions such as education, recreation, and welfare that were once lodged within the family begin to be taken over by specialized agencies. In the political arena one finds differentiation in the rise of bureaucracy, etc.

To some extent, one can argue, such a theory overlaps the concept of "structural requisites." There are two differences. One is in perspective. The idea of structural requisites is from the viewpoint of the government, i.e. the minimal concerns of any government. The second is that a theory of structural differentiation implies some ordered sequence in the creation of more complex and more specialized agencies for the handling of tasks.

In the new states one has a great laboratory for predicting and testing such hypotheses. In many of these countries, basic functions of the society are concentrated in family and village groups. The onset of industrialization means a transfer of such functions to new and more specialized agencies. Can one say that logically or sociologically such development can be plotted?

10. Accounting Schemes

By accounting schemes, I mean those efforts to sum up in a single case, or nation, or relatively closed social system, a "trial balance" which arrays all the major factors that play a role within that unit.

The *Futuribles* essay of Professor Edmund R. Leach, "The Political Future of Burma," affords an illustration of this method. Leach begins with the proposition that the existing situation in Burma ("or for that matter in any other country") may, in principle, be analyzed as the sum of a series of independent factors, a, b, c, . . . n. Social development is then seen as a series of progressions of a' through a to a'', and b' through b to b'', etc. But not all factors progress at the same pace, and a profile of the country at time II will have some but not all the factors of the country at time I.

In constructing a future profile of the country, some factors which are designated as constant could be predicted with a high degree of certainty; other factors are designated as probable, and still others as pure speculation. If one takes the speculations as a range of alternative possibilities and combines each with the constants, one would have a series of delimited conjectures ordered on some scale of probabilities.

In his empirical analysis, Leach distinguishes four groups of factors:

A. Factors with a high degree of built-in stability which, for any short-run historical period, can be treated as constant. These include, for Burma, climate and topography, language, religion, the bureaucratic structure of the internal administration, and certain culturally-defined expectations.

B. Factors which are subject to more or less linear change, either in in-

crease or decrease. Such rates of change are not immutable, but they do tend to be relatively stable over defined periods. This would include size of population and labor force, the state of communications (roads, railways, waterways), educational level of the population, numbers of trained personnel, capital resources available for investment.

C. Factors which are cyclical. Here the idea of a cycle becomes ambiguous. In business cycle theory one assumes a regularity of peaks and downturns, either long-wave (Kondratieff or Juglar) cycles or short-run cycles, based on an identification of specific determinants (rate of innovations, demand for money, etc.). In politics, the idea of a cycle is more a metaphor. This seems to be the case in Leach's examples: foreign policy ("the allies of yesterday are the enemies of today and the friends of tomorrow"); ruling types (using Pareto's metaphors of the "lions" and the "foxes," Leach assumes an alternation of "the politicians" and "the men of decisions"); age of government ("the longer an administration has been in office, the less vigorous its action"); age in government ("young men are vigorous, radical; old men incline to caution and conservatism"). Is there, here, truly a cycle?

D. Factors which are wholly fortuitous and unpredictable. These include, in Leach's itemization: the short-term objectives of active politicians; the coercive pressures of foreign powers; natural calamities, including international wars.

The historian, says Leach, tends to emphasize factors of the fourth class. But it may be, he says, that these day-to-day actions have only a "superficial and transient influence upon longer-term developmental sequences." Just as Durkheim sought to predict the rates of suicide in various systems, by seeking general causes (e.g. degree of cohesion) which were independent of any individual case, in a comparable way, says Leach, "those who seek to make political predictions can and should ignore completely the whole class of short-term political events." And Leach seeks to justify such exclusion on the ground that, seen over a pattern of decades, it is the "long-term developmental sequences" which matter, while the day-to-day events are of minor significance.

Two broad methodological questions can be raised. Can one dismiss so easily the role of decisions, or what historians call turning points? The annexation of upper Burma by the British in 1885 and the consequent destruction of the existing governmental system down to the village level do not fall, as a factor, under the other classes. It was not wholly fortuitous, yet it was external to, and decisively transformed, the system. One can say that such classes of events, because they are outside the system, cannot be taken into account. But if this is so, then a crucial problem in the area of prediction has no place in the accounting scheme. One would have to exclude, therefore, from the possibility of prediction such events as the occurrence of the October Revolution (many people expected February), the rise of Tito, and similar turning points in the history of the countries of Europe.

Secondly, do we want to stop at an "inventory of factors"? Do we not need to specify in some way the skein of relationships so that we know not only classes of factors but their functional dependencies as well? In what way does a joint family system (a constant?) act to constrain certain types of economic development? Under what conditions do the constants change? Is there an ordering principle which can specify the relationship between the groupings as classes of functional relationships?

11. Alternative Futures: The Writing of "Fictions"

One of the simplest and oldest ways of conceiving, if not predicting, the future was to envisage the possibilities open to man and then create a fiction which in extreme form men call "utopia." (In a somewhat different and systematic sense, the construction of fictions was used by Jeremy Bentham to enlarge the mode of abstractions available to speculative minds, and, quite independently, more than a half-century later, Hans Vaihinger was to elaborate this method in his famous book, *The Philosophy of "As If."* The "as if" was a construct, or fiction, which served a heuristic function. It allowed us to simplify our assumptions.)

In recent years, the writing of "alternative futures" has been a systematic technique of Rand and former Rand theorists, particularly Herman Kahn. (Curiously, and quite independently, apparently, of Bentham and Vaihinger, they have called their fictions "scenarios.") What these theorists do is to sketch a paradigm ("an explicitly structured set of assumptions, definitions, typologies, conjectures, analyses, and questions") and then construct a number of explicitly "alternative futures" which might come into being under stated conditions. Thus the alternative futures become guides to policy makers in sketching their own responses to the possible worlds that may emerge in the next decade.

The writing of a "scenario" is not itself a prediction: it is an explication of possibilities. What it is, in effect, is the step beyond the "accounting scheme" in the construction of a number of plausible profiles, and the explication of the assumptions which underlie each of these alternatives.

Herman Kahn, for example, has sketched a number of alternative world futures for the 1970s. He has constructed what he has called Alpha, Beta, Gamma, Delta worlds and indicated the kinds of international orders or equilibria which might obtain in each. Working from an "accounting scheme" of constants, relatively predictable sequential developments, constraints, and the like, he tries to assess current political factors (e.g., a degree of U.S.-Soviet detente, the strains in NATO, etc.), the present and future military technology, and possible political factors, and then sketch the alternative results.

His Alpha world is one of arms control agreements; the U.S.S.R., Europe, Japan, and the U.S. relaxed and ideologically slack, China maintaining only a defensive military posture, etc. In a variant, Alpha-1, Japan has become the implicit guarantor of South Korea, Formosa, Malaysia and India, and Western Europe is united. In Alpha-2, there is a strong Franco-German Europe, and a rearmed Japan is tending to neutralism. But the basic condition is one of high stability and peace.

The Beta worlds are one of defined structural strains. For example: the U.S.S.R. is losing dominance over the world communist movement; Peking has a low-grade nuclear force; E.E.C. pursues moderately exclusionist trade policies, Japan, Germany and France have independent nuclear deterrents, the *Tiers Monde* develops hysterical and aggressive political movements, etc.

The Gamma worlds, of extensive multipolarity, see the breakup of the old alliances: China, France, Germany, Japan, and India develop or procure nuclear weapons, E.E.C. does not develop into a political community, middle-sized countries are on the verge of becoming nuclear powers because of the development of cheap fission (i.e. atom), though not yet expensive fusion (e.g. hydrogen) bombs.

In these projections, few sophisticated techniques (game theory, systems analysis, cost-effectiveness ratios) are employed to sketch the future worlds. But what we do have is a systematic identification of relevant factors, and the combination of these, to create a coherent fiction or a set of alternative futures. And, to the extent that these alternative futures are realistic possibilities, one has a surer foundation for policy formulations to meet the various contingencies.

A different kind of experiment in conjecture is attempted by the writer in a forthcoming book, *The Post-Industrial Society*. It is, in essence, not a forecast, but a dissection of the recent past—the "prophetic past," in Chesterton's phrase—in order to identify the structural trends and structural possibilities in the society and to create an "as if" about the future. The study deals with the new role of military technology as constitutive of political decisions, the rise of scientists as a new constituency in the political process, the creation of a new "intellectual technology" (a short-hand term I use for cybernetics, decision theory, simulation, and other intellectual techniques that allow us a new way of dealing with the planning process) and other elements of structural change in the society. These changes are then projected forty years as an "as if" in order to see their impact on the composition of the labor force, class structure, elite groups, and the like. Clearly *that* world, forty years hence, will not materialize, for there are many unforeseen and "uncontrollable" variables (particularly the political weights of the new nations and their own commitments) which will shape the reality of that time. But if the "as if," as a rational projection of structural possibilities in the society, does have some heuristic validity, by comparing that model with the reality, one might then be able to gain a clearer sense of the actual agencies of social change that were operative in that time.

12. Decision Theory

One includes in decision theory a wide assortment of new techniques: linear programming, utility preference theory, game theory, simulation, etc. Strictly speaking, decision theory is not predictive because it is normative: it seeks to specify probable outcomes if one or another choice is made. The problem, then, is its adequacy as a tool for the policy-maker. M. de Jouvenel has indicated one of the problems in game theory, the problem of agreement on relative values (the assignment of utilities). Any adequate discussion would have to go far beyond the length

of this paper. The singular point to be noted, however, is that any concern with prediction eventually must explore in detail the formalization procedures of decision theory and seek to assess in what way they are useful in the art of conjecture.

In the political realm—where one seeks to assess the intentions as well as capabilities of one's opponents—where does one begin? One technique worth exploring—though not strictly within mathematical decision theory—is "political gaming" or "simulation." In effect, these are political mock wars. One can, using the Rand technique, set up actual teams and allow them to work out a political game as armies work out a war game under simulated conditions of diplomatic negotiations, or one can, with a computer, simulate various situations and work out the alternative strategies and likely outcomes under hypothecated conditions. As with any formalization technique, the added knowledge comes from a specification of the likely variables and an awareness of the range of outcomes, rather than from new "wisdom."

Most of the difficulties of politics—unlike probability situations, which are based on repeated experiments—is that decisions often have a "once-in-a-lifetime" consequence. A crucial question, therefore, is whether probabilistic methods can be used for political decision-making. In practice, one does this roughly by asking a number of "experts" and then weighing their advice. Is it possible, as L. J. Savage, for example, believes, that one can take expert opinion as a form of experiment and calculate *a priori* probabilities as a result?

But it is at this point that one runs

the risk of the rationalist fallacy of believing that there is a true optimal path for any decision. One of the most heartening developments is the recognition of the "existentialist" element which has entered into modern utility theory, itself the foundation of so much of the work of rational prediction. It used to be that in choosing a strategy in a "game against nature" (i.e. uncontrolled situations), one could follow a maximin path (i.e. go for broke) or a minimax route (i.e. seek to cut one's losses). Now a third strategy has appeared: one can choose, depending on temperament and values, a maximin or a minimax throw, but then, statistically one can hedge one's bet by an added probability which has been termed so neatly, "the criterion of regret." Now clearly, the man who invented that has learned the lessons of love and politics.

II

Why does one seek to predict? This is an era in which society has become "future-oriented" in all dimensions: a government has to anticipate future problems; an enterprise has to plan for future needs; an individual is forced to think of long-range career choices. And all of these are regarded as possible of doing. The government of the United States, for example, makes national estimates in which the intentions and capabilities of opponents are evaluated, and policy is formulated on the basis of these short-run and long-run estimates. Business firms now make regular five-year budgets and even twenty-year projections to anticipate future capital needs, market and product changes, plant location, and the like. Individuals at an early age begin to consider occupational choices and plan for university and later career life. If none of us can wholly predict the future, what we do in these actions, in the felicitous phrase used by Dennis Gabor, is seek to "invent the future."

In the light of all this, what is remarkable is how little effort has been made, intellectually, to deal with the problems of conjecture. In few of the cases are there genuine predictions of the order: these are the changes that I think will take place; these are the reasons why I think these changes will occur, etc. Most of the works analyzed above seek to specify the problems which countries confront, but only rarely is the further effort made such as: if the problems are solved this way, then the following might happen; or: these are the probabilities that the problem will be handled in this fashion. Yet one should not derogate such efforts. The correct identification of relevant problems is obviously the first step in the conjecture about the future; it is easier to make because it tends to be an extrapolation of the present.

I would like to put forth some problem areas for future investigation which, on the basis of the works surveyed, seem most promising. These are simply some suggestions, necessarily brief, of the productive leads derived from the works analyzed. (Necessarily, too, I cannot within the limits of space and competence detail the scope of these proposals; what I can do is to argue briefly their rationale.)

1. The Planning Process

A future-oriented society necessarily commits itself more and more to the idea of planning. This is the chief means of inventing the future. Most of the new states that have come onto the world scene in the last decade have ambitious planning schemes; most of the older societies, to some degree or other, are engaged in planning.

One plans, of course, for different ends; one plans in different ways (from centralized administrative to "indicative" planning); one uses different techniques (input-output schemes, systems analysis, shadow prices, simulation). One plans proportions between economic sectors; one does physical planning, as in the layout of cities; one plans for "guided mobility," i.e. the planned transfer from farms to cities. In all these instances, there is an attempt to direct human actions with different kinds of coercions, manipulations, persuasions and cooperations.

Can we, with full awareness of the problem of choosing between conflicting values, each of which may be cherished, find some way of choosing the *best* planning process that is consonant with our belief in liberty? The function of planning is not only to set forth goals and alternatives and means of achieving these. Equally important, and usually neglected, are the specification of costs and benefits, the reallocation of burdens, and the probable consequences of different kinds of actions. The true function of the planning process is not to designate the most appropriate means for given ends, but to predict the possible consequences, to explicate the values of a society and make people aware of the costs of achieving these.

Surprisingly, there are few studies extant of the planning process. There are some theoretical studies of how nations should plan and the principles of city planning, but few critical studies of how nations and groups actually plan and what can be done to improve both methods and procedures.

2. The Standardization of Social Indicators

Over the past decades, economists have developed different series of indicators to anticipate and evaluate trends in the economy. There may be differences in the conclusions drawn from time-series, but by and large there is a consensus of what should be observed.

One need not recapitulate here the obvious difficulties in establishing social and political indicators. Some of the difficulty arises from a failure to agree on what should be observed. Most of the writing on the new states, for example, concentrates on such general concepts as "modernization" or "political development" or "new elites," the dimensions, let alone the indicators, of the concept are still to be formulated. But one of the consistent themes of the recent writings in modern sociology (cf. Aron, Parsons) is that "industrial society" produces a series of common effects, has an "internal logic" in its creation of a new occupational structure, and with the rise of affluence creates new, presumably common attitudes, despite differences in traditional culture. And the work of Inkeles, Lerner, Pye, and others indicates that the break with tradition, the new patterns of urbanization, the exposure to the mass media and education all tend to create common patterns of thought in the new states.

The function of indicators is not to replace analysis or to act as predictors, but to allow comparisons over time within a country, and between countries, and more important, to allow one to *anticipate* certain likely occurrences. It is only when the indicators and the concepts are relatively precise that we could hope that indicators would be predictive of specific events.

In rough ways, we tend to use certain indicators as predictive of events. We say that rising unemployment rates presage a swing to radical groups in voting, that migration rates may be coupled with crime and divorce rates, etc. But clearly the present need is for some coherent effort to create sets of social indicators dealing with social and political change.

3. Models of Political Structures

The most difficult of all proposals is the heart of the social science enterprise itself, the construction of models of political systems.

The creation of a model allows us to do two (of a large number of) things. It may allow us to understand the "value-relevance" of a statement; it may allow us to see whether a predicted change is one which simply affects the actors in a system (e.g. a shift of power between groups), or affects the nature of a system itself. To illustrate the two points:

1) From the standpoint of a Mohammedan, all Christians are alike. The involved theological disputes between Catholics and Protestants may have little meaning for him because both are "children of Jesus." To a Catholic, the differences between a "hard-shell Baptist" and a Quaker may have little relevance for him since both are "enthusiasts." In a similar fashion, to a

confirmed Marxist, the difference between a Democrat and a Republican in the American political system has little meaning since both are capitalists. But to understand any analysis or criticism, one has to identify the standpoint from which it is made. One function of a model, therefore, is to indicate the value-relevance and level of analysis from the standpoint of the observer.

2) The analysis of power in a society can only be carried on adequately if one has a scheme to identify the relevant actors, the arena, the orientations of the actors, and their relationship to the underlying system which defines the politics of the society. By a system, I mean here the basis of renewable power independent of any momentary group of actors. Most of political analysis today, I would argue, concentrates on the "intermediate" sectors (e.g. parties, interest groups, the formal structure) or, as in the case of Soviet politics, through Kremlinology to deal with the "small units" (what I have called only half-jokingly the "small c's") of politics, but rarely is there an attempt to specify, as a Marxist analysis does, the underlying system of renewable power.

There are few operating models of political systems, on the descriptive or the analytical level, extant. Gabriel Almond and his associates have sought to establish a framework of concepts which would lead to the creation of such a model. Many years earlier, Harold Lasswell and Abraham Kaplan set forth comprehensive definitions of power, but they did not seek to combine these into a system. C. Wright Mills created a mechanistic image of a "power elite." Maurice Duverger, in his book *Political Parties*, at a lesser level has put forth a useful typology.

Most recently, Raymond Aron, in his magisterial book, *Paix et Guerre entre les Nations*, has formulated certain models of diplomatic systems. But we still lack any comprehensive analyses of different systems of power.

But here, in this entreaty, one comes full circle. For in the preoccupation with prediction one risks the hubris of the historicist mode of thought which sees the future as "pre-viewed" in some "cunning of reason" or other determinist vision of human affairs. And this is false. One seeks "pre-vision" as much to "halt" a future as help it to come into being, for the function of prediction is not, as often stated, to aid social control, but to widen the spheres of moral choice. Without that normative commitment the social sciences become a mere technology rather than humanistic discipline.

10.2 THE FUTURE AS THE BASIS FOR ESTABLISHING A SHARED CULTURE

Margaret Mead

I The Present Situation

The world today is struggling with many kinds of disjuncture. Some derive from the progressive fragmentation of what was once a whole—as higher education has broken down into a mass of separate specialties. Some have come about with the development of world views that parallel and often contradict older and displaced—but not replaced —ways of viewing the world. Others result from a juxtaposition of vastly different and extremely incongruent world views within the national and also the world-wide context provided by our contemporary press and television coverage. Within the framework of the United Nations we have balloting for representatives both from countries with many hundreds of years of high civilization and from countries just emerging from a primitive way of life. Still others are the effect of changing rates in the production of knowledge, which bring about unexpected discrepancies between the young and the old. In a sense, these different kinds of disjuncture can also be seen as related to the very diverse ways in which the emergent, changing world is experienced by people of different ages—particularly young children—who are differently placed in the world, the nation, and the community.

Discussion of this tremendous fragmentation and of the agglomerations of partly dissociated, historically divergent, and conceptually incongruent patterns has been conducted, too often, in a narrow or a piecemeal fashion which takes into account only certain problems as they affect certain groups.

Margaret Mead, "The Future as the Basis for Establishing a Shared Culture," reprinted by permission from *Daedalus*, published by the American Academy of Arts and Sciences, Boston, Massachusetts. Vol. 94, No. 1, *Science and Culture*.

The recent "two cultures" discussion is an example of such an approach, in which neither the arts nor the social sciences are included in what is essentially a lament about the state of communication within a small sector of the English-speaking world, whose members for various reasons of contemporary position or achievement think of themselves as an elite. In another context it is demanded that children's textbooks should portray "realistically" the conditions in which many American children live, because the conventional house pictured in advertisements and schoolbooks is unreal to the underprivileged children who live in cabins and coldwater flats and tenements. Even though the aim was to rectify the consequences of social and economic fragmentation at one level, a literal response to this demand would result in further fragmentation of our culture at another level. Wherever we turn, we find piecemeal statements, each of which can be regarded as a separate and partial definition of the basic problem of disjuncture, and piecemeal attempts at solution, each of which, because of the narrowness of the context in which it is made, produces new and still more complicated difficulties.

Yet these partial definitions and attempts at solution point in the same direction. We are becoming acutely aware that we need to build a culture within which there is better communication—a culture within which interrelated ideas and assumptions are sufficiently widely shared so that specialists can talk with specialists in other fields, specialists can talk with laymen, laymen can ask questions of specialists, and the least educated can participate, at the level of political choice, in decisions made necessary by scientific or philosophical processes which are new, complex, and abstruse.

Models for intercommunication of this kind—poorly documented but made vividly real through the treatment given them by historians—already exist, in the past, within our own tradition. One model, of which various uses have been made, is the Greek city, where the most erudite man and the simplest man could enjoy the same performance of a tragedy. Another, in which there has been a recent upsurge of interest, is medieval Europe, where the thinker and the knight, the churchman, the craftsman, and the serf could read a view of the world from the mosaic on the wall, the painting above the altar, or the carving in the portico, and all of them, however far apart their stations in life, could communicate within one framework of meaning. But such models are not limited to the distant past. Even much more recently, in Victorian England, a poet's words could be read and enjoyed by people of many different backgrounds, when he wrote:

Yet I doubt not thro' the ages one increasing purpose runs,
And the thoughts of men are widen'd with the process of suns.[1]

Whether or not the integration of culture which we construct retrospectively for these golden ages existed in actuality is an important question scientifically. But thinking about models, the question of actuality is less important. For the daydream and the vision, whether it was constructed by a prophet looking toward a new time or by a scholar working retrospectively, can still serve as a model of the future. Men may never, in fact, have attained the integration which some scholars believe characterized fifth-century Athens. Even so, their vision provides a challenging picture of what might be attained by modern men who have so many more possibilities for thinking about and for controlling the direction in which their culture will move.

However, all these models—as well as the simpler model of the pioneering American farmer, dressed in homespun, reared on the King James version of the Bible, and sustained by simple foods and simple virtues—share one peculiarity. In each case the means of integration is a corpus of materials from the past. The epic poems of Homer, the Confucian classics, the Jewish and the Christian Scriptures—each of these, in giving the scholar and the man in the street, the playwright and the politician access to an articulate statement of a world view, has been a source of integration. But the community of understanding of what was newly created— the poem, the play, the set of laws, the sculpture, the system of education, the style of landscape, the song—still depended on something which had been completed in the past. Today there is a continuing complaint that we have no such source of integration, and many of the measures which, it is suggested, would give a new kind of order to our thinking are designed to provide just such a body of materials. There is, for example, the proposal to teach college students the history of science as a way of giving all of them access to the scientific view of the world. Or there is the related proposal to teach all students evolution, particularly the exist-

ing body of knowledge about the evolution of man and culture, as a way of providing a kind of unity within which all specialists, no matter how specialized, would have a common set of referents.

But such suggestions place too much reliance on the past and necessarily depend on a long time span within which to build a common, shared view of the world. In the present crisis, the need to establish a shared body of assumptions is a very pressing one—too pressing to wait for the slow process of educating a small elite group in a few places in the world. The danger of nuclear disaster, which will remain with us even if all stockpiled bombs are destroyed, has created a hothouse atmosphere of crisis which forces a more rapid solution to our problems and at the same time wilts any solution which does not reflect this sense of urgency. For there is not only a genuine need for rapid solutions but also a growing restiveness among those who seek a solution. This restiveness in turn may well become a condition within which hasty, inadequate solutions are attempted—such as the substitution of slum pictures for ideal suburban middle class pictures in slum children's textbooks—within too narrow a context. Speed in working out new solutions is essential if new and more disastrous fragmentations are not to occur—but we also need an appropriate framework.

Measures taken at the college level to establish mutual understanding between the natural scientist and the humanist, the social scientist and the administrator, men trained in the law and men trained in the behavioral sciences, have a double drawback. The cumulative effect of these measures would be too slow and, in addition, they would be inadequate in that their hope lies in establishing a corpus based on something which already exists—a theory of history, a history of science, or an account of evolution as it is now known. Given the changing state of knowledge in the modern world, any such historically based body of materials becomes in part out of date before it has been well organized and widely taught. Furthermore, it would be betrayed and diluted and corrupted by those who did the teaching, as they would inevitably have to draw on their own admittedly fragmented education to convey what was to be learned. One effect of this fragmentation can be seen in attempts to express forms of new knowledge in imagery which cannot contain it, because the imagery is shaped to an earlier view of the world. In a recent sermon, for example, the Bishop of Woolwich presented a picture of dazzling contemporaneity in disavowing the possibility of belief in the corporeal ascension of Christ; but then, in proclaiming a new version of the Scriptures, he used the image of the sovereignty of Christ—an outmoded image in the terms in which he was speaking.

In the last hundred years men of science have fought uneasily with the problem of their own religious belief, and men of God have hardened their earlier visions into concrete images to confront a science they have not understood. Natural scientists have elaborated their hierarchical views of "true" science into an inability to understand the nature of the sciences of human behavior, welcoming studies of fragmented aspects of human behavior, or an inappropriate reduction in the number of variables. Human scientists have destroyed the delicacy and intricacy of their subject matter in coarse-grained attempts to imitate the experimental methods of Newtonian physics instead of developing new methods of including unanalyzable components in simulations or in developing new methods of validating the analysis of unique and complex historical events. As a result we lack the capacity to teach and the capacity to learn from a corpus based on the past. The success of any such venture would be comparably endangered by the past learning of the teachers and the past learning of the students, whose minds would already be formed by eighteen years of exposure to an internally inconsistent, contradictory, half-articulated, muddled view of the world.

But there is still another serious drawback to most current proposals for establishing mutual understanding. This is, in general, their lack of inclusiveness. Whether an approach to past knowledge is narrowly limited to the English-speaking world or includes the whole Euro-American tradition, whether it begins with the Greeks or extends backward in time to include the Paleolithic, any approach through the past can begin only with one sector of the world's culture. Inevitably, because of the historical separation of peoples and the diversity of the world's cultures throughout history, any one view of any one part of human tradition, based in the past, excludes other parts and, by emphasizing one aspect of human life, limits access to other aspects.

In the newly emerging nations we can see clearly the consequences of the efforts made by colonial educators to give to distant peoples a share in English or French or Dutch or Belgian or Spanish culture. Ironically, the more fully the colonial educators were willing to have some members at least of an African or an Asian society share in their traditions and their classics, the more keenly those who were so educated felt excluded from participation in the culture as a whole. For the classical European scholar, Africa existed mainly in very specialized historical contexts, and for centuries European students were concerned only with those parts of Africa or Asia which were ethnocentrically relevant to Greek or Roman civilization or the early Christian church. Throughout these centuries, peoples without a written tradition and peoples with a separate written tradition (the Chinese, for example, or the Javanese) lived a life to which no one in Europe was related. With the widening of the European world in the fifteenth and sixteenth centuries, Europeans treated the peoples whom they "discovered" essentially as peoples without a past, except as the European connoisseur came to appreciate their monuments and archeological ruins, or, later, as European students selectively used the histories of other peoples to illustrate their own conceptions of human history. Consequently, the greater degree of participation felt by the member of one of these more recently contacted societies in a French or an English view of the development of civilization, the more he also felt that his own cultural history was excluded from the history of man.

It is true that some heroic attempts have been made to correct for this colonial bias. Looking at a synchronic table of events, a child anywhere in the world may sit and ponder what the Chinese or the Mayans or the ancient canoe-sailing Hawaiians were doing when William the Conqueror landed in England. But almost inevitably this carefully constructed synchrony—with parallel columns of events for different parts of the world—is undone, on the one hand, by the recognition that the New World and the Old, the Asian mainland and the Pacific islands were *not* part of a consciously connected whole in A.D. 1066, and, on the other hand, by the implications of the date and the dating form, which carry the stamp of one tradition and one religious group within that tradition. It is all but impossible to write about the human past—the movements of early man, the building of the earliest known cities, the spread of artifacts and art forms, the development of styles of prophecy or symbolism—without emphasizing how the spirit of man has flowered at different times in different places and, time and again, in splendid isolation. Even in this century, the efforts of scholars to integrate the histories of the world's great living traditions have led, in the end, to a renewed preoccupation with each of these as an entity with its own long history.

Today, however, if we are to construct the beginning of a shared culture, using every superior instrument at our command and with full consciousness both of the hazards and the possibilities, we can stipulate certain properties which this still nonexistent corpus must have.

It must be equally suitable for all peoples from whatever traditions their present ways of living spring, and it must not give undue advantage to those peoples anywhere in the world whose traditions have been carried by a longer or a more fully formulated literacy. While those who come from a culture with a Shakespeare or a Dante will themselves be the richer, communications should not be so laden with allusions to Shakespeare or Dante that those who lack such a heritage cannot participate. Nor should the wealth of perceptual verbal detail in distinguishing colors, characteristic of the Dusun of Borneo or the Hanunóo of the Philippines, be used to make less differentiated systems seem crude. The possession of a script for a generation, a century, or a millennium must be allowed for in ways that will make it possible for all peoples to start their intercommunication on a relatively equal basis. No single geographical location, no traditional view of the universe, no special set of figures of speech, by which one tradition but not another has been informed, can provide an adequate base. It must be such that everyone, everywhere can start afresh, as a young child does, with a mind ready to meet ideas uncompromised by partial learning. It must be cast in a form that does not depend on years of previous learning— the fragmented learning already acquired by the college student or the student in the high school, the *lycée*, or the *Gymnasium*. Instead, it must be cast in a form that is appropriate for small children—for children whose fathers are shepherds, rubber tappers in jungles, forgotten sharecroppers, sailors or fishermen, miners or members of the dispossessed urban proletariat, as well as for the children whose forebears have read one of the world's scripts for many generations.

If this body of materials on which a new, shared culture is to be based is to include all the peoples of the world, then the peoples of the world must also contribute to it in ways that are qualitatively similar. If it is to escape from the weight of discrepant centuries, the products of civilization included within it must be chosen with the greatest care. The works of art must be universal in their appeal and examples of artistic endeavor whose processes are universally available—painting, drawing, carving, dancing, and singing in forms that are universally comprehensible. Only after a matrix of shared understanding has been developed will the way be prepared for the inclusion of specific, culturally separate traditions. But from the first it must have the character of a living tradition, so it will be free of the static qualities of older cultures, with texts that have become the test of truth and forms so rigid that experimentation has become impossible. And it must have the qualities of a natural language, polished and pruned and capable of expansion by the efforts of many minds of different calibres, redundant and sufficiently flexible so it will meet the needs of teacher and pupil, parent and child, friend and friend, master and apprentice, lawyer and client, statesman and audience, scientist and humanist in their different modes of communication. It is through use in all the complexity of relationships like these that a natural language is built and, given form and content by many kinds of human beings, becomes a medium of communication that can be learned by every child, however slight its natural ability. This projected corpus should not be confused with present day *popular culture*, produced commercially with contempt for its consumers. Instead, by involving the best minds, the most sensitive and gifted artists and poets and scientists, the new shared culture should have something of the quality of the periods of folk tradition out of which great art has repeatedly sprung.

A body of materials having these characteristics must bear the imprint of growth and use. Yet it is needed now, in this century, for children who are already born and for men who either will preserve the world for a new generation to grow up in or who, in failing to do so, will doom the newly interconnected peoples of the world to destruction by means of the very mechanisms which have made a world community a possibility. The most immediate problem, then, is that of producing, almost overnight, a corpus which expresses and makes possible new processes of growth.

We believe that the existing state of our knowledge about the processes of consciousness is such that it is necessary for us only to ask the right questions in order to direct our thinking toward answers. Today engineering and the technology of applied physical science have outstripped other applied sciences because in these fields searching questions have been asked urgently, sharply, and insistently. This paper is an attempt to ask questions, set up a series of specifications, and illustrate the order of answer for which we should be looking. There will be better ways of formulating these questions, all of which have to do with communication, and better ways of meeting the criteria which will make answers possible. In fact, it is my assumption that the creation of a body of materials which will serve our needs will depend on the contribution and the participation of all those who will also further its growth, that is, people in every walk of life, in every part of the globe, speaking every language and seeing the universe in the whole range of forms conceived by man.

II The Future as a Setting

I would propose that we consider the future as the appropriate setting for our shared world-wide culture, for the future is least compromised by partial and discrepant views. And I would choose the near future over the far future, so as to avoid as completely as possible new confusions based on partial but avowed totalistic projections born of the ideologies of certainty, like Marxism and Leninism, or the recurrent scientific dogmatisms about the possibilities of space travel, the state of the atmosphere, or the appearance of new mutations. But men's divergent dreams of eternity might be left undisturbed, providing they did not include some immediate apocalyptic moment for the destruction of the world.

Looking toward the future, we would start to build from the known. In many cases, of course, this would be knowledge very newly attained. What we would build on, then, would be the known attributes of the universe, our solar system, and the place of our earth within this system; the known processes of our present knowledge, from which we shall proceed to learn more; the known treasures of man's plastic and graphic genius as a basis for experience out of which future artists may paint and carve, musicians compose, and poets speak; the known state of instrumentation, including both the kinds of instrumentation which have already been developed (for example, communication satellites) and those which are ready to be developed; the known numbers of human beings, speaking a known number of languages, and living in lands with known amounts of fertile soil, fresh water, and irreplaceable natural resources; the known forms of organizing men into functioning groups; and the known state of modern weaponry, with its known capacity to destroy all life.

These various kinds of knowledge would be viewed as beginnings, instead of as ends—as young, growing forms of knowledge, instead of as finished products to be catalogued, diagrammed, and preserved in the pages of encyclopedias. All statements would take the form: "We know that there are at least X number of stars" (or people in Asia, or developed forms of transportation, or forms of political organization). Each such statement would be phrased as a starting point—a point from which to move onward. In this sense, the great artistic productions of all civilizations could be included, not as the splendid fruit of one or another civilization, but on new terms, as points of departure for the imagination.

The frenetic, foolhardy shipping of original works of art around the world in ships and planes, however fragile they may be, can be looked upon as a precursor of this kind of change— as tales of flying saucers preceded man's first actual ventures into space. It is as if we already dimly recognized that if we are to survive, we must share all we have, at whatever cost, so that men everywhere can move toward some as yet undefined taking-off point into the future.

But if we can achieve a new kind of consciousness of what we are aiming at, we do not need actually to move these priceless objects as if they were figures in a dream. We can, instead, take thought how, with our modern techniques, we can make the whole of an art style available, not merely single, symbolic examples, torn from their settings. Young painters and poets and musicians, dancers and architects can, today, be given access to all that is known about color and form, perspective and rhythm, technique and the development of style, the relationships of form and style and material, and the interrelationships of art forms as these have been developed in some place, at some time. We have all the necessary techniques to do this. We can photograph in color, train magnifying cameras on the inaccessible details of domes and towers, record a poet reciting his own poetry, film an artist as he paints, and use film and sound to transport people from any one part to any other part of the world to participate in the uncovering of an ancient site or the first viewing of a new dance form. We can, in fact, come out of the "manuscript stage" for all the arts, for process as well as product, and make the whole available simultaneously to a young generation so they can move ahead together and congruently into the future. Given access to the range of the world's art, young artists can see in a new light those special activities and art objects to which they themselves are immediately related, wherever they are.

Working always within the modest limits of one generation—the next twenty-five years—and without tempting the massive consequences of miscalculation, we can include the known aspects of the universe in which our continuing experimental ventures into space will be conducted and the principles, the tools, and the materials with which these ventures are beginning. Children all over the world can be given accurate, tangible models of what we now know about the solar system, models of the earth, showing how it is affected by the large scale patterning of weather, and models showing how life on earth may be affected by events in the solar system and beyond. Presented with a clear sense of the expanding limits of our knowledge, models such as these would prepare children everywhere to participate in discoveries we know must come and to anticipate new aspects of what is as yet unknown.

Within these same limits, we can bring together our existing knowledge of the world's multitudes—beginning with those who are living now and moving out toward those who will be living twenty-five years from now. The world is well mapped, and we know, within a few millions, how many people there are, where they are, and who they are. We know—or have the means of knowing—a great deal about the world's peoples. We know about the world's food supplies and can relate our knowledge to the state of those who have been well nourished and those who have been poorly fed. We know about the world's health and can relate our knowledge to the state of those who have been exposed to ancient plagues and those who are exposed to "modern" ambiguous viruses. We can picture the ways of living of those who, as children, were reared in tents, in wattle and daub houses, in houses made of mud bricks, in tenements and apartment houses, in peasant houses that have survived unchanged through hundreds of years of occupancy and in the new small houses of modern suburbs, in the anonymity of urban housing, in isolated villages, and in the crowded shacks of refugee settlements. We can define the kinds of societies, all of them contemporary, in which human loyalties are restricted to a few hundred persons, all of them known to one another, and others in which essential loyalties are expanded to include thousands or millions or even hundreds of millions of persons, only a few of them known to one another face to face. In the past we could, at best, give children some idea of the world's multitudes through books, printed words and meager illustrations. Today we have the resources to give children everywhere living experience of the whole contemporary world. And every child, everywhere in the world, can start with that knowledge and grow into its complexity. In this way, plans for population control, flood control, control of man's inroads on nature, plans for protecting human health and for developing a world food supply, and plans for sharing a world communication system can all become plans in which citizens participate in informed decisions.

None of this knowledge will in any sense be ultimate. We do not know what form knowledge itself will take twenty-five years from now, but we do know what its sources must be in present knowledge and, ordering what we now know, we can create a ground plan for the future on which all the peoples of the earth can build.

Because it must be learned by very

young children and by the children of very simple parents, this body of knowledge and experience must be expressed in clear and simple terms, using every graphic device available to us and relying more on models than on words, for in many languages appropriate words are lacking. The newer and fresher the forms of presentation are, the greater will be the possibility of success, for, as in the new mathematics teaching, all teachers—those coming out of old traditions and having long experience with special conventions and those newly aware of the possibilities of formal teaching—will have to learn what they are to teach as something new. Furthermore, parents will be caught up in the process, in one sense as the pupils of their children, discovering that they can reorder their own knowledge and keep the pace, and in another sense as supplementary teachers, widening the scope of teaching and learning. Knowledge arranged for comprehensibility by a young child is knowledge accessible to all, and the task of arranging it will necessarily fall upon the clearest minds in every field of the humanities, the sciences, the arts, engineering, and politics.

There is, however, one very immediate question. How are we to meet the problem of shared contribution? How are we to ensure that this corpus is not in the end a simplified version of modern western—essentially Euro-American —scientific and philosophic thought and of art forms and processes, however widely selected, interpreted within the western tradition? Is there any endeavor which can draw on the capacities not only of those who are specially trained but also those with untapped resources—the uneducated in Euro-American countries and the adult and wise in old, exotic cultures and newly emerging ones?

A first answer can be found, I think, in activities in which every country can have a stake and persons of every age and level of sophistication can take part. One such activity would be the fashioning of a new set of communication devices—like the visual devices used by very simple peoples to construct messages or to guide travelers on their way, but now raised to the level of world-wide intelligibility.

In recent years there has been extensive discussion of the need for a systematic development of what are now called *glyphs*, that is, graphic representations, each of which stands for an idea: male, female, water, poison, danger, stop, go, etc. Hundreds of glyphs are used in different parts of the world—as road signs, for example—but too often with ambiguous or contradictory meanings as one moves from one region to another. What is needed, internationally, is a set of glyphs which does not refer to any single phonological system or to any specific cultural system of images but will, instead, form a system of visual signs with universally recognized referents. But up to the present no sustained effort has been made to explore the minimum number that would be needed or to make a selection that would carry clear and unequivocal meaning for the peoples of the world, speaking all languages, living in all climates, and exposed to very different symbol systems. A project for the exploration of glyph forms and for experimentation with the adequacy of different forms has been authorized by the United Nations Committee for International Cooperation Year (1965—the twentieth anniversary of the founding of the United Nations). This is designed as an activity in which adults and children, artists and engineers, logicians and semanticists, linguists and historians—all those, in fact, who have an interest in doing so—can take part. For the wider the range of persons and the larger the number of cultures included in this exploration, the richer and the more fully representative will be the harvest from which a selection of glyphs can be made for international use.

Since meaning is associated with each glyph as a unit and glyphs cannot be combined syntactically, they can be used by the speakers of any language. But considerable experimentation will be necessary to avoid ambiguity which may lead to confusion or the adoption of forms which are already culturally loaded. The variety of meanings which may already be associated with certain forms can be illustrated by the sign $+$ (which, in different connections, can be the sign for addition or indicates a positive number, can stand for "north" or indicate a crossroad, and, very slightly modified, can indicate a deceased person in a genealogy, a specifically Christian derivation, or stand for the Christian sign of the cross) or the sign $\bigcirc$ (which, in different connections, may stand for circumference or for 360°, for the full moon, for an annual plant, for degrees of arc or temperature, for an individual, especially female, organism, and, very slightly modified, can stand for zero or, in our alphabet, the letter O).

Work on glyphs can lead to work on other forms of international communication. In an interconnected world we shall need a world language—a second language which could be learned by every people but which would in no sense replace their native tongue. Contemporary studies of natural languages have increased our understanding of the reasons why consciously constructed languages do not serve the very complex purposes of general communication. Most important is the fact that an artificial language, lacking the imprint of many different kinds of minds and differently organized capacities for response, lacks the redundancy necessary in a language all human beings can learn.

Without making any premature choice, we can state some of the criteria for such a secondary world language. It must be a natural language, chosen from among known living languages, but not from among those which are, today, politically controversial. Many nations would have to contribute to the final choice, but this choice would depend also on the outcome of systematic experiments with children's speech, machine simulation, experiments with mechanical translation, and so on. In addition, it would be essential to consider certain characteristics related to the current historical situation. Politically, it should be the language of a state too small to threaten other states. In order to allow for a rapid development of diverse written styles, it must be a language with a long tradition of use in written forms. To permit rapid learning, it must be a language whose phonetic system can be easily learned by speakers of other languages, and one which can be easily rendered into a phonetic script and translated without special difficulty into existing traditional scripts. It should come from the kind of population in which there is a wide diversity of roles and occupations and among whom a large number of teachers can be found, some of whom are already familiar with one or another of the great widespread languages of the world. Using modern methods of language teaching, the task of creating a world-wide body of readers and speakers could be accomplished within five years and the language itself would change in the process of this world-wide learning.

Once a secondary world language is chosen, the body of knowledge with which we shall start the next twenty-five years can be translated into it from preliminary statements in the great languages, taking the stamp of these languages as divergent subtleties of thought, present in one language and absent in another, are channeled in and new vocabulary is created to deal with new ideas.

One important effect of a secondary world language would be to protect the more localized languages from being swamped by those few which are rapidly spreading over the world. Plans have been advanced to make possible the learning and use of any one of the five or seven most widespread languages as a second language. Fully implemented, this would divide the world community into two classes of citizens—those for whom one of these languages was a mother tongue and those for whom it was a second language—and it would exacerbate already existing problems arising from differences in the quality of communication —rapid and idiomatic among native speakers and slower, more formal, and less spontaneous among those who have

learned English, French, or Russian later. In contrast, one shared second language, used on a world-wide scale, would tend to equalize the quality of world communication and, at the same time, would protect the local diversity of all other languages.

Another important aspect of a shared culture would be the articulate inclusion of the experience of those who travel to study, work, explore, or enjoy other countries. One of the most intractable elements in our present isolating cultures is the interlocking of a landscape—a landscape with mountains or a desert, jungle or tundra, rushing cataracts or slow flowing rivers, arched over by a sky in which the Dipper or the Southern Cross dominates—and a view of man. The beauty of face and movement of those who have never left their mountains or their island is partly the imprint on the human form of a complex relationship to the scale and the proportions, the seasonal rhythms and the natural style of one special part of the world. The experiences of those who have been bred to one physical environment cannot be patched together like the pieces of a patchwork quilt. But we can build on the acute and vivid experiences of those who, reared in a culture which has deeply incorporated its environment, respond intensely to some newly discovered environment—the response of the countryman to the city, the response of the city dweller to open country, the response of the immigrant to the sweep of an untouched landscape and of the traveler to a sudden vista into the past of a whole people. In the past, the visual impact of discovery was recorded retrospectively in painting and in literature. Today, films can record the more immediate response of the observer, looking with fresh eyes at the world of the nomadic Bushman or the people beneath the mountain wall of New Guinea, at the palaces in Crete or the summer palace in Peking.

We can give children a sense of movement, actually experienced or experienced only in some leap of the imagination. In the next twenty-five years we shall certainly not explore deep space, but the experience of movement can link a generation in a common sense of anticipation. As a beginning, we can give children a sense of different actual relationships to the physical environments of the whole earth, made articulate through the recorded responses of those who have moved from one environment to another. Through art, music, and film we can give children access to the ways others have experienced their own green valleys and other valleys, also green. We can develop in small children the capacity to wonder and to look through other eyes at the familiar fir trees rimming their horizon or the sea breaking on their island's shore.

In the past, these have been the experiences of those who could afford to travel and those who had access, through the arts, to the perceptions of a poet like Wordsworth in *The Prelude*, or a young scientist like Darwin on his Pacific voyage, or painters like Catlin or Gauguin. With today's technology, these need no longer be the special experiences of the privileged and the educated elite. The spur to action may be the desire for literacy in the emerging nations or a new concern for the culturally deprived in older industrialized countries. And quite different styles of motivation can give urgency to the

effort to bring the experience of some to bear on the experience of all.

Looking to the future, the immediacy of motivation is itself part of the experience. It may be an assertive desire to throw off a colonial past or a remorseful attempt to atone for long neglect. It may be the ecumenical spirit in which the Pope can say: "No pilgrim, no matter how far, religiously and geographically, may be the country from which he comes, will be any longer a stranger to this Rome. . . ."[2] It may be the belief that it is possible to remake a society, as when Martin Luther King said:

I have a dream today . . . I have a dream that one day every valley shall be exalted, every hill and mountain shall be made low. The rough places will be made plain, and the crooked places will be made straight. And the glory of the Lord shall be revealed, and all flesh shall see it together. This is our hope. This is the faith that I go back to the South with. With this faith we will be able to hew out of the mountain of despair a stone of hope.[3]

Or it may be the belief, expressed by U Thant, that men can work toward a world society:

Let us look inward for a moment on this Human Rights Day, and recognize that no one, no individual, no nation, and indeed no ideology has a monopoly of rightness, freedom or dignity. And let us translate this recognition into action so as to sustain the fullness and freedom of simple human relations leading to ever widening areas of understanding and agreement. Let us, on this day, echo the wish which Rabindranath Tagore stated in these memorable words, so that our world may be truly a world

Where the mind is without fear and the head is held high;
Where knowledge is free;

Where the world has not been broken up
  into fragments by narrow domestic
  walls;
Where words come out of the depth of
  truth;
Where tireless striving stretches its arms
  toward perfection. . . .[4]

There are also other ways in which experience can more consciously be brought to bear in developing a shared understanding. All traditions, developing slowly over centuries, are shaped by the biological nature of man—the differences in temperament and constitution among men and the processes of maturation, parenthood, and aging which are essential parts of our humanity. The conscious inclusion of the whole life process in our thinking can, in turn, alter the learning process, which in a changing world has become deeply disruptive as each elder generation has been left behind while the next has been taught an imperfect version of the new. One effect of this has been to alienate and undermine the faith of parents and grandparents as they have seen their children's minds moving away from them and as their own beliefs, unshared, have become inflexible and distorted.

The policy in most of today's world is to educate the next—the new—generation, setting aside the older generation in the mistaken hope that, as older men and women are passed over, their outmoded forms of knowledge will do no harm. Instead, we pay a double price in the alienation of the new generation from their earliest and deepest experiences as little children and in the blocking of constructive change in the world by an older generation who still exercise actual power—hoarding some resources and wasting others,

building to an outmoded scale, voting against measures the necessity of which is not understood, supporting reactionary leaders, and driving an equally inflexible opposition toward violence. Yet this lamentable outcome is unnecessary, as the generation break itself is unnecessary.

In the past the transmission of the whole body of knowledge within a slowly changing society has provided for continuity. Today we need to create an educational style which will provide for continuity and openness even within rapid change. Essentially this means an educational style in which members of different generations are involved in the process of learning. One way of assuring this is through a kind of education in which new things are taught to mothers and young children together. The mothers, however schooled, usually are less affected by contemporary styles of education than the fathers. In some countries they have had no schooling; in others, girls are warned away from science and mathematics or even from looking at the stars. So they come to the task of rearing their small children fresher than those who have been trained to teach or to administer. Child rearing, in the past fifty years, has been presented as almost entirely a matter of molding the emotional life of the child, modulating the effects of demands for cleanliness and obedience to permit more spontaneity, and of preserving an environment in which there is good nutrition and low infection danger. At the same time, we have taken out of the hands of mothers the *education* even of young children. So we have no existing rationale in which mother, child, and teacher are related within the learning process.

What we need now, in every part of the world, is a new kind of school for mothers and little children in which mothers learn to teach children what neither the mothers nor the children know.

At the same time, grandparents who, perforce, have learned a great deal about the world which has gone whirling past them and in which, however outmoded they are declared to be, they have had to maintain themselves, can be brought back into the teaching process. Where patience, experience, and wisdom are part of what must be incorporated, they have a special contribution to make. Mothers of young children, lacking a fixed relationship to the growing body of knowledge about the world, provide freshness of approach; but older people embody the experience that can be transformed into later learning. The meticulous respect for materials, coming from long experience with hand work, the exacting attention to detail, coming from work with a whole object rather than some incomplete part, and the patient acceptance of the nature of a task have a continuing relevance to work, whatever it may be. So also, the disciplined experience of working with human beings can be transformed to fit the new situations which arise when democracy replaces hierarchy and the discipline of political parties that of the clan and the tribe.

We have been living through a period in which the old have been recklessly discarded and disallowed, and this very disallowance resonates— as a way of life which has been repressed rather than transformed—in the movements of unaccountably stubborn reaction from which no civilization in our present world is exempt. Grandparents and great-grandparents—even those who are driven from their land to die in concentration camps and those who voluntarily settle themselves in modern, comfortable Golden Age clubs —live on in the conceptions of the children whose parents' lives they shaped. Given an opportunity to participate meaningfully in new knowledge, new skills, and new styles of life, the elderly can embody the changing world in such a way that their grandchildren—and all children of the youngest generation—are given a mandate to be part of the new and yet maintain human ties with the past which, however phrased, is part of our humanity. The more rapid the rate of change and the newer the corpus of knowledge which the world may come to share, the more urgently necessary it is to include the old—to transform our conception of the whole process of aging so their wisdom and experience can be assets in our new relation to the future.

Then we may ask, are such plans as these sufficiently open ended? In seeking to make equally available to the peoples of the world newly organized ways of moving into the immediate future, in a universe in which our knowledge is rapidly expanding, there is always the danger that the idea of a shared body of knowledge may be transformed into some kind of universal blueprint. In allowing this to happen we would, of course, defeat our own purpose. The danger is acute enough so that we must build a continuing wariness and questioning into the planning itself; otherwise even the best plan may result in a closed instead of an open ended system.

This means that we must be open ended in our planning as well as in our plans, recognizing that this will involve certain kinds of conscious restriction as well as conscious questioning. For example, we must insist that a world language be kept as a second language, resolutely refusing to consider it as a first language, in order to protect and assure the diversity of thought which accompanies the use of different mother tongues. We should also guard against a too early learning of the world language, so that the language of infancy—which also becomes the language of love and poetry and religion—may be protected against acquiring a too common stamp. We must insist on the inclusion of peoples from all over the world in any specific piece of planning—as in the development of an international system of glyphs—as a way of assuring a growing and an unpredictable corpus. We must be willing to forego, in large-scale planning, some kinds of apparent efficiency. If we are willing, instead, to include numerous steps and to conceive of each step somewhat differently, we are more likely, in the end, to develop new interrelationships, unforeseeable at any early stage. A more conscious inclusion of women and of the grandparental generation in learning and teaching will carry with it the extraordinary differences in existing interrelations between the minds and in the understanding of the two sexes and different age groups.

We can also take advantage of what has been learned through the use of cybernetic models, and equip this whole forward movement of culture which we are launching with a system of multiple self-corrective devices. For example, criteria could be established for reviewing the kinds of divergences that were occurring in vocabulary and conceptualizations as an idea fanned out around the world. Similarly, the rate and type of incorporation of special developments in particular parts of the world could be monitored, and cases of dilution or distortion examined and corrected. Overemphasis on one part of knowledge, on one sensory modality, on the shells men live in rather than the life they live there, on sanitation rather than beauty, on length of life rather than quality of life lived, could be listened for and watched for, and corrective measures taken speedily.

A special area of concern would be intercommunication among all those whose specializations tend to isolate them from one another, scientist from administrator, poet from statesman, citizen voter from the highly skilled specialist who must carry out his mandate using calculations which the voter cannot make, but within a system of values clearly enough stated so that both may share them. By attending to the origins of some new communication—whether a political, a technical, or an artistic innovation—the functioning of the communication process could be monitored. Special sensing organs could be established which would observe, record, and correct so that what otherwise might become a blundering, linear, and unmanageable avalanche could be shaped into a process delicately responsive to change in itself.

But always the surest guarantee of change and growth is the inclusion of living persons in every stage of an activity. Their lives, their experience, and their continuing response—even their resistances—infuse with life any plan which, if living participants are excluded, lies on the drawing board and loses its reality. Plans for the future can become old before they are lived, but the future itself is always newborn and, like any newborn thing, is open to every kind of living experience.

REFERENCES

1. Alfred Lord Tennyson, "Locksley Hall" (1842).
2. *The New York Times*, May 18, 1964.
3. From the speech by the Rev. Martin Luther King at the March on Washington, *New York Post Magazine*, September 1, 1963, p. 5.
4. From the Human Rights Day Message by (then) Acting Secretary-General U Thant, December 8, 1961 (United Nations Press Release SG/1078 HRD/11 [December 6, 1961]).

10.3 CHANGING ORGANIZATIONS

Warren G. Bennis

The Idea of Change

Not far from where the new Government Center is going up, in downtown Boston, a foreign visitor once walked up to an American sailor and asked why the ships of his country were built to last for only a short time. According to the foreign tourist, "the sailor answered without hesitation that the art of navigation is making such rapid progress that the finest ship would become obsolete if it lasted beyond a few years. In these words, which fell accidentally from an uneducated man, I began to recognize the general and systematic idea upon which your great people direct all their concerns."

The foreign visitor was that shrewd observer of American morals and manners, Alexis de Tocqueville, and the year was 1835. He would not recognize Scollay Square today. But he caught the central theme of our country—its preoccupation, its *obsession* with change. One thing, however, *is* new since de Tocqueville's time: the prevalance of newness, the changing scale and scope of change itself, so that, as Oppenheimer said, ". . . the world alters as we walk in it, so that the years of man's life measure not some small growth or rearrangement or moderation of what was learned in childhood, but a great upheaval."

Numbers have a magic all their own, and it is instructive to review some of the most relevant ones. In 1789, when

From Warren G. Bennis, "Changing Organizations," the first Douglas Murray McGregor Memorial Lecture of the Alfred P. Sloan School of Management, Massachusetts Institute of Technology. Published by M.I.T. Press, Cambridge, Mass.: February, 1966. Used by Permission.

George Washington was inaugurated, American society comprised fewer than 4 million persons, of whom 750,000 were Negroes. Few persons lived in cities; New York, then the capital, had a population of 33,000. In all, 200,000 individuals lived in what were then defined as "urban areas"—places with more than 2,500 inhabitants. In the past ten years, Los Angeles has grown by 2,375,000, almost enough to people present-day Boston. In July, 1964, the population of the U.S. was about 192 million. The U.S. Census Bureau estimates that the population in 1975 will be between 226 and 235 million and that in 1980 it will be between 246 and 260 million. World population was over 3 billion in 1964. If fertility remains at present levels until 1975 and then begins to decline, the population of the world will reach 4 billion in 1977, 5 billion by about 1990.

In 1960 when President Kennedy was elected, more than half of all Americans alive were over 33 years of age and had received their formative experiences during the Great Depression or earlier. By 1970, only ten years later, more than half of all Americans alive will be under 25 and will have been born after World War II. In one short decade the mid-age of the United States will have dropped by a full eight years —the sharpest such age drop recorded in history.

Observe the changes taking place in education. Thirty years ago only one out of every eight Americans at work had been to high school. Today four out of five attend high school. Thirty years ago 4 per cent or less of the population attended college. Now the figure is around 35 per cent, in cities about 50 per cent.

Consider one more example of social change. We are all aware of the momentum of the Scientific Revolution, whose magnitude and accelerating rate —to say nothing of its consequences— are truly staggering. By 1980 science will cut even a wider path, for in that year the government alone will spend close to $35 billion on research and development: $10 billion on arms and arms control, $7 billion on basic research, and $18 billion on vast civilian welfare programs and new technology.

"Everything nailed down is coming loose," an historian said recently, and it does seem that no exaggeration, no hyperbole, no outrage can realistically appraise the extent and pace of modernization. Exaggerations come true in only a year or two. Nothing will remain in the next ten years—or there will be twice as much of it.

And it is to our credit that the pseudo-horror stories and futuristic fantasies about *accelerations* of the rate of change (the rate of obsolescence, scientific and technological unemployment) and the number of "vanishing" stories (the vanishing salesman, the vanishing host, the vanishing adolescent, the vanishing village)—it is to our credit that these phenomenal changes have failed to deter our compulsive desire to invent, to overthrow, to upset inherited patterns and comfort in the security of the future.

No more facts and numbers are needed to make the point. We can *feel* it on the job, in the school, in the neighborhood, in our professions, in our everyday lives. Lyndon Johnson said recently, "We want change. We want progress. We want it both at home and abroad—and we aim to get it!" I think he's got it.

Changing Organizations

How will these accelerating changes in our society influence human organizations?

Let me begin by describing the dominant form of human organization employed throughout the industrial world. It is a unique and extremely durable social arrangement called "bureaucracy," a social invention, perfected during the industrial revolution to organize and direct the activities of the business firm. It is today the prevailing and supreme type of organization wherever people direct concerted effort toward the achievement of some goal. This holds for university systems, for hospitals, for large voluntary organizations, for governmental organizations.

Corsica, according to Gibbon, is much easier to deplore than to describe. The same holds true for bureaucracy. Basically, bureaucracy is a social invention which relies exclusively on the power to influence through rules, reason, and the law. Max Weber, the German sociologist who developed the theory of bureaucracy around the turn of the century, once described bureaucracy as a social machine: "Bureaucracy," he wrote, "is like a modern judge who is a vending machine into which the pleadings are inserted together with the fee and which then disgorges the judgment together with its reasons mechanically derived from the code."

The bureaucratic "machine model" Weber outlined was developed as a reaction against the personal subjugation, nepotism, cruelty, and capricious and subjective judgments which passed for managerial practices in the early days of the industrial revolution. The true hope for man, it was thought, lay in his ability to rationalize, to calculate, to use his head as well as his hands and heart. Bureaucracy emerged out of the need for more predictability, order, and precision. It was an organization ideally suited to the values of Victorian Empire.

Most students of organizations would say that the anatomy of bureaucracy consists of the following "organs": a division of labor based on functional specialization, a well-defined hierarchy of authority, a system of procedures and rules for dealing with all contingencies relating to work activities, impersonality of interpersonal relations, and promotion and selection based on technical competence. It is the pyramidal arrangement we see on most organizational charts.

Allow me to leap-frog to the conclusion of my paper now. It is my premise that the bureaucratic form of organization is out of joint with contemporary realities; that new shapes, patterns, and models are emerging which promise drastic changes in the conduct of the corporation and of managerial practices in general. In the next 25 to 50 years we should witness, and participate in, the end of bureaucracy as we know it and the rise of new social systems better suited to twentieth-century demands of industrialization.

Reasons for Organizational Change

I see two main reasons for these changes in organizational life. One has been implied earlier in terms of changes taking place in society, most commonly referred to as the population and knowledge explosions. The other is more subtle and muted—perhaps less significant, but for me profoundly exciting. I have no easy name for it, nor is it easy to define. It has to do with man's historical quest for self-awareness, for using reason to achieve and stretch his potentialities and possibilities. I think that this deliberate self-analysis has spread to large and more complex social systems, to organizations. I think there has been a dramatic upsurge of this spirit of inquiry over the past two decades. At new depths and over a wider range of affairs, organizations are opening their operations up to self-inquiry and analysis. This really involves two parallel shifts in values and outlooks, between the men who make history and the men who make knowledge. One change is the scientist's realization of his affinity with men of affairs, and the other is the latter's receptivity and new-found respect for men of knowledge. I am calling this new development *organizational revitalization*. It is a complex social process which involves a deliberate and self-conscious examination of organizational behavior and a collaborative relationship between managers and scientists to improve performance.

To you who have profited as Alfred P. Sloan Fellows here at M.I.T. from Mr. Sloan's magnificent vision, this new form of collaboration may be taken for granted. For myself, I have basked under the light of Professor Douglas McGregor's foresight and have simply come to regard reciprocity between the academician and the manager as inevitable and natural. But I can assure you that this development is unprecedented, that never before in history, in any society, has man, in his organizational context, so willingly searched, scrutinized, examined, inspected, or contemplated—for meaning, for purpose, for improvement.

I think this shift in outlook has taken a good deal of courage from both partners in this encounter. The manager has had to shake off old prejudices about "eggheads" and long-hair intellectuals. More important, he has had to make himself and his organization vulnerable and receptive to external sources and to new, unexpected, even unwanted information—which all of you know is not such an easy thing to do. The academician has had to shed some of his natural hesitancies. Scholarly conservatism is admirable, I think, except to hide behind, and for a long time caution has been a defense against reality.

It might be useful to dwell on the role of academic man and his growing involvement with social action, using the field of management education as a case in point. Until recently, the field of business was disregarded by large portions of the American public, and it was unknown to or snubbed by the academic establishment. Management education and research were at best regarded there with dark suspicion, as if contact with the world of reality —particularly monetary reality—was equivalent to a dreadful form of pollution. In fact, academic man has historically taken one of two stances toward The Establishment, *any* Establishment—that of rebellious critic or of withdrawn snob. The former (the rebel) can be "bought," but only in paperback books under such titles as: *The Power Elite, The Lonely Crowd, The Organization Man, The Hidden Persuaders, The Tyranny of Testing,*

Mass Leisure, The Exurbanites, The Life and Death of Great American Cities, The American Way of Death, Compulsory Mis-Education, The Status Seekers, Growing Up Absurd, The Paper Economy, Silent Spring, The Child Worshippers, The Affluent Society, The Depleted Society. On the basis of these titles and reports of their brisk sales, I am thinking of writing one called *Masochism in Modern America*, practically a guaranteed success.

The withdrawn stance can be observed in some of our American universities, but less so these days. It is still the prevailing attitude in many European universities. There, the university seems intent to preserve the monastic ethos of its medieval origins, offering a false but lulling security to its inmates and sapping the curriculum of virility and relevance. Max Beerbohm's whimsical and idyllic fantasy of Oxford, *Zuleika Dobson*, dramatizes this: "It is this mild, miasmal air, not less than the grey beauty and the gravity of the buildings that has helped Oxford to produce, and foster, eternally, her peculiar race of artist-scholars, scholars-artists. . . . The buildings and their traditions keep astir in his mind whatsoever is gracious; the climate enfolding and enfeebling him, lulling him, keeps him careless of the sharp, harsh exigent realities of the outer world. These realities may be seen by him . . . But they cannot fire him. Oxford is too damp for that."

"Adorable dreamer," said Matthew Arnold, in his valedictory to Oxford, "whose heart has been so romantic! who has given thyself so prodigally, given thyself to sides and to heroes not mine, only never to the Philistine! . . . what teacher could ever so save us from that bondage to which we are all prone . . . the bondage of what binds us all, the narrow, the mundane, the merely practical."

The intellectual and the manager have only recently come out of hiding and recognized the enormous possibilities of joint ventures. Remember that the idea of the professional school is new; this is true even in the case of the venerable threesome—law, medicine, and engineering—to say nothing of such recent upstarts as business and public administration. It is as new as the institutionalization of science, and even today, this change is not greeted with unmixed joy. Colin Clark, the economist, writing in a recent *Encounter*, referred to the "dreadful suggestion that Oxford ought to have a business school."

It is probably true that we in the United States have had a more pragmatic attitude toward knowledge than anyone else. Many observers have been impressed with the disdain European intellectuals seem to show for practical matters. Even in Russia, where one would least expect it, there is little interest in the "merely useful." Harrison Salisbury, the *New York Times'* Soviet expert, was struck during his recent travels by the almost total absence of liaison between research and practical application. He saw only one great agricultural experimental station on the American model. In that case, professors were working in the fields. They told Salisbury, "people call us Americans."

There may not be many American professors working in the fields, but they can be found, when not waiting in airports, almost everywhere else: in factories, in government, in less advanced countries, more recently in backward areas of our own country, in mental hospitals, in the State Department, in educational systems, and in practically all the institutional crevices Ph.D. recipients can worm their way into. They are advising, counselling, researching, recruiting, interpreting, developing, consulting, training, and working for the widest variety of client imaginable. This is not to say that the deep ambivalence which some Americans hold toward the intellectual has disappeared, but it does indicate that academic man has become more committed to action, in greater numbers, with more diligence, and with higher aspirations than at any other time in history.

Indeed, Fritz Machlup, the economist, has coined a new economic category called the "knowledge industry," which, he claims, accounts for 29 per cent of the gross national product. And Clark Kerr, the President of the University of California, said not too long ago, "What the railroads did for the second half of the last century and the automobile did for the first half of this century may be done for the second half of this century by the knowledge industry: that is, to serve as the focal point of national growth. And the university is at the center of the knowledge process."

Changes in
Managerial Philosophy

Now let us turn to the main theme and put the foregoing remarks about the reciprocity between action and knowledge into the perspective of changing organizations. Consider some of the relatively recent research and theory concerning the human side of enterprise which have made such a solid impact on management thinking and particularly upon the moral imperatives which guide managerial action. I shall be deliberately sweeping in summarizing these changes as much to hide my surprise as to cover a lot of ground quickly. (I can be personal about this. I remember sitting in Professor Mc-Gregor's class some seven years ago, when he first presented his new theories, and I remember the sharp antagonism his Theory X and Theory Y analysis then provoked. Today, I believe most of you would take these ideas as generally self-evident.)

It seems to me that we have seen over the past decade a fundamental change in the basic philosophy which underlies managerial behavior, reflected most of all in the following three areas:

1. A new concept of *man*, based on increased knowledge of his complex and shifting needs, which replaces the oversimplified, innocent push-button idea of man.
2. A new concept of *power*, based on collaboration and reason, which replaces a model of power based on coercion and fear.
3. A new concept of *organizational values*, based on humanistic-democratic ideals, which replaces the depersonalized mechanistic value system of bureaucracy.

Please do not misunderstand. The last thing I want to do is overstate the case. I do not mean that these transformations of man, power, and organizational values are fully accepted or even understood, to say nothing of implemented, in day-to-day affairs. These changes may be light-years away from actual adoption. I do mean that they have gained wide intellectual acceptance in enlightened management quarters, that they have caused a tremendous amount of rethinking and search behavior on the part of many organizations, and that they have been used as a basis for policy formulation by many large-scale organizations.

I have tried to summarize all the changes affecting organizations, resulting both from the behavioral sciences and from trends in our society, in the chart of human problems confronting contemporary organizations on ... [this page and the next]. These problems (or predicaments) emerge basically from twentieth-century changes, primarily the growth of science and education, the separation of power from property and the correlated emergence of the professional manager, and other kinds of changes which I will get to in a minute. The bureaucratic mechanism, so capable of coordinating men and power in a stable society of routine tasks, cannot cope with contemporary reali-

ties. The chart shows five major categories, which I visualize as the core tasks confronting the manager in coordinating the human side of enterprise:

1. The problem of integration grows out of our "consensual society," where personal attachments play a great part, where the individual is appreciated, in which there is concern for his well-being—not just in a veterinary-hygiene sense but as a moral, integrated personality.

2. The problem of social influence is essentially the problem of power, and leadership studies and practices reveal not only an ethical component but an *effectiveness* component: people tend to work more efficiently and with more commitment when they have a part in determining their own fates and have a stake in problem-solving.

Human Problems Confronting Contemporary Organizations

	Problem	Bureaucratic solutions	New twentieth century conditions
Integration	The problem of how to integrate individual needs and management goals.	No solution because of no problem. Individual vastly oversimplified, regarded as passive instrument or disregarded.	Emergence of human sciences and understanding of man's complexity. Rising aspirations. Humanistic-democratic ethos.
Social Influence	The problem of the distribution of power and sources of power and authority.	An explicit reliance on legal-rational power but an implicit usage of coercive power. In any case, a confused, ambiguous, shifting complex of competence, coercion, and legal code.	Separation of management from ownership. Rise of trade unions and general education. Negative and unintended effects of authoritarian rule.

Human Problems Confronting Contemporary Organizations

	Problem	Bureaucratic solutions	New twentieth century conditions
Collaboration	The problem of managing and resolving conflicts.	The "rule of hierarchy" to resolve conflicts between ranks and the "rule of coordination" to resolve conflict between horizontal groups. "Loyalty."	Specialization and professionalization and increased need for interdependence. Leadership too complex for one-man rule or omniscience.
Adaptation	The problem of responding appropriately to changes induced by the environment of the firm.	Environment stable, simple, and predictable; tasks routine. Adapting to change occurs in haphazard and adventitious ways. Unanticipated consequences abound.	External environment of firm more "turbulent," less predictable. Unprecedented rate of technological change.
"Revitalization"	The problem of growth and decay.	?	Rapid changes in technologies, tasks, manpower, raw materials, norms and values of society, and goals of enterprise and society all make constant attention to the processes of the firm and revision imperative.

3. The problem of collaboration grows out of the same social processes of conflict, stereotyping, and centrifugal forces which inhere in and divide nations and communities. They also employ the same furtive, often fruitless, always crippling mechanisms of conflict resolution: avoidance or suppression, annihilation of the weaker party by the stronger, sterile compromises, and unstable collusions and coalitions. Particularly as organizations become more complex they fragment and divide, building tribal patterns and symbolic codes which often work to exclude others (secrets and noxious jargon, for example) and on occasion to exploit differences for inward (and always, fragile) harmony. Some large organizations, in fact, can be understood only through an analysis of their cabals, cliques, and satellites, their tactics resembling a sophisticated form of guerrilla warfare, and a venture into adjacent spheres of interest is taken under cover of darkness and fear of ambush.

(The university is a wondrous place for these highly advanced battle techniques, far overshadowing their business counterparts in subterfuge and sabotage. Quite often a university becomes a loose collection of competing departments, schools, and institutes, largely non-communicating because of the multiplicity of specialist jargons and interests and held together, as Robert Hutchins once said, chiefly by a central heating system, or as Clark Kerr amended, by questions of what to do about the parking problem.)*

4. The real *coup de grâce* to bureaucracy has come as much from our turbulent environment as from its incorrect assumptions about human behavior. The pyramidal structure of bureaucracy, where power was concentrated at the top—perhaps by one person or a group who had the knowledge and resources to control the entire enterprise—seemed perfect to "run a railroad." And undoubtedly, for tasks like building railroads, for the routinized tasks of the nineteenth and early twentieth centuries, bureaucracy was and is an eminently suitable social arrangement.

Nowadays, due primarily to the growth of science, technology, and research and development activities, the organizational environment of the firm is rapidly changing. Today it is a turbulent environment, not a placid and predictable one, and there is a deepening interdependence among the economic and other facets of society. This means that economic organizations are increasingly enmeshed in legislation and public policy. Put more simply, it

* For this quote, as well as for other major influences, I want to thank Professor Kenneth D. Benne.

means that the government will be in about everything, more of the time. It may also mean, and this is radical, that maximizing cooperation, rather than competition between firms—particularly if their fates are correlated—may become a strong possibility.

5. Finally, there is the problem of revitalization. Alfred North Whitehead sets it neatly before us: "The art of free society consists first in the maintenance of the symbolic code, and secondly, in the fearlessness of revision . . . Those societies which cannot combine reverence to their symbols with freedom of revision must ultimately decay." Organizations, as well as societies, must be concerned with those social conditions that engender buoyancy, resilience, and fearlessness of revision. Growth and decay emerge as the penultimate problem where the environment of contemporary society is turbulent and uncertain.

Forecast of Organizations of the Future

A forecast falls somewhere between a prediction and a prophecy. It lacks the divine guidance of the latter and the empirical foundation of the former. On thin empirical ice, I want to set forth some of the conditions that will dictate organization life in the next twenty-five to fifty years.

1. The environment. Those factors already mentioned will continue in force and increase. Rapid technological change and diversification will lead to interpenetration of the government—its legal and economic policies—with business. Partnerships between business and government will be typical. And

because of the immensity and expense of the projects, there will be fewer identical units competing for the same buyers and sellers. The three main features of the environment will be interdependence rather than competition, turbulence rather than steadiness, and large-scale rather than small-scale enterprises.

2. Population characteristics. The most distinctive characteristic of our society is, and will become even more so, its education. Peter Drucker calls us the "educated society," and for good reason: within 15 years, two-thirds of our population living in metropolitan areas will have attended college. Adult education is growing even faster. It is now almost routine for the experienced physician, engineer, and executive to go back to school for advanced training every two or three years. Some fifty universities, in addition to a dozen large corporations, offer advanced management courses to successful men in the middle and upper ranks of business. Before World War II, only two such programs existed, both new and struggling to get students.

All of this education is not just "nice" but necessary. For as W. Willard Wirtz, the Secretary of Labor, recently pointed out, computers can do the work of most high school graduates—and they can do it cheaper and more effectively. Fifty years ago education used to be regarded as "nonwork," and intellectuals on the payroll (and many staff workers) were considered "overhead." Today, the survival of the firm depends, more than ever before, on the proper exploitation of brain power.

One other characteristic of the population which will aid our understanding of organizations of the future is increasing job mobility. The lowered cost and growing ease of transportation, coupled with the real needs of a dynamic environment, will change drastically the idea of "owning" a job—or "having roots," for that matter. Participants will be shifted from job to job and even employer to employer with little concern for roots and homestead.

3. Work values. The increased level of education and mobility will change the values we hold about work. People will be more intellectually committed to their jobs and will probably require more involvement, participation, and autonomy in their work.

Also, people will tend to be more "other-directed," taking cues for their norms and values more from their immediate environment than from tradition. We will tend to rely more heavily on temporary social arrangements, on our immediate and constantly-changing colleagues. We will tend to be more concerned and involved with relationships rather than with relatives.

4. Tasks and goals. The tasks of the firm will be more technical, complicated, and unprogrammed. They will rely more on intellect than muscle. And they will be too complicated for one person to comprehend, to say nothing of control. Essentially, they will call for the collaboration of specialists in a project or team form of organization.

There will be a complication of goals. Business will increasingly concern itself with its adaptive or innovative-creative capacity. In addition, meta-goals—that is, supra-goals which shape and provide the foundation for the goal structure—will have to be articulated and developed. For example, one meta-goal might be a system for detecting new and changing goals; another could be a system for deciding priorities among goals.

Finally, there will be more conflict and contradiction among diverse standards of organizational effectiveness, just as in hospitals and universities today there is conflict between teaching and research. The reason for this is the increased number of professionals involved, who tend to identify more with the goals of their profession than with those of their immediate employer. University professors can be used as a case in point. More and more of their income comes from outside sources, such as foundations which grant them money and industries for whom they consult. They tend not to be good "company men" because they divide their loyalty between their professional values and organizational goals.

5. Organization. The social structure of organizations of the future will have some unique characteristics. The key word will be "temporary"; there will be adaptive, rapidly changing *temporary systems*. These will be problem-oriented "task forces" composed of groups of relative strangers who represent a diverse set of professional skills. The groups will be arranged on an organic rather than a mechanical model; they will evolve in response to a problem rather than to programmed role expectations. The "executive" thus will become a coordinator or "linking pin" between various task forces. He must be a man who can speak the diverse languages of research, with skills to relay information and to mediate between groups. People will be differentiated not vertically according to rank and status but flexibly and function-

ally according to skill and professional training.

Adaptive, problem-solving, temporary systems of diverse specialists, linked together by coordinating and task-evaluating specialists in an organic flux —this is the organizational form that will gradually replace bureaucracy as we know it. As no catchy phrase comes to mind, I call this an organic-adaptive structure.

6. Motivation. The organic-adaptive structure should increase motivation, and thereby effectiveness, since it will enhance satisfactions intrinsic to the task. There is a harmony between the educated individual's need for meaningful, satisfactory, and creative tasks and a flexible organizational structure.

There will, however, also be reduced commitment to work groups, for these groups, as I have already mentioned, will be transient and changing. While skills in human interaction will become more important, due to the growing needs for collaboration in complex tasks, there will be a concomitant reduction in group cohesiveness. My prediction is that in the organic-adaptive system people will have to learn to develop quick and intense relationships on the job and learn to bear the loss of more enduring work relationships. Because of the added ambiguity of roles, more time will have to be spent on the continual search for the appropriate organizational mix.

In general, I do not agree with those who emphasize a new utopianism in which leisure, not work, will become the emotional-creative sphere of life. Jobs should become more rather than less involving; man is a problem-solving animal, and the tasks of the future guarantee a full agenda of problems.

In addition, the adaptive process itself may become captivating to many.

At the same time, I think that the future I describe is not necessarily a "happy" one. Coping with rapid change, living in temporary work systems, developing meaningful relations and then breaking them—all augur social strains, and psychological tensions. Teaching how to live with ambiguity, to identify with the adaptive process, to make a virtue out of contingency, and to be self-directing will be the task of education, the goal of maturity, and the achievement of the successful manager. To be a wife in this era will be to undertake the profession of providing stability and continuity.

In these new organizations, participants will be called on to use their minds more than at any other time in history. Fantasy, imagination, and creativity will be legitimate in ways that today seem strange. Social structures will no longer be instruments of psychic repression but will increasingly promote play and freedom on behalf of curiosity and thought.

Bureaucracy was a monumental discovery for harnessing the muscle power of the industrial revolution. In today's world, it is a lifeless crutch that is no longer useful. For we now require structures of freedom to permit the expression of play and imagination and to exploit the new pleasure of work.

One final word: While I forecast the structure and value co-ordinates for organizations of the future and contend that they are inevitable, this should not bar any of us from giving the inevitable a little push here and there. And while the French moralist may be right that there are no delightful marriages, just good ones, it is possible that if managers and scientists continue to get their heads together in organizational revitalization, they *might* develop delightful organizations—just possibly.

I started with a quote from de Tocqueville and I think it would be fitting to end with one: "I am tempted to believe that what we call necessary institutions are often no more than institutions to which we have grown accustomed. In matters of social constitution, the field of possibilities is much more extensive than men living in their various societies are ready to imagine."

Chapter 11

SOME VALUE DILEMMAS
OF THE CHANGE AGENT

VALUE considerations have appeared in discussions of planned change and the change-agent role throughout this volume, even where the focus of the discussion has been upon historical, cognitive, or technological matters. In fact, the differentiation of planned change from other modes of human change is grounded in a cluster of value commitments on the part of the agent of planned change—a commitment to collaborative ways of working, a commitment to the basing of plans for change upon valid knowledge and information, and a commitment to reducing power differentials among men as a distorting influence upon the determination of the tempo and direction of justifiable changes in human life. We have tried to be open about the value commitments of our enterprise throughout our discussion. What more needs to be said?

In the first place, the meaning of these overarching value commitments is frequently not clear in the complex and confused situations in which the change agent functions. Value considerations present themselves intertwined with cognitive and technical considerations, and it is often difficult to sort out the value component of decisions and judgments from other components when it needs most to be confronted in its own right. Confrontations of value differences and conflicts are often freighted with subjectivity and emotional heat as compared with confrontations of differences in cognitive and technical matters. And most of us are unsure of our ability to handle our subjectivity and emotional heat constructively. As a result, we tend to avoid value confrontations. This tendency is highly prevalent in behavioral-science types—and many change agents are behavioral scientists. For scientists have frequently been indoctrinated in a value-free ideal of science. In addition to the basically human difficulties in handling value confrontations constructively, behavioral scientists often suffer additional feelings of shame and guilt for being involved in value commitments at all, if these are, by definition, unscientific.

In addition, the conditions of society and culture, which were examined in the last chapter as placing processes of goal setting and direction finding in a new light, also load the value judgments and choices of change agents, where, behaviorally, values and value orientations function and perchance grow and develop, with new and wider responsibilities as indeed the choices of all men are now similarly loaded. We now know that we are no longer choosing wisely when we choose within the framework of assumed and unexamined traditions of belief and practice. We are literally legislating the future for ourselves and for others as we choose and act upon our choices. Since our value orientations are at the least partial determinants of our choices, responsibility requires that we become clear about and responsible for our actual as well as our professed ideal values as they function or fail to function in the choices we make as change agents.

The purpose of this chapter is to illuminate some of the contexts in which value clarification and responsibility are required of change agents and, by extension, of behavioral scientists in their functioning as researchers as well as in their practitioner functions. Frequently, the value quandary presents itself to the change agent as an ethical concern about manipulation of his client, about the imposition of his own value orientations upon those he is "helping," about his temptations to use his influence to narrow and foreclose rather than to widen and release the free choices of his client. And this concern is augmented rather than reduced as knowledge of the conditions of behavioral change grows and derived technologies for effecting behavioral change develop toward greater precision and power. Herbert Kelman explores this ethical quandary in "Manipulation of Human Behavior: An Ethical Dilemma for the Social Scientist." He further sees this dilemma as requiring the attention of basic researchers and applied researchers in their work as well as the attention of direct-service practitioners in their functioning. And he seeks to differentiate the ways in which the quandary presents itself for each of these functionaries within the broad spectrum of the social and behavioral sciences.

We have said that ethical quandaries and technical-cognitive difficulties present themselves together and are complexly intertwined in the life functioning of change agents and of clients. Benne, in "Some Ethical Problems in Group and Organizational Consultation," develops criteria by which change agents can distinguish and disentangle ethical from technical problems in their work. He also suggests a typology of the ethical problems encountered by the change agent and advises how abilities to identify and cope with ethical problems can be developed in the education and re-education of change agents.

Alvin Gouldner penetrates the labyrinth in which the Minotaur of value-free social science has been mythically enshrined by some contemporary sociologists and other social scientists. Gallantly utilizing the tools of the sociology of knowledge, he exorcizes the mythical monster and brings back the good news to citizens of the Athens of sociology that they need no longer sacrifice young men and women in appeasing the Minotaur. More prosaically, Gouldner urges social scientists to assume responsibility for the advancement of valid values in their research, their dissemination of research results and their teaching, and develops reasons for his urging.

11.1   MANIPULATION OF HUMAN BEHAVIOR: AN ETHICAL DILEMMA FOR THE SOCIAL SCIENTIST

Herbert C. Kelman

I

The social scientist today—and particularly the practitioner and investigator of behavior change—finds himself in a situation that has many parallels to that of the nuclear physicist. The knowledge about the control and manipulation of human behavior that he is producing or applying is beset with enormous ethical ambiguities, and he must accept responsibility for its social consequences. Even the pure researcher cannot withdraw into the comforting assurance that knowledge is ethically neutral. While this is true as far as it goes, he must concern himself with the question of how this knowledge is *likely* to be used, given the particular historical context of the society in which it is produced. Nor can the practitioner find ultimate comfort in the assurance that he is helping others and doing

From Herbert C. Kelman, "Manipulation of Human Behavior: An Ethical Dilemma for the Social Scientist," *Journal of Social Issues*, XXI, No. 2 (1965), 31–46. Used by permission.

good. For, not only is the goodness of doing good in itself a matter of ethical ambiguity—a point to which I shall return shortly—but he also confronts the question of the wider social context in which a given action is taken. The production of change may meet the momentary needs of the client— whether it be an individual, an organization, or a community—yet its long-range consequences and its effects on other units of the system of which this client is a part may be less clearly constructive.

There are several reasons why the ethical problems surrounding the study of behavior change are of increasing concern. First, our knowledge about the control of human behavior is increasing steadily and systematically. Relevant information is being developed in various areas within psychology—clinical, social, and experimental—as well as in sociology and anthropology. Personally, I do not think that the dangers from that direction are imminent. I have the feeling that the power and sensitivity of scientifically based techniques for controlling and shaping complex human behaviors are often exaggerated. Nevertheless, we are constantly working toward a systematization of this knowledge and we must at least anticipate the day when it will have developed to a point where the conditions necessary for producing a particular change in behavior can be specified with relative precision. Second, there is an increasing readiness and eagerness within our society to use whatever systematic information (or misinformation) about the control of human behavior can be made available. This readiness can be found in different quarters and in response to different motivations. It can be found among therapists and pedagogues, among idealists and agitators, among hucksters and image-makers. Third, social scientists are becoming increasingly respectable and many agencies within government, industry, the military, and the fields of public health and social welfare are becoming interested in our potential contributions. Here too there is no imminent danger. We still have a long way to go before becoming truly influential and we may find the road rather bumpy. Nevertheless, we must anticipate the possibility that social scientists will meet with a serious interest in their ideas about behavior control and have an opportunity to put them to the test on a large scale.

For all of these reasons, concern about the implications of our knowledge of behavior control is less and less a matter of hypothetical philosophical speculation. The possibilities are quite real that this knowledge will be used to control human behavior—with varying degrees of legitimacy, effectiveness, and scope. Moreover, this knowledge is being produced in a socio-historical context in which its use on a large scale, for the control of vast populations, is particularly likely. Ours is an age of mass societies in which the requirements of urbanization and industrialization, together with the availability of powerful mass media of communication, provide all the necessary conditions for extensive manipulation and control of the behavior of masses. An interest in controlling the behavior of its population is, of course, a characteristic of every society and by no means unique to our age. What *is* unique is that this is done on a mass scale, in a systematic way, and under the aegis of specialized institutions deliberately assigned to this task. Like the nuclear physicist, then, the social scientist is responsible for knowledge that—in the light of the world situation in which it is being produced—has decided explosive possibilities. It behooves us, therefore, to be concerned with the nature of the product that we are creating and the social process to which we are contributing.

In their attempts to come to grips with this problem, it seems to me, the practitioner and investigator of behavior change are confronted with a basic dilemma. On the one hand, for those of us who hold the enhancement of man's freedom of choice as a fundamental value, any manipulation of the behavior of others constitutes a violation of their essential humanity. This would be true regardless of the form that the manipulation takes—whether, for example, it be based on threat of punishment or positive reinforcement. Moreover, it would be true regardless of the "goodness" of the cause that this manipulation is designed to serve. Thus, an ethical problem arises not simply from the ends for which behavior control is being used (although this too is a major problem in its own right), but from the very fact that we are using it. On the other hand, effective behavior change inevitably involves some degree of manipulation and control, and at least an implicit imposition of the change agent's values on the client or the person he is influencing. There are many situations in which all of us—depending on our particular values—would consider behavior change desirable: for example, childhood socialization, education, psychotherapy, racial integration, and so on. The two horns of the dilemma, then, are represented by the view that any manipulation of human behavior inherently violates a fundamental value, but that there exists no formula for so structuring an effective change situation that such manipulation is totally absent.

In calling attention to the inevitability of behavior control whenever influence is being exerted, I am not suggesting that we should avoid influence under all circumstances. This is not only impossible if there is to be any social life, but it is also undesirable from the point of view of many important social values. Nor am I suggesting that we need not worry about the manipulation inherent in all influence attempts, simply because it is inevitable. The view that we can forget about this problem, because there is nothing we can do about it anyway, ignores the fact that there are important differences in degree and kind of manipulation and that there are ways of mitigating the manipulative effect

of various influence attempts even if the effect cannot be eliminated entirely. This leads me to another very crucial qualification with respect to the first horn of the dilemma that I have presented. In stating that all manipulation of behavior—regardless of its form or of the purpose it is designed to serve—is a violation of the person's essential humanity, I am not suggesting that differences between different types of manipulation are ethically insignificant. The extent to which the influence attempt—despite its manipulative component—allows for or even enhances the person's freedom of choice, the extent to which the relationship between influencer and influencee is reciprocal, the extent to which the situation is oriented toward the welfare of the influencee rather than the welfare of the influencing agent—all of these are matters of great moment from an ethical point of view. In fact, these differences are the major concern of the present analysis. But I consider it essential, as a prophylactic measure, to keep in mind that even under the most favorable conditions manipulation of the behavior of others is an ethically ambiguous act.

It is this first horn of the dilemma that Skinner seems to ignore, as can be seen from his debate with Rogers, several years ago, on issues concerning the control of human behavior.[1] Rogers, on the other hand, tends to minimize the second horn of the dilemma.

Skinner is well aware of the inevitability of control in human affairs, and argues for a type of control that is based on intelligent planning and posi-

[1] Carl R. Rogers and B. F. Skinner. Some issues concerning the control of human behavior. *Science*, 1956, *124*, 1057–1066.

tive reinforcement, and is not "exercised for the selfish purposes of the controller." He makes a number of telling points in responding to his critics. For example, he reminds us that, while we object to external controls, we often ignore psychological constraints that limit freedom of choice to the same or an even greater extent. He asks why a state of affairs that would otherwise seem admirable becomes objectionable simply because someone planned it that way. He points out that control based on the threat and exercise of punishment, which is built into our political and legal institutions, is fully accepted, but that use of positive reinforcement by government is regarded with suspicion. I find these and other points useful because they help us to focus on forms of control that often remain unrecognized and to consider forms of control that may be ethically superior to current ones but that we tend to reject because of their unorthodox nature. But Skinner fails to see the basis of many of the criticisms directed at him, because he is concerned about the control of human behavior only when that control is aversive, and when it is misused—i.e., when it is used for the benefit of the controller and to the detriment of the controllee. He seems unable to see any problem in the mere *use* of control, regardless of technique or purpose. This inability is consistent with his value position, which does not recognize the exercise of choice as a good *per se*.[2]

[2] This in turn is related to a point stressed by Rogers, namely Skinner's underestimation of the role of value choices in human affairs in general and in the application of science to social problems in particular.

My own statement of the first horn of the dilemma is predicated on the assumption that the freedom and opportunity to choose is a fundamental value. To be fully human means to choose. Complete freedom of choice is, of course, a meaningless concept. But the purpose of education and of the arrangement of the social order, as I see it, is to enable men to live in society while at the same time enhancing their freedom to choose and widening their areas of choice. I therefore regard as ethically ambiguous any action that limits freedom of choice, whether it be through punishment or reward or even through so perfect an arrangement of society that people do not care to choose. I cannot defend this value because it is not logically derived from anything else. I can, of course, offer supporting arguments for it. First, I can try to show that the desire to choose represents a universal human need, which manifests itself under different historical circumstances (not only under conditions of oppression). Second, I can point out that freedom of choice is an inescapable component of other valued states, such as love, creativity, mastery over the environment, or maximization of one's capacities. Third, I can try to argue that valuing free individual choice is a vital protection against tyranny: quite aside from the notion that power corrupts its user, even the well-motivated, unselfish controlling agent will be tempted to ignore human variability and to do what *he* thinks is good for others rather than what they think is good for themselves—and thus in essence become tyrannical—if he is unhampered by the right to choose as a basic human value. While I can offer these supporting arguments, I recognize that freedom of choice is, in the final analysis, a rock-bottom value for me. Skinner is not concerned with the dilemma presented here because apparently he does not share this fundamental value, even though he is strongly committed to certain other related values, such as the rejection of aversive control and selfish exploitation (albeit without recognizing their status as values).

With Rogers on the other hand, I feel a complete affinity at the value level. He values "man as a self-actualizing process of becoming" and in general proposes that "we select a set of values that focuses on fluid elements of process rather than static attributes." He favors a society "where individuals carry responsibility for personal decisions." He regards "responsible personal choice" as "the most essential element in being a person." But, as I have pointed out, Rogers tends to minimize the second horn of the dilemma presented here—the inevitability of some degree of manipulation in any influence attempt. He makes what appears to me the unrealistic assumption that by choosing the proper goals and the proper techniques in an influence situation one can completely sidestep the problem of manipulation and control. He seems to argue that when an influencing agent is dedicated to the value of man as a self-actualizing process and selects techniques that are designed to promote this value, he can abrogate his power over the influencee and maintain a relationship untainted by behavior control. This ignores, in my opinion, the dynamics of the influence situation itself. I fully agree that influence attempts designed to enhance the client's freedom of choice and tech-

niques that are consistent with this goal are ethically superior, and that we should continue to push and explore in this direction. But we must remain aware that the nature of the relationship between influencing agent and influencee is such that inevitably, even in these influence situations, a certain degree of control will be exercised. The assumption that we can set up an influence situation in which the problem of manipulation of behavior is removed, because of the stated purpose and formal structure of the situation, is a dangerous one. It makes us blind to the continuities between all types of influence situations and to the subtle ways in which others can be manipulated. It lulls us into the reassuring certainty that what we are doing is, by definition, good. I would regard it as more in keeping with both the realities of behavior change, and the ethical requirements of minimizing manipulation, to accept the inevitability of a certain amount of control as part of our dilemma and to find a *modus vivendi* in the face of the ethical ambiguities thus created.

II

Let me proceed to examine briefly the implications of this general dilemma for each of three roles involving social science knowledge about behavior change: the practitioner, as exemplified by the psychotherapist and the group leader or group process trainer; the applied researcher, such as the social scientist in industry or the public opinion pollster; and the basic researcher, such as the investigator of attitude change. These roles are, of course, highly overlapping, but separating them may help us focus on different nuances of the general dilemma.

The practitioner must remain alert to the possibility that he is imposing his own values on the client; that in the course of helping the client he is actually shaping his behavior in directions that he—the practitioner—has set for him. Thus, psychotherapy, even though it is devoted to what I would consider a highly valuable end—enabling the patient to live more comfortably and achieve his own goals more effectively—is definitely open to the possibility of manipulation. Psychotherapy (at least "good" psychotherapy) is markedly different from brain washing: the client enters into the relationship voluntarily; the therapist is concerned with helping the patient, rather than with furthering his own ends or the ends of some institution that he represents; influence techniques are designed to free the patient, to enhance his ability to make choices, rather than to narrow his scope. Yet there are some striking similarities between the methods of therapy and those of brainwashing to which the therapist must always remain alert, lest he overstep what is sometimes a rather thin line. The therapist cannot avoid introducing his own values into the therapeutic process. He cannot be helpful to the patient unless he deliberately tries to influence him in the direction of abandoning some behaviors and trying out others. But in doing so he must beware of two types of dangers. One is the failure to recognize that he is engaged in the control of the client's behavior. The other is intoxication with the goodness of what he is doing for and to the client, which in turn leads to a failure to recognize the ambiguity of the control

that he exercises. Only if he recognizes these two conditions is he able to take steps to counteract them.

Similar considerations hold for the group leader. Some of the principles of group leadership developed by social psychologists and variously called applied group dynamics, human relations skills, or group process sensitivity are highly congenial to democratic values. They are designed to involve the group in the decision-making process and to foster self expression on the part of the individual member. Yet the possibilities for manipulation abound. A skillful group leader may be able not only to manipulate the group into making the decision that he desires, but also to create the feeling that this decision reflects the will of the group discovered through the workings of the democratic process. This need not involve a deliberate Machiavellian deception on the part of the group leader; the leader himself may share the illusion that a group product has emerged over which he has exercised no influence. It is essential, therefore, to be fully aware of the leader's control implicit in these techniques. Some of their proponents argue that, by their very nature, these techniques can be used only for democratic ends. I would question this assumption and, in fact, consider it dangerous because it exempts the group leader from asking those questions that any practitioner of behavior change should keep before his eyes. What am I doing in my relationship to the client? Am I creating a situation in which he can make choices in line with his own values, or am I structuring the situation so that my values dominate?

When the group leader is involved in training others in human relations skills or sensitivity to group process, he is confronted with a further problem. Typically, the trainee is a member of some organization—industrial, governmental, military, educational, religious—in which he will apply the skills he is now learning. The human relations trainer is, thus, in a sense improving the trainee's ability to manipulate others in the service of the organization that he represents. Of course, this is not the goal of the training effort, and trainers always try to communicate the value of the democratic process in group life. But the fact remains that they are training a wide variety of people who will be using these skills for a wide variety of ends. It can certainly be argued that the widespread introduction of human relations skills is likely to have more positive than negative effects from the point of view of a democratic ideology. Perhaps this is true. But it is dangerous to assume that these skills carry their own built-in protection. There is no substitute for a continued attention, on the trainer's part, to questions such as these: Whom am I training? To what uses will they put the skills that I am placing at their disposal? What are the organizational processes in which I am now becoming a partner?

It is essentially these same questions to which the applied social researcher in the broad field of behavior change must address himself. I am here thinking specifically of applied research in the sense that it is done for a client. While the researcher is merely gathering facts, he is nonetheless participating quite directly in the operations of the organization that employs him. If his work is successful, then his findings will be applied to the formulation and exe-

cution of the organization's policies. There is thus the real possibility that the investigator is directly helping the organization in its attempts to manipulate the behavior of others—workers in an industry, consumers, or the voting public.

Let us take, for example, the industrial social scientist who studies factors affecting worker morale. On the basis of his recommendations, and often with his direct assistance, management may become more aware of human relations aspects of industrial work and introduce methods designed to improve morale. Ideally, these methods would consist of increased involvement and participation of workers in decisions relating to their job. Critics of this type of approach argue that the social scientist is working for management, providing them with information and introducing procedures that are designed to increase productivity at the worker's expense. The assumption in this criticism, to which I think there is some validity, is that the worker is being manipulated so that he experiences a sense of participation and involvement which is not reflected in the reality of his position within the industrial organization. In response to this criticism it can be argued that—considering the over-all lack of satisfaction in industrial work—it is a net good to give the worker some sense of participation and involvement in the work situation, to give him at least a limited opportunity to make choices and thus find some meaning in the job. To be sure, management is interested in these innovations because they expect the changes to increase productivity, but does that necessarily vitiate the advantages from the worker's point of view? This is a rather convincing defense, but in evaluating the pros and cons we must also take into account the social context in which these changes are introduced. What effect does the human relations approach have on unions, which represent the only source of independent power of the industrial worker? Does it sidestep them, and will it eventually weaken them? What are the general implications of helping the worker adjust to a situation in which he has no real freedom of choice, in any ultimate sense? These questions are not easy to answer, and every social scientist has to decide for himself whether his work in industry is doing more good than harm. In deciding whether or not—and in what way—to do applied social research in industry or elsewhere, the social scientist must ask himself: Whom am I doing this work for? How are my findings likely to be used? Will they increase or decrease the freedom of choice of the people whose behavior will be influenced? What are the social processes, both short-run and long-run, in which I am participating via my research?

Another example of applied social research that raises questions about manipulation of the population is public opinion polling, when used in connection with political campaigns or the political process in general. For instance, in a recent presidential election, computer simulation was used—based on data derived from numerous opinion polls—to predict the responses of various segments of the population to different campaign issues. Information generated by this process was made available to one of the political parties. This type of social research has some troubling implications. It raises the possibility that a candidate might use this information to manipulate the voters by presenting a desirable image—that is, saying what the public presumably wants to hear. In defense against such criticisms, the originators of this technique have pointed out that it represents a systematic way of providing the candidate with relevant information about the interests and concerns of the public, or of particular publics. He can then address himself to those issues with which the public is deeply concerned, thus making his campaign more relevant and meaningful and enhancing the democratic political process. They point out further that this is what candidates try to do anyway—and properly so; all the social scientist does is to help them base their campaigns on more adequate information, rather than on the usually unreliable estimates of politicians. Of course, what assurance do we have that opinion polls and computer simulations based on them will, in fact, be used in this ideal manner to bolster the democratic process, rather than to short-circuit it? The information can be used both to widen and to restrict the citizen's freedom of choice. But, as long as it is information that can help political organizations to manipulate the public more effectively, the researcher must concern himself actively with the question of how it is going to be used and to what kind of process it is going to contribute.

For the man engaged in "basic" research on one or another aspect of behavior change—in contrast to the man who does research for a specific client—it is much easier to take the position that the knowledge he produces is neutral. Yet, since there is a possibility that his product will be used by others for purposes of manipulation, he cannot be completely absolved from responsibility. He must consider the relative probabilities, given the existing socio-historical context, that this knowledge will be used to enhance or to restrict people's freedom of choice. These considerations must enter into his decision whether or not to carry out a given piece of research, and how to proceed with it.

Take, for example, the area of attitude change, with which I myself am strongly identified. Much of the research in this area is clearly dedicated to the discovery of general principles, which can presumably be applied to many situations with differing goals. Yet, because of the nature of the principles and the experimental settings from which they are derived, they can probably be applied most readily, most directly, and most systematically to mass communications. And, because of the nature of our social order, they are particularly likely to be used for purposes of advertising, public relations, and propaganda—forms of mass communication that are least oriented towards enhancing the listener's freedom of choice. There are, of course, many reasons for continuing this line of research, despite the probability that its findings will be used for manipulative purposes. First, one can argue that extending our general knowledge about processes of attitude change and increasing our understanding of the nature of influence are in themselves liberating forces, whose value outweighs the possibility that this knowledge will be used for undesirable ends. Second, such research may not only increase the knowledge of the potential manipulator, but also help in finding ways to counteract manipulative forces—by providing the information needed for effective resistance to manipulation, or by developing knowledge about forms of influence that enhance freedom of choice. Third, one might argue that information about attitude change, despite its potential for manipulative uses, is important for the achievement of certain socially desirable goals—such as racial integration or international understanding.

I obviously find these arguments convincing enough to continue this line of research. But the nagging thought remains that the knowledge I am producing—if it has any scientific merit—may come to be used for ever more effective manipulation of human behavior. Thus, even the basic researcher in the domain of behavior change must always ask himself: Given the realities of our present society, what are the probable uses to which the products of my research are going to be put? What are the social processes to which I am contributing by the knowledge that I feed into them?

III

The very fact that I have presented my position in the form of a dilemma should make it clear that I do not see an ultimate "solution"—a way of completely avoiding the ethical ambiguity with which practitioners and researchers in the field of behavior change are confronted. I do feel, however, that there are ways of mitigating the dehumanizing effects of new developments in the field of behavior change. I would like to propose three steps that are designed to contribute to this end. Stated in their most general form, they would involve: (1) increasing our own and others' active awareness of the manipulative aspects of our work and the ethical ambiguities inherent therein; (2) deliberately building protection against manipulation or resistance to it into the processes we use or study; and (3) setting the enhancement of freedom of choice as a central positive goal for our practice and research. In order to spell out in somewhat greater detail what these three steps might imply, I would like to examine them from the point of view of each of the three separate (though overlapping) roles that have already been differentiated: the role of the practitioner, of the applied researcher, and of the "basic" researcher in the field of behavior change. The argument that follows is summarized in Table 1.

I have already stressed how essential it is for the *practitioner* of behavior change to be aware of the fact that he is controlling the client, that he is introducing his own values both in the definition of the situation and in the setting of standards. Thus, in the therapeutic situation, it is not only inevitable but also useful for the therapist to have certain values about what needs to be done in the situation itself and what are desirable directions in which the patient might move, and to communicate these values to the patient. But he must be clear in his own mind that he is bringing these values into the

TABLE 1   Steps Designed to Mitigate the Manipulative Aspects of Behavior Change in Each of Three Social Science Roles

Desirable Steps	Role of Practitioner	Role of Applied Researcher	Role of Basic Researcher
(1) Increasing awareness of manipulation	Labelling own values to self and clients; allowing client to "talk back"	Evaluating organization that will use findings; considering on whom, how, and in what context they will be used	Predicting probabilities of different uses of research product, given existing sociohistorical context
(2) Building protection against or resistance to manipulation into the process	Minimizing own values and maximizing client's values as dominant criteria for change	Helping target group to protect its interests and resist encroachments on its freedom	Studying processes of resistance to control, and communicating findings to the public
(3) Setting enhancement of freedom of choice as a positive goal	Using professional skills and relationship to increase client's range of choices and ability to choose	Promoting opportunities for increased choice on part of target group as integral features of the planned change	Studying conditions for enhancement of freedom of choice and maximization of individual values

relationship, and he must label them properly for the patient. By recognizing himself that he is engaged in a certain degree of control—and that this is an ethically ambiguous act, even though his role as therapist requires it—and by making the patient aware of this fact, he provides some safeguards against this control. Among other things, such a recognition would allow the patient, to a limited extent, to "talk back" to the therapist—to argue about the appropriateness of the values that the therapist is introducing. A therapeutic situation is, of course, not a mutual influence situation in the true sense of the word: by definition, it is designed to examine only the patient's values and not those of the therapist. But, from the point of view of reducing the manipulativeness of the situation, it would be important to encourage mutuality at least to the extent of acknowledging that what the therapist introduces into the situation is not entirely based on objective reality, but on an alternative set of values, which are open to question. There may be particular therapeutic relationships in which a therapist finds it difficult to acknowledge the values that he brings to them, because his own motivations have become too deeply involved. There may also be institutional settings in which the therapist is required to present the institutional values as the "right" ones, in contrast to the patient's own "wrong" values. These are danger signals, and the therapist may well consider refraining from entering a therapeutic relationship or working in an institutional setting in which he is not free to acknowledge the contribution of his own values.

Second, in addition to increasing awareness of the manipulative aspects of the situation, it is important to build into the change process itself procedures that will provide protection and resistance against manipulation. For the practitioner of behavior change this means structuring the influence situation in such a way that the client will be encouraged to explore his own values, and to relate new learnings and new behavioral possibilities to his own value system. At the same time, it is important that the practitioner—be he therapist or group leader—keep to a minimum the direct and indirect constraints that he sets on the influencee. Constraints are, of course, necessary to varying degrees, both for the protection of clients and for keeping the process moving in useful directions. Insofar as possible, however, the situation should be so structured that the influencee determines the direction of the process to a maximal extent. It should be noted that what I am suggesting here is not the same as the use of non-directive techniques. In and of themselves these merely represent a set of formal techniques which may or may not have the desired effect. The crucial point is that the client's own values should be at the center of attention when change is under consideration and should be readily available as criteria against which any induced behavior can be measured. To the extent to which this is true, the patient or the group will be in a better position to resist manipulation in the service of alien values. Often, however, this will require much more than non-interference on the part of the practitioner. It may require active efforts on his part to encourage the client to bring his values to the fore and measure the induced changes against them.

Third, it is important to go beyond providing protection and resistance against manipulation that would encroach on the client's freedom of choice. The actual *enhancement* of freedom of choice should, ideally, be one of the positive goals of any influence attempt. Thus, the therapist should use his professional skills and his relationship to the patient to provide him with new experiences that enhance his ability to choose (and thus to maximixe his own values) and with new information that widens his range of choices. Similarly, the group leader should attempt to bring the group to a point where members can make more effective and creative choices, conducive to the achievement of individual and group goals. The enhancement of freedom and creativity as the positive value toward which behavior change should be directed has been discussed most eloquently by Rogers.[3]

Needless to say, it would be essential to include in the training of practitioners of behavior change and in their professional standards some consideration of these three desiderata for mitigating the manipulative aspects of their activities. If they learn to acknowledge the role of their own values in the situation, to make active efforts at keeping the client's values in the foreground, and to regard increased freedom of choice as a primary goal, they are less likely to make full use—either unwittingly or by design—of the potential for manipulation that they possess.

Now let me turn to the *applied researcher*. In deciding whether to take on a particular piece of research, he

must keep in mind that the information he is being asked to supply may be used for the manipulation of others—e.g., workers in an industry for whom he is doing a morale survey, or the voting public if he is working with poll data. The question of *who* is employing him becomes crucial, therefore. He must evaluate the organizations that will be using his findings, and consider how they are likely to use them, whose behavior they will attempt to influence, and in what context this influence will occur. He must consider the probable uses of these findings not only in the short run, but also in the long run. Thus, for example, he cannot simply rely on the fact that his contact man in an organization is someone he trusts. If this man is in a peripheral position within the organization, and if the organization is generally undemocratic and exploitative in its orientation, then the long-run prospects are not too reassuring. There is, of course, the possibility that the research itself will have a liberalizing effect on the organization; the probability that this will, in fact, happen must also be estimated. In the final analysis, there can be no foolproof guarantees, but the investigator must at least feel reasonably certain that the net effect of his research will not be a reduction in the freedom of choice of a segment of the population. Each investigator has to draw his own line, both with respect to the probability and the amount of manipulation that he is willing to tolerate. If they are likely to go beyond this line, then he must consider turning down the assignment. Once a researcher has decided to take on an assignment, he must continue to keep the manipulative potential of his findings in mind, and try to

---

[3] For example, in his debate with Skinner, *ibid.*

counteract it by the way he communicates his findings and the recommendations he bases on them. If his research is, indeed, to have a liberalizing effect on the organization, then he will have to take active steps in this direction.

In order to build some protection against manipulation into the change procedures based on his findings, the researcher should make it a rule to communicate directly with the target group (i.e., the group that is to be influenced) and to involve it in the research, and in the change process insofar as he has charge of it. Thus, an industrial social scientist employed by management might insist on informing the workers in detail about the purposes and findings of the research and the attempted changes that are likely to result from it. In giving them this information, he would try to help them protect their interests against undue attempts at manipulation and to offer them specific recommendations for resisting encroachments on their freedom of choice. Furthermore—in order to promote freedom of choice as a positive goal—he should make a concerted effort to influence the planned change that will be based on his research so that it will actually leave the target group with greater choice than it had before. In submitting his findings and recommendations to the organization that contracted for the research, he should actively seek and point up opportunities for enhancing freedom of choice on the part of the target group that can be integrated into the planned change.

The two last points both imply a rather active role for the researcher in the planning of change based on his research. I would not want to say that the researcher must always participate directly in the change process itself; there are many times when this would be impossible or inappropriate. But since he is providing information that will (at least in principle) be directly translated into action, it is his responsibility to take some stand with respect to this action. The uses to which the information is put are not only the problem of the contracting organization, but also very much the problem of the man who supplied the information. The researcher should be clear about this, and he should have the support of his profession when he takes an active part in expressing his point of view.

Let me finally, and more briefly, turn to the *basic researcher*. I have already stated my position that, even though the products of pure research are in a sense neutral, the investigator cannot escape responsibility for their probable consequences. The student of attitude change, for example, must keep in mind that his findings can be used for the systematic manipulation of the population, in ways and for purposes that would produce a net constriction in freedom of choice. In deciding whether or not to proceed with his research, he must try to make some estimate of the probabilities of different uses of his research product, in the light of existing social forces. If he expects restrictive uses to outweigh constructive ones, he would be bound to refrain from engaging in this research. If, on balance, he decides to undertake the research— and there are, of course, many good reasons for doing so—then he must continue to remain alert to its manipulative potential, and must constantly review his decision, particularly as his research emphases shift or as social conditions change.

Researchers in this area also have a special responsibility to be actively concerned with the ways in which the knowledge they produce is used by various agencies in their society. Eternal vigilance to the possibilities of manipulation is, of course, the duty of every citizen. But, as producers of knowledge about manipulation, social scientists are in a position similar to that of the many nuclear physicists who feel a *special* sense of responsibility for the ways in which their knowledge is being used.

Earlier, I suggested that research on attitude change may not only increase the knowledge of the potential manipulator, but also help in finding ways to counteract manipulative forces. So far, research along these lines has been rather limited. If investigators of attitude change and related problems are to mitigate the manipulative potential of their research, they will have to focus more deliberately and more actively on this other line of work. Thus,

in order to build some protection against manipulation into the social structure, we will have to extend our research on processes of resistance to control, and make a special effort to communicate relevant findings to the public. Such an emphasis will contribute to the development of antidotes against manipulation at the same time that research is contributing to the development of knowledge about manipulation itself. From a scientific point of view, such work will be highly germane to the study of attitude change, since it represents an exploration of its limiting conditions.

In order to promote the enhancement of freedom of choice as a positive goal, research will have to focus on the conditions favoring a person's ability to exercise choice and to maximize his individual values. Admittedly, this is a rather value-laden way of stating a problem for basic research. However, if we want our science to contribute to the liberation of man rather than to his dehumanization, this is the kind of problem to which we will have to turn our attention.

11.2 SOME ETHICAL PROBLEMS IN GROUP AND ORGANIZATIONAL CONSULTATION

Kenneth D. Benne

The purpose of this paper is to identify and clarify, from the stance of the consultant, some of the "ethical" prob-

Kenneth D. Benne, "Some Ethical Problems in Group and Organizational Consultation," *Journal of Social Issues*, XV, No. 20, (1959), 60–67. Used by permission.

lems frequently encountered in the process of consultation. Its purpose is not to offer viable solutions to such problems. Such solutions can be discovered or created only by the consultant, usually in collaboration with his client and various significant others in his associational world. A few comments on how the rigors of ethical problem-solving may be eased, but never eliminated, in the life of the consultant are offered at the end of the essay.

"Ethical" and "Technical" Problems of Consultation

How can "ethical" problems be distinguished analytically from "technical" problems? The most obvious distinction is a linguistic one. If the statement of the confronting problem involves ethical predicates—"right," "wrong," "should," "shouldn't," etc., it is primarily "ethical." If the problem is stated in terms of posited relationships between means and ends, the relative effectiveness of various means in attaining a given end, etc., the problem is primarily "technical." This distinction might be adequate were it not for two factual conditions within the current practice of consultation.

The first is a typical lack of nicety in the language habits of practicing consultants and theorists of consultation in the use of "ethical" predicates. This may or may not reflect lack of discipline in philosophical as over against scientific or clinical terminologies. A consultant may be concerned with the "right" method for presenting observational data concerning the client's behavior to the client. But this need not indicate an "ethical" quandary at all. It may be a "technical" problem of feedback—which of 2 or n possible methods of feedback is most effective in getting some desired effect under these conditions? Or the consultant may question whether he, a member of Americans for Democratic Action, can be *effective* in consulting with the board of the National Association of Manufacturers. This sounds like a "technical" problem but it need not be. It may involve a concern about what will happen to my principles as a citizen and my membership as an ADA'er, if I consort intimately with NAM'ers and help them to become more effective in achieving their program goals. If this is the concern, it involves an "ethical" quandary, though the language used in stating it is "technical." Or the consultant may settle his ethical quandaries cheaply by bootlegging in pseudo-objective terms which serve ultimately the function of normative principles—terms like "health," "growth," "learning," etc. Perhaps the language systems of consultants should be refined. But at any rate we can't depend on current consultant language usage to furnish reliable indicators of "ethical" or "technical" problems.

Second, in the practical situations faced by consultants, the "ethical" and "technical" aspects of consultation problems are complexly intertwined. Either of the queries mentioned in the last paragraph if they were to occur in the actual experience of a consultation would, whatever the nub of the difficulty presented, contain both "ethical" and "technical" considerations for the consultant. And, since "behavioral scientists" tend to favor statements of questions which will yield most readily to solution by their favored scientific methods, and since "technical" questions yield most readily to such solution, the "ethical" dimensions of problems tend to be obscured when stated by consultants who are also "behavioral scientists."

How then can "ethical" and "technical" problems of consultation be distinguished analytically? In a "purely technical" problem, the elements of the problem are externalized. The "self" of the consultant, its future career, including its ideal self-image as well as its relationships in its significant associations, are not part of what is being judged and determined in the solution of the problem. The "technical" problem is constructed in a way to exclude such considerations. The "technical" problem may involve estimates of the resources, attitudes and abilities of the consultant relative to the client and client problem to be solved. But these are seen technically as part of the instrumentation of the problematic situation and its effective resolution, not as what is centrally at stake in determining an adequate solution to the problem.

In an "ethical" problem, on the other hand, what is being judged, in conjunction with other conditions and circumstances, is precisely the future career of the self, including its future membership or non-membership in various morally significant associations. What will this or that action do to me as a person, a professional, or a consultant? Indeed, can I continue to function as the kind of person, professional or consultant I am or aspire to be, if I enter into this consultant relationship, if I perform these acts in the process of consultation? And along with these quandaries, questions about violation of the norms of present associations with various significant others, and thus of future continuance of these associations, are integrally involved. The "ethical" problem is constructed in a way to emphasize, not to exclude, such considerations.

An illustration may help to make the distinction clear. A psychologist consulting with an organization may, along with other "technical" problems, raise the question of whether other competences than his own are required to help the organization clarify and solve its confronting problem. So far, though the answer to the question involves consideration of data about himself and his competence, it is a "technical" problem. He is assessing himself as part of the instrumentation of the situation. If, however, he finds himself transgressing the bounds of his competence as a psychologist, as he and significant associations of his colleagues have defined these, the problem may take on an "ethical" shape. What will happen to *me*, as psychologist and in my colleague associations as psychologist, if I persist in this transgression? And to make it a genuine rather than a pseudo-quandary—what will happen to *me* and to other significant associations of mine, actual or aspired to, if I do not persist? The point is that in the "ethical" formulation of the problem, the future career of the self of the consultant-person, including his significant associations, are indeterminate elements in the problem and their valid determination is a part of the solution of the problem. A new commitment or a confirmed recommitment of the self to certain moral values is a part of the outcome to be achieved.

A Rough Typology of Ethical Problems of Consultation

1) Some ethical problems arise from conflicting normative expectations *within* the consultant-client relationship as to what the proper and required behaviors of the consultant *vis à vis* the

client should be. The consultant brings some more or less clear normative images of the consultant role to his associations with a potential or actual client. These are reenforced by more or less explicit consensual agreements about the central focus and permissible limits of the consultant role among the consultants' colleagues in whatever significant associations with other consultants he maintains. The client system also has images about what the helpful consultant should or shouldn't do. These may be based on previous experiences with consultants. Or they may be drawn from more "primitive" expectations with respect to the nature of "help" and the proper ways of giving and receiving "help" in the quandaries and crises of life. People have been taking difficulties to sources of "help," long before professionalized "consultation" emerged as a legitimate or semilegitimate role in contemporary society. And expectations as to proper "help" and ways of giving and receiving it are inevitably brought by clients to any "helping" situation. Out of the lack of fit between consultant's and client's normative expectations about their proper and necessary relationship, some of the ethical problems of consultation are engendered.

2) But consultants belong to associations other than those with their clients and with other consultants. Most consultants belong also to professional associations. Part of their credentials as sources of help to clients derives from their broader professional role and its supporting associations. The consultant may come to consultation as "psychologist," "psychiatrist," "anthropologist," "sociologist," "educator," "social worker," etc. And membership in

a professional association carries some weight of moral scruples and inhibitions along with it. The intrusions of these moral standards into the choices and judgments of consultants accounts for another type of ethical problem in consultation.

3) Consultants, in addition to their professional associations, are citizens, members of "the state" and often of voluntary associations which aim to influence "the state" on matters of public policy. And consultants have membership in more "personal" associations as well, families, churches, etc. Membership in these associations involves also moral identification with the norms and normative outlooks they profess and practice. Even under the most rigid regimes of role segregation within the person of the consultant, the moral commitments, scruples and inhibitions characteristic of these associations and the regions of the inner society of the consultant-person they control will intrude into choices precipitated within the consultation process. And, as they thus intrude, if they are consciously articulated, a third type of ethical problem is presented to the consultant.

The next three sections of these comments will treat one generalized ethical problem in each of these three types.

Ethical Conflicts Arising within the Consulting Relationship

I have selected ethical problems involving the virtue and counter-virtue of "flexibility" and "integrity" for treatment here. All consultants agree that there must be mutual accommodation between the initial expectations of client and of consultant in the establishment of a "healthy" and "effective" relationship. Moreover, they seem to agree that the relationship ordinarily changes over time from less dependence of client upon the consultant, through interdependence, toward eventual autonomy on the part of the client. The moral drawn from these agreements is a counsel to the virtue of "flexibility" on the part of the consultant.

Yet the consultant also has his "integrity" to maintain. And his integrity is defined by some system of values re the proper and required functioning of the consultant in helping a client. Moreover, this system of values, although ideally it has become the consultant's own, is normally supported in general outline by his "agency" and/or by the formal or informal association of consultants to which he belongs. There are thus limits of adaptability for the consultant and some of these limits normatively define what "consultation" means for him. When demands from a client for help press upon these limits, the consultant confronts an ethical problem. For his future career as a "consultant self" as well as continuance or non-continuance of his relationship with significant "consultant colleagues" are involved in the problem to be solved.

The "ethical" problem is, of course, tied up with "technical" problems. How well can the consultant predict the temporary or continuing character of some debilitating client demand upon him? Will the demand be relaxed and a more acceptable demand be substituted as the consultation proceeds? How adept is the consultant at withdrawing from a relationship which has become ethically untenable? And so the "technical" qualifiers of the "ethical"

problem run on and on. But the core "ethical" problem remains. "Flexibility" is both a "technical" and "ethical" virtue in consultation. And anxiety on the part of the consultant about "ethical" contamination from the client may at times be a neurotic rationalization for inflexibility, the personal bases of which are clouded to the consultant. But the "anxiety" is at other times a "rational fear" based upon the sober fact that both "change agent" and "client" change during a process of consultation. And change may involve disintegration of a self and its associations without valid re-integration and rebuilding.

This species of problem always presents itself in specific consultation situations. It can only be well settled in relation to such situations and not in general terms by purely dialectical methods. But it seems to me a valid demand upon the training and supervision of a consultant that he be given help in distinguishing the "neurotic" from the "rational" forms of such problems as they present themselves to him. A priori labeling of ethical concern for his integrity on the part of a consultant as necessarily a cover for some personality deficiency in relating to others hardly augurs well for the development of a body of valid ethical knowledge with respect to consultant relations.

Intrusions from Other Professional Associations

The "consultant-client" relationship is not the same in its normative demands upon the consultant as the "researcher-subject," the "clinician-patient" or "teacher-student" relationships upon social scientist, psychiatrist or educator. Yet in some of their professional associations, often their primary ones, consultants are social scientists, psychiatrists or educators as well as consultants. There is some overlap in these role-relationships. Consultants do collect and interpret data about the behavior of the client. They do help clients to clarify distorted perceptions. They do stimulate and support the learning of new knowledges and skills in the client system. This overlap in role requirements makes thorough role-segregation impossible. And in efforts to integrate discrepant but overlapping roles, ethical problems arise.

To illustrate the ethical aspects of problems precipitated by the intrusion of role images and norms from other professional relationships into the consultation situation, the "researcher-subject" versus the "consultant-client" relationship has been selected. The primary value served by the researcher's trafficking with his subjects is the testing of some hypothesis. The hypothesis originates outside the interaction between researcher and subject, usually out of some gap or discrepancy in current knowledge claims within the field of behavioral studies to which the researcher is professionally committed. The aim of the researcher is not to help the subject clarify its situation and function more adequately within it. The deferred value which the knowledge gained from the interaction *may eventually have* for the subjects figures more in the justification of the enterprise to non-scientists than in the motivational system of the researcher *qua* researcher. Since his primary aim is building knowledge, he is not concerned with his subject as a case but rather as an instance to provide con-

firmation or disconfirmation to the hypothesis he is formulating and/or testing. The collaboration between researcher and subject, while in some measure necessary, is a sharply limited and truncated collaboration. This is necessary to save the research from "contamination."

In the consultant-client relationship, the consultant is concerned centrally with the client's case. Hypotheses for guiding data collection in the process of consultation derive from the case situation of the client system and one of the principal criteria for choosing what behavior to study is immediate pay-off in terms of situational clarification for the client system. The relationship worked toward is one of "full" collaboration between consultant and client. The main psychic rewards of the consultant come from the more adequate and intelligent functioning of the client system which emerges in and hopefully follows from the processes of consultation.

The normative principles defining and guiding the establishment, maintenance and termination of the two kinds of relationships, if functionally appropriate to the differing goals, are thus at points significantly different. It is thus not surprising that the "scientist" acting as "consultant" should at times find his "scientist self" threatened by the demands upon him of "client behavior" which does not conform to the standards of "good subject behavior." Or, to use the opposite terminology—that his "consultant self" should be tempted by the demands upon him of his "unregenerate scientist self." The conflict may take the form of feelings of disloyalty to "science" for not taking advantage of the rare research opportunities which his access to the client system offers along with inhibitions imposed by the consultant ethic of not deluding the client with respect to his major motivations in probing the client system and situation. Or it may take the form of anxiety that he is losing his scientific hard-headedness in enjoying the psychic rewards of helping his client. In any event, conflict between the ethical demands of the two roles upon the self of the consultant-researcher is almost certain to occur.

The conflict is an ethical one, since its resolution involves recommitments in the self and some new inter-accommodation of the associations significant to the self and of their normative demands upon members. That non-ethical considerations also are involved is true. But it is important that the ethical dimensions of the problem be faced, clarified and dealt with as ethical problems, however difficult this may be for behavioral scientists who happen to be "anti-philosophical" in their orientation.

Intrusions from Civic and Personal Moralities of the Consultant

Particular intrusions of this type of ethical dilemmas are more disparate and harder to illustrate representatively than are instances of the other two types. For the attendant moralities in the civic, religious and other non-professional identifications of people who consult are usually both more various, as among members of this class, and less systematically articulated, within individual members, than are their professional moralities. But the norms of these non-professional associations do engender difficulties for their members who are contemplating engagement in or who are actually engaged in consultation. Where these norms have not been clearly formulated and articulated in conceptual terms, they may intrude as feelings of uneasiness or as attitudes of suspicion toward and total rejection of certain kinds of potential clients. Where they have been formulated in conceptual terms, the ethical issues between these normative principles and the normative principles involved in consultation processes can be joined and dealt with rationally. Perhaps some consultants need to work on articulating and formulating their civic, religious and personal "philosophies" as a pre-condition of adequate recognition and handling of ethical issues of this third type.

Let us assume, for illustrative purposes, a psychologist-consultant who has articulated his political philosophy. Let us assume further that he is committed to a social-democratic point of view and implements this point of view in part through active participation in Americans for Democratic Action and the Democratic Party. This psychologist is asked to consult with the management of a "reactionary" corporation on its industrial relations difficulties. Should he accept such a consultant relationship? Or, if so, under what conditions? His own social-political point of view is nearer to that of the union leadership with whom the corporation is in conflict. If he is successful in his consultation, he may be strengthening the party to the conflict whose social-political values he opposes in his political identifications. Or, perhaps, he can not be successful as a consultant in helping management in clarifying its situation, in locating weaknesses in its skills and understandings and in strengthening these, because of the ideological conflicts involved for him. Perhaps, on the other hand, his consultation may actually influence management toward fuller acceptance of unionism and toward some revision of its present social-political posture. What makes the problem of the consultant "ethical" is that it involves in its solution the future career of the self of the consultant as a political person and the future of significant political associations which he maintains, along with questions of the effectiveness and integrity of his consultant self.

If he does establish a consulting relationship, similar problems will probably dog him at points in the processes of consultation, unless he terminates or significantly modifies his previous political values and associations. The problems are not different in kind from those experienced by a Roman Catholic sociologist asked to consult with the National Council of Churches on its missionary program or an integrationist anthropologist consulting with the state department of education of a southern state on its program to maintain racial segregation in the schools. As conflicts are sharpened along ideological lines, collaboration across these lines acquires connotations of "disloyalty" and "treason." The melodramatic oversimplification of the Western divides the population into the "good guys" and the "bad guys." The "good guys" feel morally violated by efforts to help the "bad guys," and vice-versa.

That such division is always oversimplification maintains the validity of the problem of choice for the consultant. That a conflict situation fosters and reenforces such oversimplification as a social fact and requires all men, including consultants, to choose up sides lends further validity to the choices to be made. Can a consultant effectively "represent" the values of a wider mediating community to a party to a conflict with whom he consults—values of science, of impartiality, of suspended judgment, of continuing communication, etc.? This question of "can" is an empirical question which requires valid understanding of both the consultant and his associations on the one hand and the client and its situation on the other; as well as some estimate of the larger historical situation in which both function. An affirmative answer here keeps the choice open for the consultant. But the questions of "should" still remain and must be settled in their own right and by the consultant. And the valid answers need not and will not be the same for all consultants, since the self of the consultant is an indeterminate element in the solution. The realistic hope is not that these questions be abolished magically from an ideologically conflicted world. It is rather that they be answered openly, clearly and rationally rather than by processes of euphemism, drift or partisan righteousness.

Aids to Consultants in Their Ethical Quandaries

Only a few of the ethical quandaries encountered by consultants alive to such dilemmas have been illustrated. Perhaps the "facticity" of such choices has been established and a useful typology for locating principal sources of ethical frustration has been provided.

So far, the counsel to a consultant has been that he must face, recognize, articulate and "rationally" resolve his ethical conflicts for himself, if they are to be resolved at all. This, I believe, is wise counsel.

But can (and should) consultants be helped by others in facing, recognizing, articulating and rationally resolving ethical difficulties? Here too the answer is a conditional affirmative. The quest for an answer lies in two main directions—in the pre-service and in-service training of consultants; and in more effective professionalization of consultation services to groups and organizations.

Making valid distinctions between neurotic anxieties and ethical concerns is a "learned" rather than a "natural" ability. Moreover, the making of the distinction by an individual consultant usually requires the help of others more detached from personal involvement in the situations where the distinction is required. Consultants, in their pre-service training, need to be confronted by situations which involve ethical choices. They need help in sorting out and articulating these choices. They need "coaching" in the making of choices, not toward a standard solution but toward a solution which is "right" for the consultant. Such "coaching" can not be rationally separated from training processes designed to increase the self-knowledge of the consultant, including knowledge of areas of the self most vulnerable to neurotic anxieties.

Nor is it enough that consultants receive such help in their pre-service training. Consultants need such continuing help during their in-service practice of consultation too. Whether such help takes the form of supervisory conferences, periodic workshops and clinics for consultants or some other format will depend on the working situations of the consultants involved. In either pre-service or in-service training for consultants, both "technical" and "ethical" languages need to be developed and utilized. The proper choice and utilization of such languages is an important outcome of the training. If only "technical" language is legitimized in the training, this learning outcome is unlikely to be well-served.

Part of the difficulty of developing general ethical codes for group and organizational consultation is that the present practitioners of the art are drawn from numerous rather than single primary professional identifications. It is unwise and impossible for psychologist-consultants to legislate norms of appropriate behavior for psychiatrist-consultants, however attractive the prospect might be to psychologists. And the reverse is true. And so it runs for sociologists and social workers, anthropologists and educators, or any combination of these. The answer may lie in part in developing cross-professional associations of consultants who can work toward developing general "advices" concerning typical ethical problems of consultation. The answer may lie in part in specializing existing codes within particular professions to take account of special problems of group and organizational consultation.

Whichever form the development takes, and it will probably take both forms, the effect should be motivated by a spirit of inquiry into a set of difficult problems which will need to be solved eventually by consultants and clients themselves. The outcome of the inquiries is preferably general advices to consultants, the definition of broad limits of ethical and non-ethical practice, rather than detailed "shalts" and "shalt nots." For clients, approaching and engaging in consultation, also have ethical scruples and concerns, as well as neurotic anxieties and crippling ignorances. And their training and organization to be good and effective clients must eventually generate its own client wisdoms. These will have to come to terms with the professional wisdom of consultants in the actual building and handling of ethically right and technically effective consultant-client relationships.

11.3 ANTI-MINOTAUR: THE MYTH OF A VALUE-FREE SOCIOLOGY

Alvin W. Gouldner

This is an account of a myth created by and about a magnificent minotaur named Max—Max Weber, to be exact; his myth was that social science should and could be value-free. The lair of this minotaur, although reached only by a labyrinthian logic and visited only by a few who never return, is still regarded by many sociologists as a holy place. In particular, as sociologists grow older they seemed impelled to make a pilgrimage to it and to pay their respects to the problem of the relations between values and social science.

Considering the perils of the visit, their motives are somewhat perplexing. Perhaps their quest is the first sign of professional senility; perhaps it is the last sigh of youthful yearnings. And perhaps a concern with the value problem is just a way of trying to take back something that was, in youthful enthusiasm, given too hastily.

Alvin W. Gouldner, "Anti-Minotaur: The Myth of a Value-Free Sociology," *Social Problems*, IX, No. 3, 199–213. Slightly revised and abridged with the permission of the author.

In any event, the myth of a value-free sociology has been a conquering one. Today, all the powers of sociology, from Parsons to Lundberg, have entered into a tacit alliance to bind us to the dogma that "Thou shalt not commit a value judgment," especially as sociologists. Where is the introductory textbook, where the lecture course on principles, that does not affirm or imply this rule?

In the end, of course, we cannot disprove the existence of minotaurs who, after all, are thought to be sacred precisely because, being half man and half bull, they are so unlikely. The thing to see is that a belief in them is not so much untrue as it is absurd. Like Berkeley's argument for solipsism, Weber's brief for a value-free sociology is a tight one and, some say, logically unassailable. Yet it is also absurd. For both arguments appeal to reason but ignore experience.

I do not here wish to enter into an examination of the *logical* arguments involved, not because I regard them as incontrovertible but because I find them less interesting to me as a sociologist. Instead what I will do is to view the belief in a value-free sociology in the same manner that sociologists examine any element in the ideology of any group. This means that we will look upon the sociologist just as we would any other occupation, be it the taxi-cab driver, the nurse, the coal miner, or the physician. In short, I will look at the belief in a value-free sociology as part of the ideology of a working group and from the standpoint of the sociology of occupations.

The image of a value-free sociology is more than a neat intellectual theorem demanded as a sacrifice to reason; it is, also, a felt conception of a role and a set of (more or less) shared sentiments as to how sociologists should live. We may be sure that it became this not simply because it is true or logically elegant but, also, because it is somehow useful to those who believe in it. Applauding the dancer for her grace is often the audience's way of concealing its lust.

That we are in the presence of a group myth, rather than a carefully formulated and well validated belief appropriate to scientists, may be discerned if we ask, just what is it that is believed by those holding sociology to be a value-free discipline? Does the belief in a value-free sociology mean that, in point of fact, sociology is a discipline actually free of values and that it successfully excludes all non-scientific assumptions in selecting, studying, and reporting on a problem? Or does it mean that sociology *should* do so. Clearly, the first is untrue and I know of no one who even holds it possible for sociologists to exclude completely their non-scientific beliefs from their

scientific work; and if this is so, on what grounds can this impossible task held to be morally incumbent on sociologists?

Does the belief in a value-free sociology mean that sociologists cannot, do not, or should not make value judgments concerning things outside their sphere of technical competence? But what has technical competence to do with the making of value judgments? If technical competence does provide a warrant for making value-judgments then there is nothing to prohibit sociologists from making them within the area of their expertise. If, on the contrary, technical competence provides no warrant for making value judgments then, at least sociologists are as *free* to do so as anyone else; then their value judgments are at least as good as anyone else's, say, a twelve year old child's. And, by the way, if technical competence provides no warrant for making value judgments, then what does?

Does the belief in a value-free sociology mean that sociologists are or should be indifferent to the moral implications of their work? Does it mean that sociologists can and should make value judgments so long as they are careful to point out that these are different from "merely" factual statements? Does it mean that sociologists cannot logically deduce values from facts? Does it mean that sociologists do not or should not have or express *feelings* for or against some of the things they study? Does it mean that sociologists may and should inform laymen about techniques useful in realizing their own ends, if they are asked to do so, but that if they are not asked to do so they are to say nothing? Does it mean that sociologists should never take the initiative in asserting that some beliefs that laymen hold, such as the belief in the inherent inferiority of certain races, are false even when known to be contradicted by the facts of their discipline? Does it mean that social scientists should never speak out, or speak out only when invited, about the probable outcomes of a public course of action concerning which they are professionally knowledgeable? Does it mean that social scientists should never express values in their roles as teachers or in their roles as researchers, or in both? Does the belief in a value-free sociology mean that sociologists, either as teachers or researchers, have a right to covertly and unwittingly express their values but have no right to do so overtly and deliberately?

I fear that there are many sociologists today who, in conceiving social science to be value-free, mean widely different things, that many hold these beliefs dogmatically without having examined seriously the grounds upon which they are credible, and that some few affirm a value-free sociology ritualistically without having any clear idea what it might mean. Weber's own views on the relation between values and social science, and some current today are scarcely identical. While Weber saw grave hazards in the sociologist's expression of value judgments, he also held that these might be voiced if caution was exercised to distinguish them from statements of fact. If Weber insisted on the need to maintain scientific objectivity, he also warned that this was altogether different from moral indifference.

Not only was the cautious expression of value judgments deemed permissible by Weber but, he emphasized, these were positively mandatory under certain circumstances. Although Weber inveighed against the professorial "cult of personality" we might also remember that he was not against all value-imbued cults and that he himself worshipped at the shrine of individual responsibility. A familiarity with Weber's work on these points would only be embarrassing to many who today affirm a value-free sociology in his name. And should the disparity between Weber's own views and many now current come to be sensed, then the time is not far off when it will be asked, "Who now reads Max Weber?"

What to Weber was an agonizing expression of a highly personal faith, intensely felt and painstakingly argued, has today become a hollow catechism, a password, and a good excuse for no longer thinking seriously. It has become increasingly the trivial token of professional respectability, the caste mark of the decorous; it has become the gentleman's promise that boats will not be rocked. Rather than showing Weber's work the respect that it deserves, by carefully re-evaluating it in the light of our own generation's experience, we reflexively reiterate it even as we distort it to our own purposes. Ignorance of the gods is no excuse; but it can be convenient. For if the worshipper never visits the altar of his god, then he can never learn whether the fire still burns there or whether the priests, grown fat, are simply sifting the ashes.

The needs which the value-free conception of social science serves are both personal and institutional. Briefly, my contention will be that, among the main institutional forces facilitating the survival and spread of the value-free myth, was its usefulness in maintaining both the cohesion and the autonomy of the modern university, in general, and the newer social science disciplines, in particular. There is little difficulty, at any rate, in demonstrating that these were among the motives originally inducing Max Weber to formulate the conception of a value-free sociology.

This issue might be opened at a seemingly peripheral and petty point, namely when Weber abruptly mentions the problem of competition among professors for students. Weber notes that professors who do express a value-stand are more likely to attract students than those who do not and are, therefore, likely to have undue career advantages. In effect, this is a complaint against a kind of unfair competition by professors who pander to student interests. Weber's hope seems to have been that the value-free principle would serve as a kind of "Fair Trades Act" to restrain such competition. (At this point there is a curious rift in the dramatic mood of Weber's work; we had been listening to a full-throated Wagnerian aria when suddenly, the singer begins to hum snatches from Kurt Weill's "Mack the Knife.")

This suggests that one of the latent functions of the value-free doctrine is to bring peace to the academic house, by reducing competition for students and, in turn, it directs us to some of the institutional peculiarities of German universities in Weber's time. Unlike the situation in the American university, career advancement in the German was then felt to depend too largely on the professor's popularity as a teacher; indeed, at the lower ranks, the instructor's income was directly dependent on student enrollment. As a result, the competition for students was particularly keen and it was felt that the system penalized good scholars and researchers in favor of attractive teaching. In contrast, of course, the American system has been commonly accused of overstressing scholarly publication and here the contrary complaint is typical, namely, that good teaching goes unrewarded and that you must "publish or perish." In the context of the German academic system, Weber was raising no trivial point when he intimated that the value-free doctrine would reduce academic competition. He was linking the doctrine to guild problems and anchoring this lofty question to academicians' *earthy* interests.

Another relation of the value-free principle to distinctively German arrangements is also notable when Weber, opposing use of the lecture hall as an arena of value affirmation, argues that it subjects the student to a pressure which he is unable to evaluate or resist adequately. Given the comparatively exalted position of the professor in German society, and given one-sided communication inherent in the lecture hall, Weber did have a point. His fears were, perhaps, all the more justified if we accept a view of the German "national character" as being authoritarian, that is, in Nietzsche's terms a combination of arrogance and servility. But these considerations do not hold with anything like equal cogency in more democratic cultures such as our own. For here, not only are professors held in, shall I say more modest esteem, but the specific ideology of education itself often stresses the desirability of student initiative and participation, and there is more of a systematic solicitation of the student's "own" views in small "discussion" sections. There is little student servility to complement and encourage occasional professorial arrogance.

When Weber condemned the lecture hall as a forum for value-affirmation he had in mind most particularly the expression of *political* values. The point of Weber's polemic is not directed against all value with equal sharpness. It was not the expression of aesthetic or even religious values that Weber sees as most objectionable in the University, but, primarily, those of politics. His promotion of the value-free doctrine may, then, be seen not so much as an effort to amoralize as to depoliticize the University and to remove it from the political struggle. The political conflicts then echoing in the German university did not entail comparatively trivial differences, such as those now between Democrats and Republicans in the United States. Weber's proposal of the value-free doctrine was, in part, an effort to establish a *modus vivendi* among academicians whose political commitments were often intensely felt and in violent opposition.

Under these historical conditions, the value-free doctrine was a proposal for an academic truce. It said, in effect, if we all keep quiet about our political views then we may all be able to get on with our work. But if the value-free principle was suitable in Weber's Germany because it served to restrain political passions, is it equally useful in America today where, not only is there pitiable little difference in politics but men often have no politics at all. Perhaps the need of the American University today, as of American society more generally, is for more commitment to politics and for more diversity of political views. It would seem that now the national need is to take the lid off, not to screw it on more tightly.

Given the historically unique conditions of nuclear warfare, where the issue would not be decided in a long-drawn out war requiring the sustained cohesion of mass populations, national consensus is no longer, I believe, as important a condition of national survival as it once was. But if we no longer require the same degree of unanimity to *fight* a war, we do require a greater ferment of ideas and a radiating growth of political seriousness and variety within which alone we may find a way to *prevent* war. Important contributions to this have and may further be made by members of the academic community and, perhaps, especially, by its social science sector. The question arises, however, whether this group's political intelligence can ever be adequately mobilized for these purposes so long as it remains tranquilized by the value-free doctrine.

Throughout his work, Weber's strategy is to safeguard the integrity and freedom of action of both the state, as the instrument of German national policy, and of the university, as the embodiment of a larger Western tradition of rationalism. He feared that the expression of political-value judgments in the University would provoke the state into censoring the university and would imperil its autonomy. Indeed, Weber argues that professors are not entitled to freedom from state control in matters of values, since these do not rest on their specialized qualifications.

This view will seem curious only to those regarding Weber as a liberal in the Anglo-American sense, that is, as one who wishes to delimit the state's powers on behalf of the individual's liberties. Actually, however, Weber aimed not at curtailing but at strengthening the powers of the German state, and at making it a more effective instrument of German nationalism. It would seem, however, that an argument contrary to the one he advances is at least as consistent; namely, that professors are, like all others, entitled and perhaps obligated to express their values. In other words, professors have a right to profess. Rather than being made the objects of special suspicion and special control by the state, they are no less (and no more) entitled than others to the trust and protection of the state.

In a *realpolitik* vein, Weber acknowledges that the most basic national questions cannot ordinarily be discussed with full freedom in government universities. Since the discussion there cannot be completely free and all-sided, he apparently concludes that it is fitting there should be no discussion at all, rather than risk partisanship. But this is too pious by far. Even Socrates never insisted that all views must be at hand before the dialogue could begin. Here again one might as reasonably argue to the contrary, holding that one limitation of freedom is no excuse for another. Granting the reality of efforts to inhibit unpopular views in the University, it seems odds to prescribe self-suppression as a way of avoiding external suppression. Suicide does not seem a reasonable way to avoid being murdered. It appears, however, that Weber was so intent on safeguarding the autonomy of the university and the autonomy of politics, that he was willing to pay almost any price to do so, even if this led the university to detach itself from one of the basic intellectual traditions of the west—the dialectical exploration of the fundamental purposes of human life.

Insofar as the value-free doctrine is a mode of ensuring professional autonomy note that it does not, as such, entail an interest peculiar to the social sciences. In this regard, as a substantial body of research in the sociology of occupations indicates, social scientists are kin to plumbers, house painters, or librarians. For most if not all occupations seek to elude control by outsiders and manifest a drive to maintain exclusive control over their practitioners.

Without doubt the value-free principle did enhance the autonomy of sociology; it was one way in which our discipline pried itself loose—in some modest measure—from the clutch of its society, in Europe freer from political party influence, in the United States freer of ministerial influence. In both places, the value-free doctrine gave sociology a larger area of autonomy in which it could steadily pursue basic problems rather than journalistically react to passing events, and allowed it more freedom to pursue questions uninteresting either to the respectable or to the rebellious. It made sociology freer—as Comte had wanted it to be—to pursue all its own theoretical implications. In other words, the value-free principle did, I think, contribute to the intellectual growth and emancipation of our enterprise.

There was another kind of freedom, which the value-free doctrine also allowed; it enhanced a freedom from moral compulsiveness; it permitted a partial escape from the parochial prescriptions of the sociologist's local or native culture. Above all, effective internalization of the value-free principle has always encouraged at least a temporary suspension of the moralizing reflexes built into the sociologist by his own society. From one perspective, this of course has its dangers—a disorienting normlessness and moral indifference. From another standpoint, however, the value-free principle might also have provided a *moral* as well as an intellectual *opportunity*. For insofar as moral reactions are only suspended and not aborted, and insofar as this is done in the service of knowledge and intellectual discipline, then, in effect, the value-free principle strengthened Reason (or Ego) against the compulsive demands of a merely traditional morality. To this degree, the value-free discipline provided a foundation for the development of more reliable knowledge about men and, also, established a breathing space within which moral reactions could be less mechanical and in which morality could be reinvigorated.

The value-free doctrine thus had a paradoxical potentiality: it might enable men to make *better* value judgments rather than *none*. It could encourage a habit of mind that might help men in discriminating between their punitive drives and their ethical sentiments. Moralistic reflexes suspended, it was now more possible to sift conscience with the rod of reason and to cultivate moral judgments that expressed a man's total character as an adult person; he need not now live quite so much by his past parental programming but in terms of his more mature present.

The value-free doctrine could have meant an opportunity for a more authentic morality. It could and sometimes did aid men in transcending the morality of their "tribe," to open themselves to the diverse moralities of unfamiliar groups, and to see themselves and others from the standpoint of a wider range of significant cultures. But the value-free doctrine also had other, less fortunate, results as well.

Doubtless there were some who did use the opportunity thus presented; but there were, also, many who used the value-free postulates as an excuse for pursuing their private impulses to the neglect of their public responsibilities and who, far from becoming more morally sensitive, became morally jaded. Insofar as the value-free doctrine failed to realize its potentialities it did so because its deepest impulses were— as we shall note later—dualistic; it invited men to stress the separation and not the mutual connectedness of facts and values: it had the vice of its virtues. In short, the conception of a value-free sociology has had *diverse* consequences, not all of them useful or flattering to the social sciences.

On the negative side, it may be noted that the value-free doctrine is useful both to those who want to escape *from* the world and to those who want to escape *into* it. It is useful to those young, or not so young men, who live off sociology rather than for it, and who think of sociology as a way of getting ahead in the world by providing them with neutral techniques that may be sold on the open market to any buyer. The belief that it is not the business of a sociologist to make value-judgments is taken, by some, to mean that the market on which they can vend their skills is unlimited. From such a standpoint, there is no reason why one cannot sell his knowledge to spread a disease just as freely as he can to fight it. Indeed, some sociologists have had no hesitation about doing market research designed to sell more cigarettes, although well aware of the implications of recent cancer research. In brief, the value-free doctrine of social science was sometimes used to justify the sale of one's talents to the highest bidder and is, far from new, a contemporary version of the most ancient sophistry.

In still other cases, the image of a value-free sociology is the armor of the alienated sociologist's self. Although C. Wright Mills may be right in saying this is the Age of Sociology, not a few sociologists and Mills included, feel estranged and isolated from their society. They feel impotent to contribute usefully to the solution of its deepening problems and, even when they can, they fear that the terms of such an involvement require them to submit to a commercial debasement or a narrow partisanship, rather than contributing to a truly public interest.

Many sociologists feel themselves cut off from the larger community of liberal intellectuals in whose spitty satire they see themselves as ridiculous caricatures. Estranged from the larger world, they cannot escape except in fantasies of posthumous medals and by living huddled behind self-barricaded intellectual ghettoes. Self-doubt finds its anodyne in the image of a value-free sociology because this transforms their alienation into an intellectual principle; it evokes the soothing illusion, among some sociologists, that their exclusion from the larger society is a self-imposed duty rather than an externally imposed constraint.

Once committed to the premise of a value-free sociology, such sociologists are bound to a policy which can only alienate them further from the surrounding world. Social science can never be fully accepted in a society, or by a part of it, without paying its way; this means it must manifest both its relevance and concern for the contemporary human predicament. Unless the value-relevances of sociological inquiry are made plainly evident, unless there are at least some bridges between it and larger human hopes and purposes, it must inevitably be scorned by laymen as pretentious word-mongering. But the manner in which some sociologists conceive the value-free doctrine disposes them to ignore current human problems and to huddle together like old men seeking mutual warmth. "This is not our job," they say, "And if it were we would not know enough to do it. Go away, come back when we're grown up," say these old men. The issue, however, is not whether we know enough; the real questions are whether we have the courage to say and use what we do know and whether anyone knows more.

There is one way in which those who desert the world and those who sell out to it have something in common. Neither group can adopt an openly critical stance toward society. Those who sell out are accomplices; they may feel no critical impulses. Those who run out, while they do feel such impulses, are either lacking in any talent for aggression, or have often turned it inward into noisy but essentially safe university politics or into professional polemics. In adopting a conception of themselves as "value-free" scientists, their critical impulses may no longer find a target in society. Since they no longer feel free to criticize society, which always requires a measure of courage, they now turn to the cannibalistic criticism of sociology itself and begin to eat themselves up with "methodological" criticisms.

One latent meaning, then, of the image of a value-free sociology is this: "Thou shalt not commit a critical or negative value-judgment—especially of one's own society." Like a neurotic symptom this aspect of the value-free image is rooted in a conflict; it grows out of an effort to compromise between conflicting drives: On the one side, it reflects a conflict between the desire to criticize social institutions, which since Socrates has been the legacy of intellectuals, and the fear of reprisals if one does criticize—which is also a very old and human concern. On the other side, this aspect of the value-free image reflects a conflict between the fear of being critical and the fear of being regarded as unmanly or lacking in integrity, if uncritical.

The doctrine of a value-free sociology resolves these conflicts by making it seem that those who refrain from a social criticism are acting solely on behalf of a higher professional good rather than their private interests. In refraining from social criticism, both the timorous and the venal may now claim the protection of a high professional principle and, in so doing, can continue to hold themselves in decent regard. Persuade all that no one must bell the cat, then none of the mice need feel like a rat.

Should social scientists affirm or critically explore values they would of necessity come up against powerful institutions who deem the statement or protection of public values as part of their special business. Should social scientists seem to compete in this business,

they can run afoul of powerful forces and can, realistically, anticipate efforts at external curbs and controls. In saying this, however, we have to be careful lest we needlessly exacerbate academic timorousness. Actually, my own first-hand impressions of many situations where sociologists serve as consultants indicate that, once their clients come to know them, they are often quite prepared to have sociologists suggest (not dictate) policy and to have them express their own values. Nor does this always derive from the expectation that sociologists will see things their way and share their values. Indeed, it is precisely the expected difference in perspectives that is occasionally desired in seeking consultation. I find it difficult not to sympathize with businessmen who jeer at sociologists when they suddenly become more devoted to business values than the businessmen themselves.

Clearly all this does not mean that people will tolerate disagreement on basic values with social scientists more equably than they will with anyone else. Surely there is no reason why the principles governing social interaction should be miraculously suspended just because one of the parties to a social relation is a social scientist. The dangers of public resentment are real but they are only normal. They are not inconsistent with the possibility that laymen may be perfectly ready to allow social scientists as much (or as little) freedom of value expression as they would anyone else. And what more could any social scientist want?

The value-free image of social science is not consciously held for expedience's sake; it is not contrived deliberately as a hedge against public displeasure. It could not function as a face-saving device if it were. What seems more likely is that it entails something in the nature of a tacit bargain: in return for a measure of autonomy and social support, many social scientists have surrendered their critical impulses. This was not usually a callous "sell-out" but a slow process of mutual accommodation; both parties suddenly found themselves betrothed without a formal ceremony.

Nor am I saying that the critical posture is dead in American sociology; it is just badly sagging. Anyone who has followed the work of Seymour Lipset, Dennis Wrong, Leo Lowenthal, Bennett Berger, Bernard Rosenberg, Lewis Coser, Maurice Stein, C. Wright Mills, Arthur Vidich, Philip Rieff, Anselm Strauss, David Riesman, Alfred McClung Lee, Van den Haag and of others, would know better. These men still regard themselves as "intellectuals" no less than sociologists: their work is deeply linked to this larger tradition from which sociology itself has evolved. By no means have all sociologists rejected the legacy of the intellectual, namely, the right to be critical of tradition. This ancient heritage still remains embedded in the underground culture of sociology; and it comprises the enshadowed part of the occupational selves of many sociologists even if not publicly acknowledged.

In contrast with and partly in polemic against this older tradition, however, the dominant drift of American sociology today is compulsively bent upon transforming it into a "profession." (Strangely enough, many of these same sociologists see nothing contradictory in insisting that their discipline is still young and immature.) This clash between the older heritage of the critical intellectual and the modern claims of the value-free professional finds many expressions. One of these occurred at the sociologist's national meetings in Chicago in 1958. At this time, the convention in a session of the whole was considering Talcott Parsons' paper on "Sociology as a Profession." After long and involved discussion, which prompted many members suddenly to remember overdue appointments elsewhere, Chicago's E. C. Hughes rose from the floor and brought a warm response by insisting that we were not a professional but, rather, a learned society. It was at this same meeting that the American Sociological Society rechristened itself as the American Sociological Association, lest its former initials evoke public reactions discrepant with the dignity of a profession.

Another indication of the continuing clash between the critical intellectual and the value-free professional is to be found in the Phoenix-like emergence of Young Turk movements, such as SPSSI, The Society for the Psychological Study of Social Issues, which arose in response to the depression of 1929. When it was felt by Alfred McClung Lee and others that these Turks were no longer so young, they founded the SSSP, the Society for the Study of Social Problems. Both these organizations remain ongoing concerns, each characteristically interested in value-related work, and each something of a stitch in the side of its respective parent group, the American Psychological Association and the American Sociological Association.

Despite the vigor of these and other groups, however, I believe that they are primarily secondary currents whose very visibility is heightened because they are moving across the main ebb. The dominant drift in American sociology is toward professionalization, the growth of technical specialists, toward the diffusion of the value-free outlook to the point where it becomes less of an intellectual doctrine and more of a blanketing mood. American sociology is in the process of accommodating itself.

In its main outlines, such efforts at accommodation are far from new. For the doctrine of a value-free sociology is a modern extension of the medieval conflict between faith and reason. It grows out of, and still dwells in, the tendency prevalent since the 13th century to erect compartments between the two as a way of keeping the peace between them. One of the culminations of this tendency in the Middle Ages is to be found in the work of the Arabian philosopher, Ibn Rochd, better known as Averroes. Averroes had believed that absolute truth was to be found not in revelation but in philosophy, which for him meant Aristotle. He felt that revelation, faith, and the work of the theologians was a kind of footman's philosophy, necessary for those devoid of intellectual discipline and useful as a way of civilizing them.

Seeing theology as containing a measure of truth, albeit one inferior to that of philosophy and, being a prudent man, Averroes recommended that philosophers and theologians ought each to mind his own business and, in particular, that the philosophers, being intellectually superior, should show *noblesse oblige* to the theologians. He suggested that philosophers should keep their truth to themselves and write technical books which did not disturb or confuse simpler minds.

His disciples, the Latin or Christian Averroists, particularly at the University of Paris, accentuated this prudential side of their master's work; their strategy of safety was to define themselves as specialists, as technical philosophers. Their only job, said they, was to teach philosophy and to show the conclusions that flowed from it. These conclusions were "necessary" but, when at variance with the truths of revelation, it was not their job to reconcile them, said the philosophers. From this developed the so-called Doctrine of the Twofold Truth—the truths of philosophy which were logically necessary and the divine truths of revelation. If there were contradictions between the two, the philosophers merely reaffirmed their belief in revelation, and let it go at that. This sometimes took a cynical form as, for example, in John of Jaudan's comment, "I do believe that is true; but I cannot prove it. Good luck to those who can!" They thus built a watertight compartment between philosophy and faith, a separation which Saint Thomas continued and yet sought to transcend. To Saint Thomas, knowing and believing are distinct processes, each having its own separate and legitimate function and therefore not to be invaded by the other. In this view, there were two main classes of truths, both of which, however, derived from Divine Revelation. There were truths obtainable by natural reason alone, and there were truths of revelation, genuine articles of faith which elude the grasp of reason and which were susceptible neither to proof nor disproof by reason.

With the development of modern science varying efforts to accommodate it to religion continued, often taking the form of some kind of separatist doctrine in which each is assigned a different function and each is chastened to acknowledge the authority of the other in its own sphere. Weber's doctrine of a value-free sociology, which creates a gulf between science and values, is in this tradition; it may be regarded as a Protestant version of the Thomistic effort at harmonizing their relations.

The core of Weber's outlook rested on a dualism between, on the one hand, reason or rationality, especially as embodied in bureaucracy and science, and, on the other hand, more elemental emotional forces, partly encompassed in his notion of Charisma. He regards each of these forces as inimical to the other. He himself is ambivalent to each of them, viewing each as both dangerous and necessary.

On the one side, Weber is deeply concerned to protect the citadel of modern reason, the University, and fiercely opposes the professorial "cult of personality" which was the academic expression of the charismatic claim. This in turn disposes him to project an image of the university which is essentially bureaucratic, as a faceless group of specialists, each sovereign in his own cell and all sworn to foresake their individuality. Nonetheless he also hates bureaucracy precisely because it submerges individuality and dehumanizes men and is thus led to deny that he intended to bureaucratize the university in pleading for the doctrine of a value-free social science. (Yet while this, was doubtless not his *intention*, his two-pronged polemic against the cult of academic personality and in favor of the value-free doctrine does seem to drive him toward such a bureaucratic conception of the University.)

If Weber is concerned to protect

even the bureaucratic dwelling-places of rationality, he also seeks to confine bureaucracy and to circumscribe the area of its influence. In particular, he wishes to protect the highest reaches of statecraft from degenerating into a lifeless routine; he seeks to preserve politics as a realm in which there can be an expression of personal will, of serious moral commitment, a realm where greatness was possible to those who dared, persevered and suffered, a realm so powerful that it could overturn the institutional order or preserve it. He wants to safeguard high politics as an arena of human autonomy, of pure value choices, at its finest.

Yet Weber also fears for the safety of rationality in the modern world. He knows that there are powerful forces abroad which continue to threaten rationality, that there are still untamed things in men which he, more than most, had had to face. Not unlike Freud, Weber was both afraid of and drawn to these unbridled forces, the passionate Dionysian part of men. While he believed that they were being slowly subdued by an onmarching rationalization, he continued to fear that they could yet erupt and cleave modern institutional life. Although fearing these irrational forces, he also felt their disappearance from the modern world to be a "disenchantment," for he believed that they contained springs of vitality and power indispensable to human existence.

Weber is a man caught between two electrodes and torn by the current passing between them; he fears both but is unable to let go of either. He attempts to solve this dilemma by a strategy of segregation, seeking the exclusion of charismatic irrationality from certain modern *institutions*, such as the university, but admitting it into and, indeed, exalting its manifestations in the inward personal life of individuals. He wanted certain of the role structures of modern society to be rational; but he also wanted the role-players to be passionate and wilful. He wanted the play to be written by a classicist and to be acted by romanticists. Unusual man, he wanted the best of both worlds. Yet whatever the judgment of his intellect, his sentiments are not poised midway between them, but tend toward one of the two sides.

This becomes clear when we ask, if science cannot be the basis of value judgments, what then, according to Weber, was to be their basis? To answer this, we must go beyond his formal doctrine of value-free sociology, to Weber's own personal profession of belief. Weber certainly did not hold that personal values should derive from the existent culture, or from ancient tradition, nor again from formal ethical systems which he felt to be empty and lifeless. Unless men were to become inhuman robots, life, he insisted, must be guided by consciously made decisions. If men are to have dignity, they must choose their own fate.

To Weber as a man, only those values are authentic which stem from conscious decision, from a consultation of the inner conscience and a wilful commitment to its dictates. From his *personal* standpoint, it is not really true that all values are equally worthy. Those consciously held by men are more worthy than those which are merely traditional and unthinkingly repeated. Those values that men feel deeply about and passionately long to realize are better than those which are merely intellectually appealing and do not engage their entire being.

In short, Weber, too, was seeking a solution to the competing claims of reason and faith. His solution takes the form of attempting to guard the autonomy of both spheres but, most especially I believe, the domain of conscience and faith. He wants a way in which reason and faith can cohabit platonically but not as full partners. The two orders are separate but unequal. For in Weber, reason only consults conscience and perhaps even cross-examines it. But conscience has the last word, and passion and will the last deed. Here Weber stands as half-Lutheran, half-Nietzschian.

If Weber thrusts powerfully at traditionalism, nonetheless his main campaign here is waged against science and reason and is aimed at confining their influence. To Weber, even reason must submit when conscience declares, Here I stand; I can do no other! Weber saw as authentic only those values that rest on the charismatic core of the self and on its claims to intuitive certainty. Weber, too, was a seeker after certainty, the certainty that is more apt to come from the arrogance of individual conscience. For while much may be truly said of the arrogance of reason, reason always seeks reasons and is ready to sit down and talk about them.

To Weber as a Protestant, the individual's conscience is akin to the voice of revelation. He would have been dismayed at the implications of considering it as the echo of parental remonstrations. To him, individual conscience was transcendental while reason and science were only instrumental. Science is the servant of values and of personal conscience, which, like the heart, has reasons of its own. From Weber's standpoint, science and reason could only supply the means; the ends were to be dictated by values, which, even if inscrutable, were to have the final voice.

I have therefore come to believe that the value-free doctrine is, from Weber's standpoint, basically an effort to compromise two of the deepest traditions of Western thought, reason and faith, but that his arbitration seeks above all to safeguard the romantic residue in modern man. I have personal reservations not because I doubt the worth of safeguarding this romantic component, but, rather, because I disagree with the strategy of segregation which Weber advances. *I believe that, in the end, this segregation warps reason by tinging it with sadism and leaves feeling smugly sure only of itself and bereft of a sense of common humanity.*

The problem of a value-free sociology has its most poignant implications for the social scientist in his role as educator. If sociologists ought not express their personal values in the academic setting, how then are students to be safeguarded against the unwitting influence of these values which shape the sociologist's selection of problems, his preferences for certain hypotheses or conceptual schemes, his neglect of others. For these are unavoidable and, in this sense, there is and can be no value-free sociology. The only choice is between an expression of one's values, as open and honest as it can be, this side of the psychoanalytical couch, and a vain ritual of moral neutrality which, because it invites men to ignore the vulnerability of reason to bias, leaves it at the mercy of irrationality.

If truth is the vital thing, as Weber is reputed to have said on his death-bed, then it must be all the truth we have to give, as best as we know it, being painfully aware and making our students aware, that even as we offer it we may be engaged in unwitting concealment rather than revelation. If we would teach students how science is made, really made rather than as publicly reported, we cannot fail to expose them to the whole scientist by whom it is made, with all his gifts and blindnesses, with all his methods and his *values* as well. To do otherwise is to usher in an era of spiritless technicians who will be no less lacking in understanding than they are in passion, and who will be useful only because they can be used.

In the end, even these dull tools will through patient persistence and cumulation build a technology of social science strong enough to cripple us. Far as we are from a sociological atomic bomb, we already live in a world of the systematic brainwashing of prisoners of war and of housewives with their advertising exacerbated compulsions; and the social science technology of tomorrow can hardly fail to be more powerful than today's.

It would seem that social science's affinity for modeling itself after physical science might lead to instruction in matters other than research alone. Before Hiroshima, physicists also talked of a value-free science; they, too, vowed to make no value judgments. Today many of them are not so sure. If we today concern ourselves exclusively with the technical proficiency of our students and reject all responsibility for their moral sense, or lack of it, then we may someday be compelled to accept responsibility for having trained a generation willing to serve in a future Auschwitz.

Granted that science always has inherent in it both constructive and destructive potentialities. It does not follow from this that we should encourage our students to be oblivious to the difference. Nor does this in any degree detract from the indispensable norms of scientific objectivity; it merely insists that these differ radically from moral indifference.

I have suggested that, at its deepest roots, the myth of a value-free sociology was Weber's way of trying to adjudicate the tensions between two vital Western traditions: between reason and faith, between knowledge and feeling, between classicism and romanticism, between the head and the heart. Like Freud, Weber never really believed in an enduring peace or in a final resolution of this conflict. What he did was to seek a truce through the segregation of the contenders, by allowing each to dominate in different spheres of life. Although Weber's efforts at a personal synthesis brings him nearer to St. Thomas, many of his would-be followers today tend to be nearer to the Latin Averroists with their doctrine of the twofold truth, with their conception of themselves as narrow technicians who reject responsibility for the cultural and moral consequences of their work. It is precisely because of the deeply dualistic implications of the current doctrine of a value-free sociology that I felt its most appropriate symbol to be the man-beast, the cleft creature, the Minotaur.

INDEX